NATURAL RIGHT AND POLITICAL RIGHT

Natural Right and Political Right

Essays in Honor of Harry V. Jaffa

edited by
Thomas B. Silver
Peter W. Schramm

CAROLINA ACADEMIC PRESS
Durham, North Carolina 27707

Published by Carolina Academic Press
Post Office Box 8795
Forest Hills Station
Durham, NC 27707

First Published 1984
Printed in the United States of America

Library of Congress Catalogue Card Number 84-70180
ISBN 0-89089-279-2 (cloth)

Contents

NATURAL RIGHT AND POLITICAL RIGHT

INTRODUCTION

IMAGINE YOURSELF MAROONED ON A DESERT ISLAND WITH ONLY TEN BOOKS to read, but in this case books *not* of your own choosing. Suppose them all to be books written by behavioral political scientists during the past twenty years. Question: Do you think that you would die first of boredom, or of self-inflicted wounds?

This was the situation of many undergraduate students of political science in the 1960's, including some of the contributors to this volume. Except that we didn't realize that we were living on a desert island. And although we had been intellectually starved to death, we never realized that we were dead.

Never realized, that is to say, until we were born again. Those who have undergone the religious experience of being born again often describe it as private and ineffable. Our rebirth, on the other hand, was an experience shared by friends, susceptible to a precise articulation. As young political scientists we had had drilled into us the central tenet of positivism: the distinction between facts and values, according to which reason is powerless to guide human life. Qua political scientists, we were islands unto ourselves in the midst of the ferocious and bloody political controversies of the sixties, cut off from the citizen's perspective on political questions. But because the central tenet of our science was a recent discovery, allegedly unknown to earlier political thinkers, there was hardly any incentive to read books published much before our own generation. Cut off from the citizen's perspective, we were also cut off from what has been called "the conversation among the greatest minds." The exact moment of our rebirth was when we were pulled into that conversation, and the man who pulled us in was Professor Harry V. Jaffa.

Literally within moments of our first meeting with Jaffa there was a stunning enlargement of our horizons. Young "scholars" who, the day before, had not known a polis from a poultice, were suddenly listening avidly as Professor Jaffa read aloud from the Greek text of Plato's *Phaedo*. Soon after came Shakespeare's Roman plays, seen from an entirely new perspective. And then Aristotle's *Ethics*, and Aquinas's commentary, and the *Republic*, and *Tom Sawyer*, and the Lincoln-Douglas debates, and Churchill's *Marlborough*, and *Natural Right and History*, and the *Politics*, and . . . but enough. Here were ten books, any one of which we gladly would have taken to a desert island in place of a whole library of our

previous fare. Books which would have repaid endless study and produced endless delight.

Professor Jaffa did not introduce us to a conversation in which he
himself had no part. He mixed his labor with the great books and made
them his own. His classes were almost never lectures or systematic pres-
entations. They were conversations, marvelous conversations, which demonstrated our teacher's incessant search for clarity and resolution. He
had the ability to make lucid, simple formulations of philosophical positions and to show their plausibility and significance, but then to soar off
into the most imaginative conversational flights in which the dialogue
between these philosophical positions was illustrated in original and
nonformulaic ways. His conversation, more than that of any other teacher
in our experience, sowed sparks in the minds of his students.

He was combative as hell, of course, from the moment he walked
into the classroom and wrote "NO SMOKING" on the blackboard to the
final bell or the final TKO, whichever came last. But never mean spirited,
or condescending, or resentful, or cruel. Never happier, in fact, than
when his students in class discussions were stalking him, or laying traps,
or baiting him, like dogs rushing at a great bear, hoping to do together
what they could only rarely do as individuals: bring him down in the
argument. ("What do you mean 'rarely,'" we can imagine him saying,
"when did you *ever* bring me down, either together or alone!")

These conversations often spilled over into after-class gatherings;
indeed, they spilled over into our whole lives. Jaffa was constantly accessible and constantly talking about political philosophy: on the telephone,
at his house, in the gym, at parties, at chance meetings on the street. It
was not only that he was extremely gracious about receiving students and
talking with them for hours on end, but that he actually sought them
out, for long conversations, again and again over the years.

The surest place to catch him was at dawn or at dusk, on his bicycle.
Riding with the Old Man was an experience to harden both the muscles
and the mind, for even while pedaling at a breathtaking pace, at a
godforsaken hour, he would continue to discourse in his habitual way
about all manner of things, right up to the last quarter mile of the ride,
when suddenly he would accelerate in a determined effort to leave his
young students in his dust, with no consideration for the fact that the
students' conduct the previous evening, in the company of wine, women,
food, song, and cigars, might not have been completely up to Aristotle's
specifications in Book III of the *Ethics*.

But his conversations were not the only way in which Professor Jaffa
participated in the conversation of the greatest minds. No one, friend or
foe, who has ever read *Crisis of the House Divided* has denied that it is the
work of a master. The judicious tone, the extraordinary learning, the
moral seriousness, the crisp and sometimes beautiful prose of the book

have established it as a masterpiece of American political history. It is as well a model of argumentation, a dialectical tour de force, a logical juggernaut. And because its powerful arguments are focused upon the first principles of the American political order, it may fairly be called a work of political philosophy, if by political philosophy we mean the rigorous and systematic attempt to replace our opinions of fundamental political questions with knowledge of those questions.

Although *Crisis of the House Divided* was widely recognized as a work of genius, many regarded its author as an evil genius. In such circles, the thesis of the book was not well received. Some conservatives, for example, decried the book's vindication of Abraham Lincoln and the principles of the Declaration of Independence, whether because of their attachment to the doctrine of states' rights, or their suspicion of rational arguments in moral matters, or their hatred of the teaching of equality, or their denial of the necessity of prudence in political life. The reaction to the book by these conservative spokesmen was not unimportant politically, because conservatism was just then gathering strength as a national political force, and groping for self definition. It was well understood on all sides that a conservative movement shaped by the thought of a Willmore Kendall, an Ayn Rand or a Friedrich Hayek would not be the same as a conservative movement shaped by the thought of Harry Jaffa.

Crisis of the House Divided is set apart from most other political histories of our day by its assertion that natural right remains the standard for political life. In its discussion of this theme, as we have said, the book ascends from political history to political philosophy. But political philosophy is not merely the philosophical discussion of politics but the political discussion of philosophy. The dialectic within *Crisis* therefore takes place within the horizon of the American political tradition. At the center of *Crisis* is the argument that all healthy political life vibrates with the tension between nature and convention, and that political health ceases when a definitive attempt is made to resolve that tension. On the center page of *Crisis* is the aphorism:

Those who believe anything sanctioned by the law is right commit one great error; those who believe the law should sanction only what is right commit another.

In the broad sense our "law" refers to our "way of life" and that way of life is democratic. Accordingly, conservatism has been most constructive and successful in American political life when it has been able to link itself to the democratic principles of the Declaration of Independence. Lincoln is the supreme example of this. When conservatives make explicit their scorn for the demos, or attempt to put distance between themselves and the Declaration, they tend to become ineffectual. Their conservatism sours into an apolitical, a merely literary or a merely money-making, conservatism. Lincoln did not make this mistake, because he chose to understand what is low in American life in light of what he regarded as high, namely, the Declaration of Independence.

According to Jaffa, "Lincoln . . . understood the logical and moral implications of the Declaration of Independence as well as, if not better than, any man who has attempted to live by that noble testament." But Lincoln believed, contrary to what has been asserted by some recent interpreters, that the Declaration implied popular government, however troublesome or problematic that notion may be.

The American dilemma is embodied in the Declaration of Independence itself. If the dilemma exists at all, it is in the structure of the ideal, which issues in a dual imperative. For the Declaration of Independence does indeed say that all men are created equal. But by reason of this very equality governments are said to derive their just powers from the consent of the governed. Now the meaning of the expression "consent of the governed" is open to much interpretation. However, if the consent of the governed may rightfully be withdrawn from any government which the people do not believe secures their unalienable rights in a satisfactory manner, we believe that the consent of the governed cannot be interpreted in a merely hypothetical sense; it cannot be merely passive; it must embody the *opinion* of the governed. There is no question, at any rate, that for Lincoln . . . a government which did not, in the manner of a representative democracy, embody popular opinion was not a legitimate government . . . Consent meant for him, as for any Jeffersonian Democrat, active participation, an "equal voice in the government."

And again:

If the only thing that counted, the only thing that created obligation for the statesman, was the goal of equality of condition—i.e., equality of security for the unalienable rights of man—then the idea of popular government would be an absurdity. To see that each man received his "equal" measure we would have to have philospher-kings, endowed with absolute power, to decree and enforce what metaphysicians alone would know how to expound.

. . . to turn to oligarchy, as a means of enforcing equality, would itself involve a repudiation of equality in the sense of the Declaration.

Many of those who are suspicious of democracy are fearful that it represents a lowering of the tone and the goals of political life. But at the heart of Lincoln's project, according to Professor Jaffa, was the attempt to justify America's democratic principles and institutions on high, rather than low grounds.

The Lyceum speech demonstrated how the highest ambition of the loftiest souls, hitherto believed capable of gratification only in a monarchic order, might be achieved in the perpetuation of a democratic one. It recorded the discovery in the soul of "towering genius" that the highest ambition can be conceived as consummated only in the highest service, that egotism and altruism ultimately coincide in that consciousness of superiority which is superiority in the ability to benefit others. But what is true of the superior individual is also true of the superior nation; and Lincoln argues in the course of his debates with Douglas that the freedom of a free people resides above all in that consciousness of freedom which is also a consciousness of self-imposed restraints. The heart of Lincoln's case for popular government is the vindication of the people's cause on the highest grounds which had hitherto been claimed for aristocratic forms.

Here we come around to the connection between democracy and the conversation among the greatest minds. It will be admitted that a sovereign cannot rule well if he is intellectually unfit. Because in a democracy the people are sovereign, there is a grave question whether democracies can be ruled well. Surely no one is fit to rule if he is altogether deaf to the conversation among the greatest minds. If we say that liberal education consists in listening to the conversation among greatest minds, then we must say that liberal education is necessary to a healthy democracy. As Leo Strauss said:

> . . . democracy, even if it is only regarded as the hard shell which protects the soft mass culture, requires in the long run qualities of an entirely different kind: qualities of dedication, of concentration, of breadth, and of depth. Thus we understand most easily what liberal education means here and now. Liberal education is the counterpoise to mass culture, to the corroding effects of mass culture, to its inherent tendency to produce nothing but "specialists without spirit or vision and voluptuaries without heart." Liberal education is the ladder by which we try to ascend from mass democracy to democracy as originally meant. Liberal education is the necessary endeavor to found an aristocracy within democratic mass society. Liberal education reminds those members of a mass democracy who have ears to hear, of human greatness.

Under the tutelage of Professor Jaffa, many of us took the first step up the ladder of liberal education. It is not to be supposed that we are now much advanced in our studies, even after many years, for the ascent is difficult, and most who start it are disqualified by preoccupation or inability from getting very far. But the effort to learn, however incomplete, is not for that reason worthless. So long as the high confers dignity upon the low, the many who cannot achieve greatness can at least be graced by the few who do. In philosophy and politics, in history and poetry, our world seems to have forgotten what is high. It needs reminding. To study with Harry Jaffa is to be reminded constantly of human greatness, and to incur a debt beyond recompense.

The essays in this volume are written by students, colleagues, friends and peers of Professor Jaffa, who wish to do him honor on the sixty-fifth anniversary of his birth. We are grateful to Henry Salvatori and Carlton R. Appleby, whose friendship for Professor Jaffa is longstanding, and whose contributions have made this book possible.

T.B.S.
P.W.S.

1

DANTE AND THE REDISCOVERY OF POLITICAL PHILOSOPHY

Ernest L. Fortin

POLITICAL PHILOSOPHY IS A RELATIVE NEWCOMER TO THE INTELLECTUAL tradition of the Christian West. As late as the early decades of the four-teenth century, Dante could still bemoan its neglect on the part of his contemporaries and plead for its restoration to the place of honor that it once occupied among the human disciplines. Only through it would a proper solution be found to the nagging dilemmas of a society governed by two distinct and often competing authorities, one spiritual and the other temporal. It and it alone could teach his fellow countrymen to live, not as the "Babylonians" whom they had chosen to follow, but as the noble "Romans" whose descendants they claimed to be.[1] Yet Dante him-self was not without knowing that sooner or later the newly rediscovered science was bound to come into conflict with biblical revelation, that other great guide to life and the one to which most of the western world had been committed for centuries. With the Latin translation of Aristotle's *Politics* in the 1260s, the Middle Ages was introduced for the first time to a fully developed view of human existence that not only owed nothing to divine revelation but could plausibly be construed as a viable alternative to it. Just how the two rivals were to be reconciled is the theme of virtually all of Dante's major works, including his poetic masterpiece, the *Divine Comedy*. Unfortunately, the numerous exegetical problems created by the *Comedy's* use of the allegorical mode make it extremely difficult to determine his exact position in regard to this matter. If a careful reading of the poem suggests anything, it is that that position may be less conven-tional than the one that is most often ascribed to him by modern scholars.

It is generally taken for granted by admirers and critics alike that Dante's views on this as well as on all other important issues, however personally expressed, were in substantial agreement with the common beliefs of his time. The majority of the studies devoted to him in recent years fall into two broad categories answering roughly to the two most

9

prevalent forms of contemporary historical scholarship, which for want
of better terms I shall label theoretical historicism and active or radical
historicism. The first of these, represented pre-eminently in this country
by Charles S. Singleton, argues that the only valid approach to Dante's
works is the one that leads through the great theological literature of the
Middle Ages, with which Dante himself could not fail to have been acquainted and by which he presumably took his bearings. This implies
among other things that the content of the body of literature in question
can be apprehended with strict objectivity and that, by adopting the
methods of modern research, one is able to arrive at an understanding
of it which is not essentially different from that of its authors. Singleton's
aim is thus to retrace the pattern of Dante's thought "as established in the
theology of Dante's day." It is assumed from the start that "the poet did
not invent the doctrine," for "what (he) sees as poet and realizes as poet"
is nothing other than "what (was) already conceptually elaborated and
established in Christian doctrine."[2]

The second widely held position is the one articulated by D.S.
Carne-Ross on the occasion of a critical assessment of Singleton's work
which appears in the May 1, 1975, issue of *The New York Review of Books*.
Following Gadamer's hermeneutics, Carne-Ross questions the feasibility
of a detached and self-forgetful appropriation of Dante's thought of the
kind advocated by Singleton. Any endeavor to speak "as though from
inside Dante's world" is illusory and self-annulling, inasmuch as the interpreter is himself one of the structural elements in a game that could
not be enacted without him. What Singleton and his fellow travelers have
naively mistaken for a genuine recovery of the past is at most the product
of an unavoidable "fusion of horizons," entailing both a creative reinterpretation of Dante's cultural horizon and a corresponding expansion of
our own. There is in fact no such thing as *the* correct interpretation of the
Comedy since, once severed from the contingencies of its origin, the text
"has been freed for new relations of meaning exceeding those which may
have been intended by the author" (Th. Kisiel's phrase).

For all his misgivings about our ability to recapture Dante's thought
world in its primitive form, Carne-Ross, like Singleton, is convinced that
Dante's works mirror faithfully the Christian orthodoxy of the Middle
Ages. The only point at issue between the two interpreters is whether we
as moderns can reinstate in our minds the global outlook that the poet
shared with his age and, if not, on what ground his thought could still be
an object of legitimate concern to us. The answer is again given in terms
of hermeneutical theory. Our own world, we are reminded, is neither
identical with nor totally different from the premodern world out of
which it evolved by a series of gradual rather than cataclysmic changes.
In so far as the process allows for the survival of numerous elements
handed down to us from the old and now abandoned universe of dis-

course, some glimmer of recognition remains possible and the medieval text is free to address us without forfeiting its historical identity or exacting from us a "conversion" that, in our present socio-cultural context, could never be anything more than a mockery or a pretense.

No one seriously doubts that Dante dealt with the problems of his time in a spirit which was likewise that of his time, and that both the problems and the terms in which they are posed are as far removed from us as the assumptions of modernity are from those of Dante and his contemporaries. But this still leaves open the questions as to whether the general principles in the light of which he discussed those problems apply only to his time and as to whether it ultimately makes any more sense to speak of an elusive insight into the inescapable "historicality of all understanding" than it does to speak of principles whose universality transcends the particular horizon of experience from which all inquiry necessarily begins.

Be that as it may, both Singleton and Carne-Ross are a good deal more confident about the unimpeachable orthodoxy of Dante's views than an older and longer tradition of Dante scholarship whose origins can be traced back to the time of the poet himself. The fact of the matter is that, although Dante enjoys the reputation of being perhaps the greatest of all Christian poets, his status in the Christian world was from the beginning and has always remained somewhat ambiguous. To this day he is more often praised than read and more likely to be admired from a distance than studied at first hand, except perhaps by a small band of dedicated Dantophiles who have long since claimed him as their special preserve. Relatively few people have had the urge or the patience to accompany him all the way on his lengthy journey through hell, purgatory, and heaven, and fewer still have allowed themselves to be profoundly influenced by his teachings. Like Pascal, albeit for different reasons, he was never fully absorbed into the mainstream of Christian thought or fully integrated into its curriculum of studies. Pascal was blamed for denigrating human reason and for having contributed to the demise of the cosmology in which Christianity had traditionally sought its rational underpinnings. If Dante was suspected of anything, it was not of underestimating the power of reason but of placing too much trust in it. The differences run deeper however. Whereas Pascal's Christian faith was never in question, doubts have frequently been voiced concerning the sincerity of Dante's religious convictions. Not long after his death he was accused of Averroism by some of his contemporaries. The charge was never substantiated, but that it should have been made is itself symptomatic of the kind of mistrust he was capable of arousing. His *Monarchia* was, after all, condemned by the Church in 1329 and we know that copies of it were burned in a number of Italian cities at the time. The record also shows that, had it not been for the patriotic zeal of the Italian clergy, the *Comedy* itself would have been placed on the *Index of Prohibited Books* by the Council of Trent.[3]

The chief reason for the mistrust is not so much that people disagreed with him as that they did not know whether they should agree with him or not. For, the *Comedy*, as anyone who delves into it soon discovers, is not an easy book to decipher. In his short but illuminating *Life of Dante* Boccaccio tells us that it was not written solely for the purpose of "charming" its readers but of "instructing" them as well and, furthermore, that the teaching which it imparts was addressed to two distinct classes of persons: (a) the "prelates, priests, and preachers" whose duty it is to look after the "frail souls" entrusted to their care, and (b) "the people of excellent learning who, either by reflecting on what the men of the past have written or by supplementing their writings on points that may have been neglected or that beg for further clarification, seek to inform the minds and souls of their hearers and readers."[4] Accordingly, Dante's work is open to two different and at times widely divergent interpretations, one "theological" and the other "moral." In one and the same act it is able to "discipline the wise" and "strengthen the foolish." Its poetry is thus comparable to a river "wherein the little lamb may wade and the great elephant freely swim."[5] This means however that its deepest meaning is not necessarily or not always its most obvious meaning. Dante, in short, is an esoteric writer. Part of his teaching remains submerged and hence inaccessible to the casual or uninformed reader. To be more precise, his work contains not just one but two or more teachings all of which have been intended by the author, but for specifically different and, one might add, unequal audiences.

The views set forth by Boccaccio did not in any way originate with him. They merely echo and clarify Dante's own well known statements about the "polysemous" character of his writings in the *Letter to Cangrande*, the *Convivio*, and the *Comedy* itself. These statements are often taken to mean that Dante has deliberately set out to give concrete and even mystical expression to the dogmas of Christian theology by clothing them in a veil of allegory. On that telling the nucleus of hidden truth in the *Comedy* would be coextensive with the sum of the truths expounded discursively and nonmetaphorically in the theological treatises, sermons, and liturgical texts of the period. It cannot be denied of course that all or most of the great religious doctrines of the Middle Ages reappear in some form or other in the *Comedy* and Dante himself occasionally suggests as much. The basic question is whether one can come to an adequate understanding of the poem by reading it simply as a document of the age or an allegory of the Christian faith.

The issue is further complicated by Dante's frequent remarks to the effect that the matters with which he deals had not yet been touched upon or, as he puts it, that the waters on which he moves had never been sailed by anyone before (cf. *Par.*, 2, 1–6). If he means what he says, and there is no reason to doubt that he does, one may be even more inclined to think that the doctrinal substance of the *Comedy* does not coincide in all particulars with the generally accepted views of his day. In order to be sure of it, however, one would have to have a better idea of what these supposedly novel truths are. But then where does one begin to look for them?

The answer to that question can only be, "within the *Comedy* itself," for there would be no point in calling attention to the presence of some mysterious teaching in the text if that teaching were destined to remain forever beyond our reach. Assuming that Dante wrote with the hope of being understood by at least some of his readers, he could not leave them without any inkling as to what his real meaning might be; and assuming that he wrote for future generations as well as for his own, as we know he did, he could hardly rely on such information as would be available only to the people of his time. It was therefore incumbent on him to provide us with all of the clues necessary to a proper interpretation of his work or see to it that no important piece of evidence was left out which could not be supplied by the judicious exercise of one's reason or imagination.

Furthermore, the thematic discussion of poetry in the *Convivio* makes it clear that inner meaning and outer form are so bound up with each other as to constitute an organic whole from which no element, however trifling in appearance, can be dissociated without some loss of intelligibility.[6] Within the purviews of Dante's vast realm, "nothing indeed is left to chance" (*Par.*, 32, 52–3).[7] As one critic has recently stated, "Each new form of address, figure of speech, method of proof, or event is in itself purposive and subsumes, contributes to, or augments the effects of smaller, larger, and collateral divisions."[8] The reader may sometimes fail to perceive the relevance of this or that detail, but unless he prefers to think that the author was negligent or confused, he has no choice but to proceed on the assumption that each one is consonant with the rest of the text and designed to reveal, enhance, or otherwise qualify its meaning.

This is as much as to say that one cannot approach the *Comedy* as one might approach any other book and certainly not as one tends to approach most modern books. If, for reasons of his own, Dante has chosen to conceal his intention, we are constantly left to wonder whether or not what he says is to be taken at face value. The likelihood is that upon inspection some of his statements will turn out to be ironic and hence expressive of ideas that are contradicted by their literal sense. True, it would never occur to us to speak of these statements as ironic if we had not begun to detect the irony or see beyond what is actually said; but this only proves that the person who reaches this stage has already overcome his initial indifference or the merely "historical" curiosity that had attracted him to the *Comedy* in the first place and has assumed the role of a

silent participant who is compelled to take sides on the issue at hand.[9]
The experience in store for him is unique. It involves nothing less than
his transformation into an accomplice who raises himself to the level of
the author's thought by reproducing within himself the genesis of that
thought. Thanks to the collusion thus forged between the two minds,
what may have started out as just another pleasant foray into Dante's
fanciful "other world" rapidly develops into a strange spiritual adventure
in which one is willy-nilly caught up with no clear foreknowledge of
where it could lead and no guarantee that he will still be the same by the
time he reaches his destination.

With these ideas in mind let us turn, not to the whole of the *Comedy*,
to which one could not possibly do justice in a few pages, but to one
particular episode that has thus far eluded every attempt at an interpretation, namely, the meeting between Virgil, Dante, and the Latin poet
Statius in Cantos 21 and 22 of *Purgatorio*.[10] The enigma posed by these
two cantos is all the more tantalizing as the role assigned to Statius in the
action of the *Comedy* is second in importance only to those of Virgil and
Beatrice. Once introduced, Statius figures in no fewer than thirteen cantos and is, along with the other two, the only character to move from one
level to another. The reader has been prepared for what is about to happen by the allusion in the preceding canto to an earthquake that has just
caused the mountain to tremble. Nowhere else in the *Purgatorio* is there
any mention of such an event. We soon learn that the quake heralded
Statius's release from purgatory, to which he had been confined for upwards of nine hundred years in order to atone for his sins. It is worth
noting that Canto 21, where Statius makes his first appearance, marks
the mathematical mid-point of purgatory proper, through which the
travelers have been moving since Canto 9, and hence the ideological center of the whole of Dante's figurative odyssey. What exactly is the significance of Statius's presence in the overall economy of the poem and to
what does he owe the high honor conferred upon him by Dante? We may
begin by recalling the salient details of the initial encounter between the
three poets.

In the course of their journey toward the top of the mountain of
purgatory, Virgil and Dante come upon Statius on the ledge of the avaricious. Statius, still ignorant of the identity of the pilgrims, proceeds to
give a brief account of his literary career and especially of his admiration
for Virgil, to whom he graciously acknowledges his debt as a poet. There
follows a touching recognition scene in which, forgetting for a moment
that they are shades, Statius rushes to embrace his revered master.

Virgil's first reaction is one of surprise at the thought that a man of
Statius's "wisdom" should foolishly have allowed himself to be carried

away by avarice; whereupon Statius explains that the sin for which he was just now being punished was not really greed but its no doubt less contemptible opposite, prodigality, and that he was associated with the avaricious because vices opposed to the same virtue, in this case liberality or moderation in the use of wealth, are purged together on the same ledge (22, 25–54).

We are subsequently informed by Statius himself that, enlightened by the famous prophecy of the *Fourth Eclogue*, he had converted to Christianity but that, out of fear of being persecuted, he had refrained from any public profession of faith, remaining to the end of his life a "secret Christian," *chiuso cristian* (22,90), and eschewing any reference whatever to Christianity in his two epic poems, the *Achilleid*, which had not yet been written, and the *Thebaid*, which was only half completed at the time of his conversion.

Since there are no traces anywhere in the literary tradition of Statius's prodigality or avarice, whichever it may be, or for that matter of his pretended Christianity, we must assume that both details have been invented by Dante for some definite though as yet unknown purpose which would have to be taken into account in any final or reasonably complete interpretation of the relevant passages. It is likewise obvious that, in the total absence of independent witnesses, any such interpretation will have to be derived from the *Comedy* itself. Fortunately there is in Dante's text sufficient evidence to show that Statius had indeed been the victim of the vices to which he confesses, but not in the way in which one would normally have anticipated.

If we take a closer look at the matter we notice, first of all, that the initial letters of the four tercets in which Statius's avarice is described, V-L-O-E, form an acrostic spelling the word *velo* or "veil," a standard device employed by Dante to signal the existence of a covert meaning in the text.[11] We also observe that the first of these four tercets specifically adverts to the knowledge by which the doubtful or the amazing is rendered intelligible and thereby ceases to be an object of doubt or amazement: "Truly, things often take on appearances that excite false wonder because their true causes are hidden" (22, 28–30). The antithesis between the truth and its deceptive semblances is further accentuated by the manner in which the terms designating the true and the false—*veramente, falsa, vere*—are intertwined in the phrasing of the sentence. In typical Dantean fashion a correspondence has been established between the intention of the passage and its literary form.

There comes next a brief but equally mysterious statement in which Statius grossly misinterprets the following verse from the *Aeneid*: "To what (extreme of wickedness) dost thou not drive mortal hearts, accursed hunger for gold!"—*Quid non mortalia pectora cogis, / Auri sacra fames!* (3, 56). The exclamation is called forth by Aeneas's accidental discovery of the crime perpetrated by the Thracian king, Polymestor, a one-time ally of the Trojans who had later shifted his allegiance to the Greeks, treacherously murdered Priam's son, Polydorus, and confiscated the treasure entrusted to him by his father. Statius gives to Aeneas's words a meaning that is plausible if one takes the sentence by itself but which is clearly ruled out by the context and is in fact the very opposite of the one intended by Virgil. Instead of excoriating the loathsome desire for gold that lurks in the hearts of people, he laments the fact that it should have so little power over them. "Why," he says, "O blessed hunger for gold, dost thou not govern mortal appetite!" The misreading is all the more striking as Statius is at pains to explain that he has finally "understood" what Virgil wanted to say. The verb that he uses is *intendere*, which in the *Comedy* often signifies "to penetrate the hidden meaning of a text."[12] Since Dante had intimated on a previous occasion that he was cognizant of all the sordid details of the story,[13] one is loath to accuse him of inadvertence. The error in all probability is deliberate. Like the acrostic detected in the preceding verses, it points to the possibility that his own text could lend itself to more than one interpretation.

Assuming, as Virgil unmistakably does, that miserliness is not the characteristic vice of a "wise" poet, one is prompted to look for some other type of avarice or prodigality to which Statius could have succumbed. The nature of this new vice is perhaps not all that difficult to imagine. If a poet qua poet is called lavish or stingy, it is most likely to be in regard to what he has to say. The poet's coin, as everyone recognizes, is not gold or silver but words, and words, too, like money, can be dispensed or withheld inappropriately, along with the thought they convey. The little that is said about Statius in the *Comedy* suggests that, while there is no reason to suspect him of having been a spendthrift in the ordinary sense, he had fallen prey to a less common but no less important form of prodigality. As the author of two epic poems notable for their unabashed paganism —*lungamente mostrando paganesmo* (22, 91)—he may be said to have been prodigal in words, a defect from which in time he sought to cure himself, only to fall by reaction into the antipodal vice of taciturnity. Having once spoken too much, he ended up by saying too little and incurred the blame of thrift.

The suggestion, farfetched as it may sound at first hearing, becomes more credible when we consider the likely connection between the avarice gratuitously imputed to Statius by Dante and his presumed hidden Christianity. It could well be that the two fictions belong together and are intended to illumine each other. By shunning any open avowal of his newly found Christian faith, Statius practiced what was known in the Middle Ages as the "economy of truth," *oeconomia ueritatis*. His avarice is of a piece with, if not actually identical to, the "lukewarmness" (*tepidezza*) with which he reproaches himself in the same passage (22, 92). An ardent Christian would doubtless have been less fearful and more forth-right, even at the risk of his life. Not so with Statius. The subterfuge to which he resorted guaranteed his survival, but by the same token it robbed him of the one opportunity that he might have had of leading others to the truth. No one reading his poems would have learned anything about the Christian faith. His position is the exact opposite of that assigned to Virgil, who, "like one carrying his light behind him at night," showed the way to those who came after him but was unable to help himself (22, 67–9).

Our suspicion regarding Statius's verbal avarice and prodigality is confirmed in retrospect by the peculiar interplay of silence and speech with which the preceding canto had ended. Statius has just declared his unbounded esteem for Virgil but is as yet unaware that one of his interlocutors is that same Virgil, for the pleasure of whose personal acquaintance he would gladly have spent an extra year in purgatory (21, 100–2). Dante is about to reveal Virgil's identity but is restrained by a sign from his master and suddenly sees himself pulled in opposite directions by the two poets, one of them begging him to speak, the other urging him to remain quiet. Observing Statius's eagerness to know, Virgil finally relents and the disclosure takes place. What this playful and apparently idle tug of war signifies is not altogether clear. If we recall however that the composition of the *Comedy* exhibits a sequence of interlocking scenes that parallels the scheme of interlocking rhymed verses within each canto, we are given a hint as to its possible meaning. The otherwise unexplainable interlude is a subtle but direct anticipation of the next and crucial episode in the drama. Its function is to ready us for the curious blend of speech and silence or boldness and reserve which, as we have seen, constitutes the focus of the ensuing canto.

Even if, for the sake of argument, one were to grant the validity of the foregoing interpretation, one might feel that little has yet been done to dispel the obscurity in which the whole incident is shrouded. What does it matter after all that Statius should have been a coward who demonstrated his lack of courage by purposely withholding the truth about his conversion to Christianity? His role in the *Comedy* could still strike us as purely adventitious and add nothing to our understanding of either the internal structure or the doctrinal content of the poem. There is more to the story however. A moment's reflection will edge us closer to the reason that accounts for the lofty position to which Statius, a relatively minor poet compared to Virgil, is elevated at this critical juncture of Dante's voyage.

Statius's most obvious function is to serve, along with Virgil, as Dante's guide in the upper regions of purgatory. His role in this respect is analogous to the one that Virgil alone had fulfilled throughout the earlier part of the journey. But if such is the case, the composition of the poem is bound to impress us as strangely asymmetrical. Given Dante's fondness for symmetry, one would normally expect a third epic poet to assume the role previously discharged by the other two poets once the threshold of heaven is reached. No doubt Beatrice will be on hand to accompany Dante on the rest of his journey; but as a shadowy figure who cannot by any stretch of the imagination be thought to belong in the same category as Virgil and Statius, she hardly qualifies as the missing guide.

The key to the riddle is furnished in part by the positions which the three poets who travel together occupy in relation to one another and which Dante is always careful to note with the utmost precision. In the scenes that immediately follow the first encounter with Statius, both Virgil and Statius are shown leading the way and Dante, who is still in need of a guide, walks reverently behind them (22, 127; 24, 143). As they prepare to cross the wall of fire, the positions shift: Dante moves ahead of Statius and is portrayed comically as a goat between two shepherds, with Virgil in front and Statius bringing up the rear (27, 46–8 and 85–6). By the time they reach the end of purgatory a second change occurs and we notice that without much fanfare Dante has all of a sudden taken the lead (28, 82 and 145). The third canticle, it turns out, will not be without its epic poet, to wit, the author himself, who has now become so to speak his own guide. It is significant that at this moment Dante is referred to by name for the first and only time in the poem, and with particular emphasis at that, inasmuch as we are told that this was done out of necessity—*di necessità* (30, 63).[14]

In light of these observations and bearing in mind what was said earlier about Statius, we can at last address ourselves to the unresolved problem of the symbolic value attached to each of the three major poets. The simplest case is undoubtedly that of Virgil, the non-Christian who writes a non-Christian epic. The case of Statius, the poet par excellence of purgatory, is slightly more complex but no longer as bewildering as it once seemed to be, since on the basis of Dante's literary fiction he now stands for the Christian who produces what must likewise be described as a non-Christian epic. Dante's own case would appear to exhibit a simplicity analogous to that of Virgil, for one immediately thinks of him as a Christian who sets out to write a Christian epic. By this elementary procedure the symmetry that was originally thought to be lacking is restored and the three parts of the poem are adjusted to one another without any discernible hiatus. Or are they?

The only trouble with that explanation is that it again confronts us with an incomplete enumeration. One fascinating possibility has been tacitly passed over and thereby brought in a forceful if somewhat roundabout way to our attention, namely, the hypothetical case of the non-Christian who writes a Christian epic. At this point the reader is thrust in the situation of having to re-examine the various alternatives. Since neither Virgil's nor Statius's position appears subject to revision, Dante's own status is cast in a rather more dubious light. Could it be that he, too, felt the need to resort to a strategy similar to the one that he fancifully ascribes to Statius? It would be interesting to say the least if Dante, the author of the most famous Christian poem in our tradition, had slyly refused to pronounce himself on so crucial a matter.

Needless to say, the contention that the deeper layers of the *Comedy* leave room for doubt concerning the religious convictions of its author runs counter to the bulk of contemporary opinion and is apt to be greeted with a fair amount of skepticism by most readers. Even if it could be proved to everybody's satisfaction that Dante had reservations about the truth of the Christian faith, one wonders why he should have gone to such great lengths to veil his thought. We forget all too easily the severe restrictions imposed by the societies of the past on the public expression of ideas and opinions judged to be at odds with their most cherished beliefs. Statius's crypto-Christianity, which finds its rationale in the open hostility of the pagan rulers to the new Faith, has its parallel in the reticence displayed by his medieval counterpart, who lived at a time when heretics and apostates had since become liable to the harsh penalties once reserved for avowed Christians.

We know by now that there is at least one expedient to which a confirmed rebel can resort in order to avert a head-on collision with the established authority without abdicating his freedom or jeopardizing his power to act, and that is to conform in deed and speech to the conventions of the society in which he happens to live. By deftly covering his tracks he automatically creates a presumption of innocence in his favor and shifts the burden of proof to the offended party. From then on it is no longer up to him to exculpate himself but up to others to demonstrate his guilt. Even if he remains suspect, there is little likelihood of his being convicted; for it is virtually impossible to impeach someone for holding or propagating subversive views which he has never actually voiced and which, moreover, can be shown to be at variance with numerous other statements that he did make.

That Dante was keenly aware of the dangers that he faced is readily established from a variety of texts and allusions scattered throughout the *Comedy*. One of the literary devices that he utilizes in the *Purgatorio* consists in relating the seven deadly sins to the beatitudes of the Sermon on the Mount. Each time a "P" (for *peccatum*, "sin") is removed from the pilgrim's forehead, the corresponding beatitude is chanted in the background. No sooner has Dante undergone a series of tests calculated to rid him of, say, pride or anger than he is reminded of the blessedness promised to the "poor in spirit" or the "peacemakers" (cf. *Purg.*, 12, 110; 15, 38; 17, 68–69; 27, 8). In general the parallelism between sin and beatitude poses no major problem. The situation becomes a bit more complicated when we reach the fourth beatitude, "Blessed are those who hunger and thirst for righteousness," which the poet has split into two parts, one dealing with the "hungry" and the other with the "thirsty" (*Purg.*, 22, 6 and 24, 151–4). According to Grandgent, echoed by Singleton, the separation was necessitated by the desire to obtain the requisite number of beatitudes. Why that should be so is not all that evident, especially since by availing himself of all eight beatitudes Dante would already have ended up with one too many. It is more to the point to observe that in the process two other beatitudes have been silently dropped, the "meek" and the "persecuted," the praise of whose virtues would have been out of place in a discussion bearing precisely on the means by which one can escape oppression and persecution.

Nor is this all. The lacuna created by the omission of these two beatitudes is remedied by the addition of a new one, taken not from the Sermon on the Mount but from Psalm 31:1 (Vg.): "*Beati quorum tecta sunt peccata*, "Blessed are they whose sins are covered" (*Purg.*, 29, 3). The trick this time lies in the poet's having quietly suppressed the first part of the verse, which speaks not of the "covering" of one's sins but of their "remission": *Beati quorum remissa est iniquitas*. One is tempted to infer that Dante was more intent on not being caught than on being forgiven. It should be added at once that the veil which "covers" his own sins is not such as to preclude the possibility of their being uncovered by the wise, just, and sympathetic reader (cf. *Par.* 17, 104–5).

The same concern is evinced with even greater clarity in the famous Canto 17 of *Paradiso*, in which the course of the poet's life is foretold. The prophecy, oddly enough, is uttered, not by Beatrice, as we had first been led to expect (cf. *Inf.*, 10, 130–2), but by Dante's ancestor, Cacciaguida, to whom he simply refers as his "father." Dante has just listened to Cacciaguida's account of the internal strife that has long racked his native city and immediately proceeds to inquire about his own future, for which he rightly fears. The reason alleged is that if he is apprized beforehand of the misfortunes that lie ahead, he may find them easier to bear than if they were to fall upon him abruptly; for, as he says, "an arrow foreseen comes more slowly" (v. 27).

From Cacciaguida he learns first of all that he will be banished from Florence and experience the unremitting harshness of a life lived in exile (v. 48), He will discover for himself "how salty bread tastes in other people's houses and how hard the path leading up and down other people's stairs can be" (v. 58–60). He is also told that in his misery he will be able to count on the benefits of an unnamed savior whose noble deeds will bring about a reversal in people's fortunes and, finally, that notwithstanding the grave perils to which it is exposed "his life has a future far beyond the punishment of his enemies" (v. 97–8).

If this were the whole of Cacciaguida's prophecy we should have every reason to be disappointed, since practically all of the events referred to either had already come to pass or never materialized. The real burden of the prophetic speech, one surmises, lies elsewhere. It has to do neither with the known past nor the uncertain future but with that part of the future whose outlines may be discerned by a man of wise counsel. Hearing that his fame is assured, Dante is perplexed. Upon reflection, however, he gradually comes to understand that, once Florence is taken away from him, he must not "by reason of his songs" risk the loss of other cities that might still be open to him. The things that he has learned in the course of his journey, if he were to relate them, would most certainly arouse the antagonism of many of his hearers. The alternative is to remain silent; yet to do so would be to forego any chance of being remembered by posterity. A "timid friend of the truth" would have no trouble preserving his own life now, but only at the price of losing it among those "who will call this time ancient" (v. 118–20).

The effect of Dante's remarks is to elicit a smile of approval on the part of his illustrious ancestor. The opening lines of the canto had alluded ominously to the plight of Phaëton, whose failure to heed the advice of his father, the sun, was the occasion of his downfall. Only once Cacciaguida is convinced that his own advice will not be misused does he encourage Dante to lay all falsehood aside and reveal what he has seen. Some people will inevitably be offended by what he has to say, but if that should happen, they and not he will be the ones to suffer: "Let there be scatching where the itching is" (v. 129). His words, however bitterly resented, will provide a vital nourishment for those who can digest them and, without prejudice to his present sitaution, win him the acclaim of future generations.

Cacciaguida's obscure prophecy, inserted at the very center of the *Paradiso*, is a commentary on what Dante had previously described as "the art of coming back" (*Inf.*, 10, 49–51, 77, 81).[15] Its significance may be summed up by saying that if Dante wishes to avoid being persecuted for his impiety, he must accomodate his speech to the religious beliefs of his contemporaries, and if he has any hope of living beyond his time, he must in some subtle way let it be known that his own horizon is not defined by those beliefs. Therein lies the superiority of his "wisdom" to that of Statius. By steering a middle course between verbal avarice and verbal prodigality, the *Comedy* demonstrates the kind of "measure" that was still wanting in the works of his allegedly Christian predecessor. Unlike Statius, Dante cannot be blamed for saying too much or too little. He neither completely reveals nor completely conceals the inner depths of his thought. The strategem was doubly successful in that it enabled him not only to save himself and his reputation but at the same time to instruct others regardless of what their level of understanding, degree of preparedness, or personal dispositions may have been then or were likely to be in the centuries that followed.

Whether or not one accepts this general interpretation will depend in large measure on how well it squares with the rest of the poem and how much it contributes to the elucidation of its numerous and seemingly insoluble enigmas.[16] In the meantime, we have at least some evidence that Dante, who so oftern speaks of himself by indirection in the *Comedy*, had learned to wear the mask of orthodoxy, lifting it occasionally, to be sure, but only as much as was necessary to carry out his purpose. The history of the recovery of this ironic mode of communication is not without its own brand of irony. Having at last triumphed over the enemies by whom it had long been threatened from without, the Christian society of the Middle Ages will henceforth harbor in its midst an increasingly large number of thinkers bent on pursuing a course of action that would lead them further and further away from the path that clerical officaldom had marked out for itself. The adversary this time will be the more dangerous as he will be hidden within the ranks of the faithful and, so to speak, invisible to the naked eye.

What this strange adversary may have been like is hinted at in a variety of ways by Dante himself. Readers of the *Comedy* have long been puzzled by the presence among the blessed in *Paradiso*, Canto 20, of an obscure Trojan hero named Riphaeus, who, as it happens, is the only unconverted pagan to be canonized by the author. Riphaeus is of course praised for his exceeding righteousness in the *Aeneid*,[17] but there were other equally virtuous and more renowned pagans who could just as easily have been selected to illustrate the unfathomable mystery of divine predestination that the *Comedy* makes bold to explore at this point. What we notice is that, in addition to being just, Riphaeus was part of a small band of Trojans who, in the thick of the battle, disguised themselves as Greeks in order to fight against the Greeks.[18] Riphaeus's justice was not his only title to the eternal glory of Dante's heaven. It went hand in hand with a certain craftiness or duplicity similar to the one that would be used to good advantage by the new spiritual warriors of the late Middle Ages.

To speak of adversaries or warriors in this connection may not be wholly appropriate; for, unlike their early modern successors, the political writers of the Middle Ages never mounted a direct attack on Christianity and never tried to discredit it publicly. Most of them recognized both its grandeur and its usefulness and had no qualms about lending their support to it. In accordance with the tradition of classical antiquity whose spirit they sought to revive, they would have considered themselves amply rewarded if, by renouncing its worldly ambitions, the religion under which the West had lived for so long and with which it could not conveniently dispense were to become at once more spiritual and more humane.

Admittedly, the thesis defended in these pages oversimplifies matters and leaves untouched a number of equally important strata of the *Comedy*. If it should prove to be substantially correct, however, a Christian might well be tempted to write Dante off as an archvillain the study of whose works bodes nothing but ill for his faith. Yet to draw this conclusion would be to fall into an even greater oversimplification. It is certainly not a matter of chance that each of the three canticles of the *Comedy* ends with the word "stars" and that the work as a whole is brought to a fitting close with a reference to "the love that moves the sun and the other stars." The mood generated by this constant reminder of what is divine in the universe again invites a comparison with Pascal, "that strange Christian who did not find his Father in the heavens,"[19] whose modern eyes could no longer perceive anything splendid, lovely, or enchanting in a world that had lost its center along with its circumference,[20] and for whom the spectacle of the starry sky above was a source of frightened anguish rather than of serene wonder.[21] If the religious core of Dante's poem is to be discovered anywhere, it is in its concentration on the single most profound longing of the human soul, a longing once described by the author himself as "the inborn and perpetual thirst for the godlike kingdom" (*Par.*, 2, 19–20). To that longing the *Comedy* bears what is beyond the shadow of a doubt one of the most exquisite testimonies ever given. As such, it poses in all its force the problem to which, for a Christian, Christianity alone offers the ultimate answer.

The modern theologian is ordinarily inclined to view things in a rather different perspective. Chastened by a long history of religious feuds and pious cruelties, he is more likely to challenge Christianity's claim to exclusivism and demand the same measure of sympathetic consideration for all religions or at the very least all great religions. Whether this goal of universal sympathy is achievable and how much one stands to gain by pursuing it are nevertheless questions that bear careful scrutiny. The problem with which it confronts us from a confessional as well as from a nonconfessional viewpoint is that it not only tends to dilute the substance of the faith but precludes any genuine encounter between people of different religious persuasions. The seeming humility from which it draws its appeal necessitates a bracketing of one's attachment to one's beliefs in favor of a provisional espousal of another's attachment as one's own. To that extent it may be said to operate on the principle of an histrionic rather than a serious identification with the other. Like Descartes's methodical doubt, to which it bears an epistemological affinity, it must begin by negating what it seeks to preserve without being able to guarantee its subsequent retrieval. As a consequence, it inevitably misses what is most vital in the other, for only the totally committed person is in a position to appreciate the depth of someone else's commitment. Its end result would thus appear to be a subtle demotion of, and hence an implicit disrespect for, all religious positions. Upon close examination, it reveals itself as more superficial than profound, more arrogant then humble, and more provincial than truly universal.

Where Dante stood on this issue of belief versus unbelief will probably never be known with any degree of finality and is at best a matter of idle curiosity. What can be asserted with some assurance is that he himself took Christianity and its claim to truth more seriously than many and perhaps most of its latter-day advocates or critics and that he was painfully aware of all that was to be won or lost by embracing it or giving it up. For that reason if for no other, the probing of the *Comedy's* disquieting underside has more to teach us about what it means or once meant to be a Christian than any naive but comforting acceptance of its Christian surface. The faith to which such a probing can lead will be all the stronger as it is tempered in the blast furnace of the most searching critique to which it has ever been subjected.

Our own generation does not take well to the idea of an irreducible though possibly creative tension between revealed religion and philosophy of the kind that is adumbraded in the *Comedy*. It generally prefers either Etienne Gilson's attractive thesis, which collapses these two originally independent components of Western thought into the notion of a "Christian philosophy" (for the more broad-minded a "religious philosophy"), or else an older, "enlightened" theology, most familiar today in the guise of Tillich's concept of "ultimate concern," which obliterates the distinction between them altogether. The basic perplexities remain however. Against the first alternative one might urge, as Heidegger does, that the idea of a Christian philosophy is just another stillborn attempt to square the circle,[22] and against the second that, under pretense of transforming us into "rational Christians," the enlightened theology of the modern period has only succeeded in making us "extremely irrational philosophers," as Lessing predicted it would.[23]

The objection that was thought to compel the abandonment of the position taken by Dante is that it seemed to foreclose the possibility of a final reconciliation between biblical faith and philosophic reason. Even so, one is entitled to ask whether in the last analysis the unbelief occasionally engendered by that position is more offensive to the religious mind than such present-day forms of unbelief as respectful indifference or a kind of nostalgia for lost faith that goes hand in glove with the inability to distinguish between a theological truth and a pious myth.

Notes

1. Dante, *Epist.* VI. 2, 5–8, *Opere Minori*, ed. A. del Monte, (Milano: Rizzoli, 1960) pp. 764–65.
2. Ch. S. Singleton: *Dante Studies 2: Journey to Beatrice* (Cambridge, MA.: Harvard University Press, 1967), p. 7.
3. Cf. G. H. Putnam, *The Censorship of the Church of Rome* (New York: G. P. Putnam's Sons, 1909), II 308.
4. G. Boccaccio, *Life of Dante*, in F. Basetti-Sani ed., *The Earliest Lives of Dante* (New York: Frederick Ungar, 1963), pp. 74–75.
5. *Ibid.*, p. 50.
6. Dante, *Convivio*, II. 1, 9–15.
7. The point is acknowledged by Carne-Ross, who adds wistfully, *New York Review of Books*, (May 1, 1975), p. 6: "The trouble is that nothing in the *Comedy* is finally problematic …More than any other great work of the imagination, the *Comedy* confronts us with a world that is ordered and meaningful from top to bottom. A recurring phrase of Singleton's is 'It is no accident that…' One sometimes wishes it were. What Dante says in paradise, *'casual punto non puote aver sito'* (32, 53) is true of his poem as a whole: there is no place there for a particle of chance, for the randomness of things. No place, then, for the unexplained gift of the moment when, in Stevens's words, 'Life's nonsense pierces us with strange relation.' The relations are all there, plotted in advance, waiting only for reason to discover them or grace to reveal them."
8. R. S. Haller, *Literary Criticism of Dante Alighieri* (Lincoln, Nebraska: University of Nebraska Press, 1973) p. xxxix.
9. See, on the subject of irony, the remarks by J. Klein, *A Commentary on Plato's Meno* (Chapel Hill: The University of North Carolina Press, 1965), pp. 5–6.
10. An earlier and shorter version of the interpretation that follows was published under the title "Dante and Averroism," in *Actas del V Congreso Internacional de Filosofía Medieval*, (Madrid: Editora Nacional, 1979) II 739–46.
11. *Purg.*, 22, 28–39. The cryptogram follows the customary rules of the genre, which require that the proper order be restored by taking the first letter first (V), then the last (E), the second (L), and the next to the last (O). Cf. W. Arensberg, *The Cryptography of Dante* (New York: A. A. Knopf, 1921), p. 50.
12. Dante Alighieri, *La Divina Commedia*, edited and annotated by C. H. Grandgent, revised by Ch. S. Singleton, (Cambridge, MA: Harvard University Press, 1972), p. 506, *ad* v. 38.
13. Cf. *Purg.*, 20, 114–5.
14. Dante appears to be apologizing for speaking about himself in such a personal way in his own book, thus violating the rules of decorum; cf. *Convivio*, I, 2. Even as he does so, however, he manages to poke fun at the reader. The expression *di necessità* contains the poet's name in the form of a cryptogram, which is to be deciphered in accordance with the rule explained above: *D[i] NEcessiTA*. In the present case the Italian spelling of the letter "d" (*di*) has been used. We are told how to read the cryptogram by the accompanying verses, in which Dante, startled by the sound of his name, looks to the left and to the right, like the captain of a ship who rushes "aft and fore" (*di poppa in prora*) to see what the men of his crew are doing (30, 58–60). The poet puts himself forward again in the unusual rhyme scheme displayed in this passage. Of the fifteen verses that it comprises, twelve end in "a"; the remaining three, which stand out that much more prominently, end in *io*, the Italian "I."
15. The art in question is the theme of one of Boccaccio's stories, *Decameron*, III 7, which has sometimes been interpreted as a secret life of Dante.
16. For further details on this point see my *Dissidence et philosophie au moyen âge: Dante et ses antécédents*, (Montreal: Bellarmin, and Paris: Vrim, 1981), pp. 147f.

17. Virgil, *Aeneid*, II, 426–7. Riphaeus and his companions come upon this tactic accidentally when they are mistaken for Greeks by their opponents at nightfall.

18. *Ibid.*, II, 386–97.

19. P. Valéry, "Variation sur une pensée," in *Oeuvres*, (Paris: Gallimard, Bibliothèque de la Pléiade, 1957), I, 461.

20. Pascal, *Pensées*, frg. 199.

21. *Ibid.*, frg. 201.

22. M. Heidegger, *An Introduction to Metaphysics*, trans. R. Manheim (Garden City: Doubleday, 1961), p. 6.

23. G. E. Lessing, Letter to his brother Karl, 2 Feb., 1774, in *Gesammelte Werke*, ed., P. Rilla (Berlin: Aufbau Verlag, 1956), IX. 596–97.

2

JEFFERSON AND THE PRACTICE OF EMPIRE

David Tucker

IN THE EARLY YEARS OF THE REVOLUTIONARY WAR, WHEN JEFFERSON heard a rumor that Britain might seek peace or, as he put it, "come to her senses," he wrote to Benjamin Franklin, our representative in France, and to Richard Henry Lee, a delegate in Philadelphia, to describe what he thought we should get in a peace treaty.[1] Everyone knew that the peace terms would determine the future of the country. Jefferson and a few others understood that a vision of the country's future ought to decide the terms of the peace. Jefferson had already envisioned the country's future. When he looked out from Monticello he looked West and saw a Nation, a republic safe in the strength of its Union, spreading the blessings of equality and liberty. In his vision farmers occupied a preeminent position, for they were the most virtuous and independent men. Public and private happiness depended on their way of life dominating the republic.

With this vision of his country's future in mind, Jefferson planned the peace before the Revolutionary War had ended. He told Lee that we needed fishing rights off Newfoundland. Fishing was an important livelihood for northeasterners but principally important, according to Jefferson, as a nursery for seamen. We needed this training ground because America could never be simply an agrarian republic. Americans had commercial habits and Jefferson believed that the attempt to break these habits would be tyrannical.[2] Moreover, farmers needed to sell their surplus and acquire what they could not produce for themselves. Consequently, Jefferson instructed Lee that the United States ought to seek commercial relations with the countries of southern Europe. Our exports and theirs were complementary.

Jefferson's republic required more than a trained merchant marine and beneficial trade relations. If the republic lacked sufficient land to absorb its growing population, then the landless would crowd the cities, threatening republican government. The dependent and vicious "mobs of great cities add just so much to the support of pure government, as sores do to the strength of the human body."[3] To provide his republic with the land it needed, Jefferson turned his attention to the west early in his career. In 1779, while governor of Virginia, Jefferson wrote to the Spanish Governor of Louisiana—Spain having entered the struggle against Britain—about American interests in the Mississippi valley. He noted that despite war and the threat of Indian attack, people from the seaboard continued to move west of the mountains. Jefferson sketched a plan for supplying from New Orleans these people and the soldiers sent to protect them in return for goods that New Orleans would receive from the interior.[4] Jefferson wanted to protect and provide for the westerners because that would keep them attached to the original states and would keep the way to the west and the future open.[5] With western lands secured and a thriving commerce established, the republic would approach what Jefferson envisioned.

In the aftermath of the Revolutionary War, however, the future that Jefferson anticipated, and planned the peace to provide, remained far off. The country would have to struggle just to stay alive. Nothing makes clearer the difficult position in which the nation found itself in its early years than the Treaty of Paris of 1783 that brought to a close the War for Independence. The treaty established the boundaries of the United States, but each of the boundaries—at the Atlantic, the Great Lakes, the Mississippi, and along the 31st parallel between Georgia and the Floridas —was disputed in one way or another. The separate peace worked out between the United States and Britain gave the United States a boundary to the south at the 31st parallel and the right to navigate the Mississippi. Having received the Floridas from Britain as part of the general adjustment following the war, Spain was then not asked if the boundary that would separate the new republic from her Florida possessions could be set at the 31st parallel. Nor had Britain or the United States asked Spain about using the Mississippi, a river nominally controlled by the Spanish through their possession of New Orleans and the territory at the river's mouth. For her part, Britain granted Americans fishing rights off Newfoundland but, in deference to the interests of her fishermen, in language so vague that the status of these rights remained controversial. In addition, in order to satisfy her fur traders and to put pressure on the United States to fulfill its treaty obligation to restore Loyalist property, Britain refused to give up, as the treaty required, her forts in the Northwest Territory. Finally, no one was quite sure where to find the source of the Mississippi, which marked the northwest boundary of the United States, just as no one was quite sure where Maine ended and Canada began.

This list of obscurities and problems in the Treaty of Paris might make one doubt the intelligence of its drafters. In fact, the treaty was the result, at least on the American side, of both intelligence and cunning.

Its difficulties were only what one should expect given the situation in Europe. France had allied herself with the rebellious colonies because the alliance might allow her to damage her great rival Britain. France had lost her North American empire in 1763 at the conclusion of the Seven Years' War, but not her hope of recovering it. The rebellion in America offered France an opportunity to avenge herself and to serve her interests. Spain came to the aid, if one can call it that, of the new states with great reluctance. Republics and rebellion dismayed the Spanish court and Spain worried about antagonizing the British. But Spain wanted to regain British-controlled Gibraltar and to inhibit the growth of American and British power in North America, growing power she understood correctly to threaten her possessions in that part of the world and to the south.

France and Spain stood on common ground in the attempt to limit both American and British power in North America. France hoped to regain an empire and Spain to tighten a weakening grip on her own. Even as the war progressed, France looked to her own interests. The foreign minister Vergennes instructed his representative in the United States not to support American pretensions to Canada. If Canada remained in British hands the Americans would "feel to an even greater extent the need which they have for the ... [French] King."[6] Several years later the next French representative in America suggested to his superiors in France that the French should seize Cape Breton Island in order to give France a claim on fishing rights off Newfoundland, fishing rights that the French knew vitally interested the Americans. In order to draw the Spanish into the war against Britain, France ignored American demands about navigating the Mississippi, so worrying to Spain.

As diplomats, couriers, and secret agents scurried between Paris, London, and Madrid, John Adams and John Jay developed deep suspicions about the French and Spanish. Benjamin Franklin, the third of the American negotiators, trusted the French; but when contacted by a British agent about the possibility of a separate peace, Franklin responded favorably and notified Adams and Jay of the British offer. After Yorktown, the British looked to end the war and could do so most advantageously for themselves by separating the Americans from their allies. Better to contend with one set of demands than with two or three. The American envoys were compelled to seek a separate peace by evidence, some of it merely circumstantial, that Britain and France would reach agreement without consulting the United States.

In the United States, some indignation greeted the separate peace; many felt that such ingratitude to France was inexcusable. Yet the negotiators in Europe knew that the willingness of the French to sacrifice American interests excused the peace they made. France had served America well but could not sacrifice her vital interests for the sake of

America. For their part, the Americans could not allow their country to sacrifice its interests to advance those of France. The United States required independence along with boundaries and rights to make this independence safe. The Americans made their separate peace in order to make their newly independent country safe.

Jefferson aimed in the post-war settlement he planned for something more than safety. An understanding of happiness and good government guided his prescriptions for the peace treaty. But the conditions that he demanded in order to realize his vision of the country's future were also demanded by national security. Jefferson and everyone else knew that the security, indeed the very survival, of the union required that the peace treaty protect the original colonial boundaries and provide Americans the right both to navigate the Mississippi and to fish off Newfoundland. The livelihood of the northeastern states depended in part on this fishing. If it were not secured, the New England states might seek a separate peace of their own. The geography of eastern North America made the right of navigating the Mississippi a necessity.

The original states clustered along the eastern seaboard. At varying distances from the coast rose mountains that ran parallel with the coast the length of the states. In the eighteenth century, these mountains posed a formidable obstacle. Several gaps and a few rivers cut through them but they presented a barrier nonetheless. Neither British orders not to settle on the western side of the mountains nor the threat of Indian attack had prevented settlement. As the population west of the mountains grew and as that population struggled past the level of subsistence, it required an outlet for its excess crops and a means to acquire what it could not produce for itself. The passage to the East across the mountains was difficult and expensive, the passage down the Mississippi less so. Navigation of the Mississippi thus became vital to the interests of the westerners.

In 1783, when the Treaty of Paris was being negotiated, the principal areas of western settlement were Kentucky and Tennessee, the former a part of Virginia and the latter a part of North Carolina. Georgia also had claims on western lands. Thus the fate of the westerners was of paramount interest to the southern states. Just as northerners tested the ability of the Confederation government to protect their interests by how well that government protected the fisheries, so southerners tested the ability of that government to protect their interests by how well it protected the navigation of the Mississippi.

The union of the states under the Articles of Confederation probably would not have survived the sacrifice of fishing rights or navigation of the Mississippi. Thus recognition of independence, navigation of the Mississippi, and fishing rights became the requirements of a treaty to end the war of independence. Through cunning and compromise the negotiators achieved these minimum conditions. Yet the new republic was so weak and its interests so little anyone else's that the achievement of these minimum conditions could not help but be precarious. Struggling with the problems bequeathed by the treaty that granted us independence, the foreign policy of the American Founding sought to render our newly acquired independence less precarious and the young Union more secure.

The problems were tremendous. Great Britain granted us independence with bitterness and resentment, determining that we must remain as commercially dependent on her as we had before the Revolution. The British restricted our trade where they could, impressed our seamen, and held onto territory the Treaty of Paris had granted us. But British hostility to the United States was tempered by a grudging yet growing awareness that our markets were vital to her economy and American supplies to her military. After the revolution in France, Britain entered the final episode of her century-long struggle with her great continental rival. War broke out between the two countries in 1793. Under these circumstances American markets and supplies became all the more important to Britain. At first, the necessities of war impelled the British to harsh measures against those trading with the French, measures that harmed Americans most of all. In addition, the British appeared to be responsible for a treaty between her client Portugal and Algiers that would have freed the Barbary pirates to prey upon American shipping. At approximately the same time, the British governor of Lower Canada sent troops toward Detroit in order to pre-empt what he considered aggressive movements by Americans in the Ohio Valley, and another British official addressed an Indian delegation suggesting to them that a war was imminent and that they would have lands returned to them from the Americans when the British won.

War did indeed seem imminent, but it did not break out. Alexander Hamilton suggested a diplomatic solution and John Jay was dispatched to Britain. The British, for their part, recognized American anger and changed course. They did not want a war with America while fighting the French, and they needed American markets. Even before Jay arrived, they eased the most severe restrictions on trade, disavowed the provocative actions of British officials in Canada, and proclaimed their innocence in the Portugal-Algiers affair. The result of this change of attitude was Jay's Treaty. The treaty removed two of the greatest irritants in Anglo-American relations by providing for British evacuation of the northwest territory and for some compensation for damages done by the British navy. But the treaty said nothing about impressment, or new commercial arrangements, or repaying southerners for slaves stolen during the revolutionary war; nor did it say anything to ease the fears of westerners that the British would intrigue with the Indians in the future

as they had in the past. Moreover, the treaty accepted British interpretations of neutral rights and freedom of the seas. The Americans thus,
as one historian has put it, "acquiesced in Britain's war of attrition
against France."[7]

Many condemned the treaty because it would alienate the French
and for very little in return from the British. Washington reluctantly
signed it in August 1795, feeling as did Hamilton that it was the best we
could expect and that to avoid war with Britain was more important than
to avoid irritating France. Irritate the French is just what the treaty did,
acquiring British friendship at the price of French enmity. Not wishing
to fight the French, the Americans sent a delegation to France, but it did
not offer what the French considered amends for Jay's Treaty. The
French met the delegation with a request for a loan and bribes. When
news of the mistreatment of the American delegation reached the
United States, the affront to national honor produced a cry for war. War
was not declared because President Adams eventually judged it unwise
and suspected the French did not want it. Reverses in their continuing
war with England led the French to seek renewed negotiations. Adams
responded by sending representatives to France.

The result of these discussions was the Convention of Mortefontaine.
By this convention, signed on September 30, 1800, the United States
officially absolved itself of ties to France dating to the American
Revolution. By the time the convention moved through the channels of
the American government to the President, John Adams no longer held
the office. The election of 1800 put Jefferson in the White House and
although he had long been the champion of France, he did not attempt
to block the dissolution of our ties to France. Jefferson recognized that
the United States, if it were to survive, had to disentangle itself from
European politics. Jefferson originally had high hopes for the Revolution
in France but its course toward the tyranny of Napoleon encouraged him
to turn his back on Europe. Commerical relations were necessary but
alliances were not. In his first inaugural, stating his "political creed" and
echoing the sentiments of Washington's Farewell Address, Jefferson
declared "peace, commerce, and honest friendship with all nations
—entangling alliances with none."

Jefferson's hopes for America as he took office rested in part, as he
put it in his inaugural, on America's kind separation "by nature and a
wide ocean from the exterminating havoc of one quarter of the globe."
Jay's Treaty and the Convention of Mortefontaine had done much to
improve our security; but if Americans were separated from the
exterminating havoc of one quarter of the globe, they were not separated
from that quarter's threatening conspiracies. British Canada lay to the
north and her agents moved about the United States, as did those of
France. Spain contributed her share to the conspiracies, in defense of her
territory to the south and west of the new union.

Until Vermont joined the Union in 1791, the British tried to use the discontent of Vermonters, generated by the Federal government's inability to declare Vermont independent of the several states that claimed its territory, to attach Vermont's sympathies to Canada. After Jay's Treaty, conspiracies by the British aimed directly at the United States ceased. Yet the British pursued other conspiracies unfriendly to American interests. The British intrigued with United States Senator William Blount to seize Louisiana, which would have given them control over America's western commerce. Although the British government denied knowledge of the conspiracy, the British minister to the United States knew of it, and Blount had communicated with Whitehall.[8]

Having given up Louisiana in 1763, the French had no official place in North America but desired one. Their hopes may have been unfounded and their plans unlikely to succeed but still they hoped and planned. For instance, in response to Jay's Treaty, the French in 1796 sent a general, Victor Collot, on a "scientific expedition" to the Mississippi. Along the way, the general stopped to inquire how the people liked the government in Washington and to survey the terrain for military purposes. He reported that the French in St. Louis were loyal to France and that many non-French inhabitants west of the mountains were disaffected from the United States.[9] He also offered his superiors a lesson in geopolitics, instructing them that "when two nations possess, one the coast and the other the plains, the former must inevitably embrace or submit." He then applied this principle to North America. "I conclude [that] the western stages of the North American republic must unite themselves with Louisiana and form [in] the future one single compact nation."[10] To this nation under French control, according to Collot's geopolitical analysis, the original states on the coast would have to submit.

Collot's trip and its purpose were known to American officials but other French plans were not. On the day after France and the United States signed the Convention of Mortefontaine, which ended the Quasi-War, France signed in secret a treaty with Spain that gave France Louisiana. Shortly after this signing, an article appeared in the semi-official *Gazette de France* arguing that Fench possession of Louisiana would be a "counterpoise to the domination of the United States," a country that threatened "to rule over the new world, and to place under its yoke all [of France's valuable] West-India colonies."[11] This article was reprinted in the United States in 1802 and confirmed American fears about French-intentions in North America.

Although the weakest of the three European powers with an interest in North America, the Spanish were not outdone by the British or French when it came to conspiring against the interests of the United States. The Spanish feared the ever increasing numbers of Americans in the Mississippi valley. The Americans had even pushed across the

Mississippi to trade with the Indians in defiance of Spanish restrictions. The Americans controlled the commerce of New Orleans, giving the town an increasingly American character. In response to this growing American power, the Spanish did what they could. In 1784 they closed the Mississippi to Americans. The Spanish did not rest with this measure. They sought out Indians to the north and east of New Orleans and organized them into a confederacy to resist American expansion. The Spanish representative to the Federal government pursued a policy of divide and conquer by offering northeastern merchants trading advantages in Spanish ports if they would support self-imposed restrictions on United States use of the Mississippi. The resulting battles between the northern and western sections of the United States, Spain thought, would help secure the Spanish position in Louisiana. In addition, the Spanish did what they could to entice Kentucky and Tennessee into the Spanish empire. James Wilkinson, who had been a general in the Revolutionary War, secretly entered Spanish service at this time and remained a Spanish agent for many years. He agitated for statehood in Kentucky, hoping to frustrate Kentuckians enough when this was refused to make them look favorably on Spanish protection and offers of free use of the Mississippi.

These various Spanish measures and intrigues proved unavailing, primarily because of American commercial power. New Orleans could no longer survive without the goods that came down the Mississippi, and if they could not come down legally they would just have to come down illegally, and so they did. The Spanish recognized this and in 1788 opened the river to Americans in a restricted manner. Spain had not given up her hopes of containing the Americans in order to isolate her empire from the spreading contagion of republicanism. What Spain could do in this regard was limited, however, by her lack of power. When the United States and Britain began negotiating what eventually became Jay's Treaty, Spain feared an Anglo-American attack on her territories and attempted to placate the United States. In Pinckneys's Treaty, Spain accepted the boundary between Georgia and the Floridas at the 31st parallel, where it remains to this day; granted navigation of the Mississippi; and promised to leave the Indians alone. With Pinckney's Treaty Spain tacitly acknowledged her weakness in North America, including her inability to protect her South American possessions from the expanding North American republic. Ultimately Spain attempted to protect her American empire with a French buffer. Thus, at San Ildefonso, one day after the French signed the Convention of Mortefontaine ending the Quasi-War with the United States, France accepted Louisiana from Spain. In exchange, Spain received a small Italian kingdom.

In his first inaugural address, Jefferson spoke of Americans "possessing a chosen country, with room enough for our descendants to the thousandth and thousandth generation." By treaty and, Jefferson would say, by right Americans did possess their territory. But those treaties and that right ran counter to the interests of other nations, two of them among the most powerful on earth, who saw in North America a chance to increase their power. In addition, Spain saw in North America a chance to build a buffer between the United States and the rest of her empire. Amid the clash of these interests, claims of right would not be heard. Indeed, to secure favorable boundaries and navigation of the Mississippi, the United States had ignored the treaty rights of France and Spain.

Everyone involved in the contest for North America—the British, the French, the Spanish, and the Americans—realized the importance of controlling the Mississippi and New Orleans. General Collot's analysis was correct. Whoever controlled New Orleans would control North America and the states on the eastern seaboard; whoever controlled New Orleans would acquire a territory of great wealth and thus a great accession of power. This was the prize for which the European powers contended and which involved them in our affairs even if, as was true of Jefferson, we did not wish to be involved in theirs.

Shortly after his inaugural, Jefferson knew that he could not help becoming entangled with the European powers. By May 1801, Jefferson had learned that the Spanish had given Louisiana back to the French by the previously secret Treaty of San Ildefonso, although the retrocession would not become official until October 15, 1802. Jefferson understood that this changed the situation in North America. The Spanish were a weak declining power; the French a strong and growing one, led by a man who had destroyed a republic. French control of Louisiana threatened the vital interests of the United States and could not be ignored. For example, the French did not announce until November 1802 that they would abide by the terms of the Spanish-American treaty governing navigation of the Mississippi. Moreover, a French force arrived at Santo Domingo in the Caribbean in January 1802 to suppress a revolt against French rule. Rumors reached Jefferson through diplomatic channels that the suppression of the revolt had been undertaken with a large force because the French planned to use Santo Domingo as a base for their occupation of Louisiana. In March 1802, the French and British achieved a precarious peace, which freed Napoleon to involve himself in North America. In April, Napoleon gave orders to prepare an expedition to Louisiana. Fighting on Santo Domingo continued through 1802, as did preparations for the French expedition. Not until October 1802, however, did a crisis occur. On the eighteenth day of that month, the Spanish suddenly terminated the right of deposit that Americans had enjoyed at New Orleans. American goods could still move through the port; but, following the events in Europe and on Santo Domingo, the closing of the deposit looked ominous.

War and the forcible seizure of New Orleans was the response many Americans demanded to this year-long series of events involving Louisiana. Jefferson prepared for war but deplored its possibility. By temper and principle devoted to peace, Jefferson knew in addition that in the circumstances he faced war was most likely to ruin all he strove to establish. The Federalists cried for war. Jefferson feared that they might take advantage of it to regain power, an ascendancy that in his opinion would threaten republican government. The outcome of the war, of course, no one could foretell. Would the British sit idly by? Would not the war present them golden opportunities in North America? Jefferson contemplated an alliance with Britain, writing to Robert Livingston, his representative in France, that should France take "possession of New Orleans...from that moment we must marry ourselves to the British fleet and nation."[12] This alliance, if more than a bluff on Jefferson's part, might have assured a favorable outcome to the war; but would the stronger partner have acceded to the post-war demands of the weaker or respected its rights?

War promised greater harm than good, so Jefferson pursued peace. Abroad he threatened war; at home he advised peace but prepared for the worst. His plan was to buy time, maneuver into as favorable a position as circumstances permitted, and take advantage of the uncertain situation in Europe. After threatening France with war he suggested compromise and a purchase of New Orleans. He used his party's majority and its organization in the House and Senate to parry partisan thrusts and appointed as special envoy to France James Monroe, a man esteemed by westerners, the men most directly threatened by events in Louisiana. This appointment both gained him public support and moderated public opinion.

In time, Jefferson's use of threats and diplomatic initiatives with both France and Spain combined with events to grant him the end he pursued. On April 20, 1803 the Spanish announced renewal of the deposit at New Orleans. On July 3, 1803 Jefferson received news that Monroe and Livingston had agreed to purchase all of Louisiana. The *National Intelligencer*, a newspaper friendly to Jefferson, made the news public, as was fitting, on July 4.

On October 21, Jefferson proclaimed the Louisiana Treaty the law of the land, bringing the republic closer to what he had envisioned twenty-five years before. For 15 million dollars the United States had purchased from France land that doubled its existing territory. The future states of Louisiana, Arkansas, Missouri, Iowa, Oklahoma, Kansas, Nebraska, North and South Dakota, and parts of Minnesota, Colorado, Wyoming, and Montana were carved out of this acquisition, which gave to the United States wealth upon which it still lives. Robert Livingston said at the treaty's signing that "from this day the United States take their place among the powers of the first rank." Time would prove Livingston right. The purchase did not at once solve all the problems the young country faced; indeed, it created some that future generations struggled to resolve. Yet the purchase did assure our safety which, in the words of John Jay, is first "among the many objects to which a wise and free people find it necessary to direct their attention"[13] because it makes possible everything else.

Jefferson's diplomatic efforts were skillful but chance was his great ally. The renewed war between France and Britain, which kept Napoleon occupied in Europe; the resistence of the former slaves on Santo Domingo; the malaria that decimated the French troops there—all of these chance events that forced Napoleon to give up Louisiana made possible the success of Jefferson's statecraft. In another sense, however, the purchase of Louisiana was far from a chance event. All of the principal actors in our early national history, whatever may have been their differences on other points, recognized the importance of the Mississippi and of Louisiana. Leading American statesmen, Jefferson among them, were thus prepared to have Louisiana and simply awaited their chance. In this sense, chance did not dominate the Louisiana Purchase. Rather, chance merely supplied the means that men seized to achieve their carefully conceived ends.

A leading historian of our early national history has censured Jefferson's acquisition of Louisiana, noting that "the Jeffersonian concept of empire did not emerge suddenly or haphazardly a full-blown success. It reflected a well-developed expansionist tradition and a conscious vision of a national future."[14] Whether Jefferson's practice of empire merits censure we must yet consider. What is indisputable is that Jefferson did have a carefully thought out vision of an American empire.

Both the detail and grandeur of Jefferson's imperial vision are evident in the only book he wrote, *Notes on the State of Virginia*, begun during the Revolutionary war and published in 1787. In the second query or chapter of that book, Jefferson described Virginia's rivers. As is often the case in this book, in query 2 he expanded the meaning of Virginia. Jefferson began with the rivers that emptied into the Atlantic along Virginia's coast and then proceeded westward, not stopping until he had described the Mississippi and Missouri. Throughout his description, Jefferson emphasized the distance the rivers were navigable, whether they could be opened for navigation, and whether canals or portages could connect them to other rivers. Jefferson noted the confluence of a river and a body of water important for navigation and commerce. He reported that the Illinois ran into lake Michigan and the Kaskaskia into the Mississippi. He noted that a short portage connected the Tanisee with the "river Mobile, which runs into the Gulf of Mexico."

Jefferson, in the second query of *Notes on Virginia*, as John Jay would do in the second number of *The Federalist*, described an intracontinental waterway. The waterway did not exist outside Jefferson's description, but as described it showed that America had the potential for extensive commercial connections. The rivers of the east reached out to the west and with man's help could break the barrier of the mountains and unite east with west. Jefferson knew that men in New York and Pennsylvania already planned to open waterways to the west. Jefferson recognized that this commercial connection would secure the political ties upon which the safety of the Union depended.

Only when Jefferson turned to the discussion of the Missouri did the grandeur of his vision become apparent. Jefferson knew little about the river, except for the area immediately adjacent to its confluence with the Mississippi. His ignorance is evident in his suggestion that at some point the waters of the Missouri and the North River, or as we know it, the Rio Grande, flowed near each other. In fact, they are separated at their nearest point by about 700 miles. But the point here is not Jefferson's ignorance but his speculation about how easily the Missouri and the North River, like eastern rivers better known to him, might be connected. The North River passes through Santa Fe in what is now New Mexico. Jefferson stated the distance from the mouth of the Ohio to Santa Fe and then calculated the distance by river from Santa Fe to New Orleans and from New Orleans by road to Mexico City. Jefferson's vision of empire encompassed territory that would not achieve statehood until 125 years after his book was published.

Given the extent of Jefferson's vision, what are we to make of his mention of Mexico City? In 1786, Jefferson wrote a correspondent that rumors that the inhabitants of Kentucky wished to separate from the union worried him. Jefferson claimed that the limits of the nation were "not too large for good government." Jefferson continued by remarking that "our confederacy must be viewed as the nest from which all America, North and South, is to be peopled." He argued that Spain was the best proprietor until our population grew because she was the weakest European power. "My fear is that [the Spanish] are too feeble to hold them till our population can be sufficiently advanced to gain it from them piece by piece."[15]

As early as 1783, Jefferson contemplated the exploration of the vast territory that should one day belong to the United States. He heard that some people in England planned an expedition from the Mississippi to the Pacific. In a letter to George Rogers Clark, who had commanded Virginia's forces in the west during the Revolution, Jefferson wrote that "they pretend [the expedition] is only to promote knowledge. I am afraid they have thoughts of colonising into that quarter....How would you," Jefferson asked Clark, "like to lead such a party?"[16] The expedition, of course, did not occur until twenty years later and then it was Clark's younger brother William who travelled, under the command of Merriweather Lewis, to the Pacific. But this letter shows that the Lewis and Clark expedition, like the Louisiana purchase, fulfilled an intention formed early in Jefferson's public career. Jefferson did indeed have a well-developed vision of empire.

Jefferson was content to realize this vision of empire piece by piece: the Mississippi now, Santa Fe later. He expressed the principles that guided his creeping imperialism in a letter to James Monroe. The empire must grow only by doing justice to each of its parts, northeast, south, and west. Jefferson told Monroe that the best way to promote the true interest of the United States was to make "all the just claims of our fellow citizens, wherever situated, our own." This demanded exercising "a just government in their concerns and making common cause even where our separate interests would seem opposed to theirs. No other conduct," Jefferson concluded, "can attach us together; and on this attachment depends our happiness."[17]

The safety of the Union required the attachment of its parts one to another and this attachment made possible the happiness of the Union. In speaking of happiness, Jefferson had in mind the peaceful co-existence of the parts but also the happiness of the people who populated the Union. Jefferson's grand imperial designs served the simple farmers. Living on the land his imperialism provided they would dominate the United States, strengthen its governments, and find for themselves the best life available to man. Jefferson's empire was the new order of the ages because it served not the appetites of tyrannical kings, scheming clergy, and warring nobles but the happiness of common men. Jefferson's foreign policy, of which the Louisiana Purchase is the highest achievement, sought first to procure safety but ultimately to provide happiness.

We may now ask whether Jefferson's imperial designs deserve censure. Certainly the Spanish thought so. The Spanish ambassador to France before the purchase of Louisiana once commented that the United States is born a pigmy. A day will come when it will be a giant, even a colossus, formidable in these countries.... In a few more years we shall watch with grief the tyrannical existence of this same colossus."[18] One must admit that the Spanish ambassador had reason to complain. In the treaty of 1783 we simply presumed that the Spanish would give us the rights we demanded. As a people, if not as a government, we ignored Spanish attempts to limit our influence in the Mississippi valley. When the Spanish tried to organize the Indians against us, we undersold the British who were to supply the Indians and thus turned our enemies into our customers. We scurried across the Mississippi and down into Texas looking for a good deal and soon controlled commerce in New Orleans. Not all of our onslaught had such a peaceful aspect. At one point, the

Spanish representative in the United States halted his efforts to convince the northeast votes in Congress to sacrifice control of New Orleans for a favored position in Spanish ports because he feared what the frontiersmen might do if he succeeded. He did not care to bring on his fellow country-men in Louisiana what he called "the vexations of such a naturally robust people, trained to war and accustomed to the last degree of hardships."[19] No doubt this description of the frontiersmen would have gratified Jefferson. To the Spanish, however, the Americans must have looked like a gang of thieves ready to beat their rivals in a business deal or in a fight, whichever was easier, and ready to steal what, according to international law, belonged to Spain.

Were the Spanish right? Did Jefferson's vision of empire deserve censure? Jefferson penned documents that provide a defense of his imperialism and the principle of right upon which it rested. In 1793 Jefferson set down his thoughts on whether the United States ought to honor its treaties with France. Men were obliged to keep their agreements by the moral law and the same law obliged the nations composed of these individuals to keep theirs. Yet the obligation was not absolute. "When performance...becomes *impossible,* non-performance is not immoral. So if performance becomes *self-destructive* to the party, the law of self-preservation overrules the laws of obligation to others."[20]

Between nations the right of self-preservation ruled. To follow it was not immoral and Jefferson followed it in building his empire. The boundaries of Louisiana were open to interpretation and Jefferson pressed them east and west—particularly to the east, so that control of Mobile and the rivers that emptied into its bay would pass to the United States. Spain claimed this land, but the same necessity that compelled America to control New Orleans compelled us to control Mobile. Spain was weak; and when war erupted in Europe, Jefferson was sure that he would get what the country needed. We will "push [our claims] strongly with one hand, holding out a price in the other" and "obtain the Floridas...In the meanwhile, without waiting for permission, we shall enter into the exercise of the natural right we have always insisted on with Spain, to wit, that of a nation holding the upper part of streams, having a right of innocent passage through them to the ocean. We shall prepare [Spain] to see us practice on this, and she will not oppose it by force."[21]

However indefeasible and legitimate the claims of self-preservation, they did not exhaust Jefferson's understanding of natural right. A gang of thieves could appeal to the natural right of self-preservation; but the United States pursued a noble end. In 1780 Jefferson wrote to George Rogers Clark instructing him to launch a preventive attack against a rumored massing of British and Indian forces on the western frontier. If the expedition succeeded, wrote Jefferson, it would prevent "the dangerous extension" of British Canada and, he concluded, would "add to the Empire of Liberty an extensive and fertile country thereby converting dangerous enemies into valuable friends."[22] Jefferson's empire was to be an empire of liberty that converted enemies into friends. Through that aim it acquired the sanction of nature, for as God created men equal, he created them free. Equal and free men, respecting each other's rights, could become friends. Jefferson's empire aimed to provide for the safety of its citizens and their freedom and happiness as well.

Jefferson's vision, unlike the designs of thieves, reached to the happiness of all men and elevated his empire above the necessities it carefully respected. More than once Jefferson proclaimed that the American Revolution had been fought for all men. Like Lincoln after him, Jefferson understood that the Declaration held out the hope that "in due time the weights should be lifted from the shoulders of all men, and that *all* should have an equal chance."[23] "That we should wish to see the people of other countries free, is as natural, and at least as justifiable," Jefferson wrote Albert Gallatin, "as that one king should wish to see the kings of other countries maintained in their despotism."[24] When minister to France Jefferson suggested that John Adams, who was minister to Britain, propose that Britain and the United States grant reciprocal rights of citizenship. If the British agreed, then their citizens in America would have full rights of citizenship, as would American citizens in Britain. Jefferson hoped to establish such reciprocal arrangements with other countries. "As the circle of friendship widened, men would truly become citizens of the world."[25] Although Adams did not follow Jefferson's suggestion and Jefferson did not pursue it, his suggestion shows that Jefferson did indeed intend the Empire of Liberty to grow by turning enemies into friends.

Jefferson understood the ground of friendship and peace among men. The "peculiar character" of an idea "is that no one possesses the less, because every other possesses the whole of it. He who receives an idea from me, receives instruction himself without lessening mine; as he who lights his taper at mine, receives light without darkening me."[26] While the republic of letters could remain at peace, more material republics could not.[27] Even though it did so with justification and with the hope of extending justice to all, the American republic could grow only by darkening the light of others. This was a melancholy circumstance. The Declaration of Independence directed the republic beyond its borders toward justice for the men of all nations but at each of the young republic's borders stood an implacable foe. Committed to the rights of man and the freedom and happiness of all men, Jefferson, directed by stern necessity, often had to settle for less.

His republic's relationship to the rest of mankind displayed at once both the heights of Jefferson's aspiration and the limits to what men could do. For example, Jefferson would have preferred to treat benevolently the Indians—so easily our enemies and subject to dangerous foreign influences—to civilize them, to convert them to friends and to absorb them into the growing Empire of Liberty. But circumstances would not allow this. In his second inaugural Jefferson said that "endeavors to enlighten [the Indians] on the fate which awaits their present course of life, to induce them to exercise their reason, follow its dictates, and change their pursuits with the change of circumstances, have powerful obstacles to encounter; they are combated by the habits of their bodies, prejudice of their minds, ignorance, pride, and the influence of interested and crafty individuals among them." Faced with these obstacles and with the prejudices of whites, Jefferson was often reduced to such devices—one might be tempted to call them Machiavellian—as encouraging government trading houses among the Indians with the intention of burdening them with a debt that they could repay only with the exchange of their lands.[28]

Part of Jefferson's greatness lay in his distaste both for the necessity that compelled the use of such devices and for the devices themselves. He often voiced a preference, which seems to have been sincere, for a realm apart from such necessities where "we ride," as he once put it, "serence and sublime, above the concerns of this mortal world, contemplating truth and nature, matter and motion, the laws which bind up their existence and that eternal being who made and bound them up by these laws."[29] An equal part of Jefferson's greatness is that he did not remain in this distant realm, this republic of the mind, or allow it to blind him to the concerns of this mortal republic and its necessities. To this we owe the Louisiana Purchase and much else that continues to benefit us to this day.

We should depart from this discussion of the Louisiana Purchase with this sobering thought. While the purchase provided us with security and set us on the road to national greatness, it set in motion forces that could have destroyed that greatness. Into much of the land secured by the purchase moved slave owners. As their power grew, the character of the republic Jefferson did so much to found and protect came into question and made necessary a battle over slavery. It was not Jefferson's task, perhaps it was beyond his ability, to conduct this battle. The task fell to Lincoln who, within the security first provided by Jefferson's attention to necessity and on the basis of Jefferson's words, fought the decisive battle of our domestic policy and insured that Jefferson's republic would remain an empire of liberty.

Notes

1. Jefferson (hereafter TJ) to Benjamin Franklin, August 13, 1777, *The Papers of Thomas Jefferson*, ed. Julian P. Boyd (Princeton: Princeton University Press, 1950–), I, 26–27; TJ to Richard Henry Lee, August 30, 1778, ibid., II, 210–211.

2. TJ to John Jay, August 3, 1785, ibid. VIII, 426 and *Notes on the State of Virginia*, ed. William Peden, (New York: W. W. Norton and Co., 1972), p. 175.

3. Peden, p. 165.

4. TJ to Bernardo de Galvez, November 8, 1779, Boyd, III, 168.

5. TJ to James Madison, December 20, 1787, ibid. XII, 442.

6. Quoted in Lawrence S. Kaplan, *Colonies into Nation: American Diplomacy, 1763–1801* (New York: MacMillan, 1972), p. 119.

7. Ibid, p. 247.

8. J. Leitch Wright, Jr., *Britain and the American Frontier, 1783–1815* (Athens: University of Georgia Press, 1975), pp. 108–17.

9. R. R. Palmer, *The Age of the Democratic Revolution*, (Princeton: Princeton University Press, 1964), II, 517.

10. Kaplan, p. 257.

11. Quoted in Alexander DeConde, *This Affair of Louisiana*, (New York: Scribner, 1976), p. 102.

12. TJ to Robert Livingston, April 18, 1802, in *The Portable Thomas Jefferson*, ed. Merrill D. Peterson (New York: The Viking Press, 1975), p. 486.

13. Alexander Hamilton, James Madison, John Jay, *The Federalist*, ed. Jacob E. Cooke, (Middletown: Wesleyan University Press, 1961), pp. 13–14.

14. DeConde, p. 249.

15. TJ to Archibald Stuart, January 25, 1786, Boyd, IX, 218.

16. TJ to George Rogers Clark, December 4, 1783, ibid VI, 371.

17. TJ to James Monroe, August 11, 1786, ibid. X, 223–224.

18. Kaplan, p. 168.

19. Ibid, p. 170.

20. Jefferson's "Opinion on the French Treaties," April 28, 1793, *The Writings of Thomas Jefferson*, ed. Andrew A. Lipscomb and Albert Ellery Bergh, (Washington, D. C.: Issued under the Auspices of the Thomas Jefferson Memorial Association, 1905), III, 228 (emphasis in original).

21. TJ to John Breckenridge, August 12, 1803, *Portable Jefferson*, p. 495.

22. TJ to George Rogers Clark, December 25, 1780, Boyd, IV, 237–38.

23. Abraham Lincoln, "Speech in Independence Hall, Philadelphia, Pennsylvania," February 22, 1861, *The Collected Works of Abraham Lincoln*, ed. Roy P. Basler, (New Brunswick, N.J.: Rutgers University Press, 1953), IV, 240 (emphasis in original).

24. TJ to Albert Gallatin, June 16, 1817, Lipscomb and Bergh, XV, 132.

25. Merrill D. Peterson, *Thomas Jefferson and the New Nation*, (New York: Oxford University Press, 1970), pp. 309–10. Cf. Plato, *Republic*, 335d, 375c, 469b-471b 443d-3; TJ to Benjamin Rush, April 21, 1803, *Portable Jefferson*, pp. 490–94; and Harry V. Jaffa, *Crisis of the House Divided, an Interpretation of the Lincoln-Douglas* Debates, (Seattle: University of Washington Press, 1973), pp. 327, 344–45.

26. TJ to Isaac McPherson, August 13, 1813, *Portable Jefferson*, p. 530.

27. TJ to John Hollins, February 19, 1809, Lipscomb and Bergh, XII, 253.

28. TJ to William Henry Harrison, February 27, 1803, ibid. X, 370.

29. TJ to Maria Cosway, October 12, 1786, Boyd, X, 449.

3

ELEMENTS OF ANCIENT AND MODERN HARMONY*

John Adams Wettergreen

The way up is the same as the way down.
TRADITIONAL MOUNTAINEER'S CHANT

MUSIC PERVADES AMERICAN LIFE, BUT ITS EFFECTS ARE SELDOM A MATTER OF serious concern. However, in the 1950's, "rock 'n roll," with its violent rhythms and retarded melodies, alarmed the intellectuals. Then President Eisenhower said of it, in effect, "Let the kids have their fun." Overnight, the General's opinion—about matters musical—became the enlightened opinion. Except among professional musicians, nothing is thought to be more a matter of private taste, and less a matter of political concern than music.

This attitude is unusual. Shostakovich and Stalin agreed that music had the power to sustain or undermine the regime. Accordingly, one of his compositions contains a secret melody celebrating Stalin's death.[1] The view of Shostakovich and Stalin is authorized by the tradition of political philosophy from Plato to Nietzsche. It is adequately summarized by Socrates' remark in the *Republic*: "Never are the ways of music moved without the greatest political laws being moved." In this essay, I shall entertain the truth of this remark.

Contemporary social science and contemporary musical science have failed, so far, to understand "the ways of music." Theodore Adorno

*When I first met Harry Jaffa, in 1962, he was engaged in a controversy. He maintained, against some English professor, that political scientists could, with propriety, study poetry. So I thought I could celebrate Harry Jaffa's life with this discussion of another fine art. Mr. Jaffa tried to dissuade me from the study of music. Despite the remarkable weakness of his arguments, I have abandoned this study with the completion of this essay. Thus is it the mark of a good, and kindly teacher that he helps his students find the right way for themselves.

attacked, and Max Weber defended, the diatonic major/minor mode, the way of almost all modern Western music: Adorno, because he thought the mode was part of the superstructures of modern capitalism; Weber, because he thought it expressed the progress of Western values.[2] Similarly, Heinrich Schenker, the student of Brahms, defended this mode, showing it to proceed quite rationally from a simple musical thought, while Arnold Schoenberg, a composer alarmed by such hierarchical rationalism, argued for its abandonment.[3] All these German scientists, the most intelligent critics of music in the past few generations, beg the question posed by Socrates' remark. However great their differences in point of view, conclusions, and method, all four take for granted the existence of the contemporary Western musical mode, and of modern Western society, as the beginning point of their analyses. That is, they never raise the question of the origin of the dominant contemporary order: what is musical mode? Or, more radically, what is music?

What Music Is.   Almost everyone hears music when he hears it, but what is it that is heard? The common definition, "a pleasing (or moving and beautiful) combination of sounds," is inadequate. Almost any combination can please in some circumstances; even a siren is a delight, when one's house is afire. A more adequate definition is "a pleasing combination of tones," for tones are the creation of human art, and music is a human art.

Do the tones produced by human art really differ from other sounds? So far as the modern science of acoustics knows, music moves the human ear in the same way that the noises produced by birds, bombs, and breaking glass do.[5] Yet modern science also reports the discrete, natural phenomenon of musical hearing.[6] Just as the ability of some humans to see certain colors is imparied from birth, so is the ability of some to hear music. The tone-deaf do hear tones, insofar as they are merely sounds, for they can repeat them upon request; indeed, their ears do not appear to be materially deficient. They do not hear that tones are tones. That is, they cannot perceive that, somehow, some tones, but not others, ought to sound together. So they can never judge independently of whether a tone or a composition is "out of key," no matter how much training they are given. On the other hand, some human beings have an extraordinary natural ability to hear musical tones. And, as soon as those who have this gift of perfect pitch can speak, their genius becomes obvious, even if their ears are left untutored. Between these extremes lie the abilities of most of us: we perceive, somehow, that one tone sounds aright with only some others; with training, we can hear this necessity in the tones even better. It seems that musical tones are, by nature, a discrete kind of sound.

Musical art creates sounds—tones—such that one tone accepts some and rejects others, as though it had a life, will, or intention of its own.

This proposition is not so strange as it sounds. Every human being produces something like musical tones—living sounds, sounds with meaning—when he speaks. By varying tones of voice, we express intention, or meaning, apart from the words we say. For example, the words "that," "is," "a," "dog" can have precisely opposite meanings, can be an assertion or a question, or can even be gibberish, by the variation of tone and nothing else. Vocal tones can themselves be heard, for example, when human beings, like dogs, conclude that a speaker is angry, excited, or sad, even though they do not understand the language in which he speaks. Of course, perception of tone cannot always be distinguished from understanding of words. For example, there exists an ironic tone, but irony cannot be heard unless the words of the speaker are understood. So dogs, no matter how obedient (their ears are very sensitive), cannot hear their masters' dissembling. The ability to vary vocal tone is inseparable from the ability to speak.

However, it is distinguishable. The ability to vary tones is called voice. Voice is possessed by all animals that breathe in, and move through the open air. It is a distinctive capacity of the animal soul. By voice, animals give outward, audible sign of their inner tendencies (or intentions). The human voice differs from that of the other vocal animals only by the fact that it moves voluntarily; for example dogs cannot choose to dissemble their anger, but must growl. Indeed, without vocal tone, no animal, except man, could make known its inner tendencies.[7] Music is the imitation of voice.

Today, this definition is more than controversial: all experts reject it. And we can admit that modern music—Beethoven's *Ninth Symphony* or Bach's *Well-Tempered Clavier*—is not obviously an imitation of voice. Yet, strangely, all contemporary experts agree that music began *historically* by the imitation of voices, i.e., that musical instruments were first made to imitate singing. Nietzsche only radicalized this thought, when he argued that man sang before he spoke, or that tones preceded words. Now, the speaking voice does differ from the singing voice, but not by the presence or absence of tones or words. Tones and words are present in both, but, relative to speaking, singing emphasizes tones. It does so by producing each tone discretely. In speaking, voice slides freely from tone to tone without stopping; words and sentences are distinguished by silence. In singing, tones are separated by silence; the normal characteristic of the speaking voice, *portamento*, is used for special emphasis in music. It is only with a view to the movement of tones that music, including singing, is defined as the imitation of voice.[8]

Those who suppose that music began when man tried to imitate birdsongs have some truth, because the voice of birds, alone among the non-human animals, surrounds its tones with silences. Of course, because birds cannot speak, they do not *emphasize* tones when they sing. Birds do not actually sing. We say they do, because their natural voice resembles music's definitive characteristic, the separation of tones by silence.[9] Therefore, the objection to this definition—that musical art can produce effects impossible for the human voice—is founded upon a misunderstanding both of imitation and of voice. The fact that voice cannot imitate some music—for example, very high and very low or very long and very short notes—is no proof that music does not perfect the tonality of voice.[10] This fact proves the opposite: art perfects nature by imitating it.

A tone set off by silence, even the chord that opens Wagner's *Tristan and Isolde*, is not yet music. We begin to hear music when one tone sounds after another, and then only if we hear also that, somehow, those tones make sense together as a whole. When the tones make sense together, the music is "in key," or "harmonious." The whole in terms of which a particular tone makes sense is called its scale. The whole of which every scale is a part is called its "mode." At least in the West, there has always been controversy about modes, and so about scales: for example, do there exist one, few, or many modes, scales, and tones? Are modes, scales and tones homogeneous or heterogeneous? A common opinion today is that all modes and scales are irrational, merely conventional, or arbitrary. Thus the composer's choices appear, at best, as acts of blind will, and any possible collection of tones is said to be a scale. But no musician denies that music consists of tones (distinguished from and by silence). Of course, on the frontiers of mindlessness, in American universities, the shrieks of sirens are put together with the rattle of tommyguns in the name of an anti-tonal music. This demonstrates that music disappears— we hear mere sounds, if not noise—when the sound characteristic of soul ceases to be imitated.

Ancient Harmony. The ancient science of harmonics is the attempt to describe, universally or rationally, the movement of musical tones, melody. The ancient harmonists understood music to be the imitation of voice. Since voice is the audible effect of soul, a scientific account of melody, many ancient harmonists concluded, would also be a scientific account of the movements of the human soul. For well over a millenium, the investigation and definition of musical tones, scales, and modes was undertaken as the study of the states, motions, and conditions of the soul. Strangely enough, writings of the ancient harmonists, which are marked by vitriolic contentions matching anything in ancient literature, have survived, but almost nothing of the ancient melodies. Recently, tunes from various nations and historical periods were performed for professional musicians. All present agreed that "while the music of the less civilized nations was often crude, barbarous, and monotonous in the highest degree, the [ancient] Greek hymn stood quite alone in its abso-

lute lack of meaning and its unredeemed ugliness."[11] The West has preserved much of its theory of ancient music, but little of the practice, and
that not good.

According to the tradition, Pythagoras the philosopher was the first
harmonist. He is credited with the discovery of the octave, and of the
fourth and the fifth. These are, even today, thought to be the most important tonal relations. Every civilized people, and many an uncivilized one,
understands at least the octave. But the facts that strings (or columns of
air) in a ratio of 1:2 produce tones of perfect concord, and that lesser
concords are produced by strings related by simple numerical ratios (our
fifth by 2:3, our fourth by 3:4) were interpreted philosophically by the
Pythagoreans. The octave was heard to be the limit of a tone's motion,
and the fourth and fifth to be the most important parts of the motion
within that limit. For when a tone moves down through its fourth and
fifth to its octave, its changes are heard to have a beginning, a middle,
and an end. Because living voice and dead string produce tones whose
changes are determined by numerical ratios, the Pythagoreans concluded
that the universe is ruled by number.

Not all ancient harmonists were Pythagoreans, but all agreed that
Pythagoras was the first to make musical motion intelligible: the octave
demonstrates that musical tones move. Music begins, we hear sounds *qua*
music, when the sound of the keytone is followed (or accompanied, in
more complicated cases) by other sounds—notes—defined by that keytone and its octave. It ends when we hear that the tone has returned to
itself. In this way, the motion of the keytone through the notes of its
octave actualizes the keytone's potential to be what it is. And melodic
motion through the scale defined by the octave is perfect, i.e., rotary,
motion; it begins from and returns to its beginning. The keytone was
called *archē* (beginning and ruler). Accordingly, every ancient harmonist
wrote the scales from the higher tone to the lower, just the opposite of the
way of modern theory and practice. The tones only sounded aright to
the ancients when the higher ruled the lower.

Not only is the motion of tone in an octave perfect, it is also primary,
i.e., it is locomotion. The place of any note is defined relative to its *archē*
(and the octave of the *archē*, of course). Thus, when a note other than the
keytone sounds, it sounds more or less wrong—out of place. But when
the tone moves on to its end (*teleios-archē*), it arrives in its proper place.
Similarly, if a note not in the octave in which a melody is composed
chances to sound, harmony is destroyed: when melody has no ruler, all
notes sound out of place. Music, therefore, is motion from place to place.
Moreover, the place of musical motion as such is the cosmos, not any
particular place. That is, it is in the nature of musical hearing that we do
not understand tones *qua* sounding from a particular locus: they fill up
all—the air, if not the aether—that surrounds us.

The discovery that tonal motion within the octave is perfect and primary inspired ancient harmonists to discover the musical mode. They supposed they were inquiring for the principle of perfect primary motion. The inquiries of the first harmonists centered on the nature of the *archē*, as the cause of all tonal motion. First was the question of how many keytones exist. Is there only one, from which all the others have descended? Or a few, say six or thirteen? Or are there many, such that every one could be generated from every other? Second was the question of the motion of the *archē* within its octave. How many notes does a keytone generate? Hence, does the *archē* move in only one way—generate only one scale—from which any other scales (if they exist) can be derived, or are there a few ways? No ancient harmonist, I think, held that there were many ways of motion within the octave: the motion of the octave could never be accomplished, if there were an indefinite number of notes in it.

Once the number of *archai*, and the motions proper to each were established, all possible scales—every keytone, note, and their relations—would be known. With harmonics thus completed, it was thought that each scale would be found to possess a characteristic *ethos*, the habitual motion of a ruling tone. An *archē*, then, could be thought to correspond to a virtue and the mode to the motion of the soul educed by each virtue. Moreover, the mode of any given *archē* produces several other *archai*, but not all others, as notes to its scale. The system of musical tones, therefore, could be thought of as the order of the virtues. Each scale would correspond to a (desirable) human type, and the discovery of every possible scale would be the discovery of the moral order of the human species. All the ancient harmonists held that music is ethically relevant. At their most extreme, they held not only that listening to music composed according to a particular scale would habituate the soul to certain virtues, but also that musical refinement would be moral refinement.

The ancient harmonists' notion of *ethos* is mysterious to moderns; even the most thoughtful deny that the character of the keys is anything more than conventional.[12] So the natural phenomenon, which the old-fashioned harmonists investigated, ought to be noticed: correctly or incorrectly, human beings judge that tone of voice has moral meaning. For example, Americans conclude that the British are servile, when they hear them inflect strong assertions as though they were questions. So long as musicians (self-consciously) imitate voice, a people's accent will be preserved in their musical modes.

The ancient harmonists' attempt to discover a musico-ethical order, founded upon number, was theoretically difficult. Simply stated, there were two problems.

First, if the musician proceeds downward by octaves, i.e., by the most fundamental musical motion, he arrives, even within the range of the human voice (two octaves, plus a fifth), at a tone different from the *archē* (to the double octave). For the ancients, unlike the moderns, held that the octave is no simple musical equivalent of the *archē*; it is lower, so it must sound differently. The descent by octaves demonstrates the existence of more than one *archē*, but it generates no scale, no notes between *archai*. Because the motion of such a descent is discontinuous, it cannot demonstrate the relation between *archai*.

So, second, the ancient harmonists searched for the absolute *archē* by means of the next most fundamental motions, the fifth and the fourth. Proceeding downward by either of these means, the musician can discover an eight note (seven step) scale within the octave of any *archē* (if he transposes these descents upward by octaves). However, two more difficulties arise. The scale produced by a descent of fifths is slightly flat. The *archē* is a bit too low, and must be raised. But every *archē* will produce the same effect, of course. So the descent by fifths—and presumably its scale —results in a vain search for ever higher causes. So to speak, a noble atheism. The descent by fourths produces an even more repulsive, and opposite effect. The scale is sharp, the *archē* too high, and another infinite regression results: a systematic, but necessarily vain lowering of the *archē*. For reasons like these, the Pythagorean harmony sounded impracticable. Certainly, it was incapable of explaining *ethos*.

The other school of ancient harmonics was founded by Aristoxemus, a student of Aristotle. Aristoxenian harmonics is marked by its moderation, but its attention to the musical phenomena themselves, and by its lack of ethical absolutism, not to say its relativism. For each *archē*, Aristoxenus proceeded downward by one fourth, one fifth, and one octave —all three together, but only once. This procedure gave him what he regarded as the fixed notes (*estotes*) of the scale of any *archē*. It also produced what he regarded as the measure of musical motion. He defined the interval in the middle of the octave, between the fourth and the fifth, as one whole tonal step.

Against Aristoxenus, the Pythagoreans noted that the ratio producing the tonal step is irrational: it is a step that could never be taken, because it has no limits. Against this, the Musician, as he was called in the ancient times, noted that "it is self-evident that the senses rule in these matters." That is, we hear the concordance, not the ratios of the octave, fourth, and fifth.

We also hear that the motions from *archē* to fourth or fifth, and from fourth or fifth to octave are discontinuous. Insofar as it has been preserved to us, Aristoxenian harmonics is concerned with supplying the additional steps that would make the motion of the keytone continuous, i.e., harmonious. These notes were called the "movables" (*kinoumenoi*), because they did not have any one place within the octave. They had no one place, because they were not the effect of any determinate (concordant or natural) interval. Their proper place is a locus, not a point, within the interval of a fourth. The placement (*skema,* or *eidos*) of the movables determines *ethos.*

Because there is no one proper place for the movables, they are —considered in the abstract, or mathematically—uncountable: every finite magnitude is capable of unlimited divisions. So Aristoxenus investigated the physics of musical voice and hearing. His discoveries still stand. Although the human ear can comprehend a somewhat wider range of pitches than the human voice can produce, ear and voice are equally discriminating. The smallest difference of pitch that the human ear can perceive, and (therefore?) the smallest difference that the voice can produce is a *diesis* ("the compressed one"). Aristoxenus discovered that the voice cannot produce more than two *dieses* successively. If it tries for a third, it jumps: one tone in the descent (to the third) and two tones in the ascent (to the fourth). The size of the *diesis* varies with the training of the ear and voice. The most refined ear and voice can distinguish a quarter-tone. Any normal ear can distinguish a semitone. With moderate musical training, the ear can comprehend a *diesis* of one-third of a tonal step. Using these principles, Aristoxenus is reported to have constructed all possible scales.

One genus of scales corresponds to each of the three levels of musical comprehension. The enharmonic genus is determined by the quarter-tone *diesis.* The chromatic scales are constructed out of various combinations of *dieses* of one-third tone. The most common scales belong to the diatonic genus, whose smallest motion is a semitone. The diatonic, Aristoxenus remarked, "comes first," i.e., immediately from the nature of human beings. "Third and highest" and "most noble" of *ethos* are the enharmonic scales, for they demand the greatest refinement. In Aristoxenus' time, musicians, at best, used chromatic scales, and they usually mixed these with some diatonic. Aristoxenus explained: the musicians wished to pander to their audiences' desire for sweetness, as opposed to austerity.[13] In our time, all music is diatonic.

Aristoxenus discovered that *ethos* is not caused by the *archē* alone. The *archē* generates the fixed notes, whose existence allows the movables to sound as such. However, the movables, not the *archē* and its descendants, give each scale its distinctive characters. *Ethos* is an accident of the *archē,* because the changables are determined by the degree of refinement of the natural power of voice and ear to discriminate tonality within the limits set by the *archē.* If the harmonist abstracts from these natural human powers, as the Pythagoreans did, then the number of *ethoi* and *archai,* the number of scales, modes, and notes, will be found to be uncountable. Harmonics would not be possible. Thus Aristoxenus mocked those harmonists (some of whom were his own students) who hoped to discover a habitude of virtues for each *archē,* by means of mathematics. To attempt to discover some one *ethos* in the Dorian, Aeolian, or any other scale preferred for non-harmonic reasons is like trying to discover *the* name of the first day of the week.

In matters of traditional musical ethics, Aristoxenus must appear to be a relativist.[14] Nevertheless, I do not think that Aristoxenus held that music had no moralizing potential, or that musical ethics is merely conventional. Aristoxenus discovered the fixed principles of harmony, which are the proper concern of harmonics. Insofar as these principles are relevant to ethics, they are not the business of harmonics. Therefore, Aristoxenus, following his teacher, cautioned those of his students who believed that they could become noble and happy by listening to music: "Music has the potential to improve [character], not by listening alone." Yet it is as much an error to believe that music is unworthy of serious men as it is to believe that music comprehends all serious matters (*Elements*, 31–2). Harmonics trains memory and sense of tone. The ability to remember the proper orders of tones and the ability to distinguish by ear and by voice the most subtle variations of tone are gentlemanly excellences, if not moral virtues. The perfection of these abilities is the highest purpose of Aristoxenian harmonics.

Modern Harmony. The ancient philosophers were better able than Aristoxenus to conceal their contempt for the professionals who taught that music comprehends all serious matters. For, on one point of importance, they agreed with the experts: "'Never are the ways of music changed without a change of the decisive political laws,' so says Damon, and I," says Socrates with some emphasis, "am persuaded."[15] Socrates explains neither what "the ways of music" are, nor what the relation of political to musical revolutions is. He is persuaded only that the order of listening and vocalizing is coincident with the political order.

In the West, the ways of music were revolutionized once. By the ninth-century of the Christian era, the *archē* was established below. From then to this day, scales sound properly when they sound upwards.[16] That the scales properly sound downward was the only point upon which the ancient harmonists concurred. The reason for this revolution, and who made it, is very controversial. Yet this simple change is, as shall be shown, what made possible the unique character of modern Western music.[17]

That the *archē* sounds from below need not mean that the cause is lower than the effects. That would be atheism, or, at best, deism. Rather, the Christian interpretation must have been that the *archē* (or *kurios*, as it is now called) is now below, and that it reveals itself as *archē* by rising to the (old) *archē*. Ultimately, this leads to the musical thought, common and distinctive of the modern West, that a tone and its octave are equivalent, e.g., that cadence can be achieved by any octave of the keytone. But, for the ancient Greeks, hearing such an equivalence would be ridiculous, if not scandalous: Ought the base rule the noble, the lower the higher?

The ancient harmonists had a point: a tone and its octave sound differently, despite their very great concord. However, because they insisted that the high be the cause of the low, the ancients could not give a musical or acoustical explanation of the concord. To explain this material fact, they had to resort to psychology, ethics, physics, or even metaphysics. Of course, they saw the material phenomenon: the octave below is produced by the double string. However, if the higher must be the cause of the lower, then the fact that the double string has the potential to produce the higher tone is not decisive. For, in actuality (and as the ancients heard it), the double does not produce the tone of the single. Still the whole double string—both its halves—vibrates. Thus any normal ear can distinguish the tone of the monad sounding within the tone of the dyad: especially when the ear hears the lower tone followed by its octave above, and, above all, when it hears both sounding together. The ancients were correct: the motion of the dyad is different from (and engenders something different from) the motion of the monad. Indeed, it is different even from the motion of two monads moving simultaneously, but separately. Hearing so clearly that no dyad can move within any monad, the chaste ancients neglected the fact that the monad moves —only potentially, to be sure—within every dyad. The moderns, and even the medieval Christians, are more impressed by the potential of the dyad than by the actuality of the monad.

On this important musical question, it is hard to say who is correct. Probably it is always safer to understand the low tone in the light of the high, because this way preserves the essential melodic distinction. After all, high is higher than low. Yet, as I have demonstrated, this way of understanding is not wholly accurate. Perhaps it is a salutary way, because it rightly conceals the dependence of the high upon the low. But a price is paid for this noble deception of the ear: the agency of the high in the low is obscured, and with that the true cause of concord. However this may be, once scales can justly sound from below, all that is distinctive of modern Western music can develop.

In the ancient world, the meaning of music was investigated by theoretical men. In the modern world, all the great musical inventions—after the discovery of the *archē* below—are the works of musicians, especially composers. Or, more precisely, nothing of modern Western music can be written without a thorough education in theory of music.[18] I shall consider only the two greatest moments, after the first, in the development of modern harmony.

The first modern musical invention is polyphony (as distinguished from monophony, e.g., Gregorian chant, and from homophony, e.g., the great instrumental music of the late eighteenth and early nineteenth century). This is the discovery that, harmonically, more than one voice, singing more than one melody, can make sense musically. Old and young, men and women, tenors, basses, sopranos, and altos can all sing together, even if they do sing different tunes. Palestrina (1525–1594), the musical agent of counter-reforming Pope Gregory XIII, is the genius of this invention. He perfected the tonal art, counterpoint, by which various melodies can be put together.[19]

Prior to the development of polyphony, and its art of counterpoint, the whole West could speak with one voice regarding harmony. The definition of *de Anima* was adequate for ancient and medieval harmonists: harmony exists, Aristotle asserted, "when magnitudes having position and motion [e.g., notes] are so closely fitted together in a whole [e.g., a scale] that they do not admit anything else between them of the same genus." Harmony was that excellence of melody which result when it was composed of all those tones, and only those, of a properly constructed scale. Ancient harmonics could not, would not put together different melodies from different scales (with different *ethoi*).

Counterpoint implies a radical reformation, if not a rejection, of this traditional understanding of harmony. Tones from different scales, especially from the scales as anciently defined, cannot sound together without serious discord. Implicitly and theoretically, the discovery of an *archē* below should solve this problem; in principle, every higher tone participates in every lower one. Nevertheless, unprecedented technical accomplishment is necessary to manage the extraordinary discord that becomes possible with polyphony; in each scale alone, the number of discords (with the keytone) is greater than the number of concords. By ancient harmonic standards, polyphonic music must sound wildly discordant, because counterpoint does not manage discord either by ruthlessly repressing it or by excommunicating it. Rather, counterpoint deceives the ear: "the 'trick' consists in making each dissonance appear to the ear as a specific deviation from a consonance, the result of a departure from, and the anticipation of a return to, a specific consonance."[20] The contrapuntalists discovered that the ear can tolerate much more of "evil"—for that was how dissonance was heard—than the ancients ever expected, so long as it remains in the service of "good." Only in this century could a thoroughly trained musician admit, without blushing, that "we should know [sc. hear] that the most pleasant sounds of music are what according to all rules must be called dissonances." The invention of polyphonic music only implies the rejection of ancient harmony. The second great modern invention, Bach's well-tempered scales, makes a new harmony fully possible.

Bach's *Well-Tempered Clavier (WTC)* is widely respected as the single greatest modern work of musical art, because, for the first time (and, some say, for the last), in a single work, which can be played on a single instrument, there is a piece for every key. They can be played, that is, if the instrument is tuned properly: "well-tempered."[21] This construction of the scales requires that the natural concord of the fifth (and fourth), the concord that results from tuning by simple numerical ratios, be abandoned. In effect, a little bit of discord is spread over every note in each scale, rather than concentrating it at the second, third, sixth, and seventh. (I have been told that refined listeners have trouble tolerating the fifths of Bach's scales.) But the natural concord at the octave is tuned for every note. When discord is spread very evenly, it seems, every note can be an *archē*. Moreover, when the ear becomes accustomed to this tuning, more concordance is discovered in the musical world: The third upward (and the sixth) differs little in discordance from the well-tempered fifth upward (and the fourth), and so comes to be understood as a concord. At the extreme of this development, which comes well after Bach, the notion of concord and discord at intervals less than an octave becomes meaningless: all notes are heard as deviations from the keytone. Thus *WTC* is a practical demonstration of the equality of all notes, of the possibility that every note could be *archē* at least, in a musical world so well ordered as Bach's. Modern harmonics, as shall be shown, is an attempt to understand Bach's demonstration theoretically.

Once the ear can tolerate well-tempered scales—and what could foster that tolerance better than Bach's *WTC?*—the possibility of universal modulation appears. Melodies can be freely transposed into any key; the *ethos* of a scale no longer seems to be a problem. However, strictly speaking, universal modulation is only possible theoretically. That is, at best, it is possible for instrumental music only: for music that abstracts from *logos*. Once the modern composer chooses to include human voices in his compositions, their natural ranges and abilities to move require him to consider the characters of the keytones and scales. The ancient harmonists were always concerned with *ethoi*, though this concern drove them to bitter contentions, because they understood harmonics to be a part of a part of the science of poetics. In the final analysis, poetics must understand *logos*; ancient harmonics determines what tones are proper for what words. Only by abstracting from *logos*, i.e., only by presupposing that instrumental music is music pure and simple, does modern harmonics avoid the question of *ethos*, and achieve universal modulation. At the beginning of the seventeenth-century, this abstraction becomes characteristic of Western musical science.

Polyphony normally necessitates several notes sounding simultaneously, i.e., chords. Bach's scales, by equalizing every note *qua* keytone, legitimates chords: if every higher tone sounds equally within every lower tone, then when properly ordered, all tones can sound together harmoniously. This was a momentous discovery. This consciousness of chords as legitimate— not merely necessary or accidental—aspects of musical reality distinguishes modern Western music; chords occur only accidentally, if at all, in ancient and medieval Western music and in all non-Western music. Modern harmonics is the science of chords.

Modern harmony is the sound of the chords that go together with the melody. Relative to melody, harmony (normally) sounds from below, but, considered in itself modern harmony—chordal motion—is neither an ascent nor a descent. Ascent and descent, motion toward and away from the keytone, are properties of melody. Now if all notes are equal in their capacity to rule, melody must disappear, unless the ear can comprehend at any given moment which tone is, in fact, ruling. Chords supply that support from below which allows the ear to judge whether or not any particular note in a melody is ruling, or ruled. The more freely melodies move from key to key the more important is this support from below. At the extreme of modern harmonics, the chords overwhelm the melody; key is always ambiguous, or only anticipated. That is, according to the experts, the pleasure of Wagner's music results from the composer's never satisfying his listeners' desire for an *archē*.

Modern musicians agree that the rules of modern harmonics are easily grasped. By applying them, the deaf, and even the tone deaf could compose the chords necessary to harmonize a tune. The principle of these rules is the chord called "the triad." In its first degree, the triad is composed of the keytone, its third, and that third's third (the fifth of the keytone). When this triad sounds, especially if it sounds after the fifth degree (the fifth and its thirds above and below), the ruling key of the melody is said to be established. In short: by the assertion (and reassertion) of the third as a consonance, modern Western music achieves its distinctive character. When this assertion is accepted, counterpoint becomes obsolete; it sounds hypocritical, or precious.

Despite its mathematical certitude, modern harmonics is but a commentary on melody. Modern harmonies are unintelligible apart from their melodies, and modern harmonics cannot explain melody. So melodies, the object of ancient harmonics, are said to be "inspired," "irrational," or "subconscious" by the moderns. Melody must remain unintelligible to them, so long as the legitimacy of the chord as a part of music remains problematic. To the modern harmonists, the chord must be either one or many: either the chord is that unity of the multitude of notes below which is the necessary condition for beautiful melodies above; or it is the order of the multitude below which is called into being by the free motion of the keytones above. No third possibility suggests itself to the modern harmonists. Therefore, the soul of modern Western music is torn between absolute monarchism and radical democratism, the two extreme consequences of the fact that all higher tones sound within all lower tones.

In the twentieth-century, the democratic side of our musical way has tended to prevail, almost to the point of anarchy. "A-tonal" compositions, for example, attempt to eliminate systematically even the listener's anticipation of the *archē*. Nevertheless, these compositions are founded upon Bach's scales, in which the octave is emphatic. Even in a radically a-tonal composition, e.g., one in which no note's octave occurred, the octave would insinuate itself by its absence. The ancient notion that the perfect motion of the voice is rotary, although subject to profoundly different interpretations, cannot be eliminated from the way of Western music.

The Political and Musical Sciences. The clever Montesquieu asserted that the classical political philosopher's interest in music only appears to be paradoxical. The austere ancients took up this frivolity, he claims, because music was the only means available in the ancient political communities by which the harsh, contentious manners of the citizens could be softened. Montesquieu assumed that commerce, another softener, could never have been respectable in the ancient cities, and that the ancient philosophers shared in the prejudice against it.[23] The ancients did write more about music (and less about commerce) than Montesquieu. But Montesquieu was wrong: the ancients knew that in music, just as in commerce and politics, there is much to inspire controversy.

Not the ancient philosophers, but the moderns, and especially those after Montesquieu have an inordinate interest in music. Beginning with Rousseau, who took the time (at age 55!) to write a complete dictionary of music and who went so far as to compose an opera, the ephemera of music acquire metaphysical importance. Hegel states Rousseau's thought with his usual profundity: "The fundamental task of music . . . [consists] in giving resonant reflection, not to objectivity in its ordinary material sense, but to the mode and modifications under which the Self, from the point of view of its own subjectivity and ideality, is moved." This would sound Pythagorean, if the Self were the same as the soul. Instead, Hegel's Self is "our entirely empty ego; self, without further content."[24] Thus can music be conceived as civilized man's civilized way back to the experience of his prehistorical, pre-rational, perfectly free, and, in sum, "contentless" condition. It is the ultimate civilizer, because "it is only through music that man understands the joy [there was] in the annihilation of the individual."[25] The seriousness of music has always been asserted in proportion to the doubtfulness of the existence of any essential, or internal order of human life. But, from the fact that music's ways are *the* epiphenomena of civilizations, the followers of Rousseau concluded that they are the causes of civilizations, confusing the imitations with the originals.

According to Socrates, not music, but changes of its ways are politically relevant. As I have shown, the musicians attempt to elaborate the tonal laws by imitating their civilization's cosmology. Perhaps the very frivolity, the relatively innocent pleasures of music encourages the musicians' pretentiousness. However this might be, precisely because music is as frivolous as musicians are pretentious, changes of its ways are ominous. When revolutions approach, they are the first things to go, because the serious men, like General Eisenhower, usually believe that music is "kids' stuff."

Aristotle treats this opinion of music with perfect seriousness: the musical education of the youth of the best regime is the last topic of the *Politics*. In explicit controversy with the Platonic Socrates, the last lines of the *Politics* maintain that the musical curriculum ought to cultivate in the youth exactly the same taste as that of the fully grown gentlemen, who are the rulers of the best regime. Aristotle agrees that political education is the best security of the justice of any regime. But in the best regime, whose end is leisure, there cannot be one standard for the young and another for the mature. What the young learn from the best curriculum ought to be perpetuated in and by the leisurely activities of the mature. Of course, the difference in the natures of the young and the fully developed makes this aim problematic. Aristotle's music curriculum is intended to solve this problem.

According to Aristotle, the time available for leisure can be used for dancing, drinking, sleeping, or other activities that do not cultivate, and even do harm to prudence (*phronesis*). The professional musicians claim that, in addition to its power to entertain, please, and relax, music can improve the habits and the soul. "If that were true, then the youth ought to learn it, both by listening and by playing." It would be the best leisurely activity. Yet music has only one unqualifiedly good effect. It is the equivalent of a baby's rattle for the older youths: "Something is needed to keep the children from breaking the furniture, for it is not in their nature to remain at rest." Nevertheless, not just any musical curriculum will do: one ought not give a baby a rattle capable of disturbing one's rest, much less one that could destroy the furniture. The best curriculum requires a master who leads "a philosophical sort of life." Apparently, the music master is the only philosopher in town.

Such a master is necessary, because "citizens cannot judge well of matters, even trivial matters, in which they have no part whatsoever." Only such a master could teach the youth to be properly pleased by what they hear, both by allowing them to listen and by encouraging them to play a bit for themselves. Then, when the youth grow up, although they will no longer be able to find the time to play for themselves (for only the professional bother with that), they will still be adequate judges of what they hear. Remembering the example of their kindly music master, the citizens of the best regime will use leisure nobly; for example, they will invite the master to play for them.

In this charming way, the first political scientist indicated that the problem of the music curriculum is not different from, and no more difficult than the problem of enlightening the rulers.

Notes

1. Shostakovich as reported in Edward Rothstein, "Music: Why Dictators Fear It," *New York Times*, August 23, 1981, Sec. 2, pp. 1, 20.
2. Theodor W. Adorno, *Philosophy of Modern Music*, trans. Mitchell and Blomster (New York: Harper and Row, 1973) and Max Weber, *The Rational and Social Foundations of Music*, trans. and ed. Martindale *et al.* (Carbondale: University of Southern Illinois Press, 1958).
3. Heinrich Schenker, *Harmony*, trans. Borgese (Chicago: University of Chicago Press, 1954) and Arnold Schoenberg, *Harmonielehre* (Vienna, Universal edition; 1922).
4. This is the definition of J. J. Rousseau, *A Complete Dictionary of Music*, trans. Waring (Reprint of the London, 1779 edition; New York: AMS Press, 1975), p. 257.
5. See Jess J. Josephs, *The Physics of Musical Sound* (New York: D. van Norstrand Co., 1957), pp. 26–66; Herman L. F. Helmholtz, *On the Sensations of Tone . . .* , Trans. Ellis (New York: Dover, 1948), pp. 49–65, 362.
6. See G. Révèsz, *Introduction to the Psychology of Music*, trans. Gouroy (Norman, Ok: University of Oklahoma Press, 1954), pp. 95–111, 186–196, and his *Psychology of a Musical Prodigy*, (New York: Harcourt Brace, 1925), pp. 25–83; cf. Victor Zuckerkandl, *Sound and Symbol: Music and the External World*, trans. Transk (Princeton: Princeton University Press, 1956), p. 334; see also Helmholtz, p. 128c. So far, physiological studies of musical hearing have neglected the part of the ear in maintaining balance. Yet, universally, the same tones are described as high and low.
7. Non-human animals express how or where they are about to move (the why is obvious) only by tones. Thus, there is, so to speak, a universal language of dogs, but many human languages, dialects, and accents (and musics). Cf. Aristotle, *Problematics* X, 39.
8. There are two techniques of imitation: melody, movement among higher and lower tones; rhythm, the timing of the pause on each tone, and of the silences. In this essay, I consider only melody, the soul of music. Harmony is the excellence of melody.
9. All birdsongs are in key, but no bird is capable of melody: their "songs" are as likely to begin or end on one tone as another; Zuckerkandl, *Man the Musician* trans. Guterman (Princeton: Princeton University Press, 1973), pp. 290–291.
10. See, e.g., Charles W. L. Johnson, *Musical Pitch and the Measurement of Intervals among the Ancient Greeks* (Baltimore: Johns Hopkins University Press, 1896), pp. 10–15; Helmholtz, p. 544b.
11. *Aristoxenou Apmonika Stoixeia*, ed. with trans, by Henry S. Macran (Oxford: Clarendon Press, 1902), p. 2. (hereinafter cited as *Elements* and by section number) One-third of the surviving ancient melodies are drinking songs which some Cretan engraved in stone.
12. Helmholtz, pp. 550–551; Zuckerkandl, *Sound*, p. 33.
13. According to ancient gossip, Aristoxenus hated the sound of laughter.
14. Although he wrote hundreds of works, including an *Ethics*, only the most technical parts of his harmonics and rhythmics have survived in the West.
15. *Republic* 242c. "Damon" (Dorian for "democratically elected judge and executioner") is the harmonist to whom Socrates defers on all other matters of musical taste.
16. Zuckerkandl, *Sound*, pp. 361–362.

17. Boethius (c. 480–524 C. E.), the musical agent of Pope Gregory I, uses "A" to name the lowest note of a scale, whereas the ancients designated the highest with an alpha. However, only in 831 did the Holy Roman Empire's musical agent (Amalar of Metz, a protege of Charlemagne) discover that the musical tradition was discontinuous in itself and in relation to pre-Christian music. See the interesting summary in Gerald Abrahams, *The Concise Oxford History of Music* (Oxford: Oxford University Press, 1979), pp. 59–62. None of this happened in the Eastern Church, where the manuscripts of Aristoxenus were preserved.

18. Zucherkandl, *Man*, p. 225.

19. Polyphony was acceptable in practice for centuries before Palestrina. Hucbald (c. 840–930) in his *De Institione Harmonica*, indicates that, in principle, polyphony is possible. See also Aristoxenus, *Elements*, 57. However, it seems that prior to Palestrina, polyphony was accomplished by rhythmics, not harmonics.

20. Zuckerkandl, *The Sense of Music* (Princeton: Princeton University Press, 1959), p. 158.

21. In fact, Bach wrote two versions of *WTC*. In the first, he was careful to distinguish E flat from D sharp; he shows that he can maintain the most protestant of the traditional church modes. In the second, he emphasizes the distinction between A flat and G sharp; he indicates that he can still hear the enharmonic genus.

22. Zuckerkandl, *Sound*, p. 49; but, above all, consider John Hazedel Levis, *Foundations of Chinese Musical Art* (New York: Paragon Book Reprint Corporation, 1963), pp. 3–7, 37.

23. *Spirit of the Laws*, trans Nugent (New York: Hafner Publication Co., 1949), pp. 37–39 (I, iv, 8).

24. *The Philosophy of Fine Art*, trans. Osmaston (London: G. Bell, 1920), pp. 341–2, 344, 361.

25. *Birth of Tragedy out of the Spirit of Music*, trans. Golffing (Garden City, N.Y.: Doubleday, 1956), p. 127.

4

The Great Machiavellian Deed?
Reconsideration of Frederick II's Invasion of Silesia

Peter W. Schramm

*A King's accession is always a hopeful phenomenon to the public; more espe-
cially a young King's, who has been talked of for his talents and aspirings,—for
his sufferings, were it nothing more,—and whose* anti-Machiavel *is understood
to be in press. Vaguely everywhere there has a notion gone abroad that this young
King will prove considerable. Here at last has a Lover of Philosophy got upon the
throne, and great philanthropies and magnanimities are to be expected, think
rash editors and idle mankind.*

Thomas Carlyle

In May of 1740 the patchwork of unconnected lands called Brandenburg-Prussia had a new ruler. The twenty-eight year old Frederick's
accession was watched with interest in Europe. There was already reason
to think this young king would be unlike other rulers. As crown prince
he had been in the public eye for almost a decade. His father, Frederick
William, Elector of Brandenburg and King in Prussia, was an unlovable
bully of a man who beat his son regularly, tried to prevent him receiving
a serious education, and at one point was on the verge of executing
him for desertion. Austria and England, among other European states,
stepped in to try to prevent Frederick's murder. They did this for many
reasons, the most powerful being self-interest: Frederick already had a
reputation for being a delicate, kind and thoughtful young man. Would
it not be in their interest for such a man to rule over the fourth largest
army in Europe? Frederick not only read books, but wrote them. He
spoke of the duties of sovereigns, of virtue and the public good. He
favored the arts, and cultivated the friendship of those who were reputed
to be wise and tolerant. Many thought that he would have a gigantic and
wealthy court filled with poets, ballet dancers, and men of learning. In

France it was thought that he would go so far as to make Voltaire his first minister. The English were confident that he would reduce the Prussian army from 80,000 to 45,000 men. Many of his own officials hoped that he would let his ministers do the ruling while he devoted himself to the arts. Those who kept him company in his Rheinsberg days universally expected to be handsomely rewarded for having shared many pleasures while young and irresponsible. There was, in short, a general expectation that at least one state in Europe would have the pleasure of being ruled by a philosopher. A new age was dawning. Much was expected of this revolution.

But less than six months after his accession an opportunity arose that allowed Frederick to reveal something of his true character and of the magnitude of his ambitions. He grasped the opportunity with both hands and decided firmly and irrevocably to break with the policies and methods of his predecessors. Not wanting to be, as his predecessors apparently were, a puppet of history, Frederick did what none of them would dare to do, even had they had the opportunity. He attacked the Habsburg empire. Further, he did this without first seeking allies for the project, and he was never apologetic for the act. He was able to do this not only because he had the opportunity and the means, but also because he had, without the knowledge of most of his contemporaries, prepared himself before becoming king, for just such a moment. Although he was a man who took no pleasure in being a king, he performed this duty because he thought it was a charge of the most serious kind, and because he thought that men can choose not to perform such obligations only at great cost to themselves and to those whom they are committed to benefit.

Whether the resolves and deeds of Frederick the Great are praised or blamed, the magnitude of their consequences for Prussia, as well as the rest of Europe, may well be incalculable. By invading Silesia in December of 1740, six months after becoming King, and hence starting the War of the Austrian Succession, Frederick the Great conquered the richest of the Habsburg provinces, threatened to dismember the Habsburg possessions and the Holy Roman Empire, and increased the prestige of his country to such an extent that henceforth Prussia had to be dealt with as a great power.[1] Thus began the struggle for the mastery of Germany that was to last for over one hundred years. The name of Frederick the Great, as well as of Prussia, for good or evil, and often in contradictory ways, has come to be associated with enlightened monarchy, unwarranted aggression, and tyranny.

Historical scholarship condemns Frederick for being a tyrant, or, at best, for acting immorally. The renowned English historian A.J.P. Taylor calls Frederick "a barbarian of genius" who was "utterly savage in his aims and methods, civilized to the highest degree in his capacity for organization and for concentrating his resources on a given object."[2] G.P. Gooch, the author of a well known biography of Frederick, published in 1947, states: ". . . the rape of Silesia ranks with the partition of Poland among the sensational crimes of modern history."[3]

Although no less severe, two other condemnations of Frederick, from somewhat different points of view, are far more interesting. Frederick is accused of being a liar and a charlatan, of not meaning what he said and of not practicing what he preached. He is condemned for acting in a manner which he himself thought to be despicable and culpable. Speaking about Frederick's book on Machiavelli, the volume in which Frederick claimed to undertake the "defense of humanity against this monster [Machiavelli] who would destroy it,"[4] Macaulay states:

It was entitled the *Anti-Machiavel*, and was an edifying homily against rapacity, perfidy, arbitrary government, unjust war, in short, against almost everything for which its author is now remembered among men.[5]

The criticism continues:

Nobody had the least suspicion that a tyrant of extraordinary military and political talents, of industry more extraordinary still, without fear, without faith, and without mercy, had ascended the throne.[6]

Regarding Frederick's invasion of Silesia, Macaulay states:

Yet the King of Prussia, the Anti-Machiavel, had already fully determined to commit the great crime of violating his plighted faith, of robbing the ally whom he was bound to defend, and of plunging all Europe into a long, bloody and desolating war; and all this for no end whatever, execpt that he might extend his dominions, and see his name in the gazettes.[7]

Gerhard Ritter, the author of a respected biography of Frederick, first published in 1936, decided that the time honored view that Frederick was a "true son of the Enlightenment"[8] is the correct one. Furthermore, after stating that the *Anti-Machiavel* is filled with the "favored ideas of the age,"[9] he considers "what has always been considered strange . . . that it was the conqueror of Silesia who publicly expressed indignation about Machiavellian power politics."[10] Ritter then very perceptively asks: "Was Frederick's enthusiasm for humanitarian ideals superficial, or was it seriously felt? Was it in fact no more than a cynical work with which a man of particularly Machiavellian cunning attempted to deceive the world about his true intentions?"[11] Ritter quickly and bluntly answers his own questions: "Nothing could be further from the truth." The reason he gives is that there was "so little cunning" in Frederick that he often contradicts himself, "in one and the same breath." Not only did Frederick contradict himself, but what is more important, he "did not perceive the inherent contradictions." This demonstrates to Ritter, the "naive honesty of his beliefs."[12] If in fact Frederick did often contradict himself—and we believe that he did not often, if ever, do so—we may be tempted to ask Professor Ritter, what beliefs could Frederick have held with "naive honesty?" According to Ritter's schema he could give only one answer to this question: Frederick's beliefs were the beliefs held by his age, the Age of Enlightenment. Professor Ritter's assumption becomes his answer.

For the purposes of this essay we need not concern ourselves with an elaborate refutation of these judgments of Frederick. Our task is far less sophisticated. We shall merely attempt to show that before one may be allowed to make such general and impolite judgments and condemnations about a statesman, one must first understand the statesman, and his political situation, by his own standards, that is, by the goals which he had set for his nation, and the practical limitations upon their attainment. We certainly ought not to judge a statesman by condemning him for not attaining those goals, although good in themselves, which were clearly beyond his reach. And we certainly cannot pronounce judgment upon him if we think that he is merely a reflection of his age!

Is it sufficient to condemn Frederick's "great crime" by saying that he did it for no end whatever, except that he might expand his dominions, and see his name in the gazettes?[13] That Frederick wanted to extend his dominions is true. But before we chastise him for this should we not first ask why he thought it good or necessary to expand? Is it not possible that the history of Prussia and Frederick himself may be able to convince us that his motives and actions in those circumstances were the correct ones? It seems possible to us that the extension of one's dominions may in fact be a legitimate end, an object of policy worth pursuing or that a statesman may be compelled to pursue. It may happen that the political independence or survival of his country depends on it. And when the statesman is successful in working for the common good we should not be surprised if he is honored for his actions. Hence, we may say, his name will appear in the "gazettes." A people honors those who have contributed to the common good; it follows that the greater the contribution, the greater the honor. And the greatest honor, fame and glory, is given to those statesmen who raise their nation to a new level of importance and power. Thus, such statesmen may, through the new found independence of their states, better attempt to benefit their people.

A final understanding, and judgment, of Frederick's action must take into account the immediate circumstances in which his decision was made, his own understanding of that decision, and the forces and circumstances that constrained the statesmanship of his predecessors. This would entail a detailed examination of the history of the decisions of previous rulers of Brandenburg-Prussia, in order that we may see how necessity imposed crucial constraints on their choices, and in order to see how Frederick's situation, and his character, differed from theirs. Frederick's own understanding is available to us in his written works. He was one of the most thoughtful of all his contemporaries, and did not hesitate to write down his thoughts. We have a great deal of Frederick's material with which to work since he considered himself a student of politics, a poet, and even a philosopher.

One thing we may be sure of, Frederick did not consider himself a barbarian or a tyrant.

An account of the circumstances in which Brandenburg-Prussia found itself in 1740 would entail: an examination of the manner in which the personal power of the Electors of Brandenburg was established; the extension of the territories which they possessed in 1640; the conversion of the electorate into a kingdom; the foundation of a standing army of amazing strength in proportion to the area of the state and the size of the population; and the foundation of a highly centralized and efficient bureaucracy under the direct control of the sovereign.

In particular such an account would reveal the difficulties encountered by the three Hohenzollern rulers preceding Frederick II: the wars, not of their own making, that they were compelled to fight; the alliances that they had little choice in making; how often their rights and interests were arbitrarily discarded by the great powers, especially Austria and France; and how during this period not only was the country's well-being at stake, but its very existence. The prospect of the dissolution of their territories always lay before these rulers, and hence their decisions had less the character of statesmanship than of forced and desperate struggle with necessity.

Only when this is kept in mind, can one begin to fathom the true importance of Frederick II's decision to invade Silesia. Before Frederick used his dreadful army to his purpose, it was possible to imagine Brandenburg-Prussia, this country without shape and consisting of almost nothing but borders, not to exist. After Frederick's deed, it was not possible to imagine Europe without it. He raised Brandenburg-Prussia to the center of European affairs.

Although young, Frederick II was learned in political matters. It is clear both from his correspondence, and his works that were written before he became king, that his concerns and reflections were of the most serious kind. Frederick's father was adamantly opposed to the young man learning Latin, reading ancient history and philosophy, for he thought it would make him less practical. In fact, through heroic efforts on the part of Frederick, and his tutors (and large English subsidies with which to purchase books), the young man did what any honorable son would do under such circumstances: he immersed himself in ancient philosophy and history, among other things. And all without his father's knowledge. Frederick's reputation among the European *philo-*

sophes before he became king was that of an enlightened philosopher who would, by virtue of his learning and affection for humanity, usher in an age of enlightened rule such as never had been seen in the history of man. After all, what should the likes of Voltaire expect from a man who read and wrote much, and who thought that Marcus Aurelius was the wisest of rulers, and John Locke the wisest of thinkers? In the end those who thus hoped would be disappointed, at least regarding his foreign policy.

While working on the *Anti-Machiavel* Frederick wrote to Voltaire, in 1739:

I am at present employed on Machiavel. I am writing notes on his *Prince*, and have begun a work which will entirely refute his maxims, by the contradiction which is found between them and virtue, as well as by their opposition to the true interests of princes. It is not enough to point out virtue to men, we must also set the springs of interest in motion, without which but few will follow the dictates of reason.[14]

When the work was near completion, and after Voltaire had agreed to help Frederick get it published, Frederick wrote: "I estimate my labour at nothing, for it is but of short duration; but the produce of that labour I estimate at much, for it is intended to survive me."[15] Frederick understood that men are remembered and judged by posterity. But, as he wrote much later, "if we are prudent we shall anticipate posterity by rigorously judging ourselves." He judged himself as rigorously as anyone, and he hoped that "disinterested posterity" would agree with his judgment of himself.[16]

The best evidence we have of Frederick's opinions at an early age is the essay entitled: "Considerations on the Present State of the Body-Politic in Europe."[17] This was written in 1738, two years before he became King. A brief look at it shows that, in conscious preparation for his reign, Frederick pondered the most weighty political problems quite early in life, and that his thought had matured before his accession. His later works did nothing more than elaborate and clarify his earlier thinking. Despite what some historians have maintained, no internal contradiction in his thinking is apparent.[18]

Frederick may be said to accomplish three things in the 1738 essay. He explains what a prince ought to know in principle in order to acquire fame, distinguishes between statesmen and tyrants, and scrutinizes the present state of European politics focusing his interest, not surprisingly, on the major powers. A survey of these considerations will set the stage for a discussion of his decision to invade Silesia.

Frederick begins the essay by asserting that "Never did the public affairs of Europe merit greater attention than they do at present."[19] There is change in the air, new projects are talked of, new alliances are being formed and individual states are taking measures most in their interest, in order that "ambitious designs" may be executed.

A prince who is interested in acquiring fame must try not only to understand the actions of other princes, and what the effects of their actions are, but also must try to discover the true interest of each kingdom. And, as an able mechanic is not satisfied with looking at the outside of a watch, but opens it, and examines it with an eye to discovering what makes it work, so an "able politician applies himself to understand the permanent principles of courts, the engines of the politics of each prince."[20] With this knowledge he could, in theory, discern the source of all future actions of each kingdom, and hence be able to take precautionary measures against them.

Most princes are even incapable of understanding this, not to speak of acting according to its dictates, because they do not understand their calling. Most think incorrectly that

> God has expressly created, out of particular attention to their grandeur, their belief and their pride, that multitude of men, the prosperity of whom is committed to their charge; and that their subjects are destined only to be their instruments, and the ministers of their ungoverned passions.[21]

The reason that most princes think that their subjects are there for their pleasure is that their "first principles" are in error, and hence, all the consequences stemming from the first principles must also be mistaken. And these errors, since they relate to political practice, the highest possible activity of man, are very dangerous errors. They are much more dangerous than errors of mere speculation. It is for this reason that Frederick, in the preface to his *Refutation du Prince de Machiavel* condemns those scholars who think it more important to refute the maxims of Spinoza than of Machiavelli. It is really the latter who ought to be refuted, although they are equally in error, because he is most influential. Machiavelli has a direct and intentional influence on the political actions of man. He obfuscates the distinction between statesmen and tyrants, and gives corrupt advice to those young men who are ambitious to work for the public good. And these rulers, whose "first principles" are in error, are the cause of the greatest misery for mankind. There is nothing worse than the "vicious morals" and "unbridled passions" of rulers for they bring a lasting misery upon whole nations, while natural catastrophes, pestilence and the plagues of heaven are at least limited in their effect.[22]

Frederick now explains the true "first principles":

> Were princes to reject these erroneous ideas, were they desirous of inquiring into the end of their institution, they would then perceive that the rank of which they are so vain, and their elevation, is the work of the

people; that the millions of men over whom they are to watch did not yield themselves up the slaves of an individual, in order to render him more formidable and more puissant, and that they did not subject themselves to a fellow citizen to fall the martyrs of his caprices, and to be made sport of his whims, but that they chose the person among them whom they supposed the most just as their governor, that he might be to them a father; the most humane, that he might compassionate and alleviate their misfortunes; the most valiant, that he might defend them against their enemies; the most wise, that he might not insensibly plunge them into ruinous and destructive wars; and, in fine, the man who most effectually could represent the embodied states, and in whom sovereign power might be the support of justice and the laws, and not the instrument of committing crimes with impunity and of exercising tyranny.[23]

The right to rule, then, is inseparable from the obligation that the statesman has to his people. These "gods of the earth" have an obligation to secure the "happiness of their people" and to make government "mild and salutary."[24] The statesman not only looks after the safety and liberty of the people but tries to improve their condition and character at every turn. He is able to do this because he has been a student of political things: he has prepared himself for ruling. As a result, he has become, much like the ancient god Janus, able to look into the past and the future.[25] By virtue of his preparation, the statesman is not simply enslaved to the passions of the people; because he has greater foresight than they do, he does not simply do their bidding; he considers the long range interest of the people before he considers their immediate passions. If he would follow "the guidance of the passions and of caprice" he would be justly called a tyrant.[26] In other words, "The prince is to the nation he governs what the head is to the man; it is his duty to see, think, and act for the whole community, that he may procure it every advantage of which it is capable."[27]

The reason for the rise of government is "That general instinct in men, which leads them to procure for themselves the greatest possible happiness."[28] Because in the state of nature there is perfect liberty and equality, and because we know of no people, according to Frederick, "who have subjected themselves to a voluntary servitude,"[29] a statesman cannot enslave the people or allow his people to become enslaved without breaking the original compact. It is the duty, then, of princes and statesmen, to benefit their people; also, the people will quite naturally honor those who have benefited them.

Those princes who understand their employment properly do not look upon this duty lightly. They understand the connection between working for the public good and "true glory." The general misunderstanding and difficulty arises, according to Frederick, not because some princes seek glory and others don't—all princes really desire to have their names survive the grave—but because some men who seek eternal fame or glory do not understand that in order to achieve "true glory" they first have to love the public good.

The true merit of an excellent prince is to have a sincere love of the public good, of his country, and of fame; I say of fame, for that happy instinct which animates men with the desire of acquiring fame is the true principle of heroic actions. It is that impulse of the soul which raises it from its lethargy inciting it to useful, necessary and worthy enterprises.[30]

The love of the public good and the love of fame create a combination that will enable a man to spend all his waking hours for the benefit of people other than himself. But while the actions of statesmen may seem completely unselfish, they are not. On the other hand, their actions are not simply selfish either. Somehow the selfishness of the people is merged into the selfishness of the statesman—his desire for immortal fame—so that they become inseparable and dependent on one another; and something higher than mere selfishness is born. The *raison d'etre* of statesmen becomes "true glory"—as opposed to Machiavelli's "false glory," which leads princes only to appreciate the immediate applause of the people and makes them forget that kind of opinion that endures over the centuries—because only the quest for "true glory" has the salutary effect on the body politic which is essential for "true glory."

Frederick's ambition becomes even more clear when he discusses the present political situation in Europe. The discussion, inevitably, centers around Austria and France. The French are generally more clever than the Austrians. In the French, Frederick perceives "a uniform well-connected system of politics which never varies."[31] The French are able, because they are prudent, to take advantage of any situation that may arise, and benefit from it. The French make chance work for their own benefit. Frederick writes:

Whatever is studied in her project she conceals; and were we to judge by appearances we should imagine that fortune has taken this nation under her particular protection. Let us not deceive ourselves; fortune and chance are words without signification; the actual good fortune of France is her penetration, the foresight of her ministers, and the excellence of her measures.[32]

Frederick compares Louis XIV and Philip of Macedon by showing that Philip conquered Greece the same way that Louis tried to conquer Germany: he set the small and petty German states against one another, and by successfully disuniting them, he attempted to conquer them. Frederick also states that it is a mistake to think that merely because the great Louis is no longer alive French policy will differ. The Greeks also thought that their troubles had ended when Philip of Macedon died, but then

Alexander came to rule and proved even more ambitious than his father. France has always, according to Frederick, spoken the language of ambition, and ambition has a way of acting and thinking alike.[33] The Austrians, on the other hand, are not as well prepared. They are much less subtle and more dependent on force and the threat of force to accomplish their ends.

Besides predicting the "Diplomatic Revolution"—the alliance between the historical enemies, Austria and France, which actually occurred in 1756—Frederick also foresees that the death of Charles VI, the Holy Roman Emperor and ruler of the Habsburg hereditary lands, which is in no way expected, will be a time of great opportunity for France:

I can perceive projects more grand, more comprehensive, than those of which I have spoken, which may constitute a farther part of the system of France: and the moment which Providence has indicated for the execution of those vast designs seems to be that of the decease of his Imperial Majesty. What time can be more proper to give law to Europe? What circumstances more favorable under which everything may be risked?[34]

Charles's death will be an occasion for France to take advantage of because Charles had no male heirs. Charles tried to overcome the problem by publishing the Pragmatic Sanction in 1713. By it he attempted to ensure that his territories should pass undivided to his children in the male or female line, or, on their failure, to the two daughters of his elder brother Joseph I. These types of dynastic provisions were common in the German states, and the vastness of the Habsburg territories, their geographical dispersion, and the virtual autonomy of many of them in their internal affairs, seemed to make such an arrangement important. By the early 1720s Charles had secured the acceptance of the Pragmatic Sanction by the Diets of all his central European provinces. But as his hopes for a son vanished and it became clear that he must be succeeded by his eldest daughter, the Archduchess Maria Theresa, Austrian diplomacy centered on a series of efforts to have it guaranteed by all the major powers of Europe. He succeeded in getting their approval, so he left his daughter whole bundles of treaties guaranteeing her succession, but no means of enforcing them.

Of course the French are not the only ones who can take advantage of such an opportunity—any statesman with foresight, and sufficient resources, may do so. In Frederick's mind, however, there were no other states in Europe as penetrating as France. He assumes that the French will take advantage of the Emperor's death because

It is an unshaken principle among kings to aggrandize themselves as much as their power will permit; and, though such aggrandizement must be subject to different modifications, and infinitely varied according to the situation of provinces, the power of neighboring states, or fortunate opportunities, the principle is now the less unchangeable, and is never abandoned by monarchs.[35]

There are times, like the present, according to Frederick, when not very much can be gained: things are too quiet, settled. But the generally peaceful and constant situation of the 1730s will not last forever. "The mind of man, and the passions by which he is governed, are ever the same," according to Frederick.[36] Because this is true, "ambition continually acts and thinks alike,"[37] and the best way of "obtaining a just and exact idea of such events as happen among men" is to judge by comparison.[38] That is, one ought to select examples from history and draw a parallel between them and the present situation. It is the duty of statesmen to do this. By understanding the actions of the great statesmen of the past, one is able more fully to comprehend the present; should there be any great statesmen alive now, one could anticipate their actions.

Why is France in the best situation on the continent? Did she not lose the last major war? France is in a favorable position not because there are great statesmen at her helm—there are not—but because she had great statesmen leading her in the recent past, and the effects of their actions are still felt. Perhaps more important, however, is that "she meets with no opponents whose depth of mind, boldness, and abilities, can be dangerous to her."[39] There are *no* statesmen in all of Europe. Considering the present state of Europe, Frederick asks, what would a Richelieu or a Mazarin say were they at present to rise from the dead? Either of these men would be astonished not to find any great men alive: no Cromwell in England, no Prince of Orange in Holland, no Emperor Ferdinand in Germany, no Innocent II at Rome, no Marlborough or Eugene at the head of great armies. They would see, writes Frederick, "so general a debility among all those to whom the destiny of man is confided, in peace and in war: nor would they wonder were any one to vanquish and deceive the successors of these great men."[40]

Between his accession to the throne (May 31) and the death of Charles VI (October 20) the King of Prussia was preoccupied with domestic concerns. He introduced a number of reforms, which not only made his government more moderate but further increased his reputation in Europe. It is sufficient for us merely to list a few: he abolished torture as a mode of extracting confessions in criminal cases, ended certain brutalities in the army, established religious freedom, put an end to press censorship, re-opened the Berlin Academy of Sciences and restored a number of academicians to their chairs, and laid the foundation of a growing economic life.[41] A few days after his accession, it was brought to his attention that in addition to a poor harvest, cold weather in summer threatened a famine. He immediately opened the public granaries and ordered that grain be sold at a reasonable price, to relieve the sufferings of the poor. Perhaps the most significant change he made in domestic policy took place the second day he was in power. He gathered his ministers about him and declared to them that henceforth there would no longer be a distinction drawn between the interests of the King and those of the country: and should the two interests sometimes be incompatible, the interests of the country would be given preference. He said that this was to be the standard practice in all aspects of governmental administration, not only the personal policies of the King. After all, he told his ministers, a crown is just another hat, and not a very good one, for it allows the rain to fall in.[42] He made clear to his ministers, inherited from his father's reign, that he would keep them on, or offer them advancement, only according to their strengths and qualities. And significantly he discarded the trappings of the Holy Roman Empire, and himself took the title *Rex Borussorum*, King of the Prussians, as distinguished from the title of his two predecessors, *Rex Borussiae*, King in Prussia, that detached fragment of the Hohenzollern territories far to the east of Brandenburg and outside of the Holy Roman Empire.

Politics does exact patience, as Frederick well knew. He later wrote about this period and said: "the height of wisdom in a great man is to do all things in their proper season."[43] "Reason prescribes a rule on this subject from which it appears to me that no statesman ought to depart: which is to seize occasion, and when that is favourable to be enterprising: but neither to force occasion, nor leave everything to chance."[44] Sometimes the moment requires a prince to exert all his activity in order to profit the most from it; but there are other times when prudence requires inactivity, or the appearance of inactivity.

Nevertheless, he was continually reminded that his country had no "regular form." It consisted of small provinces scattered throughout Europe, and was virtually impossible to defend. Also, in order for Brandenburg-Prussia to conduct foreign policy in the past, she had always needed the support of one of the major powers. Before she could act she had to make sure that at least one, preferably more, of her borders was protected.[45] Other countries were more fortunate. France and Spain, for example, had one or more of their flanks covered by nature, as it were. This made them more secure and also allowed for a certain continuity in their policies. Unlike these countries, however, Prussia was not only exposed to attacks from all sides, but the very heart of the country was as exposed as its most outlying province.[46] Frederick's ancestors had left this kingdom, "a kind of hermaphrodite," neither an electorate nor a kingdom.[47] None of his ancestors had been successful in giving shape to it. Therefore, Frederick knew that

Fame was to be acquired by determing the nature of this being; and this sensation certainly was one of those which strengthened so many motives, comprising the King [i.e., Frederick] in grand enterprises.[48]

How was this to be? Frederick had a pretty good idea of how it was to be accomplished, but the momentous question was, when should the operation commence? Although the death of the Emperor Charles VI was unexpected, for he was only fifty-four years old, the general sentiment in Europe was that when the Emperor passed away and the Pragmatic Sanction came into effect, the document would fail to serve its intended purpose. Most of the European powers who had agreed to the Pragmatic Sanction did not do so out of belief that Maria Theresa's claim was the most valid, but from political motives, arising either out of negotiations which had taken place, or from a conviction that a monarchy like that of Austria was essential to the preservation of the balance of power in Europe.[49] Most eyes were on the King of Bavaria, for he would have been next in line for the Austrian succession had there been no Pragmatic Sanction and at every opportunity he was loudly proclaiming his rights and threatening Austria. It was generally thought that he would not be doing this, since Bavaria was not a very powerful kingdom, unless he had the support and encouragement of a greater power, like France.[50] And France had every reason to oppose the well being of her traditional rival. And should Bavaria have the support of France, there was reason to expect general war, as soon as the Emperor died. In fact, France did support Bavaria, but only half heartedly.[51] As it turned out, Bavaria and France were not the first to take advantage of the situation.

Other contemporaries had suggested (including Prince Eugene, who was deeply involved in the feverish diplomatic activity surrounding the Pragmatic Sanction) that the best guarantee of the unity of the hereditary lands, was to build up the army and the state finances—both were in less than satisfactory shape at the Emperor's death.[52] But this was not done. Frederick later said of the Emperor: "Charles VI had received from nature qualities which constitute the good citizen, but none of those which form the great man."[53] Under Charles VI the prestige and the power of the Habsburgs had declined greatly and in the closing years of his reign his armies had been defeated and dispirited: Austria had lost territory as a result of the War of the Polish Succession (1733–35) and in 1739 had signed the disgraceful Treaty of Belgrade with the Turks. Charles's ministers were old and incapable. And there was much discontent in the Habsburg hereditary lands, especially in Hungary, and Austrian garrisons had to be scattered for the protection and policing of distant parts of this territorial giant.[54]

Charles VI died from indigestion, caused by eating mushrooms. "This plate of *champignons* changed the destiny of Europe," wrote Voltaire in his *Memoirs*. Such a momentous event could not occur without reaction from some quarter. A few days after hearing of the Emperor's death Frederick made his decision to invade Austria's most fertile, and only Protestant province, Silesia.[55] Then he asked for the advice of his two most trusted advisors, Podewils and Field Marshal Schwerin. These two men of tried ability had no doubt that Europe would find itself in a great convulsion as a result of the Austrian succession. It appeared to them that two opposite courses were open for Prussia. And they thought that either one or the other must of necessity be followed. Prussia must either join in the inevitable attack on Austria, or better still, she might undertake her defence.[56]

They thought that it was a good possibility that Vienna, seeing itself threatened with complete destruction, would eagerly seize the opportunity of making a compromise with Prussia, as the only means of saving herself.[57] They proposed that Frederick maintain the old policy that all the Hohenzollern rulers had followed: to obtain recognition of their claims (be they in Silesia, Berg, Julich, or anywhere else) by offers of assistance. This was a policy that Frederick the Great had already thought to be insufficient, for it had always been rewarded with ingratitude.[58] It had proved, over the previous century, not to have been to Prussia's advantage. It certainly would, however, have been the safest policy to follow. Besides, his advisors told him that should Austria not be receptive to such an offensive and defensive alliance, one that would draw into it Russia and Sweden as well, then Frederick could follow the opposite course and ally himself with France, Bavaria, and Saxony. And, should this alliance be successful in the war, he could make certain that he would be awarded certain lands, perhaps even Silesia, in return for his support.[59]

What was Frederick to do? The opportunity had to be grasped immediately. But why should Frederick consider Silesia? Why not take Julich and Berg? At least Prussia had some legitimate claim to the latter two provinces, whereas she had none to Silesia—although she claimed to have rights to at least part of it. Silesia, unlike the provinces of Julich and Berg, was a large and prosperous province. It was the most prosperous province the Habsburgs possessed. Also, the majority of its inhabitants were Protestants and generally disliked the often harsh rule of the Habsburgs. The important consideration, however, was that Silesia would add shape to Prussia. That is to say, it was immediately to the south of Brandenburg, the heart of the Hohenzollern possessions, could easily be taken by Prussia for it was hardly defended by Austria, and once taken, could be defended. The same could not be said of Julich and Berg. Those provinces—even if they could be conquered easily enough—could not be defended as easily. They couldn't be defended not only because of simple problems such as distance from the Hohenzollern heartland, but also because Frederick could have been assured that once he took these provinces on the Rhine, he would immediately offend western European states whose wrath he would prefer not to incur. Neither of the maritime powers, nor France, would think well of seeing Prussia, already a power to be reckoned with in northern Germany, growing in strength at their doorstep.[60] But, should Prussia conquer Silesia, thought Frederick, she could almost certainly count on the support of some of the major powers (e.g., France) for it was in their interest to weaken Austria. Also, Silesia was of great importance for another reason. Frederick feared that Saxony and Bavaria, both having claims to the Habsburg crown, would use Silesia to sow discord between themselves and Austria. The Elector of Saxony was also King of Poland, and it was not inconceivable that Saxony and Poland could be united physically as well. Only Silesia separated them. Then Brandenburg-Prussia's rise in Europe would be prevented.[61] For there was increasingly less likelihood that Prussia would have opportunities to grow toward the west: the powers of Europe had prevented that possibility with great energy for quite some time, and there was no reason to think that they would in the future allow Prussia that chance.

The question remained for Frederick: could he allow events to take their course without trying to have some effect on them? In the words of Leopold von Ranke, whom Winston Churchill called the "most pregnant and fairest of historians,"[62]

And was Prussia to allow this, we will not say, to happen, but to become possible, when she manifestly wielded the most formidable power? What would succeeding generations have said of Frederick, had he suffered things to take their course without intervention on his part?[63]

Frederick then carefully calculated his political opportunities. The invasion of Silesia was not, despite what some historians have said, a rash act, one committed by an enthusiastic overly zealous young monarch, who did not know what he was doing, and who did not consider the possible consequences of his actions. Frederick thought about what the great powers would and could do, and he decided that none would react quickly. England, of course, would not act on her own, unless perhaps George II thought that his Hanoverian possessions were threatened, and Frederick could easily make certain that that would not be thought. France would be all too pleased to see the Habsburgs embroiled in difficulties. Instead of fearing an adverse immediate reaction from France he had reason to hope for support, once his initial advance proved successful. Russia might be a problem, but Frederick calculated that Russia so feared a possible attack on its northern flank, should it make any moves to help Austria, that the Russians would be hesitant to act. Besides, fortune became the handmaiden of design, for the Empress Anne died eight days after Charles and this caused much internal turmoil in Russia. By then Frederick had started preparations for the invasion, and when he heard of the Czarina's death, he became more than ever firmly convinced that chance was in his favor.[64] The "great Machiavellian deed," as one historian called it,[65] was going forward.

It may be said that Frederick's only miscalculation in the whole enterprise was his assumption that after his invasion of Silesia proved successful Maria Theresa would be willing to give up the province in order to have Prussia's support and protection in the even greater upheavals that were sure to follow. This support would obviously also entail supporting her husband Francis of Lorraine to be the next Holy Roman Emperor. This was not to be, for no one yet knew the noble and determined, and perhaps imprudent, character of the Queen of Hungary. As Frederick was moving into Silesia in the middle of December, he sent an envoy to Vienna to offer such terms to Austria. She resolutely replied to the ambassador, overcoming the objections of her husband and councillors who were more receptive to making a deal with Frederick, in the following terms:

Never, never, will the Queen renounce an inch of all her hereditary lands though she perish with all that remains to her. Rather the Turks in front of Vienna, rather cessions of the Netherlands to France, rather any concession to Bavaria and Saxony, than renunciation of Silesia.[66]

Prussia was able, despite tremendous odds, to hold on to Silesia. It is also significant that in the War of the Austrian Succession that followed the invasion of Silesia, it was not Austria that found immediate allies, but the aggressor Prussia: France, Bavaria and Saxony joined Prussia in the war against Austria, and they did so on Prussia's terms. England was the only power to support the Pragmatic Sanction.

The most important of Frederick's demands from his allies was that Austria itself should not be liquidated; its existence was much too important for maintaining a balance of power on the continent.[67] Despite the many opportunities Frederick would have to attack, and conquer Vienna, he refused to take advantage of them, much to the disgust of Bavaria and France.

The European powers were surprised by Frederick's invasion. Although by mid-November many suspected that Prussia would invade Silesia, they still found it hard to believe that this young king would, in the words of Guy Dickens, the English ambassador to Berlin, even contemplate such an "extraordinary undertaking."[68] For months preceding the invasion, the English made offers to Frederick trying to satisfy some of the demands Prussia had in the past. For example they tried to assure Frederick that they would do everything in their power to procure him a "reasonable satisfaction with regard to the affair" of Berg and Julich.[69] But of course Frederick was not to be satisfied with such promises. He was intent on acting alone, in the best interest, as he saw it, of his country.

On 15 November, Guy Dickens wrote to England that about twenty Prussian battalions were on the march and there was no doubt "that they have here some enterprise of consequence in view," and said that "the general opinion is, that His Prussian Majesty must have some designs upon Silesia."[70] But by November 19, Dickens no longer thought that it was only Silesia Frederick was interested in, he thought that the Prussian troops could possibly move towards Cleves, or even Poland. The situation remained ambiguous.[71] That is exactly the way Frederick intended it. As Dickens stated on 3 December, it was clear that Frederick's contacts and discussions with the Hague, as well as London, were intended to "deceive us, and to conceal, for a while, his ambitious and mischievous designs."[72] By the 6th of December Dickens was certain of Frederick's designs. In reporting to London on the audience he had had with the Prussian king the day before, he wrote that Frederick told him that he had no intention of supporting the Pragmatic Sanction because he himself had never agreed to it, and Austria—it had become clear years ago—was reneging on her promise to support Prussia's interest in Julich and Berg. Frederick also said that Great Britain had no right to enquire into his designs, for he only had the good of the public in mind, and "that he had weighed it with the greatest attention."[73] Frederick told Dickens that he had "examined all the advantages and disadvantages" which could result from his actions and now there was nothing else to do but support them vigorously.[74]

On December 16, 1740, 40,000 Prussian troops, almost half his army, with their young king leading them, crossed the border into Silesia. The banners under which the soldiers marched were to have been inscribed "Pro Deo et Patria," but Frederick, according to Voltaire, deleted the "Pro Deo," saying that there was no need to involve God in the quarrels of men.[75] In all of Silesia there were less than 7,000 Austrian soldiers when Frederick invaded. By the middle of January, 1741, practically the whole of the province was in Prussian hands. The Imperial city of Breslau, which was also the Austrian administrative headquarters for Silesia, opened its gates to the invaders, thankfully accepting Frederick's offer of neutrality in what was becoming a general Austro-Prussian war. Maria Theresa tried to collect troops from the other parts of her dominions, but this could not be done until April, 1741. On April 10, 1741, the Prussians gave the Austrians battle at Mollwitz, and despite an impressive Austrian onslaught, the well drilled Prussian infantry proved its mettle. Prussia was victorious. If possible, this battle, even more than the invasion, caused a sensation in Europe. A minor power had defeated a great power. A new great power, Frederick's Prussia, had emerged in the heart of Europe.

Frederick showed himself to be above his contemporaries. As soon as he appeared on the scene, he stood at the center of European politics and began to master it. And this domination grew almost continuously until his death. He had a purpose, and although the means by which he tried to attain it often varied he never lost sight of it: to give form to his scattered territories; to insure the survival of those lands that henceforth would collectively be called Prussia; and to free his country from the bonds of necessity that had shackled her statesmen for the previous hundred years. His contemporaries continued to be surprised not only by his actions, but by his success. Try as they might, however, they could not frustrate his ambition.

Notes

1. Otto von Bismarck, *The Memoirs*, trans. A.J. Butler (New York: Harper & Bros., 1899), Vol. I., p. 320.

2. A.J.P. Taylor, *The Course of German History* (New York: Capricorn Books, 1962), p. 27.

3. G.P. Gooch, *Frederick the Great: The Ruler, The Writer, The Man* (New York: Alfred A. Knopf, 1947), p. 13.

4. Frederick II, *Refutation du Prince de Machiavel*, "Studies on Voltaire and the Eighteenth Century," ed. Theodore Besterman, (Geneve: Institute et Musse Voltaire, 1958), Vol. V., p. 169.

    This book, a chapter by chapter analysis of Machiavelli's *Prince*, was completed a few months before Frederick ascended the throne, and published, anonymously, three months after he became King. Although Voltaire helped to publish it, Frederick later repudiated the original edition because he thought that Voltaire was singularly unfit to edit it. Frederick later republished it himself, without Voltaire's additions and deletions. The Besterman edition is the only reliable one; it includes Frederick's original as well as Voltaire's changes. A new translation by Paul Sonnino is now available: Frederick of Prussia, *The Refutation of Machiavelli's* Prince *or Anti–Machiavel* (Athens: Ohio University Press, 1981).

5. Thomas Babington Macaulay, *Critical and Historical Essays*, "Frederick the Great" (London: Everyman's Library, 1907), Vol. II, p. 128.

6. *Ibid.*, p. 129.

7. *Ibid.*, p. 131. Also see, Mark A. Thompson, "The War of the Austrian Succession," *The New Cambridge Modern History* (1966) Vol. VII, p. 417. Wherein he states: "Frederick was motivated by desire to strengthen Prussia and acquire personal glory." Also see, W.H. Bruford, "The Organization and Rise of Prussia," *Ibid.*, p. 307. Bruford says: "He caught by infection the sense of duty to something greater than himself, and when this was combined with the love of power, the same self-assertiveness which had prompted his revolt [against his father] became the desire for glory and for the reality of power which inspired his first decisive action as king, the invasion of Silesia."

8. Gerhard Ritter, *Frederick the Great: An Historical Profile*, trans. Peter Paret (London: Eyre & Spottiswoode, 1968), p. 54 and repeated p. 68. Cf. Friedrich Meinecke, *Machiavellism: The Doctrine of Raison d'Etat and its Place in Modern History* (New Haven: Yale University Press, 1962), Ch. 12.

9. Ritter, *op. cit.*, p. 65.

10. *Ibid.*, p. 66.

11. *Ibid.*

12. *Ibid.*

13. In a letter to his friend Karl Stephan Jordan, who had been his reader while crown-prince, written somewhere in Silesia, after he had conquered virtually the whole prov-

ince and shocked all of Europe, Frederick complains about all his duties, and states: "Were men wise, they would treat the phantom fame, which occasions them so much trouble, and induces them to dedicate that time to pain which heaven gave them for enjoyment, with greater neglect. Thou wilt find me more of a philosopher than thou hast imagined; for philosopher, more or less, I have always been. My age, the ardour of the passions, the desire for renown, curiosity itself, that I may conceal nothing from thee, and in fine, a secret instinct has torn me from the sweets of repose, by which I was charmed. I have been seduced by the desire of seeing my name in the gazettes, and afterward in history." Frederick II, *Posthumous Works of Frederick II, King of Prussia* (hereafter cited as *Works*) trans. Thomas Holcroft (London, 1789), Vol. VII, p. 63. The letter is dated March 3, 1741. Also note his letter to Jordan of February 29, 1741: "I love war for the sake of war; but were I not a king, I should be nothing more than a philosopher. In fine, each man must follow his occupation; and it is my whim not to do anything by halves." p. 60. And his letter of February 2, 1742 to the same: "I am a lunatic dear friend, thus to quit repose for the flivorous glory of uncertain success. But the frenzies of this world are sufficiently numerous; and I suppose mine to be one of the most ancient." p. 144.

14. Frederick II, *Works*, Vol. VI, p. 482 (May 16, 1739).
15. *Ibid.*, Vol. VII, p. 43 (January 1740).
16. Frederick, *History of My Own Times*, *Works*, Vol. I, pp. xx and xix.
17. "Considerations of the Present State of the Body-Politic in Europe," *Works*, Vol. IV, pp. 341–386.
18. Cf. Meinecke, p. 277.
19. "Considerations," p. 342.
20. *Ibid.*
21. "Considerations," p. 384.
22. Frederick II, *Refutation du Prince de Machiavel*, p. 169.
23. "Considerations," pp. 383–384.
24. "Considerations," p. 385.
25. *Refutation du Prince de Machiavel*, p. 294.
26. "An Essay on Forms of Government and the Duties of Sovereigns," *Works*, Vol. V, p. 9. (This essay was written in 1781).
27. "An Essay on Forms of Government," p. 15.
28. *Ibid.*, p. 8.
29. *Refutation du Prince de Machiavel*, pp. 223–224. Cf., "Considerations," p. 385; and "An Essay on Forms of Government," p. 24.
30. *The History of My Own Times*, p. xv. Cf., *Refutation du Prince de Machiavel*, pp. 314–315. Also note Bismarck's remark: "But this longing for applause, this love of approbation, is in a sovereign a powerful and sometimes profitable motive; when it is lacking, the monarch is more than usually prone to lapse into epicurian inactivity. Un petit roi d'Yvetet, se levant tard, se couchant tot, dormant fort bien sans glaric, does not conduce to the success of his country." Otto von Bismarck, *Reflections and Reminiscences*, ed. Theordore S. Hamerow (New York: Harper Torchbook, 1968), p. 252.
31. "Considerations," p. 349.
32. *Ibid.*, p. 366.
33. *Ibid.*, pp. 375–376.
34. *Ibid.*, p. 367.
35. *Ibid.*, p. 364.
36. *Ibid.*, p. 371.
37. *Ibid.*, p. 376.
38. *Ibid.*, p. 370.
39. *Ibid.*, p. 369.

40. *Ibid.*, p. 370.
41. Leopold von Ranke, *Memoirs of the House of Brandenburg* (London: John Murray, 1849), Vol. II, pp. 42–75.
42. *Ibid.*, p. 45. Also see, D.B. Horn, *Frederick the Great and the Rise of Prussia* (London: The English Universities Press Ltd., 1964), p. 37.
43. *The History of My Own Times, Works*, p. xxvi.
44. *Ibid.*, p. xxv.
45. *Ibid.*, p. 81.
46. Ranke, Vol. II, pp. 127–128.
47. *The History of My Own Times*, p. 90.
48. *Ibid.*
49. Ranke, Vol. II, p. 109.
50. *Ibid.*, p. 109. Max Immich, *Geschichte des Europaischen Staatensystems von 1660 bis 1789* (Munchen: Verlag von R. Oldenbourg, 1905) pp. 304–305.
51. Arthur M. Wilson, *French Foregin Policy During the Administration of Cardinal Fleury 1726–1743* (Cambridge, Mass.: Harvard University Press, 1936) p. 329.
52. Derek McKay, *Prince Eugene of Savoy* (London: Thames and Hudson, 1977) p. 223.
53. *The History of My Own Times*, p. 3.
54. Horn, *Frederick the Great, op. cit.*, p. 39. Also see, Karl A. Roider, *The Reluctant Ally: Austria's Policy in the Austro-Turkish War, 1737–1739* (Baton Rouge: Louisiana State University Press, 1972), p. 57. For a complete account of Austria's situation see Oswald Redlich, *Das Werden Einer Grossmacht: Osterreich von 1700 bis 1740* (Wien: Rudolf M. Rohrer Verlag, 1942).
55. Friedrich's des Grossen, *Politische Correspondenz* (Berlin: Alexander Duncker, 1879) Vol. I, p. 90–91.
56. Ranke, Vol. II, pp. 119–120. *Politische Correspondenz* , pp. 74–78.
57. Ranke, Vol. II, p. 120.
58. *Ibid.*, p. 134.
59. *Ibid.*, p. 121.
60. Dickens to Harrington, 6 December 1740, P.R.O., S.P. 90/48.
61. Ranke, Vol. II, pp. 123–124.
62. Winston S. Churchill, *Marlborough: His Life and Times* (London: George Harrap & Co., Ltd., 1939) Vol. I, p. 352.
63. Ranke Vol. II, p. 124.
65. *Ibid.*, p. 129.
65. Otto Pflanze, *Bismarck and the Development of Germany* (Princeton University Press, 1963), p. 22.
66. Quoted in C.A. Macartney, *Maria Theresa and the House of Austria* (London: The English Universities Press, Ltd., 1969), p. 34.
67. Dickens to Harrington, 6 December 1740, P.R.O., S.P. 90/48.
68. Dickens to Robinson, 13 December 1740, B.M. Add. Mss. 23806 (264).
69. Harrington to Robinson, 10 October 1740, B.M. Add. Mss. 23806.
70. Dickens to Harrington, 15 November 1740, P.R.O., S.P. 90/48.
71. Dickens to Harrington, 19 November 1740, P.R.O., S.P. 90/48.
72. Dickens to Harrington, 3 December 1740, P.R.O., S.P. 90/48.
73. Dickens to Harrington, 6 December 1740, P.R.O., S.P. 90/48.
74. *Ibid.*
75. J.M. Thompson, *Lectures on Foreign History* (Oxford: Basil Blackwell, 1979) p. 261.

5

THE FAILURE OF HENRY V

Larry Peterman

THE CRITICAL RECEPTION OF SHAKESPEARE'S HENRY MONMOUTH (HENRY V) is one of the more curious cases in Shakespeare studies. For his part, the poet lavishes what seems almost excessive praise upon Henry, crediting him with great feats of arms at Shrewsbury and Agincourt and saluting him, on the eve of his French campaign, as "the mirror of all Christian kings." Yet critics more often than not give Henry a bad press. Depending upon their own sensibilities, they fault him as a man, e.g., for his cold-hearted rejection of Falstaff; as a Christian, e.g., for his apparent hypocrisy in trying to appease God for the way the crown came to him; and as a king, e.g., for his disregard of the "customs" essential to a sound politics.[1] It follows that Shakespeare's treatment of Henry V presents an immediate problem. How are we to balance the laudatory depiction of Henry in the Lancastrian tetrology with the lingering impression it leaves that Henry is somehow flawed? How, in short, are we to understand what is wanting in Henry without doing a disservice to Shakespeare's overt account of him?

The epilogue to *Henry V* provides a point of departure with regard to this question. Although critics have not given it much attention—perhaps it is too obvious—it represents the one place where Shakespeare offers an explicit counterpoint to the otherwise triumphal portrait of Henry that the Lancastrian plays provide. The epilogue, for a start, reminds us that Henry's victories are illusory in the sense that they are but the prologue to the disastrous reign of his son Henry VI, and to the War of the Roses.[2] More important for our purposes, it also suggests something of Henry's involvement in these later events. Somehow the triumphal king fails to assure the perpetuation of "the world's best garden he achieved and [of which] he left his son imperial lord," i.e., Henry fails to pass on his own success to his natural successor.

In such terms, the epilogue points to two of Henry's dominant—but ultimately unrealized—hopes. First, there is his "imperial" ambition to unite England and France, initially by conquest and finally by the issue of his marriage to Katherine of France. Henry's ambition sets the stage for his regime's and his son's failure. As the epilogue puts it, there is a connection between the loss of France and the "bleed[ing]" of England.[3] Second, there is Henry's desire to create a new royal line and thereby assure that his son and his political heir will be the same. The king, as Exeter says of Henry, wants the crown for himself and "his heirs."[4]

Among other things, then, the epilogue directs attention to the way Henry's political and family ambitions intertwine. It also raises the question of a connection between his failure to create a lasting order that significantly expands the political horizons of his ancestors (one thinks of his grandfather John of Gaunt's lament for "this little world" of England) and his desire to establish a line of succession that would be in keeping with his ancestors' notions of descent and inheritance (one thinks of Gaunt's acceptance of Richard II's lineal or blood right to the throne).[5] The epilogue, in other words, leads us to ask whether Henry V's political objective, which departs from that of his predecessors, is consistent with his lineal objective, which seems more or less aligned with that of his predecessors. Does Henry's fault, then, lie in his attempt to move beyond the political horizons of his ancestors without abandoning their belief in family and blood ties?

This question helps place Henry V's reign in the context of Shakespeare's English history. As a group, the history plays chronicle England's transformation from the medieval and largely feudal world of Richard II to the renaissance and largely modern world of Henry VIII. As Allan Bloom puts it, they move from the "moribund medieval England" of Richard, where rule rests upon divine support, to the contemporary realm of Henry, where rule demands as well the support of "nobles and commoners."[6] Among the things that change in the course of this transition is the political importance of blood ties and ancestry. A lessening of emphasis upon divine support for the king's line is paralleled by a lessening emphasis upon breeding as a ground for political prominence.

Here it is useful to contrast passages from *Richard II* and *Henry VIII*. In the former, the king's "sacred blood" testifies to the two major bases of temporal position, divine sanction and bloodright. To paraphrase Bloom, Richard embodies the idea that political legitimacy combines properties associated with descent and properties associated with divinity.[7] This conception, particularly in its lineal aspect, suffuses Richard's realm and may be seen even outside matters relating directly to the crown. Bolingbroke (Henry IV) opposes royal policy by way of a lineal claim ("Therefore personally I lay my claim to my inheritance of free descent.") and York defends him on similar grounds ("Did not [Gaunt] deserve to have an heir. Is not his heir a well-deserving son?"). Again, Northumberland cautions the king's opponents to be careful lest they injure their descendents as well as themselves: "the king will severely prosecute 'gainst our lives, our children, and our heirs." Indeed, only Richard sees himself as detached from the demands of kinship and blood, a personal vision that, perhaps, is a clue to the mixture of arrogance and condescension that leads to his downfall:[8]

Were [Bolingbroke] my brother, nay, my kingdom's heir,
As he is but my father's brother's son,
Now by my sceptre's awe I make a vow,
Such neighbour nearness to our sacred blood
Should nothing privilege him nor partialize
The unstooping firmness of my upright soul.

With this self-description, Richard emphasizes his supposed difference from the less abstracted or more mortal men about him. By the same token, his extraordinary and almost unnatural hauteur with regard to the bonds of birth and common blood underscores the lineal and ancestral character of the medieval regime of which his kingdom is the last example.

By the end of *Henry VIII*, the character of the politics of *Richard II* has clearly changed. Ancestry no longer provides a sufficient—or even necessary—basis for political claims. This may be particularly illustrated by the last scene of the play, where the future Elizabeth I makes an appearance in swaddling clothes. The centerpiece of the scene is a long prophetic speech by Archbishop Cranmer—himself evidence of Henry VIII's subjugation of the clergy and the development of modern English politics—wherein we learn what the world will be like under Elizabeth and her successor, James I. Cranmer draws a bright picture of the future but he does not disguise the fact that modern England will set aside things valued in an earlier England. Modern Englishmen, for example, will measure their virtue by reference to the monarch rather than by reference to standards associated with breeding:[9]

God shall be truly known, and those about her
From her shall read the perfect ways of honour,
And by those claim their greatness, not by blood.

Cranmer reinforces this point, first by reminding us that Elizabeth will die "yet a virgin"—breaking with the tradition that a principal duty of the sovereign is to provide an heir—and second by likening the future queen to "the bird of wonder, the maiden phoenix," out of whose ashes springs "another heir, as great in admiration as herself." Elizabeth as a model monarch is thus identified with a form of succession that owes nothing to natural descent or generation.

In a similar vein, Cranmer describes the realm of James I as one that no longer heeds things which, for Gaunt and his contemporaries, represented political excellence. Gaunt's understanding of politics is consistent with the classical-medieval position that sound political associations presume men of common origin living in a common and circumscribed territory. The England whose loss Gaunt bemoans in his most famous speech represents a separable people or nation bound together by common blood and identified with a particular land. In other words, the England he admired defined itself according to its differences from other peoples gathered in their own lands and groupings:[10]

This happy breed of men, this little world,
This precious stone set in the silver sea,
Which serves it in the office of a wall,
Or as a moat defensive to a house,
Against the envy of less happier lands;
this blessed plot, this earth, this realm, this England,
This nurse, this teeming womb of royal kings,
Fear'd by their breed, and famous by their birth, . . .

Cranmer, however, reverses this view of England. As he has it, James will spread his "greatness of name" to all places under the sun and "make new nations." In contrast to Gaunt's vision of England, Cranmer looks to a world where paternal claims are diminished and rulers may aspire to create nations free of the old concern that political orders ought to be small and responsive to what is unique about particular peoples and places.

In their different ways, it follows, Gaunt and Cranmer represent political as well as historical poles in Shakespeare's English history. Gaunt tends toward the classical-medieval world's essentially parochial politics —late medievalism's romance with the idea of world empire notwithstanding—Cranmer toward modernity's universalism. Both positions are, in their own ways, consistent. Gaunt's concern for breeding and the special qualities of Englishmen conforms to a politics that emphasizes the strength and unity of homogenous peoples governed by their own kind in their "natural" settings: his England is a "fortress built by Nature for herself." Cranmer's prophecy of a world that sets aside the standards associated with ancestry conforms to an imperial politics in which differences among peoples and between lands have no more than conventional weight: his James will "like a mountain cedar reach his branches to all the plains about him," and thereby overcome the kinds of natural barriers—e.g., that between mountain and plain—so important to Gaunt—e.g., the sea which is a "wall" or "moat defensive."[11]

It is in this context, in turn, that Henry V's dilemma becomes apparent. Had Henry wholly followed the arguments of either Gaunt or Cranmer, he might, at least, have pursued a consistent political course. But by adhering to Gaunt's ancestral bias while inclining in the direction of Cranmer's imperialism, he ran afoul of the differences and tensions between ancient and modern thought. To be successful in the course he took, in other words, Henry would have had somehow to bridge the gap between the politics of the past and of the future. Conversely, his failure

may be said to represent a Shakespearean measure of the distance between the two ways and, perhaps, of their ultimate incommensurability.
What, then, we are led to ask, impels Henry to take the course he does,
which is but another way of asking what accounts for the transition from
the happy picture of Henry in the body of *Henry V* to the disappointment
of its epilogue?

To understand the sources of Henry's difficulties and, ultimately, of
his shortcomings, it is well to begin by considering the "noble change"
whereby he ceases to be identified with the ways of Eastcheap and becomes "the mirror of all Christian kings." This is the dominant theme in
Henry's career, at least prior to Agincourt, but its implications go beyond
Henry's own fortunes. In planning and bringing about his apparent
transition from wastrel prince to deserving monarch, Henry seizes an
opportunity coeval with the faith of his age. The political mutation he
"purposes" has the character of redemption in that it amounts to a secular
expression of the expectation that is the greatest source of hope for his
fellows. Thus, as has been noted before, he utilizes the terminology of
the faithful to explain his plans in his first soliloquy:[12]

So when this loose behaviour I throw off,
And pay the debt I never promised,
By how much better than my word I am,
By so much shall I falsify men's hopes;
And like bright metal on a sullen ground,
My reformation, glitt'ring o'er my fault,
Shall show more goodly, and attract more eyes
Than that which hath no foil to set it off.
I'll so offend, to make offence a skill,
Redeeming time when men think least I will.

Like the faithful, then, Henry looks to a better time ahead, but he
looks to it in this sphere rather than the next. And like them, he seems
assured that he can change or at least appear changed, although his
change will fulfill a human rather than a divine promise. This is not to
say that Henry is the only link in the Lancastrian plays between the
notions of temporal transformation and Christian redemption. It is
curious, for example, that the Archbishop of Canterbury dates history
from the "year of our redemption" in the course of devising an argument
which simultaneously denies the old Salic Law and provides Henry a new
claim to the French throne. Again, that Falstaff argues against Henry's
reformation and, at the same time, takes comfort in the parable of
Lazarus bears notice.[13] But these things notwithstanding, Henry is the
most obvious manifestation in the plays of the position that the changes
to which men look forward in the next world may, in some measure, be
reflected in this.

To appreciate the innovative quality of Henry's redemptive approach
to secular affairs—at least in the context of his own times—it may be

contrasted with the approach of Richard and his followers, for whom redemption is a matter of extratemporal rewards and punishments for temporal behavior. Richard, for example, would see his betrayers "damn'd without redemption." Moreover, both he and those around him doubt the possibilities for change in this life and suspect such changes as can occur. On the possibility for change, Mowbray's rejoinder to Richard's statement that the lion tames the leopard may be considered typical: "yea, but not change his spots." And regarding what change connotes, we may compare the thought of one of Richard's soldiers—just before he decamps—that England's troubles "whisper fearful change" with Richard's thought that his quarrel with Bolingbroke will "change the complexion of [England's] maid-pale peace to scarlet indignation and bedew her pasture's grass with faithful English blood."[14] From Richard's perspective, then, the change that Henry V personifies represents a departure from the ideas that men must wait until the next life to achieve their final forms and that the best temporal order is associated with changeless or stable qualities.

Although Henry's version of secular redemption is tied to Christian doctrine, it is heterodox insofar as it reverses the way in which doctrine and secular matters had heretofore intertwined. If Henry succeeds in the intention he announces in his first soliloquy, he will stand as an example that the secular order is not, as Richard thought, a fixed monument to divine grace. And Henry does succeed, of course. The descriptions of him at the beginning of *Henry V* by Canterbury and Bishop Ely are sufficient evidence of that:[15]

Cant.   The courses of his youth promised it not.
        The breath no sooner left his father's body,
        But that his wildness, mortified in him,
        Seem'd to die too; yea, at that very moment
        Consideration, like an angel came
        And whipp'd the offending Adam out of him,
   ⸰   Leaving his body as a paradise,
        To envelope and contain celestial spirits.
        Never was such a sudden scholar made;
        Never came reformation in a flood,
        With such a heady currence, scouring faults; . . .

Ely.   We are blessed in the change.

This exchange is illuminating in ways other than its testimony that Henry accomplishes what he had set out to do. Canterbury's allusions to the seemingly angelic quality of Henry's transformation, and Ely's on the blessing it connotes, bring home the point made above. Henry's change, which is a "wonder" to Canterbury given the prince's early "addiction" to Eastcheap, is initially explicable to these clerics in terms of the changes

usually ascribable to divine influence.[16] That is, the theological model of
change serves as a medium for explaining or describing Henry's worldly
change. Yet both Canterbury and Ely realize Henry has left the theological or scriptural model. His reformation does not, as has apparently
been the case before, depend on miracles or other kinds of divine intercession in human affairs. If Canterbury describes Henry's change in terms
of divine images, Ely accounts for it in natural terms. And if Henry's
reversal of his ways might have once been considered miraculous, it will
be so no more since miracles are "ceased":[17]

Ely.   The strawberry grows underneath the nettle
        And wholesome berries thrive and ripen best
        Neighbour'd by fruit of baser quality:
        And so the prince obscured his contemplation
        Under the veil of wildness; which, no doubt,
        Grew like the summer grass, fastest by night,
        Unseen, yet crescive in his faculty.
Cant.   It must be so; for miracles are ceased;
        And therefore we must needs admit the means
        How things are perfected.

Thus Henry's reformation provides those about him a standard for
what may be achieved in the way of changing one's temporal aspect upon
a wholly natural basis. Its theological origins notwithstanding, his redemption foreshadows two of the more pronounced features of the post-
medieval world. First, to risk the use of extreme examples, it moves us
toward the Machiavellian idea that men may, without affronting nature,
vary extraordinarily in this world, and, by extention, may be considered
extraordinarily malleable.[18] Henry, in this sense, comes as close as any
Shakespearean character to heeding Machiavelli's advice to princes to
deviate from that to which their natures incline and to change with time
and circumstances. Second, it moves us in the direction of the modern
view of man as self-maker, whereby the idea that God creates and by the
same logic may recreate man is transmuted into the idea that man creates
and may recreate himself.[19]

The unfolding of this new way of looking at things provides one of
the unifying elements in the Lancastrian plays. It also eventually leads us
back to the problems that attend Henry V's dual purposes as king. The
overthrow of Richard severs the tie between a permanent, or relatively
so, natural order and politics. That is, it at least attenuates the connection
between what always applies to men as men, e.g., natural inheritance and
age differences, and what applies to men in a specifically political sense,
e.g., position or status. As Richard puts it regarding Bolingbroke's ascent
to the throne, he is "too young" to be the new king's father but the king is
"old enough to be my heir."[20] Thus ends the correspondence between
paternity and political succession which previously decided political mat-

ters. Now men will have to look elsewhere to decide such things. On this point, it is useful to recall that historically the Lancastrian right to the throne rested upon a parliamentary or legal grant rather than upon a natural claim. The distance between the two Henries and Richard in this regard may be represented by the opposition between Henry V's consciousness of his obligation to his parliament—his last act in *IIHenry IV* is to call a parliament—and Richard's statement that "we were not born to sue, but to command."[21]

In a similar fashion, the Lancastrian ascent stands opposed to the medieval resolution of the problem of the evolution of political right, whereby men are considered alike in God's eyes but God—either directly or through His instrument nature—remains the source of the distinctions according to which legitimate rule is established. All men may be the same with respect to the heavenly sphere, in other words, but the temporal sphere is ordered by distinctions ultimately traceable to divine influence. In the absence of such a dichotomy, medieval man saw the only resort in temporal affairs would be right of arms.[22] Richard's reaction to those attempting to preempt his place is, therefore, consistent with the opinions of his time. He is willing to grant that he and Bolingbroke are alike in their capacities to "serve God," but he "cannot mend" revolt nor admit a temporal equivalence between his own "great glory" and his "puny" subjects. For all his early posture of detachment towards the ties of kinship and blood, he is at one with Mowbray—the object of his posturing—in the view that political importance is largely the result of "infused," in contradistinction to acquired, qualities. To be king was to be essentially different from other men. Conversely, to be as other men —to "live with bread like you, feel want, taste grief, need friends"—is to be other than a king—"subjected thus, How can you say to me, I am a king?" Thus, when Richard is stripped of his pedigree, he loses his sense of his place in the world, what today we might call his sense of self. With "no name, no title," he plays, with little success, at being other men but can only conclude that the world is unsatisfying to all, i.e., that he is at one with other men only insofar as he questions the satisfactions of this life:[23]

................But whate'er I be
Nor I, nor any man that but man is,
With nothing shall be pleas'd, till he be eas'd
With being nothing.

To his end, then, Richard adheres to the medieval dualism between the way of this world and that of the next. The two are aligned according to grace but the fixed distinctions of the one are to be set against the equality of the other. In turn, he handles the possible tension in this position, whereby mortal differences are set against heavenly communality, by seizing upon medievalism's separation of the flesh and spirit. His last words are a fitting testament to his life in that they offer us his view of his special place, by blood, in temporal affairs and his appreciation of the generalized Christian hope of what is to follow when physical existence ends:[24]

> —Exton, thy fierce hand
> Hath with the king's blood stain'd the king's own land,
> Mount, mount, my soul! thy seat is up on high,
> Whilst my gross flesh sinks downward, here to die.

With the advent of the two Henries, we experience a shift from Richard's positions. Although the new ruling family still is committed to the idea of blood ties—Bolingbroke worries over Hal's "degeneracy" and Hal seeks to reestablish "lineal honour"—its sense of the permanence of human and political distinctions is very much lessened in comparison with Richard's. Perhaps the best example of how far we have come from Richard is provided by Henry V at Agincourt. On the eve of the battle, he wanders about his camp in disguise and comes upon the common soldiers Bates and Williams, who ask him whether the king is aware of their perilous situation. To this, Henry, rather surprisingly, replies that it is best that the king not know lest in his fear he "dishearten the army." The reason he gives for this judgment is that the monarch is like other men—"the king is but a man, as I am"—save for "ceremonies" and that "his affections are higher mounted than ours." From Henry's perspective, only conventions and inclinations to which all men are prone separate him from his troops. That he can think this and not appear fearful before his army on the next day is evidence of his courage and ability, long since demonstrated, to take on the appearance for which circumstances call. But this aside, his view of kingship seems predicated on the idea that kings and subjects are in their "elements" the same, an idea upon which he expands in his soliloquy on ceremony later in the scene.[25]

As Henry's discussion with Bates and Williams continues, other constituents of his new understanding of rule come into view. The soldiers take comfort in the opinion that the guilt for the battle to come —"for how can they charitably dispose of anything, when blood is their argument"—will be borne by the king, who they think responsible if subjects "do not die well." Thus, their view of their relation to the king reflects what might be called the medieval trade-off between position and responsibility. For medieval as for classical thought, the rewards of office are balanced by its potential costs. Those who hold high place must expect greater punishments as well as benefits for their deeds than ordinary men. Henry, however, takes exception to this argument. He will not allow his followers the luxury of freeing themselves of responsibility for their acts by transferring it to him. The same logic that opens the way to his transformation by leading men to accept great changes and variations in this life also opens the way to arguing that men are indiscriminately responsible for their own behavior. Where men can take control, or hope to take control, of their own temporal fates, they cannot pass blame on to others for their own temporal misfortunes:[26]

> So, if a son that is by his father sent about merchandise do sinfully miscarry upon the sea, the imputation of his wickedness, by your rule, should be imposed upon his father that sent him: or if a servant, under his master's command transporting a sum of money, be assailed by robbers and die in many irreconciled iniquities, you may call the business of the master the author of the servant's damnation: but this is not so: the king is not bound to answer the particular ends of his soldiers, the father of his son, nor the master of his servant; for they purpose not their death, when they purpose their services.

In suggesting the comparability of fathers, masters, and kings, Henry, we immediately recognize, departs from the view—most notably identified with Aristotle—that forms of rule are qualitatively different and that to confuse them marks a perverse understanding of politics.[27] But Henry's position is a necessary consequence of his redemptive bias. To begin, it reflects the argument by faith whereby operating with a good will releases one for blame for one's acts; if rulers do not "purpose" bad ends for their subjects they may rest with clear consciences. More important for our purposes, however, that men can temporally transform and recreate themselves entails an end to the natural hierarchy, posited by thinkers like Aristotle, that commands human relationships, whether ruler-subject, father-son, or master-slave. By the same token, it entails an end to the particular responsibility of some in human affairs and universalizes, so to speak, responsibility. No longer must a ruler presume responsibility for all facets of his subjects' well-being, i.e., for their souls as well as their temporal sufficiency. Henry is able, as Richard was not, now to argue that "every subject's duty is the king's; but every subject's soul is his own."[28]

Henry's argument, however, raises certain problems. By virtue of his "sacred blood" Richard could claim the total dedication of his subjects. His combination of lineal and divine right meant that he did not have to worry, at least theoretically, that there might be a conflict sometime between his subjects' devotion to him and to their own souls. Henry is not so fortunate as Richard in this respect. In giving his subjects responsibility for their souls, he opens the way to their questioning him on matters where their fates might be at stake. Bolingbroke had already partially encountered this problem in the opposition of the Archbishop of York, who was followed "both with body and mind" while Bolingbroke's troops were "constrain'd" by the division of "the actions of their bodies from their souls."[29] Henry's resolution of this problem is consistent with his redemptive orientation. Indeed, it reinforces that orientation while at the same time furthering the new sense of rule he initiates.

In effect, Henry would end the possibility of divided loyalties in his subjects—i.e., loyalty to him in conflict with loyalty to themselves—by extending the promise of redemption he has realized to them. That is, he will fasten his followers to himself, and their ends to his, by equating his transformation and improvement with a kind of transformation and improvement that they too can realize. Thus, for example, he publicly says that his old Eastcheap companions can by "reform" have "advancement," and, at the other extreme, he promises his lords that the French campaign "shall be to you, as us, like glorious."[30] But to accomplish his purpose here, Henry must further erode the view that king and subjects are different. To the degree that his and his subjects' ends may be equated, to the same degree the distance between him and his subjects must be lessened. Thus, in Henry's most famous speech, he tells his troops at Agincourt that they may become as kin to kin. That which had formerly distinguished king from subjects, family from family, and nation from nation—blood—will now be considered a source of commonality:[31]

We few, we happy few, we band of brothers;
For he to-day that sheds his blood with me
Shall be my brother; be he ne'er so vile,
This day shall gentle his condition: . . .

How far Henry moves here from traditional ideas of temporal hierarchy and distinction may be seen by contrast with French attitudes at Agincourt. Whereas Henry welcomes the opportunity to shed his blood with even the most "vile," the French, still associating "blood" with "quality," are concerned after the battle to separate the bodies of "our nobles from our common men" and disturbed that "our vulgar drench their peasant limbs in blood of princes." Conversely, when Henry publicly takes care to attribute the English victory to God and to diminish his personal credit for it, he provides a counterpoint to the boasting and prancing individuality of the French camp prior to the battle. However hypocritical Henry's gift of his victory to God may appear to some—"Take it God, for it is none but thine."—it is consistent with his tendency to attenuate the senses of particular greatness, separateness, and responsibility that had once characterized rulers.[32]

This ends our short-hand account of Henry V's redemptive politics and its implications for rule. The argument that begins by secularizing Christian promises of a new life to come ends in the proposition that blood—and the flesh that accompanies it, as Shylock learns—establishes conformity rather than differences in men. It is a measure of Henry's accomplishments in this respect that upon his return to England from France, he behaves like a good Christian—"free from vainness and self-glorious pride"—and is contemptuous of the kind of triumph antiquity reserved for its heroes. The triumph, which represents public recognition of something extraordinary in particular individuals, must give way in a context where leaders make common cause with subjects in giving "full trophy, signal and ostent" to God. Thus, when Shakespeare, in the same passage, compares Henry's reception by his countrymen to that of a "conquering Caesar," he reminds us that Henry has an effect upon medieval England analogous to that of Caesar upon republican Rome.[33]

We may now restate the question with which we began. Is there something in Henry V's redemptive posture and politics that creates the conditions for the failure of his regime? Specifically, is there something about his new way of politics that makes particularly problematic, or defeats, his design for an imperial order ruled through family succession? Access to this question is initially provided by Falstaff, who challenges the assumption that stands at the heart of Henry's enterprise, i.e., that men may become something wholly new in this life. This challenge, and Henry's response to it, provides a virtual leitmotif in *IHenry IV* and *IIHenry IV*. From their first scene together, where Falstaff equates himself and his "vocation" with a fixed cosmological-natural order, to their last, where Henry commands his old companions to "reform," Falstaff and Henry—as Prince Hal—differ over the question of what is constant and inconstant in human affairs.[34] Falstaff, who uneasily combines Christian and pagan qualities, generally adheres to the classical teaching whereby character, once established, is difficult if not impossible to reverse. By character, in turn, he understands what results from birth or paternity and from education or habituation. Thus, for example, he considers that Hal, on the one hand, is to his father as the fruit to the tree and, on the other, that Hal has been irretrievably tainted by the Eastcheap company.[35] In the best classical tradition, in short, Falstaff views the prince as the product of nature, in the sense of inheritance from his natural father, and of nurture, in the sense of guidance from his surrogate father, Falstaff himself:[36]

> Hereof comes it that Prince Harry is valiant; for the cold blood he did naturally inherit of his father he hath like lean, sterile, and bare land manured, husbanded, and tilled, with excellent endeavour of drinking good and good store of fertile sherris, that he is become very hot and valiant. If I had a thousand sons, the first human principle I would teach them should be to forswear thin potations, and to addict themselves to sack.

It follows for Falstaff that Hal's plans to transform himself are counteracted by the intractable qualities that result from birth and training. As he puts it, the prince is "essentially made," even if he does not seem so. Conversely, by defying Falstaff on this point, Hal signifies his belief that he can defy both nature and habituation. Here, we might compare him to another Shakespearean challenger to the ties of natural inheritance and training, Coriolanus. For Hal to remake himself, to become "author of himself" in Coriolanus' terms, entails that he, like Coriolanus, overcome "instinct," in which Falstaff sets great store, and the more conventional bonds of honour and affection:[37]

My wife comes foremost; then the honour'd mould
Wherein this trunk was fram'd, and in her hand
The grandchild to her blood. But out, affection!
All bond and privilege of nature break!
....................and my young boy
Hath an aspect of intercession which
Great nature cries, 'Deny not'. Let the Volsces
Plough Rome and harrow Italy; I'll never
Be such a gosling to obey instinct, but stand
As if a man were author of himself
And knew no other kin.

Falstaff's objections to the change Hal has in mind do not, of course, pose insurmountable obstacles for the prince. Hal does, after all, dismiss his old companions and assume a new image, just as Coriolanus turns his back upon his family and Rome. But some of the implications of Falstaff's argument are harder to overcome. To the degree, for instance, that human behavior responds both to one's origins and education, the political association must respond both to what follows nature and what follows convention. Thus Falstaff is consistent with his view of the constituents of character insofar as he recognizes that politics answers both to what is true simply or by grace and what is true according to long usage and acceptance. He may privately doubt the value of honour but he knows the importance of having a "good name." Again, he recognizes that we bear obligations in this life as men simply and as members of a lawful order of things. His description, for example, of Hal as simultaneously "man" and "prince"—or "true prince" and "false thief"—echoes Aristotle's dichotomy between man and citizen, and his quibble upon the prince's "grace" and "majesty"—"when thou art king, as God save thy Grace, Majesty I should say, for grace thou wilt have none"—represents a Christian version of the same division.[38] Admittedly, there is a considerable distance between Aristotelian and Christian ideas about our dual commitments in this life. To put matters in the most extreme terms, the one ultimately reflects the distance between philosophy and the practical life, the other the distance between revelation and reason. But, the tenuousness of Falstaff's combination of authorities aside—how tenuous it is, perhaps, becomes most apparent in his death scene—it remains that he indicates how Hal as king will have to balance opposed demands, i.e., those that follow from what he is and those from what he must appear to be according to convention or law.[39] One of Falstaff's fascinating ways of bringing this dualism home to the prince is his frequent reference to him as "heir-apparent." This is the formal title applied to an assured inheritor, as opposed to an heir-presumptive whose claim can be intercepted by the birth of a nearer heir. At the same time, however, it suggests the different aspects of Hal's position. He is at once his father's son —Falstaff says the physical resemblence between them is unmistakable —and the potential occupant of an office inseparable from appearances— we recall that Douglas errs at Shrewsbury by thrice-killing the "appearances" of the king.[40]

As we shall see directly, this dualism creates difficulties for Henry. To begin, in exemplifying the possibilities of secular redemption, he stands for what might be called an honest approach to the world. Insofar as secular redemption is an analog to divine redemption, it calls for a return to what is true or a restoration of what is genuine. Thus Henry wants, as he tells his father, to "be more myself" when the opportunity arises, a thought that extends the theme of his initial soliloquy. The same orientation also comes forward in various other ways in the plays. In some scenes Henry expresses his distaste for having to hide his true feelings or declaims on the sterility of royal ceremonies and affectations, and in some scenes Henry seems to delight in placing himself in surroundings where he is unrestrained by the trappings of politics and need not worry about how his comments are received.[41] Finally, there is his last scene in the plays, where he courts Katherine of France. According to his presentation here, he is and will remain, above all, openly true and constant:[42]

. . . A good heart, Kate, is the sun and the moon; or rather the sun and not the moon; for it shines bright and never changes, but keeps his course truly. If thou would have such a one, take me; and take me, take a soldier, take a soldier, take a king.

That Henry's statement here goes beyond simple policy—i.e., is motivated by something more than regnal politics—becomes apparent later in the scene. Henry intends that he and Katherine will not be bound by "a country's fashion" or "nice customs," that they will be the "makers of manners"—like Cranmer's Elizabeth—with the perfect liberty that stops the mouths of "all find faults." In this respect, the royal couple will build upon the pattern set by Hal originally in *1Henry IV*. As king and queen, the two will eventually do nothing other than what is truly expressive of themselves, free from concern for the deceits and mannerisms of their world. It is one of the paradoxes of what Henry intends that his argument for the possibilities of human change is simultaneously an argument for behaving in a manner genuinely responsive to man's permanent nature.[43] And here part of the problem of Henry as king becomes manifest. To the degree that he abides by that part of his political theology that calls for him to "be himself," how is he to deal with that facet of politics which, if Falstaff is correct, calls for disguises and dissembling?[44]

Henry's situation, and his response to it, may be restated in the following terms. His father had destroyed the security of earlier rulers by severing position from lineal and sacred right.[45] Henry, in turn, furthers his father's course by rejecting the need, as specified by Falstaff, for ruling pretense. From Henry's perspective, this is but an appendage of the politics his new, more honest, redemptive orientation is to replace. Yet, Henry is not ready wholly to dismiss, or dispense with, the earlier world's sense of political security. Despite the contrary force of a political theology that ultimately leads to every man being responsible for himself in this world, Henry tries to command the future as well as the present by establishing a blood-line by which he can permanently influence events. As he puts it, he and Katherine "shall . . . compound a boy, half French, half English, that shall go to Constantinople and take the Turk by the beard," i.e., Henry would have a son who will replicate in a wider frame what he had done in his French campaign. In this sense, Henry seeks to fashion a realm that combines pre-Lancastrian inheritance rights with a new imperial or extra-national political bias. While it would reassert the "lineal honour," as Henry calls it, that provided earlier kings confidence, it would free men from the limits arising in the conventional and natural boundaries by which earlier kings defined politics.[46] Henry's response to the challenges of Gaunt and Falstaff is very bold indeed. In one stroke, he rejects Gaunt's parochialism and the stratagems and respect for conventions that, according to Falstaff, are necessitated by such parochialism.

Henry's boldness is equalled, of course, by the scope of his failure. The question of why he fails is more problematic than the failure itself, but on the basis of the Lancastrian plays it is possible, at least provisionally, to say that he is finally unable to overcome the arguments of Falstaff and Gaunt. John Alvis, for example, has demonstrated how the plays expose the strength of the ceremonies whose need Falstaff accepts but Henry would deny. Thus, when Henry violates French "fashion" by kissing Katherine, he puts at risk the underpinnings of the French, and thereby his own, order. As Charles of France says, what protects his maiden daughter also protects his maiden cities.[47] Again, Henry's apparent indifference to the national distinctions so important to his grandfather, and his implied indifference to the old argument that men of different nationalities can be allies but not fellow-citizens, is also challenged in various ways. A parallel group of scenes in *Henry V* is instructive in this regard. In III.iv Katherin struggles, delightfully—but rather ridiculously—to learn English, with the result that her maid tells her, in French, that "in truth you pronounce the words as well as the natives of England." In IV.iii Henry foresees that at Agincourt some of his men will die and be returned home "to find native graves" and be honoured while others will be buried in French "dunghills" and be the source of "a plague in France."

In V.i Gower corrects Pistol's estimation of Fluellen, "you thought, because he could not speak English in the native garb, he could not therefore handle an English cudgel: you find it otherwise; and henceforth let a
Welsh correction teach you a good English condition." The peripheries
in this sequence—IV.iii is the seventh of the thirteen scenes spanning
III.iv to V.i—contain comments, then, on overcoming the differences
between natives and foreigners, the one concerning language, the other
war. At the center, however, we come upon a comment on the seemingly
irreconcilable differences between native and foreign graves that leads
to wonder about how effective the peripheral erasure of differences can
be.[38]

But perhaps Shakespeare's most telling comment on Henry's failure
is left to the last scene of *Henry V*. As a whole, the scene gives us a trium-
phant Henry, the winner of both Katherine and France. But it is marred,
if only momentarily, by a disagreement between Henry and Charles concerning Henry's desire to be styled—in French, Latin, and English—"our
very dear son Henry, King of England, Inheritor of France." Henry's
desire, acceded to by Charles, bears home how badly he wants to reestablish a lineal claim to the throne. A few lines later, however, the hopeless-
ness of his desire is revealed. Henry, we find, knows that his realm will
stand or fall on how "well kept and prosperous" will be the "oaths" his
subjects take to him. It is a measure of how far Henry has come, and
how hard it would be to return to the world of Gaunt, that the only
"surety of our leagues," as Henry puts it, is men's faithfulness to their
own words. Henry's intention to refound a line based on blood is counter-
balanced by the fact that in his world men will take their bearings from
the oaths they take rather than from any fixed natural or sacred order.[49]
We have already noted one of the paradoxes that leads from Henry's
political theology, i.e., that men who believe in great human variability
will try to recapture or restore a sense of human genuineness. We now
come upon another traceable to the same source. The political theology
that leads Henry to reject ceremonies and customs eventuates in a regime where words or oaths are all that is left to tie men together.

We conclude, then, that Henry V's political error is a case of wanting
too much. He fails to recognize that the redemptive politics to which he
is wedded will not allow a return to lineal politics. On this point, it is
instructive to turn to the teaching of the greatest of modern statesmen,
Abraham Lincoln. Like Shakespeare, Lincoln provides us a teaching on
secular redemption. It is most directly expressed in his "Temperance
Address." As Harry Jaffa demonstrates, here we find Lincoln's secular
version of *Pilgrim's Progress*, i.e., a secular expression of the idea that we
must leave behind our "blood and kind" to attain the heavenly city.[50]
Unlike Henry V, however, Lincoln sees the political implications of this
idea. A teaching that the "vilest sinner" can improve his lot in this as the

next life leaves little room for the kind of permanence associated with descent. Thus, the message of the "Temperance Address," in political terms, is that the differences amongst levels of society must, to the degree possible, be set aside in redemptive ages, with the result that persuasion and fashion—Falstaff's tools—become essential to successful statecraft. And even more to the point, Lincoln's peroration makes clear that reason, not bloodright, is the only dependable guide to political activity in redemptives ages.[51]

Happy day, when all appetites controlled, all passions subdued, all matters subjected, *mind*, all conquering *mind*, shall live and move the monarch of the world. Glorious consummation! Hail fall of Fury! Reign of Reason, all hail!

Thus when Lincoln concludes his address by raising the name of Washington—"the mightiest name of earth"—but refuses to eulogize him on the grounds that he could not do justice to such a luminary—"to add brightness to the sun, or glory to the name of Washington, is alike impossible"—he reminds us of the implications of redemption.[52] Reason comes forward as a ruling principle and the old fathers, or ancestors, are set aside as active sources of instruction or ruling claims. In this sense, Lincoln understands better than Henry V what is most compelling where redemption has been secularized. By attempting to reestablish lineal rule, even on a new imperial basis, Henry V misreads the force of his own revolution, with tragic consequences for both his natural and political heirs. Thus, perhaps it is not to Henry VIII that we ought to look for the final resolution of the problems the Lancastrian tetrology raises, but to Elizabeth I, the "Virgin Queen."

Notes

1. *Henry V*, II. pro. 6. References are to the Arden editions of *Henry V*. ed. G. C. Smith (Boston: D. C. Heath, 1908), of *Richard II*, ed. P. Ure (Cambridge, Mass.: Harvard University Press, 1956), of *IHenry IV*, ed. A. R. Humphreys (London: Methuen, 1961), of *IIHenry IV*, ed. A. R. Humphreys (London: Methuen, 1966). For a recent treatment of Henry V that recounts the more prevalent opinions about him, see J. Alvis, "The Career of Henry Monmouth," in *Shakespeare as a Political Thinker*, eds. J. Alvis and T. West (Durham, N.C.: Carolina Academic Press, 1981), pp. 95–125. Hereafter the parts of the Lancastrian tetrology will be cited as *RII, IHIV, IIHIV,* and *HV*.

2. For the illusory character of Henry's triumph, see H. V. Jaffa, "An Interpretation of the Shakespearean Universe," in *Shakespeare as a Political Thinker*, p. 291.

3. *HV*, epil. 5–14. On the connection between England and France, see Alvis, pp. 109–10. Shakespeare's silence about Henry's death may be compared to Machiavelli's comments in *The Prince*, ch. 7, on the premature deaths of Borgia and his father Alexander VI.

4. *HV*, II.iv.81.

5. *RII*, II.i. 45–52.

6. "Richard II," in *Shakespeare as a Political Thinker*, p. 53.

7. *RII*, I.i.119; Bloom, p. 54.

8. *RII*, II.iii.136; II.i.193–4; II.i.245; I.i.116–21.

9. *Henry VIII*, V.iv.37ff.

10. *RII*, II.i.45–50.

11. Cf. *HV*, II.iv.80.

12. *IIHIV*, I.ii.203–212. See *IIHIV*, IV.v.54; V.v.57–60; A. J. Bryant, *Hippolyta's View* (Lexington, Ken.: University of Kentucky Press, 1961), pp. 62–61.

13. *HV*, I.ii.60; *IIHIV*, III.iii.29–32; IV.ii.23–4; *IIHIV*, I.ii.34.

14. *RII*, III.ii.129; I.i.174–5; II.iv.11; III.iii.98–100.

15. *HV*, I.i.24–37.

16. *HV*, I.i.53–59.

17. *HV*, I.i.60–68.

18. On Machiavellian malleability, see H. Mansfield Jr., *Machiavelli's New Modes and Orders* (Ithaca: Cornell University press, 1979), pp. 133–4, L. Peterman, "Dante and the Setting for Machiavellianism," *American Political Science Review*, Vol. 76, no. 3 (1982), 641.

19. See, e.g., M. Zetterbaum, "Self and Subjectivity in Political Theory," *The Review of Politics*, Vol. 44, no. 1(1982), 59–60.

20. *RII*, III.iii.204–205. Cf. I.i.85, 116.

21. *IIHIV*, V.v.103; *RII*, I.i.197. Bolingbroke claimed the throne by right of descent from Henry III, but his claim was weak in comparison with that of Mortimer. Short of getting involved in family trees, we may leave it at saying that Mortimer could claim the throne by way of Lionel, who was John of Gaunt's *older* brother, and thus his claim was prior to Bolingbroke's.

22. On this point, see, e.g., Dante, *Monarchy*, II.i, ed. and trans. D. Nicholl (London: Weidenfeld and Nicolson, 1954).

23. *RII*, III.ii.98–101; 83–88; 165–77; IV.i.255; V.v.38–41. See Bloom, p. 58.

24. *RII*, VI.v.109–12. Richard, in his association with the idea that the king is a special type person, may be said to be the last Shakespearean representative of the idea that the crown is not a fiction.

25. *HV*, IV.i.92–108; 220ff.

26. *HV*, IV.i.140–150.

27. *Pol.* 1052a7ff.

28. *HV*, IV.i.166–7.

29. *IIHIV*, I.i.190–209. On the "instinctual" loyalty Richard could command, see Bloom, p. 58.

30. *IIHIV*, V.v.66–9; *HV*, II.iii.182–3. Bolingbroke had solved the problem of divided loyalties in his subjects by the bloodless victory at Gaultree Forest. Henry furthers this course by, in effect, buying off his clerics, i.e., by granting the Church protections from parliament in exchange for its defense of his French claims. But silencing the Church does not wholly resolve the problem of the possibility of divided loyalties in Henry's subjects. It only removes a faction particularly well situated to take advantage of the division.

31. *HV*, IV.iii.60–63.

32. *HV*, IV.vii.65–77; viii.100–106; III.vii; IV.ii.

33. *HV*, V.pro.17–28.

34. *IHIV*, I.ii.13–15, 101–2; *IIHIV*, V.v.68.

35. *IHIV*, II.iv.393–425.

36. *IIHIV*, IV.iii.115–123. See, also, *IHIV*, I.ii. 135–7.

37. *IHIV*, IV.iv.267–296, 351–384; 492; *Coriolanus*, V.iii.22–37, ed. P. Brockbank (London: Methuen, 1976). See, too *Coriolanus*, IV.ii.2; *IIHenry IV*, I.vi.83; Bloom, p. 59, who denotes the opposition between Bolingbroke and instinct; and Jaffa, p. 291, who makes a direct comparison between Henry V and Coriolanus.

38. *IHIV*, I.ii.80–81; V.i.129–141; III.iii.145–6; I.ii.150–1; 16–18.

39. On Falstaff's twin character, see M. Platt, "Falstaff in the Valley of the Shadow of Death," *Interpretation*, 1979, 13ff. See also, Jaffa, p. 289.

40. *IHIV*, II.iv.399–400; *IIHIV*, I.i.128.

41. *IHIV*, III.ii.93; *IIHIV*, II.ii.50–65. See Alvis, p. 194.

42. *HV*, V.ii.131–63.

43. *HV*, V.ii.256–266.

44. *IHIV*, I.ii.195.

45. *HV*, V.ii.194–201.

46. Henry's interest in reasserting "lineal honour" is expressed at the precise moment he places the crown on his head at his father's bedside (*IIHIV*, IV.v.42–46):
Lo where it sits,
Which God shall guard; and put the world's whole strength
Into one giant arm, it shall not force
this lineal honour from me. This from thee
Will I to mine leave, as 'tis left to me.
See, also, V.ii.71 and III.ii.125, where Bolingbroke expresses his own interest in lineage when he accuses Hal of "degeneracy."

47. *HV*, V.ii.239–254, 302–304.

48. The Shakespearean measure of the possibility of integrating Henry's disparate forces into a common political order may be the continual play in *HV* on the linguistic differences between the French and English and among Henry's own troops. Given that language, for Shakespeare's as for an earlier time, constituted one of the more important sources of political division, it is arguable that the linguistic divisions exposed in *HV* reflect a Shakespearean view of how likely Henry V's ambitions were to be successful. On these matters, see L. Peterman, "Dante versus Machiavelli: Politics and Language in the *Dialogue on Language*," *Interpretation*, Vol. 10, no. 1 (1982), 209–11.

49. *HV*, V.ii. 310–352.

50. *Crisis of the House Divided* (Garden City, N.Y.: Doubleday, 1959), p. 257.

51. *Collected Works*, ed., R. Basler (New Brunswick, N.J.: Rutgers University Press, 1953), I.279.

52. *Ibid.*

6

WOODROW WILSON AND THE STATESMANSHIP OF PROGRESS

Charles R. Kesler

THE YEARS AFTER THE CIVIL WAR SAW NOT ONE BUT TWO NEW BEGINNINGS IN American politics. The first was to some extent a working and living out of the principles of the Founding, a resumption of old ways now eluci- dated and ennobled by the tragedy of the War and by the triumph over slavery. But very quickly this perpetuation or rebirth of the Old Freedom began to give way before the advance of a New. Hope-filled experiments in American politics began to be conducted, whose character was not altogether unlike that epochal experiment dared by our ancestors in the Garden, while God was not looking. The same pretension that found its temptation, and purpose, in the liberation of the passions reached out for knowledge of a new kind—for the wisdom of history that was at once the completion and nullification of the knowledge of good and evil. The results of that original experiment were not as happy as had been pre- dicted, but whether these latter-day political experiments portend a sim- ilar disappointment—and a like rebuke?—remains to be seen. Already they have proceeded, with occasional interruptions, for more than a century.

To begin to identify these novel undertakings, it would help perhaps to ponder the vast changes in structure and function that the federal government has undergone in the years since Abraham Lincoln was President. A standard list of innovations might include: the nationaliza- tion of commerce under the aegis of the interstate commerce clause; construction of huge federal highway systems and other large-scale pub- lic works; the establishment of independent regulatory commissions; the progressive income tax; provision of unemployment benefits, welfare relief, medical and disability benefits, and social insurance for ever- growing numbers of citizens; the broad assumption of responsibility for the macroeconomic health of the nation, even unto the redistribution of income; revenue sharing, urban renewal, and other programs for state and local governments; federal enforcement of civil and voting rights; and federal aid to lower and higher education. The list is by no means exhaustive, but it does suggest the new extent of the federal government's domestic responsibilities, and the way in which both Democrats and Republicans contributed to the expansion.

Nevertheless, none of these developments in itself—nor even several or all taken together—marks a *fundamental* change from the Founders' or Lincoln's understanding of the proper functions of government. Internal improvements, restriction of state power over commerce, and governmental protection of selected industries were all part of the nationalizing program of the Federalists and Whigs, which program was taken over by the Republican party. Every President from George Washington to John Quincy Adams urged the federal government to set up a national university. The Northwest Ordinance mandated that provision be made for schools—and churches—throughout the Northwest Territory; and federal support for state governments was manifest in ways ranging from the national assumption of the states' Revolutionary War debts to the actual purchase of the lands from which the trans-Appalachian states were carved to the Morrill Act's land grants for state agricultural colleges. Public relief measures, while not specifically undertaken by the federal government, were common in the states; Union troops were used to enforce the rights of blacks in southern states after the Civil War; and redistribution of income *and* wealth was promoted by state actions to abolish primogeniture and entail, and indirectly by the national system of tariff protection. In short, taken by themselves, there is nothing in these programs that could not be explained or defended as a continuation, *mutatis mutandis*, of the traditional practices of American government.

Which is not to deny that there has been a decisive change. What characterizes that change is the transformed understanding of the *purposes* of government, of the *reasons* given for these programs and the *uses* to which they are put. (The far-reaching "activism" of the Supreme Court has been prescinded from the discussion, but much the same interpretation could be given of its decisions since the Civil War.) This new view of the ends of government is in turn based on a new view of the nature of man; and the significance of these changes can be seen most clearly in their effect on the understanding and practice of American statesmanship. The man more than any other who prepared and effected this revolution in American politics, is Woodrow Wilson. It was he who first asserted in a comprehensive way that the traditional definition of statesmanship as the highest form of practical wisdom had become untenable —and had to be reconstructed with a view to the historical understanding of being.

Practical wisdom presumes the existence and authority of moral virtue, for prudence is the ability to deliberate well concerning the best means to the ends supplied by moral virtue. But moral virtue itself is the perfection of human being with regard to the governance of the passions, and presumes that human being is articulated in a fixed and permanent way.[1] To put it differently, moral virtue is inseparable from the notion of human nature and its perfection in accordance with "the laws of nature and of nature's God." Wilson believed that the historical school of philosophy in England and Germany had succeeded in anachronizing—and so disproving—the idea of nature as a standard for moral and political life, opening the way for the introduction of a new kind of statesmanship into American politics. The distinctive character of the "statesmanship of progress," as he called it,[2] was the requirement of historical "vision" or "sympathetic insight"—the ability to see whither history is tending and to prepare the nation to move in that direction, to move with the current rather than to struggle against it or be caught in its eddies—or be dashed by it against the rocks. Just how different the "statesmanship of progress" is from the statesmanship of natural right will be seen in Wilson's own analysis of the American situation, and in his recommendations for its improvement.

To many historians there is not one Woodrow Wilson but two—the conservative southern Democrat and dyed-in-the-wool Burkean and, after about 1910, the more familiar progressive reformer and idealistic crusader. The charitable explanation of the switch is that he finally saw the light; his detractors maintain that what he saw was how to get elected. While it is undeniable that there were important changes in his political opinions and alliances, both his defenders and his critics fail to appreciate the more fundamental continuity between the "two" Wilsons.[3] To his mind, Burkeanism and progressivism were not in the slightest incompatible. "There is nothing so conservative of life as growth," he explained in an address on the occasion of Princeton University's sesquicentennial. "Progress is life, for the body politic as for the body natural. To stand still is to court death. Here then . . . you have the law of conservatism disclosed: it is a law of progress."[4] Wilson would doubtless be complimented to know that he is today claimed in some measure by both the Left and Right, by liberals from Franklin Roosevelt to Teddy Kennedy and by conservatives from Herbert Hoover to Russell Kirk. This is a measure of how far the historical approach has penetrated American politics, for better or worse, and is a tribute to Wilson's lasting influence. At the same time it is a sign of how far our politics has departed from a true or unmediated understanding of the Founding, and of the supreme emblems of the Founding, the Declaration of Independence and the Constitution; for it was precisely the enduring authority of these great documents that Wilson sought to modify and supplant.

It is not to be wondered, then, that a critique of the Founding is central to Wilson's project both in his "conservative" and "progressive" phases. The problem with the American Constitution, according to the early *and* the mature Wilson, is that it was composed under the influence of a theory: in designing America's political institutions, the Framers looked to "the Whig theory of political dynamics" for guidance. Drawing upon the doctrines and experience of the Whigs in their successful efforts to rein in the British King, to constitutionalize the executive power, the Framers undertook to ring the American President with offsetting departments so as to secure the courts and legislature against executive encroachment. In so doing, however, the Framers "made no clear analysis of the matter in their own thoughts," for they were "practical men," and English to boot; it was not their habit to be "clear theorists." They did what any practical man would do in the same situation: they borrowed their theory, not exactly from the Whigs themselves (who being Englishmen were also not metaphysicians), but from the famous Frenchman who had explained to the Whigs what they had wrought. To Montesquieu the Framers turned, and learning from him that "it was essential for the preservation of liberty to differentiate the executive, legislative, and judicial functions of government and not to suffer them to be united in the same hands," they saw to it that "all intimacy of aim and cooperation of effort" between the branches was rendered impossible.[5]

But if the American Constitution had a philosopher, it was not itself a work of philosophy. Being practical men, the Framers were turned into "Whig theorists" only imperfectly; they did not follow Montesquieu as philosophers would have; they "had no thought of re-examining his principles to see if they really held good for all cases." Wilson may seem to be accusing the Framers of a lack of prudence, indicting their statesmanship for inattention to the peculiar circumstances of the American case. A closer inspection will show that he regards their decisive failing to be an inability to appreciate *historical* circumstances. Hamilton, Madison, and the other authors of the Constitution did not understand that Montesquieu had written "in a time which did not know the people as an actual and active sovereign authority," and that consequently he had not "hit upon exactly the right devices" for ensuring successful popular government. The fear of the executive that the Framers had absorbed from Montesquieu was characteristic of only one stage of English constitutional history, a stage even then fast receding. It would not be long before the British ministry would become a commitee of the House of Commons—a committee constituting the "working executive of the country" over which the King would wield only the formal power of appointment. Not being able to foresee that "party government by the legislative leaders of the people" was on the horizon, the Framers in effect froze our constitutional arrangements (particularly regarding the executive) "at the stage of constitutional development which England was leaving. . . ."[6]

It was not the inherent plausibility of Montesquieu's views, then, but their familiarity as part of a larger "system of thought" that accounted for their acceptance by the Framers. Behind the "Whig theory of political dynamics" was "the Newtonian theory of the universe," the paradigm according to which men of that time reasoned about "the structure or development of anything, whether in nature or in society." The political theory of the Founding was "a sort of unconscious copy" of Newtonian physics—it was not a fully conscious copy because, as we shall see, the Founders had not discovered the historicity of reason, and so could not acknowledge the sovereignty of their own paradigm. Politics was understood as a branch of mechanics, government as a machine regulated by "mechanically automatic balances"—the President against Congress, Congress against the President, Congress against the Court, and so forth. As the "nice poise and balance of forces" produce a universe of "symmetry and perfect adjustment," so the checks and balances of the Constitution result in good administration and liberty. In short, the Framers "constructed a government as they would have constructed an orrery—to display the laws of nature."[7]

Unhappily, from Wilson's point of view, the Newtonianism of the Constitution long outlived its Framers. Although American politics had never quite lived up to the "literary theory" of equilibrium among the branches of the federal government, it had come close. Most galling of all, even when a rather serious disequilibrium set in shortly after the Civil War—which derangement he analyzed in his first book, *Congressional Government*—the Newtonian balances had simply and arrestingly reasserted themselves in a new guise. To be specific, in the twenty years between Lincoln's assassination and Grover Cleveland's election, the separation of powers broke down; the executive and judiciary became subordinated to an imperious if not imperial Congress; Congress consigned its business to a system of standing committees whose squabbles, vanities, and pomposities precluded efficient legislating, distracted oversight of the executive, and doomed all schemes of party responsibility and public enlightenment. Despite these manifold departures from the writ of the Constitution, the essential spirit of the document was preserved in the new arrangements; from a system of balances between the powers of the federal government, America's constitutional existence became a system of balanced and mutually checking committees within the sovereign Congress. Newtonianism had been called down from the heavens, but its laws of motion were the same.[8]

Yet the Newtonian universe was not a cosmos of perfect and eternal spheres, not even of perfect and invariable ellipses, for it was understood that orbits would change as new bodies or forces acted upon them. Could not new or weightier congressmen—one thinks of men in the proportions of Speaker Joseph Cannon—or even the forces of public opinion, sufficiently concentrated, override or restructure the system of standing committees? Wilson was skeptical, for the reason that committee government reflected something more fundamental in the country.

"Congress in its composition is the country in miniature," he wrote in an essay published in 1893. "It realizes Hobbes's definition of liberty as political power divided into small fragments. The standing committees typify the individuals of the nation."[9] Newtonianism penetrated American society as well as American govenment, and if its political agent or intermediary was Montesquieu, its social agent was Hobbes. The "individuals of the nation," as Wilson paradoxically says, are practically in a state of nature with one another. In the virtual absence or suspension of political power at the center, this is what Hobbes would expect to happen; but also what he would *want* to happen, at least if his absolutism is in the service of a more fundamental liberalism. Wilson's criticism is that Hobbes's prescription is akin to his diagnosis, that civil society on Hobbesian principles is so very similar to the state of nature that the true inconveniences of the latter are never overcome.[10] Foremost among these is that men are encouraged to be private individuals rather than public citizens, to live on the level of material interests rather than common ideals. As a result, statesmanship is rendered nugatory; and as a result of that, the potential for social progress and individual self-development lies fallow.

Wilson is the most influential academic and political figure ever to criticize the American regime for being Hobbesian, and to connect that criticism to a program for the nation's reformation. Perhaps his closest competitors for the honor (if that is what it is) are the antebellum defenders of the positive good of Negro slavery, and in particular George Fitzhugh, who saw the contest between free society and slave society to be a reflection of the question between the social contract theorists and Aristotle: was man born free and equal, or unfree and unequal? Apart from the staggering question of how unfaithful is his interpretation of Aristotle —Fitzhugh is in any case a glaring example of applying classical principles imprudently, without making the necessary changes for the novel character of modern society—it must be admitted that his program for American salvation had a Lincolnian consistency to it: he held that slavery was beneficial not only for blacks but also for whites (at least for 19 out of 20 whites), and hence that it should be extended to the whole Union. In the event, Lincoln's statesmanship extinguished Fitzhugh's hope, and his philanthropic proposal became, so to speak, academic. Wilson's indictment of America's Hobbesianism began where Fitzhugh's had languished, in the academy, but swiftly left it to become a transforming force in American politics and, in one form or another, a staple of Democratic party rhetoric ever since. But its most sophisticated expressions are still heard in the universities, often from the least Wilsonian of scholars. Indeed it has become a kind of *obbligato* behind both liberal and conservative academics, whose voices sound discordant but in fact may be harmonized rather easily.[11]

But in criticizing American government's reliance on balancing ambitions and intersts to "supply the defect of better motives," as well as

American society's consuming individualism, Wilson did not intend to discriminate between the lower and higher parts of human nature, in order to direct the nation towards the noble and the common good. On the contrary, his purpose was to open America to the salutary influences of progress, after which nobility and the common good would take care of themselves.[12] He repaired to history, not to nature, as the standard by which America would ultimately be guided to a new moral and political dispensation. Contemporary liberals, whether in the academy or in politics, would find nothing objectionable in Wilson's undertaking, except perhaps the pedigree of his, i.e., their ideas. Today's conservatives would also see nothing wrong with the resort to history to purge our politics of the rationalism born of natural right, although they might complain of the pace of Wilson's reforms.

It is, however, surprising to find that those teachers who spend their days honoring reason and natural right, and whose lips are full of reverence for the fathers of philosophy, are at the same time energetic declaimers of Wilson's criticisms of the Founding. Acknowledging the superiority of classical natural right, many of them conceive a nostalgia for the glories of the *polis*—where politics was really *politics*—which elides over into their analysis of present-day political life. Not being able or prepared to *will* the return of the *polis*—or, perhaps, thinking it impossible—their reflections on America take on the character of a reverie, or of a reverie hidden within the portrait of a low, uninspired and uninspiring, oppressively modern (some would say, bourgeois or democratic) regime. In so many words, their premise is that classical natural right is lost, is—classical, buried under the debris of twenty-five centuries, give or take a few. When they come to study American politics, they come therefore with eyes that will not see, and ears that will not hear; for they intend to study not really American *politics* or the American *regime*, but American politics as a form of *modern* politics which means finally as a reflection of modern political philosophy and ideology. With such an intention, it is often enough to profess to study American politics by opening the books of modern writers.[13] And with such a longing for the imagined splendors of antiquity, it is easy to allow discontent with the permanent vexations of politics, whatever contemporary form they may take, to be co-opted by Wilson's conservative-sounding progressivism. Since those who hold a vision of the past wish to see it reborn as a vision of the future, they have common ground with those who specialize in such visions: The road to radical modernity is paved with well-intentioned longings for antiquity.[14]

To avoid traveling down this road requires studying American politics prudently, which does not mean "up to a certain point" but rather "in the manner proper for political philosophy." This manner of study begins and ends with the perspective of a good citizen in the highest sense of the term, not with the perspective of an ungrateful dreamer who wishes he had been born elsewhere and in another time. Insofar as the best or most loyal citizen is he who has had a choice—who, after contemplating the alternatives, has *chosen* his own regime—the perspective of the best citizen is that of a founder or of the regime's greatest perpetuators. The study of American politics, so conceived, must therefore include knowledge of the regime's matter or material conditions (its geography, social and economic circumstances, etc.), its laws and law-making, its "fundamental law," its customs and manners—but must culminate in knowledge of the works and days of its statesmen. It is they who breathe the breath of life into the cold body of the laws, who exemplify and form the way of life that betokens the regime. Genuine knowledge of such men as Washington, Webster, and Lincoln lies at the end of the difficult and unpredictable path that begins with their own self-understanding; but along that path the serious student will be able to discover the permanent, that is, the transhistorical meaning of statesmanship. For the life and activity of the statesman commands a natural horizon that is the same in the Athens of Socrates as in the America of Thomas Jefferson or Abraham Lincoln.

It was, however, precisely Wilson's intention to replace the natural horizon of statesmanship—the horizon of the human soul—with the new and constantly changing horizon of progress. The problem with constructing a government "to display the laws of nature," Wilson argues, is that it results in nothing *but* display, for the laws of nature are not laws of human freedom. "Government is not a machine" but is "a living thing," and as such it falls "not under the theory of the universe, but under the theory of organic life." Human freedom is not supported by or directed towards the nature that is above man, but inheres in the history or unfolding of lower, sub-human nature, whose development is not dependent upon anything higher. In short, government is "accountable to Darwin, not to Newton. It is modified by its environment, necessitated by its tasks, shaped to its functions by the sheer pressure of life." Not physics or metaphysics but biology is the highest science, and it is highest because it understands the low things ("the sheer pressure of life") that are the basis of the high. This is the pressure group theory of politics in embryo, but unlike Arthur Bentley, Wilson was not content with an understanding of politics confined to the level of pressures or interests.[15]

"Living political constitutions must be Darwinian in structure and practice," Wilson emphasizes. In practice this means that it is impossible to have successful government "without leadership or without the intimate, almost instinctive, coordination of the organs of life and action." However organic it may be, the state does not possess instincts, so it must make do with "leadership." Statesmanship understood as leadership is thus "the art of bringing the several parts of government into effective cooperation for the accomplishment of particular common objects." Wilson's indictment of the Framers may then be epitomized as follows, that they constructed a regime in which the exercise of statesmanship was direly necessary but peculiarly difficult. Having created their own political universe, they absconded like the god of the Newtonian universe, taking with them the need, and so they thought, the desirability, of any future acts of particular providence.[16] The legislative, executive, and judicial branches were left to ply their respective orbits, held in place by the forces of ambition and interest. But the system's very self-sufficiency cast doubt on the need for the executive power; its ordinary use came to be contemplated skeptically and its energetic use regarded as scarcely less than a miracle. It was the intrinsic weakness of the executive that led to the breakdown of the system, that allowed the legislature to satellize the other branches. Since the same forces obtained within as without the legislature, however, the display of standing committees, as we have seen, soon replaced the more magnificent display of separated powers.

In both cases the dimensions of the problem were life-threatening, for "no living thing can have its organs offset against each other as checks, and live." That the American regime *had* lived broadly suggested either that Wilson's grasp of the theory of separation of powers was faulty or that the practicality which made the Founders bad philosophers may in the end have made them good statesmen. It is well to consider the one before moving on to the other. The Framers were well aware of the folly of attempting a too strict separation of the powers of government, as any reader of *Federalist* No. 47 will recall.[17] There Publius defends the proposed Constitution against the Anti-Federalist charge that "the several departments of power are distributed and blended in such a manner as at once to destroy all symmetry and beauty of form, and to expose some of the essential parts of the edifice to the danger of being crushed by the disproportionate weight of other parts." By recurring to the sibylline teachings of Montesquieu, "the oracle who is always consulted and cited on this subject," Publius exploits the Anti-Federalists' propensity to rush to oracles for guidance only to misinterpret, out of haste and preconceived notions, the vouchsafed wisdom. Montesquieu, after all, had found in the British Constitution not political liberty itself but "the mirror of political liberty," meaning something that reflects it perhaps along with other objects' shadowy images. Publius "infers" from the facts of British constitutional life that Montesquieu had not meant to say, and did not say, that the departments of government "ought to have no *partial agency* in, or no *control* over, the acts of each other." It is only when "the *whole* power of one department is exercised by the same hands which possess the *whole* power of another department" that "the fundamental principles of a free constitution are subverted."[18] The Anti-Federalists had read Montesquieu in light of an exaggerated or misplaced love of "symmetry and beauty of form," which, as Publius proceeds to show, their own practice in the state constitutions belied.

Publius agrees with Wilson that politics is not the realm in which to look for "symmetry and beauty of form," not however because the laws of nature are Newtonian laws of necessity, but because in politics forms must be combined with imperfect matter, so that nature does not obliterate human freedom but ordains it, i.e., supports and limits it at the same time. In Newtonian science, all bodies are essentially the same, obeying the same laws of nature; form is reduced to the laws of motion that govern all bodies equally. But in politics, form is the distinctive character of a country, that which chiefly distinguishes it from other forms of government and ways of life. Publius' criticism of the Anti-Federalists is that they do not understand the intractability of matter and so do not see the problem posed for the form of republican government. They believe that politics can easily and completely live up to the "political maxim" of the separation of powers, forgetting the delicate and difficult relation between theory and practice, as well as the limitations of our theoretical wisdom. "Experience has instructed us," Publius had remarked ten papers before, "that no skill in the science of government has yet been able to discriminate and define, with sufficient certainty, its three great provinces—the legislative, executive, and judiciary. . . ."[19]

The Anti-Federalists' confident expectation that republican government could be secured by a "separate and distinct" division of powers committed to writing, with every "i" dotted and "t" crossed, is the sort of intellectual and political vanity that comes from admiring oneself in the mirror, without ever really seeing oneself. If their eyes were opened, they would see that to vindicate their claimed republicanism would require more than a formal display of the separation of powers (the theme of *Federalist* No. 48), even more than a separation secured by recurrent or regular appeals to the people (*Federalist* Nos. 49–50). It becomes clear from *The Federalist*'s argument that the Anti-Federalists' superficial understanding of the separation of powers is of a piece with their too easy republicanism: the "parchment barriers" in the state constitutions had quickly been overrun by the encroaching legislatures. These encroachments put an end to the "symmetry and beauty of form" that the foes of the federal Constitution so greatly admired, and proved that these critics did not understand the danger to republicanism posed by the people themselves.

In other words, the Anti-Federalists did not truly comprehend the *need* for the separation of powers in order to make republicanism respectable. Publius is able to show the inadequacy of simple, unrefined republicanism—rule by the whole people in name, but by the many in fact and in spirit, whether directly or through their representatives—without offending republican sensibilities by resorting to the same "mirror" or "standard" that Montesquieu had used, namely, the British Constitution. More precisely, Publius adopts the principle of separated powers that Montesquieu had extracted from that Constitution and incorporates it, with some modifications, into the American Constitution, which becomes itself a kind of mirror of political liberty. Gazing into that mirror, the American people will see not crude republicanism but republican government held to the standard of good government by virtue of the separation of powers. Not only that, but they will also discern the figure of Publius himself, whose majesty as a republican founder helps to synthesize republicanism and separated powers—and whose wisdom endures for future generations to consult. As Americans turned to Montesquieu to view the principles of the British Constitution, so they henceforth would open *The Federalist* to see the true principles of their own Constitution. In such manner the "honorable determination, which animates every votary of freedom, to rest all our political experiments on the capacity of mankind for self-government," may be vindicated, by showing that republican government is honorable and good.[20]

To *The Federalist*, the separation of powers was not a "display" of merry-go-round laws of nature but a qualification and refinement of republicanism. To effect this, the powers had to be mixed in order to be kept separate, the mechanism of the mixing being the same as the guardian of the separation—namely, the famous system of ambition counteracting ambition, so that "the interest of the man" may be connected with "the constitutional rights of the place." Wilson's objection to this system is that "government is not a body of blind forces; it is a body of men, with highly differentiated functions . . . but with a common task and purpose. Their cooperation is indispensable, their warfare fatal."[21] But Wilson's criticism of public purposelessness—which is, to repeat, a refrain common now to both the Left and the Right—is not true to the nature of each of the powers. It does not speak to the constitutional *duties* of the place, which are based on an understanding of these natures or functions. The lack of an extensive theoretical discussion of these specific natures is one of the chief mysteries of *The Federalist*, explained only partially by Publius' admonition, already mentioned, of the difficulty in distinguishing betwen them. Although "the greatest adepts in political science" may puzzle at this great question, Publius speaks consistently as if such knowledge were available, even declaring that "discriminating . . . in theory, the several classes of power, as they may in their nature be legislative, executive, or judiciary," is a less difficult task than protecting each "against the invasion of the others."[22]

His reticence may be due, then, not so much to lack of knowledge as to a desire to conceal as much as possible the non-republican origins of the separation of powers: the British constitution, though having one republican branch, is not a form of republican government.[23] Moreover, the distinctive nature of the powers is most visible in the least republican branches—the executive and especially the judiciary, with its indirect mode of selection and good behavior tenure. In the duties of these powers one does not see "blind forces" at work, however much ambition and self-interst may be counted upon to guard the independence that is the necessary condition of the faithful discharge of their duties. For the highest duty of these branches, though not always the most urgent, is to instruct the citizenry in that "veneration" for the Constitution which is necessary to ensure that the "reason of the public" will "control and regulate the government," and that the government will control and regulate the public passions.[24]

Through the separation of powers, which elevates the Constitution above the people's passions without vitiating its claim to be the highest expression of their (reasonable) will, the American regime makes provision for the formation of character in its citizens. "Veneration" of the Constitution means acknowledging that it is the "reason of the public" and not its passions that should "sit in judgment" and "control and regulate" the government. Citizens are encouraged to think of themselves as judges and executives—and since the highest embodiment of the public's reason is the Constitution, as *founders*—instead of merely as legislators who have or reflect passions and interests that must be checked and either neutralized or compromised. Respect for the Constitution translates into moderation or self-restraint and the justice that is expressed in faithfulness to founding principles. Finally, then, veneration of the Constitution and its "inventions of prudence," foremost among them the separation of powers, must be seen in light of the ends or principles to which prudence ministers. It may be true that these inventions make statesmanship slightly less necessary in ordinary times of the nation's life; but they also provide a place for statesmanship in ordinary and extraordinary seasons, and charge American statesmen with a duty to the principles of the Constitution that is neither ignoble nor light, and that is not intended to change with the times.[25]

So far as *The Federalist*'s view of the separation of powers has been sketched here, it is clear that Wilson's account of it as a deduction from Newtonianism is perverse. Separation of powers is pre-eminently a device for moderating and refining popular government, and can more truthfully be said to point the way to statesmanship than to displace or subvert it. That Wilson never undertook a serious examination of *The Federalist*'s doctrine on this point, despite many asseverations as to its teaching, suggests either that he prejudged the work as being too commonplace to merit his scrutiny, or that he considered the separation of powers, however understood, to be epiphenomenal. Perhaps the real or fundamental obstacle to statesmanship in the American regime is not the system of separated powers but the purpose the system is designed to serve. It is the sun at the center of the orbiting powers that is the cause of the problem: not the Constitution so much as the Declaration of Independence threatens the political life of the nation. For it is here that the ideas of natural right and natural law, those reflections of the Newtonian *Zeitgeist*, dwell, and reach out maleficently to stay the hand of statesmanship. "Liberty fixed in unalterable law," Wilson writes, "would be no liberty at all." Natural law, the most unalterable of laws, is inconsistent with human liberty and especially with the freedom of action of statesmen. To open the American regime to progress therefore requires of Wilson a critique of the Declaration that severs the connection between the ends ordained by natural law or right, and the means adopted to secure these rights in the Constitution.[26]

Wilson's reading of the Declaration—like his political science as a whole—begins with de-radicalization but ends in ever-greater radicalization. "We think of it as a highly theoretical document," he writes—in what is perhaps the most ironical sentence in all of American political science—"but except for its assertion that all men are equal it is not." Except for the heart of the Declaration's argument—that "abstract truth" which Lincoln celebrated for transforming "a merely revolutionary document" into "a rebuke and a stumbling-block to the very harbingers of re-appearing tyranny and oppression"[27]—except for that "assertion," the Declaration is a practical document. If Wilson means that the theoretical argument of the Declaration was in the service of a practical end, namely, declaring independence, that is one thing; it would be an inadequate account of the Declaration's purpose, but it would be at least partially faithful to the facts. But he means something very different. The Declaration "names as among the 'inalienable rights' of man the right to life, liberty, and the pursuit of happiness, as does . . . many another document of the time; but it expressly leaves to each generation of men the determination of what they will do with their lives, what they will prefer as the form and object of their liberty, in what they will seek their happiness." Search the text of the Declaration as one will, there are not words "expressly" saying this; nor do the words imply it, unless the actions of the signers themselves—beginning with the mutual pledge of their "sacred honor"—can be dismissed as mere whims or as a few glory-seekers' peculiar choice of lifestyle, inherently no more honorable than any other "pursuit of happiness." Wilson's interpretation can be reconciled with the language of the Declaration only by supposing the ideas of inalienable rights and happiness to have been emptied of all objective content, effectively disconnecting them from the "self-evident" truth of human equality. "That all men are created equal" is accordingly reduced from a self-evident truth or a Lincolnian "proposition" to a mere "assertion," as Wilson says so carefully.[28]

In fact it is the kind of "assertion" that has no place in a healthy regime, for good Burkean reasons. "If any one ask me what a free government is," Wilson quotes Burke as saying, "I reply, it is what the people think so." This statement goes "to the heart of the matter" for Wilson, inasmuch as it reveals why the American regime must be sundered from the tradition of natural right, and why political science should not be the study of human happiness or regimes, but the investigation of "constitutional government" and its development. With every generation, the ends of government or the substantial definitions of liberty and happiness change, according to Wilson; and since forms are related to ends, the forms of government change in some measure, too. It follows that forms of government "do not affect the essence of government" but merely "exhibit the stages of political development." The Declaration can therefore have no teaching concerning the best regime or even ranking legitimate regimes; it teaches only the "conception" or "large image" of what liberty is. Free government is what the people think it is, which means not that they can acquiesce in any regime (though there is some truth to that) but that they have the right "to adjust government to their own needs and interests." In Wilson's words, "government is a part of life, and, with life, it must change, alike in its objects and practices; only this principle must remain unaltered . . . that there must be the freest right and opportunity of adjustment." While this right is not grounded in human nature, it does justify itself by the fullest self-development of the individual, which is Wilson's problematic (because open-ended) replacement for natural right. "Constitutional government" is therefore not government according to the forms of the American Constitution or the ends of the Declaration, but government that respects the right of the governed to strike whatever balance may suit them between "the power of the government and the privileges of the individual."[29]

In deciding on this balance, the people must be guided by leaders, but neither the people nor their leaders should be guided by an abstract theory of rights, especially not by what Jefferson called the inherent and inalienable rights of man. At best the rights enumerated in the Declaration amount to a sort of historical outline of the people's general right to adjust government to their own satisfaction. Properly understood, the rights to life, liberty, and the pursuit of happiness are not natural but prescriptive, growing out of the long tradition of English constitutional history and of the Teutonic or Anglo-Saxon race's anciently cultivated capacity for self-government. These rights do not have to be granted or asserted because they are "taken for granted," as if no one doubted that "men should be free" or "their interests righteously adjusted to the powers of government." That they can be taken for granted is testimony to the English-speaking peoples' self-control and moderation, which is not the result of the statesmanship of the American or of any other Founders, nor of the singular way of life inculcated by a particular regime. The character of the Americans, as colonists and as revolutionaries and as citizens, is due to the historical development of their race or people. Wilson remarks the aphorism of Walter Bagehot, "that it was no proof of the excellence of the Constitution of the United States that the Americans had operated it with conspicuous success, because the Americans could run any constitution successfully. . . ." Indeed so exiguous is the influence of constitutionalism on the American character that it is possible to imagine both the Declaration and the Constitution swept away, without at all affecting the people's capacity for self-government.[30]

To state it differently, constitutional government depends upon "a definite understanding" between governors and governed, but such an understanding presupposes a *people* capable of agreement. It presupposes what Wilson calls a "community" that is self-conscious and to some extent self-directive. A community is the product of shared history and common interests and habits and standards: "We know that body of persons is not a community along whose blood the same events do not send the same thrill, upon whose purposes and upon whose consciousness the same events do not make the same impression"—and here is the Darwinian imperative—"and who are not capable, at every turn in their affairs, of forming resolutions and executing measures which will meet the exigency." The form of constitutional government fitted to such a community is a late fruit, indeed is the last fruit, of political development. It is the *terminus ad quem* of an evolutionary process that began with government the absolute master, first by force and later by intelligence; that saw government challenged by awakening peoples; and that culminated when "the leaders of the people themselves became the government," at which moment "the development was complete."[31] Resort to any abstract, i.e., unhistorical, theory of rights interferes with this long, slow process of growth, and leads either to social frustration and governmental paralysis, as was partially the case in America, or to tyrannical attempts to new-model society, as happened in the French Revolution. The latter provides ample material for Wilson's *argumentum ad horrendum* on this point, and he draws freely on the contrast between the American and French Revolutions to show the superiority of "constitutional precedents" to "democratic precepts," of "organic growth" to "discontent" and "revolution."[32]

That American government has had "a vital and normal organic growth," that it has had a *history*, proves that the Whig theory, though imbibed deeply by the founders, never left them so light-headed as to lose their "experienced eye for affairs" and "quick practical sagacity." They were, after all or perhaps before all, practical statesmen as well as devotees of Montesquieu and Hobbes. This was crucial in sparing America the trauma inflicted upon France by a class of revolutionary leaders whose devotion to abstract principle was not moderated by habits of self-control and patience and by long experience in self-government. Nevertheless, the American Founders *had* established a regime in which the people's right to adjust government to their own needs and interests—to the "felt necessities of the time," as Oliver Wendell Holmes, Jr., would later call it—was limited by the separation of powers (and committee government) in particular, and by government's duty to secure men's natural rights, in general. On Wilson's analysis, it seems that government roped to the star of natural rights must be either behind or ahead of the times, either lagging behind social and economic development or attempting to force progress upon an unready nation. Only constitutional government dedicated to the "freest right and opportunity of adjustment" can hope to keep pace with progress, to distribute its benefits evenly and efficiently. Political liberty in Wilson's definition is both the right to make this adjustment and "the best practicable adjustment." It is the gap between the two that creates the decisive need for the new statesmanship of progress.[33]

Now, the Wilsonian statesman is to be distinguished from the man of thought, although both are in some sense "leaders of men." As it is "the estimate of the world" that gives words their signification, however, Wilson accepts the view that the leader of men is the statesman who acts, rather than the man who writes books. The distinction is not, as it may at first appear, between practice and theory, for Wilson's historicism precludes there being eternal forms or objects worthy of detached (i.e., theoretical) contemplation. That "the true philosophy of government can be extracted only from the true history of government" means that the traditional effort to understand politics in light of permanent standards of right and wrong—that is, of natural right—must be abandoned, and with it the problem of mediating between what is always and everywhere right, and what is right or desirable here and now. Instead, the problem becomes to distinguish between the statesman and the "literary man," the man who writes novels, who cultivates "the nice fashions of literary dress," who adores "artistic completeness of thought and expression." Why does the problem take this form? History and poetry both advance claims to understand political things, and poetry was traditionally understood to have superior credentials, insofar as it could grasp "universals" in a way that history, being the chronicler of mortal men and perishable deeds, could not. But Wilson, denying the existence of universals (properly speaking), undercuts poetry's superiority: no longer can universals be captured in particulars, in the manner of poetry; rather, particulars *constitute* the only intelligible universal, which is the rational unfolding of history, or progress. This is the ground of Wilson's superordination of history, or the philosophy of history, over poetry; but precisely because both history and poetry deal with particulars, there remains a need to discriminate between the understandings of the man of action and the literary man.[34]

The activity of both types, Wilson writes, is a kind of "interpretation." What marks the interpretations of writers is a love of "proportion," whereas men of action are obliged to neglect proportion. The difference is not between contemplating and acting, but between having certain literary "sensibilities" and lacking them. The literary man is a "sensitive seer" whose imagination can bring to life a thousand characters with a thousand different motives not his own; this "subtle power of sympathy" affords him a "Shakespearean insight" into the hearts of individual men. By contrast, the leader of men has a "sympathetic and penetrative insight" not into individual secrets but into the motives that move men "in the mass." His sympathy is with what "lies waiting to be stirred" in the minds of "groups and masses," and is oriented to command, not to service. Wilson suggests that the one is to the other as a physicist is to a mechanic, or as a mechanic is to a good locomotive engineer. Putting the proportions together, it seems that the statesman is something in between a physicist and a locomotive runner—or to change terms, between a poet and a ward boss.[35] Again, the literary mind or "temperament" is said by Wilson to conceive "images" that are "rounded, perfect, ideal," "instrumental to nothing, sufficient unto themselves." (Of course these images have no existence independent of their conceivers; they are "outlooks," "such stuff as dreams are made of.") The leader of men, on the contrary, conceives "principles," which are "threads to the labyrinth of circumstances"—not self-sufficient "unities" that could function as arbitrary ends, but indications of where he has already been, at once bearing with them the accumulated knowledge of the past and warning him not to attempt to return to the past or to retrace his steps beyond what is necessary to open a new vista.[36]

The significance of this for statesmanship is nicely elaborated in another of Wilson's metaphors.

The captain of a Mississippi steamboat had made fast to the shore because of a thick fog lying upon the river. The fog lay low and dense upon the surface of the water, but overhead all was clear. A cloudless sky showed a thousand points of starry light. An impatient passenger inquired the cause of the delay. "We can't see to steer," said the captain. "But all's clear overhead," suggested the passenger, "you can see the North Star." "Yes," replied the officer, "but we are not going that way."

The moral: "Politics must follow the actual windings of the channel: if it steer by the stars it will run aground."[37] In Wilson's hands, the familiar ship of state becomes a riverboat, and the great ocean which provided challenge—but also immense latitude of action—to the statesman, is reduced to a meandering but confined waterway. There is a definite current, a direction of flow to the river: the great stream of time has a destination, a meaning. To be sure, it may be necessary to outpace the current sometimes in order to avoid shoals and hazards; and these hazards, as well as the sinuous course of the river itself, will have to be scouted to guard against unhappy surprises. But celestial navigation is not only useless but positively harmful to the negotiating of a mighty river whose bed has been carved from the earth by slow, steady processes at work for ages. Abstract principles or proportioned images, to bring the moral home, cannot be a proper guide to political action for a social organism that lives and grows by slow evolutionary adaptation to changing historical conditions.[38]

The work of the statesman is accordingly a kind of compromise, even as "all growth is a process of compromise" between organic forces and environmental or physical forces. Compromise in politics need be no more "dishonest" than in the biological growth of an organism, so long as this single condition is met—"if only it be progressive." Wilson's political career, in particular his great fall in the battle over the Treaty of Versailles, does not need to be clarified by psychohistory, provided that this fundamental limitation on his willingness to compromise, along with the general bearing of his political thought, is understood in its full significance. In Wilson's words, the task of the statesman is to read and interpret the "common thought" with a view to ascertaining "very circumspectly the *preparation* of the nation for the next move in the progress of politics." The object of course is not to counsel "a timid standing still for fear of possible mistakes," but "to point out the way of progress." The statesman's virtue, in a comprehensive sense, is "that wise sort of boldness which can afford to make mistakes because it knows what is essential and guards that from risk while it ventures all else for the sake of liberty and a freer course for reform." When "advance or catastrophe" is the choice, the responsible statesman must insist on advance, all the while admonishing his people in the cardinal commandment of the new morality: "*political sin* is the transgression of the law of political progress (rightly understood)."[39]

For the most part, the law of progress ("rightly understood") mandates "slow modification and nice all-around adjustment." Society is an organism, and must be vital in all its parts or else be stunted and deformed; development must therefore touch all regions, classes, and interests as equally as possible. But since the social organism is composed of a multitude of actual human beings, it is the majority that must and should rule, if only in the limited sense "that no reform may succeed for which the major thought of the nation is not prepared. . . ." A society or people being held together by habit—really by a habit of thought, a *Volksgeist*—it behooves the statesman to see that legislation stays near it. "The ear of the leader must ring with the voices of the people." This does not mean that the leader must echo what he hears: legislation can advance and modify habit, but must always harmonize with the "constituent habit." There is room for "initiative" but not "novelty," for "interpretation" but not "origination." The leader is adjured to "discern and strengthen the tendencies that make for development," to distinguish the permanent and progressive forces from the transitory and reactionary ones, and to encourage the former.[40]

Progress, however, does not always dictate that the leader should appear in the "harness of compromise." "Once and again one of those great Influences which we call a *Cause* arises in the midst of a nation." The unharnessed, the authentic leader of men is the champion of a cause, the reformer who stands for a "political or moral principle" that he demands to be recognized by the majority. The rallying point for reform, or the banner under which his principle marches, is a vision of the future—an understanding of the direction that history is about to take, at once an extrapolation from and transformation of present trends.[41] The term "reformer" is apt, for it is as spokesman for a cause that the leader exercises the highest kind of statesmanship—quickening the conscience of society and freeing it from the sluggishness of all self-interst and partial attachments, what Nietzsche called "the spirit of gravity." In the moment of freedom offered by political idealism, the leader is free to re-form the people in the image of his vision. At that moment "men are as clay in the hands of the consummate leader," and his is the "*power* which dictates, dominates." But it is not a form as such that the leader impresses on the clay; it is only "the application of force," a kind of intertia, a way of *moving* masses of men at the same time and speed and direction, like a flock of geese. "Form" in Wilson's understanding emerges from or is reducible to matter in motion, that is, in historical motion. "Get the country *moving* again" is therefore the characteristic call for statesmanship understood as, and limited to, leadership of the Wilsonian kind. But precisely in Wilson's identification of form with a law of motion (albeit historical motion), we see, to paraphrase Lincoln, that there is not such a Newtonian in the nation as Wilson, after all.[42]

Since the "forces of public thought" tend to be blind forces, it is up to the leader to give them "vision" both in the sense of the ability to see and of the "vision" given them to be seen. He stimulates their ability to see by opening them to movement, to progress—by fostering a confidence in the beneficence of change. What he presents to their view is the sharp demand for progress together with a vague description of the perfected arrangements to come, all of which is clinched by the concrete example of his own faith, and by the earnest of his moving, not to say transforming, rhetoric. Hence the leader becomes a kind of poet for a new society, the herald of a new age and freedom, whose poetry is concerned as much with himself as with the next stage in the advance, or is concerned with himself for the sake of the next stage. That is to say, the leader qua poet is indispensable to the leader qua politician: his poetry must create and sustain the "image" of leadership, for only by serving history can poetry now be justified. The leader therefore re-creates himself as an imagination-capturing avatar of the dawning spirit of the age, so that to believe in him is to have, if not eternal, at least evolutionary life. Broadly considered, leadership is thus a way to engage public passions through an appeal to the public imagination that seeks to lift men from the Hobbesian realm of interest and necessity, toward the realm of true human freedom that lies at the end of history. "That is the whole thing that we are constantly fighting with," Wilson told New York Democrats in his first presidential campaign, "to keep down, to ride down, to suppress our own ambitions and our own selfishness. In order to do what? In order to ride higher. In order to see more of the Empyrean. In order to make a longer flight."[43]

In the meantime, reform is kept from being revolution by its connection to the people. If "vision" is one of the characteristic virtues of the new statesmanship as it was conceived by Wilson—and as it continues to be understood in our time—then we have arrived at another of these modern virtues, "compassion." Leadership is a matter of "sympathetic insight," really of "a sympathy which is insight" into the heart (not the mind) of a people. Such sympathy, whether conscious or unconscious, allows the leader to move with the common impulse and to feel the common feeling, without becoming common himself. It is the function of the political party as Wilson saw it to provide the mechanism to effect this sort of fellow feeling, to sum up the concerns and desires of a vast nation so that its leaders would not become alienated from it. At the same time, the party serves as a conduit for the organizing vision of the leader—as the extraconstitutional or informal form that organizes motion in the nation as a whole.[44]

But at bottom the leader's sympathy or compassion for the led is his way of staying grounded in the evolution of the community; it is what keeps Wilson's doctrine of leadership from becoming Leninism. Sympathy or "common counsel," as he also calls it, assures the *timeliness* of reform; it ensures that "no man thinking thoughts born out of time can succeed in leading his generation," by *binding* him to his generation. Compassionate leaders are therefore "the more sensitive organs of society," the men who pick up "some principle of equity or morality already *accepted* well-nigh universally," but not yet risen to consciousness. Their task is to unlock the hearts of the people. to "formulate and make explicit" what lies "inchoate and vague" in the general sense of the community. At first society will resent the leaders's intrusiveness, even as we resent "the start and irritation of a rude and sudden summons from sleep." But once awakened, society will adjust to the situation and meet the "necessities of conduct" revealed to it.[45]

Hence "no cause is born out of time," and every reform is "the destruction of an anomaly" or "the wiping out of an anachronism." This holds great significance for the reformer himself, because however great he may be, in the final analysis his greatness has very little to do with himself. He is produced by the occasion, even if in his reforms he gives little thought to occasion. Great reformers are "early vehicles of the Spirit of the Age," but nothing more. Their particular virtues are vision and compassion, which make for excellence in interpreting the common thought, but not excellence in deliberating about the means most conducive to the common good. The words and deeds of Washington or Lincoln or, for that matter, Wilson himself, cannot be clarified or made intelligible on the basis of prudence and greatness of soul; instead, they must be understood as a form of the people's self-expression through the personality of their leader.[46] To quote Wilson in his 1912 presidential campaign: "I have often thought that the only strength of a public man consisted in the number of persons who agreed with him; and that the only strength that any man can boast of and be proud of is that great bodies of his fellow citizens trust him and are ready to follow him." "For the business of every leader of government," he declared, "is to hear what the nation is saying and to know what the nation is enduring. It is not his business to judge *for* the nation, but to judge *through* the nation as its spokesman and voice."[47]

The democratic statesman's duty, then, is not to recall the people to the "abstract truth" in virtue of which they live, move, and have their being, but to follow them as their habits and thoughts progressively adumbrate the judgments of history. Although great leaders are "born of the very times that oppose them," Wilson writes, "their success is the acknowledgment of their legitimacy." To triumph is to be right; or, at best, to be right guarantees that one will eventually triumph. The two formulations are in practice the same, since the ultimate test of justice remains success, i.e., historical vindication. As Wilson admitted before the election in which he would first become President, "I would a great deal rather lose in a cause that I know some day will triumph than triumph in a cause that I know some day will lose." There is implicit in this desire for a final reckoning and a once-and-for-all vindication not a little Christian eschatology—except that the judgment which Christianity reserved for the next world, Wilson obtrudes into the petty pace of this world. Even when seeking to deny it, he admits it. "Practical leadership may not beckon to the slow masses of men from beyond some dim unexplored space or some intervening chasm: it must daily feel under its own feet the *road* that leads to the goal proposed, knowing that it is a slow, a very slow, evolution to wings, and that for the present, and for a very long future also, Society must *walk*. . . ." Yes, society must walk, and for a very long time to come; but *someday it will fly*. The "evolution to wings" lies at the end of a long road, but society can walk that road, all the while preparing itself for the great metamorphosis. "The goal of political development" Wilson affirms, "is identical with the goal of individual development. Both singly and collectively man's nature draws him away from that which is brutish towards that which is human—away from his kinship with beasts toward a fuller realization of his kinship with God." Translated into political terms, the peaceful rule of common counsel "is an earnest of the ascendancy of reason over passion."[48]

Political development will be completed when this earnest is made good, when reason *is* finally ascendant over passion. At that moment, when the final and irreversible victory over passion has been won, the political problem, the human problem, will be solved. But with such exalted and providential ends comes an inevitable immoderation in means—or at least a principled inability to oppose those who advocate ignoble and even brutal means, who do not shrink from but glory in the opportunity to progress by antagonisms and contradictions, rather than by sympathy and adjustment, to the unimaginable paradise that lies at the end of history. Just how bitter is this fruit of the tree of historical knowledge we are only now learning. Far from containing or fulfilling the knowledge of good and evil, it has turned out to hold only moral nescience. Partaking of it, our statesmen have been left weak and uncertain when confronted by a wayward people and, what is worse, disarmed and bewildered by an enemy who proclaims history to be *his* ally, and who has the title deeds of success, at least over the past forty years, to prove it. If we are not to add to this bitterness the cup of our own degradation, we must be prepared to face the worst in a spirit of noble defiance, which spirit alone can summon forth the wisdom and courage necessary to turn defeat into victory.[49] But first it is necessary to reclaim the principles that make possible and intelligible that defiance—to return from the statesmanship of progress to the statesmanship of natural right—to be reborn in the "ancient faith" of our Fathers.

Notes

1. Aristotle *Nicomachean Ethics* 1102a5–1103b25, 1140a24–1140b30, 1142a32–1142b34, and 1144b1–1145a7.
2. Woodrow Wilson, *The Papers of Woodrow Wilson*, ed. Arthur S. Link, 43 vols. (Princeton: Princeton University Press, 1966–83), 9:130. Hereinafter cited as *Papers*. Wilson uses the term in the draft introduction to *The Philosophy of Politics*, his self-proclaimed "*novum organum* of political study," which he worked on episodically from 1885 to about 1892, never finished, but always hoped to take up again. For a description of the projected work, see the editorial note at 5:54–58.
3. See e.g., Arthur S. Link, *Wilson: The Road to the White House* (Princeton: Princeton Uni-

versity Press, 1947), pp. 31–35 and 122–132; but cf. Richard Hofstadter, *The American Political Tradition* (New York: Vintage, 1974), pp. 311–318 and 322–327.

4. *Papers* 10:22–23.

5. *Papers* 5:51–52; Wilson, *Constitutional Government in the United States* (New York: Columbia University Press, 1961; orig. ed. 1908), pp. 54–56.

6. *Constitutional Government*, pp. 41–44, 57; *Papers* 5:51.

7. *Constitutional Government*, pp. 54–56; Wilson, *The New Freedom* (New York: Doubleday, 1913), pp. 46–47; cf. Robert A. Goldwin, "Of Men and Angels: A Search for Morality in the Constitution," in Robert H. Horwitz, *The Moral Foundations of the American Republic* (Charlottesville: University Press of Va., 1977), pp. 10–12.

8. See Wilson, *Congressional Government: A Study in American Politics* (Baltimore: Johns Hopkins Press, 1981; orig. ed. 1885), esp. chs. 1–3, 6. For a description of the original constitutional balances, drawing not upon any official "literary theory" but upon John Adams, see *ibid.*, pp. 31–32. It is to be noted that Adams was the greatest American contributor to the doctrine of bicameralism, but not to the theory of separation of powers. Wilson conflates the two, in fact preferring the term "checks and balances," originally applied to the relations between the two legislative houses, to describe both bicameralism and the separation of powers. He thus gives to separation a peculiarly legislative reading, emphasizing what is common to the powers rather than what distinguishes them.

9. *Papers* 5:121; for Wilson's re-evaluation of his thesis of committee government in light of changing circumstances, see his Preface to the fifteenth printing of *Congressional Government*, pp. 19–23, and *Constitutional Government*, ch. 4.

10. *Papers* 5:345; cf. 9:102, 108–9.

11. George Fitzhugh, *Cannibals All! or Slaves Without Masters* (Cambridge: Harvard University Press, 1960), pp. 12–13, 71–72. Consider Leo Strauss, *The City and Man* (Chicago: University of Chicago Press, 1964), p. 11.

12. For a different interpretation, see Harry Clor, "Woodrow Wilson," in Morton J. Frisch and Richard G. Stevens, eds., *American Political Thought: The Philosophic Dimension of American Statesmanship* (Dubuque: Kendall/Hunt, 1976), esp. p. 217.

13. A striking example is the brilliantly oblique essay by Joseph Cropsey, "The United States as Regime and the Sources of the American Way of Life," in Horwitz, *op. cit.*, pp. 86–101. That this may not be his last word, however, may be inferred from "The Moral Basis of International Action," in Cropsey, *Political Philosophy and the Issues of Politics* (Chicago: Univ. of Chicago Press, 1977), pp. 172–188. Herbert J. Storing sticks closer to the phenomena, but in locating the dynamics of American statesmanship in the tension between populism and scientific management, views our politics through Wilson's lenses, despite the fact that he understands himself to be opposing Wilson. See "American Statesmanship: Old and New," in Robert A. Goldwin, ed., *Bureaucrats, Policy Analysts, Statesmen: Who Leads?* (Washington: American Enterprise Institute, 1980), esp. pp. 91–99. For the convergence of liberal and conservative critiques of the Founding, compare Richard Hofstadter, *op. cit.*, pp. 3–21; Benjamin R. Barber, "The Compromised Republic: Public Purposelessness in America," in Horwitz, *op. cit.*, pp. 19–38; and Frank M. Coleman, *Hobbes and America* (Toronto: Univ. of Toronto Press, 1977), with the Cropsey and Storing articles cited above, along with Daniel Boorstin, *The Lost World of Thomas Jefferson* (Boston: Beacon Press, 1960), esp. pp. 194–204; and the seminal treatment by Martin Diamond, "Democracy and *The Federalist*: A Reconsideration of the Framers' Intent," *American Political Science Review*, 53 (March 1959), pp. 52–68. Diamond states the issue plainly: in the Framers' view, "liberalism and republicanism are not the means by which men may ascend to a nobler life; rather they are simply instrumentalities which solve Hobbesian problems in a more moderate manner."

14. Consider Leo Strauss, *What is Political Philosophy?* (New York: Free Press, 1959), pp.

50–51; and cf. Wilson, *Papers* 9:131 and Wilson, *The State* (Boston: D. C. Heath, 1909), secs. 19–20, 1392.

15. *Constitutional Government*, pp. 56, 199; cf. *The New Freedom*, pp. 44–48; on the law of nature, see *The State*, sec. 1460.

16. "There is no country in the world where public statesmanship is so difficult as in this our own country," writes Wilson. *Papers* 16:12.

17. Wilson so recalls at *Papers* 7:129, but regards it mainly as an indication of how prevalent was the "radical misunderstanding" of the subject at the time. That is, he uses the fact that Publius had to make an *argument* against extreme separation as an excuse not to study that argument.

18. Alexander Hamilton, James Madison, John Jay, *The Federalist Papers*, ed. Clinton Rossiter (New York: New American Library, 1961), No. 47, pp. 301–303.

19. *The Federalist Papers*, No. 37, p. 228. On the character of Newtonian natural science, see Martin Heidegger, *What is a Thing?* (South Bend: Gateway Editions, 1967), trans. W. B. Barton, Jr. and Vera Deutsch, pp. 76–88.

20. *The Federalist Papers*, No. 39, p. 240.

21. Ibid., No. 51, p. 322; *Constitutional Government*, p. 56.

22. *The Federalist Papers*, No. 37, p. 228; No. 47, p. 305; No. 48, p. 308.

23. Ibid., No. 39, pp. 240–241.

24. Ibid., No. 49, pp. 314–315, 317.

25. Ibid., No. 49, p. 317; No. 51, p. 322.

26. *Papers* 7:367; *Constitutional Government*, p. 4.

27. Abraham Lincoln, *The Collected Works of Abraham Lincoln*, ed. Roy P. Basler (New Brunswick, N.J.: Rutgers University Press, 1953), Vol. III, p. 376.

28. *Constitutional Government*, p. 4.

29. Ibid., pp. 4–5, 22–23; *The State*, secs. 1074, 1394; *Papers* 5:304, and cf. *Papers* 7:363.

30. *Constitutional Government*, pp. 8–9, 27, 59; *Papers* 5:67–70.

31. *Constitutional Government*, pp. 25–28; *The State*, sec. 1414. For a revealingly different account of the stages of political development, see Wilson, "The Study of Administration," *Political Science Quarterly* 2 (June 1887), pp. 204–209.

32. *Papers* 6:228–231. Cf. *Papers* 5:62–67.

33. *Constitutional Government*, pp. 4–5, 57, 59.

34. *Papers* 5:304, 6:646–647. Much of the analysis which follows is based upon Wilson's address, "Leaders of Men," printed at 6:644–671, which is an indispensable document in the interpretation of his political thought.

35. Cf. the young Wilson's comment in an essay on Gladstone: "Great statesmen seem to direct and rule by a sort of power to put themselves in the place of the nation over whom they are set, and may thus be said to possess the souls of poets at the same time that they display the coarser sense and the more vulgar sagacity of practical men of business." *Papers* 1:628.

36. *Papers* 6:648–650, 662.

37. *Papers* 6:662.

38. Cf. William Graham Sumner, "The Absurd Effort to Make the World Over," in A. G. Keller and Maurice R. Davie, *Essays of William Graham Sumner* (New Haven: Yale University Press, 1934), Vol. I, pp. 105–106.

39. *Papers* 5:62, 65; 6:659, 663; 9:129; cf. 7:359–360.

40. *Papers* 6:659–660.

41. *Papers* 6:663. For Wilson's own politics of vision in the 1912 presidential election campaign, see his speeches in John Wells Davidson, ed., *A Crossroads of Freedom* (New Haven: Yale University Press, 1956), pp. 32, 34, 80–81, 92, 98, 147–148, 165, 242, 247, 270–271, 286–287, 324, 396, 401, 424, 426–428, 451, 459, 498–499, 518, and 520.

42. *Papers* 6:650; cf. 7:365.

43. *Papers* 6:661; *A Crossroads of Freedom*, p. 147; on the reformer's rhetorical strategy, see "The Study of Administration," pp. 208–209, together with *Papers* 7:359–360, 365–367 and *The New Freedom*, esp. pp. 44–45. But cf. Clor, *op. cit.*, pp. 205–207.

44. The leader, Wilson writes, "rallies about himself, not mobs, but parties. He binds men to himself not by a vague community of sentiment but by a definite and decisive oneness of purpose. The people feel a keen charm in the knowledge of the fact that, though he is powerful, his power is derived from them and is dependent upon their favour. They are conscious of being represented by him in respect to their greater and soberer aims. They gain in dignity as he gains in beneficent powers. To follow him is to realize the greatest possible amount of real political life." *Papers* 5:87. On the connection between leadership and party government in Wilson's thought, see the excellent discussion in James W. Caeser, *Presidential Selection: Theory and Development* (Princeton: Princeton University Press, 1979), pp. 188–207.

45. *Papers* 6:661, 663–4, 666; for the democratization resulting from the political discovery of compassion or sympathy, see Paul Eidelberg, *A Discourse on Statesmanship: The Design and Transformation of the American Polity* (Urbana, Ill.: University of Illinois Press, 1974), ch. 9.

46. *Papers* 5:61, 6:663–4. The first step toward the replacement of deliberation by interpretation—toward historicism, that is—can be seen in Hobbes's redefinition of deliberation as "putting an end to the Liberty we had of doing, or omitting, according to our own Appetite, or Aversion," and in his consequent redefinition of will as "the last Appetite in Deliberating." Consider Hobbes, *Leviathan*, Book I, ch. 6.

47. *A Crossroads of Freedom*, p. 187; *The New Freedom*, p. 73; Clor, *op. cit.*, pp. 195–197; cf., *inter alia, A Crossroads of Freedom*, pp. 145–147, 326, 448.

48. *Papers* 6:661, 664; *A Crossroads of Freedom*, p. 147; *Papers* 5:90; Kent A. Kirwan, "Historicism and Statesmanship in the Reform Argument of Woodrow Wilson," *Interpretation* 11 (September 1981), pp. 350–351.

49. Above all consider Lincoln's undying example of the greatness and nobility of the human spirit in confronting the worst, as, for example, in the peroration to his December 26, 1839 Speech on the Sub-Treasury, in *The Collected Works of Abraham Lincoln*, Vol. I, pp. 178–179; and Harry V. Jaffa's profound expositions of the meaning of Lincoln's lifework, both in its timeless and timely dimensions, as, for example, in *Crisis of the House Divided* (Chicago: University of Chicago Press, 1982; orig. ed. 1959), and in "On the Necessity of a Scholarship of the Politics of Freedom," *Statesmanship*, ed. Harry V. Jaffa (Durham: Carolina Academic Press, 1981), pp. 1–9.

7

ROUSSEAU AND HOBBES ON THE UNITY OF THE STATE

Edward J. Erler

What is it that makes the unity of the state? It is the union of its members. And whence arises the union of its members? From the mutual obligations which unite them. All this is agreed upon.
But what is the foundation of this obligation? Here authors are divided. Each establishes his principle and attacks those of others . . . I have myself not done otherwise, and, following the most sane party of those who have discussed these matters, I have posed for the foundation of the body politic the convention of its members; I have refuted the principles different from mine.
Independently of the truth of this principle, it is preferable to all the others because of the solidity of the foundation on which it is established; for what more certain foundation can be devised for the obligations among men than the free engagement of those who are obliged? One can dispute all the other principles, one is not able to dispute this one.[1]

ROUSSEAU IS WIDELY ACKNOWLEDGED TO BE THE FIRST POLITICAL PHILOSO-pher to attack modern political philosophy in the name of both politics and philosophy. His principal antagonist in this enterprise was Hobbes. In Rousseau's view "the horrible system of Hobbes,"[2] resting as it did on enlightenment rationalism, would inevitably lead simultaneously to the establishment of universal despotism and the end of philosophy. Consequently, Rousseau's defense of politics took the form of an attack on bourgeois morality and his defense of philosophy resulted in the "praise [of] ignorance."[3]

Rousseau was fully aware that modern political philosophy itself had begun as a defense of politics. Machiavelli, and in his footsteps Hobbes, had attacked the classical tradition—including the Christian tradition—with the specific intent of re-establishing on firmer grounds the foundations of autonomous political life that had been eroded by what he considered the influences of both classical thought and Christian theology.

Whereas Rousseau's condemnation of Hobbes is unequivocal, his references to Machiavelli are almost entirely favorable.

> Machiavelli was an honorable man and a good citizen; but being attached to the Medici household, he was forced, during the oppression of his homeland, to disguise his love of freedom. The choice of his inexecrable hero is in itself enough to make manifest his hidden intention; and the contrast between the maxims of his book *The Prince* and those of his *Discourses on Titus Livy* and of his *History of Florence* shows that this profound *politique* has had only superficial or corrupt readers until now.[4]

While Rousseau claims to be the first non-superficial, uncorrupted reader of Machiavelli, it is not entirely amiss to suggest that, in Rousseau's view, the most corrupt reader Machiavelli ever had was Hobbes. For, although Hobbes apparently accepted the Machiavellian critique of both the classical and Christian traditions, he failed to break completely with those traditions, as Machiavelli had evidently done.

Hobbes, following Machiavelli, attacked both the ancients and Christianity in the name of a revivified political order, one in which judgments about justice and injustice would no longer be derived from trans-political standards, but one in which such judgments would be represented by the person of the Sovereign—a "mortal god."[5] Hobbes undoubtedly agreed with Machiavelli that "effectual truth" rather than "imagination" was to be the strength of this new, albeit mortal, god. The ancients had understood natural right in terms of teleology. Nature was said to provide a standard of justice which was independent of human will. Both Machiavelli and Hobbes saw the classical version of natural right as an ineffectual guarantee of human political behavior. In the Christian polity the telos of human behavior had become even more radically trans-political and private, further complicating the question of the efficacy of natural right as a guide to political life.

As Leo Strauss pointed out, "Machiavelli had completely severed the connection between politics and natural law or natural right;"[6] Hobbes, on the other hand, set about the systematic restoration of both natural right and natural law, but on wholly modern and secular grounds. But as Strauss also pointed out, this restoration, although on Machiavellian grounds, was "in opposition to Machiavelli's own solution."[7] Machiavelli's "solution," whatever else it may have entailed, apparently did not depend on natural right or natural law in any form. The differences between Machiavelli and Hobbes in this regard can be highlighted by a consideration of the way they treat honor. Machiavelli, for all intents and purposes, made honor the highest goal of political life. In doing so, he represented honor as *the* most specifically anti-Christian virtue (or *virtù*). Machiavelli writes that in "ancient times people were greater lovers of freedom than in these," and this stems "from the same cause that makes men now less hardy. That I believe is the difference between our religion and the ancient. Ours, because it shows us the truth and the true way, makes us esteem less the honor of the world; whereas the pagans, greatly esteeming such honor and believing it their greatest good, were fiercer in their actions. . . . Ancient religion, besides this, attributed blessedness only to men abounding in worldly glory . . . Our religion has glorified humble and contemplative men rather than active ones."[8] Hobbes, on the other hand, seems to treat honor as "evil Pride," the source of all unreasonableness and thereby the source of all injustice. The difference is accounted for by the fact that Hobbes, as opposed to Machiavelli, sought to make his teaching appear consistent with Christian natural law. Bourgeois morality, more peaceful, and seemingly more amenable to Christian morality, would thus replace Machiavellian honor in the Hobbesian political universe.

It is well known that Hobbes regarded classical thought as "rather a dream than a science."[9] One of the interlocutors in Hobbes's dialogue *Decameron Physiologicum* states the Hobbesian view: "Yet both Greeks and Romans were more addicted to moral than to natural philosophy; in which kind we have their writings, but loosely and incoherently, written upon no other principles than their own passions and presumptions, without any respect to the laws of commonwealth, which are the ground and measure of true morality. So that their books tend rather to teach men to censure than to obey the laws; which has been a great hindrance to the peace of the western world ever since."[10] Even though Hobbes extended this general criticism to all pre-scientific thought, he was willing to make some rather unscientific distinctions among the classical "dreamers": Plato was "the best philosopher of the Greeks," while Aristotle was the "most absurd." Of Aristotle, Hobbes wrote, "I believe that scarcely anything can be more absurdly said in natural philosophy, than that which is called *Aristotle's Metaphysics*; nor more repugnant to government, than what he hath said in his *Politics*; nor more ignorantly, than a great part of his *Ethics*."[11] How was it possible for Hobbes from his modern materialistic, scientific perspective to distinguish so markedly between Plato and Aristotle?

From Hobbes's point of view, Aristotle rather than Plato was the source of the most significant political aspects of Christian theology. For Aristotle, in becoming the founder of moral virtue, found it necessary to distinguish between moral virtue and intellectual virtue. And in providing the autonomous foundation for moral virtue—a virtue complete in the person of the non-philosophic gentleman—Aristotle simultaneously provided for the non-political autonomy of the intellectual virtues. In short, Aristotle, in Hobbes's view, created the basis for private or non-political virtues, and thereby provided the impetus for some to take their bearings by trans-political or at least non-political ends.[12] In Hobbes's view, apparently, Plato never deviated in his view that the virtues consti-

tuted a unified whole which was informed ultimately by the requirements of the political. And, as paradoxical as it may seem at first glance,
Aristotle rather than Plato was regarded by Hobbes as the "utopian" philosopher who, in viewing the moral virtues as essentially non-problem-
atic, nevertheless made politics itself highly problematic.

Or, considering the question from a slightly more conventional
angle, it might be said that the power of modern "method" allowed
Hobbes to envision the possibility of transforming Plato's "utopianism"
into solid practicality. At the end of the second part of the *Leviathan*, at
the point where he concludes his arguments to non-Christian, i.e., future,
sovereigns, Hobbes makes this seemingly uncharacteristic remark:

> considering . . . how much depth of moral philosophy is required, in
> them that have the administration of the sovereign power; I am at the
> point of believing this my labour, as useless as the commonwealth of
> Plato. For he *also* is of opinion that it is impossible for the disorders of
> state, and change of governments by civil war, ever to be taken away, till
> sovereigns be philosophers. But when I consider again, that the science
> of natural justice, is the only science necessary for sovereigns and their
> principal ministers . . . I recover some hope, that one time or other, this
> writing of mine may fall into the hands of a sovereign, who . . . by the
> exercise of entire sovereignty, in protecting the public teaching of it,
> convert this *truth of speculation, into the utility of practice* (emphasis added).[13]

The "science of natural justice," a science unavailable to Plato—or for
that matter to any of Hobbes's predecessors—can thus convert Plato's
"useless . . . commonwealth" into one of "entire sovereignty." For "want of
method" Plato's "speculations" remain utopian, but with the right method
utopian speculations can be converted into effective realities. This means
essentially that the private virtues—the ultimate source of civil war and
contention—will be entirely subordinated to political sovereignty. Hobbes's
method—the "science of natural justice"—rather than philosophy, will
animate future "philosopher" kings.

In Hobbes's view there was a close connection between Aristotle, the
Christian polity and the teaching of the Schoolmen. In discussing the
"errors brought into religion from Aristotle's metaphysics," Hobbes refers to "the particular tenets of vain philosophy" as they "derived to the
Universities, and thence into the Church, partly from Aristotle, partly
from blindness of understanding."[14] "*Philosophia prima,*" Hobbes continues, "on which all other philosophy ought to depend" is the science of
definitions which serves "to avoid ambiguity and equivocation in reasoning."[15] Among the schools *philosophia prima* is "called *Metaphysics*; as
being a part of the philosophy of Aristotle. . . ." But Aristotle's metaphysics is taken by "the schools . . . for books of *supernatural philosophy,*" and
are interpreted by them in a way which "is for the most part so far from
the possibility of being understood, and so repugnant to natural reason,

that whosoever thinketh there is any thing to be understood by it, must needs think it supernatural." And, it is "these metaphysics, which mingled with the Scriptures" that form the basis of "school divinity."[16]

This "school divinity," based on Aristotelian metaphysics, was, in Hobbes's view, the foundation of the Christian politics which had transformed political life into a seemingly endless succession of civil wars inspired by sectarian disputes. For it was "school divinity" which had made politics subordinate to religion and transformed politics into merely a means for securing non-political—essentially private—ends.[17] This "vain philosophy of Aristotle," Hobbes remarks, "brought into the Church from [his] *entities* and *essence*," serves only "to lessen the dependence of subjects on the sovereign power of their countries."[18] It would thus not be an unfair characterization of Hobbes's view to say that for him Christianity was not Platonism, but Aristotelianism for the people. And, while it is true that the "Aristotelity" of the schoolmen is a much transformed —and essentially inaccurate—Aristotle, from the point of view of politics this point was unimportant for Hobbes.[19]

In the last chapter of the *Social Contract* Rousseau gives a perfectly Machiavellian account of the necessity of civil religion. He remarks that it was Christianity's establishment of "a spiritual kingdom on earth," which separated "the theological system from the political system" and "brought about the end of the unity of the State." This lack of unity, Rousseau continues, "caused the internal divisions that have never ceased to stir up Christian peoples . . . result[ing] in a perpetual conflict of jurisdiction that has made any good polity impossible in Christian states. . . ."[20] Civil religion is the only religion compatible with "a good polity" since it is the only religion which teaches the unity of the state—"the sanctity of the social contract and the laws."[21] In this regard Rousseau makes a curious and revealing remark about Hobbes:

Of all Christian authors, the philosopher Hobbes is the only one who correctly saw the evil and the remedy, who dared to propose the re-unification of the two heads of the eagle, and the complete return to political unity, without which no State or government will ever be well constituted. But he ought to have seen that the dominating spirit of Christianity was incompatible with that of the State. It is not so much what is horrible and false in his *politique* as what is correct and true that has made it odious.[22]

Hobbes was the philosopher who, above all, saw "the complete return to unity" as *the* political problem *par excellence* of modernity. This aspect of Hobbes's teaching, regarded as "correct" by Rousseau, is nevertheless the reason it has become "odious" to many. What is really "odious"in Rousseau's eyes was Hobbes's failure to deal adequately with "the dominating spirit of Christianity" which Rousseau says is a spirit "so favorable to tyranny that tyranny always profits from it."[23] And it is this apparent failure of Hobbes that leads Rousseau to include him ironically as one of the "Christian authors." Clearly what Rousseau is referring to here is Hobbes's attempt to reconcile his system with Christian politics under the aegis of the laws of nature. To be sure, Hobbes expected his secularized version of the laws of nature (subordinated of course to natural right) eventually to prevail. But Hobbes's concessions, according to Rousseau, were too great. These concessions gave the advantage to the forces of Christian disunity rather than secular unity. Abandonment of natural right and natural law is the only solution compatible with a "good polity" in a Christian world. And, although Hobbes spoke of the sovereign as the "soul of the body politic"[24] rather than the reason of the body politic, no one can fail to see the extent to which Rousseau radicalized this notion with his concept of the general will. The real question, however, is whether Rousseau himself was able to avoid what he calls "the dominating spirit of Christianity," or whether, after all, he merely made possible a new kind of sectarianism.

The extent to which Hobbes explicitly intended to modify Machiavelli is, I suggest, the extent to which Rousseau regarded Hobbes's "system" as "horrible." Hobbes's failure to break completely with natural right—a standard of politics independent of human autonomy—provides the animus for Rousseau's critique of Hobbes. Rousseau remarked that Machiavelli "while pretending to give lessons to kings . . . gave great ones to the people. Machiavelli's *The Prince* is the book of republicans."[25] Rousseau says *The Prince* is "the book of republicans" precisely because it exposed the extent to which princes must depend upon the people and convention in the absence of any independent standards of natural right.[26] In this sense at least Rousseau rejects Hobbes in favor of a more Machiavellian form of modernity.

Rousseau agrees with Hobbes about the point of departure, the necessity of providing a non-teleological foundation for politics or political right. This foundation takes its bearings, not from the disputable questions of human ends, but from the indisputable beginnings—the *archai* rather than the *telos*. Both Rousseau and Hobbes give accounts of the state of nature which are intended to supplant both the classical and Christian accounts of the *archai*. Both Rousseau and Hobbes agree that men in the state of nature are solitary, i.e., that the state of nature is pre-political, that men are devoid not only of society but sociability as well. But here the agreement between Rousseau and Hobbes is almost at an end. The indisputable beginnings, it seems, have become disputable.

Rousseau's criticism of Hobbes is a criticism that he makes initially of all philosophers:

The Philosophers who have examined the foundations of society have all felt the necessity of going back to the state of nature, but none of them has reached it . . . All of them . . . speaking continually of need, avarice, oppression, desires, and pride, have carried over to the state of nature ideas they have acquired in society: they spoke about savage man and they described civil man.[27]

According to Rousseau, Hobbes ascribed passions to man in the state of nature which develop only in civil society. Hobbes saw man in the state of nature as animated by two contradictory passions—vanity and fear of death. In the state of nature vanity was the predominate passion because it was able to deceive men into risking their lives in the belief that they were actually securing their lives. The existence of these passions, according to Hobbes, can be "inferred" from human self-consciousness (the "similitude of the passions"),[28] a self-consciousness which Rousseau claims is no part of primitive man's constitution in the "pure state of nature."

But for Hobbes vanity is the great dissembler in the state of nature which produces the *bellum omnium contra omnes*. Nature displays nothing but random bodies in random motion, each body having no other purpose than to conserve its own motion, i.e., its own being. "For nature worketh by motion."[29] And this motion has no immediately evident purpose beyond the preservation of motion itself. Human action, like the action of all bodies—and "every part of the universe, is . . . body and that which is not body, is no part of the universe . . . [and] is *nothing* and consequently *no where*"[30]—is random, purposeless motion. In the "condition of mere nature" the motion of individuals becomes a contest for power, a contest to preserve motion which is inspired by the fear of death —the cessation of motion. This is the meaning of Hobbes's most famous statement: "So that in the first place, I put for a general inclination of all mankind, a perpetual and restless desire of power after power, that ceaseth only in death."[31] In seeking power over others, individuals seek to confirm the strength of their own will to oppose or inform nature by making others live in the order they have created, to make others, as it were, confirm the "reality" of their own creations and thereby provide the basis for their own power and security. One of the characters in the *Decameron Physiologicum* conveys this meaning with the remark that "Men would have all the world, if they could, fear and obey them."[32] It is this radical egocentricity, imposed on man, so to speak, by a disordered and disordering universe, which is the source of man's vanity. Vanity is the product of the rudiments of human self-consciousness inspired by the fear of death,[33] and as such it is the root cause of the *bellum omnium contra omnes*. In this sense, man's vanity is not so much a reflection of nature but a reaction of human will or self-consciousness *against* nature.[34]

Rousseau, however, denies that original man has self-consciousness. He therefore possesses neither vanity nor fear of death. In the

primitive state, in the true state of nature, vanity does not exist; for each particular man regarding himself as the sole spectator to observe him, as the sole being of the universe to take an interest in him, and as the sole judge of his own merit, it is not possible that a sentiment having its source in comparisons he is not capable of making could spring up in his soul.[35]

For essentially the same reason, original man has no "knowledge of death."[36] Without a concept of "self," consciousness of death itself is impossible. The kind of self-consciousness that Hobbes attributed to man in the state of nature is the product of settled relationships which, forcing individuals to reflect on others, forces them to reflect on themselves as entities separate from others. From Rousseau's point of view, Hobbes's account pre-supposes the existence of political life. Rousseau's original man, on the other hand, is a being who is not only solitary but hardly recognizes other human beings as members of the same species.

For Hobbes the "fear of violent death" was the almost perfect vehicle for the restatement of natural law and natural right. Since it was a pre-rational passion, Hobbes thought it to be sufficiently non-teleological. And although the fear of violent death is pre-rational in its origins, it is the source of rationality in the sense that it is the one human passion powerful enough to dispel human vanity and make men amenable to the dictates of reason as embodied in the laws of nature. This is the culmination of Hobbes's attempt to ground natural right—and hence natural law—in some powerful beginning. Once the beginnings are conceded, the whole superstructure of natural right and the laws of nature fall into place as easily as the "theorems and conclusions" of a geometric proof. Thus Hobbes saw fear of violent death as the source of human right, a powerful means to counteract vanity—the source of all human evils—since when seen in the light of day, vanity always appears *unreasonable*. The account of the *archai* proves, for Hobbes, that nature is defective and stands radically in need of human art—reason. Rousseau concludes from this that, in Hobbes's account, "man . . . is naturally evil."[37] Hobbes, of course, never goes so far as to say that man is naturally evil, since that "cannot be granted without impiety"[38] but Rousseau's point is well taken and Rousseau's own piety is never in question on this point.

Hobbes's natural right, from this perspective, is really a revolt against nature in the sense that natural right is not so much a claim *of* nature as an indefeasible claim *against* nature.[39] Since the state of nature is indistinguishable from the state of war, men are impelled by nature to civil society. For Hobbes civil society thus remains a natural telos. Once the claims of natural right are admitted, once the beginnings are proved defective, the question of human ends seems unavoidable. Or, to say the same thing, once reason becomes the corrective of nature—even though reason is based on "arbitrary" beginnings[40]—the standard of political right remains outside man's autonomy. And, from Rousseau's point of view, even though Hobbes asserts that man is the "most excellent work of nature,"[41] he ultimately has recourse to standards that are somehow outside or independent of man. Only if the beginnings are perfect and man "by nature good"[42] can one hope to ground political right on man's autonomy.

Rousseau here, of course, disagrees with Machiavelli about the status of perfect beginnings. Machiavelli remarks that a state must be periodically brought back to its beginnings, but no beginnings—least of all the beginning of mankind—are perfect, although such periodic returns to beginnings can make a state immortal.[43] Strauss writes that

in the words of Machiavelli . . . if virtue presupposes political society, political society is preceded by pre-moral or sub-moral men and indeed founded by such men. There cannot be a moral law of unconditional validity . . . Morality is possible only after its condition has been created, and this condition cannot be created morally: morality rests on what to moral men must appear to be immorality. One can avoid this conclusion only by making one of the two following assumptions. Either one must assume that men are good, not at the beginning of republics but at the beginning simply; in that case they would not need civil society for becoming good. Or one must assume that civil society is founded by men of heroic virtue—of a kind of moral virtue which is not derived from habituation.[44]

Rousseau, of course, resorts to both "assumptions" for the ground of political morality. His resort to the legislator—the "heroic"founder—still has more in common with Machiavelli's founder than with Hobbes's sovereign who seems to be a "personification" of the people rather than its creator. On the other hand, Hobbes certainly agrees with Machiavelli about the beginnings of mankind. At any rate, it is clear enough that Hobbes's account of the state of nature made it necessary for Rousseau to take his political bearings from "perfect beginnings."[45]

For Rousseau, then, natural right must rest on a foundation unmediated by human self-consciousness. ". . . for it to be natural it must speak directly by nature's voice."[46] Two principles "anterior to reason" account for "the first and simplest operations of the human soul"—self-preservation and compassion or pity.[47] And, Rousseau continues, "it is from the conjunction and combination that our mind is able to make of these two principles, without the necessity of introducing that of sociability, that all the rules of natural right appear to me to flow."[48] Thus natural right, whatever else it may be in Rousseau, must be rooted in man's radical autonomy—"the pure movement of nature prior to all reflection."[19] And, as Rousseau remarks in his *Letter to Beaumont*, "the first movements of nature are always right."[50]

Without self-consciousness, original man could have remained in the state of nature indefinitely. "His soul, agitated by nothing is given over to the sole sentiment of [his] present existence."[51] Since natural man's needs are easily met "his imagination suggests nothing to him; his heart asks nothing of him. His modest needs are so easily found at hand, and he is so far from the degree of knowledge necessary for desiring to acquire greater knowledge, that he can have neither foresight nor curiosity. The spectacle of nature becomes indifferent to him by dint of becoming familiar."[52] Nothing in the human constitution or nature thus impels man to civil society. Not knowing the fears of death he does not exhibit the frenzied motion of Hobbes's natural man who pursues power in order to forestall the imminent terrors of death. Rousseau's natural man is "alone" and "idle;" his major pre-occupation is "sleep."[53] What characterizes man above all is his "almost unlimited" potential for "perfectability." Original man, one might say, is pure potential, a potential which is actualized by the "aid of circumstances."[54] What distinguishes man is thus his *history*, not his nature.[55] By nature man is indistinguishable from other animals. What truly distinguishes man is his capacity to react or adapt to circumstances, that is, his capacity to be formed by history. Man is therefore primarily an historical being; once the original horizons of the "true state of nature" begin to dissolve, natural right—the "pure movement of nature"—must inevitably give way to political right. True natural right exists "anterior to reason," i.e., it speaks only to original man "by nature's voice." But it is "historical" man rather than "original" man who stands in need of civil society. When the voice of nature no longer speaks to man "reason is . . . forced to re-establish [natural right] on other foundations."[56]

And while reason is necessary to "re-establish" natural right, natural right itself is not the rule of reason but of the general will. The general will is the reflection, on the level of civil society, of man's original autonomy —that is, of his independence of nature and therewith of reason. The extent to which the general will requires that man be "denatured" indicates the extent to which autonomous man rather than nature or reason is the foundation of Rousseau's political right. The reason necessary to "re-establish" natural right is embodied solely in the legislator who understands "all of men's passions" but who "experiences none of them." The legislator must be

capable of changing human nature, so to speak; of transforming each individual, who by himself is a perfect and solitary whole, into a part of a larger whole from which the individual receives, in a sense, his life and his being; of altering man's constitution in order to strengthen it; of substituting a partial and moral existence for the physical and independent existence we have all received from nature . . . The more these natural forces are dead and destroyed and the acquired ones great and lasting, the more the institution as well is solid and perfect.[57]

The unity of the state depends upon the extent to which "human nature" can be altered or "alienated." While it is true that civil society always involves coercive rule, each member of society obeys only "the law [he] has prescribed for [himself]."[58] In this way he "obeys only himself and remains as free as before."[59] That this freedom is not based on enlightenment or reason is indicated by the fact that it is not based on persuasion. Those who mistake their particular will for the general will are "forced to be free." But this, in Rousseau's terms, is merely a guarantee "against all personal dependence; a condition that creates the ingenuity and functioning of the political machine, and alone gives legitimacy to civil engagements which without it would be absurd, tyrannical, and subject to the most enormous abuses."[60] One might say that this kind of "moral freedom" in Rousseau is the antithesis of the bourgeois morality —based on enlightened self-interest—that Hobbes contemplated. At any rate, the general will precludes any appeal beyond convention, that is, beyond itself. This is the precise sense in which Rousseau understood Machiavelli's *Prince* to be the "book of republicans": that the unity of the state is greater when embodied in the general will than in the prince. The mechanism of the general will, in effect, makes any appeal to natural right or natural law not only superfluous, but impossible.

On the level of philosophy man's autonomy is reflected not in contemplation, but by the attempt to recover "the sentiment of first existence." In the midst of society, this philosophy is the exclusive preserve of "a few great cosmopolitan souls."[61] The kind of enlightenment rationalism represented by Hobbes allows into the "sanctuary" of philosophy "a populace unworthy of approaching it."[62] When the prejudices of the many are favorable to philosophy, philosophy is endangered no less—perhaps more —than when the prejudice is against it. Hence Rousseau's "praise of ignorance" can be seen not only as an attempt to replace bourgeois morality by one which is based "on the strength and vigor of the soul" (the "science of simple souls"),[63] but as an apology for philosophy as well. Hobbesian rationalism, if it succeeds, will be the end of philosophy as surely as it will eventuate in the world homogeneous state. Rousseau's refuge was the solitary promenade, and the primacy of sentiment over reason.

Whereas Hobbes refused to have his moral system based completely on modern science, deriving it ultimately from human self-consciousness, Rousseau does not hesitate to do so. But modern science means, above all, independence of nature and natural ends, to say nothing of the close connection between modern science and Christianity, a connection expressed perfectly by Bacon's statement that science was to serve "the relief of man's estate." This was a connection well known to Hobbes as well. Insofar as Rousseau completes, or attempts to complete, the Machiavellian "project," he makes possible—not indeed the end of sectarian warfare as Hobbes had hoped—but a new kind of sectarian warfare, that of scientific ideology. Hobbes's attempt to salvage natural right was an attempt to combat sectarian warfare on the only grounds available. Reason, albeit reason now understood primarily as method and subordinate to powerful passions, was seen by Hobbes as the means for restoring the primacy of politics over theology. Hobbes sought to restore the role of reason in human affairs by asserting the compatibility of reason and revelation: ". . . opinions, pernicious to peace and government, have in this part of the world, proceeded chiefly from the tongues, and pens of unlearned divines, who joining the words of Holy Scripture together, otherwise than is agreeable to reason, do what they can, to make men think that sanctity and natural reason, cannot stand together."[64] In this respect, it would not be wholly inaccurate to suggest that Hobbes attempted to do on Machiavellian grounds what Aquinas had attempted on Aristotelian grounds. As Harry Jaffa notes, "Thomas' teaching, although it culminates in purely theological doctrines, claims to have a foundation in natural reason independent of, and separable from, revealed doctrine. This foundation . . . is, substantially, the moral and political philosophy of Aristotle."[65] Machiavelli, however, had attacked both the tradition of reason and of revelation, i.e., all traditions, *ad uno tratto*. Taking the success of Christianity as his own model of *political* success, Machiavelli sought to replace the dogmas of revelation with dogmas derived neither from natural right nor revelation. In Hobbes's view, by attacking reason Machiavelli conceded too much to Christianity. Machiavellian necessity, however much subject to prudence, has more in common with Christianity than almost any formulation of natural right. Hobbes, of course, narrows the role of reason and prudence in his reformulation of natural right, but this was an unavoidable necessity, since the whole Hobbesian enterprise itself rested on grounds previously narrowed by Machiavelli.

But in Rousseau reason is replaced by sentiment or passion, above all, the passion of "commitment" or, as it might be put, "the moral pathos of 'sincerity.'" But once autonomous human will becomes the only standard of human things—once human freedom is sundered from human reason—theology, in one form or another, will reassert itself. This new sectarianism, based on a view of nature now totally devoid of self-consciousness, yet combining the methods of modern science and the essentially transpolitical ends of Christianity, seeks all the more its completion in the world homogeneous state, where both politics and philosophy become questionable if not impossible. It is clear, I think, that Rousseau ultimately contributed more to "the dominating spirit" of modernity than did Hobbes.

Notes

1. Rousseau, *Lettres Écrites de la Montagne, Oeuvres complétes de Jean-Jacques Rousseau*, ed. Bernard Gagnebin and Marcel Raymond, (4 vols.; Paris: Gallimand, Bibliotéque de la Pléiade, 1959–1969) III, 806.
2. *L'État de Guerre, Oeuvres*, III, 610.

3. *First Discourse, The First and Second Discourses*, trans. and ed. Roger Masters (New York: St. Martin's Press, 1964), p. 34.

4. *Social Contract*, trans. and ed. Roger Masters (New York: , 1978), III. 7, p. 88.

5. *Leviathan*, ed. Michael Oakeshott (Oxford: Basil Blackwell, n.d.), Ch. 17, p. 112; cf. Ch. 29, pp. 211–12.

6. Leo Strauss, "The Three Waves of Modernity", in *Political Philosophy: Six Essays by Leo Strauss*, ed. Hilail Gildin (Indianapolis: Bobbs— Merrill, 1975), p. 88.

7. *Natural Right and History* (Chicago: University of Chicago Press, 1953), p. 180.

8. *Discourses on Livy*, II.2.

9. *Leviathan*, Ch. 46, p. 438.

10. *English Works*, VII, 75–6.

11. *Leviathan*, Ch. 46, p. 439.

12. Ibid., Ch. 29, pp. 211–12.

13. Ibid., Ch. 31, p. 241. The parallel remark for Christian sovereigns who rule on the basis of Scripture (as interpreted by Hobbes) occurs at p. 339: "And as it was in the Apostle's time, it must be till such time as there are pastors, that could authorize an interpreter, whose interpretation should generally be stood to: but that could not be till kings were pastors, or pastors kings."

14. Ibid., Ch. 46, p. 440.

15. Ibid.

16. Ibid.

17. *De Cive*, VI.2.

18. *Leviathan*, Ch. 46, pp. 442, 79; cf. *Behemoth* (ed. Tonnies), pp. 42–44.

19. Ibid.

20. *Social Contract*, IV.8, p. 126.

21. Ibid., IV.viii, p. 131; cf., *Lettres Écrites de la Montagne*, pp. 694–95, 701–04.

22. Ibid., IV.8, p. 127.

23. Ibid., VI.8, pp. 127, 130; *Geneva Manuscript* in ibid., p. 198.

24. *Leviathan*, Ch. 21, p. 144.

25. *Social Contract*, III.vii, p. 88.

26. Cf. *Prince*, Ch. 20 and *Discourses*, II.27 where Machiavelli makes the case for the superiority of relying upon the "good will of the people" to the building of fortresses. See particularly the remark that fortresses are especially vulnerable to modern artillery; if modern artillery represents "propaganda", then (I believe) in this context fortresses represent natural right.

27. *Second Discourse*, p. 102; we note in passing that Rousseau here speaks of the contrast between "savage man" and "civil man" because the term "savage" is neutral with respect to the question of whether there is a natural human constitution. Cf. *L'État de Guerre*, pp. 611–12: "I have already said and I cannot repeat too much that the error of Hobbes and the philosophers is to confound natural man with the men they see, and to transfer to one system a being who is able to subsist only in another. . . . Thus this analytical method offers only abysses and mysteries, where the wisest comprehend the least . . . they know well the Bourgeois of London or Paris, but they will never know a man."

28. *Leviathan*, Introduction, p. 6.

29. Ibid., Ch. 6, p. 39; Ch. 46, p. 438.

30. Ibid., Ch. 46, p. 440.

31. Ibid., Ch. 11, p. 64.

32. *English Works*, VII, 73.

33. In at least one place Hobbes attempts to trace the fear of death to non-subjective causes: "For every man is desirous of what is good for him, and shuns what is evil, but chiefly the chiefest of natural evils, which is death; and this he doth by a certain impulsion of nature, no less than that whereby a stone moves downward." *De Cive*, I.7.

34. See below note 38.
35. *Second Discourse*, p. 222.
36. Ibid., p. 116.
37. Ibid., p. 128.
38. *De Cive*, Preface.
39. This idea was expressed succinctly by Spinoza: "whatever any man does after the laws of his nature, he does by the highest natural right, and he has as much right over nature as he has power." *Tractatus Politicus*, II.4.
40. *Elements of Law*, I.5; cf. *Leviathan*, Ch. 4, pp. 20, 24; Ch. 5, p. 26.
41. *Leviathan*, Introduction, p. 5.
42. *Second Discourse*, p. 193; *Letter to Beaumont, Oeuvres*, IV, 935.
43. Compare *Discourses* III.1 and III.22 with *Leviathan*, Ch. 30, p. 220.
44. *Thoughts on Machiavelli* (Seattle: University of Washington Press, 1969), p. 255; cf. *Prince* Ch. 11.
45. The glory loving founder—the highest example of which in Machiavelli is the founder of new religions—seems to be absent from Hobbes's account. Hobbes prefers an hereditary monarchy as the one most consistent with the unity of the state. Machiavelli, on the other hand, assigns an hereditary prince to the lowest rank because it requires no *virtú* to acquire and very little to hold such a principality.
46. *Second Discourse*, p. 95.
47. Ibid.
48. Ibid., pp. 95–96.
49. Ibid., p. 131.
50. *Oeuvres*, IV, 935–6. In *Emile* where the exact same phrase occurs, it is called "an incontestable maxim."
51. *Second Discourse*, p. 117.
52. Ibid.
53. Ibid., p. 112.
54. Ibid., pp. 114–15; cf., p. 140.
55. See below, pp. 54–55.
56. *Second Discourse*, p. 96.
57. *Social Contract*, II.7, p. 68.
58. Ibid., I.8, p. 56.
59. Ibid., I.6, p. 53.
60. Ibid., I.8, p. 55; cf. *Lettres Écrites de la Montagne*, p. 806.
61. *Second Discourse*, p. 160.
62. *First Discourse*, p. 62.
63. Ibid., pp. 37, 64.
64. *Leviathan*, Ch. 29, p. 212.
65. *Thomism and Aristotelianism* (Chicago: University of Chicago Press, 1952), pp. 5, 8, 19–20, 22.

8

JOHN LOCKE AND THE AMERICAN FOUNDING

Jeffrey D. Wallin

SCHOLARLY OPINION CONCERNING THE INFLUENCE OF JOHN LOCKE ON THE American Revolution and Constitution seems destined to undergo as many revisions as his place in the history of political thought itself. That this should be so is perplexing. The origins of few, if any, great nations are as well documented as our own. True, the Constitutional Convention of 1787 was held behind closed doors. But a clear record of the debates within those doors and the voluminous correspondence of most of the major participants have been available to scholars for more than a hundred and fifty years. Yet the pedigree of the thoughts that influenced the Revolution and the Constitution still excites controversy, both as to persons and ideas. Especially is this true in the case of John Locke.

On the surface there would appear to be no problem at all. The evolution of colonial thought from a matter of simple resistance to a revolution based on principle has been told often enough.[1] Congress's Declaration of Resolves being more of a legal notice than a theoretical justification for the act of revolution, such an account was provided by the Declaration of Independence. The Declaration, of course, was written by Thomas Jefferson, and Jefferson made no secret of his admiration for Locke. Along with Bacon and Newton, Locke formed the triumvirate in thought around which Jefferson's moral and intellectual universe revolved.[2]

Nevertheless, a substantial effort has gone into the task of reading Locke out of the American Founding, the latest example being *Inventing America* by Garry Wills.[3] It is not my purpose here to quarrel with Wills's notoriously loose scholarship. That has been done well enough by others.[4] His attempt to replace Locke by Francis Hutcheson and others, however, indicates why the question of Locke's influence still lives. Locke's famous "individualism" has, as it were, been coopted by a strand of current political dogma which goes by the name of libertarianism, the overriding concern of which is to defend the personal liberties of individuals against every encroachment, real or imagined, by government. By attributing the Founding to figures of the Scottish enlightenment rather than Locke, Wills seeks to support another current political dogma, that of the New Left, which, while at least as demanding in its claims for individual moral autonomy as libertarianism, wishes to defend an almost unlimited intrusion of government into private economic matters in the name of goals that have increasingly been described as "communitarian." (The word "socialistic" has been quietly dropped, for it has taken on unpleasant connotations in almost direct proportion to the growth of socialist governments around the world.)[5]

In short, the question of Locke's influence is animated by political as well as by historical interests. And this was, perhaps, to be expected. The Founders themselves used history quite effectively to bolster their political arguments. Certainly today the desire to present one's political program in the guise of advice from the Founders or their teachers is well-nigh irresistible. Precisely because the thought of America's past is bound up with, or is believed to be bound up with, America's present and future, it behooves us to understand that thought, and to understand, in addition, the relation it has or ought to have with ourselves.

We need to remind ourselves that insofar as America was founded on principle, the meaning of that principle is not a matter of interest to antiquarians only. The word "principle" is derived, through its Latin equivalent, from the Greek word "archē." An archē is a rule, in the sense that it governs the meaning or action of that of which it is the principle. It is also a beginning. It is both a rule and a beginning because a proper beginning exercises an authority over the development of what it begins. The embryo of a human child, for instance, does not become just anything; it becomes a man or a woman. Its end may be said to have been present in its beginning, and it is the presence of this end that allows the beginning to hold sway over the development of what it initiates. If our nation's beginning was at all principled, that is, if it contained an archē, then what we are now is in some respect due to what we were intended to become by the formulators of that principle or beginning. No wonder the debate over Locke's influence, and Locke's intention, is still with us.

With the exception of those who argue that the American regime was modelled on classical lines,[6] there is general agreement that the Founding reflects enlightenment, and more specifically, contractarian political thought. Ours is, after all, a limited form of government resting, both directly and indirectly, on the consent of the governed. Insofar as this is the case, the argument over which enlightenment thinker was most influential seems to be of little moment. I am inclined, however, to accept the traditional view that the political theory drawn on by the Founders is that of Locke more than of anyone else. For one thing, there is the matter of language. It is almost impossible not to see the hand of Locke in such phrases as in a "long train of abuses" or "all experience hath shown that mankind are more disposed to suffer while evils are sufferable than to right themselves by abolishing the forms to which they are accustomed" (cf. *Second Treatise*, para. 230). This is not to say that Jefferson merely cribbed some of his finer phrases from Locke. Jefferson's peculiar "felicity of expression" is well enough documented in his letters and other public writings. Besides, Jefferson himself claimed no great originality in either the thoughts or expressions contained within the Declaration. It was, he said, an "expression of the American mind." That the American mind, as well as Jefferson's own, was to a large extent a Lockean mind is a presupposition of this essay, as well as the problem to which this essay is addressed.[8]

Just what is, and what is not a Lockean mind or a Lockean way of looking at things is a point much in dispute. I believe the most brilliant articulation of what a Lockean America might be expected to become is Martin Diamond's "Ethics and Politics: The American Way."[9] For perhaps the same reason that Locke hesitates to refer directly to Hobbes, Diamond fails even to mention the name of John Locke in this essay. Nevertheless, in tracing the core of the Founders' thought to the distinction between a modern commercial republic and the ancient city, Diamond flushes out the Lockean, or he might say, the uniquely modern elements in the American regime. While Madison's method of dealing with factions appears to have been derived from Hume, his easy and comprehensive dismissal of the ends that animated ancient politics strongly reflects Locke's *Second Treatise of Government*.[10] (Indeed, in almost every respect Diamond's use of the term "modern" seems to be a synonym for "Lockean." The use of the more comprehensive term "modern" however, is understandably useful for examing Locke's influence, for it is precisely the "modern" elements of Locke's thought that are of most interest to the study of American political thought. As Diamond points out, what is distinctive about America is the way in which it differs from all previous polities: it is, after all, the *novus ordo seclorum*.[11]

Diamond sharpens his presentation of the American character by placing it in relief, as it were, against the high background of classical political thought, especially the Aristotelian connection between ethics and politics. For Aristotle, the purpose of politics is the formation of the highest type of human character by the inculcation of moral virtue accompanied by an opening to intellectual virtue. While the virtues, especially the moral ones, were thought to be indispensable to the survival of the polity, they were in the best cases also thought of as goods in themselves. Hence, when it came to education or the making of laws, the polis could be said to have looked to a standard or standards of human perfection as well as to self-preservation. This standard of excellence created an "upward pull" against the more immediate demands of the body, thereby creating a tension—sometimes a dangerous tension—between the harsh requirements of mere life or preservation and the pleasant allurements and satisfactions of the good life.

Rather than continue the search for a comprehensive resolution of the difficulties engendered by the presence of this tension, the moderns decided to abandon the tension itself. They took their bearings not by how men ought to live, but by how they do live. In this way they could hope to establish political stability on the sure ground of ever present self-interest rather than on a much hoped-for but seldom realized moral virtue. Instead of demanding, or even encouraging virtue, they "removed the task of character formation from its previously preeminent place on the agenda of politics." The regime would no longer concern itself with restraining or even restricting the human passions; henceforth it would merely channel them into productive and relatively harmless pursuits. Better to agree that there is nothing noble worth fighting over than to embrace a politics whose most characteristic activity was to be perpetually agitated between the "extremes of tyranny and anarchy." As Diamond, in a passage of Tocquevillian beauty and clarity put it:

"The American political order was deliberately tilted to resist, so to speak, the upward gravitational pull of politics toward the grand, dramatic, character-ennobling but society-wracking opinions about justice and virtue. Opinion was now to be ballasted against its dangerous tendency toward destructive zealoutry, or, to change the nautical figure, to be moored solidly in the principle of commodious self-preservation and economic self-interest. . . . In thus seeking to tame opinion, Madison was following the general tendency of modern political thought to solve the problems of politics by reducing the scope of politics. . . . by abstracting from politics the broad ethical function of character formation, modern political thought had begun a kind of depoliticizing of politics in general."

The result of this intentional muting of the political disputes hitherto engendered by disagreements over the good and noble is portrayed just as forcefully. Commerce replaces the comprehensiveness of statesmanship and the intensity of religion by means of emancipating "acquisitiveness and its attendant qualities." A "matrix" is created (the large commercial democratic republic) "within which such appetites and acquisitive aims can be excited and sufficiently satisfied. Put bluntly, this means that in order to defuse the dangerous factional force of opinion, passion, and class interest, Madison's policy deliberately risks magnifying and multiplying in American life the selfish, the interested, the narrow, the vulgar, and the crassly economic."

Diamond, to be sure, is quick to point out that although this vulgarity is the price we pay for the benefits of the American way of life, those benefits are real: freedom, "and the dignity enjoyed by the great many," to say nothing of unparalleled economic well-being. Diamond even goes so far as to indicate that, although it is not the purpose of the regime to encourage reflection on or a commitment to justice, the regime nevertheless, in its built-in demand for constant adjustments between the various factions it spawns, necessarily "impels man to ponder the advantageous and the harmful, and therefore also the just and unjust." Descending from the high moral ground of antiquity to the lowlands of modernity, Diamond returns to the decent foothills of moral virtue: the American regime, while not intended to encourage the soul-bracing politics or sharp-edged characters of the past, does, by a sort of technical oversight, thrust up questions of the just and the unjust. Justice, or the political, has not, it would seem, been replaced by economics after all. Yet we must wonder whether Diamond has not engaged in a sort of rhetorical sleight of hand intended more to strengthen the attachments of his readers to their country than to enlighten them regarding its principles.

Robert A. Licht has pointed out, for instance, that there is some question as to whether Diamond's argument truly allows for this decency, or whether, in an attempt to prevent his readers from turning from the American regime in disgust, he does not concede too much to Madison, at least according to his own argument in "Ethics and Politics."[12] As Licht puts it, "Diamond may . . . be said to be reticent about the case for the moderns. To be sure he is quite candid about Madison's assessment of the 'defect of better motives,' and concedes the low, passionate and self-interested account of human nature in his thought. But the power of modern thought as a solvent acting upon the older understanding of the human is also moderated in Diamond's account. All the old bonds of the human to the eternal begin to dissolve in the powerful corrosive of modern thought. The semi-divine status of reason as the governor of passion; the soul which finds its completion in virtue for its own sake, and is made whole in citizenship and piety; an immortal soul whose salvation is at stake in every human act; these no longer animate human striving." Licht's remarks are intended to be critical of Diamond's position. Yet I would argue that Licht's presentation of the consequences of modern thought can also be understood as providing a completion of Diamond's argument. If Diamond is correct in asserting that the intention of the Founders was to inaugurate a wholly modern project, then their act was replete with the consequences seen by Licht. Combining Licht's argument with Diamond's, we arrive at Tocqueville's characterization of the choice to be made in 1776 and 1787:

Do you wish to raise mankind to an elevated and generous view of the things of this world? Do you want to inspire men with a certain scorn of material goods? Do you hope to engender deep convictions and prepare the way for acts of profound devotion?

Are you concerned with refining mores, elevating manners, and causing the arts to blossom? Do you desire poetry, renoun, and glory?

Do you set out to organize a nation so that it will have a powerful influence over all others? Do you expect it to attempt great enterprises and, whatever be the result of its efforts, to leave a great mark on history?

If in your view that should be the main object of men in society, do not support democratic government: it surely will not lead you to that goal.

But if you think it profitable to turn men's intellectual and moral activity toward the necessities of physical life and use them to produce well-being, if you think that reason is more use to men than genius, if your object is not to create heroic virtues but rather tranquil habits, if you would rather contemplate vices than crimes and prefer fewer transgressions at the cost of fewer splendid deeds, if in place of a brilliant society you are content to live in one that is prosperous, and finally, if in your view the main object of government is not to achieve the greatest strength or glory for the nation as a whole but to provide for every individual therein the utmost well-being, protecting him as far as possible from all afflictions, then it is good to make conditions equal and to establish a democratic government.[13]

Democracy is prosaic, mediocre, vulgar; yet it is also solid, stable, and prosperous. Such a regime will not satisfy nobler souls, or even, as Tocqueville points out, average ones, for they will be dissatisfied with the pedestrian hustle and bustle of the aimless commercial activity characteristic of the "democratic" choice.[14] Still, given the economic and moral alternatives presented by current non-liberal regimes, there is much to commend, though of course not without reservation, in modern America. We do not devour one another here on the basis of the spurious distinctions of class, race, or caste that govern a large part of the world. Tocqueville's—and Diamond's—America may not be brilliant, but it is "sober." And sobriety, while not itself a virtue, resembles moderation well enough to pass for a close relative.

If not supplemented by a discussion of freedom, Diamond's account of modernity might lead one to believe that the movement from ancient to modern politics had no other end and no other effect than a lowering of the temperature of those heated disputes hitherto so destructive of political life. Certainly this is a plausible view of the American Founding, for Madison's remarks on the problem of faction fit it perfectly. But the replacement of ancient civic virtue with modern commercial virtue reflects an element of modern thought that goes much deeper than a merely expeditious choice regarding the means to public peace. The choice for the liberal, commercial state bespeaks a theoretical as well as a practical reason for the rejection of public orthodoxies of the pre-modern type, for the elevation of freedom as a political principle followed from profound uncertainties underlying the conviction that peace and prosperity are worthier political goals than those pursued by the ancient *polis*.

Modernity presents a curious amalgam of confidence and doubt. It is confident of the ability of man to found stable (according to Hobbes, even perpetual) regimes on the basis of a "scientific" knowledge regarding human nature; confident in its ability to conquer nature for "the relief of man's estate"; confident that it has destroyed the myths, religious and otherwise, that dominated men's lives prior to the age of enlightenment. But that confidence can easily be shaken, for it rests upon admitted ignorance. Ancient morality is repudiated not only because of a supposed new insight into man's behavior, epitomized by Hobbes's and Locke's neo-Epicurean doctrine that man acts wholly on the basis of pleasure and pain (or, in the case of religion, on the expectation of future pleasure or pain); more importantly, in modernity a new conviction emerges according to which man's place within the universe necessarily vitiates the deepest claim of classical political thought, that politics could be founded on ends natural to man. Ancient political thought claims not only that happiness is the end of human life, but that it has a substantive content knowable to man and attainable by personal conduct and political action (subject, of course, to the boundaries set by fortune, individual capacity, and the demands of the body). The thrust of modern politics toward freedom, and the consequent concern with rights and liberties as opposed to duties and with what is right in itself rests, in part, on the contrary notion that there is no knowable objective end for man capable of ordering the passionate demands of his body—an end that is higher and more consistent with human nature than his untutored passions would suggest by themselves. In this sense, the statement so often heard today, that one's "lifestyle" or "values" should be wholly a matter of personal preference accurately reflects the theoretical ignorance at the heart of the modern project. When it is said that one ought not to impose one's values on another, what is being claimed is that all choices regarding the human good are wholly subjective and arbitrary (never mind for the moment that this claim is itself couched in the vein of an imperative command). The most alarming aspect of this trend is not simply that it deadens moral fortitude by weakening the convictions that undergird such fortitude, but that it also appears to legitimate a sense of internal abandon, an unleashing of the will such that passion comes to dominate reason, which in turn is, as it were, eviscerated by the teaching that it cannot provide an adequate guide to life. Hence modernity comes full circle: having established liberal states aiming at peace, stability, and freedom, its principles gradually but steadily undermine the claim of those regimes to moral certainty and justice. Put another way, freedom at first allows for a multiplicity of decisions regarding the good life. Those decisions became so numerous that no one of them can attain the sort of preeminence that would enable it to impose itself on the whole society. Passions are multiplied, but they are thereby made less intense, which in turn leads to a more moderate or sober politics than would otherwise be the case. But, as I have indicated, modernity does not rest with the establishment of the free society. For by opening to all the question of the best way of life an emphasis comes in time to be placed on the inviolability of the groundless act of choosing rather than on whether the choice is or is not reasonable. The difficulty is that few men can live without moral and political convictions. Hence this theoretical openness leads in practice to a despotism of the will characterized in our own time by a personal commitment to one's choice (or "values"). When it is known that such commitments are the result of wholly arbitrary decisions, it then becomes evident that their worth can be measured only by their intensity. This surrender to commitment, however thoughtless, in turn threatens the very sobriety the regime was intended to foster, for it invites indifference to the conviction that liberty is superior to despotism.

In addition, the attempt to moderate passion, rooted in reason's supposed inability to guide passion, has had the paradoxical effect of inflaming a multitude of non-political passions which are, of course, no longer thought to be subordinate to natural ends. Unfortunately, whereas earlier political passions were frequently animated by conflicting opinions regarding the highest human ends, the intensity of our own disputes is often matched only by their vulgarity. Modernity's attack on reason, unlike the earlier attack by the perhaps improperly interpreted authority of revelation, has led to a trivilization of life.

Still, it is the release of a certain kind of political passion that is at once the most unlooked for and dangerous result of modernity. For the adaptability of the techniques of modern science to the ends of political power, while offering no means of adjudicating the worth of competing political passions and opinions, has enormously increased the cost of defeat to those that lose out. This can be seen not only in international politics (in the fate of "non-progressive" regimes), but also in the difficulty with which "old-fashioned" opinions regarding morality are able to defend themselves against the onslaught of more fashionable ones. Moreover, to put the matter in the starkest terms, if moral relativism and the increased intensity of autonomous individual "commitments" are the natural by-products of modernity, then insofar as our founding was modern, it would appear that moral relativism, far from being an almost alien element within the American regime, is embedded in its original principles.

The emergence of will over reason, as well as the emergence of commercial over civic virtue, can be seen in the works of any of the more substantial early modern thinkers (the exception would appear to be Rousseau: but his paeans to civic virtue only divert attention from his agreement with modernity regarding the superiority of will to reason). But as my aim is to say something about the American Founding, I turn to Locke, for his influence on the Founders appears to have been the most direct and consequential.

Whether in the nature of things reason ought to guide our passions, or whether, on the contrary, our passions ought to guide our thoughts, so that "the thoughts are to the desires, as scouts, and spies, to range abroad, and find the way to the things desired,"[15] depends, it would seem, on two questions: Are the desires susceptible to such guidance by reason, either directly or indirectly (that is, when coerced by law) and, is reason itself capable of grasping a standard superior to the demands of the passions? This latter question, of course, turns, at least in part, on whether there *are* standards independent of and superior to the promptings of pleasure and pain. Reason can only justly claim to rule the passions if there is a nature of things, and within that nature of things a nature of human things, or human nature, the knowledge of which can instruct men regarding the question, what is the best way of life? Only in this way can the admonition to resist the promptings of the body so that one may live a full and complete (and therefore happy) human life be said to be anything more than a prejudice or a "value judgment." As to the first question, there are few, if any, who would maintain that the passions are simply tractable. Similarly, there are few who would maintain that they are altogether intractable, although this view does play a significant part in modern political philosophy and science. Be that as it may, our concern here is with the second and more fundamental of these questions.

However much ancient moral and political life may have been based on pre-philosophic religious, civic, and family traditions,[16] ancient political thought was intensely alive to the question of whether common notions of decency and indecency reflected a correspondence, or the lack of one, to nature. Leaving aside for the moment the careful language in which Aristotle couched his answer to our question, we can say that the tradition stemming from the *Nicomachean Ethics* holds that a knowledge of human nature, whether gained by scientific inquiry or by the examination of thoughtful and widely held opinions, can supply a reasonable foundation to moral and political life. Indeed, it is for this reason that Aristotle's *Politics* follows or completes his *Ethics*. Moral virtue having been defined in the *Ethics*, the task of the *Politics* is to invite reflection on how politics can best nurture that virtue.

John Locke's understanding of human nature is presented in a much more theoretical work than the *Ethics*, namely, the *Essay Concerning Human Understanding*. Consequently, the connection between the *Essay* and the *Second Treatise of Government* is not nearly so clear as is the connection between the *Ethics* and the *Politics*. Moreover, the dominant view holds that the skeptical epistemology of Locke's *Essay Concerning Human Understanding* differs radically from the more traditionalist view of politics presented in his *Second Treatise of Government*.[17] While a full refutation of this view is beyond the scope of this paper, it does not seem unreasonable to suppose that a connection exists between an author's theoretical and practical works, especially when the theoretical work deals as explicitly with the subject matter of the practical one as Locke's *Essay* does. Some of the most significant terms employed in Locke's *Second Treatise*, such as nature, man, language, monarch, government, just and unjust, are treated exhaustively, not in the *Second Treatise*, but in the *Essay*.

The following attempt to draw out the implications of Locke's epistemology is undertaken for two reasons. It is necessary, I believe, to recognize in Locke one source of the unfettered moral freedom that lies behind our seeming inability to challenge with confidence the predominance of will characterizing contemporary claims to ethical autonomy. More importantly, I wish to draw attention to the depth of the chasm that separates the Founders' intentions from this hidden element in Lockean or modern thought.

On the face of it one might think that the *Essay* is in agreement with Aristotle's logical and ethical works. According to Locke, not only can we know something about morality, we can even say that "moral knowledge is as capable of real certainty as mathematics."[18] It will behoove us, however, to consider Locke's justification of this misleading claim. In a chapter entitled "Of the Degrees of Our Knowledge" (IV 2), which follows his perplexing argument that all human knowledge consists "in the view the mind has of its own ideas," Locke tells us that this statement does not mean that we cannot know anything with certainty. Quite the opposite. We can, says Locke, perceive "the agreement or disagreement of two ideas *immediately by themselves.*" The mind can easily perceive, for example, such truths as "*white* is not *black*, that a *circle* is not a *triangle*, that *three* are more than *two* and equal to *one* and *two*." Nevertheless, as Locke himself admits, this kind of certainty does not qualify his argument that what the mind knows is its own ideas only; in fact, it rests upon it. The mind can have perfect knowledge of its own ideas because those ideas are wholly or almost wholly "self-contained": they do not exist independently of the mind. There can, as a consequence, be a "science" of morals. But this is merely to say that there can be knowledge of the mind's "own ideas," and that it is possible to distinguish ideas that do not contradict one another from those that do.

As Locke himself puts the problem raised by his argument (posing a question by an imaginary interlocutor): "To what purpose all this sir? Knowledge, say you, is only the perception of the agreement or disagreement of our own ideas: but who knows what those ideas may be? Is there anything so extravagant as the imaginations of men's brains?" Or, as that same perceptive inquirer asks a few lines later: "But of what use is all this fine knowledge of *men's own imaginations*, to a man that inquires after the reality of things? It matters not what men's fancies are, it is the knowledge of things that is only to be prized: it is this alone gives a value to our reasonings, and preference to one man's knowledge over another's, that it is of things as they really are, and not of dreams and fancies" (IV 4.1).

One may gauge the weakness of Locke's answer by considering that a major part of it consists of an insistence that relations between ideas can be known, the very statement that called forth the question. Nevertheless, unlike some of those who followed him, Locke does admit that in some ways, at least, the "reality of things" can be known. Locke divides ideas into "simple" and "complex" ones. Complex ideas are made of simple ones, and simple ones can be known. Simple ideas reflect "the natural and regular productions of things without us, really operating upon us" (IV 4.4). There is, then, direct access to reality. Unfortunately, however, it is *only* simple ideas that have this quality, and simple ideas are only ideas like whiteness, or bitterness, or, in short, ideas that proceed directly from perceptions of space, extension, figure, rest, or motion (II 5.1). (There are also simple ideas of reflection, such as perception, thinking, volition, or willing, that is, ideas that result from operations of the mind concerning its other "ideas.") These are matters about which it is impossible or nearly impossible to disagree: whether an object is hot or cold, red or blue, good or bad (i.e., pleasant or painful), is something soon settled by observation, for it is observation, or speaking more precisely, the operation of the senses, that reveals simple ideas to us. The difficulty is that these simple ideas tell us nothing or almost nothing about the human and political good. This becomes even clearer in Locke's discussion of complex ideas, for notions of justice and the common good are, according to Locke, complex rather than simple ideas.

Locke's presentation of complex ideas is far too involved to present at length here. Nevertheless, he is quite clear about the problem that guides our, and his interlocutor's, question. There are three types of complex ideas: ideas of substances, mixed modes, and ideas of relation. As Eugene Miller has observed, the sentence, "The man is a just king," contains an example of each of these ideas: "man" is a substance, "justice" is a mixed mode, and "king" identifies a relation.[19] Mixed modes and relations comprise most, if not all, ideas relevant to moral and political life. Relations describe government and all the forms of political association covered by such terms as monarch, subject, citizen, sovereign, and so on. Mixed modes refer to such things as justice, virtue, vice, nobility, ignobility. (An action may, of course, be composed of two or more ideas.) Let us take ideas of relation first. Terms of association, like the terms we have previously discussed, can be known with exactitude for the very reason that such knowledge depends, not on whether such relations correspond to reality, but only on whether the simple ideas which comprise them do or do not correspond to one another in the way that the name of the relation is said to imply. Mixed modes, like relations, cannot be referred to a natural standard. This is because, while mixed modes, like all complex ideas, are composed of simple ideas which, when examined individually, may be known, the particular mix of them termed the mixed mode is not determined by nature or an archetype taken from nature, but rather from the desire men have to communicate their thoughts to one another (II 22.5). The important point to note is that "*Mixed modes* and *relations*, having no other reality but what they have in the minds of men, there is nothing more required to this kind of ideas to make them real, but that they be so framed, that there be a possibility of existing conformable to them" (II 30.4). The question of who is, or who is not a just man is, according to this argument, something that can be answered only with reference to whether the terms used to describe justice are or are not consistent and to whether there is a "possibility of existing conformable to them." As to whether one opinion regarding justice can be truer than another, in the old fashioned sense of conforming more or less to a standard to be found in nature, the question can be said to be, according to Locke's definition of mixed modes, meaningless. The "original patterns" of the terms of morality are simply "in the mind" (III 5.12); the discourse of politics, hitherto naively thought to be constituted by disputes over justice and the common good, can be better understood as a battle of wills regarding the question of whose mental image of justice is to prevail. Because this is true for Locke language takes on increased political importance in almost inverse proportion to his evisceration of its use for understanding nature. The mind is able to gather or collect into an intelligible unity things that have no such unity by nature. But this collection, since it is dependent upon the human mind for its very existence, will cease to be present as soon as it is no longer thought. Hence a crucial part of human political activity must be directed to keeping it in being. The idea must be kept alive and before men's minds and the way of doing this is to *name* the complex idea in one's mind so that it can be implanted in the minds of others. I will return later to this startling aspect of Locke's thought.

Most essential to the grounding of politics in a non-arbitrary standard is the concept of human nature. Certainly this would appear to be the case, even in Locke's own most explicitly political writing, the *Second Treatise of Government*. Hence one might expect that the word "man" in the statement, "The man is a just king," might correspond more nearly to an objective order of things than the terms just and king. And indeed, such is, with vital qualifications, the case. The term "man" is a "substance." And substances, says Locke, are an exception to his statement regarding modes and relations, that they are "archetypes of the mind's own making" (IV 4.5). Substances are the inferences, and sometimes Locke says that they are the unavoidable inferences, we draw from the fact that certain simple ideas regularly appear together in such a way as to indicate that qualities which are not themselves simple ideas underlie or form the "substratum" of these ideas (II 23.1). It seems impossible to doubt, for instance, the existence of corporeal bodies when we have direct experience of their qualities (II 23. 19). The substance or essence of what a

man is might, therefore, be expected to surface as an unavoidable inference from the simple ideas we associate with this term. The difficulty is
that simple ideas can reflect no more than the data given by the senses,
while a conception of human nature useful for political life requires the
notion of an essence of humanity not limited to or comprehended by the
sensual qualities of human beings. Does such an essence exist, according
to Locke, by nature?

Locke admits that substances can have essences or "archetypes that
exist in nature" (IV 4.5). Hence, while we exercise "free choice" in putting together modes and relations, it would appear that no such perfect
freedom exists in the case of the concept "man." This freedom reemerges,
however, when we see that Locke does deny that the mind can know the
essence of a substance and use that knowledge to distinguish between
classes or species. While substances *may* have real essences, these essences
cannot be known by the human mind. And since we cannot know the
essence of man, we cannot know what the essence of human nature might
be. Human nature is not, for Locke, a product of "nature's Workmanship." On the contrary, species are *the workmanship of the Understanding*,"
so that "the essences of species, as distinguished and denominated by us,
neither are nor can be anything but those precise abstract ideas we have
in our minds" (III 3.13; cf. III 6.37). Man can have but an imperfect idea
of the natures of things; in particular he receives no guidance from nature regarding the elements or simple ideas upon which he bases his
notion of species (III 9.13). His notion of what it means to be a member
of the human species is a subjective enterprise in which arbitrary solip-
sisms are accepted for what they cannot be: reflections of the true natures of external realities. All man can be sure of is that something outside of himself does exist.

Locke's treatment of simple and complex ideas is perfectly in keeping with the radical purpose of his *Essay*, which is to deny the existence of
innate ideas. The denial of innateness is radical because it is equivalent to
a denial of any correspondence between man and the world he lives in
except on the purely sensual level, for it is a denial that that which is
outside of man can be directly accessible to him or present in him in the
way, say, the image of an object can be present in the eye. In effect, it is to
deny that there is anything other than man of significance to man.[20] That
which is other does not exist, or cannot be known, or is limited to that
which can produce pleasure or pain. The significance of this is that it
overturns the traditional view, shared both by classical philosophy and
Christianity, that what is most important to man is that which lies outside
of himself and demands of him a response in thought and action. The
awareness that man exists in conjunction with what is other than himself
and is a given, or which does not depend on him for its being what it is,
demands a response in the sense that it forces man to ask what the rela-

tion of his partial view of what exists is to the truth of what exists. Insofar as he asks this question of human affairs, say of justice, it demands from him an awareness that what he needs most is true knowledge of what this other, justice, demands of him. It points man toward his need for knowledge about the things themselves. This in turn reveals that man is by nature a dependent being. His awareness of the significance of what is other than himself, whether of nature, gods, or justice, reveals his ignorance of as well as his openness to the truth about such matters and therewith of his dependence upon what is only partially known by him. The existence of the nature of things circumscribes his actions because it circumscribes his thoughts. His thoughts, to be true thoughts, must coincide not only with what is present to him without reflection, to what merely coincides with him, but to the things themselves. The difficulty of achieving this places man in a unique position. Unlike a god, he is not perfectly wise: he does not know the truth of things simply. Unlike the other beasts, he is aware of the possibility of a disjunction between the way he sees things and the way they really are, and therefore of the need to square what he sees with what can be truly seen. He is free from what simply coincides with him (he is not dictated to by necessity in all things) and dependent upon what exists independently of him. His freedom, although essential to his being, is the freedom to be aware of his dependence and to alleviate his ignorance. (Although, to the degree that he does so he becomes, in one sense, even more dependent. A perfectly wise man would be perfectly free only in the sense that he would be perfectly free to follow the dictates of wisdom. Pre-philosophical piety is reflected on the plane of theory by the discovery of nature and human nature.)

Moral freedom is a concept not limited to modern thought and politics. The Socratic claim to freedom of inquiry and the classical concept of gentlemanship were examples of the sort of claims for freedom which can be based upon the view that man is the animal that falls between the other animals and what is higher than animal life simply. Moral virtue requires, although it does not aim at, moral freedom; theoretical inquiry, while itself requiring freedom, rests upon the presence of a knowable external reality which by its very existence limits freedom. If, however, there is no higher or other realm, that defining sense of limitation must eventually slip into desuetude. The basis of political community then becomes most problematic. Whatever else may be said about the true character of the ties that formerly held men together, that is, the shared opinions upon which they based their community with one another, it was certainly believed by those so bound that these agreements reflected the truth of matters. What can hold men together when they no longer believe that truth is knowable?

Precisely to the degree that agreement is no longer thought to be based on a true perception of reality must that agreement be strengthened and preserved by means of artifice. Government becomes based on consent in a more explicit manner than ever before for the very reason that consent or agreement is thought to be so arbitrary. If this agreement is no longer thought to reflect the truth about the political and moral whole, and is yet still needed, a certain intenseness, hitherto missing, comes to dominate the choice of the elements of that agreement. According to Locke's argument, the most significant act of founding becomes the act of defining and preserving the ideas agreed upon. Since these ideas are complex ones, it is clear that they are taken, not from nature, but from the almost arbitrary (almost only because they are guided by a not altogether arbitrary intention) gathering of their constitutive elements in the mind of the founder. His task becomes one of definition, explication, and defense. He is a "defender of the faith." His task is even more difficult than the defense of religious faith in doubtful times, however, for he must defend what he knows to be his own creation. In the case of a Lockean founder, he is aware that such notions as just and unjust, legitimate and illegitimate rule, *are* only insofar as his definitions of them are accepted as true. Moreover, he knows that the claim that they rest upon a standard of nature or human nature independent of his will, is vitiated by the fact that the concept of "human nature" itself has no more claim to a reality independent of his own arbitrary definition than do "mixed modes" such as just or noble, or "relations" such as king, sovereign, or citizen. What counts, it would seem, is the ability of the founder to "name" his complex ideas, or in other words, to keep them alive and working in the minds of others so that his will displaces their wills, his notions theirs.

Moreover, if successful founding depends decisively on the public ratification of the founder's choice of "ideas," what is really primary is not the content of that particular idea but rather the act of choosing itself. In the beginning is not dependence or sobriety or prudence, or reasonable choice, but arbitrary freedom, truly *free* choice. The innermost thrust of a regime founded in such freedom would seem to be a return to the universal freedom that underlies the assent to the particular notion of justice at the base of the regime. At the heart of the political regimes of modernity, whether based on the open tyrannies of the twentieth century, or the subtle conformity of thought underlying liberal democratic states (i.e., the "tyranny" of opinion regarding human nature that undergirds liberal freedoms) is a moral autonomy capable of denying any act or thought that does not further this freedom. If the American regime is founded on liberal principles thus understood, it might not only be said that the replacement of classical virtue by commercial virtue should have been an expected outcome of the Founders' decision not to commit the regime to noble ends, it could also be said that the moral autonomy underlying the attack on the natural limits imposed by the concept of human nature is itself a necessary if hidden element of the Founding; indeed, one might almost say that such moral autonomy is the *archē* of the regime. If such were the case there would be no place within the regime from which one could defend the limits necessary to healthy political life.

It should be clear by now that the forgoing account differs considerably from that accepted by most readers of Locke's works, whether they be lay readers or scholars. The account is, however, in keeping with what often has been called the esoteric as opposed to the exoteric Locke. This distinction is meant to indicate that underneath Locke's exoteric teaching regarding political freedom and moral virtue lies an esoteric teaching that is essentially Hobbesian. My purpose thus far has been to flush out the esoteric aspects of Locke's thought and to indicate their significance for regimes founded wholly on Lockean principles.

Three possibilities would seem to follow from this analysis. First, it may be wrong. If so, this would appear to mean that the exoteric Locke is the true Locke. I can only say here that I think the evidence produced by others, as well as that in this essay, demonstrates the falseness of this view. The closer one reads Locke the more radical his theoretical views seem to be.

Second, one might argue that the distinction between the esoteric and the exoteric Locke is valid, but that neither Locke can stand alone. That is, one might claim that the political teaching of the exoteric Locke, which appears to be consistent with conventional views regarding nature, human nature, and natural law, is a coherent whole, and that an understanding of the esoteric Locke adds nothing to our understanding of the exoteric Locke, and therefore adds nothing to or should in no way modify our understanding of the American Founding, even if it was a perfectly Lockean founding.

A third alternative would be to grant the distinction, but deny its relevance for understanding the American regime on the ground that it was not, after all, Locke, but rather Madison, Jefferson, Hamilton, and others who founded the regime. Their own understanding of what they were about, it might be argued, is the clearest possible guide to understanding the regime they founded. According to this view, one might understand the regime perfectly adequately without ever having heard of John Locke.

My own view combines elements of these last two suggestions. Quite clearly, I believe the distinction between the esoteric and exoteric Locke to be a valid one. But I do not believe it follows that America, being Lockean, is necessarily radically Hobbesian. This is because a reading of the Founders reveals an adherence to political principles at variance with the esoteric Locke but in keeping with the exoteric one. Moreover, I think this is a difference of considerable significance, since it points to a principle, an *archē*, an understanding of nature and human freedom, capable of supporting a reasonable and just political way of life. In other words, I believe that an examination of the founding informed by, but not dominated by, an understanding of Locke would reveal a form of modernity based on the very sort of natural standards rejected by Locke and most, if not all, other modern political theorists.

Clearly, this is not the place to demonstrate such a view of the Founding. An enterprise of such a magnitude would require at the very least a book length treatment, and possibly several such treatments. But it is certainly not too much to remind ourselves that the most obvious thing about the American Founding is its disagreement with the thrust of the esoteric Locke. Hamilton, Adams, Madison, Washington, and all others usually referred to as Founders sound at the very least much more like the exoteric than the esoteric Locke. Even Thomas Jefferson, from whose writings one could find arguments in support of almost anything, never waivered in his belief that politics ought to be based on a standard of natural justice. Nevertheless, a full examination of the Founders' views is much needed, in spite of the publication of several thoughtful analyses in the last 20 or so years. In what follows I aim to do no more than indicate the direction in which a fuller examination of the thought of the founding with a view to shedding light on the Founders' understanding of freedom, justice, and nature, might take.

Unfortunately, the Founders left no theoretical works on the scale of Locke's *Essay*. Moreover, the intention of their written work was more immediately political than was the *Essay*. To examine their words without considering the political circumstances in which they were written would only be to guarantee that they would be misunderstood. Yet, however immediate and practical their goals might have been, a look at the arguments upon which their political convictions rested reveal principles sharply at variance with the esoteric Locke, and hence with the most problematic elements of modernity.

It is by no means necessary to demonstrate that the Founders were unfamiliar with or even disagreed with the whole of the *Essay*. Nor is this possible. James Madison, with whom I am concerned in this paper, indicates at least an awareness of the terms of Locke's *Essay*, if not a partial agreement with it, in his use of the term "complex idea" in *Federalist* No. 37.[21] Moreover, Locke's own presentation of the elusiveness of reality, were it to go no further than to emphasize how difficult access to the truth can be, would not in itself break with the philosophic tradition that preceded it and which was, unlike Locke's own arguments, capable of supporting, if at a distance, the dignity of political life. It was not part of Plato's or Aristotle's enterprise to promise an easy access to truth, be it ethical or otherwise. To do so would not only be to claim that wisdom is theoretically possible, it would be to claim that wisdom ought to rule political life directly: it would be to demand in all seriousness the rule of "philosopher kings." To say that politics is based on a true understanding of nature and human nature requires no such certitude; indeed, a proper understanding of both demands an appreciation of the limitations as well as the capacities of human beings. It also requires a grasp of the role of chance in human affairs. It is not for nothing that Aristotle claims that human happiness requires good fortune as well as good character.

The Federalist sometimes gives the impression of being an uncritical paean to the virtues of the proposed Constitution. The vices, petty and grand, of the present system are illuminated at every opportunity, while the blessings to be enjoyed by "a more perfect Union" are extolled with unending conviction and enthusiasm, especially over the "new science of politics" that will allow for the expected perfection. Yet, whatever may be the case regarding the blessings of the proposed form of government, Publius' new science of politics is hardly as scientific or perfect as Locke's *Essay* would indicate: a mere agreement of the terms of relation and modes that are, according to Locke, the building blocks of ethics and politics, will not, according to Publius, yield a perfect understanding of the political. While Publius again and again attempts to allay the fears of his opponents by relying upon the Constitution's grounding in the good sense of the people, his most subtle argument for not rejecting the Constitution agrees with the charge that the Constitution is less than perfect. In an unusually meditative interlude in these papers, wedged between discussions of taxation and the vital question of whether the proposed Constitution is sufficiently republican, James Madison chooses to discuss the relations between nature and convention, human thought and reality, and, more subtly, rhetoric and political life.

According to *Federalist* No. 37, many of the criticisms of the Constitution can be reduced to two headings: it is not sufficiently conducive to the liberties of either persons or states, and the institutions provided for by the Constitution are either too powerful or not powerful enough. Or, as Madison puts it, the Constitutional convention was faced with the tasks of 1) providing the new government with the "requisite amounts of stability and energy," without unduly encroaching on the liberties these properties were intended to protect, and 2) "marking the proper line of partition between the authority of the general and that of the State governments." Neither of these issues, according to Madison, either were or could have been resolved perfectly. Stability and energy, for instance, require long terms of office, while liberty demands that these offices be accountable to the people, which, in turn, requires short terms. While one may adjust the length of term of office to favor one or the other, one cannot balance these elements of good government in such a way as to provide fully for the demands of either. The history of American federalism is testament to the fact that the line of demarcation between the

States and the national government is almost as difficult to articulate as the tension between stability and liberty is to resolve.

It might be thought that Madison could rest his case with confidence after having pointed out the practical difficulties which the demand for such resolutions implies. But Madison was fully cognizant of the elements of modern utopianism that to a significant degree infected anti-federalist criticisms of the Constitution. Hence he knew that a full refutation required a refutation of the ground of anti-federalist arguments as well as of the arguments themselves. In pleading with his opponents to let the spirit of moderation guide their estimates of the Constitution he knew that this would first of all require a defense of moderation.[22] That this is not always understood to be the purpose of *Federalist* No. 37 is due as much to the difficulty of making a politically persuasive case for moderation—as is evidenced by the conclusion of the paper—as by the brevity of Madison's remarks.

Madison approaches the difficulties faced by the Convention by turning to a discussion of nature. Nature's lines of demarcation, which may be noted easily enough at first glance, are difficult to define with precision when viewed with the intention of making such a distinction. The examples given are the "faculties of the mind," sense, perception, judgment, desire, volition, memory, and imagination. Depending on how these terms are defined, it is certainly less than easy to distinguish clearly sense from perception, or desire from judgment, to say nothing of the difficulties which must be confronted when an attempt is made to distinguish with precision the elements of desire and volition. Still, this is not the best of examples, as it is by no means clear that the lines dividing the constituents of thought and action are as hazy as Madison implies. Turning to nature itself, Madison strengthens his case by remarking on the difficulty of distinguishing accurately the boundaries between "the great kingdom of nature, and, still more, between the various provinces and lesser portions into which they are subdivided." But this is true most of all in the case where one might expect the greatest accuracy due to the easily identifiable characteristics of the things to be distinguished, vegetable life, inorganic matter, and animal life.[23] Madison's observation that "the most sagacious and laborious naturalists have never yet succeeded in tracing with certainty the line which separates the district of vegetable life from the neighboring region of unorganized matter, or which marks the termination of the former and the commencement of the animal empire" rings as true today as it did in 1788. Still, there are few observers, whether scientists or laymen, who would deny the reality of the distinctions to be made. What matters here is not whether the lines of distinctions can be articulated with perfect clarity, but whether those lines are thought to originate in the objects themselves, or in the mind of the observer. On this Madison is firm: the works of nature "are perfectly accurate." The difficulties alluded to are due, not to imperfection of the object, but rather to imperfections of the observer, the "imperfection of the eye which surveys them." Were it not for this failing it would be difficult to account for the errors that attend men in their study of nature, to say nothing of the errors that ever attend the study of politics. As we will see, error, especially in political things, is exactly what we should expect.

Madison then returns from nature to convention in order to demonstrate that in the case of "the institutions of man," "the obscurity arises as well from the object itself as from the organ by which it is contemplated." Nature, though perfect, is not perfectly understood; but as man himself is imperfect, it is clear that in attempting to distinguish between, say, the proper boundaries of the legislative, executive and judiciary branches of government, or of common, statute, maritime, ecclesiastical and corporate law, the question of precise jurisdiction is a nice one. Add to this, as Madison is quick to point out, the obscurities incident to human language, due to which it can be said that no language is "so correct as not to include many [words] equivocally denoting different ideas," and it can be seen that the "science of government" is a very imprecise science indeed.[24] It is because humans and human artifacts partake of this confusion that Madison can hope his presentation of them will, when applied to the Constitution, moderate "still further our expectations and hopes from the efforts of human sagacity."[25] As Madison says, after mentioning the problems raised by the "interfering pretensions of the larger and smaller States," "the real wonder is that so many difficulties should have been surmounted."[26]

Madison hopes to temper the expectations of his critics by reminding them of the general estate of mankind, which is not so much economic poverty, as ignorance. The "relief of man's estate," which has characterized the modern project at least since Bacon, is epitomized not only by the attempt to turn nature to man's account, but also by the claim to a wisdom superior to that of the ancients. This claim is not vitiated but rather strengthened by modernity's soft core of skepticism. The belief that ideas originate in the mind rather than in nature has led to a new-found confidence regarding man's ability to know the truth about the human things: while man may not be able to know much about nature, he can have precise knowledge about what he himself makes. This raises a standard of accuracy in human affairs that replaces the less precise notion of prudence that guided classical political thought. From this perspective, modernity can be said to rest upon a utopian expectation regarding wisdom that would have embarrassed the authors of the most famous "utopian" works of antiquity. This claim of scientific political certitude, while once finding adherents among political behaviorists, is seldom seen in its pristine form today. Instead we are likely to see it in a form which emanates from the historicist wing of modernity, a wing fully faithful to its positivist origins. If the idea of human nature is wholly a solipsistic or historical creation, it soon becomes clear that the demand that politics conform to one's own idea of the good receives a terrific impetus. Indeed, as I have argued, the thrust of modernity releases an almost religious fervor for the defense of ideas. This strange political amalgam by which radical skepticism is transformed into new extremes of political and ethical righteousness is simply the other side of modernity's claim that no man's opinion is better than another's—itself a conviction opposed to the belief that since nature sets knowable standards, one opinion *can* be better than another—and that therefore the state should not "impose" a standard of moral or political rectitude.

The strength of Madison's regime can be seen in *Federalist* No. 37, where both naive certitude and radical skepticism, the theoretical antecedents of a politics of the will, are disposed of, and a politics of moderation theoretically defended. (This does not, by the way, require a passionless politics; it does, however, imply that insofar as a non-acquisitive passion has a place in American politics it must be a passion for maintaining the limits of politics.) For Madison never denies either that nature is in herself perfect and therefore capable of providing a true standard, or that nature can be known. The key to Madison's treatment of the subject is his position on whether wisdom regarding nature is difficult or impossible to attain, a position not essentially different from the traditional account rejected by Locke. It is a question of whether precise knowledge of nature and human nature is either possible or necessary to political life. It is, after all, only the *precise* delimitations of natural and human things that Madison denies. This would not be the case if such categories were wholly the product of human caprice (ethical and political concepts "having *no* other reality but what they have in the minds of men" [*Essay*, II 30.4, emphasis added]), for then there would be no reason not to expect a precise account of them based on the internal consistency of the terms employed. On the contrary, Madison's scheme is fully compatible with "the transcendent law of nature and of nature's God" that provides the theoretical underpinning of the Revolution and the Constitution.[27]

Again, the full consequences of the presence of nature and human nature in the founding, or in *The Federalist* as a whole, can not, obviously, be explicated here. What seems clear, however, is that Publius' understanding of nature differs significantly from Locke's. And on that distinction hangs the all important difference between moral autonomy and human freedom; between a regime based essentially on a flight *from* something (the lack of a "nature" of things) and one pointing *toward* something: the self-limiting freedom of constitutional politics. The character of this politics is prefigured and grounded in that conflation of passion and reason that dominates the founding documents and historical events of the republic for at least a hundred years after *Federalist* No. 37 was written. Nowhere in Madison's writings, or in the writings of the other Founders and their followers can one find the argument that nature is simply incapable of providing human standards.

Although there is much truth to the statement that the commercial republic requires an emancipation of the acquisitive appetites, there is little in the founding capable of supporting the claim that the political good is simply a matter of definition in the Lockean sense of the word. Insofar as the emancipation of the will as will is part of the Lockean inheritance, that inheritance would appear to have formed no part of the American founding. Insofar as the American Founding *is* a Lockean founding it is in keeping with the exoteric Locke of the *Second Treatise*, the repudiator of the "justly decried" Hobbes, the Locke thought to be in agreement with "the judicious Hooker" on the question of natural law. For this reason, the institutional arrangements of the Constitution as well as the resolution of the problem of faction in *Federalist* No. 10 might best be thought of as attempts to attenuate the forces of will and passion by providing legitimate outlets for them in such a way as to allow for, but not demand, the rule of reason.[28] One might even say that what is most important in the American regime is not the particular features of the Constitution but rather the presence of the Constitution, for it is the presence of a constitution based on a conviction regarding "the laws of nature" that provides for the spirit of constitutionalism, or republican self-restraint which is the characteristic feature of the limitations to its will that a people agrees to when it consents to be ruled by law. The full implications of this might not have been appreciated until Lincoln's Lyceum speech, but its presence is demanded by the founding documents and by the arguments urged on their behalf by their authors.

Freedom, as Diamond and others maintain, is the end of the American regime. But there is a variety of meanings that the word freedom can encompass and a correct understanding of where the American regime stands in relation to the ancient polity and other alternatives to it requires an examination of these meanings and the way in which only one of them is consistent with the moderation Madison asks for in *The Federalist*. A combination of doubt and conviction, rather than of skepticism and certitude, underpins the commitment to freedom. If it were the latter rather than the former that lay at the heart of the founding, radical moral autonomy, or radical individualism, or a politics of the will would be in keeping with the spirit if not the letter of the founding. Constitutionalism reflects, however, not the imposition of an idea at the insistence of an unfettered will, but the political face of a theoretical perspective inimicable to radical moral autonomy.[29]

Notes

1. See Roger D. Masters, "Hobbes, Locke, and the Foundations of Anglo-Saxon Liberalism," prepared for the annual meeting of the American Political Science Association, Washington, D.C., 1980, page seven of footnotes, n. 15.

2. See Jefferson's letter to John Trumbull, February 15, 1789, in Merrill D. Peterson, ed., *The Portable Thomas Jefferson* (New York: Vintage Books, 1975), pp. 434–435.

3. Garry Wills, *Inventing America: Jefferson's Declaration of Independence* (New York: Doubleday, 1978).

4. See, for example, Ronald Harnowy, "Jefferson and the Scottish Enlightenment: A Critique of Garry Wills' *Inventing America: Jefferson's Declaration of Independence*," *William and Mary Quarterly*, 3rd. Ser., XXXVI (1979), 503–523.

5. Harry V. Jaffa, "Inventing the Past: Garry Wills' *Inventing America* and the Pathology of Ideological Scholarship," *The St. John's Review* Vol. XXXIII, No. 1, Autumn 1981, pp. 3–19.

6. Paul Eidelberg, *The Philosophy of the American Constitution: A Reinterpretation of the Intentions of the Founding Fathers* (New York: The Free Press, 1968).

7. Whether the Founding is best marked by the Declaration or the Constitution is still hotly disputed in scholarly circles, Lincoln's remarks at Gettysburg notwithstanding. Those who hold that the Constitution marks a significant departure from the Declaration are, it seems to me, required to argue that the Constitution and Declaration rest on different principles. Yet it would appear that both rest upon the consent of the governed, the major differences between them being that the Declaration provides the theoretical grounds for government by consent while the Constitution, taking this principle for granted, seeks to define the arrangements most conducive to securing its establishment and survival. While my remarks in this essay were prompted by a reading of Madison's *Federalist* number 37, I believe my point could have been demonstrated equally well by reference to the "nature and nature's God" of the Declaration. For an extended argument on the connection between the Declaration and the Constitution, see H.V. Jaffa, *How to Think About the American Revolution, A Bicentennial Cerebration* (Durham: Carolina Academic Press, 1978), pp. 49–140.

8. Herbert Friedenwold, *The Declaration of Independence, Interpretation and Analysis* (New York: The MacMillan Company, 1904); Louis Hartz, *The Liberal Tradition in America* (New York: Harcourt, Brace Jovanovich, 1955); cf. Clinton Rossiter, *Seedtime of the Republic* (New York, 1953); Bernard Bailyn, *The Origins of American Politics* (New York: Vintage Books, 1967); Lance Banning, *The Jeffersonian Persuasion, Evolution of a Party Ideology* (New York, 1978); Robert E. Shalhope, "Toward a Republican Synthesis: The Emergence of an Understanding of Republicanism in American Historiography," *William and Mary Quarterly*, XXIX (1972), pp. 49–81.

9. Martin Diamond, "Ethics and Politics: The American Way," in Robert H. Horwitz, ed., *The Moral Foundations of the American Republic* (Charlottesville: University Press of Virginia, 1977).

10. Douglass Adair, "That Politics May Be Reduced to a Science: David Hume, James Madison, and the Tenth *Federalist*"; *The Huntington Library Quarterly*, 20, no. I (1961). For a differing view of Madison's indebtedness to Hume, see George Mace, *Locke, Hobbes and the Federalist: An Essay on the Genesis of the American Political Heritage* (Carbondale: Southern Illinois Press, 1979), pp. 136–137, n. 77.

    Of the ends not treated in the *Second Treatise*, see Robert A. Goldwin, *John Locke*, in Leo Strauss and Joseph Cropsey, eds., *History of Political Philosophy*, 2nd ed. (Chicago: Rand McNally, 1972), pp. 451–485.

11. It may seem strange to those familiar with Professor Diamond's work that I should choose it to make a point which seems to contradict his own view of the founding. I refer to Diamond's insistence that the Declaration of Independence gives "no guidance"

in the matter of choosing a form of government. ("The Revolution of Sober Expectations," in Irving Kristol, Martin Diamond et. al., *America's Continuing Revolution: An Act of Conservation* (Washington, D.C.: American Enterprise Institute, 1975), pp. 25–41.) As Diamond maintained that the specifically American character is formed not by Locke's Declaration, but by the institutions established by the Constitution, it would seem that he sees no connection between the American character and Locke. Nevertheless, Diamond's presentation of Madison's resolution of the problem of faction emphasizes the differences to be expected when a regime chooses to pursue, not virtue or wisdom classically understood, but commercial or bourgeois virtue. While elements of this "virtue" can be found in Machiavelli, Hobbes, Montesquieu, and others, it also follows from Locke's teaching. Hence, while Diamond may not—probably did not—intend to limit or even to direct his remarks to Locke, they are, insofar as they articulate the distinction between ancient and modern politics and ethics, illustrative of the implications of Locke's thought. Of course, I could have relied on authors more directly concerned with Locke's influence, but by doing so, I would have been forced to choose a less felicitous and powerful presentation of the thrust of Locke's thought (such as Hartz, *op. cit.*) Another recent treatment of the commercial features of the "American Way" may be found in Ralph Lerner's "Commerce and Character: The Anglo-American as New-Model Man." *William and Mary Quarterly*, 3rd. Ser. XXXVI (1979), 3–26.

12. Robert A. Licht, "Reflections on Martin Diamond's 'Ethics and Politics: The American Way,'" *Publius*, vol. 8, no. 3 (Summer, 1978), pp. 184–211.

13. Alexis de Tocqueville, *Democracy in America*, ed. by J. P. Mayer (New York: MacMillan, 1969), p. 245.

14. *Ibid.*, pp. 536–537.

15. Thomas Hobbes, *Leviathan, or the Matter, Forme and Power of a Commonwealth Ecclesiasticall and Civil*, ed. by Michael Oakeshott (New York: Blackwell's, 1962), p. 62.

16. Fustel de Coulanges, *The Ancient City* (New York: Anchor Books, 1955).

17. Peter Laslett, "Introduction" to Locke's *Two Treatises of Government*, ed. by Peter Laslett (New York: Mentor, 1965). The coherence of Locke's political and philosophical works is maintained by Leo Strauss, *Natural Right and History* (Chicago: University of Chicago Press, 1953), Richard H. Cox, *Locke on War and Peace* (Oxford: Oxford University Press, 1960), and Michael Zuckert, "Fools and Knaves: Reflections on Locke's Theory of Philosophical Discourse," *Review of Politics*, Vol. 36 (1974), pp. 544–564. The current state of the dispute is reviewed in Michael Zuckert, "The Recent Literature of Locke's Political Philosophy," *The Political Science Reviewer*, Vol. 5 (1975), pp. 271–304.

18. John Locke, *An Essay Concerning Human Understanding*, ed. by Alexander Campbell Fraser, 2 vols. (New York: Dover Publications, Inc., 1959), II, 232. Hereafter I will cite this work by book, chapter, and section.

19. Eugene F. Miller, "Locke on the Meaning of Political Language: The Teaching of the Essay Concerning Human Understanding," *The Political Science Reviewer*, Vol. IX (Fall, 1979), pp. 163–191.

20. The following discussion draws on Alan F. Blum, *Socrates: The Original and Its Images* (London, 1978).

21. Alexander Hamilton, James Madison, John Jay, *The Federalist Papers*, ed. by Clinton Rossiter (New York: Mentor, 1961).

22. *Ibid., p.* 224.

23. *Ibid., p.* 228.

24. *Ibid., p.* 229.

25. *Ibid., p.* 228.

26. *Ibid., pp.* 229, 230.

27. Although the immediate context of this phrase in *Federalist* No. 43 makes clear that it is a

reference to self-preservation, the fact that the wording of it is lifted from the Declaration of Independence indicates the fuller meaning and importance of nature to the founding and to constitutionalism.

28. *Federalist* No. 49.

29. The research for this article was supported by a grant from the Earhart Foundation. A shorter version of it was presented at a panel sponsored by The Claremont Institute for the Study of Statesmanship and Political Philosophy at the 1980 annual meeting of the American Political Science Association.

9

THE ABSENT EXECUTIVE IN ARISTOTLE'S *POLITICS*

Harvey C. Mansfield, Jr.

Energy in the executive is a leading character in the definition of good government.
THE FEDERALIST NO. 70

SUCH WAS THE DECIDED OPINION OF ALEXANDER HAMILTON. HE WAS SO sure of the necessity of a vigorous executive that in the Federalist Papers devoted to the proposed American presidency he wasted no time in explaining that necessity but applied himself to proving that a vigorous executive was consistent with the genius of republican government. Imagine our surprise, then, that in Aristotle's *Politics*, where the reader is not being asked to endorse a particular constitution and is presumed to have leisure, we find nothing to show that executive energy can be conceived, much less that it is required.

Although the *Politics* is a comprehensive book, and aims at the "definition of good government," it nowhere explains, or even suggests, that executive energy is a "leading character" in it. It contains only two passages that are directly relevant to executive power, one on the parts of regimes in Book IV (1297b35–1301a15) that does not mention the executive, and the other in Book VI (1321b2–1323a11), which does discuss the executive but is disappointingly short and vapid to our taste. Nonetheless, I shall examine these two passages under the supposition that they will bear a greater weight of detailed analysis and concentrated speculation than many today would suppose.[1] It is never superfluous to ask Aristotle's opinion on any matter, but for the study of executive power it is necessary to consult him at length, despite, or rather because of the fact that he discusses the executive hardly at all. He reveals to us that executive power is a modern practice arising from a modern doctrine.[2] Rather than discuss the executive, he raises the issues to which executive

169

power was intended as an answer. He raises them more clearly than did the founders of the doctrine of executive power—Machiavelli, Hobbes, Locke and Montesquieu—and thus shows us that executive power is *one* answer to them, not the only solution, as we might have concluded from our experience and from Hamilton's famous remark.

In Book III of the *Politics*, perhaps the most fundamental part of that work, Aristotle develops a definition of regime (*politeia*) that culminates in his discussion of "kingship over all" (*pambasileia*).[3] He does not speak of a philosopher-king, as does Plato. He agrees with Plato that the best regime is the kingship of the best man and that political science is essentially the study of this regime, but he proceeds differently. Rather than founding a best regime in speech and awaiting the coincidence of philosopher and king (*Republic* 473d), Aristotle, like the serious man he discusses in Book III, adopts the material given him for examination (*Politics* 1287a10, 1287b5–8, 1288a27). He turns to a discussion of actual regimes and of how they may be improved without being ruled directly by a philosopher.

This discussion takes place in Books IV-VI of the *Politics*. It is preceded by Aristotle's remark at the end of Book III that we must now attempt to speak of the best regime, in what way it naturally comes into being and how it subsists, and that it is necessary to make the appropriate inquiry about the best regime. These last words are repeated at the beginning of Book VII, which with Book VIII is expressly concerned with the best regime, whereas Books IV-VI do not consider it expressly. Commentators have thus been led to conclude that Books IV-VI are an interpolation not intended by Aristotle.[4] This may be so, but we shall proceed on the hypothesis that Books IV-VI tell how the best regime naturally comes into being, as Books VII and VIII tell how it subsists.

The Coming-into-Being of the Best Regime. The best regime naturally comes into being through the material nature provides, which is human bodies ordered in actual regimes. It is fitting, then, that Aristotle should compare the political scientist with the gymnastic coach at the beginning of Book IV (1288b18). The coach works with men's bodies as they are, and he improves them by training, not by ruling. The training of men by this coach of political science in correcting their existing regimes is no less a task than founding a regime from the beginning, Aristotle says, just as relearning is no less than learning from the beginning (1289a3–5). The practical task of improving politics to be undertaken in Books IV-VI is equivalent to the theoretical examination left over from Book III of whether nature allows men to rule in kingship. For it was neither clear nor proven that human excellence in the best regime is according to nature. It must now be shown that the "whole race" of men is capable of kingship (1288a16, 35), an examination and a task in which the improving of men as they are is carried on in parallel with the discovery of what they can be. Aristotle does not claim that what is practicable here and now is the best: that is the mistake of the ordinary political partisan. But he also seems to avoid the philosopher's mistake of despising what is practicable, because that mistake arises from or leads to both citizen and scientific irresponsibility. So while not confusing the practicable and the best, he studies them together in the realm of the practicable (1288b22–40), correcting the partisan's mistake more openly than the philosopher's.

Aristotle's discussion of actual regimes in Book IV concludes with an analysis of the three parts to be found in all regimes which the serious legislator must observe. Aristotle indicates that the three parts must be considered separately as well as in common, and since his three parts, the deliberative body, the magistracies and the judiciary, resemble the modern legislative, executive and judicial branches, his analysis has been reasonably taken for an early, if not founding, statement in the history of the doctrine of separation of powers.[5] Yet two things in it must strike us as peculiar. The magistracies are discussed in the plural without reference to the need for unity in one man that modern theories of the executive assert or to the monarch out of which the modern executive developed historically. It might be thought in excuse for Aristotle's neglect of monarchy in this analysis that he was captivated by the Greek city-state, which lacked a monarch. But then he has just discussed in Book III a particularly aggravated kingship, and he was quite familiar with barbarian monarchies and often speaks of them elsewhere.

We also need to explain the strange formality of his analysis which concentrates on the manner of composing the three parts, especially whether by choice or by lot, and on the order of forms and modes to such a degree that Aristotle seems to be carried away by theoretical enthusiasm from actual regimes not so much to the best regime as to all possible regimes. In this ordering, the extreme democratic procedure of composing bodies of government by lot seems to be given an undue prominence even with respect to Greek or Athenian experience, for lot is easy to manipulate and hence almost reducible to the choice behind the manipulation, we would think. Aristotle is more interested in the formal ordering of the parts than in their actual powers, and in the case of the magistracies corresponding to our executive he puts off discussing their powers to Book VI, for reasons we must seek. The magistracies as they appear in Book IV only correspond to our executive, and are not identical with it, because they are not said to have the power or duty of executing the law although the deliberative body seems to be concerned chiefly with legislation.

Both peculiarities can be seen to arise from the attention paid to the human body in Book IV, which is forecast in the comparison of the political scientist with the gymnastic trainer at the beginning. In the middle of the book, while introducing a very short consideration of tyranny, Aristotle remarks casually, in a subordinate clause, that "we admit that it [tyranny] has a certain share in regimes." So difficult is it to believe that Aristotle could have said something so Machiavellian, that two recent translations of the *Politics* avoid it with evident embarrassment, and surely it needs to be reconciled with a preceding remark that tyranny is the least a regime of all the regimes.[6] But in the fact that all regimes, that is, all actual regimes, have something tyrannical in them we can find Aristotle's reason for omitting monarchy from his analysis of the three parts of regimes: the share of tyranny in all regimes does not have to be embodied in the rule of a single individual.

What is the share of tyranny in regimes? Aristotle mentions two forms of tyranny, barbarian and ancient Greek, that were kingly because they ruled according to law over willing subjects, yet tyrannical because they ruled despotically according to their own opinion. Then he speaks of a third form, thought to be especially tyrannical and the counterpart of the "kingship over all" discussed in Book III; this is monarchy that rules without being held to account over similars and betters for its own benefit, not for that of the ruled. Therefore it is compulsory, Aristotle adds, for no free man willingly tolerates such rule. We see that the criterion of tyranny has been tacitly changed in the statement of what seems tyrannical to free men. From despotic rule according to the tyrant's opinion (which might also be according to law over willing subjects if that were the tyrant's desire) it has become irresponsible rule over similars and betters for the monarch's own benefit. The former is a distinction possibly without a difference, but the latter is an incomplete formulation: What is irresponsible rule over inferiors for *their* benefit? The answer implied is that for free men, this also is tyranny because they will not tolerate irresponsible rule however beneficial. Free men will insist that their rulers rule accountably as well as for the benefit of the ruled, and these two criteria do not necessarily coincide. When they diverge, free men will demand accountable rule even against their own interest.

This assertiveness necessarily understands itself as freedom and the contrary as tyranny. Thereby it admits that tyranny can be to one's benefit. Tyranny would then be the counterpart to kingship over all, with the difference that that king as opposed to the tyrant willingly adopts the freedom of his subjects. But can he, if free men reject kingship for their benefit as tyranny? The rejection of rule for one's own benefit by one's betters is a claim to rule oneself regardless of benefit, hence others, including one's betters; for in capacity to will, one's betters are one's similars, and no claim to rule oneself can resist extension to one's similars. The free man's claim to reject as he wills amounts to the tyrant's claim to rule as he wills. Hence all regimes share in tyranny when they take account of willingness without regard to benefit, as actual regimes must—precisely when they attempt to take account of freedom.

The "certain share" of tyranny in regimes may thus be traced to the need to consult men's willingness when governing them, to their recalcitrance in requiring to be consulted, to their resistant nature, and ultimately to the resistance of nature itself. As mere resistance, the human desire for freedom from nature leads back to the very tyranny of non-human nature which it resists, a connection which reminds us of the kinship in politics of democracy and tyranny (1292a18). Only human excellence can rescue human freedom from the willfulness which disguises its submission to lower nature, but this excellence seems especially to be tyrannical (1295a19). Excellence looks like willfulness to willful men, as they attribute the principle of their own conduct to the government of nature. They run from the appearance of tyranny to the reality. Tyranny in the brief discussion of Book IV recalls the Spartan King of Book III, the general for life who could exist in all regimes (1286a4) as the element of resistance we have been considering. It would be the strength of this "kingship" that calls into question the kingship over all to which the third tyranny is here said to correspond.

The Mixed Regime. Aristotle's solution to this difficulty is the mixed regime, which he makes the theme of Book IV. The mixed regime is mixed of democracy and oligarchy, or of natural necessity and human choice (1291a7–10, 24–28), or, as we shall see, of lot and choice. For the democratic principle of lot stands for what is given to us, or rather imposed on us, by purposeless nature. What comes to us by lot appears to take no account of what we would choose; so the opposition of choice to lot is the view of nature from the standpoint or battlefront of human recalcitrance. Through the notion of the mixed regime Aristotle teaches this uninstructed recalcitrance that some things are outside our choice and must be accepted, indeed that there is advantage in accepting them. In this context, speaking to this viewpoint, he does not attempt to argue directly that nature gives us more than our lot or fate or (as we would say) our environment; he does not now speak of nature's ruling principle or of its end; he avoids the question of the whole (1296a5–6). He keeps his discussion at the level of democracy and oligarchy and does not introduce kingship, for kingship, even or especially of the best, looks like tyranny to men who regard excellence as an unfair portion of the lot distributed by purposeless, willful nature.[7]

The mix of democracy and oligarchy and of choice and lot is shown, then, in a visible order, an order of bodies or of parts of the city or of governmental "organs" and "bodies" rather than in an invisible whole that must be thought. This visible order reveals the character of the mix —how much of each—in its form, enabling democrats and oligarchs to see and appreciate what is their own and what must be conceded to the other party (1294b13–18; 35–37). Thereby they receive an intimation of the reason why the mixed regime is beneficial and are given a gentle push in the direction that reasoning would take them. Aristotle uses the formality of order to represent its intelligibility. When he likens the parts of the city to the parts of an animal near the beginning of Book IV (1290b25), he implies that nature's forms indicate its intelligibility too, and that human purposefulness in the making and mixing of forms is supported by nature's intelligibility. Since formality is the outside of rationality, we are not surprised to see the formality of mixing culminate in the discussion of the three parts of regimes at the end of Book IV; for the three parts of regimes are also three functions of the rational soul, deliberating, ruling (here there is some doubt) and judging. From the analogy between city and animal, which implies many distinct cities with unmixable regimes (you never see the smile of a fox on the face of an ox), there is a movement in Aristotle's argument to the presentation of interchangeable parts at the end of Book IV, some of them mixed to create fantastic regimes.

By the order of bodies we are introduced to soul. The acquaintance is not merely for philosophers, because it is only through soul that we can understand how reform in politics is possible. There must be something in men, as opposed to other animals, that enables them to change their way of life and to overcome the lot which in the other animals decrees their fate. As Aristotle shows that bodily forms imply the existence of the rational soul, the soul so revealed is nonetheless the bodily part of the soul. It is the part Plato called *thumos* as distinct from appetite or eros; it is occupied with the spirited defense of one's own body rather than devoted to something outside oneself. But, as we have seen in the consideration of tyranny, human recalcitrance can be so ornery that it acts against a man's own interest merely for the sake of preserving his willfulness. His very willfulness, then, illustrates his freedom from self-interest. Even at their most irrational, human beings show the capacity for detachment which is required for rationality and, in politics, for reform. From Aristotle's presentation it would seem that the very basis of reform is to be found in stubbornness well understood.

Here we watch Aristotle passing up an opportunity to develop executive power. He does not enlarge upon the tyrant's share of regimes to establish a fund of arbitrariness with which to govern willful men. Nor does he construct a disguise of legality under which the executive would innocently transmit nature's arbitrary decrees to foolish men. He holds to his statement in Book III that the tyrannical skill is not according to nature but he gives effect to it otherwise than as king ruling over all. We have seen the political scientist appearing as a gym coach training human bodies; and later, when explaining the middle class between the rich and the poor, Aristotle speaks of a trusted arbitrator who mixes and as it were replaces the middle class whose best virtue is mediocrity (1297a6–7).

This arbitrator, we soon see, practices "sophisms" in order to make his mixes; he is not so truthful as the gym coach perhaps because he is not so respectful of the customer's unsuitable desires (1288b17–19; 1297a15, 35). But even with his sophisms he mixes democracy and oligarchy, and thus reasons to the factions he arbitrates, as much as he can, through the significance of order.

The Parts of Regimes. We come now to a closer interpretation of the passage at the end of Book IV on the parts of regimes. With some obscurity Aristotle says that we should speak again, both in common and separately for each, of these things consecutively, taking their appropriate beginning (*archē*). He leaves it ambiguous whether the things to be spoken about are the regimes of which he has been speaking just above, as the grammar would seem to require, or the parts of regimes he is about to enumerate, as the sense would seem to require. Let us take it that in speaking of parts of regimes he means to speak *again* of regimes, or that the parts correspond to whole regimes. The first part is "the deliberative about common things," and since deliberation issues in choice and choice is selective, the deliberative part has the tendency of oligarchy. The third part is what does the judging (*to dikazon*), for which Aristotle used the verb for the judging of democratic assemblies; and as this judging is a calling to account before the many, it is democratic. It also recalls to us the necessity of confronting human choice with bodily nature. The second part is "that regarding the offices," not said to be either deliberating or judging, or any other activity; and the offices (*archai*) are plural. We have noted that monarchy does not appear as a part and these *archai* may be referred to the "polity" that Aristotle has set forth in Book IV as the mixed regime. The oligarchic and democratic functions are separated by the offices rather than united by the single office of a monarch as in Book III, for in "polity," the particular regime whose name stands for the class of regimes, it is possible to change or reform in any direction toward any of the other regimes, especially toward either democracy or oligarchy, and not only in the direction of monarchy. Polity, as will be seen from a discussion just before this one, is the regime of the "hoplites," heavily-armed infantrymen (1297b23–25). When such a class rules, it is unclear whether they constitute a regime or are willing to defend any regime; similarly, "polity" is conceivable not only as a particular regime but also as that which enables all regimes to rule and thus to be regimes.

When the two typical regimes and the generic regime are seen as parts of all regimes, one can recognize that the three parts together form the soul of all regimes. They are found in common or together in each regime and separately in the governing bodies of each regime as well as in the dominant tendency of each regime; and each regime may be reformed by separating and recombining its parts.[8] The parts of the regimes are in fact the rational and ruling functions of an individual human soul, deliberating and judging, and the offices or ruling principles of that soul, though Aristotle does not point this out. For he is anxious now to protect human choice from the tyranny of excellence as it is exercised through the soul.[9] His presentation of every regime's regime reminds us of understanding the human soul through understanding the typically different human souls, but he must be mindful of the danger posed by the soul, that is, the most excellent soul, to human freedom. He therefore suggests that understanding the soul is possible, and political reform practicable, through the generic soul rather than the best soul, at least up to a point. Every regime has something of oligarchy and something of democracy, but also something of polity, which mixes oligarchy and democracy and yet remains separate from them, with open potential for change.[10] This analysis of the parts of all regimes shows how each regime can exist by showing "the serious legislator" what is beneficial for each.[11]

By contrast, the three parts of the modern schema, legislative, executive and judicial, do not describe rational functions of the soul. They center on the law which is to be made, enforced or judged by, but the law is understood as a product of the soul, abstracted from the activity necessary to produce it. The modern schema does not care how the law is arrived at and it especially avoids saying that legislating is deliberating: according to the modern doctrine of sovereignty, legislating may be deliberating or it may be resolving whimsically or surrendering to necessity. Perhaps something of the last is indicated. Aristotle says that when the parts of the regime are noble (*kalos*), the regime must necessarily be noble; and he has previously emphasized the difference between the necessary parts of the city ministering to bodily needs and the noble parts, such as deliberating and judging, that pertain to the soul (1291a18–27). But the modern schema is designed for limited government in the realm of bodily need or comfort, and it cannot afford to insist on the nobility of human choice in the activity of legislating; rather, it is barred from insisting on deliberation while it encourages wary calculation.

The Deliberative Part.   Aristotle has said that the first part is what deliberates about common things. Deliberating is not defined here, but in the *Ethics* he says that we do not deliberate about things we cannot affect or attain; we do not deliberate about eternal things or about things that change of necessity, by nature or through chance. We do not even deliberate about all human things, for example none of the Spartans deliberates about the best regime for the Scythians. We do not deliberate about ends but about means, and we deliberate to find the best means of the best means until we reach the first cause, which is the last to be found. This cause—last in the analysis, first in the genesis—is ourselves, and whatever is dominant in us that chooses (*Nic. Ethics* 1112a18–1113a14). Deliberating is thus primarily for one's own good, but Aristotle emphasizes its social character (he speaks of "us" and mentions deliberating with friends and in politics) because a man sharing reason with other men can do more with them than alone. His most valuable tool is held in common with other men, and so his own reason, which might be feeble or ill-informed by itself, gains access to the power of human reason generally. The topics of deliberation are similarly broadened from an individual's concerns to the common things of men, the human beings which are also reasonable things. To neglect the best regime in the Scythians, therefore, may have been a fault in the Spartans, whose regime did not permit, much less attempt, such apparently aimless philosophizing. For it means that they did not deliberate about the best regime for themselves. Not being satisfied with Spartan, oligarchic complacency, Aristotle raises the question, in this section of Book IV of the *Politics*, of the extent of the common things in our power about which we deliberate. He does it in a suitably muted way, because there is after all something sound in the Spartan contempt for the vagaries of far-off barbarians.

The deliberative part is said to be sovereign about three sets of things: first, war and peace, and alliances and dissolutions; second, the laws; third, death, exile and confiscation, and the audits. While in the modern scheme laws are paramount, for Aristotle they are only one concern of the deliberative part. They are the central concern, as one can see from the listing of this seeming miscellany;[12] but they are surrounded by topics of deliberation which reveal the limited power of human legislation to fend off war, to choose one's partners, to prevent disobedience, and to change what is past. In deliberating on foreign affairs, men deliberate in regard to other men on what they consider in regard to nature as a whole: whether man's relation to nature is war or peace, alliance or dissolution. And in deliberating on punishments, men intend the effects that may be inflicted by fortune or the gods and that one may do no more than wish or pray to escape. When Aristotle says that the deliberative part is sovereign, he finds it necessary at the same time to concede that the integrity of the human good to which men deliberate is questionable. Rather, he shows that men make this concession themselves in the very topics of their deliberation.

Earlier in Book IV Aristotle had defined deliberating as "the work of political joining," without explaining further; from this context we may suppose he means that when deliberating in politics, men join the human good they choose with the non-human necessities or goods that they must accept.[13] But he proceeds next to an analysis of the "judgments" about these topics. Necessarily, he says, all of them must be assigned to all, or all to some (that is to one office or several), or different judgments to different ones, or some to all and some to some. This formal analysis is exhaustive, but it abstracts from the actual topics and thus from the question how far men *can* deliberate. The deliberations are unexpectedly called "judgments" (*kriseis*), which for Aristotle are discriminations of one thing from another, judging between; and in Greek "to judge" has the meaning also of separating.[14] It appears that the work of joining requires separating, that deliberating requires judging, that to learn what we may deliberate about we must be abstracted from our own concerns that are the reference point of all deliberation. In particular, men must be separated from their habitual prejudice in favor of either democracy or oligarchy so that they may deliberate by joining.

For all judgments to be made by all is "demotic," Aristotle says, since this is what the demos seeks. But there are several "modes" (*tropoi*) of deliberating all on all, and he gives four. All may serve in turn rather than together, and meet in a body only for making laws, for constitutional matters, and for listening to reports from the magistrates.[15] All may assemble together, but only to choose magistrates, make laws, consider war and peace, and hold audits, the magistrates being selected by vote from all or by lot. All may assemble for these purposes, other matters to be managed by magistrates selected by vote whenever possible, such being those who must necessarily be skilled in order to rule. The "fourth mode" (Aristotle counts them for us) is for all to meet to deliberate about all things, and for the magistrates not to judge but only prejudge decisions. This is the "last," modern democracy which Aristotle asserts to be analogous to dynastic oligarchy and tyrannical monarchy. These four modes are then called "democratic." They were first called "demotic" as being what the demos seeks; but the demos must rule according to the necessities it finds, and "demotic" becomes "democratic" as we see that nowhere do all actually deliberate on all things (1298a10–34).

More than this, the four modes of the demotic deliberation correspond to the four possibilities of deliberation: the first mode of all deliberating in turn is a democracy of homogeneous parts in which none of the magistrates is chosen; the second has some[16] deliberations in the hands of some magistrates, chosen by an assembly of all from all by vote or lot—a moderate oligarchy; in the third, different (or "other") deliberations are made by different ones because the need for skill or knowledge is recognized; and the last mode is an uncertain mixture of some deliberations to all and some to some, depending on the use made of the opportunity to prejudge by demagogues.[17] When the four abstract possibilities of deliberation are brought to the men who actually deliberate, we find human material containing all the possibilities. So we must conclude that men cannot rule by one of the possibilities alone. This finding would be confirmed by the lists of several democracies, oligarchies, aristocracies and polities that Aristotle has supplied earlier in Book IV.[18] For when we remark, for example, that one democracy is more democratic than another, we imply that all the regimes are contained in each and that every regime is a mixed regime. Even the "last" or "complete" democracy is not completely demotic.[19]

For some to deliberate on all things is oligarchic, and here too there are "differences"[20] which prove to correspond to the four possibilities. In the first oligarchy there is a moderate property qualification, but since no man is utterly destitute, lacking body and faculties, this oligarchy could be understood as democratic or "political," as Aristotle calls it. The second oligarchy is composed of those chosen to deliberate, not of all those with a qualification; and this is properly oligarchic, some deliberating on all. When the sovereign deliberators choose themselves, when their office is hereditary and when they are sovereign over the laws, the order is "necessarily oligarchical" because it reflects the sovereignty of choice; but it also corresponds to the possibility of different deliberations by different men, because the choosers could be knowers educating other knowers, hence "hereditary," and as knowers sovereign over the laws. Two oligarchical "differences" remain. When some deliberate on some things, and all on war and peace and audits, and magistrates are selected by vote or lot, the regime is an aristocracy; and if some things are decided by magistrates selected by vote, others by magistrates selected by lot, and others by vote and lot in common, then the magistrates are from both an aristocratic regime and polity. This last regime (the two "differences" do not amount to different regimes)[21] is aristocratic if one understands that no regime can be more aristocratic than this: as we have seen, all men will want to defend themselves and to insist on auditing their rulers, however superior (1295a20). The actual aristocratic regime, therefore, allows some decisions to all besides reserving some to some; it could even be said to resemble the last democracy in its intimation that the most an aristocracy can do is to "prejudge" or predispose human deliberations. Every order or (as we say in our modern Greek) "system" of deliberation, even the best, is a lottery because one cannot guarantee that the best men will be placed in office. This is true especially of the last democracy in which the demogogue may be either Pericles or Cleon, but it is also true of aristocracy which is here fittingly provided with the unaristocratic, but "political," institution of lot.[22]

Having shown that the best regime has a democratic element, Aristotle is ready to advise democracies and oligarchies how to improve their deliberation by mixing their deliberative parts. He openly tells the modern democracy that it should adopt oligarchical practices in courts and assemblies to insure that the demos deliberates in common with the notables,[23] and he counsels oligarchies to allow the demos a share in deliberation—not to vote decrees as in present regimes, but to reject them. This advice to both sides should induce Aristotle's readers to think about the sovereignty of deliberation, a question which for us is connected to the necessity of executive power. The democrats forget that choosing loses its dignity when it descends to whimsical decreeing; it is no longer properly choice or distinctively human. We might also address this remark to the modern political science that has redefined deliberation as "decision-making." To protect the distinctiveness of choosing, moreover, it is necessary for the demos to deliberate in common with distinctive men or "notables" (*gnorimoi*), because the exercise of choice implies respect for the differences men find choiceworthy, especially in wealth but also in birth and in virtue (1289b34–1290a5). How can democrats condemn the notables to a dishonoring equality when they themselves would choose the things for which the notables are noted?

Oligarchs, who are too confident of the power of choice, should allow the demos to reject decrees and thus confine their own claim to the duties of preliminary councillors (*probouloi*) or law-guardians (*nomophulakes*) which already exist in some regimes, indeed in democratic regimes. In advising that the power of rejecting be conceded to the demos, Aristotle gives recognition to the nay-saying *thumos* of human beings; and also, without making a point of it, he admits the necessity of decrees. To allow the demos the power of rejecting is to concede the right of human stubbornness against the dignity of deliberate choice. More than this, it is to concede the power of nature to decree limits to human choice, for from the standpoint of deliberation a decree of nature is no more intelligible than a demotic whim. What the people reject and what the philosopher or scientist says nature will not permit converge in the political necessity of decrees. Aristotle proposes a change in current practice (ceasing to distinguish democracies from oligarchies) from the many proposing and the few rejecting to the reverse (1298b35–1299a1). This reform is sweeping but modest. It implies that all actual regimes are ruled by chance and necessity rather than choice, because they employ democrats for deliberating and oligarchs for rejecting; but as regards the sovereignty of deliberation, it suggests that oligarchs, that is, human beings in their choosing, must rest content with having the first word. Nature and human nature, that is, the democrats, have a veto power. In modern states this veto power is given to the executive to exercise in the name of the people, and if in addition the executive is granted the power of direction, and if direction is thereby understood as a function somehow executive, then we conceive the sovereignty of deliberation[24] yet more modestly than Aristotle and almost replace it with the sovereignty of decree.

The Offices. "Connected" to these things, Aristotle says, is "the distinction" regarding offices (*archai*, 1299a3), which are the second or central part of the regime. He does not say precisely what the distinction is, but we may suppose it to be that which keeps offices plural and prevents them from being subordinated under one office that would be a monarchy over all. This is the part of the regimes in Aristotle's schema corresponding to the modern executive power, but these offices lack unity at the top embodied in the single modern executive. Aristotle believes this plurality necessary in order to maintain the sovereignty of deliberation, to which the offices are "connected."

Four topics are announced for discussion: how many offices, sovereign over what, for what period of time and how appointed. The number and duration of offices were not topics forecast at the beginning of this section (1298a1), and their appearance now serves to confirm the plurality of offices. Regarding duration, Aristotle raises the queer possibility that offices might be eternal or ancient (1299a9) as well as of shorter term. This is too long for human tenure, but we can make sense of the description as a reference to the other meaning of *archē*, the beginning or ruling principle. Aristotle wishes to ensure—and this is the special task of Book IV—that human government is free and therefore no mere conduit of natural necessity or divine anger to individual men. The "distinction" he has spoken of here is that between *archē* in this sense and the human *archai* he must keep plural to protect from the *archē* in that sense. At the same time, as we have seen, men, especially in regard to their bodies, cannot ignore natural necessity; and Aristotle must manage a limited independence for them. Accordingly he raises a question which might have been unexpected as to what sort of office should be *called* an office, since the political community requires many chiefs not to be assumed to be officers (= rulers), first the priests, which he says are to be assumed to be other than political offices, and also chorus-sponsors, heralds and those chosen as ambassadors. The priests must be kept separate from the political offices, we may suppose, so that angry men cannot quickly call on angry gods, and the strange assortment of other offices not so called may be taken for a reference to the poets who should undoubtedly be chosen in order to prevent their ascendency over men through their self-appointed office of making gods.[25]

Aristotle then lists offices requiring care of men. Some are political and are exercised either over all citizens for some doing, for example a general over those serving as soldiers, or over a section, such as wardens of women or children. Some are economic, such as corn-measures, and some are aides to which well-off men would appoint slaves. The general rules those (literally) "generalling"; he rules those who perform the same activity as he behind him, which suggests ruling men who rule themselves. The wardens rule or literally "lay down the law" for imperfect men, inferior or immature, which suggests ruling men who rule themselves, but imperfectly. Men can also make an office or *archē* of an economic superintendence which treats other men merely as animals to be fed or of servile tasks that imply men are slaves. Surely all are necessary, but Aristotle does not say whether they deserve to be *called* offices; he does say that those especially to be spoken of as offices are the ones assigned deliberation about certain things, judging, and ordering, especially the last as this is "more ruling." But he directs this inconclusive discussion to a "dianoetic inquiry," perhaps in the *Physics* or *Metaphysics*.[26] He has been speaking only of the "name" of what humans call "offices." Ordering is "more ruling," it seems, because of the lack of correspondence between these offices and first principles, which must here be kept at a distance from human government. Still again we perceive the possibility of an executive power that orders or commands, but, consistent with his defense of bodily freedom, Aristotle does not mention any law to be executed and he indicates that the rulers order or command themselves (i.e., not as executives of something or someone alien to them) while ordering others.[27]

Next Aristotle opens the question of how many offices should be established by making a distinction between those necessary for the city and those not necessary but useful to the "serious regime." This distinction is still discouraging to the possibility of monarchy, but Aristotle moves to the difference between large cities and small. In large cities it is possible for one office to serve one function, but in small cities requiring the same offices and laws as the large, it is necessary to combine several functions in one office. If we carry this thought as far as it will go, we arrive at monarchy and we see that the "small city" could be the soul of one man in which all the offices would be ordered. Yet this small city suffers from "few human beings" (*oliganthropia*, cf. 1297b26) or little humanity because the offices are ordered for the necessities of the city and do not allow for human freedom. Since such freedom is useful for the "serious regime" —the soul which is serious about both natural order and human freedom, Aristotle does not himself combine offices in the small city as far as he could have nor does he mention the soul.[28] He says that if one could say how many offices every city must have of necessity, and how many it ought (*dei*) to have, one would know more easily which offices can be combined in a single office. The distinction between the necessary and the useful offices is restated in a way more favorable to the combining of all offices under a single office, but Aristotle does not say this is possible.

When combining offices, one must face three questions: which matters ought to be cared for in offices distributed by place and which by one office sovereign everywhere; whether offices should be distinguished by function or for human beings, for example, one office for good order or a different one for children and women; and does the kind (*genos*) of office vary according to the regimes? Aristotle is asking how it is possible to combine offices while preserving necessary distinctions. Pursuing the last question, he remarks that some offices are peculiar to certain regimes, such as the preliminary councillors (*probouloi*), who are undemocratic as opposed to the council (*boulē*) which is demotic. Yet there must be some such office to care for deliberating beforehand for the demos, and if its number is few it is oligarchical; and preliminary councillors are necessarily few in multitude, hence oligarchical. While previously Aristotle seemed to recommend preliminary councillors for oligarchies (1298b27–9), now he seems to confuse them with democratic councillors and to say that they are necessary in democracies. He points out to the democrats that as free human beings they are few among the demos of all things, and that to protect their humanity they must "pre-deliberate" or assume those principles which distinguish them from the rest of (unfree) nature. Such principles (*archai*) must be given recognition in political offices if they are to be effective, for as he says, the power even of the demotic council (*boulē*) is dissolved in democracies where the demos deals with all things (1299b38). In our terms, a legislative assembly is not deliberative unless it provides for offices composed of few, such as committees, in which men use their leisure to deliberate.

With this proof Aristotle indicates that we can mix regimes by combining offices, but instead of making that point and going on to discuss polity, he brings aristocracy to our attention. Wardens of children and women, and other offices sovereign in care, are aristocratic, he says; and he means to say that care, including self-care, is aristocratic because it requires education, and the democratic and oligarchical qualities of freedom and wealth, which he has just mentioned (1299b25–8), do not suffice. The distinction between the offices necessary to a city and those useful for the serious regime which the complete city ought to have, remains. It could be said on the basis of Book III that the city's necessities are identical with the elements that make it complete; for how can men deliberate on their necessities unless they have been educated to deliberate *well*? Deliberating well is a topic in Aristotle's *Ethics* (1142a31), but not in Book IV of the *Politics*, where men are supposed to deliberate well enough for their necessities in well-ordered institutions. Rather than disdain such institutions for their inadequacy, Aristotle leaves a reminder of it. This is his way of proposing practical improvements while bringing the best regime into existence.

Now Aristotle turns to the modes of appointing for offices. Referring to the topic of how many offices, he says he is putting aside the discussion for now, but in fact he advances it. He says that one should attempt to discuss the establishment of offices "from the beginning" (*ex archés*), which can also mean "from the beginning principle." The beginning principle being "attempted" (Aristotle does not say it can be accomplished) in Book IV is that of human choice. Human choice finds itself confronted with what is not chosen, which from its standpoint appears to be merely given, by chance or lot. Aristotle teaches us from actual political practices that the dichotomy between choice and lot, though initially impressive and "first for us," is inadequate. For in practice we do not choose to be governed only by choice: we choose to be governed, sometimes and in different ways, by lot. Any established office, indeed, is a kind of lottery because in establishing the office we do not know who will fill it. We do, however, have some idea of the character or nature of who will fill it, and this suggests that what first appears as chance may be, in some reliable degree, intelligible nature. Like the king over all, but more modestly, we can choose in the sense of intend this intelligibility. If intelligently contrived, an office may be a wise choice and a good bet on what cannot be chosen, as for example the American founders could not choose American presidents but could expect certain characters to be called forth by the nature of the office of presidency.[29] Thus Aristotle may preserve the difference between choice and lot while suggesting how they may be combined under one principle.

In the discussion of establishing offices that follows, Aristotle excels himself in terseness. The mathematical, combinatory character of his treatment is meant to train the "serious legislator" in looking for possibilities that are not actual or prevalent and to correct the two sorts of complacency one still finds among liberals and conservatives today: that of supposing we can choose anything we like and that of making do with what chance supplies. The text is or is thought to be corrupt, but at least some of its irregularities can be explained through cautious interpretation. Aristotle says that the differences in appointing to offices are to be found in three "boundaries" which, when combined, yield all the modes. They are: who appoints to the offices, from whom, and in what mode? Of each of the three boundaries there are three differences: either all citizens appoint or some; either from all or from some; and either by vote (= choice) or by lot.

Pausing to consider this analysis, we see three ways in which offices can be either democratic (all appoint, from all, by lot) or oligarchic (some appoint, from some, by choice). But in these three ways democracy and oligarchy have been removed from actual regimes where one or the other is established as sovereign and are presented in an abstract regime as if to a statesman with perfect freedom of choice. At the same time it is evident that this abstract regime, if it exists, must be a democracy with freedom for both democratic and oligarchic choices.[30] For though oligarchy is in need of democratic elements, it is exclusive and therefore not potentially democratic as democracy is potentially oligarchical. One must consider "some" *in* "all" rather than *opposed to* "all" in order to make all the possibilities manifest. Then one may find, for example, that in appointing from some (Aristotle gives examples only of appointing from some[31]), one achieves an oligarchic result whether or not the mode is vote or lot and whether or not all or some appoint, because "from some" is already a choice or vote. Thus all appointing by lot, if the "from all" is divided or ordered into "somes," have an oligarchic potentiality in which human choice need not be exercised to be realized. Thus, if the human race is divided into men of property and men of virtue, all appointing by lot will reflect and not suppress this distribution: these kinds of men will show up in the offices. And while ordering in the nature of the "all" from which men choose supports and even guides human choice, ordering in the appointers and the mode of appointment prevents nature from determining human choice. For the various "somes" can be scattered or fixed in a political-social hierarchy contrived to restrain them, and kept from dominating political deliberation. Human, that is, political ordering in offices (*archai*) prevents the beginning principle (*archē*) of nature from being distributed to, that is, from ruling, each individual human being. In offices, men free themselves from such determination by ordering themselves and thus regarding themselves, not nature or the gods, as the beginning principle. If we examine the "boundaries" of the three differences, it is evident that they collapse in the case of one citizen appointing himself, from all and from some and by vote and by lot: they collapse in the case of "kingship over all." Then the true boundary is in the need to escape the rule of one, when that "one" is our enslavement by bodily nature; and this need forces us to distinguish and also to mix choice and lot. Choice and lot are the plural *archai* which we can neither identify with each other nor hold separate and unmixed. We equate them at the peril of our freedom and fail to mix them at the risk of our security.

More precisely, it should be said that the differences must be "coupled" to retain both elements rather than "mixed" so that each element loses its identity.[32] The "joining" of deliberation must be arranged in the "coupling" of offices. Aristotle speaks next of "couplings" by which offices may be ordered, as some appointing to some and all to some, etc. This possibility reveals the duplex character of each ordering as a coupling of choice and lot, the deliberated and the given, the human and the natural. When men articulate their ordering, they couple their choices to nature's givens so that they can take advantage of nature's articulation of "all" into "somes" without surrendering to it. They can use the "others" who have necessary skills (1298a9, 28) without becoming enslaved to them if they couple the "others" with "all," thus transforming "others" into "somes"—or lot into nature. For the necessary "others," which first appear in contrast to what men would choose, become a "some" that men might be persuaded to couple with their choice. Now with the three differences, Aristotle says there will be four modes; and he rehearses them first from a democratic, then from an oligarchic, point of view (1300a23–33). In the democratic rehearsal, appointing to office in turn (*ana meros*) replaces appointing from some; but in the oligarchic, appointing is from some, not in turn. We seem to be advised that the fundamental issue between democracy and oligarchy, when both are moderated, is whether a group claiming to rule takes its turn or seeks to perpetuate itself in office as an exclusive "some." This statement of the case once again seems favorable to democracy for being the more moderate alternative. Oligarchy is oligarchy because if the "some" from which offices are filled is exclusive, it matters less that all appoint or that appointment is by lot. But democracy (properly understood) is a coupling of oligarchy with democracy, as is shown in the democratic practice of ruling in turn. Nonetheless, neither democracy nor oligarchy makes the other unnecessary, since democracy secures only rule in turn for the most choiceworthy regime and that most choiceworthy regime cannot perpetuate itself except with concessions to "lot." Thus the coupling of democracy and oligarchy in the ordering of offices points to the superiority of aristocracy in which the most choiceworthy regime of men is coupled with the natural principle (*archē*) which ensures that it will be chosen.[33]

There follows a list of seven modes described as to regime which confirms that aristocracy, the plural kingship of Book III, remains above this discussion. It remains, that is, and it is above. For neither democracy nor oligarchy can sustain the distinction between choice and lot on which both depend. When all appoint, the result is demotic whether the mode is by vote (= choice) or by lot, because in the demotic understanding no justification exists for choosing one man over another. In actual practice, "not all" (but not "some") appoint because democracies are swayed by demagogues or "preliminary councillors" who pre-deliberate for the demos; here a better result, which Aristotle calls "political," is possible. When some appoint, the result is oligarchical, again whether the mode is by vote or by lot. Oligarchs choose by wealth, which is often a matter of chance and anyway not a principle that can explain the dignity of choice. When the mode is both vote and lot, it is more oligarchical, Aristotle remarks. This mode is usually practiced because no difference is seen between vote and lot, or because most men (including democrats, of course) are oblivious to the element of lot in choice. For some to choose from all and some from some, or some by vote and some by lot is "political aristocratically," implying the intervention of someone, perhaps a political scientist, who mixes some and all or vote and lot consciously, with a view to the best. For this mode lot is retained because, as we have seen, from the standpoint of choice the best comes by lot. When some appoint from some, and the result from lot is not similar to that from vote, we again have oligarchy; but this time it would seem to be a self-constituted "some" (some from some), conscious of choosing. The last mode is some appointing from all, with no reservation for any "some"; and all appoint from some by vote. Aristotle calls this "aristocratic," and we interpret it as human choice that makes no presumption in its own favor followed by nature's (= all) choice of the best in accordance with human choice. It is the best result, the perfect coupling of oligarchy and democracy, of choice and lot; but does it occur? Aristotle merely leaves it for us as the boundary beyond which only monarchy remains and there are no offices to be ordered. As such, this mode need not be actual, yet it can guide the ordering of actual regimes.

At the end of this section on offices Aristotle says that the modes are so many in number and that which ones are beneficial for whom, and how appointments ought to be made, will be clear when the *powers* of offices are considered. Here he has abstracted the ordering of offices in actual regimes to place them in an abstract regime, combining modes as if they were numbers. This abstract regime is not equipped with a law to be executed, which would have to be human law generally or natural law; and so Aristotle is not called upon to produce an abstract or generalized executive power in the manner of John Locke. We may suppose that in his view a single law of this kind would make men heedless of the need to mix lot and choice.

Judging. The "remaining" part of regimes is judging or "dicasting" (the word for judging in a democratic assembly); Aristotle does not say it is "next" or "connected" as he said about offices to the deliberative part. He will consider the modes "under the same assumption," he says. That would be the assumption that he must treat the existing in order to bring the best into existence, in particular (in Book IV) the human body and the spirited part of the soul that speaks for the body in the soul. We therefore find no law stated by which men judge and no standard or *archē*, as in Book III, of "that according to which the king rules all things according to his own will" (1287a10, 35). For such a law to spirited men would seem to give support to their angry judgments, and they would misinterpret it so as to indulge their sweeping statements of democratic indiscrimination and arrogant, oligarchic assertiveness. Since Aristotle means to reform such men, he must remove that prop from their judgments temporarily until they learn to use them as a guide to moderation. This temporary unPlatonic separation of judging from the standard of judgment was also necessary, as we saw, to protect the right of human initiative in deliberation; but it is now needed all the more for the complementary purpose of enabling men to criticize what they do on their own.

The differences in courts, Aristotle says, are found in three "boundaries," from whom, about whom and how—meaning: whether they are drawn from all or some, how many forms of courts there are, and whether they are selected by lot or by vote. We note that as with the offices, the boundaries are again three; but the question of about whom men judge has replaced the question of those who appoint. Courts are distinct from

other offices or from offices in that the appointers are less important
than the judged, the end more important than the beginning. Aristotle
turns indeed to the boundary of about whom first, and answers his question of how many forms (*eidē*) of courts with curious precision: there are
eight. He lists them, and we are not surprised to see in this context that
the first is the court of audit or calling to account, the claim on one's
betters that men insist on making.

The first five forms of courts are made to form a group in Aristotle's
listing. They are, besides the court of audit, one for those who injure the
public, another for matters bearing on the regime, a fourth for rulers
and private men disputing about punishments, and fifth, disputes about
large private contracts.[34] Clearly these courts are oriented on the regime,
to suggest perhaps that men should call their rulers (or betters) to account
on behalf of the regime rather than merely to express outrage. This
standard of judgment can only be provisional, of course, because regimes
differ, but provisionally one might guess from the single example of an
Athenian court that the regime of these courts is democratic.[35] It might
be better to say, since in a sense democracy contains the other regimes,
that these courts are oriented on a non-partisan regime. Aristotle can
discuss the powers of courts and still maintain the formality of his analysis because courts, in contrast to other offices, are less relative to any
particular regime. The different forms of courts imposed by kinds of
crimes that do not at first glance appear very distinct divide the jurisdiction of a single court which might be closely identified with the regime.
They scatter judgments that might otherwise come too readily to a focus
on the safety of the regime, and they encourage moderation by requiring
the judges to attend to the kind of case. There is no court for cases of
impiety.[36]

Besides these five courts are three that are non-political, courts on
homicide, foreigners and small private contracts.[37] As regards the last,
Aristotle in his exactness believes that even small claims must come to
"judgment"[38] though not by a multitude of judges (= dicasts); the word
for judgment is now *krisis*, implying discrimination or separation. It is
noteworthy that judging as separation comes up in the least political of
the courts, for small sums have no political consequences. To judge and
to call others to account one must have a standard outside of oneself and
beyond the threat to one's own preservation. In this Aristotle disagrees
with Locke, who accorded every man a natural executive power of the
law of nature to exercise whenever he felt threatened and had no appeal
to government. For Aristotle, such an allowance does not take sufficient
account of the fact that "most are bad judges of their own interests"
(1280a16).[39] If they judge by the standard of what is good for the regime,
they achieve a certain distance from their own interest and a wider
perspective. Yet as the regime is nothing but an elaboration of their own

interest, they must be required further to judge by what is necessary for any regime, if not by the best regime. To judge by the common necessities of all regimes, however, they must have a notion of what is political and how it is related to what is non-political. For example, in judging homicide they must have a notion of the dignity of man and his place in nature; and in judging foreigners, they must have a notion of what makes men foreign to each other and therefore of what is foreign to man. These notions of the boundaries between the political and the non-political might be compared to contracts: private, because each man can judge for himself if he is free enough to call his rulers to account; and large or small according as they are commonplaces of a multitude or nice and exact understandings of a few.

Having left this reminder of the non-political, Aristotle returns to political courts and considers the "from whom" and the "how." He reminds the spirited men he is addressing that if such courts are not "nobly" conducted, regimes will suffer divisions and changes (1300b38). To avoid revolution, they must be willing to reform. As with offices, he lists modes of courts in two groups that are democratic and oligarchic but not so called. But with the courts, the oligarchical group of modes drawn from "some" is identified with the modes of those judging in turn or by section (*kata meros*); these were democratic modes of offices. When it comes to judging, that is, the oligarchs cannot be exclusive; they must regard themselves as a "some" that is a part within the whole. Aristotle concludes that the modes are divided into first the demotic, from all about all cases; second, the oligarchic, from some about all; and third, the aristocratic and political, some from all and some from some. In all this he has said nothing explicit about what judging is (though elsewhere he has[40]), but he has left something to be inferred. Judging seems to be discriminating on the basis of a standard, and that standard, if it is not merely to replicate the things being judged, if it is to allow a critical distance, must be non-political and non-human; it must be nature. In this regard, then, demotic courts would be those in which all things are judged from the standpoint of all nature; oligarchic, those in which all things are judged from a human standpoint; aristocratic and political, those in which some things are judged from the standpoint of nature, some from a human standpoint.[41]

Aristotle leaves us with the inevitability of the mixed regime, understood fundamentally as a mixture of choice and lot, or of deliberating and judging. Whereas deliberating is a social act of human initiative connected to offices, in which rulers "begin" the rule they choose for themselves, judging is a private act requiring that one separate himself from what he has begun, to achieve a critical detachment. When judging, one does not merely accept what one is given; one's "lot" may be rejected. But to reject it, one must rely on and accept some standard of judgment; so judging is accepting with the possibility of rejecting, an activity of thought that gives human recalcitrance its say but accepts the sovereignty of what is outside oneself, of nature. As deliberating implies a soul that can begin the motion of a man's body, judging implies a soul that can separate a man from his body, call him to account, and make him self-critical. While showing us that the mixed regime is inevitable, Aristotle only hints at how it might be just or noble (1300b38).

Powers and Offices. When we come to the reconsideration of offices at the end of Book VI, including Aristotle's only explicit discussion of the executive, we find the discussion of "powers" promised in Book IV (1300b8). The offices are now divided according to their powers into two main groups, the necessary offices and the noble ones. From this division we learn something more of the noble mixed regime than could be seen in the abstract modes discussed in Book IV. It appears that a noble regime must retain the distinction between the necessary and the noble. The reason, we can surmise, is that noble men distinguish themselves as noble from the ignoble, and their consciousness of the distinction is necessary to the definition of nobility. Nobility is visible because it must be visible to those defining themselves against the ignoble, and in Greek, conveniently, the word for "noble" (*kalos*) also means "beautiful."[42] But when the noble regime makes this concession to the (perhaps questionable) perception of noble men, it encounters the difficulty that the ignoble offices may be necessary because they are just. For justice can sometimes be ignoble, especially the justice of carrying out justice, of the imposition of penalties, or of the executive.

In order to retain the distinction between necessary and noble offices in the mixed regime, Aristotle must retain the distinction between choice and lot and must align the two distinctions. He must present choice as something noble, not merely deliberate, and keep it distinguished from lot in order to promote the nobility of not accepting one's lot. Thus the vulgar democratic spiritedness of nay-saying to what is good for you is transformed, or almost transformed, into a striving for the noble. In making his mixed regime noble, Aristotle allies himself with human dissatisfaction or indeed with human indignation. After the abstract regime at the end of Book IV, he takes up the regime in motion or revolution in Book V, which we must look at briefly.

Regimes are put in motion or suffer revolution for cause, and there are two kinds of cause, clearly but not explicitly marked out by Aristotle, corresponding to the difference between justice and nobility (1301a25–1301b5 and 1302a16–1303b17). The first kind is the single cause of all revolutions, which is the injustice of all existing regimes (1301a36). The imperfection of regimes would have an unfailing cause in the imperfection of human beings; and if this imperfection were viewed from a sufficient philosophic distance, one might conclude that revolutions cannot remedy human injustice and do not matter. Aristotle remarks that those superior in virtue, who would become revolutionaries with the most justice, are least inclined to do so, whereas those superior in birth (*genos*) make a claim to be unequal, and we may add, are most inclined to revolution with or without justice (1301a39–1301b5; 1304b5–6). The second kind of cause, then, describes the things that move most (non-philosophic) men to revolution, especially these noble honor-lovers.[43] In their indignation at the injustice or slights they receive the possibility of significant improvement or even perfection is implied, for it makes no sense to become angry at imperfections that cannot be corrected. This kind of cause is plural because it is occasioned by accidents (1303b17; see 1301a38; Book V abounds with fascinating examples) which are important to men. The philosophic view of revolution, from which revolutions merely exchange one system of injustice for another, must be combined with the perspective of political men striving to be noble and seeking honor, to whom changes of regime are all-important. With the philosophic view Aristotle can avoid inflating the expectations of political men, but the political view encourages reform and keeps the makers of reform occupied in wholesome or at least more constructive activity.

In Book VI the lovers of honor are presented with the noble opportunity of founding. But the regimes they are to found are democracy and oligarchy, nothing better, and democracy, which would surely be the last regime a founder would choose to found, receives first consideration and more ample discussion by far.[44] Aristotle does not bring up the mixed regime; instead, he says that since democracies and other regimes happen to exist, one must determine what is appropriate and beneficial for each (1316b39). As in Book V, where he advised how to preserve each regime (1304b20, 1307b27), so now he accepts that each regime will have what is appropriate (*oikeion*) to it and will not be required to sacrifice this to a mixed regime. This concession follows from his acceptance of the legitimacy of revolutionary indignation in Book V, for political indignation is partisan rather than neutral and detached. But in Book VI, the honor-lovers who are to bring the noble regime into existence are required, as founders, to combine the beneficial for each regime with the appropriate even if it is uncongenial to them as partisans. When the partisan takes on the responsibility of founder, he must swallow the bitter with the sweet, but he should be the more ready to do so as founding is more noble than partisanship and indeed as bitter tastes sweeter to the noble. They are confronted with the imaginary task of founding a democracy, and thus made to pretend that democracy is agreeable to them to the end that they will appreciate how it is beneficial to them as anti-democrats. The "greatest work" of the legislator is not only to construct a regime, but to make it to last, as it is not difficult to make a regime (perhaps in the dialogues of Plato?) for one or two or three days (1319b33–7). Making a regime to last, it turns out, especially requires finding resources and occupation or activity for the poor (1320a33–b16; 1267a10). In this subtle way the nobles are induced to exercise their nobility in ignoble necessities they would rather ignore. When they are at last given the opportunity of founding an oligarchy, they are merely told that oligarchy is the opposite of democracy; and in the congenial task of ordering for war, they are reminded of the political consequences of using the different military units and made to conform the order of war to the occupations of peace. As their last preparation for reconsidering the offices, Aristotle appeals to their sense of honor over their desire for profit, and he recommends to them the noble but expensive virtue of magnificence.[45]

The offices are given their powers, as compared with Book IV, now that the powers (*dunameis*) are understood as potentialities for noble men. The offices do not rule men as if they were external powers or laws from nature guaranteeing the regularity if not the perfection of human behavior. Rather, men must assume the offices and make the potentialities actual with their own virtuous activity. In their self-government, to repeat, they do not merely execute a rule or law that has its origin outside themselves. If this point seems obvious, it is because we take for granted the compatibility between ruling and freedom which Aristotle thinks necessary to connect through nobility. Noble men will be attracted by the difference between potentiality and actuality in the offices, providing what we call a "challenge." Thus they may be attracted even to the necessary offices without which it is impossible for the city to exist as well as to those providing good order and ornament without which it cannot be managed[46] nobly. Of the seventeen offices Aristotle lists twelve are called necessary, but the first two of these, offices for the market and for common and private properties in the city, have as an object additional to necessary cares the maintenance of good order (*eukosmia*). These offices, though necessary, may be ennobled or beautified to attract those who are attracted by the noble. With the executive, however, the difficulty is more severe.

On the list of necessary offices, the sixth, "almost the most necessary and the most difficult of the offices," is that "regarding deeds against the condemned and defaulters according to the lists and regarding the keeping of prisoners."[47] The office is difficult because it involves much odium; so no one undertakes it willingly except for great profit and those who do undertake it are unwilling to act in accordance with the laws. But it is a necessary office because there is no use in judgments of justice if they are not "exacted to their end" (*lambanein telos*).[48] This may be taken as Aristotle's expression for "execution." He has conceived the office and said that it was necessary, but since it cannot be beautified, he minimizes it. He does not expand it into the awesome modern executive by taking advantage of its odium to make it more powerful and more efficient. On the contrary, he counsels that this be not "one same office" but different offices from different courts, that one try to divide up offices concerning public notice of those written down as defaulters,[49] that judgments of outgoing magistrates be carried out by new ones, and that the doer (the executive) be other than the condemner. For, Aristotle says, the less odium there is for the doers, the more the deeds will be brought to their conclusion. When those who condemn and those who carry out are the same, there is twofold odium, and for the same ones to carry out all such judgments makes them enemies of all. But would they not be feared and respected by all?

It is difficult to dismiss the larger implications of the office which Aristotle admits could possibly be "one same office." If one person holds this "one same office" of condemning and executing, and of executing all judgments, and does so not until he is replaced but for all time in perpetuity, he would be a god, the chief god. Any human being who took this office with the necessary human limitations would be the imitator or executive of this god and his government a punitive theocracy. In Book III Aristotle said that ostracizing a man of outstanding virtue would be like claiming to rule over Zeus and partitioning his offices.[50] In Books IV to VI Aristotle himself does this precisely: he ostracizes the monarch in order to rule over Zeus by partitioning offices.

The difficulty in the office of executive is not merely that it is unattractive to the noble or the "respectable" because of the odium attached to it, but more that precisely because of this odium it is attractive to the "base." Speaking of one duty of the executive, the guarding of prisoners, Aristotle says that this must be kept separate from executing, and that although the respectable avoid it especially, yet it is not safe to make the base "sovereign," for rather than being capable of guarding others they themselves need a guard.[51] How could the base be made "sovereign" by being entrusted with the duties of jailers, duties which might seem particularly suited to give honest employment to disreputable characters? When Aristotle spoke of "the guards of prisoners" he said literally "the guards of bodies" (1322a2): is it not imaginable that, in keeping with the concern of Books IV to VI for the political importance of human bodies, all human government could be comprehended in the office of jailer? Here is a hint, but no more than a hint, of the outsized modern executive.

Aristotle has combatted the notion that to guard men one need only guard their bodies, and thus guard them as prisoners, but (as we have seen) there is some truth in it; and so to minimize the danger from base men—not the modest vulgar but the seekers of tyranny misled by false nobility—he minimizes the opportunities in this office. To do so he has supplied in a treatise on *Politics* an understanding of nature intended to reassure men and to moderate their angry desire to punish. Nature understood as unfriendly to men gives human justice no support and compels human government to imitate angry gods, to rely on fear as the motive for obedience, and to loose hatred against its enemies. This was Machiavelli's way but not Aristotle's. Aristotle asserted or discovered an understanding of nature favorable to human ends and the human good so as to avoid making the Machiavellian princes sovereign.

Notes

1. See the useful survey of scholarship by Renato Laurenti, *Genesi e Formazione della "Politica" di Aristotele* (Padova: Cedam, 1965), pp. 5–42. Richard Robinson says: "The fact is, probably, that the *Politics* is a collection of long essays and brief jottings pretending to be a treatise." *Aristotle's Politics, Books III and IV*, R. Robinson, ed. (Oxford: Clarendon Press, 1962), p. ix. *Cf.* Jean Aubonnet, ed., Aristotle, *Politique* (Paris: Les Belles Lettres, 1971), II 4; C. H. Rowe, "Aims and Methods in Aristotle's *Politics*," *Classical Quarterly*, 27 (1977), p. 160; and Carnes Lord, "The Character and Composition of Aristotle's *Politics*," *Political Theory*, 9 (1981), pp. 459–478. For Ernest Barker it is also a "fact" that the *Politics* is "a collection or conflation of different essays rather than a single treatise," but he warns that "differences of tone and emphasis . . . may well be merely the differences inherent in different contexts." Barker, trans., *The Politics of Aristotle* (New York: Oxford University Press, 1962), pp. xxxvii, xlvi. W. D. Ross, *Aristotle* (London: Longman's, 1923), p. 236; W. L. Newman, *The Politics of Aristotle*, (4 vols.; Oxford: Oxford University Press, 1902), II, xxix-xxxii.

2. See Harvey C. Mansfield, Jr., "The Ambivalence of Executive Power," in J. Bessette and J. Tulis, eds., *The Presidency in the Constitutional Order* (Baton Rouge: Louisiana State University Press, 1981), pp. 314–33.

3. On Book III of the *Politics*, see Leo Strauss, *The City and Man* (Chicago: Rand McNally, 1964), ch. 1; Harry V. Jaffa, "Aristotle," in Leo Strauss and Joseph Cropsey, eds., *History of Political Philosophy*, 2nd ed. (Chicago: Rand McNally, 1972), pp. 64–129; Delba Winthrop, "Aristotle and Political Responsibility," *Political Theory*, 3 (1975), pp. 406–22 and "Aristotle on Participatory Democracy," *Polity*, 11 (1978), pp. 151–71; Egon Braun, "Das dritte Buch der aristotelischen 'Politik': Interpretation," *Sitzungsberichte der Osterreichischen Akademie der Wissenschaften*, philos-hist. Kl., 247.4 (1965).

4. See note 1 above. Although the conclusion is as old as Nicholas Oresme, this has been *the* topic of twentieth-century scholarship on Aristotle's *Politics* since the publication of Werner Jaeger's study in the genetic method, *Aristoteles, Grundlegung einer Geschichte seiner Entwicklung* (Berlin, 1923).

5. M. J. C. Vile, *Constitutionalism and the Separation of Powers* (Oxford: Clarendon Press, 1967), p. 22. See Barker's warning, *The Politics of Aristotle* (p. 193n); Newman's discussion, *The Politics of Aristotle*, (IV, 236–38); and Eckart Schütrumpf, *Die Analyse der Polis durch Aristoteles* (Amsterdam: Grüner, 1980), p. 240n4.

6. *Politics* 1295a3; 1293b29. Barker does not translate it, and H. Rackham, Aristotle, *Politics*, (Loeb Library ed., Cambridge, MA, 1944) mistranslates, as do B. Jowett, *The Politics of Aristotle*, (Oxford: Oxford University Press, 1885), and J. E. C. Welldon, *The Politics of Aristotle*, (London: Longman's, 1897). Aubonnet has it correctly.

7. In our day this democratic attitude has been expressed by John Rawls: "No one deserves his greater natural capacity nor merits a more favorable starting place in society." *A Theory of Justice* (Cambridge, MA: Harvard University Press, 1971), p. 102. How then does a human being deserve his lot? "Human" rights as a whole, which depend on man's favored place in nature, must be undeserved.

8. The soul is more a part than is a body (*Politics* 1291a24) because it is a part of several possible wholes. See also 1278b8.

9. Earlier in Book IV, at 1291a27–31, he speaks of deliberating and judging as parts of the soul but not as ruling principles; here he discusses them together with the offices as ruling principles, but not as parts of the soul.

10. Again, in 1210a27–31, it is shown that deliberating and judging may be done in separate parts of the city or in the same part, but the offices, the element of polity, are lacking. In the intervening argument Aristotle shows that it is necessary to mix and how this may be done.

11. *Politics* 1297b38. Thus, as Barker says (p. 188n), Aristotle fulfills the next to last item on the program given near the beginning of Book IV at 1289b13–26. *Cf.* Newman, IV, 235.

12. To study an Aristotelian list, one must make an accurate translation with special attention to the prepositions and conjunctions that create sets. Aristotle says: "The deliberative is sovereign about war and peace and alliance and dissolution, and about laws, and about death and exile and confiscation, and the audits." (1289a4–7) The three "abouts" give three sets; the "ands" and the sense give five sets; and the items are nine. "Laws" are in the center of each.

13. *Politics* 1291a28, where the context would suggest joining the necessary and the noble.

14. See esp. *De Anima* 426b8–427a15, 432a16; *Metaphysics* 990a24, 995b2–4, 1008b2–1009a5; *Nic. Ethics* 1118a28, 1134a31, 1165a34; *Politics* 1289b11, 1291a40, 1321a30.

15. Such was the regime of the Milesian Telecles, whose political theory recalls the philosophical atomism of the far-famed Thales, also a Milesian (1298a13). Nothing is known of Telecles but this; Newman, IV, 241.

16. Not all, because all to some is in fact impossible, as is all to all. All will insist on making some deliberations but will not be sufficiently skilled, or interested, to make all deliberations. Pure democracy and pure oligarchy are impossible.

17. *Ath. Const.* 26.1, 18.1; *Politics* 1304b20, 1319b12; Thucydides, II 65.7.

18. In these lists it is shown that the several democracies and oligarchies can be understood together as either all democracies or all oligarchies, depending on the standard of judgment applied to them. Just as all regimes can be found in each, so each can be found in all. See 1291b30–1292b10 and 1292 b10–1293a35.

19. Thus a perfectly hooked or snub nose no longer looks like a nose, as Aristotle remarks in Book V, 1309b27–30.

20. *Politics* 1298a35: not "modes" (*tropoi*). "Some" are already a mode, that is, an ordering of all without reference to a whole.

21. As indicated by "if" instead of "when," 1298b7.

22. See *Politics* 1294b11 and 1273a18, 1317b21. Hobbes has it that lot (in view of the lot of primogeniture) is an aristocratic principle; *De Cive*, III, xviii.

23. *Politics* 1298b21: More precisely, the demos (philosophers) should deliberate with the notables (political men), and these with the multitude (the democracy).

24. Aristotle makes it explicit at the end of this section that his discussion has served to delimit both deliberation and sovereignty, *Politics* 1299a2–3; see *Nic. Ethics* 1112b33.

25. On priests, see *Politics* 1322b18, 1328b11, 1329a27, 1331b5; on chorus-sponsors, see 1276b5, 1309a19. Aristotle does not explain why priests et al. are not rulers (Aubonnet, II, 326n3 and Newman, IV, 256) because the matter is a delicate one.

26. *Eudemian Ethics* 1249b10–17; *Metaphysics* 982a18, 1072b2, 14; *Physics* 184a15.

27. "Ordering" is used first in the middle, then in the active; *Politics* 1299a27.

28. Aristotle says that the offices in the small city are like a spit-lampholder, a sword used by soldiers also as a lamp; perhaps an allusion to Plato's guardian who is also a philosopher, the philosopher-king; 1299b10. *Cf.* 1252b1 and Plato, *Republic* 496b (Newman, IV, 259).

29. *The Federalist* No. 72.

30. Plato, *Republic* 557d.

31. *Politics* 1300a17. Aristotle mentions that at Megara those only were eligible who returned together from exile and fought together against the demos. See *Metaphysics* 1046b29.

32. *Politics* 1300a20; *cf.* 1294a35–1294b40. See G. J. D. Aalders, "Die Mischverfassung und ihre historische Dokumentation in den *Politika* des Aristoteles," Fondation Hardt, *Entretiens sur l'Antiquité Classique*, 11 (1965), p. 209.

33. This addition is reflected in Aristotle's addition of the democratic and oligarchic modes. He says: "And so the modes become twelve, apart from the two combinations." The twelve modes can be counted with this key: 1) all 2) some 3) from all 4) from some 5) vote 6) lot 7) in turn. Thus: 135, 136, 145, 146, 175, 176; 235, 236, 245, 246, 275, 276. 145, 146, and 275, 276 are not given but ought to be counted: all from some and some from a section in turn. The two "combinations"—a) some in turn and some from all, and b) some by vote and some by lot—reflect the two standpoints of the chosen and the chooser: democracy and oligarchy. They are to be set apart because their separateness is overcome in aristocracy.

34. *Politics* 1300b20–35. On the meaning of "contracts," see *Nic. Ethics* 1131a1–9.

35. *Politics*, 1300b30. On the court at Phreatto, located in Piraeus (see *Ath Const.* 57.3), the judges were on shore and the culprits were on the ship, philosophers becoming political philosophers. *Cf.* the exiles returning to Megara, 1300a18; and Plato, *Republic* 558a.

36. Newman, IV, 269.

37. The eighth is set off from the first seven, reminding us that 8 is 7 + 1 as well as 9–1. *Politics* 1300b33.

38. Aristotle is thus much more exact in his courts than Hippodamos in his, which had exactness as their chief aim; 1268b4–22.

39. See also *Politics* 1281b31–1282a24, 1287a10–26; *Nic. Ethics* 1112b32, 1141b34. John Locke, *Two Treatises of Government*, II.7–13.

40. *De Anima* 926b8–927a15; *Metaphysics* 995b2–4, 1008b2–1009a5. *Cf.* Winthrop, "Aristotle on Parcipitatory Democracy," p. 170.

41. Aristotle does not mention what aristocratic and political courts judge *about* because in this rarefied consideration these "courts" must be about some things, though ordinary courts could be about all things as well.

42. Beauty of soul is not separable from beauty of body, and so Aristotle says, with some understatement, that it is "not so easy to see" as beauty of body; *Politics* 1254b39.

43. The two final causes given are gain and honor, but gain is indicated to be a cause by comparison with others, that is, when it is a matter of honor; *Politics* 1302a32–1302b2.

44. On democracy: *Politics* 1317a11–1320b17. On oligarchy: 1320b17–1321b3. Aristotle does not cite the example of Solon, who came from "the middle citizens" and founded a democracy; 1296a19. See *Ath Const.* 12–13.

45. *Politics* 1321a36–40; *cf.* 1318b17. Note that this virtue leads to the second necessary office of maintaining buildings that are falling down; 1321b20. It is also interesting that the gods do not maintain their own houses, and the eleventh office must be assigned this among other similar duties; 1322b22.

46. *Politics* 1321b8: *oikeisthai*, implying the management of one's own; this is something of a private task for the honor-lovers. It can also mean "settled in."

47. *Politics* 1321b41–1322a2. This office is *almost* the most necessary and difficult because the first office could be taken as that if "markets" are taken in the most extended sense as the traffic of human beings with all things.

48. *Politics* 1322a7; *Nic. Ethics* 1180a21. Newman (IV, 557) refers to Plato, *Crito*, 50b.

49. *Politics* 1322a10; *cf.* 1322a1. This strange category may include those who write about the *archai* in the more elevated sense; for in writing about the beginning principles of nature and men they can hardly avoid identifying them with the gods, as can Aristotle with his ambivalent writing.

50. *Politics* 1284b31. The eleventh office here is men caring for the gods, not executing their decrees; 1322b19.

51. *Politics* 1322a23–6. The base can make great profit out of guarding prisoners if to do this they rule, 1322a3. On the base, see 1254b1.

10

MACHIAVELLI AND CAESAR

Grant Mindle

CAESAR! NO OTHER NAME LOOMS SO LARGE IN THE ANNALS OF ROME, casting its shadow over both the republic it subjugated and the empire it fathered. It is as if the enmity between patrician and pleb, an enmity intrinsic to republican Rome, and the contest for preeminence which rent assunder the unity of its ruling class required for their resolution the phenomenon we have come to call Caesarism.

To attribute such significance to Caesar is but to follow the example of Machiavelli, for according to Machiavelli, inherent in the beginning of Rome were the seeds of Caesarism. The tumults between patrician and pleb were not just "the first cause" of Roman liberty and the ground of Roman greatness: they were also in time the cause of Roman servitude, the imposition of which coincided with the accession of Caesar.[1] Similarly, the Roman empire rested upon a foundation laid by Caesar. Writers were not permitted to speak freely of him, since to speak ill of Caesar would have been to impugn the legitimacy of those who "ruled under that name."[2]

Despite the significance Machiavelli attributes to Caesar, our theme —Machiavelli and Caesar—has attracted little attention. Although Machiavelli's thoughts on political corruption have been widely discussed, the man who epitomizes that corruption has largely been ignored. This oversight is unfortunate. Had more attention been paid to Machiavelli's treatment of Caesar, the mystery surrounding Machiavelli's intention and the manner in which he communicates that intention might have been illuminated: what Machiavelli says about Caesar is a clue to his thoughts on tyranny and ultimately morality, while how he says it is an indication of the method one should adopt when studying his works.

The principal text establishing Machiavelli's attitude towards tyrants in general and Caesar in particular is commonly assumed to be *Discourses* I, 10. And indeed, one need only consider its title—"The founders of a republic or a kingdom are as praiseworthy as those of a tyranny are blameworthy"—as well as its assertion that Caesar, as founder of a tyranny, is blameworthy, to appreciate why this assumption is so common and why this text constitutes for so many conclusive proof of Machiavelli's morality.

Indicative of the conventional approach to I, 10 are the following statements, the first by J. H. Whitfield, and the second by Quentin Skinner.

> Nevertheless in this page [I, 10] Machiavelli has let his political ide-
> als appear with exemplary candour....No chapter throws a better light
> upon the scope of a *vivere civile* than the famous *D*. I, x, which follows
> immediately on the chapter for Romulus, and which, because it is so
> typical of Machiavelli, criticism has often been anxious to deny, as irony,
> or ridicule.[3]

> Once again we find Machiavelli reiterating the same traditional
> themes. He emphasizes that no one should 'be deceived by Caesar's
> renown, since the truth about his rise to power is that 'he so successfully
> blinded the masses' that he made them 'unaware of the yoke which they
> themselves placed on their necks.' This enabled him to become 'Rome's
> first tyrant' and ensured that the city 'never again recovered its liberties.'
> ...And his ideal of civic virtue is supplied by Scipio, whose pattern of
> behavior he urges every private citizen to emulate, expressing the hope
> that each individual may learn 'to conduct himself in his fatherland
> rather as Scipio did than as Caesar.'[4]

Neither Whitfield nor Skinner analyzes the chapter as a whole, but let us
do so now.

The same subject—the criteria for awarding praise or blame—is
discussed in both *Discourses* I, 10, and *The Prince*, ch. 15, albeit with this
difference: in *The Prince*, men are said to judge one another on the basis
of certain qualities (e.g. liberality or stinginess), whereas in the *Discourses*,
these qualities or "virtues" are replaced by a list of thirteen accomplishments.[5] Most praiseworthy are the heads and orderers of religions. Second in rank are the founders of republics and kingdoms. Army commanders, writers, and those who excel in some art and its practice also
receive degrees of praise while those who overturn religions, destroy
kingdoms and republics or show themselves the enemies of virtue, letters,
and every art which brings utility and honor to mankind Machiavelli pro-
nounces infamous and detestable. In I, 10 no enumeration of the virtues
is necessary, because the preceding chapter has already established the
wisdom of judging every action according to its effects, or more precisely
"when the fact accuses, the effect excuses."[6] Not the fact that Romulus
murdered Remus, but the value of the end that murder was meant to
serve becomes the prime consideration. Besides, if Machiavelli had considered virtue, the wicked Severus might well have merited the highest
praise, for of those discussed in I, 10, he alone is called virtuous.[7]

Machiavelli's confidence in the criteria announced in I, 10 is evidenced by his assertion that no one, whether foolish or wise, wicked or
good, would—if required to choose—refrain from praising what is to be

praised or blaming what is to be blamed. Contrary to what one might expect, this consensus does not mean men are ready to avow the reasonableness of morality: "Almost all men deceived by a false good and a false glory allow themselves either voluntarily or ignorantly to fall into the ranks of those who merit more blame than praise." Knowledge of what is praiseworthy is rarely conducive to morality, because men embrace tyranny for the same reason they consider it blameworthy: the suspicion that tyrannical rule is profitable for the tyrant alone. To prove that crime does not pay, that the fate of tyrants is not to be envied, Machiavelli now advocates the reading of histories. It is from "the memories of ancient things" that the citizen of a republic learns to prefer Scipio to Caesar, and the subject of a monarchy Agesilaus, Timoleon, and Dion to Nabis, Phalarus, and Dionysius.[8] Whoever reads history, Machiavelli says, would see the former showered with praise and the latter dismissed with scorn; he would see that although Timoleon and the others had no less authority in their fatherland than Dionysius and Phalarus, they had more security.

Given Machiavelli's definition of tyranny—the wielding of "absolute power,"[9] his assertion that Agesilaus and the others had no less authority than the tyrants Phalarus and Dionysius raises more questions than it answers. Can a man who wields absolute power be called a king? Are tyrants to be distinguished from kings solely on the basis of their historical reputation and the security of their reign? And why does Machiavelli go out of his way to include examples which are to say the least inapt? Agesilaus was no paragon; Dion, the victim of a conspiracy; Nabis, with regard to security, a model for princes everywhere; and Dionysius, a tyrant who eluded his just deserts.[10] An argument relying on such examples is hardly convincing. How to reconcile absolute authority, glory, and security—and not the disavowal of that authority for the sake of glory and security—is the theme of this history. The introduction of Caesar merely adds to the confusion, for Caesar, perhaps more than any other, symbolizes the union of these ends.

> Nor should anyone be deceived by the *glory* of Caesar, hearing him especially celebrated by writers; because those who praise him are corrupted by his fortune and frightened by the length [security?] of his imperium, which being supported under that name did not permit writers to speak freely of him. But whoever wishes to know what free writers would say of him should look to what they say about Cataline (my emphasis).[11]

Tyranny was initially repudiated on the grounds that the tyrant never notices "how much fame, how much glory, how much honor, security, and tranquility of mind he is fleeing and how much infamy, blame, censure, peril, and inquietude he is incurring": tyranny was repudiated not for failing to secure the common good, but for failing to secure the private good of tyrants. But consider Caesar's private good. He acquired absolute authority, glory (though some concealed blame), and founded an empire whose longevity frightened his enemies and whose emperors were obliged to reign under his name. No wonder Machiavelli insists we compare Scipio and not Brutus with Caesar.[12]

The example of Caesar is also confusing for another reason: the doubts it raises about Machiavelli's original analysis of praise and blame. The glory of Caesar is proof that knowledge of what is praiseworthy is not as evident as we were led to believe, that many are indeed so foolish or so wicked as to praise what is to be blamed. Since corruption and fear give rise to undeserved praise, the dichotomy of praise or blame must be replaced by the dichotomy of corrupt and fearful or free. Or are the free also fearful? Free writers blamed Caesar esoterically in order to tell the truth without jeopardizing their security.[13]

How does one judge a man who has the power to command praise? Unwilling to rate Caesar according to his reputation, Machiavelli judges Caesar by the consequences of his actions, in particular by the empire he founded. This is why the remainder of I, 10 ignores the life of Caesar, and studies instead the lives of Caesar's heirs. "Whoever becomes prince in a republic" (an odd expression) is asked to consider how much more praise the good emperors merited than those who lived otherwise. But more important than praise or blame is the emperor's security; the good emperors, Titus, Nerva, Trajan, Hadrian, Antoninus, and Marcus were more secure and less dependent upon their legions than Caligula, Nero, Vitellius, and the other wicked emperors. Were this history well considered, it would be sufficient instruction to show any prince the way of glory or of infamy, of security or of fear, because of the twenty-six emperors from Caesar to Maximinus, sixteen were assassinated and ten died ordinarily. And yet goodness alone is no guarantee of dying ordinarily and wickedness entails no punishment if, like Severus, the wicked emperor enjoys great fortune and virtue. First impressions notwithstanding, "the lesson of this history" does not concern the value of goodness, but "how to order a kingdom." All the emperors who succeeded to the throne by heredity, except Titus, were wicked; all those who acquired the throne by adoption were good, as were the five from Nerva to Marcus.[14] From the foregoing we infer that "whoever becomes prince in a republic" (Caesar?) may set aside the precept to preserve republics, and found an empire provided that adoption becomes the formula for succession. Caesar merits blame not for destroying the Roman republic, but for failing to order his kingdom well.[15] Perhaps the blame is not Caesar's alone. Did the good emperors, especially Marcus, not exhibit the same lack of foresight?

To facilitate his analysis of Caesar's empire, Machiavelli divides imperial Rome into three periods, the central one comprising the times from Nerva to Marcus, the golden age when one could hold and defend whatever opinion he wished.[16] A moment's reflection upon the war, sedition, and cruelty which preceded Nerva's and succeeded Marcus' reign is said to show "how much Rome, Italy, and the world owed to Caesar."[17] So beguiling is the rhetoric employed here that no one seems to have noticed the poverty of Machiavelli's argument. How can Caesar be responsible only for the times preceding Nerva and succeeding Marcus? Why not hold him responsible for the Roman empire as a whole, for all its emperors good and wicked, all of them having ruled under that name. Having ignored the peaceful reign of Caesar's adopted heir, Augustus, Machiavelli has the audacity to hold him responsible for the misery following Marcus' death 224 years later. Is Caesar responsible for Marcus' failure to disinherit his worthless son and adopt a worthy successor?[18]

Near the end of I, 10 we are invited to compare Caesar's handiwork, the Roman empire, with Romulus' (the Roman republic?).[19] "And truly a prince looking for the glory of the world would desire to possess a corrupt city, not to ruin it altogether like Caesar, but to reorder it like Romulus." Why the creation of the Roman empire cannot be called a reordering is never explained, nor does Machiavelli explain why the good emperors did not reorder Rome when it was in their possession, especially since "the heavens cannot give men a greater occasion for glory nor can men desire anything better than this." How can Machiavelli denounce Caesar for his failure to reorder Rome without implicitly denouncing the good emperors as well? How can Machiavelli praise the times from Nerva to Marcus more highly than any other period in Roman history without casting doubt upon the superiority of Romulus' handiwork to Caesar's?

Caesar is condemned, but the inadequacy of the argument condemning him foreshadows the rehabilitation of his reputation in the chapters which follow. In I, 10 Caesar was the enemy of a just and decent populace, a tyrant who put an end to their liberty, but in I, 17 he is the people's champion, his tyranny invisible, and the people themselves are now so corrupt that "the authority and severity of Brutus with all the eastern legions were not enough to keep them disposed to desire that liberty be maintained which he in the manner of the first Brutus had returned to them." Corrupted by the party of Marius, and blinded by Caesar, the people "never noticed the yoke which they themselves placed on their necks." Responsibility for the death of Roman liberty belongs to the people as well as Caesar, his wickedness mirroring their corruption. Considering the circumstances, even a Caesar dedicated to the preservation of Roman liberty could not have prolonged that liberty beyond his lifetime, and thus it makes no sense to hold Caesar liable for what happened to Rome after his death, let alone after Marcus' death.[20]

The next reference to Caesar occurs in I, 29, a chapter entitled "Which is more ungrateful, a people or a prince?" A free city, Machiavelli observes, has two ends, conquest and the preservation of its liberty, and it errs by loving the one or the other too much. With regard to liberty, citizens err when they offend those they ought to reward or suspect those in whom they ought to have confidence, and in a corrupt republic these errors may lead to tyranny "as happened in Rome when Caesar took by force what ingratitude denied him."[21] In I, 29 responsibility for the death of Roman liberty rests exclusively with the Roman people, their corruption and ingratitude having provoked Caesar to take by force what was his by right. The reversal of Machiavelli's argument is now complete, Caesar having become the victim, and Rome, the criminal. Lest one doubt Caesar's right to punish Rome for its ingratitude the following chapter includes this acknowledgement: a victorious general who fears the ingratitude of his lord may conspire against him.[22]

Machiavelli's attitude towards tyrants and tyrannies is more complex than Skinner or Whitfield would have us believe, According to Whitfield, "Machiavelli never dreamt of giving other counsel to a tyrant than the wise one, to lay down his tyranny."[23] But where does Machiavelli offer this advice? In I, 10 he says, "And if to order well a city one had to give up the principate, one would merit some excuse for not ordering it."[24] In I, 40 the accidents responsible for the creation of the Decemvirate are discussed since they merit consideration "by those wishing to maintain a free republic as well as those designing its subjection." The discussion that follows is testimony to Machiavelli's impartiality, a demonstration of his willingness to teach the good as well as the wicked how to attain their objective, for by disclosing the "errors made by Appius, the head of the Decemvirate, which were prejudicial to the tyranny he was proposing to establish," Machiavelli shows us how Appius (or those eager to imitate Appius) could have succeeded. Even when Machiavelli takes sides one notices a certain impartiality since the target of his criticism is not the nature of a man's desires, but his ignorance of the means necessary to satisfy those desires; for example, he rebukes Appius for his inability to establish a tyranny, not for his desire to do so.[25] After observing in III, 6 the reluctance of tyrants to put aside their tyranny—this is probably the passage Whitfield had in mind—Machiavelli goes on the show how such men can protect themselves from those disposed to conspire against them.[26] In III, 8 those who desire to establish a tyranny are advised to consider what the times permit and adjust their behavior accordingly (like Caesar?).[27] Especially fascinating, however, is the last sentence of I, 25: "the one who wishes to establish an absolute power, what by authors is called a tyranny, must renovate everything as will be said in the following chapter." But instead of discussing tyranny—the words "tyrant," "tyranny," and "absolute power" never occur in I, 26—Machiavelli discusses how a new prince in a new state ought to behave, and thereby gives us to understand that this new prince is equivalent to what was customarily meant by the word "tyrant."[28] Once this relationship is appreciated it comes as no surprise that Severus, the virtuous and tyrannical emperor denounced in I, 10, should be in *The Prince* a model for founders.

> Since they were new princes, it was useless and harmful to wish to imitate Marcus....a new prince in a new state cannot imitate the actions of Marcus, nor is it even necessary to follow those of Severus; but he must take from Severus those parts which are necessary to found his state and from Marcus those which are fitting and glorious to preserve a state which is already established and firm.[29]

Since founding seems to require the kind of behavior one is tempted to call tyrannical, a closer examination of founders, in particular Romulus, the founder Machiavelli compares with Caesar, is likely to be enlightening. According to the title of *Discourses* I, 9—the only chapter principally devoted to Romulus and the one immediately preceding Machiavelli's first reference to Caesar—"it is necessary to be alone to wish to order a republic anew or to reform it altogether outside of its ancient orders." It was Romulus' recognition of this necessity which induced him to kill his brother, Remus, and later to consent to the death of Titus Tatius. But if "being alone" means, as it seems to mean here, being able to introduce new orders without the consent of others, how does it differ from the possession of absolute power or "what by authors is called tyranny?"

> However a prudent orderer of a republic who has this spirit of wishing to govern not for himself but for the common good, not for his own success but for the common fatherland must contrive to have sole authority.[30]

Because a tyrant would also contrive to have sole authority, and would, if he were prudent, profess a desire to govern for the common good, a tyrant cannot be distinguished from a "prudent orderer" by the extent of his authority, by his profession of goodness, or even by his use of violence, for both are violent.[31] This is why Machiavelli asks us to consider the end a man's violence is meant to serve, whether its purpose is to mend or to destroy as well as the degree of authority he bequeaths to his successors.[32] "The prudent and virtuous" are determined to prevent their successors from enjoying the same degree of authority they enjoyed, for they realize that men, being more prone to evil than to good, are liable to use ambitiously the authority they had used virtuously, and that the many, though incapable of ordering a republic themselves, are more disposed to maintaining those orders once they have been established.

"The prudent and virtuous" are thus doubly alone, their authority exceeding that of both their contemporaries and their successors, a feat which seems to presuppose the possibility of extending one's reign beyond one's lifetime (cf. Caesar, whose successors ruled under that name).

To be alone is to rule over not only the present, but also the future, and since this requires the cooperation of others, "the prudent orderer" must arrange his kingdom or republic so that his successors will have a stake in the perpetuation of his enterprise.[33] That Romulus should be excused for the death of his brother and of his companion, Titus Tatius, and that this was done for the sake of the common good, and not for his own ambition is demonstrated by his having immediately ordered a Senate with which he consulted and according to whose opinion he deliberated, reserving for himself merely the command of the armies and the right to convoke the senate. Indeed, Romulus' orders were so favorable to a civil and free life that when Rome became free the only innovation necessary was to replace its perpetual king with two consuls elected annually.[34]

Before we join Machiavelli in singing Romulus' praises, it is well to consider more carefully both the evidence Machiavelli adduces on his behalf and the relation of his interpretation of these events to that of his source, Livy. According to Machiavelli the deaths of Remus and Titus Tatius were the consequence of Romulus' desire to govern for the common good, for one must be alone to order a republic anew.[35] But according to Livy, having resolved to found a city, Romulus and Remus found themselves unable to agree on what its name and who its king should be. Since the right to rule could not be adjudicated on the basis of age, for they were twins, it was agreed that the gods should choose by augury. Remus received the first augury, the flight of six vultures, Romulus the second, the flight of twelve, whereupon each claimed priority, Remus because his omen was first, Romulus because his was larger. A fight broke out, and Romulus slew Remus. Also reported by Livy is the more common story that Remus "leaped over the walls in mockery of his brother whereupon Romulus in great anger slew him."[36] Machiavelli's claim that Romulus killed Remus to secure the common good is sheer fabrication, the intention and the reasoning he attributes to Romulus having no basis in Livy's text. With regard to Titus, Livy reports that his failure to punish his kinsmen for their mistreatment of some Laurentian envoys after the Laurentians sought redress under the law of nations stirred such indignation that when Titus came to Lavinium for the annual sacrifice "a mob came together and killed him." Romulus' complicity is limited to the observation that Titus' death "is said to have awakened less resentment than was proper, whether owing to the disloyalty that attends a divided rule, or because he thought Titus had been not unjustly slain."[37]

In I, 9 Machiavelli reconstructs Romulus' intention in the light of the institutions he founded. But once again, Machiavelli's account bears little resemblance to Livy's. Although Livy credits Romulus with the creation of the senate, he never indicates the extent of its powers, nor does he substantiate Machiavelli's claim that Romulus reserved for himself merely the command of the armies and the right to convoke the senate. Apart from its creation, the senate is mentioned but twice.

> So, on the advice of the senate, Romulus sent envoys round among all the neighboring nations to solicit for the new people an alliance and the privilege of intermarrying.[38]
> [Romulus] was more liked by the commons than by the senate...As [he]was holding a muster...suddenly a storm came up, with loud claps of thunder, and enveloped him in a cloud so thick to hide him from the sight of the assembly; and from that moment Romulus was no more on earth....[the soldiers] readily believed the assertion of the senators, who had been standing next to Romulus, that he had been caught up on high in the blast....There were some, I believe, even then who secretly asserted that the king had been rent in pieces by the hands of the senators.[39]

Like Caesar, Romulus was a favorite of the commons, and like Caesar he was killed by the senate. But unlike Caesar, the commons never avenged his death, for they believed the senators when they said he had become a god. If, as Machiavelli claims, the powers Romulus reserved for himself were severely limited, then his murder at the hands of the senators and the struggle they engaged in after his death "for the coveted kingship" are to say the least peculiar.[40]

Romulus was no republican, and the institutions he founded were less amenable to republicanism than an initial reading of I, 9 might lead one to believe. Near the beginning of the chapter Romulus is called "a founder of a free life," and near the end he is juxtaposed with the one who wishes "to order a republic," but in the middle Romulus' orders are characterized as "more compatible with a free and civil life than with an absolute and tyrannical one." What "compatible with a free life" means had been explained in I, 2.

> For Romulus and all the other kings made many and good laws quite compatible with a free life: but because *their end was to found a kingdom and not a republic*, when that city became free they lacked many things that were necessary to order in favor of liberty which had not been ordered by those kings (my emphasis).[41]

Not only does the account of Romulus' intention in I, 9 and 10 overlook the role fortune played in the creation of the Roman republic, but Machiavelli regularly treats the accidental as if it were the product of conscious intention. The accidental death of Titus Tatius is treated as murder, as one step in Romulus' plan to found the Roman republic though no evidence for such a plan exists. In I, 19 Rome is said to have been extremely *fortunate* to have had first a fierce and warlike king (Romulus), then a peaceful and religious one (Numa), and finally a third similar in ferocity to the first (Tullus); had the order of succession been otherwise, Rome would have become effeminate and the prey of it neighbors.[42] But if the succession of Roman kings was purely accidental, then Romulus no less than Caesar failed to guarantee the virtue of his successors.[43] Indeed, had the monarchy not been abolished, Rome would have quickly become weak and inconsequential. Had the corruption of the kings spread to the populace, the creation of the Roman republic would have been impossible, and without that republic the effect which excuses the deaths of Remus and Titus would not exist.

To appreciate just how much violence Machiavelli is prepared to excuse, one must consider the only other example discussed in I, 9: the conduct of king Cleomenes. Agis, Cleomenes' predecessor, having decided that Sparta's departure from the laws of Lycurgus was responsible for the decay of its virtue and this in turn for the decline of its power and empire, attempted to reinstitute "those limits within which the laws of Lycurgus had [once] confined them." But the ephors, Sparta's senators, fearing that Agis desired to establish a tyranny, killed him while the project was still in its initial stages.[44] Inspired by "the records and writings" of Agis, Cleomenes undertook to restore the laws of Lycurgus, but this time with the recognition that "he would not be able to do this good for his fatherland without becoming the sole authority." Since the acquisition of that authority required the extirpation of all opposition, Cleomenes began his restoration of Spartan virtue by murdering the ephors and anyone else who might conceivably oppose him. His project, though "just and praiseworthy," was never brought to fruition, because shortly thereafter Sparta succumbed to the assaults of the Macedonians. Despite Cleomenes' failure to produce the effect necessary to excuse his violence, his conduct remains a model for others. Plutarch, the source of Machiavelli's example, is less sanguine about Cleomenes' justice.

> For to use the knife, unless under extremest necessity, is neither good surgery nor wise policy, but in both cases mere unskillfulness, and in the latter unjust as well as unfeeling.[45]

One would never know from Machiavelli's summary that Agis nearly succeeded in restoring the laws of Lycurgus without resorting to violence; nor does Machiavelli report the opinion of Plutarch, that Cleomenes should be censured for resorting to violence without first ascertaining whether persuasion alone was sufficient.[46] The Machiavellian maxim, "to order a republic it is necessary to be alone," and its corollary, "when the fact accuses, the effect excuses," constitute a repudiation of speech and persuasion, and an exhortation to whoever believes his country requires reordering and believes himself capable of executing that reordering to murder those who stand in his way. In short, the founder is entitled to regard disagreement, honest or otherwise, as criminal and worthy of capital punishment. Lest we forget, Remus' only crime, at least according to Machiavelli's account, was to have been Romulus' brother, Titus Tatius' to have been chosen by Romulus to rule jointly with him.[47]

When a prince murders his rivals in order to be alone and claims such actions are necessary to promote the common good, what are we to think? Must we allow him time to consolidate his authority and produce the good effects necessary to excuse his apparent criminality? Perhaps Brutus was too quick to condemn Caesar! Suppose the prince who adopts Machiavelli's counsel misjudges his capacity to promote the common good, to produce the effects necessary to excuse his "crimes," what then? By teaching men to acquire sole authority, to ride roughshod over their opposition in the name of some common good to be established in the future, Machiavelli blurs the dichotomy of prince or tyrant since the present actions of the prince are indistinguishable from those of the tyrant. Nowhere is this blurring more explicit than in the famous eighth chapter of *The Prince*, a chapter entitled "On those who have become princes through iniquity." There we learn that Agathocles the Sicilian became king of Syracuse by arranging for the soldiers under his command to kill the senators and the richest citizens. Because the cruelties he committed were well used, that is performed all at once in order to assure his position and then converted to the utility of his subjects, Agathocles was able to remedy his position with God and man.[48]

If the murder of one's rivals may be excused by subsequent beneficence, then the prince need not take his bearings from the praise or blame of his contemporaries. The effectual truth of Machiavelli's teaching in the fifteenth chapter of *The Prince* and in I, 9 and 10 of the *Discourses* is the repudiation of praise and blame as a guide for human behavior. In *The Prince* praise and blame are repudiated in the name of the individual's self-preservation; because a man who wishes to make a "profession of good" in all things will fall to ruin among so many who are not good, a prince ought not to be concerned with incurring the infamy of those vices without which it would be difficult (though perhaps not impossible) to preserve his state. But in the *Discourses* the chapter (I, 9) advising the prince to disregard ordinary morality is followed by one (I, 10) advising him to consider the praise allotted *by historians* to the founders of a republic or a kingdom.

The culmination of I, 10 is its comparison of Romulus with Caesar, the perfect prince with the perfect tyrant. But the contrast is more apparent than real, because the argument praising Romulus and the one condemning Caesar are defective. The perspective of I, 10 is plebeian, that is, one in which praise and blame, good and evil are idealized and personified.[49] Indeed, the plebeian character of its argument is foreshadowed by its title—"The founders of a republic or a kingdom are as praiseworthy as those of a tyranny are blameworthy," a title which recognizes only three kinds of government: republican, monarchical, and tyrannical. The omission of a wicked analogue to republicanism corresponds to the chapter's abstraction from the problem posed by popular corruption.

The argument in I, 10 treats the people as if they were superfluous, assigning all praise or blame, all responsibility to the prince alone, even going so far as to hold him responsible for events transpiring centuries after his death. But to focus such praise or blame is reasonable only if the prince is indeed alone, and only if the people are essentially passive, mere material to be stamped with whatever form the prince desires. The plebeian view of the ruling class rests on the tacit premise that the people are passive, that the people never rule, that the people are absolved of all political responsibility. As a body the people are weak, acquiring strength only when they select a spokesman and delegate to him the authority to speak and act on their behalf.[50] It is because the people can only speak and act through another that all government, whether it be republican, monarchical or tyrannical, is essentially princely, and it is the princely character of all government which explains and justifies Machiavelli's use of the expression "whoever becomes prince in a republic" as well as his failure to cite a single republican founder in I, 9 and 10, a remarkable omission considering their titles.[51]

The princely character of all government is disguised when the people choose a champion to represent their interests and combat their enemies. Caesar was such a champion, although the practice antedates Caesar, and has its origin with Marius and the controversy surrounding Rome's agrarian law.[52] The plebs staked their reputation on Marius, electing him consul four times while the nobility, to combat the plebs, turned to Sulla and made him the head of their party.[53] The politics of Rome thus became a contest for preeminence between the heads of two parties, each symbolizing the interests and aspirations of his class.[54]

In time the plebs began "to worship" those capable of overcoming the nobility, completely oblivious to the danger lurking behind their desire for revenge.[55] "And when a people is induced to make this error, of giving reputation to one because he opposes those they hold in odium, and that one is wise, it will always happen that he will become tyrant of that city."[56] Blinded by their hatred of the nobility, the plebs were led to adopt a dangerous expedient, the conferral of excessive reputation or praise. So overjoyed were they by Caesar's ability to wreak havoc on the nobility that the plebs never "noticed the yoke they themselves placed on their own necks," the authority they delegated to Caesar eventually becoming the instrument of their own oppression. The nobility were no less immune from self-deception, admiration for Caesar's virtue leading Pompey and others to grant him such favor that before long that admiration turned to fear. As evidence, Machiavelli cites the judgment of Cicero: "Pompey had too late began to fear Caesar" (I, 33). Impelled by fear to devise some remedy for the authority Caesar had acquired, their attempt to retract the authority they had already given merely accelerated the republic's ruin.[57]

Rome owes its destruction as much if not more to its virtues than to its vices, the seeds of its destruction having been concealed within the virtues exhibited by its leading citizens. Not the empirical observation that praise and blame are ineffectual, but the discovery that the worship of virtue (or more precisely the authority a reputation for virtue procures) leads to oppression is the justification for Machiavelli's repudiation of praise and blame as understood by others. Perhaps this is why the list of accomplishments with which I, 10 begins fails to praise "the lovers of virtue," though it does blame "the enemies of *virtú*."[58] This point of view culminates in the assertion that there are no unmixed goods, no idealizations and personifications of good or evil, no virtue without its accompanying vice.[59] That virtue or goodness may be the cause of evil is confirmed by an unexpected source: Caesar. In I, 46 Machiavelli calls the saying Sallust put in the mouth of Caesar very true: "all evil examples stem from good beginnings."[60] Because men are easily deceived, especially by an act which appears to be virtuous, they do nothing about it when in fact they ought "to pay attention to the works of citizens, because many times under a pious work a beginning of tyranny is hidden."[61] Virtue is more akin to tyranny than many have imagined since virtue, however it is understood, and self-aggrandizement are inseparable. This is so, because even the denial of self-aggrandizement is a form of self-aggrandizement, a relation beautifully illustrated by the letter of Cicero's cited in I, 33 and mentioned above: "I am doing nothing in a spirit of self-aggrandizement, and my influence is by so much the more esteemed."[62] Classical political science tried to distinguish virtue from self-aggrandizement by defining a tyrant as one who attends to the common good only when it coincides with his private advantage.[63] But once this distinction is understood to be illusory, then politics becomes at its best the management of self-aggrandizement, the management of tyranny.

Machiavelli's rejection of the classical dichotomy is evidenced by his blending of virtue with self-preservation (ch. 15) or security (I, 10), a blending Machiavelli calls "*virtú*." Not the subordination of self-interest to virtue in the name of what is noble, but the denial that such a subordination is possible is the implication of Machiavelli's analysis of virtue.[64] Since all human action is self-aggrandizement, what matters is how that self-aggrandizement is disguised.[65] The motives and actions of Romulus and Caesar were similar, but their reputations differed, the explanation for this disparity being the power of literary men to color our interpretation of their conduct. Caesar's reputation suffered because he dominated but never transformed altogether the opinions of literary men, because his rule was less absolute, less revolutionary than necessary. Near the beginning of I, 10 literary men "are joined" to those army commanders who have increased their kingdom or fatherland, perhaps because self-aggrandizement is perfected when it is disguised and excused via interpretation: "After these are celebrated those who at the head of armies have increased their kingdom or fatherland. To these are joined literary men…"

By treating Romulus and Caesar antithetically, at least initially, Machiavelli intimates the primacy of propaganda, for the reduction of all human action to self-aggrandizement means that all interpretation, be it praise or blame, is merely propaganda. The propagandists *par excellence* are the heads and orderers of religions; the founders of republics or kingdoms are second in rank since they must bow to the regnant morality, for only those who create the standards of praise and blame by which their achievements are appraised are truly alone. The men Machiavelli calls "most praiseworthy" ("Among all men praised, the most praiseworthy are those who have been the heads and orderers of religions") are never discussed in I, 10, perhaps because the most comprehensive form of self-aggrandizement is also the least conspicuous. When a literary or religious innovation succeeds, its author necessarily appears subordinate to the standards he authors, and this subordination allows him to disguise and excuse his self-aggrandizement.

The validity of this analysis is confirmed not only by Machiavelli's strange references to writings and writers in I, 9 and 10, but also by his treatment of religion in the five succeeding chapters. In I, 11 religion is presented as a ruse legislators employ to ennoble their private judgments by cloaking them under the mantle of God's majesty, a ruse whose necessity is deduced from the observation that "many goods are known by a prudent man which do not have in themselves the evident reasons apt to persuade others." Distrustful of his own authority, Numa feigned converse with a nymph so as to induce the Roman people to adopt the new institutions he deemed necessary. Besides being a source of authority, religion is also the means by which a founder can prolong his authority beyond his lifetime and assume responsibility for "the health of a republic or of a kingdom" after his death. Finally, religion, not unlike the maxim of I, 9 ("when the fact accuses, the effect excuses") offers a doctrine about man's future well-being which serves to excuse and justify present injustices.[66] Indeed, what is most impressive about religion is its ability to excuse what men would otherwise judge inexcusable. But since religion can also excuse the unreasonable as such, it should come as no surprise that the theme of I, 12–15 proves to be the management and mismanagement of religion.

Machiavelli's judgment of Caesar is more favorable than an initial reading of the *Discourses* might lead one to believe, for the condemnation of Caesar in I, 10 is as striking as it is misleading. The truth about Caesar cannot be revealed all at once, since the deception Machiavelli practices in I, 10 is no less essential to his purpose than its subtle unmasking in the chapters which follow. The condemnation of Caesar constitutes "proof" of Machiavelli's morality, and by providing such "proof" Machiavelli makes it possible for those who cherish morality to condemn Caesar and embrace Romulus without ever realizing that the motives and actions of the two are indistinguishable. In short, the condemnation of Caesar is intended to induce the reader to sanction conduct he would otherwise condemn, while the gradual rehabilitation of Caesar's reputation allows those who need no pacifier to appreciate the truth about Machiavelli's teaching.

Machiavelli's failure to provide a principle which allows us to distinguish Caesar from Romulus or monarchy from tyranny is a sign of his impartiality. Another sign of that impartiality is the movement of *The Prince* and the *Discourses* as a whole. *The Prince* has a dry, scholastic beginning, one in which principalities are classified according to their mode of acquisition, and "the reasoning about republics" is set aside.[67] Yet despite its conservative and monarchical beginning, its final chapter is revolutionary and patriotic, culminating in a rousing quotation from a patriotic poem of Petrarch's declaring that "the ancient valor in Italian hearts is not yet dead." The celebration of principalities, princes, and princely virtues with which *The Prince* begins is eventually replaced by a kind of republicanism, by a celebration of popular virtue. Thus the movement of *The Prince* is from monarchy to a kind of republicanism. The *Discourses* mirrors this movement, beginning with a rousing exhortation to resurrect republicanism and republican virtue, since "of that ancient valor no sign remains."[68] Although that resurrection ought to culminate in an equally rousing call to arms, the *Discourses* offers instead a dispassionate conclusion, its final chapter celebrating Fabius Maximus, not the Roman people.[69] Indeed, Fabius earned the title "Maximus," because he alone recognized the need and devised the means to restrict the rights which Rome's newest citizens might enjoy. The celebration of republicanism and republican virtue with which the *Discourses* begins is eventually replaced by a celebration of one man, Fabius Maximus, and the petty oligarchical trick he devised, and thus the movement of the *Discourses* is from republicanism to a kind of monarchy.

The movement of *The Prince* and its reflection in the *Discourses* elicit the following query: Is the dichotomy of monarchy or republicanism as illusory as the dichotomy of monarchy or tyranny? Such a query might seem absurd given the opening sentence of *The Prince*: "All the states, all the dominions that have had and have imperium over men have been and are either republics or principalities." But once the awkward references to the past and the present are joined with Machiavelli's silence regarding the future the sentence acquires a new meaning. Left open is the possibility of a polity that transcends the dichotomy of monarchy or republicanism. The existence of that opening is confirmed by the catalogue of principalities which follows, for that catalogue overlooks the subject of chapter eleven, the ecclesiastical principality.[70]

> They alone have states and do not defend them; subjects and do not govern them; and the states, being undefended, are not taken from them; and the subjects, being ungoverned, do not mind it, never envisioning nor being able to alienate themselves from them.[71]

These are the only princes who retain their principality however they "proceed and live," since their "security and happiness" is a consequence of the invisibility or indirection of their rule. Machiavelli must forego discussing "the superior causes" which uphold this principality, because to do otherwise would be "the office of a presumptuous and reckless man."[72] The restraint the Church silently imposes is a sign of its authority, but since it is good to reason about everything, one must reason about this authority as well, albeit indirectly.[73] This procedure is doubly necessary because the spiritual resists direct examination, the spiritual forces of the Church becoming visible only when they are viewed through the medium of temporal things. But because the spiritual must be inferred from the temporal, the rule such principalities exercise is easily overlooked; it is easy to forget that the spiritual forces the Church commands are the ground for the temporal forces it has amassed.[74]

Christianity presides over a world that includes both principalities and republics. Indeed, one might even characterize Christianity itself as a kind of republic. Thus, Machiavelli is permitted to speak of "the princes of the Christian republic" as well as "the Christian states and republic." These phrases, to be found in I, 12, are reminiscent of the one we stumbled across in I, 10, "whoever becomes prince in a republic." Since all government is princely, the presence of a prince cannot distinguish one form of government from another. Republicanism, at least as Machiavelli conceives it, presides over a body politic that includes both princes and plebeians, or more precisely a republic is a polity in which "the name and not the royal power" has been expelled.[75] In an ecclesiastical principality the spiritual rules the temporal, but invisibly or indirectly. In a republic, "the royal power" becomes invisible or indirect. But in a temporal principality this invisibility or indirection is rarely achieved.

Recognition of the indirect rule ecclesiastical principalities exercise is the necessary precondition for a reconsideration of Machiavelli's remarks regarding writers and writings in I, 9 and 10. According to Machiavelli, Cleomenes learned about Agis' plan to restore the laws of Lycurgus from some writings he left behind; but according to Plutarch, Cleomenes owes his knowledge of Agis' plan to his wife who was also Agis' widow.[76] Machiavelli's allusion to writings which never existed is meant to intimate the possibility that a writer may also rule indirectly if he leaves behind writings calculated to inspire others to execute the plans he has devised. Similarly, the references to historians in I, 10 are meant to show how a writer's interpretation of the past can facilitate his rule over the future. This is the purpose of Machiavelli's political science, to introduce "new modes and orders," and to oblige those who succeed him to operate within the context of those "new modes and orders." The office Machiavelli seeks is spiritual or ecclesiastical, and as such it transcends the temporal dichotomy of principality or republic. This transcendence is a necessary consequence of Machiavelli's failure to distinguish monarchy from tyranny, for once all human action is regarded as self-aggrandizement it becomes possible for Machiavelli to advise one and all. It is after all not the desire to acquire, but only the failure to acquire that merits Machiavelli's reproof. In *The Prince*, ch. 3 the French king is reproved for his failure to conquer Italy, not for his desire to do so.

> It is truly a very natural and ordinary thing to desire to acquire; and always when men who can, do so, they are praised and not blamed; but when they cannot and wish to do so in every way, here is the error and the blame.[77]

The patriotic flourish with which *The Prince* concludes is misleading insofar as it obscures the impartiality inherent in Machiavelli's celebration of acquisition.

None of the foregoing is meant to deny Machiavelli's republicanism, indeed his republican bias is unmistakable. But the ground for that bias is seldom appreciated. It is not because democracy is a superior alternative to rule by the few, for there is no alternative to rule by the few, appearances notwithstanding. In every republic, however it is ordered, no more than forty or fifty citizens need be reckoned among the ranks of command.[78] Nor is Machiavelli's republicanism evidence of his justice since the "common good" republics observe is hardly common.

> And undoubtedly this common good is not observed if not in republics, because everything that serves its purpose is carried out: and however much it results in harm to this or that private man, there are so many for whom the above mentioned is good, that they can prevail over the dispositions of those few who are oppressed by it.[79]

Because even the common good is a form of oppression, the question "which government is to be preferred" is tantamount to the question "whom should we oppress". The popular answer, at least domestically, is republican. If the popular answer also seems more just, it is only because we often forget that republicanism conceals a brand of foreign oppression so barbarous that it is shunned by all civilized princes. Machiavelli is unequivocal: the hardest servitude is the subjection a victorious republic imposes.[80]

Had Machiavelli's republicanism been a consequence of his morality, he would have reserved the highest praise for those republics inclined to echew a policy of expansionism, preferring above all the orders of Sparta and Venice, two republics content to maintain the status quo. But since the necessity to acquire militates against such contentment, the highest praise is reserved for Rome, a republic ordered for empire.[81] Rome is to be preferred in spite of the servitude its aggrandizement imposes upon others since the virtue of Rome is simultaneously the oppression of its neighbors.[82] The explanation for Machiavelli's republicanism is not his morality, but the necessity to acquire; republics are superior to princi- palities because republics are more acquisitive, more fit for aggrandize- ment and empire.

The moral superiority of republican government is usually taken for granted since the patriotism its citizens exhibit invites praise while the selfishness ostensibly inherent in all principalities provokes censure.[83] When a prince reigns alone and in his own name, many are ready to suspect that self-interest and not the common good is the basis for his deliberations. To obviate these suspicions, a prince is encouraged to mask his authority either by "not disturbing the orders of his ancestors" or by instituting a senate. A prince who elects the former must renounce innovation, by confusing his authority with that of his ancestors. This strategy is effective, because the oppression that underlies subjection to custom is imperceptible as long as man equates the good and the just with the customary.[84] The obverse of this equation—that innovation is wicked and unjust—is the foundation for Machiavelli's remark that "no- thing [is] more difficult to carry out nor more doubtful of success nor more dangerous to manage" than the introduction of new orders.[85] Un- able to gainsay innovation, the new prince is obliged to devise some method to overcome the isolation and therefore the suspicion that sur- rounds all innovations. To appreciate the method Machiavelli prefers for securing the cooperation of others, it is necessary to consider first the method he impugns. How not to allay suspicion is the topic of *Discourses* III, 5.

III, 5 bears the following title: "What causes the loss of a kingdom to a king who has inherited it." Its principal example, Tarquin the Proud, is said to have "inherited" his kingdom, a Machiavellian euphemism mean- ing he killed his predecessor, Servius Tullius, and usurped his title. Livy believes the justice and legitimacy of Roman kingship perished with him; indeed, Servius is said to have ruled "so well that even a good and moderate successor would have found it hard to emulate him."[86] Machiavelli disagrees. Although Tarquin's method of occupying the kingdom was "extraordinary and odious," by itself it was hardly enough to preclude his quest for legitimacy and security, nor was the rape of Lucretia by his son Sextus necessarily menacing.[87] The enmity this "error" aroused could have been allayed had Tarquin been willing to sacrifice his son in order to divert suspicion, a sacrifice which would have enhanced Tarquin's reputation as well as stymied Brutus' conspiracy to establish the Roman republic.[88] The same mistake underlies both incidents: as a king, Tarquin arrogated all authority to himself, and relieved the senate of "the onus and envy" that necessarily accompany the exercise of political authority: and later, after the rape of Lucretia, he failed to inflict the punishment necessary to dissociate himself from his son, and thereby allowed Brutus to hold the kingship itself responsible for Sextus' "error." To allay suspicion as well as to ensure cooperation, authority and responsibility should be diffused. Or rather, since the concentration of authority is unavoidable, for it is necessary to be alone to order a city anew, diffusion must succeed concentration if the initial concentration of authority, and the violation of ancestral orders, is to be excused. By creating a senate, by arranging for others to partake in and assume responsibility for the polity he founded, Romulus was able to surmount the suspicions his actions aroused.[89]

Individual selfishness is easily and universally condemned. But when selfishness is collectivized, condemnation is rarely forthcoming, and indeed the more general the selfishness the more likely it will pass for morality. Few are ready to champion, at least in public, the slogan, "my advantage right or wrong," and yet many consider its analogue, "my country right or wrong," praiseworthy. When the freedom of the fatherland is at stake, there is no injustice, no cruelty, no ignominy that cannot be excused.[90]

To witness the application of this principle, one need only consider Machiavelli's *Prince*. The final chapter of *The Prince*, the only chapter explicitly devoted to the liberation of Italy, is generally considered proof of Machiavelli's patriotism, and this patriotism in turn proof of Machiavelli's idealism and morality. What is generally forgotten is that the patriotism Machiavelli invokes has little foundation in reality. Machiavelli would have us believe all Italy is "ready and disposed to follow a banner, provided there is someone who takes it."[91] But would the Venetians rally behind a Florentine banner?[92] Given Machiavelli's rhetoric, it is easy to forget that the French were brought "into Italy by the ambition of the Venetians;"[93] that in kingdoms like France (or Italy!) there are always some malcontents eager to invite foreign intervention;[94] that Cesare Borgia's alliance with the Pope—an alliance analogous to Lorenzo's —aroused considerable hostility;[95] that Lorenzo must extinguish all of

Italy's princes and their families to secure his conquest;[96] that Italy's republics will resist unification and therefore their citizens must be "scattered and dispersed;"[97] that cruelty is necessary to achieve union, peace, and faith;[98] and that deceit is indispensable.[99] In the name of a patriotism that does not yet exist, a patriotism Italy's putative liberator must create in order to excuse the means he must employ, the precepts Machiavelli prescribes are excused and even ennobled. Overwhelmed by Machiavelli's rhetoric, many consider Cesare Borgia's attempt to unify Italy praiseworthy and his failure tragic.[100] Cesare's devotion to the common good and his patriotism are taken for granted even though Machiavelli never ascribes a single patriotic or selfless motive to him. Not patriotism, but Pope Alexander VI's desire to make his son great, provided the impetus for Cesare's enterprise. To promote this end, the Pope was obliged to facilitate the French invasion of Italy, that is to facilitate the barbarian invasion Italy's "liberator" must repel. As for Cesare, he was moved by the following desires: "to maintain his conquest and proceed further;" to establish "good foundations for his power;" "to reduce [Romagna] to peace and obedience under the princely arm;" to induce men to ascribe his cruelty to another so that he might avoid the hatred of his subjects; "to protect himself;" to stand "on his own" and avoid dependence "upon the fortune and forces of others;" "to assure himself of his enemies, to gain to himself friends, to conquer either by force or fraud, to make himself loved and feared by the people, followed and revered by the soldiers, to extinguish those who can or must harm [him], to innovate the ancient orders with new modes, to be severe and gracious, magnanimous and liberal, [and] to maintain the friendship of kings and princes in such a mode that they must benefit [him] with pleasure or offend [him] with caution."[101] Machiavelli obscures the self-interest that underlies Cesare's enterprise by focusing attention on the union, peace, and obedience he brought to Romagna. That Cesare's actions benefited Romagna is not proof of his justice, since even a tyrant attends to the common good when it coincides with his private advantage. Furthermore, the price Italy paid for the order Cesare brought to Romagna was hardly insignificant: subjection to the French, Spanish, and Swiss. No less significant is the absence of any evidence to suggest Cesare's aim was the unification of Italy; considering the weakness of his forces, his father's inability to grant him sovereignty over the lands belonging to the Church, and the strength of his opposition, the most Cesare could have hoped for would have been "to become lord of Tuscany."[102] The patriotism of the twenty-sixth chapter is an illusion, but a necessary illusion, one that induces the deceived to excuse what they would otherwise judge inexcusable. Not the morality of patriotism, but the cruelty it excuses and even ennobles is one of the principal reasons for its invocation.

The implications of this argument may be extended to encompass domestic policy as well. In a principality, especially one in which the prince arrogates all authority to himself, severity is ill-advised, since men will attribute the prince's severity to his wickedness. To gain "the obedience and the love"[103] of the soldiers and subjects, Machiavelli offers the following counsel: obedience may be procured "by being an observer of orders and being held virtuous," while love is a consequence of the "affability, humanity, and compassion," the prince displays.[104] But in a republic such behavior is out of place, since "the particular benevolence" it inspires is prejudicial to liberty. It is "more praiseworthy and less dangerous" for a citizen who lives under a republic to employ severity as Manlius did when he killed his son to secure the obedience of his soldiers. Such severity is altogether beneficial because those who proceed in this way never acquire particular friends or partisans while those who proceed oppositely not only prepare the way for tyranny, but the suspicion their popularity arouses obliges the city to secure itself against them (like Caesar?).[105] Severity, however, allays suspicion, because to employ severity is to disavow popularity, and to disavow popularity in a republic is to disavow personal ambition.[106] Thus the very unpopularity of Manlian severity became proof of his patriotism.

Sheldon Wolin believes Machiavelli advocates "an economy of violence,"[107] but to advocate necessary violence only is little comfort when one has an expanded notion of the necessary. Machiavelli prefers the severity of Manlius to the humanity of his contemporary Valerius Corvinus, Manlius' equal in virtue, number of triumphs, and glory, because in a republic to procure obedience and victory through severity is preferable to procuring it through humanity. In short, the way of Valerius is inferior to the way of Manlius because Valerius led Rome to victory without executing his son and without subjecting his soldiers to excessively harsh commands.

Not morality, but the severity republics excuse, both at home and abroad, is the cause of Machiavelli's republicanism. Severity abroad is necessary for aggrandizement while severity at home is necessary for the perpetuation of the republic itself. Manlian severity enables a republic to return its orders to their beginning and to its ancient virtue: "And if a republic were so happy that it often had, as we said above, someone who with his example would renew the laws and not only keep it from running to ruin but pull it backwards, it would be perpetual."[108] Republics are more oppressive than principalities because the oppression they exercise, both at home and abroad, is easily cloaked in a veil of morality. Domestic oppression is ennobled when justified in the name of the common good, even though its effectual truth is majority self-interest, while foreign oppression is ennobled when justified in the name of patriotism, even though its effectual truth is collective selfishness. Machiavelli advocates not "an economy of violence," but a new view of nature, one in which the dichotomy of virtue or vice, praise or blame is no longer adequate for understanding political life. Many consider Machiavelli's republicanism proof of his morality and idealism; on the contrary, his republicanism is a consequence of his impartiality and a sign of his realism.

Of all the references to Caesar in the *Discourses*, there is only one which remains to be considered. In *Discourses* III, 13 Machiavelli asks "Where should one place more trust, in a good captain with a weak army or in a good army with a weak captain," and following in this the opinion of Caesar declares that neither the one nor the other is to be esteemed. The examples offered, however, are inapt since Machiavelli compares the behavior of an army with a captain with the behavior of that army after its captain's death. Once again Machiavelli's theme is in fact how a prince can preserve the orders he has established after his death, or more precisely how a prince can extend his rule beyond his lifetime. Although Caesar was in many respects more powerful after his death than before,[109] he never fully resolved this difficulty. This is Machiavelli's improvement over classical political science, for he believes it is possible "to trust in a captain who has the time to instruct men and the means of arming them," especially when that captain is a writer whose writings are calculated to recruit both the captains and the soldiers his enterprise requires.[110] Machiavelli aspires to be the Caesar of the modern world, but this time a Caesar who is willing to employ the severity necessary to ensure the perpetuation of his orders.

Notes

Note: Machiavelli's *Discourses on the First Ten Books of Livy* will be abbreviated to *Disc.*; his *Prince*, to *Pr.*; all page references are to the Feltrinelli edition of Machiavelli's works unless otherwise indicated, Leo Strauss' *Thoughts on Machiavelli* will be abbreviated to *Thoughts*.

1. *Disc.*, I. 4, 37, p. 218, 40, p. 229; III. 24.
2. *Disc.*, I. 10, p. 157.
3. J. H. Whitfield, *Discourses on Machiavelli* (Cambridge: W. Heffer and Sons, 1969), pp. 73, 147. The phrase *vivere civile* ("civil life") never occurs in I. 10.
4. Quentin Skinner, *The Foundations of Modern Political Thought* (Cambridge: Cambridge University Press, 1979), I. 161–62.
5. The words "praise" and "blame" occur only in the titles of *Disc.*, I. 10, and *Pr.*, ch. 15.
6. *Disc.*, I. 9, p. 153.
7. Only Severus is called virtuous in I. 10, although some of those cited in I. 10 are called virtuous elsewhere.
8. This procedure is in accord with the principle enunciated in I. 9, for whom but an historian can judge if one must judge all rulers according to the effects of their rule. Consider also the Christian parallel as discussed in *Disc.*, III. 1, p. 383. Christianity denies men the right to judge the present actions of others, insisting instead that they await the Day of Judgement, the final effect which excuses and justifies all human history.

9. *Disc.*, I. 25, p. 193.

10. Regarding Agesilaus, see Plutarch's *Lives* trans. by John Dryden (New York: The Modern Library, 1932), pp. 714, 716, 729, 731–33, 736, and 798. Regarding Dion, see pp. 294, 1155, 1172–78, 1181, 1184–85, 1220–21. Regarding Dionysius I. see pp. 1158–60, and Dionysius II. pp. 294, 302, 304, and 1175. Machiavelli's account of Timoleon is also inaccurate, see pp. 296–98, 314, and 346. Cf. *Disc.*, III. 5, p. 389 where Machiavelli intimates that Timoleon allowed the people relatively little liberty. When Machiavelli mentions security, he omits mentioning both Nabis and Dion; Dion because he was a victim of a conspiracy, and Nabis, because according to *Pr.*; chs. 9, p. 47 and 19, p. 76 *Disc.*, I. 40. p. 228 he is a model for those who seek security through the good will of the people. But according to Livy "whoever took the initiative in killing him would win the complete gratitude of the Lacedaemonians," XXXV, 35, pp. 2–3 Loeb Classical Library, trans. by B. O. Foster (Cambridge: Harvard University Press, 1976); how Nabis earned the good will of the people is recounted in XXXIV, 27: "To prevent any internal disorder he held the people in check with terror and severe punishments since he could not hope that they would wish well to a tyrant." The day after Nabis persuaded Sparta's leading citizens to lay down their arms and entrust their safety to him, he had them put to death. To cow the people some innocent rustics were driven with whips through the city's streets and then put to death. "By inspiring fear he stunned the minds of the crowd and prevented any attempt at revolution." Machiavelli's praise of Nabis in the passages cited above is especially shocking because I. 10 is proof Machiavelli knew how despicable he was. See also Polybius, *History* XIII. 6–8. The omission of Nabis is also striking, because Nabis was nevertheless the victim of a conspiracy; see *Disc.*, III. 6, pp. 398–99, 404. Nor is Agesilaus mentioned, perhaps because he lost Sparta its empire; see Plutarch, p. 736. Cf. *Pr.*, ch. 11, where ecclesiastical princes are said to be secure whether or not the prince is virtuous.

11. *Disc.*, I. 10, p. 157.

12. The original alternative in I. 10 was Scipio or Caesar, perhaps because no reasonable man would prefer Brutus' fate to Caesar's since to choose Brutus is to repudiate security. Brutus was celebrated by writers because it was unsafe to blame Caesar, and thus was never celebrated in his own right. See also *Thoughts*, pp. 33–4, 304n, 54. In *Pr.*, ch. 14 Caesar is called "an excellent man"; no personal crimes are attributed to him in either the *Pr.* or the *Disc.* Regarding Caesar's mildness, see Plutarch, p. 1220.

13. Cf. *Disc.*, III. 35.

14. Machiavelli neglects to mention that Caligula and Nero were adopted.

15. If Machiavelli did not wish the reader to draw this inference, why did he ask whoever becomes "prince in a republic" to compare the good emperors with the bad instead of leaving it to the comparison of Scipio with Caesar? Cf. also the end of I. 10 where Romulus is praised and Caesar blamed for not *reordering* Rome.

16. The untruth of this assertion of Machiavelli's is evidenced not only by his previous statement that no one was permitted to speak ill of Caesar directly, but also by Marcus' notorious persecution of Christians, a persecution he pursued more vigorously than any other emperor in the history of Rome. It is strange that Machiavelli should call this period "the triumph of the world." (I. 10) Regarding Marcus' behavior, see J. S. Mill, *On Liberty* (New York: Norton & Co., 1975), pp. 26–27.

17. Notwithstanding their virtue, Machiavelli rarely mentions or analyzes the careers of those emperors he calls good. Cf. *Pr.*, ch. 19, p. 84 where the good emperor Perinax is criticized for choosing to imitate Marcus rather than Severus. Regarding Augustus, see *Disc.* I. 52, p. 248. In I. 37, p. 218 Machiavelli calls Caesar Rome's first tyrant and claims that Rome never again recovered her liberty, thereby implying that Rome was no freer during the reign of those emperors he calls good than during the reign of those he calls wicked. Regarding the people's desire for liberty, see III. p. 5.

18. On the one hand Machiavelli says everyone would want to live during the reign of Mar-

cus and on the other than those who desire glory need crave the opportunity for displaying their virtue corrupt times provide, thereby indicating the disparity between the good of the many and the good of the few. Cf. Harry V. Jaffa, *Crisis of the House Divided* (Seattle: University of Washington Press, 1973), pp. 183–84, 210–25.

19. Cf. title of *Disc.*, I. 9.

20. Cf. the association of the invisibility of Caesar's tyranny with the extent of popular corruption in *Disc.*, I. 34, 208–09. In III. 6, p. 408 Caesar is said to have had the people as his friend. In I. 17 neither Timoleon nor Dion are held liable for the tyranny established after their deaths; given the extent of popular corruption its establishment was inevitable. Cf. also III. 18, p. 440 where Brutus' defeat is attributed to an error in judgment.

21. Machiavelli postpones his discussion of how loving conquest too much leads to tyranny, but when he does discuss it, Caesar proves to be the principal example. See *Disc.*, I. 5, p. 140; III. 24.

22. Consider *Disc.*, III. 6, p. 409 where Caesar is described as the head of an army.

23. Whitfield, pp. 34–35. Quentin Skinner, *Machiavelli* (New York: Hill and Wang, 1981), p. 88.

24. The passage seems to imply no such excuse exists, and thus the possibility of reordering a city without relinquishing absolute authority, i.e. without ceasing to be a tyrant.

25. Cf. Machiavelli's reference to "one who is wise" in *Disc.*, I. 40, p. 227. I. 40 is proof that popularity and tyranny need not be incompatible. Cf. also *Thoughts*, p. 266; Whitfield, pp. 28, 31. Whitfield does not discuss I. 40.

26. *Disc.*, III. 6, p. 392. Consider also Machiavelli's advice to Tarquin in III. 5. See Harvey C. Mansfield, Jr., *Machiavelli's New Modes and Orders* (Ithaca: Cornell University Press, 1979), pp. 314–317.

27. Cf. *Disc.* III. 8, pp. 415–16 where Machiavelli shows that Manlius' wickedness need not be a barrier to glory.

28. Cf. *Thoughts*, pp. 48–49.

29. *Pr.*, ch. 19, p. 84; quoted from Machiavelli, *The Prince*, trans. by Leo Paul deAlvarez (Dallas: University of Dallas Press, 1980), pp. 120–21.

30. *Disc.*, I. 9 p. 153.

31. Cf. the behavior of Appius Claudius who acquired authority by spreading the rumor that Rome's ten tables of law required two more to attain their perfection, *Disc.*, I. 40, p. 225.

32. But how then should one interpret Christianity's destruction of paganism? Founding presupposes destruction. *Disc.*, II. 5. See also, Mansfield, p. 65.

33. Cf. *Disc.*, I. preface where Machiavelli offers his successors a role in his enterprise, the introduction of new modes and orders.

34. Machiavelli conveniently overlooks the creation of the tribunate. Cf. *Disc.*, I. 3; I. 40, p. 224; III. 1, p. 380.

35. Cf. *Disc.*, I. 18 where Machiavelli fails to mention Romulus' or Cleomenes' desire to serve the common good. See *Thoughts*, p. 44, and Mansfield, p. 87. See also Plutarch, pp. 42, 75 where Romulus is said to have taken on a "haughtier bearing, to renounce his popular ways, and to change to the ways of a monarch" towards the end of his life.

36. Livy I. 6–7.3

37. Father Walker would have us believe "Almost all [of Machiavelli's] quotations from Livy are exact and almost all of his facts agree with the sources once one has found the right one." But Walker fails to cite any source for the facts as related in *Disc.*, I. 9. Leslie J. Walker, *The Discourses of Niccolo Machiavelli* (London: Routledge and Kegan Paul, 1975), 1975), II. 24–26, 311. Livy I. 14, 2–3. Note also that all of the institutions which excuse Romulus' homicides were already established when he consented to Titus Tatius' death. Cf. *Disc.*, I. 18 where Machiavelli now credits Romulus with killing and not merely consenting to Titus' death.

38. Livy I. 9. 2.

39. Livy I. 15. 6–16.
40. Livy I. 17. 1.
41. *Disc.*, I. 2, p. 134.
42. *Disc.*, I. 19.
43. Regarding the imperfections of Rome's political institutions see *Disc.*, I. 2, p. 134; I. 49, p. 241. See also I. 17; III. 5. *Thoughts*, pp. 271–72. Romulus never adopted his successor, Numa's selection having been inspired by the heavens (I. 11, p. 160).
44. Unlike Machiavelli, Plutarch never attributes to Agis the desire to restore Sparta's power. Because one may appear tyrannical when one is not, it is necessary to kill even those who are moved by considerations of justice to oppose the prince's endeavors. In fact, however, the ephors knew Agis' intention was not the establishment of a tyranny. Plutarch, pp. 961, 964. Cf. the references to the senate in *Disc.*, I. 9 with those in I. 10. The argument in I. 9 is symmetrical, Romulus having created a senate, Agis having been killed by one, and Cleomenes having destroyed one. See Whitfield, p. 156; Sheldon Wolin, *Politics and Vision* (Boston: Little, Brown and Co., 1960), pp. 199–200. Whitfield and Wolin unduly limit the scope of Machiavelli's teaching when they claim his advice is meant only for the new prince, Agis and Celomenes having been hereditary princes.
45. Plutarch, p. 1021. Livy calls Cleomenes Sparta's first tyrant, XXXIV. 26. 14; XXXIV. 28. 1.
46. I. 9 consistently overlooks the possibility of persuasion. Apparently Romulus need not be expected to find out whether Remus or Titus would have objected to the institutions he wished to establish before arranging for their execution. Or does Machiavelli overlook persuasion because persuasion is a kind of force? See *Disc.*, II. 13. Cf. Whitfield, p. 26; Whitfield denies one can "win favour by deceiving."
47. Whitfield claims Machiavelli never recommends "the *spegnare* (extinguishing) of citizens." (p. 65) But how does one explain Borgia's execution of Remirro (*Pr.*, ch. 7), Romulus' murder of Remus and Titus, Cleomenes' murder of the Spartan ephors, Nabis' murder of Sparta's leading citizens, and Moses' behavior (*Disc.*, III. 30)? See also I. 16, pp. 175–6 where Machiavelli shows how one may satisfy the people by destroying the nobility.
48. Skinner believes Machiavelli "insists that princely conduct must be *onesto* (honest) as well as *utile* (useful)," and therefore he "expresses contempt for Agathocles, in spite of his remarkable achievements, on the grounds that the criminal methods he invariably employed 'can win a prince power but not glory.'" This does not explain what principle enables us to distinguish the behavior of Hiero, Cesare Borgia, Nabis, and Hannibal, each of whom Machiavelli praises, from Agathocles. Hiero became prince of Syracuse by slaughtering the city's mercenaries and seizing control of the city. See *Pr.*, ch. 6, p. 33, ch. 13, p. 60. cf. *Disc.*, Ep. Ded. p. 122. Cesare Borgia eluded blame by appointing a subordinate disposed to commit the atrocities he deemed necessary. See *Pr.*, ch. 7, p. 37, ch. 17, p. 68. For Nabis, see note 10. Hannibal is praised for his "inhuman cruelty together with his infinite other vitues." See *Pr.*, ch. 17, pp. 70–71, and *Disc.*, III. 21. Hiero, Nabis, Hannibal, and Agathocles all receive praise for the security they attained. Skinner does not mention that immediately after Machiavelli says "it cannot be called *virtú* to kill one's citizens, betray friends, be without trust, without piety, and without religion," he says "because if one considers the *virtú* of Agathocles ..." Skinner does not consider Machiavelli's "apparent" blame of Agathocles in the light of Machiavelli's subsequent discussion of the obligations one owes to one's citizens, one's friends as well as the status of trust, piety, and religion as they are discussed in chs. 15ff. Nor does Skinner mention Machiavelli's assertion that Agathocles remedied his position with God and man. Given Skinner's analysis, the possibility of such a reconciliation requires explanation. Skinner notices Machiavelli's condemnation of Caesar in I. 10, but not the rehabilitation of Caesar's reputation; he notices the praise of Scipio in I. 10, but not the

criticism of Scipio in *Pr.*, ch. 17. In short, Skinner's analysis suffers because he never realizes the arguments in *The Prince* and the *Discourses* share a movement of their own. To see that movement all references to the same man, deed, or principle must be analyzed as a whole. One might also consider the references to Agathocles in *Disc.*, II. 13, and III. 6, p. 409. See Skinner, *Foundations*, I. 119, 137–38, 161–62. Machiavelli's account of Agathocles bears only the slightest resemblance to the account in his sources. See Diodorus Siculus, Loeb Classical Library, IX, Book XIX. 1–9; XX. 4, 63–89, 101; (Cambridge: Harvard University Press, 1960); Agathocles's cruelties were repeated periodically; he left his children to die in Libya; he never remedied his position with God or with man. A Latin translation of Diodorus Siculus was available for Machiavelli to read. See Walker, II. 279. See also the account of Agathocles in Justinius, *Epitome*, XXIII, ch. 2. Cf. *Thoughts*, pp. 309–10n.53.

49. *Thoughts*, p. 128. *Disc.*, I. 3.

50. *Disc.*, I. 53; I. 57; I. 58.

51. Cf. *Pr.*, ch. 3, p. 21 where the Romans are treated as "wise princes." Consider also the sense in which the tribunes were in fact popular princes.

52. *Disc.*, III. 6, p. 408. Cf. *Pr.*, ch. 9, p. 45; Machiavelli's discussion of the civic principality is reminiscent of his analysis of Caesarism. I. 37, pp. 217–18.

53. Consider Marius' seven terms as consul (*Disc.*, I. 37) in the light of Machiavelli's criticism of the prolongation of commands (III. 24).

54. Caesar of course was not a plebeian; Machiavelli seems to deny that the head of any party can completely identify his interests with that of his suporters.

55. *Disc.*, I. 5, p. 140.

56. *Disc.*, I. 40, p. 227.

57. Consider how this example affects the status of gratitude and justice as virtues.

58. Rome was destroyed because Caesar was virtuous and wise. Cf. *Pr.*, ch. 16, pp. 67–68 and *Disc.*, I. 40, p. 227. See *Thoughts*, pp. 190–91; Mansfield, p. 67 Cf. *Pr.*, ch. 21, p. 92 where the prince is advised "to show himself a lover of virtue," and not to be a lover of virtue.

59. In *Pr.*, ch. 15 *virtú* is a combination of virtue and vice. "The one alone" of *Disc.*, I. 9 is transformed by plebeian personification or worship into the two, the pure good and pure evil of I. 10; they separate what in fact is always mixed. See also *Disc.*, I. 2, p. 131; I. 6, p. 144. Mansfield, "Burke and Machiavellian Principles in Politics," in *Edmund Burke: The Enlightenment and the Modern World*, ed. by Peter J. Stanlis (Detroit: University of Detroit Press, 1967), p. 57. *Thoughts*, p. 198.

60. *Thoughts*, p. 167.

61. *Thoughts*, p. 343n.188. The word "tyranny" appears only in the chapter headings of *Disc.*, I. 10 and III. 28. Cf. the references to "false good" in I. 10; I. 53, and III. 28.

62. Cicero, *Epistolae ad Familiares*, Loeb Classical Library, trans. W. Glynn Williams (Cambridge: Harvard University Press, 1960) III, 343. Cf. Nietzsche, *Beyond Good and Evil*, no. 6; *Genealogy of Morals*, 1st essay, secs. 7–10. Cf. *Disc.*, III. 2; Mansfield, pp. 305–09.

63. Aristotle, *Politics*, 1311a2–4.

64. In *Disc.*, I. 10 army commanders are celebrated according to the extent of their success in increasing their country's dominions. The possibility that one might fail and still merit the greatest praise is implicitly denied. This does not mean, however, that all success is praiseworthy. See also *Pr.*, ch. 3, p. 12 where the desire to acquire merits blame only if it is unsuccessful.

65. Cf. reference to Caesar in *Disc.*, I. 34, p. 170 where self-aggrandizement is said to be capable of acquiring names sufficient to conceal self-aggrandizement.

66. *Disc.*, II. 2, pp. 282–83; III. 1, pp. 382–83.

67. *Pr.*, chs. 1, 2.

68. *Disc.*, I. preface, p. 124.

69. *Thoughts*, p. 16.

70. *Thoughts*, p. 63.
71. *Pr.*, ch. 11, p. 50.
72. Cf. Machiavelli's reluctance to reason about the Church in *Pr.*, ch. 11, p. 50 with his reluctance to reason about Moses in ch. 6, p. 31.
73. *Disc.*, I. 18, p. 179.
74. Cf. the reference to spiritual authority in ch. 3, p. 23. J.A.W. Gunn considers the notion that Machiavelli engaged in a kind of spiritual warfare ludicrous. But once the significance of spiritual authority is appreciated the notion that Machiavelli would engage in such warfare become eminently reasonable. See Mansfield, pp. 184–85. J.A.W. Gunn, "Review of *Machiavelli's New Modes and Orders*," *Canadian Journal of Political Science*, XIV, 1 (1981), pp. 181–83.
75. *Disc.*, I. 2, p. 134.
76. Plutarch, p. 972.
77. *Pr.*, ch. 3, pp. 23–24.
78. *Disc.*, I. 16, p. 176. Consider also the account of democracy in I. 2, p. 132.
79. *Disc.*, II. 2, p. 280. Cf. Mansfield, p. 193.
80. *Disc.*, II. 2, p. 284.
81. *Disc.*, I. 6. In *Pr.*, ch. 1 Machiavelli classifies all principalities with regard to the modes by which they are acquired, not their morality or justice.
82. Roman virtue was also the cause of Rome's own servitude. See, for example, *Disc.*, II. 2.
83. Cf. *Thoughts*, p. 11.
84. *Pr.*, ch. 2. Machiavelli treats two distinct Dukes of Ferrara as if they were one. To follow custom is to renounce individuality, or more precisely to hide under the individuality of another. Religion may also be used to conceal originality. See *Disc.*, I. 11. See also I. 45; Savanarola's failure to observe a law he made rendered his ambition and partisanship manifest to all.
85. *Pr.*, ch. 6, p. 31.
86. Livy I. 48.
87. Only Mansifeld, p. 314, considers it remarkable that Machiavelli should treat Tarquin as legitimate and Servius as a usurper. Neither Whitfield nor Walker notices this oddity. Romulus' murders were excused in the name of the common good; Tarquin's murder of Servius is excused even though no such excuse is advanced, another indication of the questionable morality of *Disc.*, I. 9. Machiavelli consistently treats rape lightly. Cf. I. 44. Machiavelli's failure to mention the rape of Virginia in I. 40 is also significant. In the *Mandragola* rape becomes the subject of a comedy.
88. Unlike Tarquin, Brutus was prepared to sacrifice his sons. *Disc.*, III. 3.
89. The praise in *Disc.*, I. 10 of those emperors who respected the authority of the senate should be understood in the light of this observation. Cf. Hamilton et al. *The Federalist*, No. 70.
90. *Disc.*, III. 41.
91. *Pr.*, Ch. 26, p. 102, Cf. *Thoughts*, pp. 63–69.
92. *Pr.*, ch. 3, p. 24, ch. 7, p. 38, ch. 11, p. 51, ch. 21, p. 92.
93. *Pr.*, *ch.* 3, p. 22.
94. *Pr.*, ch. 3, pp. 17, 20, 22, ch. 4, p. 27, ch. 7, p. 35, ch. 12, p. 57, ch. 25, p. 100.
95. *Pr.*, ch. 3, p. 23, ch. 7, pp. 35–36, ch. 8, p. 43, ch. 11, p. 51. Machiavelli excuses Borgia's crimes despite the fact his enterprise failed.
96. *Pr.*, ch. 2, ch. 3, pp. 17–18, ch. 7, p. 36, ch. 19, p. 77. That one must be prepared to kill children is evident from the final citation above.
97. *Pr.*, ch. 5.
98. *Pr.*, ch. 17, p. 68.
99. *Pr.*, ch. 7, p. 36, ch. 18.
100. Whitfield, pp. 23–25, 67–68, 107. Pasquale Villari, *The Life and Times of Niccolo Machiavelli* (London: Ernest Benin, 1929), II, 166. Allan Gilbert, "Introduction," *The*

Prince and Other Works (Chicago: Packard and Co., 1941), pp. 31–33. Charles D. Tarlton, "The Symbolism of Redemption and the Exorcism of Fortune," *Review of Politics*, 30 (July, 1968), p. 343. Alkis Kontos, "Success and Knowledge in Machiavelli," in Anthony Parel ed., *The Political Calculus* (Toronto: University of Toronto Press, 1972), p. 95. The word *"patria"* never occurs in *Pr.*, ch. 7; perhaps to underscore its absence Machiavelli uses it in chs. 6 and 8, p. 44. Its use in ch. 8 in connection with Agathocles is particularly striking.

101. *Pr.*, ch. 7, ch. 11, p. 52, ch. 17, p. 68.

102. *Pr.*, ch. 7, p. 38, ch. 11, p. 52. That Machiavelli regarded the unification of Italy under Borgia or Lorenzo as impossible is rarely appreciated. Cf. *Thoughts*, pp. 71–74. Consider the evaluation of Borgia's intention and strength in William Harrison Woodward, *Cesare Borgia* (London: Chapman and Hall, 1913), pp. 295, 322, 327, 337–38. Historians seem less likely to succumb to Machiavelli's rhetoric.

103. All quotations in this paragraph are from *Disc.*, III. 22.

104. The unspoken implication of this division is that affability, humanity, and compassion are not virtues.

105. Cf. *Disc.*, III. 22.

106. See Mansfield's interpretation of Manlius' reverence for father and fatherland, pp. 379–81.

107. Wolin, p. 22.

108. *Disc.*, III. 22, p. 450. The translation is Mansfield's, p. 381.

109. *Disc.*, I. 52, p. 248.

110. In *Disc.*, III. 13 two kinds of captains are discussed, a distinction which corresponds to the difference between Machiavelli and those who adopt his counsels.

11

YOUNG MEN IN A HURRY
ROOSEVELT, LODGE, AND THE FOUNDATIONS OF TWENTIETH CENTURY REPUBLICANISM

Patrick J. Garrity

"THE TWENTIETH CENTURY LOOMS BEFORE US BIG WITH THE FATE OF NA-tions," Theodore Roosevelt reflected in 1900. "If we stand idly by . . then the bolder and stronger peoples will pass us by, and will win for them-selves the domination of the world."[1]

Roosevelt, the all-but-inevitable Vice Presidential nominee of the Re-publican Party in 1900, took the struggle for national survival very seri-ously. In his mind, the United States stood at a crossroads: it could re-main a second-rate, divided nation, or it could master its own fate and move boldly into the new century. During the previous decade, the young Roosevelt and Henry Cabot Lodge had become the political and intellec-tual leaders of a movement that would commit the United States whole-heartedly to the latter course. Their ambition was monumental: to cap-ture the leadership of the Republican Party; to identify that party with the principles and policies of American nationalism; to use the rebirth of American nationalism to bring the United States into a position of global pre-eminence.

And by 1900, with the United States victorious over Spain and with Roosevelt soon to be one heartbeat away from the White House, the new nationalists were not far from success.

I. American Nationalism and American History. At a time when American politicians still bothered to take history seriously, Roosevelt and Lodge set about to study the past in order to discover what made nations great. They wrote political biographies of such American states-men as George Washington, Alexander Hamilton, Gouverneur Morris and Thomas Hart Benton. Heavily influenced by social Darwinism in scholarship and politics, they had come to the conclusion that the struggle

between peoples (divided among particular nations) was the driving force
of history. To struggle, and to succeed, at great and noble tasks was the
highest calling of mankind. Great men and great nations welcomed these
challenges to test and strengthen their character. As Lodge told the Senate
in March 1900:

The athelete does not win his race by sitting habitually in an armchair.
The pioneer does not open up new regions to his fellow-men by staying
in warm shelter behind the city walls. A cloistered virtue is but a poor
virtue after all. Men who have done great things are those who have
never shrunk from trial or adventure. If a man has the right qualities in
him, responsibility sobers, strengthens and develops him. The same is
true of nations. The nation which fearlessly meets its responsibilities rises
to the task when presure is upon it.[2]

The United States was certainly blessed with the material conditions
for greatness: abundant national resources, a talented and energetic
population, and a favorable strategic location. Unfortunately, in the eyes
of Roosevelt and Lodge, those material advantages had not been used
fully because of a spiritual division in the regime. American history was
characterized by an internal struggle betwen two competing factions, each
exercising a powerful hold on the American mind.

The first faction, generally but not always dominant, was that of the
true nationalist, the large Americans. These patriots had fought the War
of Independence, framed and supported the Constitution (for which the
Declaration of Independence had only cleared the way[3]), resisted foreign
influence, encouraged national commerce, expanded across the continent, and warred to preserve the Union, that highest expression of American nationalism. Its heroes were statesmen like Washington, Hamilton
and Lincoln.[4]

But true Americanism had been constantly opposed by a sentiment
at best partly American, which originated in the colonial, dependent,
particularist mind-set that opposed the Revolution. If the nationalists represented the progressive movement of the age, then the "anti-nationalists"

. . . represented the forces of conservatism, and even of reaction. . . .
They stood for the separatist as opposed to the national principle, for
strict as opposed to liberal construction of the constitution, for the rights
of States, as opposed to the powers of the Union, for the halt instead of
the march.[5]

This nationalist bill of particulars was obviously drawn up against
John C. Calhoun and the southern secessionists, but Roosevelt and Lodge
traced the lineage of anti-nationalism back to Thomas Jefferson. Jefferson had been lukewarm on the Constitution, drew his political support from the old anti-Federalists, encouraged foreign (i.e., French)

influence in American politics, and authored the Kentucky Resolutions with their anti-national doctrine of nullification.[6]

Neither Roosevelt nor Lodge offered a principled statement of democratic nationalism to challenge that of Jefferson in, say, the Declaration. Instead, they were interested in the formation of a particular national character that would serve as the basis for sound nationalistic policies. For this character, they pointed neither to a doctrine nor a document, but to a model: George Washington, who was "not even excepting Lincoln, the greatest man of modern times."[7]

Washington gained this distinction not only because of his personal virtue or his love of the Union, but because he proved to be an American at a time when there were no Americans. Washington was the Founder of the American character, and thus his superiority to Lincoln, who was merely its Preserver.

> The truth was that in 1779 our main task was to shape new political conditions, and then to reconcile our people to them; whereas in 1860 we had merely to fight fiercely for the preservation of what was already ours. In the first emergency we needed statesmen, and in the second warriors; and the statesmen and warriors were forthcoming.[8]

Since Lodge and Roosevelt regarded themselves as latter-day preservers, they stressed the importance of the warrior to their revived American nationalism. They celebrated Lincoln not for his moral opposition to slavery *per se*, but for his nationalist opposition to the threat of disunity posed by the slavery issue.[9]

II. Recovering the Party of Nationalism. Having identified the decisive conflict within the American regime, Roosevelt and Lodge next sought the vehicle that would allow them to weigh in on the side of nationalism. It seemed that, since the time of the Founding, one political party had represented the nationalist tradition, while its opposite espoused anti-nationalism. Lodge argued in 1893 that few things were more permanent than party divisions under representative government; their names might change, but the real distinctions between parties changed very little over time: "Party divisions at bottom rest on the differences, inherent in human nature, between people who desire progress and those whose controlling impulse is in favor of keeping things as they are."[10]

In the years after the Civil War, the Republican Party was clearly the national party, and so Roosevelt and Lodge were Republicans. But they feared that the character of American nationalism was being eroded "through the commercial and cheap altruistic spirit, the spirit of the Birmingham school, the spirit of the banker, the broker, the mere manufacturer, the mere merchant . . ."[11] Unfortunately, the Republican Party was also allied with business, and hence indirectly with the "adoration of money . . ."[12] Roosevelt and Lodge deeply felt the need to redirect the Republican Party toward its higher, nationalistic mission. Through their scholarship, they hoped to base resurgent Republicanism upon the restoration of the old Federalist Party to respectability. If the strength and greatness of the nation rested on fostering a vigorous American nationalism, who better to study than the original proponents of Union, the Federalists?

According to Roosevelt and Lodge, Federalist nationalism manifested itself most notably in two areas: economics and territorial expansion. Hamilton's Report on Manufactures gave birth to the protectionist policy, to Henry Clay's "American System," and to the modern (1890s) Republican economic program. In the successful establishment of industry, Hamilton foresaw the road to true independence from foreign nations. Lodge portrayed Hamilton as seeking strength and order in questions of politics and government—by properly regulating finances, Hamilton hoped to increase the strength of the national government, and hence to establish public order.[13]

On the issue of territorial expansion, both Roosevelt and Lodge took care to credit the Federalists with being the first expansionists. Washington "perceived at a glance that the key and guarantee of that future were in the wild regions of the West." In the West "lay the road to national greatness." Hamilton was thus constantly on the alert to wrest from Spain final and complete control of the Mississippi Valley. But the Federalists were hardly blind and greedy conquerors; expansion was always subordinated to the concept of national greatness. Washington, for example, took care to open the coast's inland communications with the West, in order to bind the people of that territory to the Union *before* free navigation on the Mississippi inclined them in other directions.[14]

After the collapse of the Federalists,[15] the natural political succession would seem to place the Whig Party as the torchbearer of Hamilton nationalism from Federalist to Republican times. But Roosevelt was quite reserved in his praise of the Whigs, apparently because of his admiration for the territorially expansive nationalism of such Democrats as Andrew Jackson and Thomas Hart Benton. Clay's orthodox economic nationalism alone was much less appealing to Roosevelt as a decisive political principle.[16] In fact, Roosevelt goes out of his way to absolve expansionism from the taint of slavery.

Doubtless the slave-holders worked hard to secure additional territory out of which to form new slave states; but Texas and California would have been in the end taken by us, had there not been a single slave in the Mississippi valley. The greed for conquest of new lands which characterized the Western people had nothing whatever to do with the fact that some of them owned slaves. Long before there had been so much as the faintest foreshadowing of the importance which the slavery question was to assume, the West had been eagerly pressing on to territorial conquest.[17]

III. Creating the New Republicanism. Having elucidated the guiding principle of the regime (American nationalism), and having noted the party most closely attached to that principle (the Republican Party), Roosevelt and Lodge were left with revitalizing the connection between the two.

"The Democratic party is the conservative party of today; the Republican is the revolutionary party," Roosevelt proclaimed in 1900. But in 1890, Republicanism was far from the ideal mechanism of Americanism that the Roosevelt-Lodge nationalists desired. Its foreign policy was by and large cautious. The commercial, "Old Guard" wing of the party emphasized protectionism, and not much else, as the core of its principles. Harry Thurston Peck characterized Republicans as "the party of the bankers, the manufacturers, the lords of commerce, and all those active, restless, scheming spirits who had learned that great fortunes were to be made in other ways than by legitimate industry."[18] To William Jennings Bryan, they were the plutocrats.[19] Lord Charnwood was a bit more charitable: "It was in the main also the party of solid business interests . . . A certain flatness of political tone was perhaps inevitable."[20]

That was precisely what galled Roosevelt and Lodge about the Republican Party; next to anti-nationalism, political "flatness" was the most serious offense that a large American could imagine. The new nationalists sought the issue that would transform their party back into the institutional spearhead of true Americanism.

Roosevelt and Lodge were associated with the reformist wing of the party, which sought to purify Republicanism through devices such as civil service reform. By the mid-1890s, it seemed clear that this line of attack would not suffice to gain control of the party. For political and principled reasons, neither man was inclined to support tariff reform or free silver, two other domestic issues that might have transformed the party. However, they could not rely simply on the vague rhetoric of Americanism to establish a workable, permanent political coalition.

The original Republican Party had melded rhetoric and principle on the high, nationalist policy of demanding the restoration of the Missouri Compromise.[21] The Republicans of the Gilded Age were united on the still nationalistic, but lower policy of protectionism and commercialism. For large Americans like Roosevelt and Lodge, this reflection of Hambiltonian economics was neither adequate nor politically self-sustaining. The Republican Party desperately needed a great, national idea to secure its hold on the American soul.

The answer, it seemed to Roosevelt and Lodge, was to revive the second part of the old Federalist program: Hamiltonian expansionism. But the new Republican expansionism was to take a form suited to a great world power—i.e., an intense, aggressive American foreign policy. In October 1894, while campaigning for the office of mayor in New York, Roosevelt confessed to Lodge that, on the tariff business, he had "a tinge of economic agnosticism . . . but our foreign policy is, to me, of an importance which is difficult for me to overestimate." Foreign relations were for Roosevelt "the subject on which I feel deepest . . ."[22]

Through their study of American history, Roosevelt and Lodge had become convinced that an aggressively nationalistic "large" foreign policy was both proper and politically salutary. Washington's Farewell Address and the Monroe Doctrine, those two great statements of American foreign policy, had demonstrated what was *not* obvious to the public at that time—the nationalist necessity to separate America from Europe. The great national accomplishment of the first few American generations was to insist on that fundamental division—in part by driving European powers out of the New World.[23] This process required an expansion of the territory of the United States, culminating in the creation of a continental American empire.

Roosevelt and Lodge sought to revive the expansionist spirit as the device by which the Republican Party and the United States would achieve their manifest destiny. "I believe in the expansion of the great nations," Roosevelt wrote Sir Cecil Arthur Spring Rice in 1899.[24] Expansion tested and strengthened national character.

> . . . if a nation is great, as we claim that ours is, it can remain so only by doing great work and achieving dangerous and difficult tasks. . . . If we lead soft and easy lives, concerning ourselves with little things only, we shall occupy but an ignoble place in the great world drama of the centuries that are opening. It is only through strife—righteous strife—righteously conducted, but still strife, that we can expect to win to the higher levels where the victors in the struggle are crowded.[25]

The expansionist sentiment so assiduously cultivated by Roosevelt and Lodge did not necessarily demand territorial growth. It meant above all an assertive nationalism, a passion to defend and advance American interests. True Americans demanded a massive naval buildup; they took offense at the unprovoked attack on American sailors in Chile in 1891; they watched with suspicion British encroachments in Venezuela, Nicaragua and in the Bering Sea. But if American nationalism led to territorial expansion, whether strategic (Hawaii) or accidental (the Philippines) in character, so be it. The imperialist instinct was inseparable from the spirit of national greatness. Lodge believed that an outward-looking foreign policy would simultaneously be the means for Republican political supremacy:

As an American, I regret that our opponents should insist on making a party question of this new and far-reaching problem [the Philippines], so fraught with great promise of good both to ourselves and to others. As a party man and as a Republican I can only rejoice. Once more our opponents insist that we shall be the only political party devoted to American policies. As the standard of expansion once so strongly held by their great predecessors drops from their nerveless hands we take it up and invite the American people to march with it. We offer our policy to the American people, to Democrats and to Republicans, as an American policy, alike in duty and honor, in morals and in interest, as one not of skepticism and doubt, but of hope and faith in ourselves and in the future, as becomes a great nation which has not yet learned to use the art of retreat or to speak with the accents of despair.[26]

IV. Conclusion: Nationalism Sobered.   Between 1890 and 1900, Theodore Roosevelt and Henry Cabot Lodge had seen an enormous change in the face of America. The frontier had officially been closed; former Confederate generals had led U.S. troops into combat in Cuba; the United States was emerging as the world's strongest economic and (potentially) military power. The ascendancy of the Republican Party seemed assured, and the large Americans could look forward to the day when Roosevelt himself became President. A career of scholarship in the 1880s, and politics in the 1890s, had borne fruit for the two ardent young nationalists.

Their formula for success in the twentieth century seemed simple enough. In the past, America had too often been faced with a choice between internal improvement and external expansion. (This contrast had been drawn sharply in elections such as that of 1844, when neither Clay nor Polk represented a truly national spirit.) Roosevelt and the large Americans believed that it was possible to combine the two strands, to seek internal (i.e., character) improvement *through* external expansion. This was the stuff of Roosevelt's early progressivism.[27]

It should be noted that Roosevelt, while President, came to put much more emphasis on the domestic, reformist side of progressivism. In part, this was because the sobering reality of world politics had moderated his rather bad-tempered nationalism. Roosevelt began to see America's national interest bound up in a world balance of power, and he and Lodge made a rather dramatic shift from Anglophobe to Anglophile shortly after the Spanish-American War. But Roosevelt also began to see the limitations that foreign policy had on long-term domestic political consensus. The average New York party boss, Roosevelt remarked to Lodge in 1898, was "quite willing to allow you to do what you want in such trivial matters as war and the acquisition of Puerto Rico and Hawaii, provided you don't interfere with the really vital questions, such as giving out contracts for cartage in the Custom House and interfering with the appointment of street sweepers."[28]

Of course, Roosevelt proceeded to secure the Panama Canal zone, conduct his Big Stick policy and sail the American fleet around the world. But the tremendous potential for an American empire never materialized. Imperialism was broken as a political force in the debates over the acquisition of the Philippines, when the anti-imperialists lost the vote in the Senate but triumphed in the moral arena. Fittingly, the opponents of annexation brought forth Thomas Jefferson and the Declaration of Independence as the foundation of their moral rejection of imperialism.

In the end, Roosevelt's domestic brand of progressivism lost out to an alternative form, the New Freedom. In foreign policy, Roosevelt's nationalism was supplanted by Wilsonian *inter*nationalism. This marked the ultimate defeat of Roosevelt's grand design. Despite Lodge's successful nationalist resistance to the League of Nations and the Versailles Treaty, America's ultimate rise to world power came about on principles decisively different from those of the Republican visionaries of the 1890s.

Notes

1. Howard K. Beale, *Theodore Roosevelt and the Rise of America to World Power* (Baltimore: The Johns Hopkins Press, 1956), p. 80.
2. *Congressional Record* 35, 56:1, part 3, March 7, 1900, p. 2628.
3. Theodore Rosevelt, *Gouverneur Morris* (Boston: Houghton Mifflin, 1912), p. 115.
4. See, for example, Henry Cabot Lodge, *George Washington*, 2 vols, (New Rochelle, N.Y: Arlington House, 1898), vol. 2, pp. 8, 15–16, 83, 217, 273.
5. Lodge, "Outlook and Duty of the Republican Party," *Forum* 15 (April 1893): 251–2.
6. Roosevelt, *Gouverneur Morris*, p. 109, 114, 260; Lodge, *Alexander Hamilton* (Boston: Houghton Mifflin, 1912), pp. 123, 128.
7. Roosevelt to Lodge, August 24, 1884, in *Selections from the Correspondence of Theodore Roosevelt and Henry Cabot Lodge*, 2 vols. (New York: Chalres Scribner's Sons, 1925), vol. 1, p. 9. Hereinafter cited as *Roosevelt-Lodge Correspondence*.
8. Roosevelt, *Gouverneur Morris*, pp. 42–5.
9. Ibid., pp. 142–3, 282; Roosevelt, *Thomas Hart Benton* (Boston: Houghton Mifflin, 1895), p. 95.
10. Lodge, "Outlook and Duty," pp. 250–1.
11. Roosevelt to Spring Rice, August 15, 1897, in *The Letters of Theodore Roosevelt*, ed. Elting E. Morrison, 8 vols. (Cambridge: Harvard University Press, 1951–1954), vol. 1, p. 648. Hereinafter cited as *Roosevelt Letters*.
12. Cited by William C. Widenor, *Henry Cabot Lodge and the Search for an American Foreign Policy* (Berkeley: University of California Press, 1980), p. 8.
13. Lodge, *George Washington*, 2:83, and *Alexander Hamilton*, pp. 89, 107–8, 111.
14. Lodge, *George Washington*, 2:8, 15–16.
15. Any resurrection of the Federalists required a satisfactory explanation of why the first great national party failed to hold power, and eventually declined to the point where Federalism became the vehicle of northern separation (e.g., the Hartford Convention). Roosevelt blamed the disaster on the Federalist's distrust of the people. "In a government such as ours it was a foregone conclusion that a party which did not believe in the people would sooner or later be thrown from power unless there was an armed breakup of the system." (Roosevelt, *Gouverneur Morris*, p. 280.) Lodge cited an overreaction on the part of the Federalists, who feared the link between the French revolutionaries and the Jeffersonian Republicans. "The overthrow of religion, society, property and morals,

which they beheld in Paris, seemed to be threatening their own country, and they became as extreme as their opponents in the exactly opposite direction." (Lodge, *George Washington*, 2:294.)

16. Roosevelt, *Thomas Hart Benton*, pp. 108–9, 238.

17. Ibid., pp. 173–4, 234–5.

18. Harry Thurston Peck, *Twenty Years of the Republic* (New York: Dodd, Mead & Company, 1919), p. 266.

19. Louis W. Koenig, *Bryan* (New York: G.P. Putnam's Sons, 1971), p. 326; William Jennings Bryan, *Bryan on Imperialism* (Chicago: Bentley & Company, 1900), p. 22.

20. Lord Godfrey Rathbone Berison Charnwood, *Theodore Roosevelt* (Boston: Atlantic Monthly Press, 1923), p. 78.

21. Harry V. Jaffa, *Crisis of the House Divided* (Seattle: University of Washington Press, 1973), p. 285.

22. Roosevelt to Lodge, October 27, 1894, *Roosevelt-Lodge Correspondence*, 1:139.

23. Lodge, *George Washington*, 2:130–3, and *Alexander Hamilton*, p. 152.

24. Roosevelt to Spring Rice, December 2, 1899, *Roosevelt Letters*, 2:1104.

25. Roosevelt to Becker, September 6, 1899, *Roosevelt Letters*, 1:1068.

26. *Congressional Record* 35, 56:1, part 3, March 7, 1900, p. 2617; Beale, *Theodore Roosevelt*, p. 68.

27. Jaffa, *Crisis of the House Divided*, p. 344.

28. Roosevelt to Lodge, July 1 and October 16, 1898, *Roosevelt-Lodge Correspondence*, 1:334, 357.

12

DEFENDING SOCRATES AND DEFENDING POLITICS

Thomas G. West

RARELY IS ONE'S PUBLISHED WRITING TREATED WITH THE CARE THAT STEWART Umphrey brings to his reading of my *Plato's Defense of Socrates* in his essay "*Eros* and *Thumos*."[1] It can certainly be said of Umphrey's learned and spirited critique, as I trust will also be said of my response, that ours is no merely personal exchange, but rather one that addresses the principal question facing philosophers and political men—indeed, all human beings. As it was for Plato, so today the proper appreciation of Socrates' fate may afford the best entry into the question of how one ought to live.

Because Umphrey's review provoked a rethinking of the content and purpose of my book, the present response is no mere rehearsal of old arguments. In defending what I said there, I have found myself obliged to deepen (though not to change) my critique and defense of Socrates. Moreover, I have had to make explicit why that critique and defense were appropriate in light of the contemporary crisis of the West.

Umphrey's review presents itself as a defense of Socrates against my alleged condemnation of Socrates. By defending Socrates, Umphrey seeks to defend philosophy, which, in his opinion, I am inadvertently attacking in my defense of the justice of Athens' condemnation of the philosopher. On the contrary, I maintain that the greatest enemy of philosophy today is not politics but the view that there is no essential conflict between philosophy and political life—the very view which Umphrey seems compelled to uphold in his defense of Socrates. This view appears today in two versions. The most radical version is historicism or nihilism, according to which philosophy as quest for the truth about man and the world is impossible. Therefore, philosophy, being as arbitrary and groundless at its root as any historically conditioned political ideology, does not differ in principle from the opinions at the base of every political community. The more typical version of the current view holds that Plato's cave, being open to light, can be enlightened.[2] The illusion of easy escape from the cave, the illusion of Enlightenment, certainly remains a dominant feature of the West today. As a consequence of this view we live, according to an image of Leo Strauss, in a pit beneath the cave, from which we must ascend in the first instance not to the sunlight but to the pre-Enlightenment cave in which politics and philosophy come to sight as enemies.[3] It must be seen that the typical assumption that they are easily made compatible leads in fact to an evisceration of the political. What is needed today, then, is not in the first instance a defense of Socrates but rather a defense of the dignity and authority of political life. By maintaining that Socrates is innocent of the charge brought against him by Athens, Umphrey wittingly or unwittingly contributes to the prevailing liberal prejudice.

I. Socrates Was Guilty. Let us examine Umphrey's defense of Socrates. We will focus on what I take to be the two leading points of his argument. First, Umphrey maintains that Socrates is innocent because I have not proven him guilty according to Athenian Law. He says that I should have investigated the historical evidence for laws against impiety in ancient Athens (391–392). But in fact there was no need for me to conduct such an investigation because the existence of such laws was never questioned during the trial. No one, least of all Socrates, ever suggests that impiety and corruption of the young are not illegal. Besides, later in his review Umphrey even mentions evidence external to the *Apology of Socrates* that impiety *was* against the law (419). Umphrey himself concedes that this part of his defense of Socrates is unconvincing (392).

The second point of his defense involves a broad comparison of Socrates' speeches and way of life with the convictions and traditions of Athens. He sees no real conflict between the two. I will speak to three of his chief contentions.

(a) Umphrey asserts that "West misconceives Socratic irony by overestimating the openness or publicity of Socratic philosophy" (395). I agree with Umphrey that one must distinguish Socrates' own activity from "the public *praxis* in which it occurs." But it is precisely Socrates' "public *praxis*" that is at issue here. Was not Socrates famous for publicly contradicting generally accepted opinions about "the greatest things," including the traditional stories about the gods? (*Apology* 21c-23b, *Republic* 377b-383c, *Euthyphro* 6a). Did not Socrates corrupt the young Lysis, as is demonstrated by Umphrey himself in his discussion of Bolotin's book?[4] Reading Umphrey, one sometimes wonders how the trial for impiety and corruption of the young could ever have taken place. One is reminded of Walter Berns's Socrates, who politely "went down into the cave to learn from the various imperfect opinions of men" and who "lived quietly with his fellow Athenians while hardly letting them know he philosophized."[5] This sounds more like a cautious junior professor on his way to tenure than the defiant challenger of Callicles, Anytus, and Meletus (*Gorgias, Meno, Apology of Socrates*). To be sure, Socrates did not blurt out his private opinions to just anyone at any time; I went to considerable lengths to show Socrates' circumspection in my account of the *Apology of Socrates*. But he did reveal quite a lot, and that provided the legitimate occasion for his indictment and condemnation. The least that one would have to say is that Socrates' secrecy measures seem to have been defective.[6]

Socrates' philosophic quest for knowledge of "the greatest things" necessarily comes up against the authoritative opinions of the Athenian tradition. Those opinions prove under Socrates' examination to be boastful claims to knowledge where there is no knowledge. So Socrates cannot accept those opinions. Such opinions concern not only morality but especially the gods of the city. Therefore Socrates did not believe in the gods in which the city believed. Moreover, by conducting his arguments in public, in the presence of young people, he corrupted the young in the sense that the city understood corruption.

(b) Umphrey denies that orthodoxy, the holding of correct opinions, is as important to religious "belief" (*nomizein*) as I think it is. The law is much more concerned with right action than right thought. "Civic religion consists . . . less in holding certain things to be the case—for example, that Zeus exists and cares—than in performance of certain practices (*nomizomena*)—for example, making and keeping oaths" (396). Even if Umphrey's argument is correct, it misses the point. Orthodoxy is the foundation of orthopraxy. Fear of punishment is no sufficient guarantor of right conduct; what is especially needed are deeply held convictions about the just and unjust, good and bad, noble and shameful. Although Umphrey does not deny the need for such convictions, his argument tempts the reader to think they are superfluous. He leaves one with the impression that he is a follower of the political theory of modern liberalism, which did indeed attempt to discover a new basis for political life acording to which private opinion could be left alone. It is doubtful, however, whether modern liberalism has succeeded in a single instance in providing the foundation for an enduring political order, for a regime that remains indifferent to the moral convictions of its citizens is one that invites self-contempt and eventual self-destruction: Weimar Germany, for example. The United States is certainly not a liberal regime of this sort, as is shown above all by the speeches and career of Lincoln. A liberal regime whose citizens hold opinions indifferent or hostile to free government cannot last. All the more important are the moral opinions of the citizens of other, nonliberal polities. For these reasons the Athenians were rightly concerned about Socrates' opinions regarding the gods, and so his habitual performance of prescribed religious duties was hardly enough to establish his piety.

(c) Umphrey employs an esoteric interpretation of Greek poetry to rationalize the Greek gods and thereby to make them compatible with Socratic inquiry. As poetic analysis his account is perhaps plausible if not completely convincing. But as an account of the self-understanding of

Athenian civic theology it is far off the mark. For if "the 'cosmos' of Ideas according to Plato is not dissimilar to the pantheon according to Homer" (397)—an astounding enough claim in itself—then these beautiful, remote gods of Homer are only nominally the same as the avenging gods of Athens, who affirm the authority of the laws and the sanctity of the family. On behalf of these gods the Athenians engaged in a frenzy of murderous recriminations against guilty and innocent alike following the mutilation of the Hermes-statues during the war with Sparta (Thucydides VI). And the Athenians condemned the ten generals who did not pick up the dead bodies from the naval battle partly because they were thought to have violated the sacred burial laws.[7] Because Umphrey underrates the degree to which Athens was rooted in the ancestral (397), he also underrates the degree to which their gods were understood as defenders of ancestral tradition and of the sacredness of "one's own." Umphrey conflates the readily accessible with the remote and implicit teachings of Greek poetry in the same way as he accuses me of conflating the exoteric and esoteric teachings of Socrates. But the poets were generally thought to speak the truth about the gods (*Euthyphro* 6a-b), while Socrates was generally believed to deny the city's gods (*Apology* 18b-c).

We may summarize Umphrey's defense of Socrates as follows: (a) Socrates keeps his true, subversive thoughts hidden, so there is no conflict between Socrates and the city; (b) since private convictions are barely relevant to law-abidingness, we should hesitate to conclude on the basis of his opinions alone that Socrates was guilty of impiety; (c) besides, the citizens' opinions are really protophilosophic, more or less open to a rational account of the whole, like Greek poetry.

One might wonder why Umphrey bothers to argue that Socrates concealed his thought if there is no conflict between that thought and the city. Likewise, we could continue our examination of other, less important aspects of Umphrey's defense. More to the point, we could be led to ask what significance could possibly attach to the trial of Socrates if Umphrey is right in his contention that Socrates did not make public his thoughts, thoughts seemingly harmless in any event. Was the trial, then, merely the ganging-up of some democratic politicians on a former friend of Critias and Alcibiades, those former enemies of the Athenian democracy? From the point of view of philosophy—the core of Socrates' life—was the trial only a tale told by an idiot, signifying nothing?

But it would be pointless to pursue these questions. For Umphrey lets us know that he does not believe his own arguments. He prefaces his defense of Socrates with this surprising admission: "One can say of [West's] book what Hobbes said of Spinoza's *Theologico-Political Treatise*: it disseminates the truth with bold candor" (388). More particularly, Umphrey all but concedes in the fifth and final section of his review that Socrates was indeed guilty of violating the city's laws both in the narrow and in the larger sense. The conflict between Socrates and Athens was fundamental. There *was* a law against what Socrates was doing, and Socrates' activity *did* cause disrespect for authority within the city (419).

Why then does Umphrey pretend to disagree indignantly with me about Socrates' guilt when he really agrees? The answer is that Umphrey wants to defend philosophy against what he regards as its principal enemy: the waspish, spirited pretentiousness of the political. "From the standpoint of the philosopher, [the conflict between Socrates and Athens] is a conflict between *eros* and *thumos*, between human wisdom and very great stupidity or sophistry" (417). Umphrey's whole essay, which is entitled "*Eros* and *Thumos*," may be read as a sustained attack on thumos (spiritedness) and on politics in the name of philosophy. In the first half of his essay, in which he reviews Bolotin's book on friendship, Umphrey presents an extended analysis and critique of friendship. He takes friendship to be founded on spiritedness, on the ground that friendship and spiritedness remain satisfied with being oneself and being at home with one's own (family, friends, and city) without concern for aspiring to and acquiring the good (see especially 378–379). The latter concern, characteristic of philosophy, belongs according to Umphrey to the province of eros. Plato's portrayal of the trial gives us a picture of embodied Eros (Socrates) in elemental conflict with embodied Thumos (Athens). Umphrey defends the erotic Socrates, then, against the spirited attack of West and Athens. Socrates may be guilty of breaking the law, but Athens and West are guilty of being enemies of philosophy and hence of the erotic pursuit of the good.[8]

Evidently Umphrey directs his spirited indignation (392) against me not because he is convinced of Socrates' innocence but rather in order to reprimand me for letting the cat out of the bag. Umphrey would prefer to conceal the truth about Socrates in order to defend his own "friend," philosophy. There is precedent for this procedure: Plato wrote the *Apology of Socrates* as a defense of Socrates while showing "between the lines" the deficiency of Socrates. But ancient Athens is not modern America. Athens was a city in which philosophy as a way of life known to the city was quite new. There was no public prejudice in its favor, and much against. In America today people are accustomed to defer to the claims of science and rational inquiry. Philosophy is publicly respectable. A common dogma holds that open-mindedness is one of the highest virtues. Spiritedness in its political manifestations, on the other hand, has fallen into disrepute. War and imperialism are out of fashion. Patriotism makes people uncomfortable. The notion that the country is threatened by Communist enemies is derided. Nixon's spirited partisanship was roundly hated; much more acceptable is Reagan's easygoing nice-fellow manner. Serious religious conviction is an embarrassment, particularly among teachers and journalists, who in turn are encouraging young people and older citizens to feel the same way. It is considered illiberal to express concern over the decline of traditional morality. In short, all those things which, according to Socrates and the ancients, are essential to healthy political life, are today under attack. Yet Umphrey thinks, as I judge from the way he wrote his review, that the most urgent duty of the philosopher today is to attack spiritedness and the political.

The practical problem of our time is the victory of the modern liberal critique of politics, a critique which maintains that one can and ought to do away with the intrusions of spiritedness into public life. An enlightened, sophisticated citizenry can supposedly live together peacefully without any public concern with morality, religion, hatred of enemies, or any other of the lingering relics of the Dark Ages. Such superstitions are to be relegated to the arena of private life, and there they will gradually be rendered harmless by the spreading doctrine that there is no matter of right and wrong important enough to fight over to the death. The Last Man will live in John Rawls's bureaucratic utopia in perfect contentment.

Of course, political life did not transform itself in the hoped-for manner. The promises of liberalism proved to be empty. Instead of the apolitical, purely administrative politics of a new age of civilization and peace, we in the twentieth century find ourselves subjected to a politics of bestiality—in Communism and Nazism bestial beyond the wildest dreams of tyrants of earlier ages. War and partisan contention become far more terrible than ever before because the parties of modernity compete in a common apocalyptic mission: to rid the world once and for all of the remnants of illiberalism, of spiritedness. Blind to the political character of its crusade against politics and traditional morality, modern liberalism threatens not only the survival of a civilized West but the survival of philosophy itself.

This, then, is why I attacked Socrates in my book: not because I am antiphilosophic, but because I wanted to defend against liberalism the dignity of spiritedness and of political life. From a certain point of view I am even executing Umphrey's project more faithfully than he does himself: if spiritedness causes one to be content with one's own and eros leads one away from it, then the eros that turns away from one's own calls in the first instance for a spirited critique of Socrates (who is viewed as apolitical and hence self-evidently good, according to current dogma) and a spirited defense of politics. Umphrey and I agree, I trust, that philosophy is in danger and ought to be protected. We disagree about where the current danger to philosophy is strongest. He sees it in politics, I infer, while I see it in the pseudo-philosophical opinion that views politics and the conditions of political life with indifference or sovereign contempt.

There is more hatred of what Socrates stands for beneath the easygoing praise accorded him by our liberal age than in my sympathetic critique of him. It is necessary to understand and face up to Socrates' guilt in its full scope before attempting to transcend the realm of conventional opinion by philosophizing. Indeed, except in the rarest cases, such "transcendence" is nothing more than an exchange of one convention (that of the political community) for another (that of a philosophic sect or of the "Republic of Letters").

II. Socrates' Way of Life. But what is philosophy? Umphrey seeks not merely to defend Socrates, but also to understand him. He devotes the central section of his review of my book (402–412) to the question of Socrates' "thing," his *pragma*, which, as he says at the outset, is really the main theme of his whole essay (354). Umphrey accepts much of the argument that I developed in *Plato's Defense of Socrates*, especially concerning the incomplete, questioning character of Socrates' "human wisdom." Umphrey and I agree that Socrates "must remain radically Odyssean, wandering (or falling) between goal and starting point, wisdom and ignorance, virtue and one's own, mind (or soul) and body (or city)" (405). But Umphrey disagrees with my estimate (which is shared according to him by Leo Strauss [405]), that Socrates' way of life makes sense. Umphrey believes it is *alogon*, nonrational, for "human wisdom is suppositionless." It "provides insufficient purchase for *any* inquiry. Yet Socrates inquires like *crazy*" (409, emphasis added): "there is madness in his *methodos*." Umphrey even purports to discover "the religious dimension in his thinking" in Socrates' allegedly unquestioning deference to his nonrational daimonic voice: "To the extent he is guided by it, he operates mindlessly." In light of all this, Umphrey cannot understand why "Socrates remains outwardly resolute and serene. This is but one appearance of a problem which I, for one, am unable to resolve: By virtue of what does Socrates, or anyone else, keep his head in *aporia* [perplexity]?" (410).

One is certainly surprised to encounter this disparagement of Socratic philosophizing after Umphrey has gone to such length to defend Socrates. It appears that Umphrey is a sort of Don Quixote: the noble knight battles the supposed enemy of beautiful Philosophia, yet West is no enemy to his lady, who, alas, turns out, like Dulcinea, to be no fair lady at all but merely a "beautiful illusion" (412). But in fact, Umphrey's essay as a whole goes well beyond Quixotism. For after exploding the pretensions of spiritedness (and therefore of political life generally) in the name of eros in his review of Bolotin, he proceeds to explode the pretensions of eros (and therefore of philosophy) in his review of West. Umphrey is no Don Quixote, but rather a universal pulverizer. After the dust clears, we seem to be left with nothing. How are we to understand this strange turn of events?

In the *Apology*, Socrates gradually unveils his true self in the course of his speeches to the jury. Umphrey provides a useful and sympathetic

summary of my somewhat complicated explanation of this unveiling
(403–405). There is no need here to go over this ground again. For the
main point of Umphrey's diagnosis and rejection of Socratic philosophy
and of my defense of Socratic philosophy is this: Socrates' "human wisdom" (*Apology* 20d), limited as it is to knowledge of one's ignorance of
"the greatest things" (22d), cannot provide knowledge that the philosophic life of conversational inquiry is worth living. It is not Socrates'
practice but his theory that is boastful or pretentious (410). Therefore
Socrates' affirmation and choice of his way of life is irrational at its root.
Nor does Umphrey shy away from the terrible implication of his argument. In the end, he suspects, "one cannot know the whole and be whole"
(411). In other words, knowledge and happiness are incompatible. It
must be understood that this is not an incidental point made by Umphrey
in passing. For he conceives this opposition between knowledge and happiness as an expression of the opposition within the soul of eros and
thumos. Love, which strives ultimately for wisdom, and spiritedness,
which repels everything that threatens one's own preservation and one's
being comfortably at home with himself, are implacable enemies. For
since love takes one outside of oneself, alienating one from oneself in
the quest for knowledge, spiritedness opposes love on behalf of man's
"natural," self-complacent, self-ignorant wholeness. There can be no
peace, but only war more or less concealed, between such opposite con-
tenders for sovereignty in the soul. The supposition that the erotic quest
for wisdom can restore man's natural, thumotic wholeness—that the goal
of eros and thumos is one—is false. So insofar as Socrates holds that the
life of philosophy is the greatest good for a human being, he is probably
succumbing to "a beautiful illusion without which our life would appear
unlivable" (412).

We are familiar with Umphrey's position. Let us not hesitate to call it
by its true name: nihilism. Umphrey rejects Socratism, then, because he
is a nihilist. So let us address the point in question: is Socrates' human
wisdom a sufficient foundation for a rational life? We may begin from
the fact that knowledge of one's ignorance about the greatest things is not
ignorance altogether. Such knowledge implies that one knows what the
greatest things are, that is, what the most important problems or questions are. One knows this by a reflection on one's human condition: one is
alive, one's way of life is a matter of choice, and that choice is urgent and
inexorable. How to live, or, in a typical Socratic formulation, "What is
virtue?" comes to sight as life's primary question. But how is this question
to be answered? Since people hold different opinions about it, Socrates
examines their opinions by conversing with them. He quickly discovers
that those opinions are incoherent. So he tries his own hand at thinking
out in conversation with others the question of how to live. As he pursues
this inquiry, he finds that it is long, arduous, and apparently inconclusive

—though always pleasant. He does make some progress in clarifying and deepening his understanding of the problem. He even derives a certain satisfaction from his awareness of this progress. But he acquires no final answers. In spite of that fact, or because of it, he finds himself in possession of a tentative answer to his question: the best life is the life of inquiry. Of course Socrates cannot be absolutely certain that this is the best life; as long as the inquiry remains incomplete, his serenity will be tempered by a sober recognition that against all likelihood his whole life could be a mistake.

We may consider the *Republic* as exemplary of Socrates' procedure. Confronted at the beginning with Cephalus' paternal authority and, behind it, the authority of "divine revelation," Socrates points out to Cephalus an apparent contradiction in its prescription. Instead of continuing the discussion, Cephalus abruptly departs, laughing. Is his laughter a sign of genuine superiority to Socrates' paltry *logos*? Or is it only a more or less conscious cover for his inability to respond sensibly to Socrates' question? For almost all practical purposes Socrates must assume that the latter is the correct explanation, or else he would be left in helpless perplexity and the conversation could not reasonably continue. Still, he cannot *know* that this is the case. Maybe against all odds, and against the evidence of Cephalus' character (which comes to sight as defective), Cephalus' authoritative, poetic, "revealed" wisdom *is* the way to truth. The memory of Cephalus' brief appearance and exit, then, hangs over the subsequent discussion like a looming question mark. But that does not intimidate Socrates—far from it. He inquires, not "like crazy," as Umphrey asserts, but soberly, tentatively assuming that the opinions of himself and his interlocutors contain divinations, or partial glimpses, of the truth they are seeking, and that the refinement and enlargement of those opinions will bring them closer to the idea of justice. And that is exactly what seems to happen. For although the conversation reported in the *Republic* fails to provide a simple, unambiguous definition of justice, it does succeed in showing forth the full scope of the problem of justice. It does so, in brief, by showing that whenever we speak of justice we have two different things in mind: complete dedication to the common good of one's own community, and perfection of one's own soul. If we take the *Republic* as a whole, including the Cephalus episode, we may even say that the *Republic* itself, as it is read and thought through by the reader, *is* the idea of justice. Through it we see what justice is, how the problem of justice reveals itself in all its aspects. Is that achievement knowledge or ignorance? It cannot be knowledge strictly speaking, because of the necessary reservations we have mentioned. But it is more than ignorance. And so, by virtue of his resourcefulness (*euporia*) in inquiry, Socrates is able to "keep his head in *aporia* [perplexity]" (410) when others are overwhelmed and dumbfounded by the prospect of indefinite prolongation of the argument. For some Socrates may be only a torpedo-fish who stuns them into lethargy, but for others he is a gadfly who awakens and prepares them to think.[9]

III. Socrates, Classical Political Philosophy, and Modernity. Umphrey's verdict, in sum, is that "while the difference between his [Socrates'] philosophizing and his human wisdom is greater than West makes it seem, the pretentiousness of Socrates' practice is less than West makes it seem" (410). My contention, of course, is just the opposite: while Socrates' philosophizing is nothing more than the continual exercise of his human wisdom, his practice, his patent and persistent challenge to the foundations of Athenian morality and piety, is political dynamite. We have seen that Umphrey secretly agrees with me concerning Socrates' guilt; but I do not concur secretly or openly with Umphrey's nihilistic disparagement of the Socratic enterprise.

At the foundation of modern liberalism lies the conviction that there is nothing serious at stake in the quarrels of political life and that philosophy as the quest for the Right and the Good is impossible.[10] Umphrey's account of Plato appears to agree, for according to Umphrey political life is founded on an illusion, and Socratic philosophy is "madness" (410). One might have expected an assiduous student of the classics like Umphrey to enlist as an ally in my effort to counteract the reigning liberal prejudices of our day. Instead, he does not seem to mind placing the Socratic-Platonic citadel at the disposal of the forces of modernity. Is it not more fitting to defend Socratic philosophy *and* civic piety against the liberal trivialization of both?

Socrates and Athens—philosophy and politics—both agree that knowing and doing what is right matters more than anything else in life, while modern liberalism denigrates both by denying publicly that the question of what is right is answerable. We have all grown up with these opinions, and we are infected by them. The political cowardice of the West, as well as the virtual collapse of political philosophy since Nietzsche, may both be traced to the victory of such opinions. For if life is meaningless at its heart, then there is no point either in defending oneself or in thinking for oneself. It is gradually dawning on people that the victory of modernity means not the joyful liberation of man from the last remaining chains of the dark ages, but rather the utter disappearance of significance from human life.

If an ideological liberalism which reduces to nihilism is the current view, and if, as I think, this view ought to be attacked for the sake of the life of inquiry as well as for the sake of morality, then we should not be told to look down on political concerns, but rather to pay them a due respect. We are less in need of reminders of the deficiency of political morality than of lessons in its nobility and strength. We do not need to hear that classical natural right gives little or no guidance to political life, but rather that natural right is the indispensable foundation of sound politics.

It was this concern—and not any gratuitous "taste for manliness and subtle thought," as Umphrey seems to think (421)—that moved me to try to understand the peculiar way in which Plato portrays Socrates in the *Apology of Socrates* and elsewhere. Sometimes Umphrey seems unaware of this concern of mine (for example, 392, n. 50); at other times he dismisses what I had to say about it rather rudely (420–421); elsewhere Umphrey presents in his own name a view about the relationship of Plato and Socrates that concurs with my own (395, 399). Since Umphrey seems not to have grasped my intention in this matter, I will state more clearly what I understand to be the difference between Plato and Socrates, for this is one of the most distinctive features of *Plato's Defense of Socrates*.

Plato wrote the *Apology of Socrates* in such a way that the surface impression of Socrates' innocence contradicts the true teaching of the work, Socrates' guilt. Plato proceeded in this way not because he wished to denigrate political life but rather to lay the foundation for a new political morality. Plato fashioned from Socrates a new hero in a new, post-Homeric "poetry" in order to provide the best of the Greek youth with a standard by which politics could be measured and ordered. In reading Plato it is necessary to contrast Socrates as he appears to the characters within the dialogues with Socrates as he appears to us, the readers. To the jury before whom he speaks, Socrates is an ugly, offensive old man who annoys the citizens and threatens the city. To the readers of Plato's *Apology of Socrates*, Socrates is a noble truth-seeker wrongfully condemned to death by ignorance and villainy. Plato rejuvenates and ennobles Socrates (*Second Letter* 314c) by blunting his harsh edges, his persistent questioning of conventional opinions. The Platonic Socrates comes to sight for us as a defender of morality and political responsibility.[11]

For example, it is characteristic of Plato that he (and not Socrates) should bring into the light of day the reverential, almost patriotic speeches of Socrates in the *Crito*, a most private dialogue conducted secretly in prison in the dark, where it otherwise would have remained. For the *Crito* is a "performed" dialogue, that is, one that *Plato* reports directly to his readers; it is not narrated by Socrates or anyone else. When it is read together with the *Apology of Socrates*, the *Crito* mitigates for Plato's readers the lingering effects of Socrates' defiance of Athens in his defense speech. In the same spirit as my remarks here, Alfarabi goes so far as to say that the *Crito* is the *Apology of Socrates*—that is, Socrates' real defense speech is the *Crito*, not the speech he delivered at the trial, which Alfarabi appropriately renames the *Protest of Socrates against the Athenians*.[12]

The key to Plato's transformation of Socrates into a figure of impeccable moral and political credentials is to be found in the new image of philosophy put forward in the dialogues. The philosophic life, which might seem to be the enemy of morality because of its uncompromising insistence on knowledge as the only acceptable basis for thought and action, is painted in beautiful tones by Plato in his portrait of Socrates as hero, so that philosophy itself takes on the color of morality.[13] Philosophy becomes an object of respect and love in the pious eyes of spirited lovers of the noble. Philosophy becomes as it were the peak of moral virtue, including in its sweep all or most of the demands of morality in the traditional understanding.

Plato proceeded as he did because of the danger to sound politics, as well as to philosophy, that arises when philosophic inquiry is conducted openly and continuously in any society. For all societies, even modern liberal societies, exist in the element of opinion. The bond that holds them together is the shared convictions about the things that truly matter, the things about which one dares not make jokes in public. Undiluted Socratic philosophy is dynamite for civil socity:[14] it explodes these convictions by throwing them and everything else into question—everything except the rightness of the philosophic life itself. From the jury that was about to vote on his condemnation to death, Socrates demanded public recognition of the philosopher as the city's greatest benefactor. (According to Alfarabi, Plato corrected his predecessor Socrates on this point by omitting any provision for exalting the philosophers in the city, as opposed to exalting the "virtuous" and the "princes."[15]) But the philosopher cannot be recognized as the greatest benefactor without undermining the moral conditions of political life and of philosophy itself. Here is the larger ground of Socrates' guilt. The public expression of his philosophizing endangers philosophy, the best way of life. Aristophanes' *Clouds* shows how the Socratic critique of the Athenian gods destroys the sanctity of the family, on which the city depends for the moral education of its children.

Philosophy presupposes morality, for philosophy begins from the moral stance that there is nothing more needful than justice and truth. Unless the souls of the young are imbued with an ardent longing for these things, there will be no philosophy, for those souls will be incapable of taking themselves or anything else seriously. At their core they will be frivolously nihilistic, for although they will experience all sorts of things in life as exciting, entertaining, and interesting, they will never ascend to the central question of philosophy because they will not feel the inescapable primacy of the question of what is the right way of life. They may study philosophical books, and they may pride themselves on their philosophic openness to all the serious questions. But when they take up works of political philosophy, they will view those works in a detached way, aesthetically, so to speak, as though they were working on an elegant sort of crossword puzzle or mathematical game. The ultimate consequence of a public critique of morality is the same as the effect of contemporary liberalism in academic life, namely, to eviscerate philosophy by turning it into an easygoing moral relativism presided over by various in-groups of cognoscenti who applaud each others' refined interpretations of great books and ideas while they live the quite ordinary life of liberal intellectuals.

Ours is a time of serious revival of the study of classical philosophy, achieved through the efforts of Jacob Klein, Heidegger, and above all Leo Strauss. But that revival has occurred against the background and the opposition of radical modernity. Both Heidegger and Klein have been affected, probably against their intentions, by this radical modernity. The challenge, then, is to persist in this revival by aspiring to liberate ourselves not from morality but from the chains of modernity in which all of us are bound from childhood on. Of the three thinkers mentioned, Strauss most successfully resisted this enslavement, and he was able to do so because he never forgot that as a Jew living among non-Jews he was ruled by those who, if it came to a fight, would destroy him because of his political and religious heritage. Strauss called this problem "the theologico-political predicament"[16] and he devoted his life to the study of that problem.

It appears that few of Strauss's students—or the students of his students—are alive to the primacy for political philosophy and political life of the "theologico-political predicament." One set of students, who may be likened to ancient Epicureans, preoccupy themselves with the study of Great Books as an end in itself—a pleasant activity that is the best that life can offer. For them, political philosophy has apparently come to mean not thoughtful confrontation with the conditions of philosophizing in the world of radical modernity, but rather an exceedingly private, scholarly concern with the exegesis of leading texts in the history of philosophy. Another set of students, more bold, and spirited, continues by new means the long war waged by modern liberalism against politics and philosophy. This group—to which Umphrey may belong—enlists the authority of Strauss's authority, classical political philosophy, and discovers in it—modernity. Against the intention of Strauss's life work—see especially the tremendous attack on modern liberalism in the Schmitt review and his remarks on that review at the end of the Spinoza preface[17] —these scholars are teaching in effect that the one apparently serious alternative to modernity, classical political philosophy, provides in fact a covert endorsement of modern liberalism and ultimately of nihilism.

One of the typical features of both these kinds of students, it must be said, is a secret or open contempt for America and American politics. This is so in spite of the fact that the American regime is one of the few regimes of the modern world whose principles (rightly understood) and conduct are defensible on the basis of the classics. One must indeed admit with Strauss that "the theory of liberal democracy originated . . . in the first and second waves of modernity" and that liberal democracy cannot be defended by a "return to the earlier forms of modern thought: the critique of moden rationalism or of the modern belief in reason by Nietzsche cannot be dismissed or forgotten." Yet "the theoretical crisis [of liberal democracy] does not necessarily lead to a practical crisis, for the superiority of liberal democracy to communism, Stalinist or post-Stalinist, is obvious enough. And above all, liberal democracy, in contra-distinction to communism and fascism, derives powerful support from a way of thinking which cannot be called modern at all: the premodern thought of our Western tradition."[18] Strauss points here to the most im-portant task of contemporary American statesmanship, whether prac-ticed by scholars or political men: to explain and defend America as a polity springing from and aspiring toward the highest purposes of West-ern civilization. For "the coming of the universal and homogeneous state will be the end of philosophy on earth."[19]

Notes

1. "*Eros* and *Thumos*," *Interpretation* 10 (May & Sept. 1982), 353–422. Pp. 354–382 ad-dress David Bolotin's *Plato's Dialogue on Friendship: An Interpretation of the "Lysis," with a New Translation* (Ithaca: Cornell University Press, 1979); pp. 382–422 address my essay *Plato's Defense of Socrates*, in Plato's *"Apology of Socrates': An Interpretation, with a New Translation* (Cornell University Press, 1979). Umphrey studied with Seth Benardete at the New School for Social Research; I studied with Harry V. Jaffa in Claremont.
2. It is true that Plato's cave *is* open to the light (*Republic* 514a), but the whole city literally turns its back on that light and denies that it is there at all. Umphrey overstates the cave's openness and understates its closedness (p. 398). Citations in the text will be to Umphrey's review.
3. *Persecution and the Art of Writing* (Glencoe: Free Press, 1952), pp. 154–158.
4. Trying to defend Socrates from the charge of corrupting Lysis, Umphrey concludes that "These defenses are admirable even if not entirely successful" and that Socrates' investi-gation in common with Lysis and the others is "communal dynamite" (380).
5. Walter Berns, "A Reply to Harry Jaffa," *National Review*, January 22, 1982, p. 45 (res-ponding to Jaffa's "In Defense of Political Philosophy: A Letter to Walter Berns," pp. 36–44 of the same journal). This Jaffa-Berns exchange bears directly upon the princi-pal question at issue between Umphrey and me.
6. A point noted by Aristophanes in the *Clouds*: see Leo Strauss, *Socrates and Aristophanes* (New York: Basic Books, 1966), p. 14.
7. *Apology of Socrates* 32b-c and my note to that passage.
8. Umphrey amuses his readers by suggesting that his defense of Socrates is at the same time an urgently needed defense of me, for since I am a "Socratic philosopher," my "explicit condemnation of Socrates is implicitly a condemnation of [myself]" (388). More likely to get me into trouble in the contemporary world of liberal academia is my forthright, "conservative" defense of the political. Consider the case of Willmoore Kendall, a predecessor of mine at the University of Dallas, who was hardly beloved for *his* defense of Athens against Socrates. See "The People versus Socrates Revisited," in *Willmoore Kendall Contra Mundum* (New Rochelle: Arlington House, 1971).

    On spiritedness as *the* characteristic of the political, see also Umphrey's useful essay "On the Theme of Plato's *Laches*," *Interpretation* 6 (Fall 1976), 1–10.
9. He has the former effect on Meno (*Meno* 80a-b) and Critias (*Charmides* 169c), for example.

The whole of the present essay, but especially the section just concluded, also responds to two other intelligent critics, both of whom objected to the absence of a thematic discussion of Socrates' "human wisdom" in my book: David L. Levine's review appeared in *Philosophical Topics* 12 (Spring 1981), 261–265; Michael Davis' in *Independent Journal of Philosophy* 3 (1979), 151–152.

The quotation from Umphrey in the next sentence is taken from his typescript. There appears to be an omission in the printed version on p. 410.

10. See, for example, Locke's *Essay on Human Understanding*, II.21 ("Of the Idea of Power").

11. Umphrey, p. 395, mentions that "*Plato's* Socrates comes to sight as a moral man" (my emphasis). But he does not notice or rather admit that the way Socrates comes to sight to Plato's readers is not the way he comes to sight to the citizens of Athens.

12. *Alfarabi's Philosophy of Plato and Aristotle*, trans. Muhsin Mahdi (Ithaca: Cornell University Press, 1969), p. 63.

13. West, *Plato's Defense of Socrates*, pp. 220–221.

14. The expression is from Leo Strauss, *Natural Right and History* (Chicago: University of Chicago Press, 1953), p. 153; Umphrey alludes to it on p. 380 (see my n. 4 above) and discusses it on p. 395.

15. Alfarabi, pp. 67, 37.

16. Strauss, *Spinoza's Critique of Religion* (New York: Schocken Books, 1965), Preface, p. 1.

17. *Spinoza's Critique of Religion*, pp. 31 and 331–351.

18. Strauss, "Three Waves of Modernity," in *Political Philosophy*, ed. Hilail Gildin (Indianapolis: Bobbs-Merrill/Pegasus, 1975), p. 98.

19. Strauss, *On Tyranny* (Glencoe: Free Press, 1963), p. 226.

13

THE PEACEFUL PURPOSES OF WINSTON CHURCHILL

L. P. Arnn

THE REPUTATION OF WINSTON CHURCHILL IS HELD IN A CURIOUS AND UN-flattering contradiction by modern historians. Students are taught— especially in the schools, but to a lesser extent in the universities, too —that Churchill was the savior of his country, and even of the whole West. They are shown photographs of him with a cigar jutting from his mouth, with his fingers thrust into a defiant "V," and with a caption selected from among his many pugnacious sayings. Against the lunatic Hitler, there rose up a man of extraordinary stubbornness, ambition, audacity, and, yes, even courage. Here was an unusual man for an unusual time.

Churchill once wrote of something he believed Calvin Coolidge to have said: "True, but not exhaustive."[1] That is how the experts look upon this most obvious aspect of Winston Churchill's reputation. "Of course," they admit, "he saved the country, but . . . ." Of course, he saved the country, but he interfered with the generals. Of course, he saved the country, but he loved war for its own sake. Of course, he saved the country, but he was dominated by an "intense personal ambition." Robert Rhodes James, a fine writer and a noted authority on the subject, puts it well:

> In domestic politics, this failure to illuminate the future or to envisage a new, changed society was not an advantage; it also goes far to explain why he leaves no message and no vision for the new rising generation today. He is regarded by them as a fascinating historical personality, but essentially a man of his time.[2]

We must understand the significance of this judgment. The unsubtle observer, when he hears the tale of 1940, will think to himself, here was a man with all the qualities. But this, it turns out, is a crude error, and we are rescued from it by the best students of the past, who teach us that the towering figure of 1940 is somehow irrelevant to us or to the future that has succeeded him. Elsewhere, Rhodes James explains further: "The dispassionate observer can hardly fail to be struck by the absence in Churchill's career, until the mid-1930s, of any great identifiable cause, and by his preoccupation with the immediate." [3]

The indictment boils down to this: Churchill was good for war, bad for peace. He had no domestic policy, or none based upon a connected set of principles. He had a fiercely driven character that made him just the man for a situation created by a lunatic. Always spoiling for a fight, he was ready when the big fight came. But when rationality can or must prevail, another type than that of Churchill must take the lead.

It seems a little odd, then, that Rhodes James also writes: "He shared —and perhaps believed in it more than many Conservatives—the fear of Socialism and Bolshevism. Belief in private enterprise lay in the core of his being."[4] We do not know why, in Rhodes James' mind, this belief in private enterprise at the core of Churchill's being did not constitute "an identifiable cause." Rhodes James does not explain.

Perhaps Rhodes James wishes to imply that this attachment to private enterprise was unworthy of the Churchill who, in the mid-1930s, at last found a cause in anti-National Socialism. In one sense, there is plausibility in this. We think of Churchill as a hero, summoning his countrymen and their allies to heroic virtue. We think of Churchill demanding "blood, toil, tears and sweat." We think of Churchill telling the Cabinet that there would be no surrender until "everyone one of us lies choking in his own blood."[5]

How unfitting to the subject, then, to rifle among the petty interests spawned by commercial democracy in search of the great peacetime cause of Winston Churchill. When we speak of private enterprise, we speak indeed of such virtues as industry and thrift, but these virtues shine with a duller lustre than the glory of the hero. When we speak of private enterprise, we accept *a fortiori* an element of self-interest or, as some would say, of selfishness as one of the mainsprings of society. There would seem to be a contradiction in trying to make Churchill out as a true believer in that kind of liberalism.

We feel it necessary, however, to confront this difficulty. Churchill was not a general. He was a statesman; he left the army and a soldierly career to become a statesman. In doing so, he deliberately involved himself in much thornier questions than face the purely military functionary. It is true, for example, that the martial virtues have a status independent of the issues involved in any, or at least in most any, particular war. We can think of many instances when it has been appropriate for a soldier in one army to compliment the courage of a soldier in another—Churchill, for example, paid a fine tribute to Rommel during the North Africa campaign—and this can be appropriate even when the enemy fights for a cause that is unjust. But statesmanship involves a higher principle. War is waged in service of victory, and victory is therefore a higher object than war. Victory, in turn, is sought ultimately for the happiness that the victor will have the opportunity to win, in the peace that follows the conflict. The happiness of the people is a subject that falls within the ken of domestic policy. Happiness is a higher object for a nation than victory, and therefore, in the end, home affairs is higher and more important than foreign policy, to the extent that there is a distinction between them.

If Churchill had been a general, it would be possible to preserve to him the one corner of greatness which most historians now grudgingly afford him. But a statesman who excelled only in fighting, and who had little or no sense of the cause in which he fought, is hardly any statesman at all. Think, for example, of Hitler, who was unable to understand the distinction between the aims of peace and the aims of war, and who denied the final superiority of the former. Hitler's politics revolved around the triumph of the will. The strength of the will—in his view the measure of the greatness of a people—is best tested in war. We think, though it is a point of controversy, that Churchill had a different and a better understanding of politics than this. In denying that he did, the established historians argue more than is immediately apparent. They argue not only that Chuchill was suited solely for one, unprecedented, unrepeatable situation; they argue not only that Churchill is irrelevant to the present. They argue, it must be realized, that Churchill was the Hitler of the western allies.[6] This is what we think it necessary to dispute.

As is often the case, Rhodes James himself provides the framework upon which we can build our investigation. We begin by agreeing that Rhodes James is right, or nearly right, in his assertion that "belief in private enterprise lay at the core" of Churchill's being. But there is more to the story than that, as we can see by examining the period in Churchill's life when his attachment to those causes was least prominent in his politics.

The first decade of Churchill's parliamentary career is a story of steady, though not uninterrupted, movement toward the left. He began as a Conservative, intending to advocate Tory Democracy within the party in which his father had carried the same banner. By 1904, he had broken with the Conservative leadership on Army reform, on tariffs, and on social welfare legislation. He became impressed with the pitiable condition of the working poor in England's greatest cities. During 1904, he left the Conservative Party, crossed the floor to join the Liberals, and immediately became an unrelenting critic of his former party colleagues. He portrayed them as representative of the rich and the powerful and as exploitative of the poor and the unfortunate. He adopted, straight out of the *Fabian Essays*, the idea that land takes its value only in a minor way from the exertions or the merits of the landlord. The phrase "unearned increment"—a socialist watchword—became frequent in his speeches. He called for discrimination by the tax collector between the earned and the unearned increments in various kinds of wealth, and he called for a much heavier taxation of the latter. He spoke of society as a pyramid, and he believed the job of the Liberal Party was to melt down the peak of the pyramid and to widen the base. These positions, which he maintained with a vigor worthy of his efforts in his most glorious years, won for him the lasting enmity of many in the Conservative Party. This was eventually to cost him dearly.

It is easy to think that Churchill took these radical views solely because of his apprehensions about the effect of socialism upon a mass electorate, recently enfranchised. To some extent, he *did* do it precisely in order to cut the ground from beneath the socialists. However, Churchill believed himself to be fighting on two flanks. On the left he saw a socialist enemy, but there was another foe on the right. On his birthday in 1899, when a prisoner of war in a Boer camp, Churchill wrote to his American friend, Bourke Cochran:

> The economics of former days are on your side. But capitalism in the form of Trusts has reached a pitch of power which the old economists never contemplated and which excites my most lively terror. Merchant-Princes are very well but if I have anything to say to it, their kingdom shall not be of this world. The new century will witness the great war for the existence of the Individual. Up to a certain point combination has brought us nothing but good, but we seem to have reached a period when it threatens nothing but evil. I do not want to see men buy cheaper food and better clothes at the price of their manhood. Poor but independent is worth something as a motto.[7]

Churchill was alive to the potential evils of commerce, or of commerce regarded more highly than it deserves. This was a common enough observation in his time, frequently made, for example, by the Fabians. Moreover, like the Fabians, Churchill saw an element in the Conservative Party—at that time still his own party—devoted to giving political expression to the power of these "merchant-princes."

When Churchill left the Conservative Party, he believed that he had gravitated to the center of the political spectrum.[8] He saw in the Conservative doctrine of protection a counterpart—similar in principle, but transferred bodily rightwards—to the progressive doctrines of the socialists. He said on April 21, 1908:

> The socialists have a plan for putting this world right; Mr. Joynson-Hicks and his friends the Tory protectionists go even further. They have four great social reagents of society—by tariffs, alcohol, gun powder, and denominational teaching they claim to be able to provide alike for the body and soul.[9]

These "four reagants" have reference to four elements of Conservative policy: protection; legislation favoring publicans, who tended to vote Conservative; legislation to expand and reform the army; and education policy. Much of this is little more than ordinary party chaff. Political parties always have certain groups that, partly for accidental reasons, come to vote consistently in their favor. Seldom are parties so short-sighted as to forget these groups when they design their legislative programs. Seldom are opposing parties so discreet as to avoid criticism of these alliances of interest—except when they make their own. The shifting back and forth of such alliances—whether of publicans, priests, shipowners or shipwrights—is the normal stuff of party controversy.

However, Churchill saw in the Conservative policy of protection a problem of a different magnitude. The protectionists believed that by a simple adjustment of taxation two prizes could be won: greater employment and prosperity at home, and greater union in the Empire. The mother country and the colonies and dominions would place duties on imports of food and manufactured goods from non-Empire nations. For the mother country, this *might* mean higher food prices (the protectionists admitted this sometimes, and sometimes did not), but it *would* mean a larger market for her manufactured goods at home and in the Empire. For the colonies and dominions, this *might* mean higher prices for manufactured goods, but it *would* mean improved markets for food exports to the Empire. There would be a net profit for everyone because employment and trade at home would improve, the revenue from the tariff would be useful, and the Empire would be bound together by practical ties of common advantage.

Thus far, we have the makings of a policy that crosses class boundaries, or seems to. Workers and management have a common interest in protection, because—and this was explained in great detail by the protectionists—as the trade goes, so goes the man who toils in the trade. Joseph Chamberlain, who provided the motive force for protection, had been before his Conservative days a Radical within the Liberal Party. He represented and dominated Birmingham, seat of the great Midlands manufacturing region, which had been solid for Gladstone before the Home Rule Bill of 1886 that drove Chamberlain and the Whigs out of the Liberal Party. Chamberlain believed that he could make the great urban regions, previously considered fertile ground for socialism, safe Conservative country. The masses and the industrialists could vote together for Imperial unity and domestic prosperity. The result would be a Britain safe from socialism at home and an Empire powerful enough and united enough to dominate the world.

Here, then, was an elaborate scheme to cope with enormous constitutional changes. Here was a plan to create a sound democracy in a nation with an aristocratic tradition. Chamberlain wished to found a modern, cosmopolitan, free Empire, large enough to circle the globe, powerful enough to grasp and hold the gateways to continents and the passages to oceans. He wished to knit with steel bonds of interest and advantage what was already connected by sympathies and opinions of ancient line-age. He wished to secure a lasting, if not a perpetual, prosperity at home; to enroll masters and men in the same cause; to win the cities for the Tory party; to win Democracy for Imperial Splendor.

We cannot help but wonder, why did not Churchill join? Nay, why did he not simply remain with his father's old allies, in whose ranks he had already enlisted? Joseph Chamberlain had been a Radical; his Liberal credentials were impeccable. When he had decided to make his pilgrimmage from Radical to Tory, who other than Lord Randolph, Churchill's own father, torchbearer of Tory Democracy, had welcomed him to the Carlton Club. Churchill said he wished to make a constitutional, proud, virtuous Democracy. Surely Joe Chamberlain was the man to follow. Surely this Churchill, who—it is said—had no cause to serve but ambition, would fall in with these protectionists.

The facts, however, are inconvenient. Churchill left the Conservative Party, defied the protectionists, and joined the Liberals. He left, he claimed, in order to stand up for "the left-out millions," but at the same time—and here is what we must understand—to stand up for free enterprise. He left because someone would have to pay the bill for this great scheme, and the people who would pay the bill were not the people who would reap the benefits.

In Churchill's mind, the effect of protection would be this: the consumer would be made to pay a higher price for a home-made item, an item that before the tariff he had been unwilling to purchase. The many consumers would be compelled to pay a tax to support in greater plenty the few manufacturers (or, by the same token, the few farmers in the Empire). Churchill believed this to be unwise and unfair: unwise, because it supported by taxation the production of goods that were not really economical to make; and unfair, because it compelled the many to pay for the betterment of the few.

For this reason, Churchill believed protection to be a political movement parallel to socialism. On November 10, 1904, he said:

Many people are frightened at the Independent Labour Party. There is much more to fear from the Independent Capitalist Party. Nothing is esteemed except money, nothing counted except a banking account. Quality, education, civic distinction, public virtue are valued less and less. Riches unadorned are cherished more and more. The Unionist Party has degenerated so far that every interest in it fights for its own advantage regardless of the common interest of the State.[10]

Churchill believed that protection, like socialism, was based on materialism. It aimed to distribute wealth—admittedly throughout the broad masses—without reference to the service performed by the recipients. There would be freedom to earn and to gather lucre, but it would be divorced from the moral value of labor and ingenuity. Like socialism, protection turned its back on private enterprise and private initiative. Like socialism, it favored the interests of one class above another. Like socialism, it held that by exalting the claims of that class, the whole community could move forward to a near perfect, if not a perfect era. When the socialists called out, "Make the rich pay!," the protectionists called out, "Make the foreigner pay!" (but really meaning, Churchill argued, "Make the poor pay!"). Both promised something for nothing, and both made their promises to a growing electorate, increasingly of a middle and working class character.

Churchill believed that the protectionists, like the socialists, would engender class hatred. And in this kind of class strife, the socialists ultimately held all the cards. The protectionists might for a time convince the people that tariffs were making new jobs and greater prosperity for everyone. But eventually, the people would see the true result: higher food prices and higher profits in certain manufacturing trades. Even if the workers in those trades were paid higher wages, the benefits of protection would be confined to a relatively small portion of the population. The reaction against this injustice, Churchill believed, would bring in the socialists.

Churchill set himself to ensure that the reaction would never come, by ensuring that the plan would never be tried. In fact, it never was. Instead, the Liberals won the General Election of 1906, and in the first Liberal Cabinet there appeared Winston S. Churchill, Undersecretary of State for the Colonies. He had, in his opposition to the protectionists and eventually to the Conservative Party itself, taken on a considerable responsibility. He had left his party, and his name alone had ensured that his defection would injure his former colleagues. He had compounded the injury by sparing almost nothing in his polemics against his ex-allies. He had rejected a Great Design, propounded by one of the great Parliamentary figures, aimed to secure many of the purposes to which Churchill had paid at least lip service. Now it remained for him to propose an alternative.

Propose it he did. To begin with, let us state precisely what it was that Churchill claimed he set out to do. He set out, he said, to support democracy in Great Britain. On May 30, 1923, he said to Sir Robert Horne, "I am what I have always been—a Tory Democrat."[11] "Tory Democracy" has always been a curious combination of terms. The Tory Party was, on the face of it, the least democratic party. It was the party of the constitution, including the sovereign hereditary monarch and the hereditary chamber in Parliament. It was the party of the Church of England, established as the official religion, led by the same monarch who ruled the temporal realm. It was the party of hallowed custom, preserving closer connections than any other party with Britain's aristocratic, undemocratic background.

Churchill was certainly aware of this. During December 1909, when a Liberal and in the midst of the fiercest attacks of his life upon the Tory Party, Churchill scathed the Conservative Party for its attachment to aristocracy. Churchill quoted in particular Lord Curzon, about whom one can read in Churchill's *Great Contemporaries*,[12] to have said: "All civilization has been the work of aristocracies." In his response, Churchill gave one of his must lucid and compelling explanations of what he meant by democracy. "What," Churchill replied, "does Lord Curzon mean by aristocracy?"

It is quite clear from the argument of his speech that he did not mean nature's aristocracy, the best and most gifted beings in each generation in each country, the wisest, the bravest, the most generous, the most skilful, the most beautiful, the strongest, and the most virtuous. If he had meant that I think we should probably agree with him. Democracy has been called "the association of us all through the leadership of the best."[13]

Tory Democracy was, for Churchill, "the association of us all through the leadership of the best." We must remember that Churchill gave this definition at a crucial moment, the most radical moment, in his career. He was in full rebellion against the House of Lords. He was completely engaged in the fight against the Conservative Party, which had been routed in a General Election, but which was using its power within the hereditary chamber to thwart the Liberal Government. Churchill published extracts from this speech in a special electioneering volume that contains his most democratic statements. It is appropriately called *The People's Rights*.

Yet, he engages in a curious advocacy of democracy. Democracy means the rule of the many, the rule of the great masses. The principle that justifies the rule of everyone is equality. Churchill said on May 30, 1911: "The whole foundation of our political system is the equality of rights and the equal importance and value of the political rights enjoyed by persons in every class."[14] On the other hand, aristocracy, the rule of the best, is founded upon the inequality of various characters, and upon the justice and the wisdom of allowing the best to rule. Aristocracy is literally "the leadership of the best." But the questions arise, in regard to aristocracy, how are the best to be identified, and who is to make the identification. Lord Curzon and the defenders of the House of Lords argued that the great many cannot be, without qualification, relied upon to select their superiors to rule. But Churchill responded that the Lords were wrong, both as to what constitutes excellence, and as to how to ensure that excellence be chosen. His criticism of Lord Curzon continued:

But the context of Lord Curzon's quotation and the argument of his speech, which was designed entirely to prove that the House of Lords was a desirable institution for us to maintain in its present form, clearly shows that by aristocracy he meant the hereditary legislators, the barons, earls, dukes, etc., and their equivalent in other countries. Again I say that this has only to be stated to be dismissed as absurd. All civilization has been the work of aristocracies. It would be much more true to say "the upkeep of aristocracies has been the hard work of all civilizations."[15]

Churchill admitted that checks on the immediate passions of the people were necessary to preserve freedom and justice. But the Lords, who claimed that they were supplying such checks, had become in his view nothing more than a high-toned party caucus, protecting its own interest. The Lords were predominately Tory protectionists, and Churchill argued that their object was to secure an advantage for themselves and their class. Admittedly, many aristocrats were unselfish people who understood the aristocracy to embody the traditions and the glory of England. Churchill was to some extent in agreement with them. But he insisted that they must pay their own way and they must not violate the "equality of rights" that was the "whole foundation of our political system."

This brings us to the real sense in which Churchill was, even in his most radical days, a supporter of free enterprise. Churchill responded to Lord Curzon, "the upkeep of aristocracies has been the hard work of all civilizations." This is reminiscent of Abraham Lincoln's terse definition of slavery, "you work, I'll eat." For Lincoln, the Great Emancipator, the alternative to slavery, or forced labor, was what he called "free labor." Lincoln once said:

Free labor has the inspiration of hope; pure slavery has no hope. The power of hope upon human exertion, and happiness, is wonderful. The slave-master himself has a conception of it; and hates the system of *tasks* among slaves. The slave whom you cannot drive with a lash to break 70 pounds of hemp in a day, if you will task him to break 100, and promise him pay for all he does over, he will break you 150. You have substituted *hope*, for the *rod*. And yet perhaps it does not occur to you, that to the extent of your gain in the case, you have given up the slave system of labor.[16]

Compare with Churchill:

I venture to say that if the capitalist system is to survive, it must be continuously refreshed by enterprises produced by the genius, the inventiveness, the calculation, the sacrifice and the audacity of individuals. We must not disparage or hinder new businesses making new work for the old unemployed . . . . the House of Commons, where all classes and all interests are represented, ought certainly not to take a view against the equity shareholder or against the bold pioneer who, pushing through the crowd, reaps as his just reward what look likes an enormous prize.[17]

In Churchill and in Lincoln, men are said to work best and live best when they have hope, when they have a goal for which to strive and the prospect of a better life if they are diligent. The impetus for production is supplied by "bold pioneers," who work and who take risks in their own interest. Such people are entitled to a just reward, which will in some cases look like an "enormous prize." This may seem an open encouragement to selfishness among the people, but Churchill, like Lincoln, believed that it was "the only system that has ever been devised for regulating the economic relations between man and man . . . apart from slavery." Both socialists and the protectionists, Churchill argued, would abandon free enterprise, and in the same motion they would abandon justice. The socialists would replace the boldness of the pioneer with "enormous offices filled with bureaucrats," and with "compulsion, the conscription of labor in place of freedom which now exists, and in place of the incentive of private profit." This, Churchill believed, was the whole substance of the "socialist scheme of state slavery." But the protectionists, with their favoritism of manufactures, and their heavy but invisible taxation of the working classes, were proposing in fact a system of slavery in a different form.

Admittedly, the socialists and the protectionists were, on the surface, poles apart in their opinions about property. The former wished to eliminate completely the holding of private property, and the latter wished, or said they wished, to encourage the holding of property among all classes. Churchill claimed, however, that the protectionists, like the socialists, would ultimately concentrate the holding of property in the hands of the governing few. Certainly the protectionists were seeking to protect private property, and many of them claimed that protection would generate wealth, which would be spread about, and which would win converts to capitalism wherever it went. This, Churchill agreed, would be a good thing, but it was only the necessary, not the sufficient, condition of the effect intended. In December, 1909, Churchill said:

The security of property depends upon the wide diffusion of property and its increasing spread year by year among new classes and over great numbers of people. That is the first security . . . . But property will not be secure for many years merely because it is gradually diffused more and more widely throughout the nation. There must be another guarantee besides that. It must be supported by the moral convictions of the people, and if the moral convictions of the people are to be retained, then there must be a constant and successful effort to reconcile the processes by which property is acquired with ideas of justice, usefulness, and services to fellow men. Just laws regulating the acquisition of wealth are the essential foundation, and only permanent foundation, by which the security of property can be based. A society where property was insecure would quickly degenerate into barbarism. A society where property was secure irrespective of the methods by which it was acquired or retained—such a society would be degenerating not to barbarism, but to death.[18]

In their failure to understand that private property exists in the interest of justice, but is not automatically or always synonymous with it, the protectionists would become, Churchill argued, the unwilling cause of its destruction.

It is true that Churchill did not himself make an unqualified defense of capitalism or free enterprise. He favored, throughout his life, heavier taxation upon accumulated wealth than upon wages. He favored, throughout his life, elaborate schemes of social welfare to support those who faltered or who were the victims of accident. He favored compulsory insurance and the nationalization of railways. He understood that, in his support of these policies, he was departing from a policy of pure or perfect equality of opportunity. On January 13, 1909, he said:

> We shall be all the stronger in the day of battle if we can show that we have neglected no practicable measure by which these evils can be diminished, and can prove by fact and not by words that, while we strive for civil and religious equality, we also labour to build up—so far as social machinery can avail—tolerable basic conditions for our fellow-countrymen. There lies the march, and those who valiantly pursue it need never fear to lose their hold upon the heart of Britain.[19]

The ultimate dictate of capitalism, if it is taken as the highest principle of action, is that each individual should pursue the goods of the earth, and the security that follows upon them, to the exclusion of all else. He may indeed be willing to live under a legal system that accords property rights to others, but his actions, including his actions in support of the law, would be governed solely by concern for himself. Of that "last full measure of devotion," of the sacrifice of "blood, toil, tears and sweat," the pure capitalist, if he existed, would be incapable. Churchill, we know, in his later years, was certainly willing to demand such sacrifices. But they are implied no less in his early career. On October 10, 1908, Churchill said:

> "Few," it is written, "and evil are the days of man." Soon, very soon, our brief lives will be lived. Soon, very soon, we and our affairs will have passed away. Uncounted generations will trample heedlessly upon our tombs. What is the use of living, if it be not to strive for noble causes and to make this muddled world a better place for those who will live in it after we are gone? How else can we put ourselves in harmonious relation with the great verities and consolations of the infinite and the eternal?[20]

For Churchill, capitalism or free enterprise was not a replacement for virtue or for aristocracy. It was a means to both. He was a statesman in a nation with many ancient customs, some of which could be drawn upon to moderate the emerging democracy and to elevate its temper, but others of which were grave dangers to democratic life. The same history that gave England the blessing of a rich, aristocratic heritage, reaching back toward Roman antiquity, gave it also the curse of class division. The structure of English society was always potentially rigid, always potentially brittle. Churchill believed that any economic system—any system for distributing the goods, political or economic, of the nation—that recognized or reinforced existing class distinctions raised the supreme danger to the state. Free enterprise was commendable in his eyes precisely because it would—if monopoly were prevented, and if taxation were evenly levied—operate in such a way as to mitigate class distinctions.

Rhodes James observes that, even in this radical period in his life, Churchill's "basic conservatism" is noticeable.[21] Indeed it is. Churchill the Liberal was attacking his former Conservative colleagues in the name of a conservative cause. But first one must know what is meant by "conservative." Churchill's vehemence against Chamberlain and the protectionists derived in large part from the natural appeal their position had for the people. Chamberlain represented a manufacturing district. He and his associates in the protection movement were under constant fire from the socialists, often in league with the trade unions. They needed a weapon with which to fight, and protection was a way to retaliate in kind. It appealed to the strong passion in any people to have more without going to more trouble. At the same time it assuaged their conscience, by assuring them that the whole arrangement was good for their country and its Empire. The foreigner, who had been reaping excess profits anyway, would pay the cost.

In reply, Churchill spoke incessantly and, we believe, sincerely, about the rights of the people, and the interests of the people, and the betterment of the left out millions. But with the same breath he warned them that, if they were to demand to reap the fruits of their own labor, they would be taking on an obligation *to do* the labor, and to suffer if they did not. Justice is a two-edged sword. In a memo about tax policy written while he was Chancellor of the Exchequer, Churchill observed: "A premium on effort is the aim, and a penalty on inertia may well be its companion."[22] However much Churchill may have wished to mitigate through social reform the consequences of failure, he did not seek to remove them, nor did he believe it possible to do so. On April 2, 1908, Churchill said:

Evils there are in our society today, great elemental evils, but they are not due to the maxims of sound finance which this association has so long sustained, and they will not be remedied by any quack treatment at the hands of any party in the State. There is no royal road, it has been said, to knowledge, and there is no shortcut to national prosperity. There is no conjuring trick, no feat of legerdemain, no talisman, no incantation, no wave of the magician's wand by which you will in a moment alter the hard and stubborn facts of life; but there are principles of policy, of economics, and of morals which have been discovered by the great men of the past and which are open to us more widely by the science of the present, by following which the millions who are left out . . . may gradually and surely arrive at better and brighter days and happier and nobler lives.[23]

Private enterprise was for Churchill a method to achieve a distribution of goods in proportion to work done and burdens borne. To him, its main implications were moral, not economic. Within the wide realm in which it operated, it directly opposed and combated socialism and protection, which he saw as two aspects of the same tendency. Protection and socialism encouraged the people to drop their steady habits and to indulge their wildest hopes. Private enterprise —properly managed— reminded them constantly of the difficulty involved in getting a living. This reminder conjured up the necessity of prudence and thrift to prosperity. It brought back into the public notice the necessity of virtue to good living. It must be admitted that free enterprise could not, in Churchill's mind, achieve the salvation of the state. Taken to extreme, held up as a supreme principle, free enterprise led to the desire for monopoly, and under those circumstances it encouraged greed and selfishness. The salvation of the State must be effected, not by merchant-princes, but by princes, or rather by statesmen. On May 4, 1923, Churchill commented on the relative lack, in Britain, of checks or controls upon the popular will, and upon the heavy responsibilities the people bore in ruling an empire and in sustaining a great nation on an island. He could see, he said, only one solution for Britain's many problems:

Our task is, therefore, one of extraordinary difficulty. How can we do it? How have we done it hitherto? Only by giving the masses of the people true leadership and guidance with great and acceptable authority; only by spreading political education everywhere with energy and conviction; only by giving to the people a feeling of association with the conduct of affairs, the feeling that they own the Government and are responsible for the national fortunes. That is the only way by which we have maintained ourselves in the past; and, if it is successfully followed, it will afford a far better security than many of those safeguards and checks upon which Continental Governments rely.[24]

Free enterprise was, Churchill believed, a tool which a statesman might use in the service of virtue, including of course the smaller virtues, but not excluding even the higher virtues. The virtue of the statesman may, in fact, be said to consist precisely in the abililty to bring the lower virtues connected with getting a living and seeing after one's own, into harmony with the higher virtues inseparable from great action on a large scale.

Though it may seem at first glance ridiculous to mention in this context another great war leader, we have in Churchill's portrait of John Churchill, the first Duke of Marlborough, a microcosm of how Churchill saw this statesman's art to function. The Duke is appropriate, because on the one hand his courage is unquestioned and his achievements are unmatched, and on the other, he is accused—and in some instances guilty—of petty avarice unworthy almost of a scrimping fishmonger, a vice to which Winston Churchill was in no way prone. But Churchill wrote:

> It would have been more agreeable to the Muse of History if Marlborough had refused all honours and rewards, and had met the addresses of the Commons by saying that owing to the heavy charges upon the public he had resolved to fight the next campaign on half-pay. But then he would not have been the Marlborough who gained the victories. For certain it is that this same matter-of-fact care for his own interests and desire to found a powerful family in an enduring State was an inherent part of his great deeds. He was a builder for England, for posterity, and for himself. No one of these purposes could be removed without impairing the others, and part of his genius lay in their almost constant harmony.[25]

We believe that Winston Churchill's "identifiable cause," in his early, his middle, and his later years, was to achieve just such harmony as this in the great mass of the British people. In that object can be found the ground of his devotion to free enterprise, no less than the cause of his steadfastness in war and crisis.

Notes

1. Winston S. Churchill, *The Second World War*, Volume I: *The Gathering Storm* (Boston: Houghton Mifflin, 1948), p. 24.
2. Robert Rhodes James, "The Politician," in A.J.P. Taylor, ed., *Churchill Revised* (New York: The Dial Press, 1969), pp. 127–28.
3. Robert Rhodes James, *Churchill: A Study in Failure, 1900–1939* (New York: The World Publishing Company, 1970), p. 381.
4. Rhodes James, "Politician," p. 97.
5. Martin Gilbert, *Winston S. Churchill*, Volume VI: *Finest Hour, 1939–41* (Boston: Houghton Mifflin, 1983), p. 420.
6. We must except Martin Gilbert, the official biographer of Churchill, from this criticism. His sober, careful, and yet massive researches into Churchill's career have already prepared the way for a better understanding. See in particular his *Churchill's Political Philosophy* (Oxford: Oxford University Press, 1981).
7. Churchill to Bourke Cochran, November 30, 1899, reprinted in Randolph Churchill, *Winston S. Churchill, Companion Volume I, Part 2* (London: Heinemann, 1967), pp. 1082–83.
8. On October 24, 1903, Churchill wrote to his friend, Lord Hugh Cecil: "It would be far better for the country in the long run if you were to face the real facts of the case and help to preserve a reconstituted Liberal Party against the twin assaults of capital & Labour. And wherever you go you can only do your best for those religious causes which care about—and your efforts would be more effective on the Liberal side, than on these

Tory materialists." Churchill to Lord Hugh Cecil, October 24, 1903, reprinted in Randolph Churchill, *Churchill, Companion II, 1*, p. 244.

9. Churchill, speech in the Grand Theatre, Manchester, reprinted in Robert Rhodes James, ed., *Winston S. Churchill: His Complete Speeches*, Volume I, (New York: Chelsea House Publishers, 1974), p. 996.

10. Churchill, speech in St. Andrews Hall, Glasgow, reprinted in ibid., p. 381.

11. Martin Gilbert, *Winston S. Churchill*, Volume I, *Prophet of Truth* (Boston: Houghton Mifflin, 1977), p. 8.

12. Winston S. Churchill, *Great Contemporaries* (Chicago: University of Chicago Press, 1973).

13. Winston S. Churchill, *The People's Rights* (London: Jonathon Cape, 1970), pp. 53–54.

14. Churchill, speech in House of Commons, reprinted in Rhodes James, *Speeches*, Volume II, p. 1824.

15. Churchill, *People's Rights*, pp. 53–54.

16. Richard N. Current, ed., *The Political Thought of Abraham Lincoln* (New York: Bobbs Merrill, 1967), pp. 328–29.

17. Churchill, speech in House of Commons, reprinted in Rhodes James, *Speeches*, Volume VI, p. 5860.

18. Churchill, *People's Rights*, pp. 93–94.

19. Churchill, speech in Birmingham, reprinted in Winston Churchill, *Liberalism and the Social Problem* (London: Hodder and Stoughton, 1909), p. 224.

20. Churchill, speech in Kinnaird Hall, Dundee, reprinted in Ibid., p. 210.

21. Rhodes James, *Failure*, p. 36.

22. Gilbert, *Prophet*, p. 74.

23. Churchill, speech in Sun Hall, Liverpool, reprinted in Rhodes James, *Speeches*, Volume I, p. 929.

24. Churchill, speech at the Aldwych Club, London, reprinted in Rhodes James, *Speeches*, Volume IV, p. 3387.

25. Winston S. Churchill, *Marlborough: His Life and Times*, Vol. I, (London: George Harrap, 1934), p. 620.

14

ANOTHER PEEK AT ARISTOTLE AND PHYLLIS

THE PLACE OF WOMEN IN ARISTOTLE'S ARGUMENT FOR HUMAN EQUALITY[1]

Ken Masugi

Nor is there any legislator, however wise or powerful, who could maintain free institutions if he did not take equality for his first principle and watchword.
TOCQUEVILLE, DEMOCRACY IN AMERICA, VOLUME II, PART IV, CHAPTER 7

COMMENTATORS THROUGHOUT THE AGES HAVE DAMNED OR PRAISED ARIStotle for his alleged advocacy of slavery and his denial of human equality. Today, not surprisingly, we find "feminists" charging the Philosopher with advocacy of female subjugation and male superiority. His alleged misogyny plays an important role in Susan Moller Okin's *Women in Western Political Thought,* an undertaking so shoddy that one may rightly ask why it merits mention, much less discussion.[2] But Okin's polemic against Aristotle is a good place to begin a serious discussion of his view of women, for her misinterpretations are actually a more boldly stated form of conventional scholarly views. Such falsifications—whether in their radicalized feminist garb or in more staid dress—prevent one from understanding not only Aristotle's view of women in politics but his whole approach to politics.

The misunderstanding of Aristotle's views on these questions arises from what we can call his method or rhetoric, his political manner of addressing controversial questions. Aristotle has a surface teaching which reflects the conventions of the day but which nonetheless points toward female and male similarities even while it acknowledges differences. At his depth, however, Aristotle argues for women's status as freemen— *eleutheroi.* Of all the beings on earth men and women are most similar to each other. Although this fundamental equality does not mean they are the same, it does allow that they can exercise the same virtues and share in the human good of happiness. Thus, Aristotle is far from the apologist for despotism or misogyny Okin and others take him for—he is indeed western civilization's profoundest and most subtle teacher of human equality.

Okin's Aristotle. In *Women in Western Political Thought* Okin argues that "the great tradition of political philosophy consists, generally speaking, of writings by men for men, and about men."[3] These writings, she maintains, have systematically denied women the status of political and "real" equality with males. But if the western tradition is to remain "relevant," it must be able to speak to the current Western trend toward formal and "real" equality between men and women.[4] Okin omits Marx and other socialist thinkers, who view the abolition of the family with relative equanimity or approval, and who look toward a "humane" future rather than a repressive nature for their standards.[5] Indeed, her book is a preliminary destruction intended to clear the way for a socialist future for the Western world. Swept away would be the unfortunate legacies of the political philosophers Okin does examine—Plato, Aristotle, Rousseau, and Mill —each of whom regarded women primarily in terms of the function they play for males and the family. Such a "functionalism" continues to inform contemporary thought and practice. And it was Aristotle who first articulated this functionalism that epitomizes all that is wrong with the western tradition's view of women.[6]

Okin's condemnation of Aristotle, which echoes throughout the text, develops two major claims—that he establishes a functionalism which informs his approach to everything in the cosmos, and that consequently he directs his philosophy of human affairs to "redeeming prevailing moral views and standards."[7] Citing Aristotle's recapitulation of his procedure in Book VII, Okin concludes:

> Aristotle's ethics is, to a large extent, traditional ethics clarified and justified (that is, saved from inconsistencies and vagueness). Unlike Plato, he does not argue . . . that the world should be different from the way it is, but starts from a basic belief that the *status quo* in both the natural and the social realm is the best way for things to be.[8]

Aristotle hardly appears to be in any serious sense a philosopher at all. Instead he seems scarcely to be more than a creature of his times who, moreover, consciously sought to be nothing other than that.[9]

In the remainder of the book Okin proceeds to argue that Aristotle looks at the entire cosmos and man within it in terms of a functionalism and a concomitant notion of hierarchy which have disastrous consequences for the treatment of slaves and women. He understands what things are, she maintains, by considering their respective functions.[10] And a "strict hierarchy" of functions exists. She concludes that for Aristotle the "Greek *polis* is the natural, and therefore best, form of political association, and that the Greek family—with its subordination of wife, children and slaves—is the natural, and therefore best, form of household and family structure."[11] Aristotle identifies the natural with the conventional simply. Now, she continues, man's function is the highest activity of thinking.[12] Thus, animals and the "vast majority of humans as well . . . are intended by nature to be the instruments" which allow the few to contemplate. "[P]resumably to make his functionalism appear more palatable Aristotle argues that relationships between superior and inferior partners are for the sake of a mutual or a common benefit.[13] But in fact, Okin contends, women are to be understood simply in terms of the function the males insist they carry out. To support her point —she admits that "the subject of women's function . . . is on the whole implicit in the *Politics*"—she cites several passages from *The Generation of Animals*.[14] Based on her citation of this source, she returns to the *Ethics* and *Politics* to contend that women are regarded as inferiors. "All the moral standards applied to women . . . are determined by her function as the bearer of new citizens and the guardian of the household."[15] Thus, Aristotle accords women lower physical, mental, and moral potentials and standards than those of males.

Book I of the *Politics* indeed stresses the great differences between human beings. At the beginning Aristotle examines the first human relationships in order to determine the grounds for distinguishing among the types of rule in the *polis* and the family.[16] These first human relationships are the male-female and the ruler-subject relationships. Aristotle maintains that the first coupling (*sunduazesthai*) occurs from necessity. (He does not speak of a *koinōnia*, which implies a common good.) Male and female do not choose (*prohairein*) to propagate the species, but nature makes them seek to leave behind another. The other relationship is one of natural ruler and natural subject, for survival (*sōtēria*). As distinct as thought and body, the natural master and the natural slave find a mutual advantage in their unity. Thus the first examples of human association arise from the natural drives for sex and mastery.

Dramatic inequalities characterize members of both pairs. It would seem that Aristotle agrees with Calhoun's contention that the statement, "All men are created equal," is a "self-evident lie." If this is the nature which makes the city natural (1252b 31), then any equality between man and woman based on nature alone is scarcely conceivable. Consider too Aristotle's resort to poetry to belittle women: "Silence is a woman's crown (*kosmos*)" (1260a 30). That is, a woman's universe should be encased in silence. Weak in *logos* anyway, she should not bother men with her opinions. This should suffice to confirm that Aristotle thought the worst of women.

Against the background of such statements and remaining true to her historicism, Okin maintains:

> A large part of Aristotle's "social teleology"—that is, his functional treatment of most men—is no longer acceptable. Given the development . . . of modern concepts of equality and the rights of man, it is no longer regarded as justifiable to designate some men as by nature the instruments of others, or to set up different moral standards for different classes. Thus, those who wish to redeem Aristotle's political and moral philosophy as a whole are obliged either to go out of their way to argue anew for his treatment of slaves and workers, or else explicitly to dissociate themselves from this part of his thought, in order to free the remainder from its taint.[17]

Moreover, according to her,

> the injustice of his treatment of slaves, women and workers is all of a piece. . . .
> His system of politics is so extensively based on inequalities that to deny any aspect of the inequality jeopardizes the entire structure.[18]

Nonetheless, Okin laments, those who decry Aristotle's treatment of slavery continue to overlook his treatment of women. Okin correctly argues that the slavery and women issues represent a single theme, but we maintain, contrary to her conclusions, that Aristotle intends a defense of human equality indistinguishable from that of Abraham Lincoln, one which includes both slaves and women. Moreover, the Aristotle-Lincoln argument for women's equality is far better grounded than that of Okin, whose historicism would embrace equality because it had become a widely "acceptable" notion. Thus, our discussion of Aristotle will attempt to show that he is not the captive of his times or the functionalist she charges him as being. We seek not only to salvage Aristotle's view of women but his view of mankind in general.

The Rhetoric of Equality. The rhetorical problems an advocate of equality faces are evident in Aristotle's reputation in the Middle Ages, as indicated in the Aristotle and Phyllis story, and in Lincoln's argument against the spread of slavery prior to the Civil War. A favorite subject of medieval legend, the tale (or "libel", as one scholar calls it)[19] of Aristotle and Phyllis describes Aristotle's embarassing tryst with an Indian seductress, Phyllis. Alexander the Great, the tale goes, began devoting too much time to his wife, the beautiful Phyllis. Told to discipline his former pupil, Aristotle succeeded in the task through the force of argument. The angry

Phyllis then resolved to humiliate Aristotle. Even the Philosopher was unable to resist her charms and declarations of fondness. To prove his love for her, she insisted that he permit her to ride his back (complete with saddle and bridle). This the mooning Aristotle consented to do, in what he thought was a private encounter in a garden. The fiendish Phyllis, however, had arranged for Alexander to come to the garden on another pretext. Upon seeing the spectacle, the indignant Alexander was to hear the Philosopher's explanation:

"'. . . if the woman's cunning and malice have so much power, that she deceived an old man and the most prudent among all mortals . . . how much more will she prevail, attract, deceive you, unless you take caution from my example.' Having heard these things, the king abated his anger and spared his teacher for answering promptly."[20]

Now undoubtedly the tale served Christian interests in its medieval war against philosophy. One scholar even contends that the story re-emerged with the rise of a neo-Thomist movement in the sixteenth century.[21] Here we see how a mere woman debunks philosophy's claim as the highest human activity! But I would also conjecture that yet another basic motive in ridiculing Aristotle lay in his—that is the real Aristotle's—argument for the humanity of women. It is my hope that such an apparently improbable interpretation of the Aristotle and Phyllis saga will seem more than plausible by the end of the paper.

Let us next consider another example of the rhetoric of equality. Reflect on Abraham Lincoln's interpretation of equality:

There is a natural disgust in the minds of nearly all white people to the idea of an indiscriminate amalgamation of the white and black races; and Judge Douglas evidently is basing his chief hope, upon the chances of being able to appropriate the benefit of this disgust to himself . . . He finds the Republicans insisting that the Declaration of Independence includes ALL men, black as well as white; and forthwith he boldly denies that it includes negroes at all, and proceeds to argue gravely that all who contend it does, do so only because they want to vote, and eat, and sleep, and marry with negroes! He will have it that they cannot be consistent else. Now I protest against that counterfeit logic which concludes that, because I do not want a black woman for a *slave* I must necessarily want her for a *wife*. I need not have her for either, I can just leave her alone. In some respects she certainly is not my equal; but in her natural right to eat the bread she earns with her own hands without asking leave of any one else, she is my equal, and the equal of all others.[22]

Observers oblivious to the rhetorical necessities of Lincoln's situation have interpreted his remarks as being racist. But the observation about "natural disgust" indicates the context within which his remarks will have to be taken. Without acknowledging the politically inexpedient and then impracticable policy of making political and civil equals of ex-slaves who happen to be black, Lincoln can still argue that, though they remain unequals in other regards, he and a black woman are equals in at least one natural right. Keep in mind that white women then did not have the same civil rights as white men. Lincoln plays on this difference to give the appearance to some that he does not favor total political and civil equality for black men—an unpopular opinion which would have branded him an abolitionist and hence prevented him from advancing beyond a country lawyer. Thus, Lincoln found it prudent to compare himself with a black woman, who is "in some respects . . . certainly not [his] equal."[23] He then proceeds to give an interpretation of the Declaration which can and should inspire political life today. Equality permits unavoidable inequalities—those of "color, size, intellect, moral developments, or social capacity"—to have their due weight. Aristotle, we will argue, is just as strong an advocate of human equality as Lincoln. And like Lincoln he too employs a cautious rhetoric. For both Aristotle and Lincoln the teaching of human equality is essential to the formation and perpetuation of healthy political life, as their notions of equality ultimately include women as well as men.

Human Equality. In order to understand Aristotle's argument for women as freemen and in some sense the equals of men, we must first attempt to understand the problematic notion of human equality. With extraordinary subtlety Aristotle's *Politics* promulgates a political science based on human equality. His explication of political life is above all dedicated to defending its worthiness, on its own terms, and not necessarily for any trans-political (e.g., philosophy) or sub-political (e.g., friendship) goods. Man's political nature makes his political activity good for its own sake, though, of course, man may have trans- and sub-political aims as well. But Aristotle understands political rule as something apart from despotic or even monarchical rule. To understand this distinction one must consider the significance of human equality in his political science. That political rule can be a separate realm worthy of such deference rests in turn on the notion of human equality—can and ought all human beings treat each other in *some* sense as moral and political equals? Equality of course does not mean egalitarianism, the equal distribution of capacities and honors. Rather, the Aristotelian notion of human equality stresses the fact that all men share in a common nature—part soul, part body, part divine, part bestial—which in turn provides the true basis for the diversity of a single humanity. Only forms of political rule, which point toward the recognition of human equality, can be seriously considered as decent political possibilities, assuming men have some choice.

In *Politics* I Aristotle attempts to persuade the reader of human equality by de-emphasizing bodily differences, so that differences of soul

—that is, of character and intellect—can have some weight in political affairs. And as Aristotle makes this argument the status of women inevitably rises. He wryly observes, "beauty of soul is not as easy to see as beauty of body" (1254b 38–55a 1). Tall and handsome men are, after all, even in this most egalitarian of ages, more successful than short and homely ones in political and other careers. And racial and ethnic appeals are a permanent part of political life. Of course the ultimate denial of human equality is the notion that some "men" are really gods, and that other "men" are in fact beasts. But men created the gods in their image, Aristotle tells us (1252b 26–7). (Recall Genesis 6:4.) Nonetheless, man will always use physical characteristics as a handy, rough and ready means of judging qualities of the soul. Yet, qualities of soul, such as intelligence, cannot be given absolute deference either; philosopher-kings are as great a threat to Aristotle's project as is the rule of brute force. The provision for the banishment of men who exceed in virtue out of all proportion (1284a 3–34) underlines his commitment to equality. Thus, by stressing the soul's importance—through his "invention" of moral virtue—Aristotle takes account of common sense in its typical manifestations of common decency.

As we will see, Aristotle will begin his arguments for human equality and political rule by arguing against the absolute justice of conventional slavery. Despotism as a mode of rule is suspect, outside the household and, implicitly, within it. After having thus allowed for as much equality as conceivable between conventional master and conventional slave, Aristotle will elevate the female half of humanity. But here the differences are too great for equality to be argued simply. Aristotle will have to concede distinctions, which, however, need not necessarily betray a fundamental difference. For women to be in any way the equals of men, it would seem that they would have to show a superiority of soul which would override the bodily differences. Yet Aristotle appears to increase the inequality by ascribing inferior mental capacities to women.

With this difficulty in mind, let us observe for now that Aristotle raises both slaves and women above the status of property (1252b 5–6). Only natural slaves, whose number he carefully circumscribes, are inferior and deserve to be ruled by those naturally superior, and women, though different from men, are still regarded as half the free population (1260b 19). As we examine Aristotle's adumbration of the status of women, we will consider his arguments for their political, moral, and intellectual dignity. He will eventually describe women as half the free population (*eleutheroi*) (1260a 18–19). Indeed, if both partners are decent (*epieikēs*), they can have a friendship of virtue (*di' aretēn*), moral and intellectual. It seems that women can participate in the highest of human relationships, in the political community and in private life.[24] Let us make these the peaks of *telē* as we investigate the place of women in *Politics* I.

We will attempt to show Aristotle's elevation of women from the status of mere property to that of a crucial political element. How is it that those whom the barbarians regard as slaves (with differently shaped and functioning bodies) become freemen by the end of *Politics* I?

However, before we can reach these peaks we must justify the existence of deep valleys. How does the defender of Aristotle, the Abraham Lincoln of Athens, as it were, make sense of statements which would give to women less of the human-defining trait of *logos*, and demand silence of them as their ornament or crown (1260a 30)? It would seem most difficult to defend Aristotle against the charge of denying the full measure of humanity to women.

Aristotle's Methodos *in the* Ethics *and the* Politics. As Okin has charged, and as some of Aristotle's most ardent enthusiasts have lamented, it appears undeniable that he is a Greek chauvinist, an apologist for slavery, and an unabashed upholder of male dominance over the female.[25] A closer inspection reveals, however, that each of these alleged Aristotelian positions presents a resolution of contradictions leading to a rather different conclusion than the surface portrayal had originally suggested. This, and not a relativism or "ethnocentrism," is the true meaning of Aristotle's "methodology" of taking seriously prevailing options. He moves from observation to prejudice back to yet another prejudice, propelling the reader on to yet other steps which Aristotle himself does not explicitly make. It is above all this dialectic which constitutes the core of Aristotelianism. Thus a superficial account retains some of its veracity, while pointing to a profounder argument. Let us reflect on Aristotle's *methodos* and then note how his surface teachings concerning barbarians, women, and slaves ought to be refined.

Contrary to scholars such as Okin, Aristotle engages in neither a "functionalist" view of the world nor an apology for contemporary Greek practices. Rather, his approach is literally a phenomenology, that is, a *logos* or explanation of appearances. But unlike Husserlian phenomenology or its variants, Aristotle's procedure points one toward a natural good, the activity of thinking or philosophizing.[26] In other words, without the precedent of Plato, Aristotle could not have attempted such a phenomenology. His procedure presupposes the worthiness of philosophizing. Without this qualification, his undertaking would in fact justify the prevailing practices in any society, however wicked. Aristotle's procedure is not an attempt to preserve every institution and practice of Greek society (note his virtual dismissal of the gods, who were all-important to the historical *polis*[27]) but an attempt to preserve the best aspects of the conventional and then point beyond to what is truly noble and good: philosophy; friendship, which transfigures the virtues; and statesmanship, which preserves and promotes these goods. Thus, as we read the *Ethics* and *Politics* Aristotle invites us to reflect on how the ordinary understanding of human life can be refined—refinement being the key concept in his phenomenology—to bring about these natural human goods.[28]

Now some would insist that the loss of the *polis* means that all of Aristotle's political philosophy is no longer relevant to modern concerns. True, size does play some role in his regard for the *polis*. However, the compelling reason for his attention to it, other than the fact that it is "one's own," and one must begin from one's own if one is to make sense of the world, is that the historical *polis* was the only haven for civilization and freedom in ancient times. Everywhere else brutish practices, unrelieved superstition, and despotism prevailed. The fact that at least some men were free in the *polis* made it a more desirable place than the harsh empires of Persia and Egypt and the rude village of the Europeans. Thus, Aristotle's concern is for those in any political situation who care for philosophy and politics.[29]

Nature: Greeks, Barbarians, and Women. Aristotle's political science has universal application because of its concern with nature. The focus on nature stands for the "objectivity" of the inquiry. (Consider in this light the vague discussion of natural right in *Ethics* V. 7.) Nature indicates the objective existence of the external world; nature does not give man directions as certain as the commands of divine revelation. Men refine nature through their conventions, as the *Politics* makes evident.[30] Thus, it is not the crude nature described at the *Politics'* beginning to which civilized human beings should seek to attain. While the *Ethics* initially disavows a naturalistic ethic (1103a 23–26, 1114a 31–b 25), the argument of IX. 9 indicates a natural good, existence or life, which consists of sensing (*aisthanesthai*) and thinking, which are in turn refined into friendship and politics, and philosophizing.[31] In the *Politics* various arguments concerning nature reinforce a judicious sobriety about political possibilities. One sees this teaching on nature and its sobriety in what might be taken as a simple assertion of Greek superiority over barbarians.

As he quotes Euripides, "it is proper that Greeks rule barbarians" (*Iphigeneia in Aulis* 1400). The barbarians err in failing to recognize the natural distinction between female and slave, for they do not recognize nature as offering a standard; hence barbarian men and women are as male and female slaves. If thought (*dianoia*) defines the natural ruler, the implication is that the barbarians lack *dianoia* and hence the notion of nature.[32] There is no principle of authority within the barbarian family other than force, the strength of body. (Consider our comments on Tecmessa, below, and consider what Aristotle says in the *Ethics* about the Persian family: the father is a tyrant and the children are slaves [1160b

27–31].) Civilization requires that they be distinguished. Both realms must be ordered before civilization can exist. This refinement of the crude nature of the *Politics'* initial description of human beings (the desire for mastery and coupling) culminates in the description of man as a political animal (that is, one who requires political life for his humanity and for his perfection) and the definition of man as the animal with *logos*.[33] Thus Greeks are superior to barbarians, but by virtue of a principle which qualifies that superiority. The standard which nature sets up is one that can diminish the Greeks as well as raise them. (Compare the American notion of equality as a two-edged sword.)

Now, the Greeks are distinguished from the barbarians by virtue of their elevation of women. Still, women would seem to have a circumscribed place. The three relationships comprising the household are mastership, marriage, and fathering (the latter two have no particular name, Aristotle adds) (1253b 4–11). The anonymity of these relationships indicates their dependence on the conventions of civilized society. Convention refines nature, so that women rise in status from their primeval relationships with men to their place in families, which nourish and educate the young. The various familial relationships correspond with various forms of rule—the ruler of the household rules the slave despotically, as father rules his children royally, and a husband rules his wife politically. (It is of course important to keep in mind that the male rules over wife and children "as freemen" [1259a 39–40].) But the latter relationship is a modified political one in which the partners do not simply exchange roles as ruler and ruled. The male is "by nature more suited to command than the female," except when the union is "against nature" (1259b 1–3). (Similarly the more venerable and complete command the young and incomplete.) Aristotle then elaborates on the type of political rule which obtains between male and female.

> Now then in most cases of political rule ruler and ruled change places. For political rule wants nature to be equal and to differ in nothing, but nevertheless whenever one rules and the other is ruled they tend to seek differences in *schēmata* [forms, garments, insignia, mere appearances, fashions, figures, or manners], in speech, and in honors, just as Amasis told of in his story of the footbasin. The male always had this trait in relation to the female. (1259b 4–10)[34]

Thus Aristotle indicates that the male desire to rule (which he evidently accepts as natural) prevents the male-female relationship from being one of perfect political rule, in which the partners exchange places. The male insists on making his difference in *schēma* further evidence of superiority.[35] Nature may desire equality, but human beings, always aware of their bodies, create conventions which deny it.[36]

Each member of the family displays a certain virtue. The art of household management is more concerned with humans than with soulless property, virtue than with property or wealth, and freemen rather than slaves (1259b 18–21). Yet even the slaves are to possess moral virtue at least to some extent; having *logos* they certainly have the capacity for virtue. Hence by emphasizing what slaves and freemen have in common Aristotle reduces the difference between them. And Aristotle would argue "nearly" (*schedon*) the same point concerning women and children. But by nature there are ruler and ruled, in whom virtue differs. (At this point Aristotle includes the rule of males over other males as well as over slaves, women, and children, to remind the reader that the arguments he gives can apply to free males as well as women, slaves, and children [1260a 7–10].) As in the case of rule, so regarding *logos*: Men, women, slaves, and children possess *logos* in different ways. The slave lacks the capacity to deliberate (*bouleutikon*), the female has it without full authority (*akuron*), and the child has it in incomplete form.[37] Yet, would it make sense to say that all males have the capacity to deliberate with full authority? Surely this is something learned and not simply natural. Intellectual virtue is needed to perfect the *logos* of each human being. Each sex must possess both intellectual and moral excellences to the extent necessary for its respective *ergon*. To elaborate on the different degrees to which each member of the family exercises virtue, Aristotle chooses the male-oriented example of courage (*andreia*). In a man this involves leadership, in a woman service (*huperētikē*) (1260a 23). (Recall that courage is a virtue exercised on the battlefield.) Thus, even in the most masculine of virtues women can have some share.

In *Politics* III Aristotle will remark that as justice differs in the different regimes, so do the virtues for the different sexes. A brave woman would be a cowardly man. A woman is the chatterer (*lalos*) if she is as ordered (*kosmia*) as a good man, "since even the *oikonomia* of man and woman are different, for his work is to take and hers is to guard" (1277b 24–5).

But however virtue may be apportioned between the sexes, the male possesses the greater share of it. Why should the females of today— including of course those with nobler motives than the mythical Phyllis —tolerate such a second-class status? Does not the higher educational status of women today belie Aristotle's evident contempt for them? Or does this contemporary elevation merely reflect the sad condition to which modernity has brought both men and women? To respond thoughtfully to these queries, let us consider Aristotle's most comprehensive response to the human equality question—his discussion of slavery and in particular his distinction between natural and conventional slavery.

In the course of presenting the distinction between natural and conventional slavery Aristotle reflects on the meaning of nature. Aristotle contrasts natural things with those in a state of corruption. Presumably the nature of man is to be found in that human being who is best in both body and soul.

Can it be that birth may convey such a boon, apart from one's city? But if this were true the family might raise itself above the city. Politics would thus lose its dignity, its claim to being a high or even the highest human activity. To preserve the dignity of political life, which is rooted in a particular city, nobility of birth must not be allowed such an extreme claim. Aristotle must prevent the sub-political from overwhelming the dignity of the political sphere on its own merits. Thus it is appropriate that he quote Helen in a tragedy by his friend Theodectes, referring to her divine parentage:

Of divine roots from both sides an offspring,
Who could dare call me servant?

Yet such claims of divine origin are precisely what sensible politics must strive to deny. Helen will have to be judged on her body and soul, not on alleged divine origins. Aristotle thus underlines his commitment to basing politics on human equality. Politics must not become the search for divine roots; rather, it must orient itself by nature, in all its modes, refining for the best.

How then can we judge superior and inferior? Just as soul is superior to body, so is male to female, and tame animal to wild beast. It would be disadvantageous for both if the inferior were to rule the superior. The natural slave would be a human being who differed as much from other men as body does from soul or man from beast (1254b 16–20). Such a man can only apprehend *logos* but cannot be said to possess it. In a passage filled with irony Aristotle declares:

Accordingly, nature wants to create a distinction between the bodies of freemen and of slaves . . . but often the opposite comes about: [Slaves] have the bodies of freemen, and freemen the soul only. Since this is certainly plain, that if freemen were born as gods [from human figures; cf. 1252b 26–27], all would say that those who are "left behind" (*hoi hupoleipomenoi*) would be much more just to differentiate concerning the soul. But it is not as easy to see the beauty of soul as that of body. Hence it is plain that by nature some men are free, and some are slaves, and for them to be slaves is advantageous and just. (1254b 27–55a 2)

In presenting the other side of the question Aristotle explores the notion that all slavery is conventional (*nomikon*). Yet in a way this argument returns to the one supporting the notion of natural differences (1255a 30–31), that is, the standards of virtue and vice (cf. 1094b 14–16). In summary "Aristotle is emphatic that those who are called slaves, but who are in fact competent, are not slaves, but by law and convention only, and the slavery of such men does rest, at bottom, upon force."[38] Despite the enormous difference between master and slave resting on convention, Aristotle does not absolutely deny the possibility of friendship, at least in

the case of natural master and natural slaves, in its way a friendship of
two bodies, one soul.

> For the same thing is advantageous for the part and for the whole, both
> for the body and for the soul. The slave is a kind of part of the master, a
> sort of ensouled part of the body, though it is separated. Hence there is
> a kind of advantage (*sumpheron*) and friendship for each other in those
> who deserve these positions by nature, but for those who are not in these
> positions in this way but rather through convention (*nomos*) having been
> forced (*biastheis*), the opposite obtains. (1255b 9–15)[39]

Thus the only just form of slavery is the natural one, *in which the slave
benefits*. Since the natural slave only perceives *logos* but does not have an
active command of it, he would only be able to carry out commands but
could not bear any responsibility for his actions.[40] Of course political life
can never be completely just, and conventional slavery will continue to
prevail—even the best regime of Book VII.[41] And so women will continue
to have a markedly inferior status in society, until modern technology
and conditions permit their rise.[42]

Women as Equals? Aristotle seems to have reversed himself at the end
of Book I, when he allows women the status of freemen. But how then are
we to understand what freemen are and how it is that women—inferior
as they evidently are—can be freemen? More to the point of our argument, how does this description affirm women's equality with men? If
women are not as low as the barbarians make them—that is, mere slaves
—are they equals with men, as Socrates in the *Republic* makes them?
That Aristotle is dissatisfied with the contemporary treatment of women
is plain in his critique of Sparta, the contemporary city he cites for its
attention to virtue (1102a 10–11, 1180a 24–26). Aristotle maintains that
in Sparta half the city may be said to be badly legislated for, since the wom-
en are improperly treated (1269b 15–19). The Spartans do not oppress
their women; rather, they do not rule them properly. The women own
almost two-fifths of the land, and thus rule their husbands as heiresses
(1270a 23–25). "What difference," Aristotle asks, "if the women rule or
the rulers are ruled by women?" (1269b 32–34).[43] But if it is bad for
women to rule, how is it proper to consider them freemen?

Certainly it is difficult enough for men (*andres*) to qualify for citizenship. In addition to requirements of birth, citizens must contribute to
the common good in terms of military service or the production of
wealth. (Military service is the leading criterion of citizenship in a democracy, wealth of citizenship in an oligarchy. Democracy and oligarchy are
the two fundamental types of regime, at least in that era.) The city is
formed as a defensive alliance and a trading partnership and, Aristotle

insists on adding, for the sake of *eu zēn*, the good life, which means a conception of human excellence. Now a woman could not directly participate in a nation's military obligations, and, except in an a-typical situation (such as Sparta), she could not acquire or produce wealth in the same way a man could. But with the aid of technology, including the rise of modern warfare, which fails to distinguish between combatant and noncombatant, it became reasonable for regimes to grant women more of the political and civil rights of men. Nothing in Aristotle denies to women the rights of citizenship under modern conditions. Indeed, the arguments of *Politics* V would seem to urge their eventual inclusion in the regime as citizens, under modern conditions. Nonetheless, given the ancient situation it would have been foolish for women to have the citizenship rights of men.

But defense and wealth are necessary conditions of the city. What of the city's sufficient condition, virtue? Here women, as mothers, play an absolutely crucial political role. Recall Coriolanus' mother, Volumnia. She would have been insulted by an offer of suffrage, but she—and all Rome—was aware of her political significance. Women are properly called freemen to the extent that they promote the exercise of virtue. The rise in women's status can be explained by the fact that Aristotle refers to the regime, that is, the city's way of life, substantively for the first time, at the end of Book I of the *Politics*. Women, like men, are more than just parts of families; they are also members of a regime, even though they may not be complete citizens (at least under ancient circumstances). But despite women's need to care for virtue it may still be argued that they are inferior in virtue. But a closer reading of two citations of poetry in Book I often adduced to support this position denies such a simplistic view of women.[44]

Let us reconsider his quotation from Euripides, "It is proper that Greeks rule barbarians." A closer examination of its context undermines both its chauvinism and, as well, support of male superiority.

Euripides' *Iphigeneia in Aulis* concerns Agamemnon's sacrifice of his daughter Iphigeneia to appease the gods, who would then allow the becalmed Greek fleet to sail for Troy to bring back the wife of his brother Menelaus, Helen. Though now tergiversating, Agamemnon had deceived his wife Clytemnestra into bringing Iphigeneia to Aulis by falsely proclaiming a marriage between her and Achilles. (Menelaus prevented Agamemnon's countermanding order from being sent.) When Agamemnon hears of the arrival of his wife and daughter he discovers Menelaus' stratagem. Even though Menelaus subsequently relents on his insistence that the prophet's advice be followed and Iphigeneia sacrificed, Agamemnon laments that he is controlled not only by justice (the commitment to the oath given to Helen's father, admonishing all suitors to defend the marriage) but self-interest as well (the Greek army will kill him and his family if they are denied the women and other booty of Troy). Clytemnestra, upon arriving, and then Achilles discover the deception. Enraged at being used by Agamemnon, who told him nothing about the betrothal scheme, Achilles vows revenge for the humiliation (not, of course, to prevent a human sacrifice). Confronted by his wife, Agamemnon protests that he acts with the interest of Greece in mind. Iphigeneia, who first presented herself as a young girl excited at the prospect of marriage to the vaunted Achilles, bewails her fate. Then, Achilles announces his powerlessness before the entire Greek army (led by Odysseus), who will demand the sacrifice of the girl. At this point, Iphigeneia, in a startling change of attitude, resolves to die, to sacrifice herself for Greece and her own glory. It is in this context that she remarks "It is proper that Greeks rule barbarians, not barbarian Greeks." The barbarians, she explains, are slaves and the Greeks are free. In two extraordinary speeches (1404–15, 1421–32) Achilles expressed his envy of Iphigeneia, who now threatens his pre-eminence in valor. Indeed, he now offers to come to her defense. (Again, it is evident that his motive is the preservation of his own glory; the mighty Achilles—feeling threatened by a mere girl!) But she is unrelenting in her resolve to die a glorious death, and she goes to the altar to be sacrificed. A messenger announces to Clytemnestra that as the sacrificial knife thrust home, her daughter was transformed into a deer. Agamemnon supports this account, which places their daughter with the gods.

Aristotle intends the reader to keep this play in mind throughout the remainder of Book I. We see that in a way a young girl—one who is extremely clever —can be the superior of the greatest Greek warrior. Her mind rules her actions, whereas mind does not rule the Greek camp. Iphigeneia can earn a reputation as a preserver of Greece almost impossible to better, and Achilles and the other Greeks in attempting to gain glory at Troy will only help to preserve hers. Moreover, she cunningly manages to denounce the Greeks even as she elevates herself. Of course it should not be forgotten that Iphigeneia's valor consists in making the best out of a most unfortunate situation. Yet surely the late fifth century Athenian audience which viewed the play could not but feel revulsion at their ancestors when hearing her urge that the sacrifice proceed, so that Greeks could rule the barbarian Trojans. As if any activity could be more—in a not unrelated sense—barbaric than human sacrifice! Thus, the quotation Aristotle cites allegedly to support Greek superiority over the barbarians in fact does nothing of the kind; it shows rather that barbaric practices, including human sacrifice, can occur even among the Greeks, who hold themselves to be the superiors of all others.[45]

As this example indicates, Aristotle does not recklessly challenge any prevailing Greek prejudices; he allows the reader to educate himself to his teaching. Aristotle is indeed a "conservative" in appearance, but be-

neath the surface which the careful reader refines exists that most revolutionary of all activities, political philosophy.

Consider now the context of his slighting reference to women, from
Sophocles. "As the poet said concerning a woman, so it should be held
(*echein nomizein*) of all: 'Silence gives a woman a *kosmos*'" (*Ajax* 293). The
case for women makes the case for all humans. Virtue differs from human to human. But is there not something called human virtue? Citizen virtue, it is true, is masculine (1276b 30). After all, men fight the
wars. So Aristotle disputes the Socratic account given in the *Meno* (71e
ff.) and even cites Meno's friend and teacher, Gorgias, in support of this
view. With a sophist and a tyrant as his authorities Aristotle proceeds to
quote a poet, Sophocles, to justify this distinction between male and female virtue. But again, as with the quotation from Euripides, Aristotle's
citation of poetry proves instructive. This old saying is spoken by an in-
sane Ajax to his sensible slave-mistress, Tecmessa. Aristotle has apparently chosen one of the most inappropriate of all passages in Greek literature to support the conventional belief that women (and slaves) are simply
creatures to be ruled. In fact, as an examination of the play shows, it is
the bellowing Ajax who should have been silent. Tecmessa, a well-born
Phrygian (and hence not a Greek but a barbarian), bears herself with
nobility and grace (as well as a sensible self-interest). She is *kalēkagathē*,
the perfect lie to the contention that all slavery is just. Thus the most
striking instances of female inferiority prove to be not only ambiguous
but affirmative of the opposite—in given instances women can be the
equals and indeed the superiors of even exceptional men. Of course,
Ajax's advice might make sense were it spoken by a sensible man—one
who recognized the limits of the statement's veracity. Women may speak
the truth, but they are not often in a position to make their truths
effectual. And so it is they should often remain silent, if only for their
own sake. Thus the surface and the deep meanings of the quotation
make sense. It seems that in dealing with women, men must be prepared
to speak with moderation.

Thus we see the possibility of women exercising the virtue which is
the object of civic education in ways which seem more than mere poor
imitations of male actions. But by making the strongest case for women's
equality with men through poetry Aristotle indicates that only in rare,
controlled situations can such equality prevail. (Compare the similarly
qualified defense of women by Shakespeare, especially in his portrayal of
Lucrece and the Portias.) As the fates of the two heroines Iphigeneia and
Tecmessa indicate, their political efficacy would be limited indeed. And
all of this again points to Aristotle's concern for politics.

Our focus on women in this essay serves to clarify the differences
between ancient and modern views of politics. Aristotle's obsession with
remaining on the political level brings about his surface slighting of

women. In the *Politics* Aristotle is uninterested simply in understanding women; women are of interest insofar as they are politically relevant. Thus, an "Aristotelian" today would in no way desire restoring the conditions of Aristotle's times. Given modern conditions and the modern science of politics, it make sense for women to possess equal political rights. And under ancient conditions it was perfectly appropriate for them to be denied such rights. For the ancient city oligarchy and democracy were the fundamental forms of which the city is constituted. And these reflect the body, and hence inequality. In the modern state ideology becomes essential for the purpose of unification. In a curious way modern politics makes the mind of greater importance than did ancient politics. With its stress on thought, modern politics permits women to have a greater political place.[46] The family fades in significance, and the phenomenon of the individual arises.[47] An Aristotelian understanding of politics today would attempt to work with the modern condition and its assumption of equality and attempt to refine that into the proper sorts of inequalities essential for human happiness. In this essay we attempted the reverse process: refining the equality out of the inequalities which manifested themselves on the surface of political phenomena. Thus we see that Aristotle's political philosophy is not bound by historical circumstances. Those of us today who would continue to be guided by his thought should regard him as one of western civilization's women's liberators—one who would have doubtless admired a Phyllis for her mind.[48]

Notes

1. This is a substantially revised version of a paper first given at the 1981 Annual Meeting of the Pacific Northwest Political Science Association, Reed College, Portland, Oregon, April 30–May 2, 1981. The idea for this paper came from a confrontation with feminist political theorists at an American Political Science Association-sponsored seminar on citizenship directed by Nannerl O. Keohane, who suggested I write a paper on Aristotle's view of women.
2. Princeton: Princeton University Press, 1979.
3. Okin, p. 5.
4. Ibid., pp. 3–4.
5. Ibid., pp. 8–9.
6. Her studies of Plato, Rousseau, and Mill all make the same historicist error of her Aristotle study. That is, she assumes that the historical situation of each thinker fairly well defined his understanding of politics.
7. Okin, p. 74.
8. Ibid., pp. 73–74.

One should, as in other matters, present the phenomena and first, having gone through the perplexities, bring to light all leading opinions (*endoxa*) concerning these conditions (*pathē*), or, if not all, most of them and the most important. For if the difficulties are dissolved and the leading opinions remain, they would be proven sufficiently. (1145b 2–7)

Okin falsely identifies the location of this passage, at the beginning of Book VII, as "at the outset of the discussion of one of the virtues." The discussion of the virtues was concluded in Book VI. Throughout the notes she cites the "*Nichomachean*[sic] *Ethics*," evidently from the misprinting of Nicomachean on the cover of the Bobbs-Merrill edition. (The text, however, contains the correct, accepted spelling.)

9. There is hardly a sentence in the entire chapter on Aristotle which we believe to be either correct or even interesting albeit wrong. But in this essay Okin is not our primary concern.

10. What Okin translate as "function"—following scholars suich as G. E. R. Lloyd—is *ergon*, which is in fact better translated as "work," in the sense of action.

11. Okin, p. 76.

12. But man is unique among the animals, for he has two *energeiai*—thinking as well as generation. Man is the only animal with *logos*—a fact which at least modifies in his case the general observations Aristotle makes about male and female in the lower animals. Incidentally, in this argument (pp. 76–77) Okin assumes that Aristotle believes in the Olympian gods. *Ethics* X compares the contemplative life to the activity of *ho theos*. He is careful to distinguish between *hoi theoi* (meaning the Greek gods) and *ho theos* (his notion of the divine, ultimately the thought-thinking-thought of *Metaphysics* L.)

13. Okin, p. 78.

14. Ibid., pp. 81–83. *Generation of Animals* 727B-732A (*infra*), 738B, 766A, 767B, 775A. Cf. W. W. Fortenbaugh, "Aristotle on Slaves and Women," in *Articles on Aristotle*, vol. 2: *Ethics and Politics*, ed. Jonathan Barnes, Malcolm Schofield, and Richard Sorabji (London: Duckworth, 1977). "It is striking that in the *Politics* Aristotle all but ignores biological explanations of female inferiority" (p. 139, footnote 8). Okin assumes that, in studying diverse phenomena, the observer can cross disciplinary boundaries and transfer statements appropriate in one science or discipline to the realm of another. Such a procedure violates the most fundamental elements of Aristotle's thought. Each discipline is to understand phenomena at their own level. It may very well be the case that on the biological level Aristotle argues for the inferiority of the female to the male. But one must take the greatest care in extending biological principles to the political realm.

15. Okin, p. 90.

16. As we will see later, he is not thereby attempting to explain politics solely from the perspective of sub-political life but rather to indicate the enduring persistence of the sub-political within the political.

17. Okin, p. 95.

18. Ibid., p. 95, p. 277.

19. One scholar, following Jean Adhemar, *Influences antiques dans l'art du moyen-age francais* (London: Warburg Institute, 1937), pp. 297–99, attributes the inclusion of Aristotle in a tale of Arab and ultimately Indian origin to a cleric Jacques de Vitry, "who was quite raid about the dangers of reading classical philosophy." (Jane Campbell Hutchison, "The Housebook Master and the Folly of the Wise Man," *The Art Bulletin* 48 [March 1966]:75.)

20. Jakob Von Vitry, *Die Exempla aus den Sermones feriales et communes.*, Joseph Greven., ed. (Heidelberg: Carl Winter's Buchhandlung, 1914), p. 16. Translated by J. Jackson Barlow. I follow the elaboration given by George Sarton, "Aristotle and Phyllis," *Isis*, 14 (1930), Number 1, pp. 8–19. See also Emile Mâle, *The Gothic Image*, trans. Dora Nussey (New York: Harper and Row, Harper Torchbooks, 1958), pp. 332–5. He supplies "Campaspe" for "Phyllis." Most scholars give the early thirteenth century as the flourishing period of the Aristotle and Phyllis legend. It was later in that century when Aquinas succeeded in legitimizing Aristotle. On the tension between piety and philosophy see Ralph Lerner and Muhsin Mahdi, eds., *Medieval Political Philosophy* (New York:

The Free Press, 1963). See especially "The Condemnation of the 219 Propositions," pp. 335–54.

According to Henry Adams, "the bishops in 1209 burned no les than ten in Paris for too great intimacy with Arab and Jew disciples of Aristotle." *Mont-Saint Michel and Chartres* (Garden City, New York: Doubleday and Company, Doubleday Anchor Books, 1959), pp. 190–91.

21. Hutchison, pp. 77–78.

22. *Collected Works*, ed. Roy P. Basler (New Brunswick, New Jersey: Rutgers University Press), 3:405. Lincoln, whose understanding of the equality principle reminds one of the classical notion of the best regime, goes on to derive representative democracy, government by consent, and the separation of powers from it. Unfortunately the impoverished Roger Taney-Stephen Douglas reading of the Declaration by and large obtains today.

For another example of Lincoln's rhetoric consider the opening remarks of his fourth debate with Douglas, at Charleston:

I will say then that I am not, nor ever have been in favor of bringing about in any way the social and political equality of the white and black races—that I am not now nor ever have been in favor of making voters or jurors of negroes, nor of qualifying them to hold office, nor to intermarry with white people; and I will say in addition to this that there is a physical difference between the white and black races which I believe will forever forbid the two races living together on terms of social and political equality.

The great emphasis here is on Lincoln's past and present beliefs, not what a future following emancipation might bring (ibid., pp. 145–46). But Lincoln's only accounted policy then was to put slavery "in the course of ultimate extinction." Lincoln's Aristotelianism is demonstrated by Harry V. Jaffa, *Crisis of the House Divided* (Chicago: University of Chicago Press, 1982; reprint ed., Garden City, N. Y.: Doubleday & Co., 1959).

23. Note that, taken strictly logically, "not being equal" could mean superior as well as inferior. Consider Lincoln's 1836 proposal to extend suffrage to women.

I go for all sharing the privileges of the government, who assist in bearing its burdens. Consequently I go for admitting all whites to the right of suffrage, who pay taxes or bear arms, (by no means excluding females.) (*Collected Works* 1:48.)

24. Note that the third of the five natural means of acquisition is brigandage, that is, the use of violence for the sake of gain. In what is one of only two uses of natural right in the Aristotelian corpus, he maintains that warfare "should be used against both beasts and men who are by nature to be ruled, though unwilling, since this warfare is by nature just (*phusei dikaion*)" (1256b 24–26). This "pre-political" natural right reflects the superiority of the males with the strongest bodies and the hardiest spirits. While political life and presumably the political natural right of *Ethics* VI. 7 attempt to balance these traits, they can never be totally eliminated.

That the arguments against private property and for the abolition of the family are the opposite sides of the same coin is made absolutely clear in Okin's argument. Both are rooted in the love of one's own, which Aristotle seeks to refine and which socialists wish to extirpate.

25. See my review of Mortimer Adler, *Aristotle for Everybody* in *The Claremont Review of Books* 1 (March 1982):4.

26. See Thomas G. West, "Phenomenological Psychology and Aristotelian Politics," revi-

sion of a paper delivered at the 1976 Annual Meeting of the American Political Science Association. (Photocopied).

27. Fustel de Coulanges, *The Ancient City*, trans. Willard Small (Garden City: Doubleday & Co., Doubleday Anchor Books, n.d.).

28. For perceptive comments on Aristotle's *methodos* see Bernard Bosanquet, *The Principle of Individuality and Value—The Gifford Lectures for* 1911 (London: Macmillan & Co., 1912), pp. 393–403. Invaluable is Harry V. Jaffa, *Thomism and Aristotelianism* (Chicago: University of Chicago Press, 1952).

29. The *Ethics* does not lead us to conclude that the size of the city has any effect on the acquisition or exercise of the virtues. See Leo Strauss, *What is Political Philosophy?* (New York: Free Press, 1959), p. 65; and *Liberalism—Ancient and Modern* (New York: Basic Books, 1968), p. viii.

30. Cf. Jacob Klein, "The Nature of Nature," *The Independent Journal of Philosophy*, 3 (1979): 101–9.

31. Consider the challenge of 1094b 16–17; are all judgments concerning what is noble and just merely conventional? At its most elementary level "nature" stands for the objectivity of the external world. The notion of nature makes it possible to have the world outside our minds as an object of study. Aristotle leads his readers through various questions concerning nature in *Physics* II. Invaluable for its study is Heidegger's essay on II. 1 in *Wegmarken* (Frankfurt am Main: Vittorio Klostermann, 1967), pp. 309–71. The modern reader must understand that nature means both form (*eidos*) and matter; besides the other three causes nature is "an end (*telos*) and a forsake-of-which" (*hou heneka*) (194a 28–29). To ascribe naturalness to a being and then to proceed to understand its nature is to study that being's perfection or *telos*.

32. On the barbarian ignorance of nature see Lerner and Mahdi, *Medieval Political Philosophy*, p. 306.

33. Relying again on poetry to illuminate the household, Aristotle quotes Hesiod as saying: "First of all a house and a woman and an ox for plowing." But Aristotle omits the remainder of Hesiod's line—"a slave women and no wife, to follow the oxen as well . . ." (1252b 10–12; *Works and Days*. 404–5.) The plowing (*aroter*) can refer either to agriculture or sexual intercourse (cf. Sophocles, *Antigone* 569). (See W. L. Newman, ed. *The Politics of Aristotle*, 4 vols. [Oxford: Clarendon Press, 1887], 1:112.)

34. But if gold footbasins can become gold statues of gods, so can the latter be transformed into the former. Substance, not form, is crucial. (Herodotus II. 172.)

35. *Republic* V, 454 c–e.

36. Throughout *Politics* I conventions refine nature, which always falls short of its wish or intention. In *Ethics* VIII. 10–11 the inequalities between man and woman, master and slave, and father and child all point toward a fundamental human equality. Though the husband is said to rule the wife aristocratically, the differences between male and female are further reduced. Men should rule women but not in all matters. When women are heiresses, they might rule oligarchically. Yet if heiresses can rule oligarchically, might they not also be able to exercise liberality? If so, might they not practice other virtues as well?

 A fine portrayal of the difference between weak and dominant *logos* in women is Portia before and after Bassanio takes her for his bride. Marriage to even the frivolous Bassanio gives her *logos* a starting-point and thus strengthens it. Consider too Brutus' wife Portia in Shakespeare's *Julius Caesar*.

37. In this light compare Elinor and Marianne, the Sense and Sensibility, respectively, of Jane Austen's fine novel.

38. Harry V. Jaffa, "Aristotle," in *History of Political Philosophy*, ed. Leo Strauss and Joseph Cropsey, 2nd ed. (Chicago: Rand McNally, 1972), p. 76. Thus, Okin's charge that "Harry Jaffa . . . is content merely to summarize what Aristotle says about women, and actu-

ally seeks to justify his argument that there are natural slaves" (p. 93) grossly distorts his presentation, which is in any case more than a mere summary of Aristotle's views about the family. (See Jaffa, pp. 76–78.) Okin evidently assumes that "natural slave" is a euphemism for anyone who is enslaved.

39. Recall Thrasymachus' definition of justice as the advantage of the stronger (*kreitton*) or better. The ambiguity of the Greek strengthens his position, while it leads to his downfall. Cf. Newman, *The Politics of Aristotle*, 1:145, at 13.

40. Thus, conventional slavery injures the master as well as the slave, for it undermines his concern for political virtue.

41. The *Ethics*' reiteration of human equality is made even more explicit in its treatment of slavery.

But neither is there friendship for a horse or an ox or a slave *qua* slave, for there is nothing *koinon*: The slave is an ensouled tool, and a tool is a soulless slave. In that he is a slave, there can be no friendship in itself, but in that he is a man (*anthrōpos*), it is possible. For it seems that there is something just between any man and any other who are capable of sharing in law and agreement. (1161b 2–7)

Despite the range of political and other conventions, human beings are human beings by virtue of a certain common nature, which in principle permits any one to become a friend and hence a fellow citizen of any other human being. (Consider J. A. Stewart, *Notes on the Nicomachean Ethics of Aristotle*, 2 vols. [Oxford: Clarendon Press, 1892]2: 316–19. Although he points to this passage as a source of the Roman teaching of the "natural equality of all men," he also insists that Aristotle was essentially an apologist for slavery.)

A fine modern elaboration of this argument is found in Lincoln's Wisconsin State Agricultural Society Address. Reflecting on the utility of fairs as a means of promoting friendship, Lincoln remarks:

From the first appearance of man upon the earth, down to very recent times, the words *"stranger"* and *"enemy"* were *quite* or *almost*, synonymous. Long after civilized nations had defined robbery and murder as high crimes, and had affixed severe punishments to them, when practices among and upon their own people respectively, it was deemed no offence, but even meritorious, to rob, and murder, and enslave *strangers*, whether as nations or as individuals. Even yet, this has not totally disappeared. The man of the highest moral cultivation, in spite of all which abstract principle can do, likes him whom it *does* know much better than him whom he does *not* know. To correct the evils, great and small, which spring from want of sympathy, and from positive enmity, among *strangers*, as nations, or as individuals, is one of the highest functions of civilization. (*Works* 3:471–72)

42. Afterward Aristotle will note that, though a freeman, the mechanic is said to be under a sort of slavery (*douleia tis*) (1260a 33–26). Here he does describe the slave as *tōn phusei*, while neither the shoemaker nor the other artisans are so. But I would take Rackham's translation as correct: "of the natural classes." Insofar as the *polis* is natural, every *polis* (which does not of course know modern technology) requires "by nature" people like slaves. But this is a far cry from maintaining that all slaves are natural ones. And slaves, Aristotle observes, have more reason than the children who will be future freemen.

43. Of course it might not be impossible to attribute Sparta's relative goodness to the predominance of its women.

44. As with Plato, so with Aristotle one must check all quotations from other sources and match them with the context from which they are taken. Our curiosity should be raised whenever a philosopher chooses to cite another's words—especially those of a poet —rather than speak in his own name. Aristotle uses poetry for heuristic purposes, not simply for ornamentation.

45. On the difference between Greeks and barbarians consider his remarks on the Europeans, Greeks, and Asians in Book VII (1327b 18–28a 16). This is more than a mere depiction of ethnic or racial stereotyping as it may first appear. In this passage he reduces ethnic or racial traits to character traits, which are in fact found in varying combinations among the Greeks. That Aristotle did not believe in barbarian inferiority is made evident in Book II's praise of Carthage (1272b 24ff.), emphasized by his previous criticisms of Sparta and Crete and his silence on the merits of Athens. Note how Aristotle's analysis makes us shift our attention from body to character.

46. Reflect on Hobbes's arguments for the equality of mind (as well of body) in the *Leviathan*, chapter 13.

47. "Let reverence for the laws be breathed by every American mother, to the lisping babe, that prattles on her lap . . . ," (Lincoln, *Works*, 1:112). Consider Tocqueville's argument in chapter 12, part 3, volume II of *Democracy in America* and the context: In the European situation

    the sort of equality forced on both sexes degrades them both, and . . . so coarse a jumble of nature's works could produce nothing but feeble men and unseemly women . . . .

    . . . American women, who are often manly in their intelligence and in their energy, usually preserve great delicacy of personal appearance and always have the manners of women, though they sometimes show the minds and hearts of men . . . .

    . . . If anyone asks me what I think the chief cause of the extraordinary prosperity and growing power of [America], I should answer that it is due to the superiority of their women.

48. What the Aristotle of the medieval tale represents is the failure of the knower of the universal to reflect on the particular. Aristotle cannot rule his own passions and hence is ruled by Phyllis. (Alexander, the political man, would at least be ruled by Aristotle.) Both Alexander and Phyllis are spirited, but Aristotle here is spiritless. A properly cultivated male spiritedness carries men beyond their own particular bodies to the city—consider the phenomenon of patriotism—and for a rare few beyond politics to philosophy. (Female spiritedness, on the other hand, binds women closer to their families, as we saw in the example of Bassanio's [Not Brutus'] Portia.) Spiritedness links the care for the particular to the love of the universal. This is why political philosophy is the core of philosophy. (For a different interpretation of *thumos* see Mary Pollingue Nichols's thoughtful review of Okin in *The Political Science Reviewer* [forthcoming].)

15

THE HERO ABROAD
TOWARD AN INTERPRETATION OF
TOM SAWYER ABROAD

Dennis J. Mahoney

TOM SAWYER, HERO OF MIDDLE AMERICA, COMES BACK TO LIFE IN A NOVEL written nearly two decades after the original. *Tom Sawyer Abroad* is explicitly a sequel to *The Adventures of Tom Sawyer* and *The Adventures of Huckleberry Finn*, taking up the narrative where the latter leaves it. Tom is once again accompanied by Huck Finn, the untutored natural democrat, and Jim, delivered from slavery in the previous book, a naively pious Christian.

This book is, chronologically, a sequel to *Huckleberry Finn*, but the main characters more closely resemble their original incarnations in *Tom Sawyer*. The characters are not, in this novel, connected with their native soil; the reader encounters them, as it were, up in the air. There are more famous books where the action is made possible by a descent; in this book the action is made possible by an ascent.

The book opens with Tom's shameless exploitation of his gunshot wound, a wound itself genuine, and one received heroicly (though needlessly) in the course of the rescue of the slave Jim. Tom works the bullet wound for all it is worth, but, after a time, "Tom's glory got to paling down," and that left him "sick and disgusted." Finding himself no longer the center of attention, and with his youth, as he imagines, slipping away, Tom sets "to work to get up a plan to make him celebrated."

That work is described in the title of the chapter as the seeking of new adventures. It is precisely the novelty of Tom's adventures that lead to his celebrity. Only in the continuous seeking after *new* adventures can Tom retain his status as hero of middle America.

Not for the first time, Tom's scheme for celebrity involves capitalizing on religion, for his plan is to conduct a crusade against the "paynim" —Tom's old-fashioned word for infidels—to liberate the Holy Land. When Huck and Jim protest the injustice of making a war against innocent people in order to take their land from them, Tom loses patience with those who "ain't got any more sense than to try to reason out a thing that's pure theology by the laws that protect real estate."

Tom is, of course, the most unlikely of theologians. His enthusiasm for a crusade is not inspired by holy zeal or by any other sentiment connected with conventional piety. The new crusade will be waged not to regain the Holy Land for the Church but to regain the celebrity status of Tom Sawyer. Huck's and Jim's objections—on legal and economic grounds—offend Tom because they are objections to a scheme devised for the greater glory of Tom.

Tom's loss of celebrity and his plan to regain it by a crusade make up the first of the thirteen chapters in *Tom Sawyer Abroad*. Nevertheless, the ensuing chapters do not explicitly recount either a crusade—although there is a conquest of Mt. Sinai—or the recovery of Tom's lost celebrity. The whole of the book must be regarded as Tom's crusade, insuring that upon his homecoming (the last sentence of the book finds the gang "shov[ing] for home") his celebrity will indeed be greater than ever.

There is another conquest: Tom's new theology triumphs in violent struggle to gain control over the new holy ground of science and technology. The role of the paynim—that is, of the unbelievers—is played out by a scientist who is no devotee of Tom's new religion. That infidel, however, is expelled from his own property, and the expulsion is heartily welcomed by the disciples Huck and Jim.

In the second chapter, Tom, whose design it was in the first chapter to rise *in* the world, contrives to rise *from* the world, by means of a balloon (or, rather, an airship). Tom, who has already managed to stage his own resurrection without the necessity of dying now stages his ascension without the necessity of a crucifixion.

Tom and his companions go to the exhibition of the balloon because a connection with that novelty seems sure to regain for Tom some of his lost celebrity. Unfortunately, Tom's archrival, Nat Parsons, is also present; hence, the success of Tom's scheme depends upon his remaining aboard the craft longer than Parsons. Tom and the gang conceal themselves in the gondola and are trapped when the balloon takes off.

In his attraction to the balloon, Tom proves himself the intellectual superior of his fellow-townsmen, who can only jeer at the scientists whose invention and construction it is. The balloon appears to Huck, who is thoroughly under the spell of Tom, as "noble"; but to the townspeople it is an object of ridicule. Huck's assessment of the scientist himself also diverges from the crowd's, for while the townspeople are contemptuous of the scientist he appears to Huck as a "genius."

In a sense, however, by ridiculing the scientist and his invention, the crowd asserts its own power. The scientist expected, because of his native superiority, to achieve such fame that his name will be remembered for more than a thousand years and he will be renowned as a benefactor of mankind; the crowd knows that fame is bestowed by the many, and laughs at the scientist's expectation. The scientist's name does not appear in the book.

Tom understands fame better than the scientist does. Tom actively strives for that which the scientist believes will come to him as of right. The scientist seeks to do great things, and expects that a reputation for doing great things will follow. Tom is more direct, he seeks for the reputation in the first instance. And Tom's ascension is a product of that search for reputation: he and his gang had no intention of becoming part of the scientist's experiments; they were aboard the airship because there was a potential for notoriety, within their small village, in having seen and boarded the airship.

Not only does the scientist not understand the crowd, he does not understand Tom. When the stowaway gang is discovered, Tom is immediately selected as the protege. The scientist teaches Tom how to steer and control the airship, and no sooner has he done so than Tom begins plotting a revolution. To remain under the authority of the scientist once Tom has "got used to this balloon and over the scare of being cut loose from solid ground" is, as Tom says, "no good politics." But for Tom there is little, if any difference, between what is "good politics" and what is good for the preservation of Tom's skin.

Chapter III is the second chapter that includes Tom's name in its title as the subject of active verbs. (The others are Chapters I, VII, and IX.) Chapter I is called "Tom Seeks New Adventures" and Chapter III is called "Tom Explains"; these are linked by the chapter describing the balloon ascension and containing Tom's assertion concerning "good politics."

What Tom first explains in the chapter is the absence of visible borders on the ground over which the balloon passes. Huckleberry Finn observes, as subsequent generations of aeronauts and and astronauts have done, that from the air it is difficult to say where one state ends and another begins. Of course, borders exist by convention, and not by nature; but Huck, who is apparently ignorant of this distinction expects to see the states arrayed below him in the same colors they wear on his map. The instrument of science has revealed to Huck the distinction between nature and convention; but it is Tom—not the scientist—who explains, that is, who interprets the distinction for Huck. That is one of the requirements of good politics.

Tom also explains, this time for Jim, the concept of time zones. Clocks are a conventional interpretation of a natural phenomenon— ("Ger-reat Scott, it's the *longitude!*" exclaims Tom) and Jim, like Huck, is innocent of the distinction between nature and convention. It "grieves" Jim to hear Tom assert that time is not everywhere the same "arter the way [Tom has] been raised." Jim supposes that Tom's education would have equated the conventions of the community to the law of God. Jim is

not so easily explained to as Huck, because his objections to Tom's explanation are theological. And, unlike Huck, Jim is not converted by Tom's
explanation.

Chapter III is Tom's opportunity to show his comprehension of the
human soul, or of human nature. Successful explanation depends upon
a correct understanding both of the thing explained and the person to
whom it is explained. Tom is more successful explaining to Huck than to
Jim, perhaps because Huck's soul is less affected by revelation.

In Chapter IV, the adventurers confront the hostile elements of the
physical universe. While crossing the Atlantic Ocean, their balloon is
tossed about by a fierce storm. The scientist, whose mastery of the elements of the physical world enabled him to construct the fantastic airship,
is seemingly powerless in the face of the storm. But the powerlessness
was self-induced through the consumption of alcohol; and the alcoholic
haze brought with it both the necessity and the possibility of a revolution
in the politics of the airship. In the same chapter, Tom, Huck, and Jim
face the hostility of the scientist in whose balloon they are passengers.
After a search and a struggle, the drunken scientist attempts to throw
Tom overboard and by means of a clever ploy (Tom clings to a trailing
rope ladder), Tom causes the scientist to hurl himself into space and into
the ocean below.

For some time after his nemesis falls, Tom remains dangling below
the gondola, but, in due course, he climbs back aboard the airship, assuming command of the vessel. The democratic force on the balloon has
overthrown the scientist and has claimed the balloon, which the scientist
created for the purpose of investigation, turning the invention to the new
purpose of promoting the pleasure of the non-scientists.

The good politics that Tom establishes is no mere nose-count majoritarianism. In the very next chapter, Tom is able to resist a two-to-one
vote in favor of returning home immediately. He resists by appealing
once again to the "glory" that can be achieved by acceding to his scheme.
The gang, or at any rate Tom Sawyer the Erornort, would "be heard of
all round the world."

The travellers' original destination was England, and when, in the
fifth chapter, they arrive over land they assume that they have arrived in
England. In fact, however, the storm has blown the balloon off its course
and the gang finds itself over North Africa. Although the terrain is flat
and sandy, the travellers assume that they have only to come close to the
ground to inquire the way to London. Only when they are pursued by
lions is this impression dispelled.

It is Tom, of course, who in the sixth chapter deduces from the
presence of sand and lions that the party has reached the great Sahara.
His surmise is confirmed when the balloon passes over a caravan. Even as
they watch, the caravan is attacked by robbers, and an opportunity for
real heroism presents itself. The gang rescues a child who has been kid-

napped by the robbers. Real heroism does not present itself any differently from mock heroism.

The seventh and central chapter of the book is entitled "Tom Respects the Flea." In that chapter, Tom delivers two lectures to his companions: the first on the strength of a flea relative to its size, the second
the retelling of a tale from *Arabian Nights*. The connection between the
two is not immediately apparent, nor is it apparent why the second
lecture—drawn from "right in the midst of the *Arabian Nights*" should
be included under the heading "Tom Respects the Flea."

Between Tom's two lectures, at the center of this chapter and, therefore, at the center of the book, the travellers experience a rebirth:

> It didn't seem like we was the same lot that was in such a state . . . We was
> used to the balloon now and not afraid anymore, and didn't want to be
> anywheres else. Why, it seemed just like home; it 'most seemed as if I
> had been born and raised in it, and Jim and Tom said the same.

Huck Finn, as narrator, describes his own rebirth and informs the reader
that Jim and Tom felt the same way. But there is nothing in the words or
actions of Tom to indicate that he has, indeed, shared Huck's experience.
Indeed, Tom has engineered the circumstances that brought about the
rebirth of his companions. Tom was not, himself, in need of regeneration.

Chapter VIII links the second pair of chapters with Tom's name in
their titles: "Tom Respects the Flea" and "Tom Discourses on the Desert."
The chapter is itself entitled "The Disappearing Lake," and concerns the
relationship of appearance and reality.

At the beginning of the chapter, the gang comes upon an entire
caravan dead and mummified on the desert. After landing to inspect
this phenomenon, the travellers help themselves to certain possessions of
the dead caravaneers: some weapons and a box containing coins and
jewels. When his companions later regret having stolen from the dead,
Tom introduces them to the moral theology of the New Calvinism: to
return the stolen goods to their dead owners would be to put temptation
in the path of potential thieves, and would therefore be sinful. Huck
learns the lesson well, for he wishes "we had took all they had, so there
wouldn't 'a' been no temptation at all left."

Between the discovery of the caravan and the decision against replacing the stolen goods, the party observes a mirage. Overcome with thirst
while flying over the desert, the travellers spot a lake on the horizon. The
lake proves to be a mirage, the image of an actual lake refracted in the
hot air and so appearing where there is no lake. Tom's exposition of the
theological justification for keeping their stolen treasure, which occurs
immediately thereafter, is the moral equivalent of the mirage.

The ninth chapter is entitled "Tom Discourses on the Desert." The
title has a double significance, for the discourse is about the desert and it
is also conducted in a desert environment. Moreover, despite the title, it is

not only Tom who discourses, but Jim and Huck as well. Tom's discourse concerns the size of the desert, and has two parts. In the first part, Tom gives an empirical description of the desert, comparing the number of square miles in the Sahara with the number of square miles in the United States; in the second part, Tom argues that even though the Sahara is large, it is not important, because importance is not a function of size. To illustrate this, Tom says that Great Britain is small but important. Between the two parts of Tom's discourse is a discourse by Jim on the process of creation, according to which the Sahara was not created but was merely a pile of the rubble left over from creation.

Chapter X, the central chapter of the second half of the book, comprises a parable, ostensibly a tale from the *Arabian Nights*, narrated by Tom, and a commentary in the form of a dialogue among the travellers.

In Tom's version of the story, a dervish annoints the eyes of a rich merchant with a salve that enables him to find a great treasure, agreeing to split the treasure with him; but the merchant's greed is such that he demands the whole amount and even then is unsatisfied. The dervish accomodates the man's demand for another application of the salve, warning him that it will make him blind. And when the merchant becomes blind the dervish takes the whole of the treasure for himself.

The dervish is clearly a prototype of Tom Sawyer. As Tom points out, the dervish is a sucessful swindler because "he know'd the man's character." Tom, too, succeeds as a swindler by knowing men's characters. Tom reckons "there's a lot of people like that dervish. They swindle, right and left, but they always make the other person *seem* to swindle himself."

Indeed, Tom demonstrates his capacity for knowing others' characters even as he speaks, for he has convinced his companions that a certain hill upon which they light is the very hill where the events of the story took place. But, seemingly, there is no reward for this swindle, except that Tom becomes in Huck's eyes a hero equal, except in age, to George Washington and Captain Kidd. One recollects Tom's earlier plan to run off and become a pirate, for glory's sake, and now sees Tom enjoying a pirate's share of glory.

In Chapter XI Tom and his gang encounter a second storm, this time a sand storm. Like the wind and rainstorm of seven chapters earlier, this storm results in the death of non-members of the gang (in this case a caravan on the desert floor) while sparing the gang members; and, like the earlier storm this one causes the travellers to become disoriented. This time, their delivery is truly miraculous, since the gondola of the airship is filled with sand—twenty tons of it—and yet they are not forced to the ground and buried along with the caravan, but are able to continue hovering some thousand feet in the air.

When the storm is spent, Tom is obliged to undertake an exercise in distributive justice. The task of shoveling the sand is to be apportioned "according to fairness and strength." Because Jim is not only stronger than his younger associates but also less fair, that is, darker hued, he is assigned three-fifths of the sand.

The chapter also shows Tom's potential as a capitalist. The most immediate result of the sandstorm was that the gondola of the airship was filled with sand, "genuwyne sand from the genuwyne Desert of Sahara." Tom immediately spots the money-making potential of this situation. Surely for something as novel as real Sahara sand people will be willing to pay good money. Only the prospect of having to pay customs duties to each of the dozens of countries they would pass over on the way deters the young entrepreneurs from bottling the sand and taking it home to sell in Missouri.

The twelfth chapter is the only one in which a person other than Tom Sawyer is named in the title. The chapter is called "Jim Standing Siege." The chapter recounts the arrival of the balloon and its passengers in Egypt. Jim rejoices at being in the place where so many biblical events took place; but Tom is more excited to be at the locale of stories from *Arabian Nights*. Biblical history is not "in Tom's line," perhaps because Tom acquired his reputation for biblical knowledge without opening the Book.

Jim is forced to stand seige when Tom, in order to contemplate the proportions of the Sphynx, sails off into the distance while Jim stands on its head "with an American flag to protect him, it being a foreign land." The flag, unfortunately, fails in its duty when the Arabs attack, and Tom and Huck must rescue Jim from his station. Tom assures his companions that the Arabs cannot get away with this insult to the American flag: not only will they have to apologize, they will have to pay a cash indemnity, which they all agree is a more satisfactory reparation for the insult done — especially as the government will get the apology, but the travellers will get the money.

Only in the thirteenth and final chapter does Huck reveal to his readers that he is wise to the secrets of Tom Sawyer. The pair arrives in Cairo and Tom demonstrates his superior knowledge by pointing out a number of landmarks, including the granary where the biblical Joseph stored Pharaoh's grain and the ruins of a house where certain incidents recounted in the *Arabian Nights* took place. From the latter Tom secures a brick, which he intends to donate to a museum—"with his name on it," of course. Huck determines to test Tom's knowledge by substituting a similar brick from another location. Needless to say, Tom is deceived.

Huck correctly concludes that Tom acts on the basis of instinct, not knowledge, and Jim concurs in that conclusion. What they misconceive is the object of Tom's unerring instinct. Tom's instinct does not, as they suppose, lead him always to the truth (as his knowledge cannot), but rather it leads him to what others can be made to accept as the truth.

Huck does not deviate far from Tom's own position when he maintains that the incident "shows that for all the brag you hear about knowledge being such a wonderful thing, instink is worth forty of it for reall unerringness."

Immediately afterward, the gang recruits a new member, an Arab who offers to guide them. Even as Tom has found the exact site of Joseph's granary, the new guide discovers the exact locations of Israel's crossing of the Red Sea and of Moses's talk with God. The gang appears to take for granted the efficacy of the guide's knowledge.

The journey of Tom and his companions comes to an end on the slopes of Mt. Sinai—not because that is the limit of the balloon's range, but because it is the limit of Aunt Polly's apron strings. Before he can cross from Sinai to the promised land, Tom is overcome by a desire to smoke tobacco. For this purpose the scientist's Meerschaum and the strange pipes of the Arabs are unsuited, only a Missouri corncob pipe will suffice. Tom and Huck remain camped on Mt. Sinai, sending Jim and the Arab back to Misouri—notwithstanding that Tom alone has mastered the science of aeronavigation and that Tom could smoke his pipe at least twenty-four hours sooner if he went himself and lit up on the return journey.

Tom is still subject to Aunt Polly's governance, and cannot risk being caught. When Jim is caught retrieving the pipe, Aunt Polly commands him to bring Tom home, and her command is law. The book ends with the gang shoving for home; and even the prospect of the celebrity Tom knows must attend his return cannot make him gay in the fact of Aunt Polly's righteous wrath.

Tom Sawyer Abroad was written in 1892, when Samuel Clemens, plagued by financial woes, was living in Europe. Literary critics and Twain scholars generally dismiss the book as a piece of hack work unworthy of serious analysis. This underestimate Clemens probably foresaw and accepted; nevertheless, there was more in his mind than making a few easy dollars. Writing about the half-completed novel, then tentatively entitled *Huck Finn in Africa* or *Huckleberry Finn Abroad*, Clemens declared:

I have started Huck Finn and Tom Sawyer (still 15 years old) and their friend the freed slave Jim around the world in a stray *balloon*, with Huck as narrator, and somewhere after the end of that great voyage he will work in the said episode and then nobody will suspect that a whole book has been written and the globe circumnavigated merely to get that episode in . . .[1]

A previous communication in which Clemens described the main episode to Hall is no part of Clemens's published correspondence; and so the reader is left to determine which of the several revealing incidents in the novel was so important as to justify the writing of a whole book and the originally intended circumnavigation of the globe.

We scarcely need this enigmatic epistle to justify a more careful reading of *Tom Sawyer Abroad* than that work has heretofore received. In Tom Sawyer, Clemens created the hero of middle America. Wherever Tom travels, and whatever his adventures, he reveals the character that appeals to those men who were educated in the regime of the Declaration of Independence. To understand that character is to understand something about those men, and so to understand the regime. Texts that are neither philosophic nor explicitly political may nevertheless teach us about both natural right and political right. How they may do so has been explained by Professor Harry Jaffa.

Notes

1. Letter to Fred J. Hall, 10 August 1982, in Hamlin Hill, ed., *Mark Twain's Letters to his Publishers, 1867–1894* (Berkeley: University of California Press, 1967), pages 313–315.

16

EQUALITY, LIBERTY AND CONSENT IN *A THEORY OF JUSTICE*

Thomas Engeman

ALTHOUGH THE SECONDARY LITERATURE ON JOHN RAWLS'S *A THEORY of Justice* is already considerable, no apology for the addition of another study appears necessary. In spite of the analysis and criticism Rawls's work has received, it seems to thrive on opposition, and continues on from success to success; *A Theory of Justice* is by any estimation far from a dead letter.[1]

More serious for the intention of this study is Rawls's stated indifference to the practical implications of his work.[2] He is, he says, modestly attempting to develop a theory of justice, independent of politics. Here, one might quote Montaigne on Rawls's behalf. "It is quite easy," Montaigne observed, "upon accepted foundations, to build whatever one pleases."

The interest in Rawls's work, however, seems to be as great among political "practitioners" as among academic philosophers. The sprawling edifice of "ethics in public policy" studies, for example, is already partially undergirded by the "Rawlsian" principle of the "maximin."[3] The unstated connection between Rawls's theory and practice is suggested by Stuart Hampshire: "Professor Rawls arrives...at the principle of justice which social democrats have always groped for."[4] Professor Allan Bloom also sees a connection between Rawls's theory and political practice. Bloom argues that *A Theory of Justice* "amounts to a restatement of American Constitutional arrangements, reinterpreted to include the implications of the welfare state."[5] Brian Barry, another celebrated critic, reiterates Bloom's view. Barry suggests that Rawls is offering a defense of American liberalism in referring to the United States and "similar types of society" as nearly just because there is "a previous overruling desire to preserve justice."[6]

Without questioning Rawls's apolitical intention, I propose to reflect on the connection suggested by Bloom and Barry between Rawls's theory and the theory and practice of American liberalism. This study is confined to American liberalism, for while this country is a "social democracy," it has certain unique features, which we will explore, separating it from its European cousins.

Contrary to Bloom's and Barry's view, a reading of *A Theory of Justice*, along with Rawls's later works, raises a question about Rawls's fidelity to American liberalism. While others, including Marc Plattner, David Schaeffer and Harvey C. Mansfield, Jr., have questioned Rawls's liberalism, none of them has identified and elaborated what I believe to be the three central questions.[8] (1) What function does consent play in making political choices? (2) What is the place of federalism and private association in American political life? (3) What should be the proper distribution of power in American society? I will argue that these three questions are at the core of American liberalism and that Rawls answers them all in an essentially illiberal manner.

The first part of this study will examine the problem of the "old" liberalism. I will argue that in concentrating on the problem of equality, Rawls ignores, and hence may exaggerate, other more fundamental problems centering on the problem of consent, the status of private associations, and therefore the distribution of power in American society. Finally, I conclude that the solution to the problem of inequality presented by *A Theory of Justice* offers a greater challenge to existing "American Constitutional arrangements" than is suggested by either Bloom, Barry, or indeed, Rawls himself.

The problem Rawls sees in the "older liberalism" is related to the inequality resulting from competitive individualism. If, as Locke believed, the rational and industrious have a right to acquire disproportionate rewards because their selfish activity contributes to the general welfare, a degree of oligarchy will result through their accumulation of wealth and power. The old liberal response is that under the usual social configuration—many poor and few rich—political democracy, or universal, active consent, would naturally insure an increasingly equal income distribution. With everyone favoring policies beneficial to himself, the poor majority would express a clear preference for greater wealth and use its electoral power to achieve it.[9] Universal consent thus modifies the tendency to oligarchy. This situation changes, however, when the many are rich, at least relatively, and the few poor.[10] A dominant middle class actively expressing its preference for greater wealth and privilege will encounter moral difficulties in relation to the poor minority, who cannot successfully compete with the middle class on an individual, or political, basis.

As the most numerous and, collectively, the wealthiest class, the American middle class rules society and effectively controls public policy.

Any ruling class naturally fills the offices of the state with those whom they like, respect, and trust—those who can lead them and who seem to be able to improve the lot of the average voter.

Every class justifies its rule by praising its claim to justice. The claim of the middle class rests on its productivity and openness (equality of opportunity). The presence of virtually unlimited opportunities for advancement through education, the military, and job training seemingly guarantees that those with any semblance of motivation and ability can succeed.

Of course every such claim to justice is only partially true, and therefore, partially false. All societies, even modern technological ones, no matter how free and open, are both fortuitous and discriminatory. Unanticipated changes in market conditions, techniques of production, and credit may lead even the most deserving to failure. Ethnic, racial, and sexual bias may deny equality to others. Moreover, even if all of these limits to achievement could be eliminated, the inherent barriers remain to the congenitally unequal who can never succeed under any conceivable free condition.

According to the old liberalism, those who do not succeed should be protected through private and public charity. But the unsuccessful have no right or "entitlement" to equal treatment, although one might wish to treat them well out of reasons of compassion. Equal treatment by right would be unjust to those who have achieved acceptable goals, while it would also destroy the incentive to achieve for others. However, to become the object of charity, not justice, would seem to deny the fundamental perception of human equality which underlies the system. Seemingly, the relation between equality of "opportunity" and of "result" must be drawn closer if the claim of equal human dignity is to be maintained.

The recognition of the weakness of middle class justice to deal with the dissimilar and disadvantaged did not originate with Rawls. In American society it was thoroughly analyzed by Tocqueville.[11] In relation to the blacks, as slaves or free men, Tocqueville offered this formula. The white majority considers the blacks inferior and seeks social distance from them. Since middle class opinion determines social policy, no solution to racial discrimination is possible without, 1) a change in white opinion, or 2) external compulsion from some power insensitive to public opinion. Tocqueville was pessimistic, believing as he did, that the first alternative would prove glacial at best, while the second would elevate the blacks only at the expense of the freedom and self-rule of society as a whole.[12]

A theoretical solution to the problem of reconciling morality and consent was first offered by Jean Jacques Rousseau. In order to counteract the selfishness of enlightened individualism, Rousseau separated the general will from the will of all. The will of all is what is generally called the will of the majority, "the private interest and sum of particular wills."

The general will, on the contrary, is the sum of the deliberation of individuals without the interference of associations or parties.

By this mechanism, Rousseau felt the animosity between groups, and the gap between private interest and public good could be eliminated or reduced. But, Rousseau argued, the realization of the general will must be a rare event, depending, among other things, upon a small community of equals governed by a strict morality and a "divine" legislator.[13] Realizing the unlikelihood and perhaps impossibility of founding such a community, Rousseau maintained that a government could be judged as a moral one insofar as it is guided by the principle of the equal freedom and dignity of each of its members. But in practice, he wisely refrained from insisting that that morality had to be the basis of practical choices. Rousseau realized with perfect clarity that unless a self-governing people could be persuaded to make a free moral choice, the consequences of forcing them to do so would be unimaginable. This can be seen in Rousseau's practical identification of the general will with the majority will.[14]

If I understand him correctly, Rawls gingerly embraces the moral or illiberal alternative Rousseau presents: Namely for Rawls, the theoretical and practical bases of justice, i.e., equality *and* consent, take place in the same action. They come together in the "original position" where individuals rationally calculate life chances. The result of this calculation can be summarized in Lincoln's judgment, "As I would not choose to be a slave, so I would not choose to be a master." Ignorant of their ability, and of what to expect in civil and contingent society, rational individuals in the original position soberly consent not to be subjected to the worst possibilities—mental or physical incapacity, or other handicaps—rather than speculate on possible good fortune—being born with a "silver spoon" or above average ability.[15]

Having established by means of rational consent man's equality, Rawls proceeds to argue that those in society who are in fact disadvantaged are being treated immorally, for they, too, chose in the original position to be treated equally.

In so far as inequalities exist for the advantaged, however, they can be justified by Rawls's second, or "difference principle". The difference principle states: "The higher expectations of those better situated are just if and only if they work as part of a scheme which improves the expectations of the least advantaged members of society."[16]

As has been noted, the difference principle is a restatement of the anticipated economic development of the older liberal economics. Adam Smith, in some sense a follower of John Locke, was proud of the observation that, "The accommodation of an European prince does not always so much exceed that of an industrious and frugal peasant, as the accommodation of the latter exceeds that of many an African king."[17] In other words, the wealth generated by modern economies will be beneficial to all—however, not to all equally. The position of the modern worker, while inferior to that of the owner, is vastly superior to that of a primitive monarch or his own previous condition. Rawls, like Smith, maintains the legitimacy of inequalities, but he makes more explicit the moral basis upon which these inequalities rest: the fundamental equality of the original position.

According to Rawls, all politics, in the usual sense—who should rule? for what end?—is subordinate to these two principles of justice. Although there will be periodic elections in the just society, the deliberation of the elected representatives will be circumscribed by the demands of impartial justice demanded of the "rational legislator" judging public policy on the basis of the two principles of justice.[18]

Given the principles of justice, the range of policy choices will be limited. For example, one of the primary goods the least advantaged should enjoy is self-respect; all public policy, therefore, should enhance their respectability. As a result, Rawls argues that a narrow or group-interested standpoint indifferent to this policy goal should be restricted: non-disadvantaged groups pursuing their own self-respect will find a poor reception in the legislative halls. "The aim of constitutional design," Rawls says, "is to make sure, if possible, that the self-interest of social classes does not so distort the political settlement that it is made outside the permitted limits."[19]

Although Rawls concedes that majority rule is an "effective legislative procedure," he goes on to add that "the procedure of majority rule, however it is defined and circumscribed, has a subordinate place as a procedural device."[20] The consequence of its "subordinate place," as Rawls shows, is seen when a majority opposes policies determined by the principles of justice: the latter policies are to be preferred to the will of the majority. We will return to this point later (Part IV).

Rawls, however, argues that his is essentially a liberal view of justice. How does he understand the requisites of political liberty in modern societies? At the risk of confusing it with the "difference principle" and the "original position," let us begin with Rawls's "first principle" of liberty. "Each person," he asserts, "is to have an equal right to the most extensive total system of equal basic liberties compatible with a similar system of liberty for all."[21] Rawls indicates that considerable individual liberty is compatible with equal liberty for all. To put it in an American idiom, Rawls includes in his just society the "Bill of Rights," as generously interpreted as one might wish. The freedoms of speech, press, association and so on are clearly protected in his social thought. In recommitting himself to the "Bill of Rights," Rawls does not differ from the old liberalism. However, Rawls hastens to add these are not natural rights and hence they may be limited by circumstance.

The second aspect of Rawls's liberalism is found in his defense of civil disobedience in those situations where it becomes clear that one is not receiving the basic liberties promised in the "first principle" of liberty.[22]

Civil disobedience is a theoretical problem in any society, no matter how liberal. The principle of civil disobedience is politically explosive because it threatens the community's ability to take measures necessary for its preservation, measures which may in turn threaten the rights, interests, or moral conscience of individuals. The central problem: under what conditions is conscription tolerable in a society sworn to protect the life and liberty of its citizens? To understand this difficulty, let us go back to the tradition to which Rawls claims allegiance and consider the approach of John Locke and its reflection in the American political experience in Thomas Jefferson's Declaration of Independence.

In his chapter on "Prerogative," Locke argues that the executive has the power to do what is in the public interest, even if it requires illegal acts.[23] The corrective for the abuse of prerogative is the right of the people to judge when such power is not used for the public good. Locke sees that in certain situations, usually involving prerogative, the injustice of the government is so great that it should no longer be considered a government. In this case, the people collectively may organize a new government, using force against the old one if necessary.[24]

The Declaration of Independence also reflects the collective nature of civil disobedience to established governments. The people, after long experience of injustice—not for light and transient reasons—can withdraw their allegiance to their "government."

Further evidence of the same approach can be seen in Lincoln's reaction to the *Dred Scott* decision, which he thought unconstitutional, but which had to be obeyed until Constitutional means could be found to change it.[25]

The demand for collective action insures, insofar as possible, that individuals will not resort to civil disobedience because of personal vagaries or the prejudices resulting from judgments made in one's own behalf.[26] While there will be cases where an individual or group may be treated unjustly and cannot legitimately oppose the injustice done them through civil obedience, this risk is run in the older liberal tradition in order to prevent the more common political problem of individuals refusing obedience on moral grounds when obedience is not only legitimately demanded but politically imperative.

In determining the proper ground for civil disobedience, Rawls admits that the ideal procedure would be for everyone to undergo the restraint of having to think of the common good, more or less required by

Locke and Jefferson, but this procedure seems impractical. As an alternative, Rawls argues that individuals should simply imagine the outcome of such deliberation and act according to their reflection on that process. By ignoring the fact that individuals may often be wrong as well as selfish, Rawls's solution becomes sufficiently anomic that it would probably reduce law abidingness to simple coercion.[27] For example, Rawls suggests, "In these cases (involving the proper rate of savings), there is no reason why a democrat may not oppose the public will by suitable forms of non-compliance, or even as a government official try to circumvent it."[28] This is certainly the opposite pole from the tradition from which Rawls claims authority.

The "first principle" of rights and the teaching of civil disobedience are the core of Rawls's liberalism. How effectively do they serve as the basis of a contemporary liberal society? Is there something he has left out? Are there other principles at work which may reduce these two to insignificance? Or may these two principles prove so effective that government may cease to operate reasonably even for the sake of the least advantaged?

The first thing to notice is that both principles are passive or reactive. The first principle of justice may be expected to make legislative and executive policies expansive, for the courts can be relied upon to protect the individual's basic liberties, after the fact. Civil disobedience will have the same effect. In both cases the individual's ability to escape the law becomes a judicial right.

Although Rawls's "Bill of Rights" and appeal to civil disobedience may be reassuring to individuals, will they have any effect on the direction of public policy? Or, do they simply allow the public sector to expand while making the execution of the law more difficult? Is liberalism as a political theory exhausted by the negative protection of rights? Or, does it also require a positive ability to influence public policy through active participation in the public choices of society? If liberalism requires such consent, then a theory of liberal justice must include a reflection on political participation. But, to repeat, no commentator has adequately accounted for the reason Rawls's conception of consent is so weak in comparison with existing "American Constitutional arrangements."[29]

According to the older liberalism, if freedom and equality are the standards, everyone should have a right to consent to and, if possible, the ability to participate in, governmental decisions. What is characteristic of American society is that most forms of consent are not explicitly public —working in political campaigns, voting, and holding public office —but revolve around what Peter Berger and Richard Neuhaus have recently called mediating structures.[30] These mediating structures are the non-economic parts of what Tocqueville originally called private associations, e.g., families, churches, neighborhood organizations, to which Tocqueville added business, labor (if they had existed), professional and charitable organizations. Mediating associations are important in every society but in America they are of fundamental importance, according to Tocqueville, because participation in them constitutes the major means both of consent and of community in a highly individualistic culture formed by mass immigration, without the traditional social orders found in Europe.[31]

The place of mediating associations is strengthened not only by the overall separation of the public and private spheres in American society but also by the separation of national from state and local public authority. In crucial areas such as criminal and civil justice, education, workman's compensation and unemployment, the states and localities under the current federal arrangement maintain considerable power. The combination of federalism and limited government is the basis of private association in American Constitutional arrangements.

Berger and Neuhaus argue that mediating associations preserve private as well as public life:

Such institutions have a private face, giving private life a measure of stability and have a public face, transferring meaning and value to the megastructures...Their strategic position derives from their reducing both the anomic precariousness of individual existence in isolation from society and the threat of alienation to the public order.[32]

The voluntary organizations provide an important basis of private morality and of public consent to the larger society. Without them, public association (e.g. bureaucracy) is extended to fill the void created by the weakness of the private realm. However, the continuing relevance of private associations requires the viability of the older liberal view of justice, in contrast to Rawls's original position.

The older view saw the public good as "self-interest rightly understood," a moderate reasonableness in pursuing one's individual goals.[33] Private associations were considered one of the major devices by which individual, private interest could become collective, moderate, and purposeful. In the old liberalism, there was no fundamental distinction between "economic" and "moral" passions: the desire to found General Motors or a Temperance Union were equally moral. However, as a result of Rousseau, this conception of a scientifically neutral politics was decisively challenged—taken off its head, so to speak, and put back on its moral feet. To act morally, it was no longer enough to respect the equal rights of others while pursuing one's self-interest rationally and moderately. Political morality now meant disinterested action for the common good, and the common good increasingly came to mean the relief of the impoverished, or the least advantaged, to use Rawls's phrase.

Naturally, the self-interested partisanship of the private associations had to be reduced or abandoned.

For Rawls the private associations are based on questionable moral grounds. Moreover, they reinforce their amorality with powers adverse to those that underlie a *Theory of Justice*. The power of the private associations depends on their numbers—their votes—and upon their wealth, which can in turn influence votes. Rawls has taken care of the first problem by reducing consent to a secondary consideration. Votes are almost worthless. Moreover, Rawls has also transformed property ownership from one based on individual natural right to one based on the social calculation of reward based on the "difference principle." Individuals no longer own wealth as a result of labor but under Rawls's plan receive pay in proportion to the benefit of the least advantaged. Wealth becomes social or public, no longer individual or private.[34]

Practically, Rawls's redefinition of public good as the maximum support for the least advantaged will result in the growth of public institutions necessary to administer this policy. These public spirited institutions are the bureaucracies, which are national in scope as well as general in morality. Fairness knows no regional or sectarian bound. Without a self-interest of their own, at least no private pursuit of profit, the bureaucrats can act rationally and morally for the whole.

In contrast to the older liberalism, Rawls sees associations not as private entities helping to make public choices, but as literally, or wholly, private; they are important only in reinforcing the individual members' sense of purpose and self-identity. Everyone, he says, should have "a community of shared interests to which he belongs and where he finds his endeavors confirmed by associates." Associations aid individuals in the formation of their private selves by creating the opportunities for social relations with other like selves. The connection between the private interest and the public purposefulness of such associations is absent. Private associations lose their quasi-public function and are permanently reduced to the level of social clubs.[35]

As a result, private associations have increasingly become perceived as "special interests" parochially defending limited views of the "common good," i.e., their self-interest. As such, they morally distort the commitment to the "original position." The most characteristic example of the application of such generalized morality in contemporary society is the unraveling of the political parties. The principle of continuing political partisanship based on either class or group interest is unjust on the basis of the morality developed by Rousseau, and now Rawls, whereas the independent voter can rationally and morally decide for himself what is in the public interest.[36]

Rawls's demotion of the social, private sphere can be most clearly seen in his critique of Robert Dahl's pluralism:

A just constitution must rely to some extent on citizens and legislatures adopting a wider view and exercising good judgment in applying the principles of justice. There seems to be no way of allowing them to take a narrow or group-oriented standpoint and then regulating the process so that it leads to a just outcome.

Rawls continues to sharpen his point.

The pluralist account of democracy, in so far as the rivalry between interests is believed to regulate the political process, is open to similar objection. See R.A. Dahl, *A Preface to Democratic Theory*...and more recently, *Pluralist Democracy in the United States*...[37]

Behind Robert Dahl, of course, stands a greater figure, who is also refuted by Rawls's critique of pluralism. James Madison, the principal architect of "American Constitutional arrangements," argued in *Federalist Ten* that the pernicious effects of faction—the greatest disease of popular government—could only be effectively controlled by extending the sphere of government, and creating a plethora of interests. "A greater variety of parties and interests," Madison argued, "makes it less probable that a majority of the whole will have a common motive to invade the rights of other citizens." Moreover a variety of interests tends to guarantee that any consensus will of necessity be a broad one and, as such, generally benevolent.[38]

Madison thought the alternative to "pluralism" was either the destruction of political liberty or giving to everyone the same opinions. The first possibility is folly in Madison's view, while the second is impractical. "As long as the reason of man continues fallible," Madison says, differing opinions about economic rights, religion, "ideology," and political leadership will agitate the political community. While each of these differing opinions is a potential source of faction, "the regulation of the various and interfering (economic) interests forms the principal task of modern legislation."[39]

Madison was well aware of the limits of using sect to forestall faction. He describes the continuing need for statesmen, actuated by "indirect and remote considerations," affecting the public good. However, knowing that such statesmen would rarely be "at the helm," Madison settled for the congress of interests.

Rawls, contrary to Madison, appears content to give to everyone the same political opinions through the original position.

Each citizen wants everyone to act from principles to which all would agree in an initial situation of equality. This desire is regulative, as the condition of finality on moral principles requires, and when everyone acts justly, all find satisfaction in the very same thing.[40]

Moreover, Rawls seems more sanguine that truly disinterested statesmen or "rational legislators"—not "representative legislators"—can be found to insure that the principles of justice are carried into practice.[41]

Rawls thus effectively curtails both the public and private modes of consent—that of electoral majorities and of private associations. By thus reducing the essential question of consent to that of the "original position," Rawls substitutes a formal liberty for an actual liberty. In place of a functioning liberal society, dominated by an apparently moderate middle class, Rawls lays the theoretical ground for a bureaucratic state which merely promises to protect individual rights. Experience suggests that it is often difficult to guarantee either economic or political rights where there is bureaucratic control—except through effective electoral pressure.[42] Just where consent is most needed, Rawls reduces it to a "subordinate position."

To deny the majority's right to make fundamental decisions, as Rawls seeks, transfers sovereignty to the "rational legislators" ruling according to the moral principles established by the "original position" and the "difference principle," "circumventing" the "public will" when necessary.[43] This transfer effectively disenfranchises the middle class, putting in its place a rational elite ruling in the name of the disadvantaged. But this elite's disinterested rule is itself problematic. Every ruling class rules first in its own interest (as does the contemporary middle class). A ruling class becomes just when it is willing to encourage, or tolerate, the interests of the other classes. But it rules with an eye to its *own* conception of justice and self-preservation.[44]

An American government of "rational legislators" leads to a theoretical contradiction and to an impolitic consequence. First, the theoretical contradiction can be seen in that the rule of the advantaged few, the "rational legislators," ignores the principle of equality underlying Rawls's contract (as well as that of his professed masters Locke and Rousseau) requiring majoritarianism.[45] Second, the impolitic consequence is generated by the reflection that a regime is generally defined by the economic and political strength of the strongest class. When a particular class is clearly stronger, political wisdom dictates that one seek to modify its injustice by persuasion, not seek its subordination, as Rawls seems to suggest.[46] The latter course leads to reaction, diminishing the willingness of the dominant class to compromise even for the least advantaged. Therefore, Rawls's theoretical solution to the problem of American justice may foster the problem he seeks to solve.

Although moderate, Rawls's liberal equalitarianism, seen from the populist perspective of American democracy, is essentially illiberal. However, seen from the traditional, elitist perspective of European liberalism—fundamentally different from the free middle class of the American experience—Rawls is more liberal.

Rawls, of course, is not altogether mistaken in his perception of the moral dilemmas of American society. Inequality is a problem for those who cannot compete because of prejudice, chance, or nature. However, without the social communities and the individual freedom found in the private sphere of American society, the problems of alienation and mediocrity in the middle class would probably be exaggerated as power was withdrawn from the traditional sources of middle class power—the private associations—and given to those general, public institutions seeking to aid the least advantaged.

What can be done to moderate existing inequality without beoming entangled in the problems encircling Rawls? Obviously, no easy answer is at hand, for at one extreme the liberal egalitarian is faced with the seemingly impossible task of defending the equality not only of the victims of prejudice, chance, or nature, but of those who have, or choose, "lazy genes." Arthur Okun, a follower of Rawls, offers a slightly comical defense of their equality.[47] But this difficulty should not blind us to the fact that at the other extreme one arrives at the laissez-faire policies of a crypto-oligarchy ruling through a free market. It seems the middle class depends on legislation regulating power (from public and private elites) inimical to its rule.

Recent experience suggests that the American polity can produce popular support for effective social welfare policies.[48] The majority seems sufficiently fair and reasonable to compromise its immediate economic interest for the benefit of the least advantaged. In other words, through public education and effective leadership (social as well as political), it appears possible to maintain a popular consensus for a reasonable economic redistribution.

Indeed, the maintenance of this middle class (not elite) consensus seems fundamental. For this reason, theories like Rawls's, insensitive to the popular self-rule of a middle class regime, may prove counter-productive. The increasing disaffection of the middle class from the "rational legislators" of the modern bureaucratic state suggests the choice of equality over consent is even now issuing in practical results counter to those intended by Rawls. The majority appears to be trying with increasing determination to recapture political and economic power from the "rational legislators."

However, the middle class is politically moderate. Therefore, it is probably too much to expect that Rawls's crypto-elitism will eventuate in a middle class reaction. The rational bureaucratic state is already too well established, even here and now, to be compromised fundamentally by a wrathful middle class. Rather, the questions seem to be (1) whether policies implemented without effective majority consent can be moral, and (2) whether the majority, sensing its loss of effective control, will not become even more politically apathetic. The latter is the result forecast by Tocqueville in the antepenultimate chapter of *Democracy in America*.[49]

John Rawls's stated indifference to the question of democratic theory and practice makes him insensitive to the cause of the people's attachment to their government. A *Theory of Justice*, it seems, will necessarily prove threatening to "American Constitutional arrangements" for it apparently ignores the basis of American political psychology issuing from the people's belief that it enjoys *self*–government through active participation in open, decentralized institutions.[50]

Notes

1. Robert Nozick, *Anarchy, State, and Utopia* (N.Y.: Basic Books, 1974), p. 183. Brian Barry, *The Liberal Theory of Justice* (Oxford: Clarendon Press, 1973), p. ix. Robert K. Fullinwider, "A Chronological Bibliography of Works on John Rawls's, *A Theory of Justice,*" *Political Theory*, (1977), pp. 561–70.

2. John Rawls, *A Theory of Justice* (Cambridge: Harvard University Press, 1971), pp. 226–27. See Stuart Hampshire, "A New Philosophy of the Just Society," *The New York Review of Books*, February 24, 1972, p. 39. "He (Rawls) is not concerned with the particularities of political science or with the theory of democracy." As I will try to show, this is an artificial distinction, which founders on the tension between equality and the right of citizens to consent to, and participate in, public policy choices.

3. Henry Shue, *Basic Rights: Subsistence, Affluence and U.S. Foreign Policy* (Princeton, NJ: Princeton University Press, 1980), pp. 127–29. Shue ultimately breaks with Rawls over the inability of the "maximin" to guarantee the "basic rights" of the least advantaged in undeveloped nations. Mark T. Lilla, "Ethos, 'Ethics,' and Public Service," *The Public Interest*, 63 (Spring, 1981), pp. 3–17. Norman Furniss and Timothy Tilton, *The Case for the Welfare State: From Social Security to Social Equality* (Bloomington: Indiana University Press, 1977), pp. 26–27, 50. Ronald Dworkin, *Taking Rights Seriously* (Cambridge MA: Harvard University Press, 1977), p. 149, as quoted in John Hart Ely, *Democracy and Distrust: A Theory of Judicial Review* (Cambridge, M.A.: Harvard University Press, 1980), p. 58, writes: "Constitutional law can make no genuine advance until it isolates the problem of rights against the state and makes that problem part of its own agenda. That argues for a fusion of constitutional law and moral theory, a connection that, incredibly, has yet to take place. It is perfectly understandable that lawyers dread contamination with moral philosophy, and particularly with those philosophers who talk about rights, because the spooky overtones of that concept threaten the graveyard of reason. But better philosophy is now available than the lawyers may remember. Professor Rawls of Harvard, for example, has published an abstract and complex book about justice which no constitutional lawyer will be able to ignore."

4. Hampshire, "A New Philosophy," p. 37.

5. Allan Bloom, "Justice: John Rawls vs. The Tradition of Political Philosophy," *The American Political Science Review*, 69 (June, 1975) pp. 648–62. Bloom also argues that Rawls creates an enormously active government, whose goal is to provide the primary goods, including the sense of one's own worth.

6. Barry, pp. 50, 141. But, see Robert Amdus's criticism of Barry on this point in *Political Theory*, 3 (February, 1975) pp. 100–03.

7. John Rawls, "Fairness to Goodness," *Philosophic Review*, 84 (October, 1975), pp. 536–54. ———. "The Independence of Moral Theory," *Proceedings and Addresses of the American Philosophical Association*, 48 (1974–1975), pp. 5–22. ———. "The Basic Structure as Subject," *American Philosophical Quarterly*, 14 (April, 1977), pp. 159–165. The greater emphasis in his recent work on the "background" of justice, especially the "basic structure," indicates that Rawls is increasingly cognizant of the actual conditions or limits of political justice. However, the relation between practice and theory, especially seen in the relation between equality and consent, has still not found a place in his theory of

justice. Rousseau remarked that the serious Romans refused to believe the Christian claim that the Kingdom of Heaven had no relation to the empire of Caesar.

8. Marc F. Plattner, "The Welfare State vs. the Redistributive State," *The Public Interest*, 55 (Spring, 1979), pp. 28–48. David L. Schaefer, "The Sense and Nonsense of Justice," *The Political Science Reviewer*, 3 (Fall, 1973), pp. 1–41. Michael Zuckert, "Justice Deserted: A Critique of Rawls's *A Theory of Justice*," *Polity*, 13 (Spring, 1981), pp. 446–83. Harvey C. Mansfield, Jr., *The Spirit of Liberalism* (Cambridge, MA: Harvard University Press, 1978), pp. 99–101. See also Robert Paul Wolff, *Understanding Rawls* (Princeton, N.J.: Princeton University Press, 1977).

9. John Locke, *Second Treatise of Civil Government*, Chapters IX-XII. M. Seliger, *The Liberal Politics of John Locke*, (London: George Allen & Unwin, 1968), pp. 146–67, 267–323.

10. Aristotle, *Politics*, 1279b-1280a, Alexis de Tocqueville, *Democracy in America*, ed. J. P. Mayer (Garden City, N.Y.: Doubleday and Co., 1966), pp. 250–55, 551–55, 634–45. For a contrasting view, see Michael Parenti, *Democracy for the Few* (New York: St. Martin's Press, 1980). Kenneth M. Dolbeare and Murray J. Edelman, *American Politics* (Lexington, Mass.: D. C. Heath, 1981 (1971), pp. 125–54. However, a critical appraisal of the data offered by Dolbeare and Edelman would only slightly alter the framework we are using. "Middle class" as used here is a self-definition and a general term referring to income and wealth and, most importantly, to "middle class" attitudes toward competitive achievement.

11. Tocqueville, pp. 355–63.

12. Ibid., pp. 342–44.

13. Jean Jacques Rousseau, *On the Social Contract*, II. 1–7: III. 4.

14. Ibid., II. 7; IV. 4; IV. 8. On the basis of the previous consent to the "original position," Rawls believes it is possible to divorce a theory of justice from a theory of consent in a community of equals. This Rousseau emphatically denied, although, to say the least, Rousseau explored every possibility—fair and foul—to make the will of all identical to the general will. For the necessity of choice for moral action, consider Aristotle, *Nicomachean Ethics*, 1109b-1115a.

15. Rawls, *Justice*, pp. 11–22.

16. Ibid., pp. 60–83.

17. Adam Smith, *The Wealth of Nations*, I, i.

18. Rawls, *Justice*, p. 357.

19. Ibid., p. 362.

20. Ibid., pp. 353–54, 356, 383.

21. Ibid. p. 302.

22. Ibid., pp. 382–91.

23. John Locke, *Second Treatise of Civil Gove rnment*, XIV.

24. Ibid., XIV, 168; XIX. Seliger, pp. 124–29.

25. "Speech at Springfield, Illinois" (June 26, 1857) in Roy P. Basler, ed., *The Collected Works of Abraham Lincoln* (New Brunswick, N.J.: Rutgers University Press, 1953), II, 400–09.

26. This account of civil disobedience is deliberately skewed. One should consider the thought of Henry David Thoreau, Martin Luther King, Jr., and Michael Walzer to understand some of the complexities involved. However, as sophisticated as Rawls's solution is, it is still fraught with theoretical difficulties. Why should the same individual be presumed to be rational and moral when considering whether to obey a law already made, but be presumed to be incompetent to make a law through the process of consent? Isn't it more reasonable to assume individuals should consent to law and then be bound to what they have consented to? For an opposite view, see Daniel M. Farrell, "Dealing with Injustices in a Reasonably Just Society: Some Observations on Rawls's Theory of Political Duty" in H. G. Blocker and E. H. Smith, eds., *John Rawls's Theory of Social Justice* (Athens, Ohio: Ohio University Press, 1980), pp. 187–210. Also, David L.

Schaefer, *Justice or Tyranny?: A Critique of John Rawls's A Theory of Justice* (Port Washington, N.Y.: Kennikat Press, 1979), pp. 60–3.

27. Rawls, *Justice*, pp. 296, 389, 381, on conscientious refusal: "The conduct and aims of states in waging war, especially large powerful ones, are in some circumstances so likely to be unjust that one is forced to conclude that in the foreseeable future one must abjure military service altogether."

28. Ibid., p. 296.

29. Vernon Van Dyke is aware of this problem. See, "Justice as Fairness: For Groups?," *The American Political Science Review*, 69 (June, 1975). Moreover, this tendency has been noted, if not explored, by several commentators who have identified Rawls with an illiberal or bureaucratic Rousseau. Benjamin R. Barber, "Can America be Democratic?," *Discourses* (Chicago: Loyola University of Chicago, 1981), pp. 1–17, typifies this view: "John Rawls's *A Theory of Justice*, brings with it a number of premises which are in the long run dangerous to democracy." See, ibid., "Justifying Justice: Problems of Psychology, Politics and Measurement in Rawls" and Milton Fisk, "History and Reason in Rawls's Moral Theory" in Norman Daniels ed., *Reading Rawls* (New York: Basic Books, n.d.), pp. 292–318, 53–80.

30. Peter L.Berger and Richard J. Neuhaus, *To Empower People: The Role of Mediating Structures in Public Policy* (Washington, D.C.: American Enterprise Institute for Public Policy Research, 1977).

31. Tocqueville, pp. 503–30.

32. Berger and Neuhaus, p. 3.

33. Tocqueville, pp. 667–79.

34. Plattner, p, 48.

35. Rawls, *Justice*, pp. 442, 467–71, 520–29. But, also, pp. 309–10.

36. See above note 13. Everett C. Ladd, Jr., *Where Have All the Voters Gone? (New York: W. W. Norton, 1978)*, pp. 3, 5, 57. David Broder, *The Party's Over* (New York: Harper and Row, 1971), pp. 199–201.

37. Rawls, *Justice*, pp. 360–61.

38. Alexander Hamilton, James Madison, and John Jay, *The Federalist Papers* (Middleton, Conn.: Wesleyan University Press, 1961), pp. 64–65.

39. Ibid., pp. 58–59. Mansfield, pp. 17–19.

40. Rawls, *Justice*, p. 527. Jefferson insisted that fair majorities must be "reasonable," i.e. must respect the equal natural rights of all. However, one can respect rights, while still believing in relevant human inequalities. The natural aristoi, as Jefferson called them, should receive unequal treatment, e.g. education. They would become moral by serving the general interest. Rawls denies human inequality except that as certain individuals prove more efficient, their efficiency should be rewarded by more wealth.

41. Ibid., pp. 231, 294, 518–19. Rawls differs from Madison in his belief that a rational and moral politics is possible. Rawls's faith accounts for his willingness to trust the rational legislators and, at the same time, to believe they will govern in cooperation with an enlightened majority. But Rawls cannot free himself from his suspicion of the actual majority. He remarks: "As things are, legislators must reckon with strong public feelings. Men's sense of outrage, however irrational, will set boundaries upon what is politically possible."

42. Henry James Ford, *The Rise and Growth of American Politics* (New York: MacMillan, 1898), p. 322. See Moise Ostrogorski, *Democracy and the Organization of Political Parties*, translated by F. Clarke (New York: MacMillan, 1902). In contemporary literature there is considerable skepticism about the role of elections. See, for example, Dolbeare and Edelman, pp. 485–86, for a frequently expressed view. However, for an alternative, see John L. Sullivan and Robert E. O'Connor, "Electoral Choice and Popular Control of Public Policy: The Case of the 1966 House Elections," *American Political Science Review* 66 (December, 1972), 1256–68. See note 50 below.

43. Rawls, *Justice*, p. 337.

44. Aristotle, *Politics*, III, IV. Since every polity is governed by its strongest social class, it is inevitable that that class will rule in its own interest if for no other reason than to maintain the stability of the laws, i.e. to resist revolution. Of course, the same necessity, according to Aristotle, should encourage justice in dealing with other social classes.

45. See above notes 9, 13, 14. Rawls, of course, is aware of the problem of equality and consent. However, because consent leads to results he apparently finds noxious, he opts for the original position, i.e. formal consent and the practical rule of the rational legislators.

46. Tocqueville, pp. 515, 530.

47. Arthur M. Okun, *Equality and Efficiency: The Big Tradeoff* (Washington, D.C.: The Brookings Institution, 1975), p. 45. Okun's work rests primarily on Rawls.

48. Everett C. Ladd, Jr., pp. 32–34. Ladd shows the consistency of majority opinion supporting traditional welfare policies, at least until the mid 1970s.

49. Tocqueville, pp. 690–695, 695–end.

50. See, for example, the writings of Gerald Pomper, especially the *Voter's Choice: Varieties of American Electoral Behavior* (New York: Harper and Row, Inc., 1975). For a contrasting view, see Dolbeare and Edelman, pp. 469–72, 493–97.

17

THE ORTHODOX
JOHN DICKINSON

Christopher Flannery

*And can the liberties of a nation be thought secure when we have removed their
only firm basis, a conviction in the minds of the people that these liberties are the
gift of God? That they are not to be violated but with his wrath?*
THOMAS JEFFERSON

IN THE DECADE PRECEDING THE DECLARATION OF INDEPENDENCE JOHN
Dickinson was "recognized as the chief spokesman for American rights
and liberty."[1] Dickinson wrote voluminously during this period, defending and defining the American Cause. In the literature of the revolution,
according to Paul Leicester Ford, Dickinson was "as pre-eminent as Washington in war, Franklin in diplomacy, and Morris in finance."[2] He won
this distinction chiefly by a series of twelve letters written in response to
several acts of the British Ministry and Parliament alleged to be in violation of the rights of the American colonists. Of the twenty-three newspapers published in the colonies in the winter of 1767–68, nineteen printed
all twelve of these *Letters from a Farmer in Pennsylvania to the Inhabitants of
the British Colonies.* Pamphlet editions were immediately published in
Philadelphia, Boston, New York, Williamsburg, London, and Paris. Dickinson was called "the American Pitt." In Paris salons "the Farmer" was
compared with Cicero. Not until Paine's *Common Sense* appeared in 1776
was any product of an American pen so acclaimed, on both sides of the
Atlantic, as the *Farmer's Letters.*

Dickinson played a leading role in the successive continental assemblies that carried forward the American Revolution and forged the thirteen separate colonies into one nation. He was a representative of Pennsylvania at the Stamp Act Congress in 1765, and was chief author of the
"Declaration of Rights and Grievances" and the petition to the king
adopted by that Congress. He was a member of the First Continental
Congress, and again had a hand in drafting the official proclamations of

that assembly, including the "Declarations and Resolves," whose list of grievances would be echoed in the Declaration of Independence. In the Second Continental Congress, Dickinson authored the famous "olive branch petition" to the king and, with Jefferson, the "Declaration on the Causes and Necessity of Taking up Arms," intended to be read by the new commander in chief, George Washington, to his assembled troops in Cambridge.

Dickinson wrote the original draft of the Articles of Confederation, submitted to Congress on July 12, 1776. A decade later he was chosen president of the Annapolis Convention, which was the immediate catalyst of the Constitutional Convention convened in Philadelphia in May, 1787, to amend the Articles of Confederation. As a delegate from Delaware to the Constitutional Convention Dickinson led the fight for equal representation of the states in the senate. In the following struggle for ratification Dickinson wrote a series of letters, signed "Fabius," in support of the new constitution.

Only a handful of the greatest Americans can be said to have evoked the spirit and molded the form of the American Revolution and Founding as tellingly as did John Dickinson, the Pennsylvania Farmer. And yet, what his contemporary, Ezra Stiles, prophesied of Dickinson in 1776 has —for some two centuries at least—largely proven true: "He now goes into oblivion or a dishonorable reminiscence with posterity."[3]

"Until the year of Independence," writes Milton Flower, the Farmer's recent biographer, "John Dickinson, apart from Benjamin Franklin, was probably the American known to more colonists than any other."[4] In the century following the year of American independence, more biographies were written of Benjamin Franklin than of any American statesman, including the Father of the Country, George Washington. In the same century John Dickinson was the subject of not one biography. Not until 1891 was a biography written of the illustrious Farmer. Following this, almost another century would expire before the second biography should appear, Flower's *John Dickinson: Conservative Revolutionary* (1983). In a brief (somewhat inaccurate) recollection of the most historic moment in the deliberations of the Second Continental Congress, Thomas Jefferson reveals the cause of the "oblivion" into which the name of Dickinson would fall. Of that Congress, Jefferson recalled, the American Declaration of Independence was "signed by every member present except Mr. Dickinson."[5]

If the love of fame is the ruling passion of the noblest minds, then John Dickinson's was a mind strongly tinctured with nobility. He held, with Tacitus, that "To despite Fame is to despite the Virtues by which it is acquir'd." He was avid of the good opinion of his countrymen, and spoke and wrote repeatedly of his gratitude at winning and his desire not to forfeit their esteem. He was, according to his biographer, "ever mindful of his 'reputation.'"[6] Yet in the crowning act of his political career, the act above all others for which he knew he would be remembered, and by which all his other words and deeds would be measured, Dickinson willingly and with full deliberation cast his celebrated name into obscurity and ill repute.

On July 1, 1776, the members of the Continental Congress sat as a committee of the whole to consider Richard Henry Lee's resolution: "that these United Colonies are and of right, ought to be, free and independent States. . . ."[7] Support for this resolution was by no means unanimous. The New York delegates were restrained by their Provincial Congress from voting for independence. A similar restriction on the Maryland delegation was removed only on the day the resolution was considered. South Carolina was leaning against the measure. The Delaware and Pennsylvania delegations were divided. And the votes of nine colonies were needed for passage. In rising to oppose this resolution, Dickinson nonetheless knew that he was leading a lost cause, that independence would come, if not with this vote then with another, and that his name would forever be enrolled among the opponents of this historic step. "My Conduct, this day," he said in the exordium of his fateful speech, "I expect will give the finishing Blow to my once too great . . . [now] too diminished Popularity."[8] That his cause was a lost cause, one which, far from enhancing his fame, would win for him immediate and enduring opprobrium, did not mean to Dickinson that it was a cause unworthy of the last full measure of devotion. As he had said in another forum just the day before Lee introduced his resolution: "The loss of life . . . or of what is dearer than life itself, the affection of my countrymen shall not deter me from acting as an honest man. . . . I can defy the world . . . but—I defy not heaven: nor will I ever barter my conscience for the esteem of mankind."[9] If true glory is reserved to those who do not seek final vindication at the bar of changing public opinion, but before a higher seat of judgment, then such was the ruling object of John Dickinson's mind.

Following Dickinson's speech there ensued nine hours of exhausting debate during which, as Jefferson recalled, "all the powers of the soul had been distended with the magnitude of the object."[10] Finally a vote was taken. New York abstained, Delaware was divided, South Carolina and Dickinson's Pennsylvania were opposed. Congress had, but barely had, the nine votes necessary to pass the resolution for independence. In the hope of passing this momentous resolution more resoundingly, Congress postponed the official vote until the next day, July 2. The New York delegates, bound by their restrictive instructions, could do no more than abstain. South Carolina changed its vote to affirmative. A new delegate arrived at the last minute to swing Delaware's vote in favor of independence. John Dickinson and Robert Morris abstained from voting and thus made possible an affirmative vote for Pennsylvania. America had chosen independence without a single dissenting vote.

An admirer of John Dickinson has written that "All of Dickinson's career is summarized in his refusal to affirm the Declaration [of Independence]."[11] This judgment is confirmed, with remarkable uniformity, by the arbiters of that posterity with which Dickinson courted so dishonorable a reminiscence. In the eyes of his most recent biographer, Dickinson's opposition to the Declaration of Independence epitomized the "conservative stance" the Farmer took toward all the great issues of the revolutionary and founding periods. His spirited opposition to the oppressive measures of the British Ministry and Parliament won the applause of the "radicals" in the early days of the Revolution. His constitutional reluctance to cast off old traditions, institutions and attachments caused him to be called a traitor by 1776. But it was changing times and circumstances that made Dickinson appear to his countrymen in such contrasting lights. "Dickinson never changed his principles." He was from beginning to end—what his new biography is entitled—a "Conservative Revolutionary."[12]

This is the firmly established tradition. Dickinson's first, and only other biographer, Charles Stillé, wrote of his subject as "always an intense conservative."[13] James Truslow Adams, in the *Dictionary of American Biography*, describes Dickinson, in almost exactly the same words, as "always intensely conservative."[14] "By temperament and breeding Dickinson was a conservative," writes V.L. Parrington in his famous *Main Currents in American Thought*.[15] "Both by nature and by culture, John Dickinson was a conservative," according to Moses Coit Tyler.[16] More recently (1962), as editor of a new edition of the Farmer's Letters, Forrest McDonald repeats that "Dickinson's view is . . . conservative."[17]

"Conservative" is, of course, a broad term with a long history and a wide variety of possible meanings. Edmund Morgan, in his popular history, *The Birth of the Republic 1763–1789*, offers a generally accepted definition of the term in the relevant context:

> There were in 1776, as there always are, conservative men who thought the overthrow of a government, however evil, must entail worse consequences than submission. They had come this far in seeking what they considered their legal and constitutional rights, but to go where [Tom] Paine was leading was to abandon both law and constitution and risk all in the untried and unrigged ship of "natural" rights. Rather than board such a vessel they would give up the contest and accept whatever King and Parliament chose to give them.[18]

Whether dishonored or honored, John Dickinson has apparently become, in the eyes of posterity, almost literally the very definition of a conservative in the American Revolution.

Dickinson is praised by his first biographer for understanding that the rights and liberty of the American colonists "were built, not, as many afterwards contended, on some vague theory of natural rights, but upon a much firmer and surer foundation, immemorial custom. . . ." In contrast to those revolutionaries who claimed to "follow the light of nature," Dickinson was ever "guided by the lamp of experience." He "had a horror of any changes brought about by revolutionary means." From first to last, Dickinson is said by Stillé to have resisted the measures of the British ministry because these acts were "violations of English, not of natural, law." Dickinson's "horizon was always bounded by the legal aspects of the situation."[19] Parrington, with less admiration for Dickinson, nonetheless agrees wholeheartedly with Stillé that the Farmer's arguments were directed not only against the British ministry, but against "the natural rights advocates." He "little understood the spirit of liberalism that was stirring in many minds." Dickinson's "appeal was to the law and the constitution; never to abstract principles."[20] Dickinson had, according to Tyler, "an uncommon horror of all changes that violated the sequences of established law. His philosophy of politics was practical, rather than merely speculative . . . [I]n all his writings, whether official or personal, his endeavor was to place the American claim on historic constitutional grounds."[21] McDonald writes that "Dickinson's view is historical, pragmatic, and in the Burkean sense, conservative." "Throughout his life, Dickinson explicitly rejected the rationalism of the eighteenth century," which held that "men are born with certain rights, whether they are honored in a particular society or not."[22]

To prefer submission to revolution; to be bounded wholly by the legal horizon; to discover the ultimate foundation of American rights in prescriptive law and "immemorial custom"; above all, explicitly and emphatically to reject vague theories of natural right: if these were essential elements of conservatism in 1776, nothing would appear to be a more complete and precise example of it than the statesmanship of John Dickinson.

There is, indeed, a strong thread of consistency running through Dickinson's words and deeds from the earliest stirrings of resistance in the 1760s to the securing of that "more perfect Union" in 1789, and beyond. On the evidence of his extensive writings over this critical quarter century one could make a case for the claim of his biographer, that he never changed his political principles. But were these principles what posterity has so consistently said them to be? The Pennsylvania Farmer will not be troubled in his long sleep over our answer to this question, so far as it concerns merely his own good name. As it happens, however, Dickinson's good name is to a degree bound up with the good name of the country in whose destiny, as he wrote, "I was resolved by every impulse of my soul to share."[23]

Some who would resurrect the name of Dickinson from the relative oblivion into which it has fallen, would raise it above the names of those Founding Fathers who have come to embody the very idea of America. M.E. Bradford, for example, writes:

The very fact of Dickinson's influential career undermines cherished theories of our national origins. If he is more useful in telling us what his times signified than are some of the Fathers we have been taught to reverence as the true progenitors—more useful than Paine, or Madison, or even most of Jefferson (the "advanced", private opinions)—then the authority of many components of what we now recognize as the American political religion or *telos* and the manner of thinking which has generated these ends is called into question. *And he is!* [24]

Dickinson, as opposed in particular to such speculative proponents of natural rights as Thomas Jefferson and Thomas Paine, "embodies the American political prescription."[25]

To make Dickinson again—what he was before 1776—the spokesman for American rights and liberty, is under the terms of the orthodox scholarship to cast off those cherished theories of our national origins which are the rock on which the American political religion is built; it is to disavow the *telos* or end of American political life which is inherent in our national origins as commonly understood; and to refound American rights and liberties, not on specious theories of natural right, but on the firm and sure foundation of "immemorial custom."

For all that Dickinson sought the honor of his countrymen, he would rather, I think, his name were consigned to oblivion than to win immortality on such terms. Throughout the American Revolution and Founding, whatever conventional order he was defending, Dickinson always aimed to inculcate in the minds and hearts of the American people the conviction that their rights and liberties were not theirs by mere convention, but were "the gift of God" bestowed upon all men by nature.

In an early speech before the Pennsylvania Assembly the young Dickinson succinctly expressed his understanding of the relation of customary to intrinsic right, of the conventional to the natural order—an understanding that informed his statesmanship to the end of his life. A majority of the Assembly, led by the already formidable Benjamin Franklin, sought to change Pennsylvania from a Proprietary to a Royal colony. There were grievances (shared by Dickinson) against the proprietors of Pennsylvania, and it was thought that relief could be found if the British monarch would "take the People of this Province under his immediate protection and government."[26] Dickinson, taking what his biographer describes as the conservative side in the issue, opposed the change of government.[27] The rights and liberties of Pennsylvania, in his opinion, would be placed in equal or greater peril under the Crown than under the proprietors.

No man, sir, amongst us hath denied, or will deny, that this province must *stake* on the event of the present attempt, liberties that ought to be immortal—*Liberties!* founded on the acknowledged *rights of human nature*; and restrained in our mother-country, only by an unavoidable necessity of adhering in some measure, to long established customs. Thus hath been formed between old errors and hasty innovations, an entangled chain, that our ancestors either had not moderation or leisure enough to untwist.

In risking a change of government, he feared:

The people of *this society* will lose the exercise of those rights, which, tho' they ARE INTITLED TO AS MEN, YET SUCH IS THE SITUATION OF HUMAN AFFAIRS, they with difficulty can find a spot on the whole globe where they are allowed to enjoy them. (emphasis in original)[28]

Dickinson never in the long course of his career lost sight of the "unavoidable necessity of adhering in some measure to long established customs." Nor did he ever cease to measure established customs and institutions against "the ackowledged rights of human nature"—rights the exercise of which Pennsylvanians or Americans might be deprived of by chance or necessity, but which they would always be "intitled to as men." Reckoning by the rights of human nature, Dickinson's statesmanship always sought to ply a middle course between old errors and hasty innovations.

In September 1765, the Pennsylvania Assembly issued several "Resolves upon the Stamp Act, and other late acts of Parliament," so that "their Successors may be acquainted with the Sentiments they entertain of those unconstitutional Impositions." Dickinson wrote a draft on which the official resolutions drew heavily. The first words of his list of resolutions were:

That the Constitution of Government in this Province, is founded on the natural Rights of Mankind, and the noble Principles of *English* Liberty . . .[29]

These words were repeated, without change, in the official resolutions as "unanimously agreed to by the House."[30] In October Dickinson went to New York as a Pennsylvania delegate to the Stamp Act Congress where, "Throughout the debates Dickinson echoed much that was in the Pennsylvania Assembly's resolutions upholding 'the Natural Rights of Mankind, and the noble Principles of English Liberty.'"[31]

In the Stamp Act crisis, and throughout the crises of the coming decade, Dickinson considered the British constitution the best security for the rights of the colonists. Transgressions of those rights he always held to be transgressions of that constitution. But this was not a view bounded wholly by the legal aspects of the situation. This was not an appeal to laws and constitutions as ends in themselves. Such abject legalism Dickinson considered the constitutionalism of slaves. He did not defend the rights of the colonists for the sake of the British constitution, but the constitution for the sake of the rights.

In the months following the Stamp Act Congress Dickinson wrote an impassioned defense of American opposition to that Act, in the form of a letter to the committee of correspondence of Barbados. Here is the man who appealed to laws and constitutions and never to abstract principles:

> To talk of your "charter" *gentlemen*, on this occasion, is but weakening the cause by relying on false aids . . .
> Kings or parliaments could not *give* the *rights essential to happiness*, as you confess those invaded by the Stamp Act to be. We claim them from a higher source—from the King of kings, and Lord of all the earth. They are not annexed to us by parchments and seals. They are created in us by the decrees of Providence, which establish the laws of our nature. They are born with us; exist with us; and cannot be taken from us by any human power, without taking our lives. In short, they are founded on the immutable maxims of reason and justice.[32]

The Stamp Act having been repealed, Dickinson next took up his pen against the establishment of vice-admiralty courts which deprived the colonists of trial by jury, the Quartering Act, the Restraining Act suspending the New York Assembly, the Townshend Acts, and the Declaratory Act asserting the authority of Parliament to make laws for the colonies in "all cases whatsoever." On December 2, 1767, appeared the first of the series of letters that would launch Dickinson into immediate fame as the Pennsylvania Farmer.

In his *Farmer's Letters* Dickinson continued to seek reconciliation with Great Britain. As always he insisted that such reconciliation could be possible only if the rights of the colonists were respected. And, as always, Dickinson appealed to the British Constitution and to British history only as that constitution and that history supported rights derived from a higher and prior source. The right of property was the right of most immediate concern to the colonists, and the now famous cry—"No Taxation without Representation"—was a theme on which the Farmer rang countless variations throughout the letters.

In these letters, as in many of his other writings, it was Dickinson's habit to quote extensively from statutes and histories, and from the speeches of statesmen and the writings of philosophers and jurists, to buttress his arguments. Often his footnotes are lengthier than his letters. Introducing a long quotation from a speech by Lord Cambden, the Farmer indicates with absolute clarity where he looks for the source and original of the rights for which he spiritedly contends. "The following extracts," he apologizes, "so *perfectly agree with, and confirm the sentiments avowed in these letters*, that it is hoped the inserting them in this note will be excused."[33] (my emphasis) The heart of the quotation is:

... TAXATION and REPRESENTATION are inseparable—this position is founded on the laws of nature; it is more, it is itself AN ETERNAL LAW OF NATURE; for whatever is a man's own, is absolutely his own; NO MAN HATH A RIGHT TO TAKE IT FROM HIM WITHOUT HIS CONSENT ...

"It is impossible to read this speech," wrote Dickinson, ". . . and not be charmed with the generous zeal for the rights of mankind that glows in every sentence."[34]

Such a zeal glows throughout the Farmer's Letters, as it animated his statesmanship during the coming years in which he, as much as any American, gave shape to the "American mind" that Thomas Jefferson sought to express in the Declaration of Independence. Conservatives like John Dickinson, we are told, were loath to abandon law and constitution for the vague theories of natural rights espoused by Thomas Jefferson or Thomas Paine. But so long as John Dickinson supported the British Constitution, he did so always and only on the basis of such vague theories of the natural rights of man. Upon the same grounds, once the colonies had secured their independence, Dickinson would defend the *American* constitution. In his "Fabius" letters written in 1788 to support ratification of the Constitution, Dickinson followed the practice of extensive quotation as in his earlier letters. Three years after the first appearance of the "Fabius" letters, appeared Tom Paine's *Rights of Man*. When the "Fabius" letters were reprinted with additions, in 1797, Dickinson took the occasion to draw directly upon Paine for his lucid expression of what Dickinson had always conceived as the character and source of those rights on which constitutional government is founded. Paine speaks for Dickinson thus in Letter III:

The error of those who reason by precedent, drawn from antiquity, respecting the rights of man, is, that they do not go far enough into antiquity. They do not go the whole way. They stop in some of the intermediate stages of an hundred or a thousand years, and produce what was then done, as a rule for the present day. This is no authority at all. If we travel still further into antiquity, we shall find a direct contrary opinion and practice prevailing; and if antiquity is to be authority, a thousand such authorities may be produced, successively contradicting each other: but if we proceed on, at last we shall come out right: We shall then come to the time when man came from the hand of his Maker. What was he then? *Man*. Man was his high and only title, and a higher cannot be given him—We are now got at the origin of man, and at the origin of his rights.[35]

If the Pennsylvania Farmer would not defend the British, so much less would he pretend to defend the American Constitution, by appeals to "immemorial custom."

If, then, John Dickinson was not hobbled by slavish worship of antiquity, if he—with Jefferson and Paine—was a zealous advocate of the rights of man, how could he oppose these "radicals" on the question of American independence? How could he keep his name from that document in which the rights of man would be so nobly enshrined as the rights of Americans?

"All honor to Jefferson," wrote Abraham Lincoln,

> to the man who, in the concrete pressure of a struggle for national independence by a single people, had the coolness, forecast, and capacity to introduce into a merely revolutionary document, an abstract truth, applicable to all men and all times, and so to embalm it there, that to-day, and in all coming days, it shall be a rebuke and a stumbling-block to the very harbingers of re-appearing tyrany and oppression.[36]

Of John Dickinson, Paul Leicester Ford writes: "But for his disapproval of a Declaration of Independence at the time it was moved, he would have been the framer of the vindication of that step."[37] So Abraham Lincoln might have written, as the crisis of the Union impended, "All honor to Dickinson." "The principles of Jefferson," wrote Lincoln, "are the definitions and axioms of free society." The principles of Jefferson were the principles of Dickinson as well. He agreed wholeheartedly with the "abstract truth" that made the Declaration of Independence applicable to all men and all times and a stumbling block to tyranny in all coming days. Had Dickinson had the honor of framing the vindication of American independence, there can be no doubt that he would have justified that step by appeal to that same abstract truth. What Dickinson disagreed with was the concrete, merely revolutionary act of a single people.

Dickinson understood—as did Jefferson—that, while Americans were *entitled* to the rights of human nature *as men*, they could only *secure* those rights as a single people, as *Americans*—in a particular time and place, through particular customs, laws and institutions. That Americans possessed these rights, as human beings, and that these rights were the foundation of all other rights, was a self-evident truth accessible to human reason. How to secure these rights was, and is, a practical question, to be decided by political judgment, or what ancient philosophers called prudence, the specific virtue of the statesman. Whether or when to declare independence was a practical, not a theoretical question. And it was precisely on this concrete, practical question that the fame of John Dickinson foundered.

By July 1776, Dickinson maintained that he did not even entertain any doubt *whether* America should declare independence, only when. He opposed, in his words, "only *the time of the declaration*, and not *independence itself*."[38] His reasons for this opposition were weighty, and shared by many:

"It was acknowledged in the debate, that the first campaign would be decisive as to the final event of the controversy . . . . [T]he declaration would not strengthen us by one man, or by the least supply . . . We ought not [therefore], without some prelusary trials of our strength, to commit our country upon an alternative, where, to recede *would be* infamy, and to persist *might be* destruction . . .

"It was informing our enemies what was the ultimate object of our arms, which ought to be concealed until we had consulted other powers, and were better prepared for resistance . . .

"It might . . . unite the different parties [in Great Britain] against us, without gaining anything in counterbalance.

". . .it might occasion disunion among ourselves . . .

"Foreign aid would not be obtained by the declaration, but by our actions in the field . . .

"We ought to know the disposition of the great powers, before such an irrevocable step should be taken . . .

". . . the formation of our governments, and an agreement upon the terms of our confederation, ought to precede the assumption of our station among sovereigns . . . but the relation one citizen was to bear to another, and the connection one state was to have with another, [the people] could not know . . .

"the boundaries of the states ought to be fixed before the declaration . . ."[39] (emphasis in original)

Those who favored independence in July 1776, distending all the powers of the soul, answered these arguments point by point and carried the day, but barely. They did not have to convince their countrymen of the abstract truths that animated their cause. John Dickinson, among others, had successfully established these truths as the common sense of the nation by this time. They had to convince their fellows of the concrete, merely revolutionary measure to be taken by a single people on behalf of these abstract truths.

Politics, the philosopher tells us, is concerned with matters that might be otherwise. Neither John Dickinson nor Thomas Jefferson could foresee the outcome of the struggle they were beginning. Actions, chances and decisions that would determine the success or failure of their cause were locked in the impenetrable future. Yet a concrete decision was called for now. The achievement of independence "has proved," wrote Dickinson in retrospect, "that the national council was right" in declaring independence when they did, and that he was wrong in opposing it.[40] Even this may be saying too much, before first determining whether declaring independence, when they did, advanced or impeded their achieving it on satisfactory terms. Nevertheless, it must be said that Thomas Jefferson deserves all the honor that Lincoln and posterity generally have bestowed on him, in considerable part because of the "merely revolutionary" measure that he took. John Dickinson, on the other hand, for opposing that concrete and merely revolutionary step, cannot and would not complain if posterity shuffled him off somewhat to the shadows as it has done. For the voice that spoke in taking that merely revolutionary step, as Dickinson believed, was "the sacred voice of my country . . . a voice that proclaimed her destiny."[41] And John Dickinson stood silent when that voice spoke.

What John Dickinson would complain of, and what he does not deserve, is to be remembered—by some to be "honored"—as the enemy of those abstract principles and axioms, those self-evident truths, on which his country was founded. For the Pennsylvania Farmer there could be no more "dishonorable reminiscence with posterity" than this.

John Dickinson would have wished—as he deserved—to be remembered, as he was remembered, by the author of the Declaration of Independence which he never signed:

Among the first of the advocates for the rights of his country . . . he continued to the last the orthodox advocate of the true principles of our new government . . .[42]

Notes

1. Milton E. Flower, *John Dickinson: Conservative Revolutionary* (Charlottesville: The University Press of Virginia, 1983), p. 69.
2. Paul Leicester Ford, ed., *The Political Writings of John Dickinson 1764–1774* (New York: DA CAPO Press, 1970), p. ix.
3. Flower, p. 166.
4. Ibid., p. 69.
5. Julian P. Boyd, ed., *The Papers of Thomas Jefferson* (Princeton: Princeton University Press, 1950), Vol. I, p. 315. This problematic recollection has been the center of historical controversy for a century. See Boyd's discussion of this issue in the volume cited, pp. 299–308. This unquestionably inaccurate recollection by Jefferson is, nonetheless, a fair reflection of how Dickinson has been remembered by his country.
6. Flower, p. 182.
7. Ibid., pp. 158–159.
8. Ibid., p. 162.
9. Ibid., p. 156.
10. Jefferson to the Editor of the *Journal de Paris*, August 27, 1787, Boyd, XII, p. 63.
11. M.E. Bradford, "Penman of the Revolution," *National Review*, June 10, 1983, p. 699.
12. Flower, p. ix.
13. Charles J. Stillé, *The Life and Times of John Dickinson* (New York: Burt Franklin, 1969), p. 43.
14. James Truslow Adams, *Dictionary of American Biography*, Allen Johnson, ed., (New York: Charles Scribner's Sons, 1930), p. 222.
15. Vernon Louis Parrington, *Maincurrents in American Thought* (New York: Harcourt, Brace and Company, 1930), p. 222.
16. Moses Coit Tyler, *The Literary History of the American Revolution 1763–1783* (New York: G.P. Putnam's Sons, 1905), Vol. II, p. 28.
17. Forrest McDonald, ed., *Empire and Nation* (New Jersey: Prentice-Hall, Inc., 1962), p. x.

18. Edmund S. Morgan, *The Birth of the Republic 1763–1789* (Chicago: The University of Chicago Press, 1956), p. 74.
19. Stillé, pp. 25–43.
20. Parrington, pp. 222–223, 231.
21. Tyler, Vol. II, p. 28.
22. McDonald, p. x.
23. Stillé, p. 204.
24. M.E. Bradford, *Better Guide Than Reason: Studies in the American Revolution* (La Salle, Illinois: Sherwood Sugden & Co., 1979), p. 79.
25. Ibid., p. 93.
26. Flower, p. 35.
27. Ibid., pp. 38, 54.
28. Ford, pp. 34, 39.
29. Ibid., pp. 173–174.
30. Ibid., p. 171.
31. Flower, p. 53.
32. Ford, pp. 261–262.
33. McDonald, p. 44.
34. Ibid., pp. 44–45.
35. Paul Leicester Ford, ed., *Pamphlets on the Constitution of the United States, Published during its discussion by the People 1787–1788* (New York: 1888), p. 177.
36. Lincoln to Henry L. Pierce and others, April 6, 1859, *The Collected Works of Abraham Lincoln*, Roy P. Basler, ed. (New Brunswick, New Jersey: Rutgers University Press, 1953), Vol. III, p. 376.
37. Ford, *Political Writings*, p. ix.
38. Stillé, pp. 367–375.
39. Ibid.
40. Ibid.
41. Ibid.
42. H.A. Washington, ed. *The Writings of Thomas Jefferson* (New York: Derby & Jackson, 1859) p. 249.

18

PHENOMENOLOGY AND POLITICAL PHILOSOPHY

John Zvesper

MODERN PHENOMENOLOGY APPEARS TEMPTING TO THOSE STUDENTS OF politics who recognize that the assumptions and methods of modern natural science are less than perfectly adequate for political philosophy and political science. But is modern phenomenology able to provide real aid as well as mere comfort to such students? Is modern phenomenology capable of serving not only as an explanation and confirmation of the inadequacy of modern natural science in understanding human and political things, but also as an adequate alternative way of pursuing this understanding and of guiding political judgment? The answer can be yes only if phenomenology can help provide a philosophical understanding of ethics, as a basis for politics. It can do this only if it avoids the tendency to collapse into existentialism, but it is arguable that this tendency is inherent in modern phenomenology. If this argument is sound, it would seem reasonable to conclude that the phenomenological temptation deserves a wary response.

The phenomenological movement[1] has been one of the most powerful currents in twentieth-century philosophy. Its prime mover, Edmund Husserl, was not primarily concerned with ethics and politics, but he did see—or at least after the First World War he came to see—that the ethical and political indifference of modern natural science was part of the modern scientific crisis. He hoped phenomenology would eventually lead toward a philosophical science capable of addressing ethical questions, and meanwhile he believed that individuals could feel the happiness of solidarity with the rest of humanity in its possibly endless progress toward this end.[2]

The promised ethical and political fruits of phenomenology have not yet appeared. Insofar as phenomenological methods have been used in the ethical and social sciences, the results (apart from such dubiously rigorous attempts to revitalize ethics as that of Max Scheler[3]), have been faithful to Husserl's caution without progressing as he had hoped, and have been limited to meta-ethical studies of the genesis and structure of ethical and social worlds. These studies have not attempted to examine the merits of particular ethical and social phenomena. They have examined the way human consciousness creates and maintains everyday, prescientific life-worlds;[4] they have mapped the social geography of relations among members of life-worlds;[5] and they have investigated the structure (avoiding the content) of moral judgments.[6] They have failed to rise above ethical and social relativism. This failure makes the transition from phenomenology to existentialism seem permissable or even necessary. Stanley Rosen's characterization of this transition is roughly just:

The "pre-rationalists," after an abortive experiment with descriptive, scientific or phenomenological positivism, in which they sought to combine the purity of mathematical speech with the spiritual edification to be derived from speaking about the spirit, admitted their failure by repudiating the old ways and attempting to found a new speech or thinking in which the sense or significance of speech emerges not from speech but from presence before or communion with, the silent source of speech.[7]

The rapid development of phenomenology into existentialism suggests that certain features of Husserl's phenomenology may have pointed in this direction from the beginning. Jacob Klein's account of Husserl's philosophy emphasizes one of these features, namely Husserl's concern with problems of origin, that is with *rizomata*, not with *arche* (which is "more directly related to...perfect shape").[8] Concern with origin naturally leads away from questions of natural and moral ends. (Consider the subtitle and the doctrines of Hobbes's *Leviathan*.)

A related feature of Husserl's phenomenology, one with comparable effects on its ethical and political significance, is its Cartesian and Kantian dualism. Husserl was more empirical than Descartes; rather than deducing the world by meditating on the ego, Husserl focused on the actual experience of the ego thinking thoughts. But Husserl still thought of Descartes as phenomenology's "genuine patriarch."[9] The contrast between the human mind and the material world, or between spirit and nature, remained overwhelmingly significant for Husserl. Although he sought a unified view—for example, he wished to see the modern physical sciences understood as "ramifications" of the basic spiritual science of phenomenology[10]—he remained an idealist, contrasting nature with spiritual humanity, and subordinating the former to the latter. The tendency to subjectivism and relativism inherent in this position is visible in Husserl's criticism of the naturalistic study of human affairs. For example, in his lecture on "Philosophy and the Crisis of European Man," he insisted that the "innate entelechy" of humanity is not at all a natural, biological fact. There is no human zoology: "From the point of view of soul, humanity has never been a finished product, nor will it be, nor can it ever repeat itself."[11] "Nature is eternal;" psychic phenomena appear "in an absolute flow."[12] The repetitious character of nature is alien to the human world, which lacks natural definition and direction. Human nature is not natural.[13] The conduct of human life can find no guidance in nature. Human life itself creates the world of nature. Nature is "a spiritual accomplishment."[14]

Although Husserl credited Descartes with the fundamental insight which made phenomenology possible, his immediate teacher was Franz Brentano, whose empirical psychology taught Husserl that "the fundamental characteristic" of human, psychic life is intentionality.[15] Intentionality is the word used to express the observation that mental activities always refer to non-mental objects. For Brentano and Husserl, this observation sharply distinguished human, psychic phenomena from physical phenomena; for Husserl, it also made it seem plausible to concentrate on the psychic, as the fundamental way of understanding both psychic and physical, which after all are both phenomena, that is, appearances experienced psychically.

However, it is doubtful that the observation of intentionality can bear all of the weight which Husserl, or even Brentano before him, placed on it. Brentano traced his thesis that "the reference to something as an object, is a distinguishing characteristic of all mental phenomena," and that "no physical phenomenon exhibits anything similar,"[16] back through scholastic doctrines to Aristotle's *De Anima* and *Metaphysics*. But the passage on which Brentano most relied (*Metaphysics* 1021a 29) does not suggest such a sharp distinction as Brentano draws between psychic and physical. Aristotle includes in the class of relative terms that Brentano says are all mental not only the relativity between knowable and knowing and between perceivable and perceiving but also between measurable and measure. Aristotle simply observes that perceiving and knowing are related to things perceived and known in the same way that a measure is related to something measurable, but differently from relations expressed in comparative terms or in terms of activity and passivity. Comparative relations and relations between agent and something acted upon are relations of mutual reference; for example, larger and smaller, and washable and washer, are mutually relative. There is not such an equality in relations of the former kind, for while perceivable, knowable, and measurable things are relative to perceiving, knowing, and measures, the reverse is strictly speaking not the case, because these already refer to, and thus embody their objects: as Brentano remarked, perceiving and knowing are already perceptions *of something* and knowledge *of something*. As he failed to remark, the same is true of measurable and measures. Aristotle gives no examples here, but his meaning seems to be that a measurable quantity of something incorporates that thing in the same way that a thought or a sight of something incorporates that thing. A ton must be a ton of something, just as a thought must be a thought of something. A ton of concrete thus illustrates intentionality as well as purely mental activities illustrate it. There seems little basis for building on Aristotle's classification of relativities a strict distinction between physical and psychical phenomena.

In any case, as Brentano himself was aware, Aristotle did not make such a sharp distinction.[17] In Aristotle's philosophy, psychology is closely related to physics (and metaphysics) on the one hand and to ethics (and politics) on the other. They are all distinct disciplines, but within shouting distance of each other. Psychology links the study of nature to the study of humanity. By breaking the Aristotelian link between psychology and physics, modern phenomenology breaks the link between psychology and ethics. A well-considered phenomenological approach to ethics might be "consonant with metaphysical, psychological, and sociological theses." But it demands "that the solution to the problem of ethics must not be dictated by a prior acceptance of hypotheses drawn from these other fields."[18] Carving up knowledge into such discrete spheres reduces the ability of efforts in one field to assist those in another. In particular, it prevents the psychologist or anthropologist from helping the moralist and the politician. The conduct of the lives even of scientists themselves is refused the assistance of their science. The role of reason in ethics and politics is constricted. Moral and political philosophy become impossible. It is instructive to notice that with Brentano, ethical science, although intended to be anti-relativistic, was already an appreciation of the self-evident correctness of certain emotional experiences, divorced from any consideration of intelligible reasons for the experienced rightness or wrongness.[19]

When one's own conduct is thus treated as the experience of an ego, the phenomenologist as social scientist becomes the "detached," "disinterested spectator"[20] or "disinterested observer"[21] of the ego's naive life-world. The danger of self-forgetful positivism does not seem to be altogether avoided by the phenomenological approach. But more characteristically, phenomenology maintains that it can recover for science subjects that positivism removes from scientific inquiry: phenomenology "can salvage and reveal a richness of qualities which the impoverished talk about values as merely a matter of likes or dislikes misses completely."[22] However, having dismissed nature as a limiting, moderating guide to moral and political opinion, phenomenology invites the existentialist predicament, where there is no reasonable way to decide among contradictory opinions. The "richness" of moral and political life then easily becomes a loquacious but unpromising war of everyone against everyone.

The doctrines of Brentano and Husserl may be regarded as the seeds rather than merely the roots of twentieth-century phenomenology. Still, to combat any suspicion that we have been too Husserlian by being too preoccupied with the origins of phenomenology, it may be useful now to consider a more contemporary specimen: the interesting and ambitious essays in phenomenological biology and psychology by Hans Jonas. These writings (published in two collections called *The Phenomenon of Life* and *Philosophical Essays*) develop a "philosophy of organism," which is meant to counteract "the focus on mentality" of "the idealism of consciousness" of the kind evident in Husserlian phenomenology.[23] Therefore they may correct or at least test our observations on the ethical and political usefulness of phenomenology, observations which focused on the Husserlian seeds. Jonas would have philosophy try "for a stand beyond the quarrel of the ancients and the moderns," by "stretching from physics and biology to theology and ethics."[24] Analysis of his thinking will also, therefore, test our contention that phenomenology logically leads to a damaging compartmentalization of different philosophical inquiries.

In the first book of the *Metaphysics*, Aristotle describes wisdom (*sophia*) as the knowledge of causes, in four senses: the definition, formula, or essence—the formal cause; the matter or substratum—the material cause; the source of motion or change—the efficient cause; and the purpose, good or end—the final cause. In a survey of previous philosophical schools, he suggests that the recognition of these four different senses developed in an ascending, dialectical fashion. The first philosophers recognized only material causes. Later thinkers were led to inquire into efficient causation, because material causation could not explain the generation and corruption of things. Plato was the first to deal rigorously with formal causation, but he did this to the neglect of efficient and final causation, with the result that "philosophy had become identical with mathematics for modern thinkers"—a situation Aristotle aimed to challenge with his own philosophy, with its due and clear recognition of all four senses of causation and of their interrelations.

As with Brentano and Husserl, comparison of Jonas's position with Aristotle's is revealing. *The Phenomenon of Life* is a collection of essays "toward a philosophical biology." Jonas opposes this philosophical biology to modern "materialist" or "mechanical" biology: he writes at a time when thinkers concern themselves with material and efficient causes. The philosophy as mathematics of his day is connected not with forms, but with mechanics and efficient causality (thus it is algebra rather than geometry).[25] The philosophical advance of Jonas's biology and psychology consists in his reintroduction of formal causality, and reconsideration of efficient causality in the light shed by this reintroduction. In his emphasis on forms Jonas is rather Platonic; he opposes his arguments to "the anti-Platonic movement of the modern mind" (43, 45, 48).[26] From an Aristotelian point of view Jonas's philosophy is insufficient in the same way as Plato's: it neglects final causality, because of or in spite of its concentration on forms, which to Aristotle imply ends.

Jonas is reluctant to accept Aristotle's correction of Plato and his connection of forms and ends, with all the ethical and metaphysical implications of that connection. He declares that "the nondogmatic thinker will not suppress the testimony of life; he will accept it today as a call to a revision of the conventional model of reality inherited from a natural science which may well itself be passing beyond it." However, he also claims "that such a revision need not mean a return to Aristotle." (2; cf. 206, 209) In fact, in spite of Jonas's call for a "stand beyond the quarrel of the ancients and the moderns," his own stand remains in the modern camp. He claims to depart from modernity in his insistence that "the organic even in its lowest forms prefigures mind," and from antiquity in his contention that "mind even in its highest reaches remains part of the organic" (1). He seems to regret the rise of modern materialistic monism, which reduces all of nature to non-life in order to understand it. But he also wishes to build on this mortalistic foundation. "Materialism is the real ontology of our world since the Renaissance, the real heir to dualism, . . . and with it must be our discourse" (20). He distrusts "the idealism of the philosophy of consciousness," which is too easily evasive of life and forgetful of death, and too easily self-satisfied (26); and which is, in any case, "but a complementarity, an epiphenomenon as it were, of materialism" (20). Yet the degree to which he accepts existentialism as the other major focus of his discourse is evident in his characterization of his work as "an 'existentialist' interpretation of biological facts" (ix). He continues to hope that some combination of existentialism and materialism will make it possible to understand life, even as he displays the inherent and related weaknesses of these twin schools of thought. He hesitates to allow psychology to straddle ethics and metaphysics, in Aristotelian fashion. The ultimate reason for that hope and this hesitation may be his retention of the modern principle—no mind without organism—in his protest against modernity. He wants to insist on the intelligibility of the world without admitting the possibility of reasoning that intelligence somehow rules the world: "where the divine itself is said to enter, . . . phenomenology ceases to have a say" (261).

Jonas notices that the latest form of idealism, the dualism-without-metaphysics of existentialism, is only the Scylla to the Charybdis of materialistic monism (234). He wishes to avoid this dualism-without-metaphysics. But perhaps partly in order to accept evidence from modern biology, but also because modern phenomenology and existentialism seem compelled to give way to myths when metaphysical questions arise, he avoids rational metaphysics as well. He must therefore try to avoid dualism altogether. Nevertheless, he wishes to retain "enough of the dualistic insight," "the discovery of the distinct concept of mind," "to uphold the humanity of man," and to avoid "a monistic naturalism which...would abolish...the idea of man as man." The fear that humanity will become invisible if dualism is not allowed to leave an "indelible mark on the ontological landscape" (234, 55n.8) would seem to be the basis of Jonas's reluctance to rest his protest against modernity on anything but certain elements of modernity.

Aristotle's analysis of causation shows that the question "why" includes the questions "what" (matter and form), "how" (efficiency), and "what for" (teleology). Because the phenomenon of life exhibits itself in the phenomena of life—the activities of living things—the question raised by a philosophical biology or psychology—the question "why life?" —becomes a question of the what, the how, and the what-for of living beings and their activities. Jonas recognizes that whatness involves two principles—matter and form—and this recognition kindles his departures from modern natural science. The potency of organization or form "must...be included in the very concept of physical 'substance'..." (2). This departure is crucial in biology and psychology. Living things are qualitatively different from lifeless things because "with life...the difference of matter and form, in respect to lifeless things an abstract distinction, emerges as a concrete reality. And the ontological relationship is reversed: form becomes the essence, matter the accident" (80). In other words, "in living things...form for once is the cause rather than the result of the material collections in which it successively subsists" (79). Jonas shows how mere materialism leads to a biology ignorant of *bios* and a psychology ignorant of *psyche*. Reintroduction of the consideration of the formal essence of life should reverse the theoretical trend of post-Cartesian science, the "ever-increasing expansion of the extent of the lifeless—until this...became coextensive with being" (20).

Jonas refers to the mysterious detachability of form from matter in sight, imagination and intellect (147). This would seem to be his friendliest gesture toward antiquity. Much of his essay on "The Nobility of Sight" is reminiscent of Platonic and Aristotelian thoughts on sense perception (e.g. *Phaedrus* 250c; *Metaphysics* I,i; *Nicomachean Ethics* I, vi). However, Jonas adds a distinctly modern qualification: not sight but touch provides humans with their primary and most certain evidence of reality. With this qualification Jonas is trying to combine contrary points of view: the ancient one that would understand hearing, smell, taste and touch by using sight as a model (*De Anima* II, vii-xi); and the modern one that uses touch as the model for understanding all sense perception, and ridicules Aristotelian absurdities like "audible species" (Hobbes, *Leviathan*, ch. 1; *English Works*, IV, 390–391; cf. Machiavelli, *The Prince*, ch. 18).

Departing from Hobbes's crude but more common modern view, Jonas and other modern phenomenologists rely on the body and the sense of touch as the most certain means of at least the beginnings of self-knowledge as well as knowledge of the world: "in feeling my own reality by some sort of *effort* I make, I feel the reality of the world," because of the "resistance" that objects offer "to my efforts to displace" them (148). Hobbes emphasizes the passivity of the senses and the fanciful illusion of external reality caused by the passive, mechanistic "resistance, or counterpressure" of the individual to objects, which are themselves (in their "several motions") the cause of sense perception. Jonas's "phenomenology of the senses" emphasizes the voluntary activity of the individual and the resistance of the world. It is the practical, materially sensing part of ourselves, or rather "our body exerting itself in action," and not "the theoretical self" or even any part of "sense perception" that provides evidence of causality (22–33). For this reason, touch retains a certain nobility: "touch is the sense, and the only sense, in which the perception of quality is normally blended with the experience of force, which being reciprocal does not let the subject be passive; thus touch is the sense in which the original encounter with reality as reality takes place" (147–148). The felt effort involved in moral or intellectual projects is not given such attention. From an Aristotelian point of view, the knowledge of oneself as a cause is a crucial part of ethics and politics; virtues are praiseworthy, and praise implies voluntary activity, with the efficient cause in the virtuous human being, aware of the relevant circumstances (*Nicomachean Ethics* III, i). But this means voluntary activity not of the body but of the soul; more precisely, of the parts of the soul that possess or can defer to reason and knowledge (*ibid.*, I, vii; III, ii). Jonas's materialistic qualification to his rediscovery of formal causation shows why modern phenomenology may be unable to "stretch" from psychology to ethics, to supply a psychological basis of ethics and politics. Even the apparently more idealistic Husserl displays this materialistic bent, for example by finding the origins of geometrical knowledge in the experience of actually handling material objects.[27] Husserl also finds that perception and knowledge are active rather than passive.[28] The materialism of modern phenomenology is able to account for a subjective efficient causality which supports an existentialist freedom and responsibility, but seems unable to relate efficient causality to final causality ("the end of all generation and change": *Metaphysics* I, iii), or to specify the good and the work proper to human beings, as a foundation for ethics and politics (cf. *Nicomachean Ethics* I, vii).

In the Aristotelian view, a natural end or purpose appears at the temporal end of the accurate operation of natural efficient causation, the accuracy of which is defined in the light of the purpose. In the modern mortalistic view, ends are not a subject for inquiry; what happens

happens by the necessities of the properties of matter and motion, not because of natural ends. Even efficient causation is tainted with anthropomorphism, and precise modern science properly avoids both kinds of explanation and restricts itself to the description of sequences of positions in space and time (36). Jonas (in the spirit of Socrates: cf. *Theaetetus* 169d-171d) turns the tables on the modern view as it appears in behaviorism, cybernetics and Darwinism, to show how it is self-contradictory "in disowning itself as evidence of its subject matter" (125, 134). He also suggests that scientists no longer need to be so wary of anthropomorphism, since science no longer radically separates man and nature, *res cogitans* having been reduced to *res extensa*. In the face of the success of materialistic, mortalistic monism, the alternatives are to ignore the presence of inwardness in man, or to accept it "as a valid testimony to the nature of that wider reality that lets it emerge, and to accept what it reveals in itself as part of the general evidence" (37). Not wishing to "deny genuineness to the self-experience of life," Jonas chooses the latter alternative, and reopens the question of teleology. However, he is not prepared to appeal to an "impersonal teleology" of the Aristotelian kind. Instead, he appeals generally from materialism to existentialism, in particular to the subjective and intersubjective knowledge of human purposiveness, seen or felt in the phenomena of effort and the burden of decision. There are moments (6, 7, 106, 127) when he almost suggests that the Aristotelian connection of natural forms with natural ends may be right, but there remains a large element of indeterminacy and relativistic subjectivity or individualism in Jonas's teleology. This individualism can be seen in his sustained effort to seize identity from the clutches of materialistic reductionism, when he insists on the notion of the individual as a knowable (4, 82–83; *Philosophical Essays*, Essay 9). The possibility of knowledge of individuals is doubtful from an Aristotelian point of view, but also less urgent, because whole species—including the human species—have recognizable looks and works. This recognizable human nature is a burden rather than a source of moral guidance to the phenomenologist and existentialist. For example, Simone de Beauvoir complains that women are more enthralled than men to the species of humanity; they have greater difficulty emancipating themselves from human nature. Jonas is wary of facile existentialism, but he too complains of "the poverty and even boredom" of the view that humanity has a fixed essence (*Philosophical Essays*, p. 240). Just as Jonas remarks that "cybernetics is an attempt to account for purposive behavior without purpose" (120), one could object that his phenomenology produces a teleology without *teleos*, according to which the purpose of life—of all life, although humans enjoy and suffer a greater degree and a greater awareness of it—is freedom, defined as self-identity through an escalating degree of detachment from the world. This freedom is balanced by corresponding degrees of dependence on exchange between the self and the world, and in the end by death, but it is not otherwise directed to any particular end. Accordingly, not until the metaphysical myth which concludes *The Phenomenon of Life* does there appear any explanation of the phenomenon of guilt. Consciousness of guilt (*aitia*) would seem to be directly linked to the possibility of being a cause (*aition*). But Jonas's myth attributes the possibility of man's consciousness of guilt to an awareness that man is the trustee of god in the process of becoming:

In the beginning, for unknowable reasons, the ground of being, or the Divine, chose to give itself over to the chance and risk and endless variety of becoming. And wholly so: entering into the adventure of space and time, the deity held back nothing of itself; no uncommitted or unimpaired part remained to direct, correct, and ultimately guarantee the devious working-out of its destiny in creation (275).

As the "last twist" of evolution, man is charged with "responsibility under the disjunction of good and evil" (277; cf. 186–187). Does not this responsibility appear so "awesome" and burdensome to Jonas at least partly because it is so vague and indeterminate ("endless")?

But what is good and evil for man? Perhaps Jonas overestimates the extent to which ancient thinkers thought they had answered this question. This overestimation, and the reason for Jonas's reluctance or inability to produce any substantial guidance on ethical and political questions, appears most clearly in his essay on "The Practical Uses of Theory" (188–210). Because modern theory, following Bacon, has become an unending process of discovery after discovery, identical with a technology of "unceasing dynamism," Jonas rules out "a return to the classical position," which would not be "open to honesty and logic." Although Jonas is aware that the metamorphosis of scientific theory into technology prevents science from raising "the question of ends" (208), he nevertheless accepts the essentially progressive and practical bent of science, and the infinity of knowable things this involves, in contrast to the ancient view that "the number of truly knowable things is finite" (206; but cf. *De Anima* 409b 25–30). Jonas contends that "the modern discovery that knowing nature requires coming to grips with nature...has permanently corrected Aristotle's 'contemplative' view of theory" (205). But is this not a narrow interpretation of the basis of the ancient argument that philosophy is the end of man? Even if commitment to modern, practical theory is practically or theoretically necessary, this does not lessen the force of the argument—admittedly perhaps more Socratic than Aristotelian—that discourse about what Jonas himself says is the "the supremely useful and much-needed knowledge of ends" (205) is, until this knowledge is won, the proper human work and good. Even this limited ancient definition of the "image of man" (205) can form a substantial basis for ethical and political science; to see this, one only needs to recall the place in Aristotle's thought of the doctrine that man's argument about what is good and bad makes him political (*Politics* I, ii).

In his *Philosophical Essays*, published seven years after *The Phenomenon of Life* (which still contains, however, the more fundamental reflections), Jonas confesses that his earlier essays had been written when he was somewhat too optimistic and Baconian in his reliance on technology. But in spite of his second thoughts on the beneficence of technology, he continues to defer to the ethical significance of technology, because he believes it changes the questions so much that no known ethical principles are able to provide answers. In particular, he worries that the development of the human power to damage nature and to change "human constants" like genetic unpredictability and death make any ethics assuming such constants irrelevant.

In fact, the ominous technological developments that he notices do not much alter his ability to reach ethical conclusions. He is still inclined to the view that "the depth of historical change in man" makes incredible any ethically useful "definition of man." This remains the most difficult problem, "where we all get stuck," whether before or after the raising of our ecological consciousness (*Essays*, pp. xv-xviii, *Essays* 1, 3 and 12).

Jonas's metaphysical myth suggests that man—possibly man with the opportunity to become overman—is now the highest form of life and the most important being in the universe, whose actions will complete, save or spoil "the image of God, haltingly begun by the universe" (277). (If god is not exactly dead, he has gone incommunicado, by adopting an immanent mode of being.) This, and Jonas's fear that humanity will become indefinable if dualism is not accepted to a degree, indicate his adherence to—in spite of his efforts to break away from (ix)—a distinctly modern humanism or anthropocentricity. Here is the heart of the modernity of phenomenology. The modern principle is not "no mind without organism" so much as it is the radical humanism which is exhibited in modern thought from Machiavelli to existentialism. Modernity begins with Machiavelli's attempt to understand man on his own, without reference to a higher context. (As T. S. Elliot put it, "Machiavelli was no fanatic; he merely told the truth about humanity...without the addition of superhuman Grace.")[29] This was a protest against what one could call the ancient phenomenology of Aristotle, which tried to let lower things come to light without ruling out before investigation any higher possibilities in these things. Jonas, like other modern phenomenologists, brilliantly demonstrates the dangers of the reductionism of modern thought, in which the lower is always used to explain the higher and therefore always emerges as "the effectual truth" (*The Prince*, ch. 15) of the higher (200–201). But modern phenomenology is modern precisely because it does not avoid that primary modern reduction of the horizon of the realm it studies so thoroughly. Modern phenomenology is too unpolitical because it is too merely political. It does not look at man and politics in the context of anything greater or higher.

The most immediate remedy for phenomenology's political incompetence may be not metaphysics, but the more mundane task of developing the psychological insights that are produced, for example, by the less existentialist strand of Jonas's meditations on the possibility of understanding humans and their history. Even without a phenomenological metaphysics, phenomenological psychology and anthropology can be expected to provide evidence relevant to political philosophy, if they resist the relativistic and existential tendencies we have noticed: an overdrawn opposition between humanity and nature, a distrust of reason in practical affairs, a preoccupation with origins and historicity and an inattention to unchanging ends, a refusal to admit the connection between forms and ends, a somewhat concealed but controlling materialism, and an activist, subjective epistemology. Resisting these tendencies, Jonas's own anthropology occasionally reaches a politically relevant conclusion, for example, that "the fact of language belongs to the timeless essence of man" (*Philosophical Essays*, p. 254). Erwin Straus has shown that a sound and thorough phenomenological anthropology is pregnant with ethical significance.[30] Wise midwifery may yet deliver a political branch of the phenomenological family. But such a child may be difficult for its parents to recognize.

Notes

1. The phrase comes from Herbert Spiegelberg, *The Phenomenological Movement* (2 vols. The Hague: Martinus Nijhoff, 1969). A recent anthology of phenomenological writings, *Existential Phenomenology and Political Theory*, ed. Hwa Yol Jung (Chicago: Regnery, 1972), designed to promote "vigilance and serious attention" to phenomenology among political scientists (p. xiii), illustrates my argument by being true to its title: the only thematically political section of the book is on "The Existential Conditions of Politics."

2. Marvin Farber, *Phenomenology and Existence* (New York: Harper & Row, 1967), p. 190; Spiegelberg, I, 76–85; Edmund Husserl, *Phenomenology and the Crisis of Philosophy*, tr. Quentin Lauer (New York: Harper & Row, 1966), pp. 168–69.

3. Spiegelberg, I, 228–68.

4. Aron Gurwitsch, "Problems of the Life-World," in *Phenomenology and Social Reality*, ed. Maurice Natanson (The Hague: Martinus Nijhoff, 1970), pp. 54ff.

5. Alfred Schutz, *On Phenomenology and Social Relations*, ed. Helmut R. Wagner (Chicago: University of Chicago Press, 1970); Herbert Spiegelberg, *Doing Phenomenology* (The Hague: Martinus Nijhoff, 1975), pp. 260–63.

6. Maurice Mandelbaum, *The Phenomenology of Moral Experience* (Glencoe: Free Press, 1955), pp. 32–43, 135–40, 308.

7. "Nihilism," in *New Essays in Phenomenology*, ed. James M. Edie (Chicago: Quadrangle Books, 1969), p. 152.

8. "Phenomenology and the History of Science," in *Philosophical Essays in Memory of Edmund Husserl*, ed. Marvin Farber (New York: Greenwood Press, 1968 [originally 1940]), pp. 141, 147, 149.

9. Edmund Husserl, *The Paris Lectures*, tr. Peter Koestenbaum (The Hague: Martinus Nijhoff, 1964), p. 3.

10. *Ibid.*, p. 38.

11. *Crisis*, pp. 157–58.

12. "Philosophy as Rigorous Science," in *ibid.*, pp. 105–08.

13. That this is still the opinion held in phenomenological accounts of ethics is suggested by the fact that "human nature ethical theory" can so readily be contrasted with ethical theories based in realms other than that of humanity: "God, nature, or reason." Robert J. McShea, "Human Nature Ethical Theory," *Philosophy and Phenomenological Research*, 39 (1978–79), p. 386.

14. *Crisis*, p. 190.

15. *Ibid.*, pp. 189–90; *Paris Lectures*, p. 31.

16. *Psychology from an Empirical Standpoint*, ed. Linda L. McAlister (London: Routledge & K. Paul, 1973), pp. 88–91, 97, 271–75. Brentano found a "suggestion of this view in Aristotle...especially *Metaphysics*, Book V, Chapter 15, 1021a29." *The Origin of Our Knowledge of Right and Wrong*, ed. Roderick M. Chisholm (London: Humanities Press, 1969), p. 14n.29.

17. *Psychology*, p. 87.

18. Mandelbaum, pp. 16–26, 31–35. Mandelbaum argues (pp. 33–34) that Aristotle, for example, made the mistake of jumping too quickly from an analysis of moral experience in its own contradictory terms to an appeal to the "most authoritative" opinions, thus begging the question. But for Aristotle the ultimately "authoritative" opinion is that of the philosopher, whose contemplation of physical and psychological truths improves his moral reasoning; ethics cannot long be "self-contained." (p. 31)

19. *Origin*, pp. 19–20, 76–90.

20. Husserl, *Paris Lectures*, pp. 14–16, 36–39.

21. Alfred Schutz, "Phenomenology and the Social Sciences," in *Philosophical Essays*, ed. Farber, pp. 184–85.

22. Spiegelberg, *Doing Phenomenology*, pp. 59–60.

23. *Philosophical Essays: From Ancient Creed to Technological Man* (Englewood Cliffs, NJ: Prentice, 1974), p. xii.

24. *The Phenomenon of Life: Toward a Philosophical Biology* (New York: Greenwood, 1967), pp. x, 1.

25. See Jacob Klein, *Greek Mathematical Thought and the Origins of Algebra* (Cambridge, MA: M.I.T. Press, 1968).

26. Unless otherwise noted, numbers in parentheses refer to pages in *The Phenomenon of Life*.

27. Klein, "Phenomenology and the History of Science," pp. 152–53.

28. *Paris Lectures*, pp. 16–29.

29. "Niccolo Machiavelli," in *For Lancelot Andrewes* (Garden City, NY: Doubleday, Doran & Company, 1929), p. 62.

30. See particularly the essays on "Awakeness," "The Upright Posture," "Man: A Questioning Being," "Shame as a Historiological Problem," and "The Sigh," in *Phenomenological Psychology* (New York: Basic Books, 1966). However, Straus himself might regard a project to provide philosophical guidance to ethics and politics as a sign of pathological compulsion. See "The Pathology of Compulsion," in *ibid.*, p. 321, where religious devotion, tradition, and resignation are seen as the healthy responses to the human condition, opposed to "an impotent interrogation of the final meaning of everything."

19

THE POLITICAL ODYSSEY OF HERBERT WEHNER

Wayne C. Thompson

WILLY BRANDT, FORMER CHANCELLOR OF WEST GERMANY, WROTE IN 1971 that "Herbert Wehner's greatest strength is the unity of theory and practice, of principled orientation and practical handling, of conviction and action."[1] This unity was extremely important for the Federal Republic of Germany (FRG), the Social Democratic Party of Germany (SPD) and Wehner himself, who from 1949 until his retirement in 1983 was probably the most consistently powerful and influential political figure in the SPD. More than any other person, he shaped and guided the SPD for its role as the major ruling party in the FRG from 1969 until 1982. As former SPD vice-chairman. Minister of All-German Affairs, and after 1969 leader of the governing SPD's parliamentary party. Wehner displayed tactical genius in elevating and maintaining his party as West Germany's major ruling group.

Yet, since the end of the Second World War, his brilliant political maneuvering, which revealed a sharp recognition of a constantly changing political situation, always aimed toward, and was limited by, certain overriding principles and goals: 1) that all Germans ultimately have the chance to live in freedom and in a unified Germany; 2) that all citizens have an equal chance to develop their full potential; 3) that the needs of workers and the socially weak be recognized and that these groups not be pushed to the periphery of the state; 4) that reformers not lose sight of what reforms are truly necessary, the degree to which they can be realized, the values and groups which would be negatively affected by them, and whether the reforms could work and be financed; 5) finally, that the free and democratic order be protected at all costs. As he reminded his colleagues at the 1959 SPD party congress in Bad Godesberg, "everyone can talk about freedom, but only within a free political order!" Wehner himself admitted that he "made radical mistakes in the radicality of youth," but that "I have sufficient experience of my own. . . . One cannot be permitted to destroy nor see destroyed the foundations which one needs in order to construct something better." Again in 1970 he told delegates at the Saarland SPD party congress that there is nothing wrong with "showing the flag" of reform and change; "but one should never forget that one must be able to place the staff into firm ground in order that it be able to stand upright and be carried on by others."[2]

Wehner's political rise in West German politics was especially difficult because of a particular handicap, which made it impossible for him to be considered as a chancellor candidate: before and during Hitler's rule, Wehner was one of the highest ranking members of the Communist Party of Germany (KPD). His past hangs over him like a dark cloud casting shadows over his motives and actions. He has never been able to avoid charges that he left his country in order to serve an anti-democratic enemy of Germany or that he, unlike former West Berlin mayor, Ernst Reuter, neither voluntarily broke with the KPD, nor publicly denounced the Communist movement and its agents until after his reentry into the work of the party was no longer possible. It is understandable that he entered West German politics with great trepidation. When asked by Kurt Schumacher to seek a seat in the first Federal Parliament (Bundestag) in 1949, Wehner predicted that his future political enemies "will skin me alive."[3]

Mere opposition to Hitler has by no means been an undeniable political advantage to aspirants of political power in Germany's first successful democratic regime. In order for earlier opposition to be considered entirely acceptable to most West German voters, the individual must: 1) not have left Germany for the duration of the Hitler years and therefore not have practiced resistance to Hitler from the safety of foreign soil; 2) not have been a member of any group which apparently supported a foreign power fighting against the *Wehrmacht*, in which Germans' own relatives and loved ones were serving and dying; 3) not have been a member of political groups which openly advocated a post-war political order which would have been totalitarian and which therefore would have been entirely opposed to the norms and principles of the new West German democratic order.

Willy Brandt, who left Germany in 1933 and who returned to occupied Germany in a Norwegian officer's uniform, was plagued for almost a quarter of a century by the charge of having been a traitor. Nevertheless, because he had not been a member of a political party which was directed by a foreign power and which sought to replace a liberal democratic political order with a totalitarian one, the charges gradually lost most of their significance, and he was able to become West Germany's chancellor.

Brandt's success in overcoming most doubts about his past was not shared by Wehner. Very few of Wehner's political opponents were able to resist the temptation to remind the German public of his past. For Adenauer, who was a master at deriving political advantages from West Germans' justified fears of Moscow and East Berlin, Wehner was a useful whipping boy. His past could mislead many voters to equate the party in which such a ranking former Communist could now operate with the Moscow-oriented "Socialist Unity Front of Germany" (SED), which was serving Soviet interests in the German Democratic Republic (GDR). Also, in 1966 an anonymous group of SPD dissidents charged Wehner in a venomous article with attempting to transform the SPD into a Bolshevik party, for which Wehner had been well schooled in Moscow.[4]

Even after thirty years of manifest democratic engagement, Wehner had not freed himself from the past. In 1976 two West German army generals were dismissed for refusing to withdraw their invitation to a highly decorated flying ace of the Third Reich, who remained a public advocate of National Socialist principles, to speak to an assembly of West German soldiers. The generals had justified their stand by announcing that such a person could certainly be invited to speak today, "so long as former Communists such as Wehner sit in the Bundestag." Speaking before the Bundestag in February of 1977, in defense of his dismissal of the generals, Defense Minister Georg Leber directed a rhetorical question toward the opposition: "Who is responsible for the fall of the Weimar Republic?" A young Christian Democratic member of parliament, Wolfgang Sauer, reacted to this provocative and incorrect implication that the opposition were direct descendants of the political forces which destroyed the Weimar Republic, by announcing: "Also Herbert Wehner!" The parliamentary and press tumult which followed lasted several weeks before dying down.[5]

Scarcely a year passed before Wehner's past was again dragged before public scrutiny. When Wehner was invited to give the address at the annual memorial service in Plötzensee (West Berlin) on July 20, 1978, to honor those who died in the attempt to overthrow Hitler on July 20, 1944, the Christian Social Union (CSU) member of parliament, Graf von Stauffenberg, the son of the plot's famed leader, objected. Stauffenberg argued that in evaluating a person's role in the resistance to Hitler, it is necessary to consider not only what a person had "fought against," but what a person had "fought for." The KPD had indeed opposed Hitler at times, but it had never supported the establishment of a liberal democratic order which respected human rights. Not wishing to drag the memory of those who died resisting Hitler into an ugly political controversy, Wehner declined the invitation. His past had again returned to haunt him.[6]

Wehner was one of the few political leaders in Bonn who had bitter enemies in all political camps on both sides of the wall which separates the two Germanys. Almost every issue of the ultra-conservative newspaper, *Deutsche National Zeitung*, contains an attack against this former Communist who, in its words, "was during a large part of his life the chief terrorist of the German branch of the Soviet gangster syndicate;" the comparison of Wehner, who in his youth had embraced both anarchism and militant communism, with West Germany's contemporary terrorists is obvious. The East German Communist party organ, *Neues Deutschland*, on the other hand, described Wehner as an opportunist who constantly refused to submit to "proletarian discipline." He allegedly "hated the masses" and remained both an elitist and an anarchist. Indeed, after the war, Wehner feared that his life might be threatened by his former party comrades who were in power in East Berlin. In his response to a letter published on May 7, 1957, in the Swedish newspaper, *Dagens Nyheter*, accusing him of having been a Soviet spy, he wrote that after the war the KPD and the organs of the SED had tried "through slander and physical threats to bring me to political capitulation."[7]

Wehner was never sure how much he should say about his own past. Soon after his entry into West German politics, he considered publishing 216 pages of *Memoirs* which he had written while he was still in Swedish exile. In this remarkable document, he described his experiences in the KPD, and he reflected on those experiences in the hope that he would be able to draw from them the right conclusions for his future political activity. It contains many close and valuable insights into Bolshevik theory and practice which have lost none of their immediacy.[8]

Wehner has permitted a few of his pre-war speeches and writings to be reprinted, but he is still not inclined to say very much about his political activity before 1946. No examination of his past can discredit his enormous contribution to West German democracy, but the student of theory and practice can greatly benefit from a brief look at Wehner's early political life and from the lessons which Wehner himself drew from · it. For a decade and a half, Wehner operated at the center of a political movement which always invokes the principles of human liberation and social egalitarianism. But whenever it is in full power it establishes in practice a totalitarian political system and a social order characterized by sharp distinctions and privileges for the few. Wehner thus had the opportunity closely to observe the human costs which must be paid when political action becomes largely unhinged from political principles and oriented instead primarily toward power and privilege. He emerged from his experience determined to link politics in postwar Germany with the principles of democracy and individual freedom, principles which in the KPD were degraded to mere propaganda. He had come to realize that those principles give meaning to, and place limits upon, political action.

His early political life provides important insights into Bolshevism. Although Moscow's hold on Communist parties of the world has in many cases been loosened or broken, the Bolshevik theory of revolution and party organization remains valid for most of the world's Communist parties. This fact has made it very difficult for non-Communist parties to maintain trustworthy political relationships with Communist ones. In pluralist, democratic regimes, Communist parties are always difficult coalition partners, and where they have gained control of police and military forces, they have always destroyed the pluralistic character of the regime. Wehner's experiences indicate that these difficulties are not merely a recent problem, and they certainly help to strengthen the SPD's long-standing policy not to maintain party-to-party relations with Communist organizations.

His experiences also shed light on the political background of most of the GDR's leaders, whom he knew intimately, and on the GDR's own interpretation of the past, which the regime uses to justify its own existence. He discredits its idealized portrayal of its heritage as a consistent force for peace and democracy and against fascism. In fact, it was his intimate familiarity with East German political leaders' aims and *modus operandi* which prompted Schumacher, the SPD's first post-war leader, to select him as a close adviser and thereby to launch Wehner's meteoric rise in the SPD.

The examples of West Germany and of Wehner both demonstrate that a direct involvement with totalitarian politics can sometimes strengthen the democratic character of a state or of an individual. The institutions of West Germany were carefully constructed by persons whose own confrontation with totalitarianism showed liberal democracy to be highly desirable, even essential, for human beings. Likewise, Wehner's own experiences with totalitarianism (in his words: "forty-nine percent under Hitler and fifty-one percent under Communism") played a crucial part in the political education of this German democrat. He wrote from his Swedish prison cell in the winter of 1942–3 that he was a man "who has collected some experience in the course of the political struggle."[9]

Wehner himself associates the violent events in 1923 surrounding the overthrow of the SPD-KPD coalition government in his native Saxony with his turn from the moderate reformist path which German Social Democracy had long taken. He still remembers vividly the needless killing by *Reichswehr* troops of more than forty workers in the small town of Freiberg. Such events helped to create an atmosphere in which many young Germans could, in Wehner's words, "no longer understand how we should fit all these things together in our minds in some meaningful order." Wehner remembers that "we weren't filled with hatred, but we were thrown off the track. I know youth protest and youth opposition from my own experience."

The son of a seamstress and an unemployed cobbler, Wehner began to perceive the crisis of Weimar increasingly in terms of a dominant possessing class using naked state power to oppress the working class. He also became convinced that any state, as an exploitative instrument, should be destroyed. Anarchism, the young Wehner began to believe, was the proper medicine against the political crisis. Late in 1923 the adult adviser of his socialist youth group came to his mother and told her that her son would end "on the gallows" if his thinking toward anarchism continued to develop. "He is an idealist," the adviser said, "but this is dangerous." His mother implored her son "not to stumble into political byways," but he chose not to follow that advice. His activities soon brought him into conflict with the law, and he was charged in a federal court with attacking President Paul von Hindenburg and the Weimar constitution. Because of a timely amnesty, the charges against him were dropped.[10]

In 1926 he went to Berlin in order to collaborate with the anarchist Erich Mühsam, but he soon became uneasy about the anarchist position and desired to "do something in an organized way." Therefore, in 1927, he joined the increasingly rigid KPD. Because of his intelligence, diligence and rhetorical talents, he rose rapidly in the KPD organization in Saxony. By 1930, (at age 24) he was a member of the KPD district leadership and a vice-chairman of the KPD in the Saxon State Parliament.

Given his position, his publicly expressed views toward the crisis facing Germany were quite predictable. In a scathing speech before the Saxon State Parliament on October 7, 1930, he revealed rhetorical talents which would make him one of the most provocative and colorful figures in the West German parliament after 1949. He rejected parliamentary government and all cooperation with Social Democrats (whom he accused of being handmaidens of the fascists) and heaped lavish praise upon the Soviet Union. In characteristic Marxist fashion, he argued that parliamentary democracy was a mere instrument of "bourgeois dictatorship" and could never produce policies which could benefit workers; it was, he argued, "an old program, an old melody" which had to be swept away along with the entire Weimar "exploiters' republic." The organization allegedly most responsible for creating the "exploiters' republic" in Germany was the SPD. Far from being a protector for the working class, the SPD superbly carried out the task allegedly assigned to it by the bourgeoisie —that of protecting the bourgeoisie against the working class and of "systematic hindrance of the workers' struggle." By performing this function, the SPD, according to Wehner, was actually producing the conditions in which fascism could grow in Germany. "Their policy is social fascism embellished with radical phrases."

For Wehner, the immediate steps which had to be taken were obvious. First, an extra-parliamentary, revolutionary struggle was indispensable: "What is necessary is not loose talk, not pacifist attitudes toward the bourgeoisie, but a clear formation of fronts in the revolutionary struggle." Second, this revolutionary struggle would have to be organized according to the principles of Bolshevism, "under whose banner such grandiose successes have been achieved in the Soviet Union."[11] German Communists were later to pay a heavy price for their attacks on the feeble liberal democratic institutions and for their almost blind support of Soviet interests.

At the end of the year 1931 Wehner was transferred to Berlin in order to become the "Technical Secretary" of the Politburo; he had been selected as party chief Ernst Thälmann's right hand man. Although he performed all his duties with characteristic energy and persistence, he remembered with displeasure the "apparatus atmosphere" in which he operated; he looked back on it as an atmosphere of distrust and mutual spying and one in which all creative thought was effectively smothered. He wrote that a genuine intra-party intelligence service had developed which came to view itself as the soul of the organization. In fact, he noted that the number of the KPD's intelligence files on its own members grew to such size that following Hitler's assumption of power they could not even be transported unnoticed to a secure hiding place. The files were therefore easily captured by the Gestapo, which used the material to black-mail or convict arrested Communists. In such a setting one soon discovered that it was most important for any party member to unmask and pin blame on others, not to discuss and respect honest opinions. Wehner noted that most new party secretaries saw their first and primary task as that of establishing that the assertions of their predecessors were untrue or exaggerated. "The result was a war of all against all and of cliques against other cliques. One either adjusted to this reality or was driven to passivity."[12]

Wehner recalled that no criticism could ever be directed from the bottom up, and no discussions about fundamental strategy or principles (which party leaders tended to regard as "petty bourgeois needs" or "Social Democratic residue") could take place unless the party leadership ordered it. This prevented the constructive exchange of opinions and, for that reason, the emergence of a more realistic evaluation of the crisis in which Germany found itself. "If one understands this apparatus hierarchy, then one understands not only the actual political impotency of the party when facing the burning problems of the day, but also the inner collapse of the comrades' capacity to think and of their power of mental resistance." Wehner became convinced that not only the individual party members, but the entire party itself suffered from such a stultifying atmosphere: "Seen from the outside, the KPD appeared to be a strong, fighting party, which understood how to employ its power effectively. On the inside, however, it was a machine which was capable of carrying out decisions, but which was incapable of creatively forming opinions and of deciding among diverse views." He added: "Only robust non-thinkers or cynical strivers can prosper and ultimately succeed in such an atmosphere. The party practice which emerged from this was more than a hindrance to preparing the working class for independent thought and action. It was poison."[13]

One might ask why Wehner remained in the KPD if he were actually so critical of an organization in which creative thinking was so unwelcome. He himself claims to have seen no constructive alternative to supporting the KPD in the last months before the collapse of the republic. He noted three decades later that "it was then a question of Hitler, and there was therefore no choice for me." As he began to discover what the KPD was like in reality, he felt bound to the party by a "feeling of obligation," the obligation to rid Germany of the cancer of fascism before turning his attention to changing the KPD itself.[14] Wehner, like too many politically active Germans, saw the choice facing the German people as being between National Socialism or Communism. In the politically polarized environment during the final years of the Weimar Republic many Germans chose to support one or the other as "the lesser of two evils." Like Wehner, they were blind to any third alternative.

After January 30, 1933, Thälmann assigned Wehner the specific task of improving the party's capacity to function under conditions of illegality, for which little preparation had been made before 1933. This was not an easy assignment, Wehner remembered. The whole party apparatus was so over-centralized and so infected with cliques, intrigues and ideological inflexibility that Wehner found it impossible to do more than "to keep it barely in operation." Following the Reichstag fire on February 27, 1933, Thälmann, who was clearly unable to adjust to clandestine activity, and many other leading Communists were arrested, and a twelve year period of harsh repression of all opposition to the Nazis commenced. The KPD's illusions of being able to operate even quasi-legally after Hitler's take-over were dashed as the party's headquarters, presses and other facilities were seized by the police.[15]

Among the major problems which prevented the KPD from concentrating its full attention on the newly established dictatorship was a familiar one within Communist parties: the personal struggles for power within the organization. Wehner later condemned this continuous internecine intriguing, but it cannot be doubted that he was deeply involved in these struggles himself. Thälmann's arrest had been the signal for Walter Ulbricht's bid for leadership in the party. Wehner recalled that Ulbricht, who until 1971 was the East German state and party chief, was a born intriguer and gave the impression after Thälmann's arrest of "extraordinary freshness." It had become clear almost immediately that Ulbricht was attempting "to centralize all the strings into his own hands." Wehner remembered:

> Ulbricht's strength consisted in an untiring busyness . . . He kept his collaborators and subordinates (he needed subordinates) constantly in movement and controlled their work relentlessly. His superiority stemmed neither from deeper perception nor greater maturity, but from his capacity always to be better informed than others and to take care of details much more obstinately . . . Ulbricht consumed cadre in large numbers but trained only blind adherents and bunglers.[16]

By the end of 1933, virtually all Politburo members had either fled into exile or had been arrested, and Wehner became the leading KPD figure still operating within Germany. "For several years I . . . had in my hands the entire illegal work within Germany." From the beginning friction existed between the KPD leadership outside of Germany and the KPD organization within Germany. The latter, operating under dangerous circumstances, needed greater flexibility; but the Politburo refused to abandon Stalin's principles of party organization and instead demanded even greater centralization. This was a formula for impotence. Calls from within Germany for more sympathetic support toward those who were risking their lives fell on deaf ears. KPD leaders in Paris were, in Wehner's words, too involved with "hypocrisy, fawning, and arrogance of power." With no regard for the safety of the organization within Germany, they sent entire trunks full of newspapers and brochures, written by persons with no familiarity with the existing conditions within Germany. Wehner reported that party members in Germany were indignant at having been degraded to the level of mere delivery and distribution agents of this dangerous and often entirely naive material. The KPD was never able to solve the fundamental problem of uniting initiative and independent activity at the lowest level with the principle of democratic centralism.[17]

Finally realizing in 1934 that the KPD's virtual political isolation in Germany had contributed in considerable measure to Hitler's assumption of power, Moscow reversed its policy of isolation by supporting the French Communist Party's participation in a popular front with French socialists and other left of center parties, even though this new policy represented a radical break with Lenin's doctrine of the dominant role of Communist parties. Although Wehner supported the new policy, he expressed in his *Memoirs* annoyance about

the haste with which questions were now suddenly decided whose solutions would earlier have been of crucial importance for the country. I was sickened by the campaign-like treatment of the problem of cooperation with the Social Democrats; one could only expect new conflicts to emerge from the purely tactical treatment of this problem.

He was learning fast that "tactical maneuvering . . . in reality forms the living content of the Communist functionary and politician." He sensed absolutely no interest in a genuine rapprochement with Social Democrats or other opponents of Hitler. Nevertheless, until 1937 he dutifully operated in the Saar (where he worked together with Erich Honecker, Ulbricht's successor as East German state and party chief), Paris, Prague and Moscow in order to attempt to create some unity in the resistance against Hitler.[18]

In February, 1935, Wehner was arrested in Prague, and after spending five weeks in jail, he was expelled to the Soviet Union. In Moscow Wehner prepared for the Comintern detailed oral and written reports on his illegal conspiratorial work in Germany. The Comintern's leader, Georgi

Dimitrov, was so impressed with those reports that he arranged to have Wehner give lectures and seminars on conspiratorial work at the Lenin School, a training institute for Communist cadre from all over the world. During this time Wehner resisted all efforts to send him away from Moscow until after the Comintern world congress and the KPD party congress had been held. Wehner, who undoubtedly had ambitions to improve his own position within the KPD, wanted to be present wherever important political and personnel decisions were to be made. He realized that in a movement in which the struggle for personal power was perhaps the most essential activity for the individual member, it was not only unwise, but potentially dangerous, to be absent and therefore unable to protect oneself from intrigues.

On July 25, 1935, the Seventh Comintern World Congress opened in order to sanction the new policy of Communist participation in popular front governments or movements. Dimitrov publicly stated that "the Communist Party is not the sole representative of the workers" and that "an alliance whose purpose is to cheat and deceive one's partner is fundamentally unstable and not particularly effective." Nevertheless, it is certain that the new policy was in no way construed as a rejection of world revolution under the leadership of the Communist parties. Dimitrov told one comrade in private not to forget "that we Communists struggle for the world revolution. When it triumphs, the steely columns of the Communists will march over the people who today offer us their support. One cannot change that; that is inescapable." Also, the leading KPD Politburo member, Wilhelm Pieck, warned against the misunderstanding that the traditional Communist goals of world revolution should be given up; instead, he emphasized, the traditional goal must be achieved with new methods. Ulbricht spoke with even greater clarity when he announced to the Congress that the creation of anti-fascist popular fronts would in effect "create better conditions for the establishment of Soviet power and prepare better the struggle for the dictatorship of the proletariat."[19] Thus, the Seventh Comintern Congress adopted the very formula for the takeover of power which was used successfully in Eastern Europe after the Second World War. Wehner's observation in 1946 appears to be entirely correct that Moscow's and the KPD's popular front policies were purely tactical and were never grounded in the conviction that Communists could in the long-run cooperate with non-Communists without seeking to dominate them.

In October, 1935, after the Comintern Congress had ended, thirty-eight KPD delegates assembled for a KPD party conference in Kunzevo, outside Moscow. In order to mislead the Gestapo, this conference was called the "Brussels Conference." At this KPD party congress, Wehner and four others, including Ulbricht, were assigned to the Operational Leadership, and Wehner was elected to the Central Committee and to candidate status in the Politburo. Thus, he had become one of the highest ranking leaders within the KPD. The major item of business was to adopt officially the new popular front policy ordered by Moscow. Wilhelm Pieck, in his address, stated the obvious: It had been wrong "that the KPD had fought the Prussian [SPD] Government of Braun and Severing, that it had failed to see the imminent threat of the fascist terror reign and that it had thereby been prevented from pursuing a truly broad united front policy focused above all on the defense of democratic rights and freedoms."

None of the assembled delegates dreamed of criticizing the new policy. In his *Memoirs*, Wehner recalled how party members scramble whenever the signals from Moscow are clear and a new policy direction is necessary: "Everyone collected material and witnesses which could support the correctness of the one or the other policy. Everyone was for the unity front, had always been for it; everyone explained the unity front differently." East German scholar, Klaus Mammach, summed up the conference's conclusion in good Aesopian language: "Every sectarianism *vis-à-vis* Social Democrats must be overcome; at the same time, however, every attempt of right-wing Social Democratic leaders to sabotage the unity of action must also be resisted." Shortly after the "Brussels Conference" Pieck certainly gave potential allies reason to doubt the sincerity of the KPD's shift of policy. He noted publicly that the "masses" would "considerably determine the content of democracy in the new regime," but that it would be the Communist parties which would help those masses to "draw the right conclusions more quickly and clearly." Ultimately, such statements, the purges (which were in full swing in the Soviet Union), Stalin's obsession to root out Trotskyite influences wherever they might be found, and Ulbricht's crude attempts to establish Communist controlled "popular front friendship circles" all placed intolerable strains on the popular front idea and made its realization impossible.[20]

In January, 1937, after having spent an additional year in Western Europe, especially in Paris, where he organized a German Communist brigade to fight in the Spanish Civil War, Wehner was ordered to return to Moscow, where he spent the next four years. He and his wife were quartered in a single room in the rat-infested Hotel Lux, formerly a merchants' hotel, where foreign Comintern representatives were housed. The hotel was under strict control by the Soviet secret service, and no Russian was permitted to enter the hotel without a special permit. A former Hungarian Communist, Julius Hay, remembered that "nothing about that rambling, unassuming, even slightly dilapidated building betrayed the fact that within its walls the cauldrons of the world revolution bubbled and seethed non-stop." Nevertheless, those international Communists living in the Lux enjoyed a far higher standard of living than the normal Soviet citizens at that time. Wehner noted with disapproval how the leading German Communists had managed to secure for themselves special allotments of food, clothing, free theater tickets and coupons for purchasing exclusive wares in the special shops for high Soviet officials. Such a relatively high standard of living stimulated in the minds of normal Soviet citizens both envy and disgust toward this international revolutionary aristocracy. Such distrust was not diminished by familiarity. Residents in the Lux had almost no contact with Russians unconnected with the Comintern, and Hay had the impression that most of the German Communists "regarded the Russians as little better than aborigines," whose language they would never have "dreamt of learning." Wehner was one of the few Germans who at least tried to learn some Russian.[21]

Nor was the Hotel Lux a refuge from the fear and uncertainty which had gripped all persons living in the Soviet Union since the purge trials had begun in 1934. In his *Memoirs* Wehner described the prevailing atmosphere:

A panic-stricken horror spread itself at that time, a hysterical fear of an incomprehensible, but nevertheless almost inescapable danger. If a colleague did not appear for work at his office, his other colleagues assumed that he had been arrested in the night by the organs of the NKVD [secret police]. Immediately countless questions popped up in the minds of every individual: Probably everyone silently asked himself—How will the arrested colleague's relationship to me be interpreted by the NKVD? Outwardly everyone tried either to appear unconcerned or to pretend that he had expected this arrest for a long time. No one pretended to have had close personal contact with an arrested colleague. And since . . . every individual's personal relationships or connections were talked about mercilessly and shamelessly, were later evaluated, and were made objects of discussion for weeks, all persons strived to reduce their personal connections with others to the necessary minimum. Everyone tried to keep a safe distance from most others. After every visit, one sensed that the visitor's intent was to find something out. Almost everyone renounced earlier friends, trembled at the possibility that one of his relatives could be accused or arrested, as a result of which one would automatically become the object of investigations and accusations. In private everyone sought acceptable explanations for earlier friendships, meetings and happenings from which personal dangers could emerge.

Wehner recalled that "Bolshevik self-criticism" grew to "flaggelantism" and that "informing, provocation, cowardly throwing the blame for one's own mistakes onto others all raged in this sick atmosphere. No one wanted to assume any responsibility." Perhaps most inexcusable was the prohibition against talking to any "so-called enemy of the people" or to their families. Spouses and other relatives of an accused comrade lost their apartments and their jobs, and some wives were compelled to resort to prostitution in order to stay alive in this desperate and hostile situation. Two Austrian Communists, Ruth von Mayenburg and Ernst Fischer, found only one refuge from the hysterical atmosphere of Moscow: Wehner's room—". . . here was an oasis, where the sincere, human word prevailed among comrades who did not constantly behave like functionaries. Here one found the sarcastic joke, unconventional thinking, courage to doubt, even to despair." Although they knew neither Wehner's real name (he used the cover name Kurt Funk) nor anything about his earlier activity, they dared to become very close friends.[22]

Like most foreign Communists in Moscow, Wehner did not know the actual motives behind the purges. They appeared to have no foreign political logic, coming as they did at such an inopportune time: when Moscow was trying to breathe life into the popular front policy. It made some sense for the Communist Party of the Soviet Union (CPSU) to attempt to establish absolute party dominance within the country after the convulsive and ruthless agricultural program. Also, it was not difficult to see that Stalin was determined to establish his own absolute dominance over the party. However, the individual who lived in this atmosphere of "lawlessness, uncertainty which rose to a point of panic-stricken fear, cynical fatalism, bureaucratic unscrupulousness, impotency of the individual human being in the face of an incomprehensible, powerful machinery" (Wehner's own words) could never credibly pretend to see a system or inner logic in the mass of arrests which were made. The result was "isolation of every individual in the midst of a chaos of individuals fighting openly and secretly against each other." This, it later seemed to Wehner, was "characteristic of the consequences of totalitarian dictatorship."[23]

The purges claimed victims for reasons not comprehensible even to thoroughly dedicated Communists. Julius Hay reported the arrest of a young Hungarian Communist, Elga Schweiger: "It was discovered, and reported in the appropriate quarter, that if four of the ashtrays Elga had recently designed for a Leningrad factory were placed together in a particular way, the resultant shape was not unlike the Fascist swastika." Despite her protestations that "neither she nor anyone else was in the habit of placing four ashtrays together either in the incriminating arrangement or in any other arrangement," she was kept in prison for months. No one could remain aloof from such inexplicable and arbitrary behavior on the part of Soviet secret police officials.

A few persons, in order to divert attention from themselves, lavished praise on those unknown figures who were ordering the arrests. Wehner remembered, for instance, that Ulbricht had openly and frequently proclaimed that the purges were "a brilliant example of how the Socialist state, without regard for the status or earlier service of the person, ruthlessly eradicates its 'fifth column' before it can do any harm." This was the statement of a frightened, desperate person. While the information gathered by the secret police from denunciations was used against countless German Communists, the Soviet secret police had no respect whatsoever for leading German Communists and never consulted with them about who should be arrested.[24]

It is not surprising that an investigation, which lasted for a year and a half, was conducted against Wehner. He never knew exactly why the investigation had been initiated against him. He was informed once that he and others had been reported for allegedly singing German national-ist songs in their rooms at the Lux. One comrade, Hans Kippenberger, claimed that he had heard people singing "Deutschland über alles" one night and assumed that Wehner was one of those who was involved. Wehner also gained insight into the low niveau of denunciations when he was confronted in one of two interrogations with such a question, which he recorded in his *Memoirs*: He was reminded by interrogators that at one point when the train had stopped during an earlier trip from Paris to Saarbrücken he had paid the wine bill for five Communist functionaries. Where, he was asked, had he gotten so much money? Wehner was per-haps justified in his impression that the motive of the interrogators had been to "bring me to the gallows by means of all rules of the art." Inno-cence or guilt seemed to play no role whatsoever in the frightful wave of arrests and liquidations. Also, he clearly had some rivals in the KPD. Nevertheless, he was possibly in less danger than he had imagined at the time. During the entire investigation, he continued to perform all his duties as chief of the Comintern's Central European section. Dimitrov, who along with Wilhelm Pieck, perhaps intervened to have the investiga-tion concluded, continued to place a high value on Wehner's work. No charges were ever brought against him, and he was never subjected to any form of physical torture. It is entirely possible that the purpose of his investigation was to gather incriminating evidence against other German Communists in Moscow.[25]

Only a minority of German Communists in Moscow emerged un-scathed from the purges, which had begun in 1934 after the Kirov assassi-nation and which lasted roughly until Bukharin's trial in March, 1938. In the end, the Soviet Union proved to be a more dangerous place for Ger-man Communist leaders than Nazi Germany. While two Politburo mem-bers lost their lives at the hands of the SS and Gestapo, four Politburo members were liquidated in the Soviet Union. While nine members of the Central Committee of the KPD lost their lives in Nazi prisons or concentration camps, ten KPD Central Committee members were mur-dered in the Soviet Union. Despite all that had happened, Communists were expected to continue to serve the cause. Wehner noted that the contradiction between reality and the expectations raised and fed by the official propaganda was "devastating for the individual." The individual Communist could expect neither solidarity nor succor from the Soviet regime. Nevertheless, the Soviet dictatorship "demanded that even the person who had been trampled on the ground place himself again in its service. Many did just that. As soon as they believed they could see even a glimmer of personal hope, they again attached themselves to their for-

mer conceptions and again took their places in the ranks of the movement."[26]

In such a setting, it is scarcely surprising that Wehner's published
writings from that time, which appeared chiefly in *Die Kommunistische
Internationale* (which he coedited) under the name Kurt Funk, did not
veer obviously from the dominant political line. It was impossible, he
admitted in his *Memoirs*, to escape "Moscow's Procrustean bed." He remembered his work during this time as a "fight against windmills." Indeed,
several persons who worked with him recalled that Wehner disagreed
with Moscow's optimistic assessment of revolutionary conditions in Europe
and of Hitler's allegedly decreasing popular support within Germany.
Julius Hay remembered Wehner's impatience with misleading descriptions of the political environment within Germany, excessively dictated
by both ideology and by Soviet foreign policy interests. The requirement
to support Soviet foreign policy unconditionally was never easy to fulfill
because foreign Communists never knew whether that meandering policy might change radically just before or after a broadcast or publication.
Foreign Communists were never informed or asked to comment in advance
on policy directions decided upon within the thick walls of the Kremlin.

This was manifest on the occasion of the signing of the Hitler-Stalin
Pact on August 23, 1939. Although, as Wehner noted later in his *Memoirs*,
in the months before the pact the Comintern's press section had been
instructed to tone down its attacks against Germany, the KPD was caught
completely by surprise, despite the fact that it should already have become
accustomed to seeing its own objectives trampled underfoot by those of
the CPSU. After working for more than three years under orders to establish an alliance of anti-fascist forces against Hitler's Germany, German
Communists were now expected to defend an entirely different kind of
alliance, one which laid the foundation for large-scale German and Soviet
territorial expansion in Europe and for the outbreak of the most destructive war in history. Subsequent events in Poland, the Baltic states, Bessarabia,
Northern Bukovina and Finland revealed that these two major powers
were pursuing objectives which went beyond the mere defense of their
homelands. The preservation of peace was certainly not among Stalin's
primary objectives in 1939 and 1940.[27]

Peace is, however, a magical word. After Hitler and Stalin had partitioned Poland in September, 1939, German Communists supported the
public effort to salvage the slogan of peace and to turn it against those
powers, particularly France and Britain, which were now allegedly conducting an "imperialist war" against Hitler's Germany. On October 9,
1939, the official Soviet government newspaper, *Izvestia*, scorned the Western press's campaign against the "Hitler ideology" and called the blood-
letting "senseless and absurd cruelty" which allegedly reminded one of
the wars of religion in the Middle Ages. Wilhelm Pieck described the

struggle against "Hitlerism" as "hypocritical" and an attempt in reality to "starve the German people and to expand the war against women, children, the sick and the aged." The high-point of this astonishing attempt to discredit the struggle against German expansionism was reached in an article by Ulbricht in *Die Welt* on February 2, 1940. Ulbricht branded "British imperialism" as the "most reactionary force in the world" and British democracy as worse than Nazi totalitarianism.[28]

The peace which the KPD advocated would have left most of central and western Europe under fascist control. This disastrously inopportune call for peace stands in glaring contradiction to the Communist propaganda claim since the Second World War that European Communists were the consistent bulwark of the anti-fascist movement. In actuality, European Communists opposed fascism only when the Soviet Union's state and party interests were threatened by Hitler's Germany. Whenever Soviet interests could be furthered through cooperation with fascists, then such cooperation was welcomed. This was the foreign political equivalent of the KPD's policy within Germany before the rise of Hitler: the KPD had preferred fascist totalitarianism to liberal democracy in the disastrously mistaken belief that the former would be a prelude to a Communist revolution (an illusion apparently shared by leftist terrorists in West Germany today). While there were no formal agreements between the German National Socialists and Communists, whenever they sought common objectives, such as the destruction of liberal democracy, German Communists offered no serious opposition to National Socialism. Only when the KPD organization itself was threatened by the Nazis did the KPD offer resistance.

Since clearly no criticism of Soviet policy was possible inside the Soviet Union, one must ask why anyone could continue to support Stalin with any kind of conviction or inner enthusiasm. In his *Memoirs*, Wehner claims never to have been under the illusion that the Soviet Union was a "socialist or democratic ideal state," or that "the development toward socialism must be carried out this way and no other way." He was aware that the nationalist tendency of Soviet policy drove a wedge between the Soviet Union (and those Communist parties loyal to it) and the other "directions of the working movement." Nevertheless, he believed that the terrible reality of fascist dictatorship required that socialists stand alongside the Soviet Union, which he continued to consider as the "essential protector of the international working class against reaction." He still hoped that the Soviet Union, despite its obvious shortcomings, would complete its revolution and "as a democratized land with socialist tendencies serve as a significant support for all progressive forces on earth." By the time he wrote these lines, Wehner already knew that such thoughts had been illusory.[29]

In January, 1941, Wehner was able to leave the atmosphere of fear and intrigue in which he had been living for four years. He was sent to

Stockholm in order to investigate reported irregularities in the Communist underground organization and to build up a new party organization in Berlin. He recalled: "By the time I left the Soviet Union, I had learned much, but there was one thing which I had not yet learned: what conclusions to draw from my experiences." He was happy to leave Moscow: "I wanted to be free of all ambiguity; I wanted to be in direct confrontation with the enemy, about whose real character I believed I knew more than many of those in high political office." While he did not contemplate a break with the KPD as long as that party could still play a role in the resistance to Hitler, he claims in his *Memoirs* to have wanted to attempt to change the working class movement, to establish its independence from Moscow and to introduce inner democratization after the war.

What I did not yet recognize was that all efforts to create independent centers of a free socialist workers' movement would be doomed to failure as long as Moscow had the opportunity to assert its influence to bring all elements into its tow and to distort and finally to paralyze all revolutionary initiative.[30]

His hopes to help recreate an independent, democratic workers' movement were dashed a few months after his arrival in Stockholm.

Wehner set about to reorganize the Communist resistance organization. He sent a few agents into Germany and was planning to go there himself when an event occurred which remains unexplained and which changed the direction of his political life altogether. In February, 1942, Wehner, who was regarded as the KPD's master of conspiratorial activity, was arrested by Swedish police in the apartment of a comrade who had been arrested after returning from Germany a few weeks earlier. Wehner surely knew that the apartment was under constant surveillance by Swedish police. He later explained his arrest as momentary laxness to which any human being is subject, but was such laxness intentional? Did this revolutionary veteran who had grown increasingly disillusioned with his own party secretly want to come in from the cold? This question remains unanswered.[31]

The investigation and trial which followed his arrest could hardly have pleased this passionately political man. He spent the next two and a half years in unheated Swedish prison cells and in Swedish labor camps with insufficient food and no opportunity to exchange letters or to read Swedish or foreign literature. Worse, his arrest and trial created political problems for him which he could never entirely overcome.

His arrest led to an irreparable rupture with his own party, the KPD. Reports of Wehner's arrest and of his alleged betrayal of KPD agents operating in both Germany and Sweden were sent by KPD comrades to Ulbricht in the Soviet Union. Indeed, a number of Communist agents were arrested both in Germany and Sweden within a few weeks of Wehner's arrest. Moreover, the Swedish Social Democrat, Georg Branting, whom the KPD had asked to defend Wehner, declared after reviewing the transcripts of Wehner's initial interrogations that "this man is neither a Communist nor an anti-fascist. Wehner is a provocateur and a traitor" (a declaration which Branting later recanted). Apparently without waiting for further details, Ulbricht acted quickly to eliminate this potential challenger to his control of the KPD. Wehner was expelled from the party although he was not informed of his expulsion until after his release from prison in 1944. He was a victim of the kind of personal rivalries which are always so important in this kind of party. Branded as a traitor, Wehner was ostracized by his former comrades, and his reentry into the work of the party was no longer possible.[32]

Not until more than thirty years later were the records of his interrogation and trial released to the public by Swedish authorities. These records indicate clearly that he had been as successful as could ever have been expected in shielding the identity of his comrades at least until they could either escape or destroy any incriminating materials. Not until four weeks after his arrest and not until Swedish police threatened him with extradition to Germany, which would have meant death, did he reveal his address. Wehner was well aware that the Swedish government, which had chosen to maintain Swedish neutrality by avoiding all antagonism with the Germans, had ordered the Swedish police to cooperate with the Gestapo.[33]

For many of his future political adversaries in West Germany, the very fact that he did not initiate his break with the KPD is proof that he never completely broke with Bolshevism. The charge for which he was convicted proved to be especially embarrassing for him. He was sentenced for engaging in intelligence activities for a foreign power, namely the Soviet Union. Wehner's insistence that he was a German patriot, struggling to liberate his country from National Socialism was not accepted by the Swedish court. Of course, the precarious diplomatic situation in which Sweden found itself at the time was such that Swedish officials were extremely hesitant to appear to condone or encourage any resistance activity against Hitler from Swedish soil. It could not be denied that he had been sent to Sweden to perform a mission for the Comintern, an organization which was undeniably an instrument of Soviet power. Therefore, Wehner's work in Sweden no doubt would have served Soviet state interests. On the other hand, judging from his intense concern after 1945 that Germany be reunified and independent of foreign control, it is likely that Wehner was indeed guided primarily by patriotic motives. His problem is the familiar one for any former Communist in West Germany today: he can never demonstrate beyond a doubt that his major objective had been to serve his own country, not the Soviet Union.

In 1946 Wehner returned to Germany and entered the SPD, which he had defamed so many times since the late 1920's. Schumacher was initially skeptical of him, and only his careful reading of Wehner's *Memoirs*, together with the intervention of several SPD associates, could convince him that Wehner could be trusted. Schumacher decided that Wehner's intimate knowledge of the new East German leaders and their methods could be very useful in the struggle to prevent those Germans in the Western zones from suffering the same fate as their compatriots east of the Elbe.

Wehner's subsequent career as a Social Democrat showed that Schumacher's judgment was entirely correct. In his first test Wehner persuaded Hamburg's dock workers to support West Germany's Social Democrats, not the KPD, and he vigorously opposed the SPD's joining with the KPD in the Western zones to form a Socialist Unity Front. Based on his experience, he suspected that such a unification would amount to virtual Communist control, and developments in the GDR have proven him to be correct.[34]

Since 1946 he has consistently used his undeniable political skill to support the most democratic political order which Germany has ever known. He has never renounced his basic socialist persuasion, nor his conviction that no democratic order can ignore the needs of workers or the socially weak. However, his own experience taught him to be skeptical of ideologies, which, in his own words, "can be so inhibiting for human beings who must live with one another." He especially mistrusts those ideologies which assume that a revolution which radically changes economic relationships is a precondition for dealing with the concrete problems of workers or of any other citizens in a democratic state. He learned that totalitarian movements and those states which are created by such movements stifle creative and realistic thinking and in no way liberate human beings. Looking back on his and the KPD's failure in 1933, he wrote that "not until I had had the help of later experience was I able to recognize that the basic evil is rooted in the totalitarian teaching of the party." That is, he had become convinced that the political practices of Marxist-Leninists, while making a mockery of democratic principles, are shaped in large part by Marxist-Leninist theory itself. Finally, he learned through bitter experience that liberal democracy is not a subtle and disguised instrument for class exploitation, but rather a necessary condition for human dignity.[35]

In 1959 at the SPD party congress in Bad Godesberg he was chiefly responsible for achieving the overwhelming majority for the adoption of the non-Marxist, reformist "Godesberg Program," which transformed the SPD from a working class party to a mass reform party. Contrary to widespread opinion in Germany, Wehner was not the "father" of this program. But he realized that such a change was absolutely essential if the SPD were ever to escape from the "one-third ghetto" in West German elections and to attract enough votes either to win a majority or to become the strongest party in a governing coalition. It took only ten years for the SPD to obtain this goal. He had thoroughly learned that what is demanded in relatively prosperous democratic countries is not parties which preach flights of revolutionary fantasy with little relation to the citizens' perceived needs, but pragmatic parties which seek by constitutional means to achieve the basic needs and desires of the citizenry. In the debates over the adoption of the new program, as in other critical political debates after 1949, Wehner impressed upon his listeners his own past in order to strengthen his arguments. He told the delegates at the party congress: "I know from bitter experience during the Weimar Republic—I learned much through the blows of dictatorship and have a heavy debt to pay for it today and pay it gladly for this party—exactly because I am among those who were burned badly, who once due to dissatisfaction and falsely conceived radicalism . . . were forced to gain bloody experience."[36]

Notes

1. Willy Brandt, "Einheit von Theorie und Praxis," *Die Neue Gesellschaft*, July, 1971, p. 445. I am very grateful to the Alexander von Humboldt-Stiftung, without whose generous support I could not have written this piece.
2. *Ibid.*, pp. 445–47. Wehner, "Die Arbeiter nicht vom Staat trennen," *Christ und Welt*, Feb. 8, 1963, and Reinhard Appel, *Gefragt: Herbert Wehner* (Bonn: Berto Verlag, 1969), p. 41.
3. "Wehners Traum von der Einheit," *Der Spiegel*, Nr. 28, 1977, p. 31. See also Appel, p. 8.
4. "Die Anklage der SPD-Fronde gegen Herbert Wehner," *Die Zeit*, March 11, 1966.
5. For the debate, see Henri Nanning, "Das alles wegen Wehner?," *Stern*, Nov. 11, 1976; "Wehner, Weimar and die Bundesrepublik," *Bayern-Kurier*, March 12, 1977; "Sauers Attacke auf Wehner erhitzt die Gemüter," *Süddeutsche Zeitung*, Feb. 5, 1977; "NSDAP und KPD zerstören Weimar," *Die Welt*, June 15, 1977.
6. For the debate, see Peter Boenisch, "Der 20. Juli und Wehner," *Die Welt*, July 22, 1978; Alois Mertes, "Der 20. Juli und die kommunistische Vergangenheit von Wehner," *Die Welt*, July 29, 1978; and "Tradition in Zwielicht," *Vorwärts*, July 27, 1978.
7. "Strauss oder Wehner—Wer ist terrorist? Wehners Vergangenheit als Verbrecher," *Deutsche National Zeitung*, March 21, 1975. Excerpts from *Neues Deutschland* in *Dokumentation der Zeit*. Informationsarchiv. Deutsches Institut für Zeitgeschichte Berlin. Heft 222, Sept., 1960, pp. 30–33. Wehner's response appeared in *Dagens Nyheter* on March 11, 1957. See also, Gerhard Jahn, ed., *Herbert Wehner, Beiträge zu einer Biographie* (Cologne: Kiepenheuer & Witsch, 1976), pp. 15, 185. Also Günter Gaus, "Der Schwierige. Versuch über Herbert Wehner," *Der Monat*, Heft 244, Jan., 1969, p. 51.
8. This crucial document for this study, dated July 23, 1946, and hereafter referred to as *Notizen*, can be read by scholars in the United States at the Hoover Institution on War, Revolution and Peace, Stanford University. All page numbers cited in these footnotes will refer to the original document. In 1982 it was finally published in Germany under the title of *Herbert Wehner Zeugnis*, ed. by Gerhard Jahn (Cologne: Verlag Kiepenheuer und Witsch, 1982).
9. Gerhard Jahn, ed., *Herbert Wehner, Wandel und Bewährung. Ausgewählte Reden und Schriften 1930–1975*, 2nd ed., (Frankfurt/M., Berlin, Hannover: Verlage Ullstein und Dietz, 1976), pp. 35–47. Also, Wehner, "Die Arbeiter."
10. Herbert Wehner, "50 Jahre danach," *Die Neue Gesellschaft*, Nov./Dec. 1968, p. 452. Günter Gaus, *Staatserhaltende Opposition oder Hat die SPD kapituliert? Gespräche mit Herbert Wehner*

(Reinbeck bei Hamburg: Rowohlt Taschenbuch, 1966), p. 52. Appel, pp. 10–13. Jahn, *Beiträge*, p. 98.

11. Jahn, *Wandel und Bewährung*, pp. 1–2, 4–6, 8–12.

12. Siegfried Bahne, *Die KPD und das Ende von Weimar. Das Scheitern einer Politik* 1932–1935 (Frankfurt/M.: Campus Verlag, 1976), pp. 13–14, 34, 40–41, 71. *Notizen*, pp. 7–8, 12, 21–22. Babette Gross, *Willi Münzenberg. A Political Biography* (E. Lansing: Michigan State Univ. Press, 1974), pp. 214–16. Appel, p. 28. A Freudenhammer and K. Vater, *Herbert Wehner. Ein Leben mit der Deutschen Frage* (Munich: C. Bertelsmann, 1978), pp. 43–44.

13. *Notizen*, pp. 13, 19–21, 24–25, 27–28. Julius Hay, *Born 1900. Memoirs*. (LaSalle, Ill.: Open Court, 1975), p. 112.

14. Wehner, "Die Arbeiter."

15. *Notizen*, pp. 31, 33–37, 42. Bahne, *Weimar*, pp. 40–42, 49, 58, 61. Gross, *Münzenberg*, pp. 237–38, 259. Richard Crossman, ed., *The God That Failed*, (New York: Harpers and Brothers, 1949), pp. 48, 51–52.

16. *Notizen*, pp. 22–23, 38, 40–41.

17. Freudenhammer/Vater, pp. 46–47, 51, 57. Bahne, *Weimar* pp. 49–50. *Notizen*, pp. 61–62.

18. *Notizen*, pp. 10, 27, 70, 75–76, 79. Bahne, *Weimar*, pp. 58–59. Freudenhammer/Vater, *Ein Leben*, pp. 48–51. Gross, *Münzenberg*, p. 273.

19. *Notizen*, pp. 3, 82, 84–85, 92, 96–97. Freudenhammer/Vater, *Ein Leben*, pp. 59–61. Ernst Fischer, *An Opposing Man* (London: Allen, 1974), pp. 267–68. Gross, *Münzenberg*, pp. 277, 282. See Hartmut Soell, *Fritz Erler–Eine Politische Biographie* (2 vols.; Bonn-Bad Godesberg: J.H.W. Dietz, 1976), II, 1130.

20. Freudenhammer/Vater, *Ein Leben*, pp. 54, 63–71. Gross, *Münzenberg*, pp. 279: 282–86, 296. Klaus Mammach, ed., *Die Brüsseler Konferenz der KPD (3.-15. Okt. 1935)* (Berlin: Dietz, 1975), pp. 29, 33–34. Bahne, *Weimar*, p. 63. *Notizen*, pp. 106, 126, 128–29, 132.

21. Hay, *Memoirs*, pp. 158, 160, 165. Freudenhammer/Vater, *Ein Leben*, p. 58. Fischer, *Opposing Man*, p. 280. Ruth Fischer, *Stalin and German Communism. A Study in the Origins of the Party State* (Cambridge: Harvard Univ. Press, 1948), p. 542. Ruth von Mayenburg, *Blaues Blut und Rote Fahnen. Ein Leben unter vielen Namen* (Vienna: Fritz Molden, 1969), and *Hotel Lux* (Munich: C. Bertelsmann, 1978). See also Margarete Buber, *Under Two Dictators* (London: Victor Gollancz, 1949), part I.

22. *Notizen*, pp. 140–41, 147. Mayenburg, *Blaues Blut*, pp. 264–265.

23. *Notizen*, pp. 135, 151, 173. Horst Duhnke, *Die KPD von 1933 bis 1945* (Cologne: Kiepenheuer & Witsch, 1972), p. 261.

24. Hay, *Memoirs*, p. 162. Carola Stern, *Ulbricht: A Political Biography* (New York: Praeger, 1965), pp. 74, 79. Freudenhammer/Vater, *Ein Leben*, p. 74. Fischer, *Opposing Man*, p. 294. Gross, *Münzenberg*, p. 290. *Notizen*, p. 167.

25. *Notizen*, pp. 100, 151–57. Freudenhammer/Vater, *Ein Leben*, pp. 76–80. Appel, p. 29. Hay, *Memoirs*, p. 263.

26. Stern, *Ulbricht*, p. 78. Buber, *Two Dictators*, p. 9. *Notizen*, p. 173.

27. *Notizen*, pp. 108, 174, 179, 184. Hay, *Memoirs*, p. 209. Fischer, *Opposing Man*, pp. 287–88, 343, 348–50. Duhnke, *KPD*, pp. 286–87, 294, 333–34, 347. Freudenhammer/Vater, *Ein Leben*, pp. 81–84. The pact destroyed what few chances remained to establish a popular front, and it led to the arrest and deportation of as many as 3,000 of the 4,000 German Communists in the Soviet Union.

28. Duhnke, *KPD*, pp. 341, 344. *Notizen*, pp. 167–68, 181–82. Freudenhammer/Vater, *Ein Leben*, pp. 85–88. Jahn, *Beiträge*, pp. 100–01. Buber, *Two Dictators*. Fischer, *Opposing Man*, p. 350.

29. *Notizen*, pp. 135–36, 183. Fischer, *Opposing Man*, p. 261. For difficulty of breaking with Communist movement, see Gaus, *Gespräche*, p. 53; Klaus Harprecht, "Lutheraner-halb links. Ein Portrait Herbert Wehners," *Der Monat*, Heft 220, Jan. 1967, p. 14; Jahn, *Beiträge*, pp. 101–02; and Gustav Regler, *Owl of Minerva* (New York: Farrar, Straus and Giroux, 1960), pp. 256–57, 363.

30. `Notizen*, pp. 189–191, 194.

31. *Ibid.*, pp. 192, 205–07. Freudenhammer/Vater, *Ein Leben*, pp. 96–139.

32. *Notizen*, pp. 206–07. Freudenhammer/Vater, *Ein Leben*, p. 115.

33. *Notizen*, pp. 206–08. See "Anhang: Der Prozess Wehner in Dokumenten," in Freud-enhammer/Vater, *Ein Leben*, pp. 274–394.

34. *Notizen*, p. 215. Freudenhammer/Vater, *Ein Leben*, p. 149. Wehner, "Die Arbeiter."

35. "Wehners Traum," *Spiegel*, p. 36. *Notizen*, pp. 7, 30–31. For his own elaboration of those elements of Leninism which lay the foundation for totalitarianism, see Wehner, "Nachdenkliches Gedenken an W.I. Lenin," *Die Neue Gesellschaft*, Heft 5, Sept./Oct. 1970.

36. Soell, *Fritz Erler*, I, 289–329. Freudenhammer/Vater, *Ein Leben*, pp. 202–03. Jahn, *Wandel und Bewährung*, p. 214.

20

POLITICAL PHILOSOPHY OR NIHILIST SCIENCE
EDUCATION'S ONLY SERIOUS QUESTION *

Harry Neumann

Harry Jaffa did not learn from his teacher, Leo Strauss, that moral indignation is the greatest enemy of philosophy.

WALTER BERNS

ENEMIES AND FRIENDS HAVE SOUGHT CLARIFICATION OF RECENT CHANGES in my outlook. In the last decade it has changed three times. The first two changes still assumed that thoughtful men were confronted with fundamental alternatives between which choice was difficult, if not impossible. I saw these alternatives first as ancients or moderns, then as philosophy or politics. The third and deepest change led me to see truth as scientific. I no longer believe that an alternative exists to science. If one were available, it would be philosophy. Civilization, culture, humanities are parts of science, its window-dressing. Scientific knowledge, the only real knowledge or wisdom, is rare, although nothing is more easily acquired.

Science emerges when anyone, from cavemen to contemporaries, declares his independence from philosophy. Prior to this declaration of independence, there is no science as such. Instead there is aristotelian or epicurean or thomist or newtonian or einsteinean or christian science, etc. Each of these pseudo-sciences is subordinated to some more or less

Author's note: The research for this article was assisted by grants from the Earhart Foundation and the John Brown Cook Association for Freedom. It was read at the annual meeting of the American Political Science Association in Denver, Colorado in September, 1982.

clearly articulated philosophic (or theological) theory about the universe. Each subordinates science's radically personal, incommunicable core to a hypothesis or theory, a philosophic effort to communicate something common to the whole universe. In the next section of this paper, I will clarify science's incommunicable, because apolitical, essence. Here I want just to note that communicable science really is philosophy. Not science, but philosophy is political and therefore communicable. Unlike philosophy, science does not delude itself into the belief that it has any redeeming social value.

The differing pseudo-sciences are guided by different, often opposing, philosophies (or theologies). Genuine science eliminates this proliferation of pseudo-sciences. Its independence from philosophy means destruction of all moral-political-religious restraints. It denies that any limits exist to its experience or experimentation.

Sometimes I ask students if any real restraints, limits set by something like nature or gods, exist to curb scientific experimentation. Can science, for example, make men immortal or transform them into eagles? Most students deny that anything is intrinsically impossible. They acknowledge that some things *probably* will not happen tomorrow and even in a century, but, in principle, nothing prevents anything imaginable from happening at any time. Like good liberals, these same students usually cling to a groundless faith that science's uncurbed experimentation ought to be used for liberal goals—to promote freedom rather than slavery, peace rather than war. As if that made any difference in the nihilist world revealed by science! The faith that science's omnipotence can be restrained in the name of some non-arbitrary moral obligation is unscientific. It is relapse into the philosophic illusion from which science liberates itself. Interpreted scientifically, any such relapse, any moral-political commitment, springs from the tyrannic decision to have it so: all moral-political demands are efforts to tyrannize over reality, to replace nature or truth with the propaganda dearest to one's heart.

I use "science" in its original meaning, *scientia*, knowledge of the way things really are. It is the only genuine knowledge and it is readily available always and everywhere. Science is prior to the usual distinctions —right and wrong, truth and falsity, death and life, freedom and determinism, beast and man, dreaming and wakefulness. It is prior to all distinctions. At bottom, there is nothing complicated or sophisticated about science. Not science, but its window dressing or propaganda has sparked so-called knowledge explosions requiring complicated machinery and ever greater specialization.

Science itself is the simple realization that whatever is experienced —a self, a world, the law of contradiction, a god or anything else—is nothing apart from its being experienced. Science's reality is nothing but empty experiences, impressions as Hume called them. From a scientific point of view everything high or low, including the distinction between high and low, becomes a way of experiencing, a point of view, an interpretation, a method, a way of thinking or perceiving. Heidegger's "Age of the World-View" rightly notes that "world view" understood scientifically "does not mean a view of the world, but the world understood as a view (or picture). Existence as a whole is now understood in such a way that it only exists in the first place insofar as it is produced by man who perceives or produces it (*durch den vorstellend-herstellenden Menschen*)...Wherever existence is not interpreted in this way, the world cannot become a view or picture; there cannot be a world view." Heidegger rightly insists that a previously unscientific world-view does not change into a scientific one, but this very thing, "that the world itself becomes a view" is the essence of science. In this regard, Nietzsche's *Will to Power* (481, 466) claims that, for science there are no facts, only interpretations or methods—methods of experience, points of view. There is nothing inherently rigorous or mathematical in scientific method which, rightly understood as it rarely is, means nothing more than nihilist experience, any way (or method) of experiencing—whether it be that of a tiger, an infant or an Einstein. Science is the realization that reality is nothing but mere experience, methods of perceiving or thinking. This "definition" of science, like all theories or thoughts, is no more than another empty experience or method.

It is illusory to believe that words or thoughts, "scientific" or unscientific theories, are anything more than empty experiences, empty because they are not definable or limited by anything. Experience is its own reason or lack of reason, its own cause and its own effect. This reality revealed by science is nihilist consisting quite literally of nothing, of empty, interchangeable nothings, experiences or methods. In his *Reveries of the Solitary Walker*, Rousseau called them reveries. He meant that reality provides no grounds for distinguishing (private) dreams or reveries and the (public) state of wakefulness. Both are only scientific methods.

All science is nihilist. The expression "nihilist science" is as much a tautology as "scientific method" or "scientific reveries." Science is nihilist precisely because the reality grasped by it is nothing but methods or reveries. In *What is Political Philosophy?* (p. 178), Leo Strauss deplores Hobbes' scientific reduction of human life to phantasmagoria: "In the light of Hobbes' natural science man and his works become a mere phantasmagoria. Through Hobbes' natural science, 'the native hue' of his political science 'is sicklied o'er with the pale cast' of something which is reminiscent of death but utterly lacks the majesty of death...It seems that if we want to do justice to the life which vibrates in Hobbes' political teaching, we must understand that teaching by itself and not in the light of his natural science." This philosophic segregation of, or abstraction from, Hobbes' scientific core informs the method of interpretation common to Strauss and to Harry Jaffa, his main student. It is meant to rescue those so interpreted from their conscious or unconscious nihilism, to make them philosophic insofar as possible instead of scientific. Insofar as it is meant to be more than another scientific method, I consider this rescue mission unrealistic both in itself (since philosophy is illusory) and in contemporary regimes which foster nihilist-scientific self-knowledge.

Unaware of science's nihilism, pseudo-scientists emphasize science's proofs and discoveries, especially its potential or actual redeeming social value. They mistake science's window dressing for its core. Except for realization of life's nihilism, there are no scientific proofs or discoveries. This simple, unsophisticated realization—and it alone—is science. No other truth is provable or discoverable in a universe where nothing prevents anything from changing into anything else or into the nothingness which everything always is. For example, there would be no real change if, as in Kafka's *Metamorphosis*, men should become insects. Such transformations would be no changes in reality since neither men nor insects nor anything else is anything but the nothingness of phantasmagoria.

In the essentially private, incommunicable world of scientific reveries or methods, there is no place for philosophic seminars or symposia. For science is not a cooperative enterprise in which scientists work for each other and with each other, building on previous scientific findings. Science neither progresses nor regresses. It requires no complicated equipment or intricate specialization. Its beginning and end is realization of life's nihilism. Once that is realized scientists can, to pass the time, champion any "scientific" theory or moral-political cause. So long as they exempt nothing from reality's nihilism, they can promote war or peace, evolution or creation, a stationary or a mobile earth, dictatorship or anarchy—or anything else. However they never forget that these philosophic-propagandistic conflicts between mankind's moralities have nothing to do with science, genuine knowledge of reality.

To win propaganda victories, men make distinctions between good and bad, true and false, right and wrong. Reality is not propagandistic; it makes neither these nor any other distinctions. No reason exists to want one thing rather than another. All efforts to make something out of reality's nothingness are merely other forms of that nothingness. As Goethe notes at the beginning of his *Faust*, all striving is the work of the devil, the tyrannic attempt to alter a reality which provides nothing for which to strive.

Like most men, Faust is philosophic in that he needs the illusion of a self and a universe which exist as something more than phantasmagoria. Philosophy is the desire to grasp and to communicate such a non-nihilist reality. It is love of wisdom or science, not science itself. If it were scientific, it would realize that truth is indifferent or repulsive, but hardly lovable. In a nihilist universe, nothing exists to love or to be loved; nothing exists to be anything but reveries or methods.

I do not know why most men cling so desperately to philosophic illusion. Reasons why anything exists are unavailable in a nihilist world. Reasons actually are nothing but more or less persuasive propaganda. Since philosophy is essentially political, its chief illusion is that valid, non-propagandistic grounds support the distinctions crucial to moral-political life: freedom and slavery, justice and injustice, good and bad.

Among contemporary academics, only Harry Jaffa consistently defends philosophy as a moral-political enterprise. It is therefore surprising that Jaffa's guidance is not sought by all professors and students yearning for a reality in which their appeals to justice and freedom are more than propaganda. Their usual unwillingness to seek it reveals a nihilism destructive of those appeals. This nihilism is hidden from them by their deficient self-knowledge. Propelled by this deficiency, Jaffa's enemies often denounce his thought as too political to be philosophic. Their "philosophy" is remote from moral indignation, the hatred of enemies responsible for political partisanship. Jaffa knows better: any non-nihilist effort to know oneself and the universe is radically political and, as such, unthinkable without that hatred.

If there were any serious contemporary opposition to my scientific rejection of philosophy, it would be Jaffa or his best students. I am grateful for their help in clarifying that rejection. Other academics can provide little, if any, help. Although they usually imagine themselves opposed to my scientific orientation, they actually are not. They are nihilists whose poor self-knowledge is responsible for their ignorance of both science and philosophy. They assume that science or philosophy are what is taught in science or philosophy departments. Nothing could be further from the truth!

In those departments, as in academic life generally, there is hopeless confusion about science and philosophy and therefore about education. Neither science nor philosophy are academic departments. Nor are they part of culture or civilization or the humanities. Neither is part of anything. Understood in its own terms, each claims that it alone comprehends all reality. I believe that no alternative exists to science; philosophers are scientists whose deficient self-knowledge is responsible for apparently ineradicable illusions about themselves and consequently about science.

Only one question exists for genuine education: which of the two, science or philosophy, comprehends reality for what it is? Everything in schools not moved by the determination to answer this question is the usual academic trivia, not education. In this introduction, I sketched the grounds for my being a scientist rather than a philosopher. The rest of the paper further distinguishes science from philosophy, apolitical from political thought.

Philosophers are unrealistic because their self-knowledge is political. This self-knowledge blinds them to life's nihilism. Philosophy springs from common sense or what Nietzsche, more nihilistically, called the herd instinct. The herd instinct's essence is its being common or communal, an instinct which makes political sense out of life. This instinct inspires the faith that one has an identity distinguishing one from other things in a universe shared with them. It creates the illusion that reality is a coherent, intelligible world, not merely a chaos of empty reveries or experiences.

Although it obviously is impossible to experience anything but experiences, herd instinct faith makes men believe that they grasp things which exist as more than mere experience. However much the herd instinct may vary in different bestial and human herds, it never is democratic. For it always inculcates one chief care in all herd members. That care is to get what is good for oneself, to live the good life. This care is informed by the moral-political orthodoxies of one's herd. Unlike unphilosophic herd members, philosophic herd members turn this care into a question whose answer is not self-evident. Philosophers, that is, philosophic herd members, spend their lives striving to answer what they see as their herd's chief question. Consequently philosophers always are radically political. There are no apolitical philosophers, only philosophic herd members.

The primacy of the moral-political question, the question of the good life, is revealed not by rational inquiry, since it sets the goal of all rational inquiry. Faith in its primacy is forced upon both philosophic and unphilosophic herd members by what Nietzsche in his *Joyful Science* (1,354) calls the strongest instinct of any herd. In his *Zarathustra* (II:8) he rightly discerns enslavement to the herd instinct as the hallmark of all "the famous wise men," the philosophers.

Philosophers do not interpret their herd instinct orientation scientifically, as faith in an illusion (*Credo quia absurdum*), but philosophically, as a kind of seeing through a glass darkly which they strive to clarify (*Credo ut intelligam*). Blinding philosophers to life's nihilism, this faith creates the conviction that they inhabit a universe in which their (internal) selves and the (external) world exist as something more than phantasmagoria.

The self-knowledge created by herd instinct faith compels philosophers to see themselves as radically political. The philosophic way of life is a never ending dialogue (with fellow citizens) aimed at discovering what is good; not what is good for some nihilist individual who as such has no good or evil, but what is good for oneself as a citizen, a herd-member. Consequently, the question of the good life is the question of the best regime or political order. It is not even a serious question for scientists, but then, what can be serious in science's nihilism? Nothing apart from arbitrary willfulness, the tyrannic resolve to force seriousness on nihilism's indifference. In a book aptly entitled *Beyond Good and Evil* (9), Nietzsche describes philosophy as the most tyrannic form of this will to overpower reality's nihilism.

Herd instinct faith permits, indeed compels, philosophers to perceive themselves as herd members, not as nihilist individuals. This political orientation is responsible for the philosopher's trust in a universe in which he and what is good for him exist as something more than nihilist experience. Without the illusions inspired by this faith, he would regard his self and his desire to get what is good for it as no more than reveries. In science's nihilist reality there are no goods to seek or selves to seek them. Consequently scientists can, like Humpty-Dumpty, say or mean anything about anything, including their selves and what is beneficial to them. They are not bound by their herd instinct imperative to obtain what is good.

Non-nihilist goods and evils always are political. Private, apolitical goods or evils exist only as nihilist methods. That is why any serious concern with good or evil, right or wrong, truth or falsity always is radically political. Such concerns move men insofar as they are citizens, not insofar as they have achieved scientific liberation from civic or familial ties. Only philosophic or unphilosophic herd members, not scientists, are moved by a serious need to distinguish right from wrong, truth from lies.

Philosophy's political faith is unavailable to men not born into herds sanctifying that faith, herds in which there is no separation of church and state, religion and politics. Only the piety fostered by such herds makes possible philosophy. Consequently nihilism is inevitable when self-knowledge comes to citizens of contemporary regimes which encourage the faith that government exists to serve the individuals governed. Such nihilist regimes teach that the rights of individuals are primary. Behind this nihilism is the scientific realization that no herd is more than the will of its members that it be: "political" life, the concern with right or wrong or with truth or falsity, is grounded in nothing but nihilist will or reveries.

Politics in these contemporary regimes is scientific and therefore radically apolitical. It consists of nihilist individuals doing what Humpty-Dumpty does, persuading and/or forcing others to accept their reveries as authoritative. This unpolitical politics at bottom is more or less effective propaganda created by nihilists who are, and who seek, nothing but scientific phantasmagoria.

Marxist withering away of the state, the death of politics, is not something that will occur only in a future classless society in which hatred and desire for revenge between men finally is eradicated. It occurs here and now whenever men see themselves primarily as individuals with individual rights not as pious fathers and citizens with political and familial duties. When this individualism is rightly understood, as it rarely is, it is seen to issue from scientific realization of life's nihilism. Depending on their tastes or "values," nihilists may prefer democratic, communist or nazi reveries. In each case, politics is reduced to radically apolitical phantasmagoria.

The more scientific enlightenment is permitted in contemporary regimes grounded in nihilist-individualistic rights, the more herd members realize that nothing holds their herd together except force and/or propaganda. To prevent the resultant anarchy from dissolving all political ties, effective propaganda is required. Since (philosophic) propaganda cannot be effective in scientifically enlightened herds, police and military terror is the only resort there. It is appropriate that the old Greek word for political community (*polis*) comes down almost unchanged to our modern-nihilist regime as "police." In scientifically enlightened herds, the police are the heart of politics. These herds —that is, all contemporary regimes—become police states once they see their nihilism for what it is. The only difference is that liberal democratic propaganda more effectively prevents scientific self-knowledge. Contrary to appearances, liberal democracies are more immune to scientific enlightenment than tyrannies. Less immunity is responsible for brutal suppression of individualism by fascists and communists.

On the day the Russians began their extirpation of Polish freedom, a liberal newscaster in America, appalled by their brutality, gave this example of it at its worst: the communists forced cancellation of a play glorifying a lesbian mother's struggle to raise her sons. In private, familial matters communist morality is traditional, finding lesbian mothers abhorrent. Convinced that only terror and propaganda can make men seriously moral or political, the communists are not prepared to sanction dialogues about the merits of lesbian motherhood. The newscaster hoped that sometime in the future the communists would see the error of their ways. For him, political life is essentially a life of Socratic dialogue, the free exchange of ideas, not violent suppression of the immoral and the dissident.

The newscaster valued individual freedom above all. Like most liberals, he failed to see that communist suppression occurs precisely because communists share his view that by nature men are individuals liberated from all moral-political ties and, therefore, free to choose their own morality, however dissident it might be. As Rousseau's *Social Contract* (II:7) claims, one must be a god or superman capable of destroying man's true (individualist) nature, if one is to transform men into citizens. In the absence of superhuman power, what except terror and propaganda can compel men to be moral or political once scientific enlightenment succeeds? Its lack of success in contemporary liberals permits them still to cling to the deficient self-knowledge responsible for their insistence upon the political desirability of individual freedom, the withering away of the state.

Scientific self-knowledge necessarily translates into tyrannic politics. Consistent opposition to nazism or communism arises not from liberalism, but from the political faith informing philosophy. This faith inspired the illusion necessary to non-tyrannic politics, convincing ancient herd members that their being born a citizen of their particular herd was not an accident occurring to individuals free from all moral-political ties. The political faith at philosophy's core was sanctified by the particular gods of one's herd. Otherwise being born in this herd rather than another one will indeed seem merely accidental as it does in all contemporary-scientific herds. In these herds, neither non-tyrannic rule nor philosophers are possible.

Birth must seem sanctified to support non-tyrannic politics. This sanctification could be experienced only in ancient herds whose gods, moral-political authorities, were political not cosmopolitan. In these herds, there was no separation of church and state, morality and politics, conscience and society. Their citizens considered it impious to share moral-political ties with foreigners.

Nothing is less realistic than the self-knowledge inspired by those pre-scientific herds. Yet it is crucial to realize that philosophy could emerge only in them. Science is unhistorical; it surfaces wherever reality's nihilism is grasped. Philosophy's emergence requires rare historical conditions no longer available today. Its serious pursuit was limited to ancient herds without scientific enlightenment. To be sure, philosophic herd members questioned their herd's claim to answer its main question, to know what was good for its members. However in the decisive respect, philosophic herd members sided with their unphilosophic brethren by embracing the faith that such a good exists as something more than scientific reveries. The philosopher's pestering of fellow citizens with his questioning seemed disloyal only to those unable to discern its patriotic core. His job was twofold: 1) Questioning his herd's moral-political faith. 2) Defending that faith against scientific-nihilist enlightenment.

The philosopher was only a seeker after wisdom. Achievement of wisdom was precluded by philosophy's dependence upon faith, not knowledge. Without their political faith, philosophers would have had no self and no goal in life, no reason to be or not to be. Philosophers saw themselves as political philosophers because philosophy's heart and soul was political. On philosophic horizons, politics did not present itself as something vile, generating passions hostile to free inquiry. The chief political passion, hatred of enemies and desire for vengeance against them, springs from the herd instinct faith that one has or needs goods without which life is not worth living. Hatred is the natural reaction to whoever threatens those goods. Consider Psalm 137.

In ancient, pre-scientific herds, that fury was sanctified by familial and civic piety. Without this sanctified hatred, there can be scientists but neither serious philosophers nor citizens. In the contemporary absence of that sanctification, hatred of enemies usually is justified by liberal propaganda's apolitical wars to end all wars, to establish peace on earth, good will to all men.

No one realized better than Nietzsche the commanding role played by that hatred in philosophic or pre-scientific thought. Its destruction, the elimination of what he called the spirit of revenge, would elevate those few capable of it to supermen. The need to transcend all philosophic, that is political or hateful, thought is at the core of his *Zarathustra* (II:7, 20) and *Will to Power* (765): *"That man be saved from the desire for revenge:* that is for me the bridge to the highest hope...*The spirit of revenge* that has been [in philosophic, pre-scientific thought] man's best reflection...Everywhere where responsibility or reasons were sought, it was *the spirit of revenge* doing the seeking. Over millenia this spirit of revenge has achieved such a mastery over mankind that all metaphysics, psychology, conceptions of history, but above all morality, is stigmatized with it. As far as man has thought, he has dragged the bacillus of revenge into things...We others who wish to win back for becoming its innocence wish to be the missionaries of a purer thought: that nothing has given man his qualities, neither god, nor society, nor his parents and ancestors, nor he himself—that nothing is responsible for him. There is no being *(Wesen)* that could be made responsible for anyone's existing or being the way he is...There is no purpose, no sense for our being...This is a great solace, in this lies the innocence of all existence."

21

THE MAN WHO WALKED
WITH GOD

Thomas B. Silver

WILLIAM JAMES IS SAID TO HAVE CALLED HIM "THE GREATEST TEACHER IN
the United States."

"The greatest teacher of philosophy?" someone asked.

"No, no," said James, "the greatest teacher."[1]

His greatness as a teacher was attested to by other prominent contemporaries, including Arthur Lovejoy and John Dewey.

He was, in the whole history of the college where he taught, "the
most famous and mysterious of . . . teachers," "a man around whose romantic personality legends gathered even in his lifetime."[2]

To a colleague, he was "a keen student of psychology, a wise philosopher."

> He had a passion for truth. He sought it eagerly as a man digs for
> hid treasure. He sought it in all places and at all times. When he was a
> student in college few of us knew when his lamp went out at night, or
> was relighted in the morning.[3]

To his students, the greatest teacher was "one of the greatest of
men."[4] Until the end of their lives, all remembered and most revered
him. They remembered his resonant voice and hypnotic eyes—the eyes
"coal black . . . deep, cavernous, glowing."[5] "Lustrous eyes," that "looked
straight at men and sometimes through them."[6]

He devoted himself to his students, publishing almost nothing. His
career unfolded entirely within the walls of his classroom. There his
method was Socratic. Every student was exposed to a cycle of argument
and destruction, discussion and reconstruction, the chief purpose of
which was to inculcate the habit of critical and independent thought. To
be sure, he did write thin pamphlets—short arguments or dialogues
—that he himself printed in his cellar. But these pamphlets were not for
public distribution, because they contained partial, incorrect, or inconclusive arguments that might be misconstrued or do harm. They were distributed only to his students, who had to pledge to return them without
copying them or showing them to outsiders.

Visitors to his classroom were few.

The outsider, curious to get a glimpse of the ways of this man who could so wield philosophy as to stir the student soul to its very depths, was not made welcome. In his opinion, a stranger tended to introduce a disturbing element into the atmosphere, and . . . tended to make it seem that philosophy and its methods were on exhibition . . . If sometimes this attitude . . . seemed too esoteric to comport well with the modern teaching of philosophy, sufficient justification was felt to exist in the fact that thereby the student was made to feel that he was on sacred ground at the very portals of the inner shrine of truth.[7]

Misinterpretation was always a danger as well. One college Trustee would not let his son take the philosophy course, because he was afraid the boy's religious faith would be undermined. But "although foolish men occasionally suspected him of heresy, he had given his classes before the course was ended a foundation for a firm religious conviction."[8] He believed that "philosophy is the mount of transfiguration of human nature."[9] His students looked upon him as "a man who walked with God."[10]

For twenty-five years, Professor Charles E. Garman taught philosophy at Amherst College, during one of the most fertile periods in the college's history. ("It will not be denied that Amherst graduates of the period 1870–1910 achieved distinction out of proportion to their numbers.")[11] There an opportunity came to Garman that comes to few teachers: the opportunity to influence deeply several of the leading statesmen of a generation. Three of these statesmen were born within a few months of each other, in 1872 and 1873. They were destined to meet at Amherst College in the 1890s and to become students of Charles Garman. Later they occupied prominent places in the nation's political life. One achieved greatness as a diplomat, and later was elected a United States Senator; one reached the United States Supreme Court; and one became President of the United States. They were, respectively, Dwight Morrow, Harlan Stone, and Calvin Coolidge.

Plato says, in the most famous passage of the *Republic*, that evils shall not cease from the world until philosophers become kings or kings philosophers. Charles Garman never became a king, nor did his three students become philosophers; nor for that matter did evils cease from the world. But Garman did impart to his students a structure of ideas, which they took with them into the political world and which informed their political actions during one of the three or four most pivotal decades in American history.

Students of the American political tradition rightly focus on the great turning points in our political history; for it is at moments of greatest national trial that the American character becomes most fully revealed, as the importance of the event summons forth a passionate, articulate, and pointed debate which invariably comes to involve the architectonic principles of the regime.

Unfortunately, these revelations are sometimes lost, even on scholars, who, being human after all, are subject to the same blinding partisan passions as their fellow citizens. In some cases, neither the passion for truth, nor the passage of time, has enabled some scholars to conquer their own partisanship.

Certainly much partisan blindness has characterized the historiography of the struggle between the New Deal and the "old order" that it replaced. One indication of this partisanship is that the pedigree of the New Deal has been traced in a thousand books, whereas until recently scholars have been content not to probe behind the standard one dimensional accounts of Presidents Coolidge and Hoover. So complete, in fact, was the victory of the New Deal court historians, that it not only silenced but also persuaded many of its academic adversaries. Even today, many liberal and conservative scholars have a common view of the decade leading up to the election of 1932, namely, that the Republican Party, presided over by Coolidge and Hoover, was a tool of class interest or bourgeois acquisitiveness. To quote an example of this view that lies right at hand:

[American conservatives] have not been conservative enough. Their insubstantial heroes have been Coolidge, Hoover, Taft. Their very advocacy of a *materialist capitalism* has been but a negative reaction to socialism—they have overlooked, among other things, the fact that capitalism and industrialism were the great anti-conservative forces of the nineteenth century and after . . . 'Buying, selling, investing are the moving impulses of our life. The inhabitants of our country must be stimulated to new wants in all directions.' These were the words of Calvin Coolidge, often seen as the sour New England saint of thrift and probity instead of what he was, a man soaked in the practice of public relations and a proponent of inflation. (emphasis mine)[12]

Coolidge in particular, for liberals, is an object of disgust; for conservatives—excepting those who are unabashed advocates of unrestrained capitalism—he is a source of embarrassment; for both he is an object of ridicule.

But there is more to the matter than just the opprobrium attaching to a minor politician who fell through the trap door of history fifty years ago. William Allen White, for one, believed that Calvin Coolidge was the perfect embodiment of the spirit of his age. Far from being an accidental or insignificant figure, he was president by design and destiny. Coolidge, born on the fourth of July, was the quintessential American, and America —at least during its first century and a half—was the quintessence of the modern commercial age. America during the twenties, as the preeminent modern commercial republic, had largely discarded the baggage of moral and religious sentiments with which it had begun its journey, and had not yet acquired the baggage of Rooseveltian idealism. To many liberal and conservative scholars, this America, no less than Calvin Coolidge himself, is an object of disgust, embarrassment, and ridicule.

America, understood in this way, is a product of modern political philosophy, in particular the political philosophy of Hobbes and Locke. The purpose of that philosophy was to create modern man: selfish, individualistic, materialistic, bourgeois. According to Locke, man is radically selfish. The individual, prompted by self-interest alone, is the originator of property. Civil society comes into being solely to protect property and the rights of individuals to acquire property. Civil society is a deduction from individual selfishness.

In the Lockean scheme, selfishness replaces virtue as the ordering principle of the human soul, or rather, the meaning of virtue is transformed. Good character is no longer an end but a means. Virtue, whether moral or intellectual, becomes instrumental. Wealth is no longer an occasion for the exercise of virtue; virtue is a tool for acquiring wealth. Virtue, in short, has been degraded into bourgeois virtue.

If virtue is no longer the ordering principle of the human soul, neither is it the ordering principle of civil society. The parts being prior to the whole, the so-called common good is the by-product of individual self-seeking. If we say that chance is crossed intentions, then the common good is a chance sum. The common good is collective selfishness.

It is said that Locke, knowing the power of the tradition he opposed —and perhaps even fearing for his personal safety—presented his new teaching in a cautious, subtle, even esoteric way. He was confident that the corrosive power of acquisitiveness would after while eat away the foundations of the old order, and that new foundations in accord with an enlightened understanding of man's true place in the universe would replace them. Calvin Coolidge, the man who exalted the bourgeois virtues and said that the business of America is business, was a Lockean freed from the need for caution. Coolidge was the reductio ad absurdum of Locke's joyless quest for joy.

That Calvin Coolidge understood himself to be a disciple of Garman there can be no doubt. "It always seemed to me," he said in his autobiography,

that all our other studies were in the nature of a preparation for the course in philosophy. The head of the department was Charles E. Garman, who was one of the most remarkable men with whom I ever came in contact.[13]

According to William Allen White, Coolidge "continued to apply the Garmanian philosophy . . . to all matters, great and small, through his career."[14]

Although Charles Garman wrote little for publication, his students compiled after his death a volume of his letters, speeches, pamphlets, and notes of class lectures, entitled *The Letters, Lectures, and Addresses of Charles Edward Garman.* This collection Coolidge kept next to the Bible at the head of his bed throughout his life.

Several of the selections in the volume are grouped under the titles, "The Political and Social Order" and "Social Progress," and they represented what Garman considered his "most important contribution."[15]

Given the fragmentary state of Garman's meager written legacy, it is not possible to reconstruct fully his moral and political teaching. Nor is it important to do so. For the present purpose it will suffice to lay out briefly the main themes of his teaching—themes which (I assert without stopping to prove) run through the speeches of Calvin Coolidge.

It was no accident that Charles Garman had students who, decades after his death, "continued to apply Garmanian philosophy in all matters great and small." For this was Garman's intention. He was highly conscious that the boys coming into his classroom at the end of the nineteenth century were the products of a materialistic and relativistic age. "As the students come to me they are as 'children tossed about by every wind of doubt, by the sleight of man, and cunning craftiness.'"[16]

Garman knew that decent political life required a theoretical or rational defense against the powerful and respectable teachings of relativism and materialism. He knew that inherited religious faith—soft and slack in many boys, doctrinaire and brittle in others—was by itself insufficient protection.

For ages the ancestors of the American people have been inspired and quickened by their religious faith. They believed in verbal inspiration of the Scriptures. The church laid the greatest possible stress on this life as a preparation for the future, with its awful rewards and punishments of heaven and hell. We can hardly imagine the strength of these motives. What a check they were to wrongdoing . . . All this has changed now. Whether rightly or wrongly, the higher criticism is working havoc with the doctrine of inspiration in the popular mind. . . It is clear that the public have not the old motives for action that shaped the early history of our country. Now, what motives are you going to put in the place of the old. . .?[17]

Of course, the motive that had begun to fill the vacuum in men's souls was acquisitiveness. Garman knew that this motive, ever present in human nature, was in modern times dangerously abetted by science.

The progress of science not merely increases the power of the lion over the lamb; it increases also the ferocity of his nature. The more he has the more he wants. The Greek meaning of the word covetousness is not a desire for little, not a desire for much, but a desire for more.[18]

In terms of the American political order, we may state the problem Garman confronted as follows: at the time of the American founding, dynamic young modern technology was yoked uneasily with an aged moral tradition. The passage of a century found the latter desperately weakened, while the former, gathering strength, began to tug America powerfully off course. That Garman regarded this as a profound difficulty meant that for him the political problem began where Locke's teaching ended.

But if Garman was critical of unchecked and open-ended capitalism, he was no less a critic of humanitarian reform, of the view that the equalization or democratization of wealth and political power is the solution to the problem of justice. He rejected equally the short term selfishness of the many and the shrewder long term selfishness of the few, because he wished to transcend altogether the plane upon which the few and the many fought. (". . . slavery of the short-sighted to the long-sighted has always existed and always will exist as long as quantity is the aim of each.")[19]

The radical attack on property, and the conservative defense of property, gave to property an undeservedly central role in men's affairs. The "standard recognition in society," said Garman, should be "merit and manliness instead of wealth."[19] In a word, Garman did not believe that the solution to the economic problem was the solution to the human problem.

In all the schemes that are proposed by politicians, labor agitators, statesmen, and scholars, we are able by careful study to discover that there are only two distinct trends. Antagonistic as these writers are to each other in details, there is only one comprehensive antagonism. We can overlook particular differences and give our attention to the fundamental distinction that sharply outlines the position of all writers as belonging to either one party or the other. The first party, including by far the larger number, is devoted to the great effort of bringing about the millennium through a variety of contrivances, all of which reduce to attempts of a purely quantitative character. Just as in music you get harmony or discord, treble or bass, by a quantitative increase or decrease in the number of vibrations, so that the whole scheme of music can be worked out in terms of mathematics; so there are writers and critics who aim by simply quantitative devices for distributing wealth, or suffrage, or wages, to change the great national discord to be found in each country to a grand anthem of contentment and prosperity.

The other great party, while not undervaluing the efforts for quantitative justice, yet feel that the labor problems, the political evils, the corruption of municipal politics, are but symptoms of deep-seated disease in human nature for which there is no remedy of a superficial character that is seriously worth experimenting with. We must go to the very source of the whole trouble and seek a change in the quality of human life. There must be truer conceptions of human nature and less selfishness. These thinkers are never tired of reechoing the words of Christ to Nicodemus as the great hope for the evils of our time, "YE MUST BE BORN AGAIN." This is true not merely of individuals, but of institutions and of society itself. The time has come when business and social organizations must be regenerated; when the aim of life shall no longer be simply to get, but to be heroic and noble, and to achieve great things.[21]

"To be human is to be intelligent; to be intelligent is to look at the part in the light of the whole."[22] Starting from this premise, Garman was obliged to reject a certain version of the social contract theory.

It will be seen, then, that the whole is very different from an aggregation of parts. The civil compact theory affirms that because one man has no prerogative over another, society can have no prerogative over the individual, because society is made up of individuals and the whole cannot be greater than the sum of the parts. Nothing is more ridiculous than this system.[23]

Against the view that the individual, prompted by self interest alone, is the originator or property, and that civil society comes into being solely to protect the individual's right to originate property; against the view that civil society is a deduction from individual selfishness; against the view that the common good is the by-product of atomistic self-seeking; against the view that virtue is instrumental, Garman held out for the view that men realize themselves only in and through a whole composed of their families and friends and fellow citizens; that the end of civil society is not wealth and property, but that wealth and property serve the ends of society, namely, the cultivation of the intellectual and moral virtues; that man's destiny does not lie in the joyless quest for joy but in moral duty, in the first instance in service to his family and friends, later to fellow citizens and fellow human beings.

We have laid great stress in the past on wealth and social position, but we are coming to a time in our history when all cannot hope to be wealthy in the new sense of that term; when there will be an impassable barrier between the great fortunes and the common people. Now, the result may be the formation of classes in society with antagonistic interests. If this occurs there will be some chance of realizing the prophecy of Macaulay [that democracy is self-destructive]. But we hope for better things; the ethical conception of human life must be pushed to the front. Then service, not wealth, will be the standard of honor. If the great fortunes are used for the service of the community, if machines are made to do mechanical work and laborers are no longer hands but heads, if their whole time is not spent in barely winning a livelihood, but through education and religion fair emphasis is given to the moral, social, and intellectual nature, Macaulay's prophecy will seem shortsighted and narrow.[24]

Such, in outline, are the very un-Lockean political views of Professor Charles Garman, which views drew upon older moral traditions and attempted to adapt them to a world that had been profoundly reshaped by the teaching of John Locke and other modern philosophers. Garman's opinions and formulations permeate the speeches of Calvin Coolidge. If we look to a country's leaders for authoritative expressions of the country's self-understanding, then we must say that America in the nineteen twenties did not understand itself as many scholars say it understood itself. And if we assert that a serious study of the past begins with an appreciation of how the past understood itself, then we may justly wonder whether most scholars have even yet begun to study seriously America on the eve of the New Deal.

Notes

1. Walter A. Dyer, "Garman of Amherst," *Sewanee Review*, April 1935, p. 146.
2. Claude Fuess, *Calvin Coolidge, The Man From Vermont* (Boston: Little Brown and Co., 1940), p. 57
3. Charles E. Garman, *Letters, Lectures, and Addresses* (Boston:Houghton Mifflin Company, 1909), p. 555.
4. Ibid., p. 567.
5. Harlan Stone, quoted in William Allen White, *A Puritan in Babylon* (New York: MacMillian Co., 1938), p. 38.
6. Garman, p. 564.
7. Garman, p. 585.
8. Fuess, p. 58.
9. Garman, p. 382.
10. Calvin Coolidge, *Autobiography* (New York: Cosmopolitan Book Corporation, 1929), p. 65.
11. Thomas Le Duc, *Piety and Intellect at Amherst College, 1865–1912* , p. 148.
12. John Lukacs, "The American Conservatives," *Harpers*, January 1984, p. 46.
13. Coolidge, p. 63.
14. William Allen White, p. 282.
15. Garman, p. 315.
16. Le Duc, p. 111.
17. Ibid., p. 348–349.
18. Ibid., p. 359.
19. Ibid., p. 356.
20. Ibid., p. 372.
21. Ibid., p. 354.
22. Ibid., p. 358.
23. Ibid., p. 328.
24. Ibid., p. 378.

22

THE RELIGION OF ROOTLESSNESS*

Sanderson Schaub

Nothing passes belief when a god's intention wills it.
Against necessity not even the gods can fight.
                                    TWO GREEK ROOTS[1]

WHAT IS THE ESSENTIAL CHARACTER OF MODERN SOCIETY? THIS QUESTION IS
not merely timely, nor is it by any means merely academic. It is therefore
rather incidental that this essay deals with a recent article by Stephen
Taylor Holmes of Harvard University and the subsequent scholarly inter-
change to which it gave rise.[2] In his article Holmes admits and even stresses
that the ancient sophist Aristippus may help us to understand the character of modernity. But he does so in order to attack Leo Strauss among
others for suggesting the application of the principles of classical political
philosophy to the study of modern society. In Holmes's view classical
principles are not only useless, but indeed dangerous to the perpetuation
of modern liberal societies. What is essential is that Holmes's attack on
the classics readily leads to a clarification of the roots of the question
about modernity. For in Holmes's attack we can discern the old confrontation between ancient piety and Socratic reason. We think that Holmes
shows plainly, if inadvertently, that modernity in its extreme form stands
not on the principles of reason, but on those of ancient religion.[3] Since
these were nothing, however, if not the ancient gods themselves, this es-

---

*In studying this modern phenomenon it is helpful to recall that at one time the study of
the roots was thought to be identical with the study of first principles, with either theology
or philosophy. Cf. "Albo: *Book of Roots," Medieval Political Philosophy* Ralph Lerner and Muhsin
Mahdi, eds. (New York: Free Press, 1963) p. 238; Joseph Cropsey, *Political Philosophy and the
Issues of Politics* (Chicago: University of Chicago Press, 1977) p. 141; and Aristotle, Metaphysics, 981b 27–29, 1071b 26–27.

say might be said to lead up to the question: without such gods can extreme modernity ultimately stand at all? At the same time, we maintain the crucial importance of the alternative standpoint, that of classical reason, for understanding and preserving modern political freedom.

It was Leo Strauss who above all attempted to revive in modern times the thought of the classical political philosophers, and it is Strauss against whom Holmes primarily directs his attack. Yet Holmes repeats the failure of modern liberalism by obscuring the pious element in man while grounding his own position on that element. Modern liberalism, to paraphrase Strauss, has not killed piety, but merely killed understanding of piety, and sincerity regarding piety. The danger to the perpetuation of liberalism in our time Holmes traces to the principles of the classics, not to modern romanticism. Yet even as he accuses the defenders of the classics in the name of the radically free individual's radically free will, he himself defends, as did the accusers of Socrates, the principle of the ancient Greek religion, which he allows us to see as the principle of romanticism: "Nothing passes belief when a god's intention wills it."

The main reason that Strauss turned to the classics was the failure of modern liberalism.[4] In Germany in particular the failure of modern liberalism generated the rule of the Nazis, and Strauss was a German Jew. Modern liberalism seemed to be rooted in modern rationalism, in the enlightenment. Tracing its course from the thought of Hobbes and Spinoza to its disruption in Nietzsche, not to mention Heidegger, who supported the Nazis at least at first, Strauss came to suspect that modern rationalism was self-destructive. He doubted whether it could, having come to be viewed in Germany especially as merely one among many possible ideologies,[5] defend its *raison d'etre* reasonably or whether the enlightenment, ultimately, could defend its superiority to romanticism. Certainly in Germany the Weimar democracy's enlightenment liberalism had surrendered to Hitler's triumph of the will. The rhetoric of the enlightenment had become for Strauss a questionable piece of propaganda, albeit high-class Machiavellian propaganda. Holmes seems to be unimpressed by the failure of modern liberalism in Germany and to be unaware of the questionability of the enlightenment.

At the core of the enlightenment was the modern critique of religion. Strauss expressed doubt that the enlightenment could unquestionably assert its superiority to the religious, in particular the orthodox Jewish, interpretation of the world. Ridicule was not a sufficient refutation, however politically effective. Holmes, on the other hand, sees himself as a defender of the enlightenment and modern liberalism. Only somewhat paradoxically, one could say that Holmes is a pious defender of modern liberal orthodoxy, for if the enlightenment has not succeeded, it is but one more orthodoxy, and if the enlightenment has succeeded, it is the established or *the* orthodoxy. Accordingly, Holmes makes the appropriate orthodox enlightenment jests about Strauss having remembered "the ancestral pieties" and about his "piety toward Greece." Now we ought not to fault Holmes's piety at least before we have learned from it. His concern for liberalism is admirable. Strauss favored liberalism under modern circumstances as Holmes appears to see. But he thought that the classics presented a sound defense for it, as Holmes does not quite see. I propose to treat Holmes's discussion of the classics by concentrating on those points which, to me at least, seem to reveal how Holmes's orthodox enlightenment contempt for piety, which Strauss did not share, misleads him.

To begin with, Holmes cannot find a Greek equivalent to our word "legitimate."[6] He suggests *orthos*, right, and *kata phusin*, according to nature. The moderns by comparison, he concludes, are "quite moderate." He sees only extremism in the classics because he does not emphatically confront the piety of Greek politics to which the classics made large concessions. *Archai nomo*, to rule by law, is easy to say in Greek. In *On Tyranny*,[7] a book which Holmes cites, Strauss points out that while theoretically there might seem to be no difference between Hiero and Cyrus, between a ruler who is called a tyrant and a ruler who is called a king, Xenophon preserves the difference because of its practical importance, since he is aware of the "blessings of legitimacy." Cyrus, unlike Hiero, was the legitimate heir to the throne, not a usurper. Practically speaking, the just is the lawful: any alternative offends piety.

For the same reason, Holmes does not notice Plato's antipathy to radical political change. He maintains that "Plato was doubtless more strongly attached to the *stratopedou politeia* or 'garrison state' than certain pro-democratic Athenians."[8] This guarded statement is misleading because, in his *Seventh Letter* (324 D), Plato says that the Athenian oligarchy, a Spartan garrison state erected on the shambles of the Peloponnesian War, made the democracy look like the golden age. In the *City and Man*,[9] another book which Holmes cites, Strauss points out that the presence in the *Republic* of victims of this same oligarchic regime suggests that through that dialogue reform is not meant to take place on the political level or that human ills will always remain. When the pious Cephalus, whose family suffered the violence of that oligarchy, leaves the dialogue, the possibility for political persuasion is in some degree removed, if not entirely lost, because in sound politics reason must be tempered with piety. Holmes, confusing philosophic notions with Greek piety, believes that in classical Greece "there was a widespread belief in some kind of 'natural law' capable of lending moral legitimacy to the regime."[10] This is incorrect. There was a widespread belief in *divine* law (cf. Thucydides III 82.6). He is right that Plato was no modern liberal, but he fails to bring out the turn to nature, which issued in Socratic natural right, as a form of liberation.

Holmes claims that "by associating, for example, Nazism with modern scientific detachment, Strauss has helped promulgate the myth that twentieth-century autocracy is *basically* a result of our having stopped brooding over old books and having therefore forgotten the ancestral pieties."[11] Holmes has difficulty comprehending the movement from modern rationalism to romanticism. When the Greek poets or the Jewish prophets taught the ancetral pieties they "brooded" over man's purpose. Classical political philosophy, in replacing the divine will with the standard of nature, learned from the old piety to keep man's purpose as its theme: *"quid sit deus?"* Modern rationalism, in radically rejecting any piety whatsoever, dissevered reason and purpose and thus had no reason to oppose Hitler's perverse purpose. Holmes suggests that Strauss has deflected attention away from the possibility "that modern 'totalitarian' regimes[12] rely for ideological legitimation on a diffuse rancor against modernity and on an anachronistic nostalgia for the integrated and heavily politicized life of the Greek city-state."[13] Now Strauss, to the contrary, has quietly but firmly drawn our attention in *Natural Right and History,*[14] another book which Holmes cites, to the fact that Rousseau, the founder of modern romanticism, appealed to ancient political life against modern enlightenment, but not to classical political philosophy. In other words, ancient piety, not the classical view of nature, is what is attractive to romanticism. The clearest illustration of this point is Heidegger's remark: "only a god can save us." Moreover, in *Liberalism: Ancient and Modern*, a book which Holmes cites, Strauss, after mentioning Rousseau, traces Hitler Germany to romanticism, especially the longing for the Middle Ages and the Crusades against the Jews.[15] It is appropriate to note in this regard that longing for antique piety is not the same thing as possessing it.

Holmes accepts the thesis of Benjamin Constant "that the most appalling form of modern tyranny may actually contain a distorted echo of ancient freedom."[16] Holmes could also have appealed to the conservative Burke, the great opponent of Rousseau and the French Revolution. Perhaps such an appeal would seem impious to an orthodox liberal. Macaulay, who admired Burke, disliked Plutarch, who was Rousseau's favorite author, for reasons similar to Constant's and out of a distaste for ancient politics and its political heroes; but, like Burke, he admired the classical political philosophers and their liberal or generous sentiments. Ancient piety was too severe. On the other side, while there were no "Greek liberals" "for Plato to attack," there was indeed license, which Burke and Macaulay deplore along with Plato. The trouble with "liberal 'forgetfullness' toward Greece," which Holmes wishes to "encourage,"[17] is that it causes us to forget what Macaulay repeatedly urges us not to forget, that Greece was *not all one.* Thus Holmes blurs the distinction between religion and reason on which liberalism was founded. Accordingly, he seems unaware when he criticizes "the imprudent importation of doctrines" espoused in

the *Republic*, the *Laws*, and the *Politics*,[18] that he is in some respects literally repeating the charge made against Socrates of "carrying in new gods"
—*importation*—and of corrupting the youth by "teachings"—*doctrines*—
the charge originally made by, of all things, ancestral piety![19]

When Holmes speaks of "pro-oligarchic philosophers like Plato and
Aristotle," we can hear Socrates on trial before the *demos*. Holmes notes
that "the institution of ostracism revealed to what extent citizens had no
'subjective rights' against the city."[20] Yet the case of Socrates demonstrates
this point even more conspicuously! Unlike Holmes and the ancient piety,
Plato made room for Socrates in the political society of his *Laws*. "Participation, as Plato admired it," says Holmes, was *"to ta hautou prattein,"* mind-
ing one's own business,[21] not political deliberation.[22] Here Holmes simply confounds Spartan or ancestral piety with Plato's own views. Yet, if his
contention that Plato "was an enthusiast of political participation" "must
be modified,"[23] other impressions that he has of Plato must be modified
as well. "Participation in the mixed constitution or *politeia* favored by Aristotle has a great deal more to do with collective deliberation and policy
making than does the chore-minding of Plato's ideal city."[24] But, since
Plato's alleged enthusiasm for politics requires modification, surely his
ideal city and so too his chore-minding must be taken with a grain of salt.
Aristotle at any rate could be said to be pro-oligarchic only from a strict
partisan democratic standpoint, since he favors a mixed regime, which is
no less pro-democratic, as in fact Plato does also in his *Laws*.

In an interesting comment, Holmes relates Plato's and Aristotle's use
of *to morion*, the part, to *"moros* and *moira,* one's appointed and fore-
ordained destiny."[25] Holmes thus indicates without bringing fully to light
the similarity between ancient political philosophy and ancient piety, both
of which meant to articulate man's end or purpose. But there is a difference as well. Whereas according to Homer man's destiny is willed by
Zeus, Plato and Aristotle understand man as a part, the microcosm, of
the cosmos overarched by natural necessity. Man's purpose appears in
the natural order rather than in Zeus' will. In this context, Holmes refers
to "incorrigible nature," which ancient piety would have recognized as
Zeus' unalterable will (compare the character Strepsiades in Aristophanes'
Clouds). The classics indeed make use of poetic notions to teach their
point, but such notions do not precisely constitute their point. "Against
necessity not even the gods can fight." Theoretically to dispel the thought
of Plato and Aristotle, Holmes would have to show that modern liberalism has overcome "incorrigible nature" or, put differently, man's concern
with piety. Holmes dismisses "the whole/part interpretation," chiding the
belief that "the kind of soul I indelibly have can only unfold its potential
in the context of a beehive division of labor."[26] He mocks and resents any
hint of the need for restraint in the face of the natural order. By "comparing the city to the soul" the classics unhappily remind us "that 'reason'

must surely rule over the passions and appetites because it is 'higher' than they are."[27] May we not infer by his use of inverted commas that the rule of reason in the soul, which is the main point of the comparison, is what he especially resents and wishes to forget? Strange as it may appear, Holmes could seem to prefer the willfullness of Zeus to the natural order.

Accordingly, Holmes seems to question Aristotle's reasoned view of politics whereby the "middle-class citizens *should* dominate the city since they can avoid the ingrained hubris and contempt of the wealthy as well as the ground-in servility and envy of the poor."[28] He states this moderate viewpoint quite fairly. But this moderate view was shared by Locke, Montesquieu, Adam Smith, and James Madison, to whom Holmes appeals in justification of liberal forgetfulness toward Greece. These moderate modern political thinkers, inasmuch as their doctrines of natural right relied on man's natural reason in contradistinction to the brutes and so on the natural order, not only displayed their preference for reason to the River Lethe, but *imported* classic principles.

Nevertheless, inasmuch as Aristotle's claims "sound wildly implausible" to moderns, we must "try to explain exactly what made them seem convincing to Aristotle."[29] One cannot do so, however, without starting from ancestral piety. That the *polis* is prior to the individual "depends on a sharp contrast between actions which take place in an *oikos* or household and actions which take place in the political sphere."[30] But one cannot grasp the full force of Aristotle's argument if one "forgets" that this means the subordination of the Greek domestic religion to the common good, to political needs, and at the least to Greek civic religion.[31] From this vantage point, one can most plainly see the polemical character of Aristotle's account, how the modern state-society distinction was already present in rudimentary form in ancient Greece—the city as a federation of old families[32]—how Aristotle opposes that distinction as composing an incomplete or inferior form of association, and why Stephen Taylor Holmes objects so strongly, i.e., in a polemical manner, to the use of the Aristotelian framework for the comprehension of modernity. It is not merely a theoretical issue, but a practical and polemical struggle: the common good versus the old families and their household gods.

Ancient Greek examples of glorified *oikoi*, quite different from the modern "shrinkage of the basic kinship unit to the small and increasingly one-generational nuclear family,"[33] would be the House of Pelops, a wealthy Oriental, the Heracleidae, a race descended from a hero who became a god, the Peisistratidae, who for a time ruled Athens as tyrants (with Athena's help), and the Eumolpidae, whose control over the Eleusian rites secured for them the predominant religious influence in Athens. In modern society, what stands in lieu of the domestic religions is a multitude of denominations, but also art for art's sake and vulgar hedonism. "Without insight into actions which are simply choiceworthy for their own sake, *phronesis* or prudence would tumble into an abysmal infinite regress."[34] If modern society is not overarched by the recognition of the superiority of political honor and nobility, prudence degenerates into a "Benthamite"[35] calculus of utility. Accordingly, Nietzsche, who opposed modern society as the realm of the last man, of mere aesthetic comfort, devalued prudence as a virtue.[36] In such a situation, one must either try to establish the validity of low purposes or, if this should prove unsatisfactory, one is thrown into the despair and existentialism of the consciousness of an "infinite regress." Not with, but precisely without the Aristotelian framework, the longing for the most ancient piety then makes itself felt. Such would be life in accordance with divine law. The higher alternative, Aristotle implies, is life in accordance with political law, what Holmes calls "the positive side" of freedom: "the chance for peers to rule and be ruled in turn."[37] If, as Holmes argues, modern society fails to offer that chance or, rather, offers it only to a limited extent, this would merely mean that modern society is in certain respects inferior to the best regime. Perhaps Holmes cannot accept such a conclusion. Or perhaps he fears that the youth will be corrupted or lured into romantic idealism by such a conclusion. In any event, the presupposition of his argument is that liberalism depends on the belief that the modern alternative to ancestral piety, the "differentiated society," is in the decisive respect humanly satisfactory. Thus we say that he piously defends that belief as a "non-trivial" contention, as the poet who accused Socrates at his trial, Meletus, his name meaning "he who cares," defended a similar belief against Socrates.

Holmes notes that Aristotle is cognizant of a higher form of life than that devoted to politics. He wonders about the consistency of this position with the assertation of the priority of the *polis* to the individual, and with its correlate, that man is a political animal. The theoretical life, according to Aristotle, is "the complete happiness of man."[38] Holmes fails to ask, however, whether the openness of modern liberalism—to the extent that it is open—to the philosophic life would not a provide a certain justification for modernity in Aristotle's eyes. But he notices Aristotle's consistency. "In one sense, at any rate, Aristotle never swerves from his definition of man as a political animal. He specifically calls *theoria* a divine and not human *arete* [virtue]."[39] Holmes's neglect of the ancestral pieties might seem to indicate his disinterest in the question of what the divine is. In the *City and Man*,[40] which, again, Holmes cites, Strauss points out that: "In asserting that man transcends the city, Aristotle agrees with the liberalism of the modern age. Yet he differs from that liberalism by limiting this transcendence only to the highest in man." Holmes cares passionately about the lower elements in man, even the sub-political ones, from the Aristotelian standpoint. It is perhaps fairer and surely more enlightening to say that Holmes disagrees with Aristotle about what is highest in man or about what is divine. But he does not make the ground of his disagreement clear. For obviously he would not maintain that the will of Zeus is primary.

Holmes repeatedly refers to what he thinks was Plato's "oligarchic dream."[41] The trial of Socrates was suffused with fear and resentment on the part of the *demos* of his tie to the oligarchy and its dream which came to naught.[42] But Plato tells us that he himself refused to participate in this "dream," that Socrates refused to obey the rulers of this oligarchy, and that it made the former democracy look like the golden age.[43] Holmes is hard put to see the sympathy with liberalism on the part of the classics and certain of their defenders. Again, this is because he overlooks the problem of piety. He quotes Fustel de Coulanges:[44] "The state allowed no man to be indifferent to its interests; the philosopher or studious man had no right to live apart." Holmes "forgets" to mention what appears, as it were, on every page of Fustel's book, that the explanation behind this fact was the religious bond and the ancient religious duties, not classical political philosophy. "When a decision like the condemnation and summary execution of the generals in command at Arginusae violated formal procedure, it was justified by appeal to the security and prosperity of the city."[45] Xenophon (*Hellenika* I. 7), whom Holmes cites here, makes clear that it was primarily justified by appeal to ancestral piety. In the midst of a storm the generals had failed to collect the corpses after the battle at sea. As Fustel de Coulanges shows,[46] ancient peoples feared the *daimonia* or wrath of the ancestral gods, unleashed by improper burial. Xenophon further underlines the fact that in this instance Socrates stood alone against the decision—how could Holmes have overlooked this fact?—on the ground that the problem of the divine law be taken up within the bounds set by the political law: the generals, who allegedly did not recover all the corpses from the sea, ought to be tried individually. More than did the old piety the political law respected individuals.[47]

Holmes simply obscures such important distinctions. "A *koinonia*," in Latin "*societas*," he notes, "was ordinarily understood as an organic association expressing a corporate bond."[48] This definition is too vague. As Fustel de Coulanges stresses,[49] a *koinonia* was ordinarily understood as the common worship of the same gods. Yet the "conventional Olympian religion" does not prove the "Greek identification of the polity with total society."[50] The Olympic religious festivals were pan-Hellenic, as was the Delphic oracle, to give another illustration. Put simply, there were tensions within the ancient Greek pantheon between the pan-Hellenic gods and the peculiar gods of the different cities, and between these and the various domestic or household gods.[51] In addition, Plato discusses the importance of the cosmic gods, such as the sun and the moon. Anaxagoras was persecuted for impiety in Athens for suggesting the sun was a stone.

We should not lose sight of the fact that the ancients never represented God to themselves as a unique being exercising his action upon the universe. Each of their innumerable gods had his little domain; to one a family belonged, to another tribe, to a third a city.... As to the god of the human race, a few philosophers had an idea of him; the mysteries of Eleusis might have afforded a glimpse of him to the most intelligent of the initiated; but the vulgar never believed in such a god. For ages man understood the divine being only as a force which protected him personally, and every man, or every group of men, desired to have a god.[52]

Holmes is altogether correct that "impiety was a crime against the state."[53] But he fails to consider, first, the different forms of piety, second, that Socrates was put to death on a charge of impiety and, third, that Aristotle in his *Ethics* does not even treat piety as a virtue. The "city-state, as an ideal type," may have been "*relatively* undifferentiated,"[54] but in actual fact Greek society embodied a clash of differing pieties among themselves and with impieties. Greek political life was therefore far more differentiated than Holmes suggests. It seems fair to say that Holmes, the defender of differentiation, shares with ancient polytheism a fear of classical political philosophy because of its interpretation of the divine. Is Holmes as lacking in piety as he seems to believe or to wish to have us believe?[55]

Holmes argues that "the vague politicization of most spheres of social life lent a degree of everyday plausibility to Aristotle's otherwise obscure philosophical claim that all (subordinate) communities are 'parts' of the political community."[56] Yet it was above all the manifest pervasive influence of religion throughout social life, not "the vague politicization of most spheres" that provided the backdrop for Aristotle's claim. The poetic hierarchy of the relations among the gods and their relations with men was replaced by the *novel* philosophic claim of a hierarchy for the most part strictly human. If political participation "had the force of a direct moral imperative"[57] to the Greeks at large, which, if we are to believe Pericles, it did not (Thucydides II. 40. 2), this was grounded in the perception of *civic* piety as the foremost concern of man.[58] Since Holmes strives to counter this civic orientation, and since he seems to disagree with Aristotle's conception of the divine, it looks, from the classical perspective, as though he is, as were most Greeks, mainly concerned with the protection of the domestic gods.

Holmes surely likes the private realm opened up by the modern, ultimately Christian distinction,[59] "so important to Kant, between morality and legality, between inward conviction and outward conformity."[60] In this matter he for once properly distinguishes between Socrates and the Greeks. Yet he fails to clarify the implications as to the liberalism of the classics. He wishes instead to bring out the fact that, according to Aristotle, the importance of habituation to politics justifies the priority of the city. Actually, this is not "yet another justification," but fundamental.[61] Law, understood as political freedom—ruling and being ruled—is the beginning from which and the end to which habituation is directed. Man is the political animal because *nomos*, law or convention, is part of man's *physis* or nature. But if one pays no heed to the pious element in man, to his habitual concerns, this is hard to see. By contrast, Holmes's notion of freedom, of liberalism, is that of the sophist Aristippus, "the alien or rootless freeman" to whom freedom (equals happiness) is "incompatible with both ruling and being ruled."[62] While he sees Aristippus as "vicious" and "self-seeking" (he owned and ruled slaves), his problem was his asociality. Today this problem has been overcome. One can be habituated like Aristippus to an apolitical existence without thereby becoming asocial. Following Kant or Christianity, one can be moral without becoming greatly concerned with law or politics. Moreover, there is apparently no need to be concerned even with domestic conventions, unlike Aristippus, because there is no need to own slaves, presumably thanks to modern technology. Thus Holmes replies to Socrates' rebuttal that "a life without friendship"[63] is quite wretched by pointing to what he suggests is the near self-sufficiency of modern society. Yet, while a handful of Aristippuses could perhaps live in modern society among friends, how could one distinguish a society full of Aristippuses from anarchy? Furthermore, how could such a society avoid turning friendship into slavery? Those who were habituated to ruling and being ruled would become the slaves of the "drones," to use a Platonic expression. The goal of Aristippus is to be irresponsible, even at the cost of rootlessness.[64] I doubt whether Holmes seriously believes that a society of rootless, irresponsible drones could long survive.[65] At any rate, one is forced either to explain Holmes's conception by a naivete similar to that of certain religious believers who live in another world or to assume that Holmes is playfully joking with us, since, on the level of society, responsibilities (*aretai*), conventions (*nomoi*), traditional habits, ruling and being ruled, return. For whether in businesses, universities, churches, families, governments or armies, such empirical facts appear every day. If the scale of politics in certain domains is less broad, less free, or less noble than that of the most enduring political and strategic conceptions, this in no way detracts from, but only accentuates the supremacy of the sphere of a Jefferson, a Lincoln, a Roosevelt, or a Churchill.[66]

Holmes thinks that there is "such a plurality of choices" today that the political versus apolitical alternative is "simplistic."[67] Yet he does not show that the result of these choices differs from an "infinite regress." Nietzsche's charge against the banality of the last man is scarcely refuted. Modern sympathy "for apolitical ideals is based not *so much* on philistinism and superficiality of attitude *as* on a specific set of historical transformations."[68] Does Holmes then admit that such sympathy is *partially* based on unthinking insipidity? Then perhaps such sympathy needs rethinking or thinking. Moreover, Aristotle's theory of politics comprehends both aspects of law or convention, which is hardly surprising. Changing atti-

tudes, i.e., habits, mores and opinions, can cause structural transformations, i.e., changes in formal institutions, just as "structural changes" affect conventions and habits. Holmes has not offered a single reason to
reject the freedom to evaluate Western societies in terms of the extent to
which they are directed to the rule of law, to political freedom and virtue,
and the extent to which they are succumbing to the "religion" of rootlessness and apolitical ideals.

Holmes contends that the rise of Christianity created the "successful
integration" of religion and politics. One secret of "political rationality"
in the West was "the historical unlikelihood of a double totalization" of
religion and politics such as occurred under "Byzantine caesaropapism."[69]
In a similar context, he quotes a modern sociologist to the effect that the
political and religious spheres "are essentially prone to 'totalistic' orienta-
tions."[70] The classics would attribute this to the fact that both spheres are
concerned with man's purpose or that What is just? What is noble? and
What is pious? are essentially controversial questions.[71] Holmes refers us
to Greece and Israel as the model alternative answers to these queries.
Since Holmes is apprehensive of the response of Greece, at least that of
the philosophers, it might seem that he inclines toward the answer of
Israel. But of course he is apprehensive of both alternatives and would
seem to prefer some kind of synthesis. Yet he fails to provide a reasoned
view of the ground or purpose of such a synthesis, one which would
partly reject both crude alternatives. "Bourgeois rights are valued neither because they mysteriously 'inhere' in transhistorical *natura humana*
nor because they 'reflect' our innermost essence, but rather because they
help solve a specific social problem…maintaining and protecting social
differentiation."[72] But if men possess no natural and inalienable rights, if
men are not by nature free and equal, then "social differentiation," a
watered down term for the more lucid *political freedom*, is no problem at
all. "If slavery is right," said Lincoln, "all words, acts, laws and constitutions against it, are themselves wrong, and should be silenced, and swept
away."[73] Like German romanticism, Holmes transforms the natural right
doctrine into a mere ideology, into an untrue or non-serious purpose, in
fact, into an instrument without purpose. Why is political freedom superior to or more choiceworthy than any other ideology? One cannot point
to the "murderous brutality which accompanies fascist and communist
regimes," because for one thing, murder depends on the distinction between either dead or alive and Holmes considers "either/or reasoning"
to entail a "weakness for melodramatic disjunctions."[74] And, for another
reason, since murderous brutality is not against man's nature, nothing
rules it out, unless, according to Holmes, it is against God's will, which
may, thank God, for all we know, be less "mysterious" to him than natural
reason. However that may be, the rise of ideology, the secularization of
religion, the "forgetting" of piety, has made possible and actual—whatever

the "historical unlikelihood"—the "double totalization" of both Fascism and Communism: the partisan political rule of "ideological" priests.

The phrase "double" totalization is of course misleading, because it expresses the balance which Holmes seeks, namely, a question mark. What he fears is single totalization, that is to say, a solution. Yet who has given a deeper analysis of the problematic character of human life than Plato? Holmes is quite mistaken in his belief that the classics thought that politics "can solve all human problems" or that "politics can solve all of humanity's fundamental problems."[75] The *Republic* "solves" the political problem, the question of justice, in a ridiculous, mad, or Aristophanic manner, by obliterating the "subsystem" of the family,[76] which manages only to leave the erotic problem, the question of love, for Plato to take up in his *Banquet*. In this dialogue two gods manifest themselves or, at any rate, a tension shows up between apolitical aesthetic communion generated by eros, which is defended by the poet and accuser of Socrates,[77] Aristophanes,[78] and apolitical noetic communion generated by eros, which is defended by Socrates.[79] Moreover, Aristotle says quite plainly that "it is utopian if one supposes that political wisdom or prudence is the most serious, if man is not the best of the beings in the cosmos."[80] But clearly he considers the problem of the divine being to be of a higher order. As for Strauss's view, it is helpful to reflect on his statements about the insolubility of the Jewish problem, such as the following: "The German-Jewish problem was never solved. It was annihilated by the annihilation of the German Jews."[81] Yet in actual practice, double totalization would mean civil war.[82] Either the rule of politics or the rule of religion must prevail and the other sphere take a subordinate place: the more humane, generous, liberal the rule, the freer the society. Which of these spheres is to predominate, which indeed is more likely to be liberal and to nourish genuine human freedom, constitutes the quarrel between the classics and moderns like Holmes.

Holmes is simply at a loss to say anything about purpose. He makes the classics' "emphasis on duties instead of rights"[83] a function of relative undifferentiation, i.e., relative unfreedom, but he does not demonstrate that rights are more important than duties. During World War II Churchill remarked in regard to the matter of a few weeks' holiday for civil servants (let us paraphrase): how can anyone in such a crisis bear to be away from his duties for an hour? The classics of course would have admitted that especially without crises holy days would arise: thus Aristotle's admonition to make the divine a concern as much as possible. Holmes seems to think that the purpose of a "whole" (community) is to give "moral security and 'warmth' to its constituent parts."[84] Security, according to the classics, is surely one aim of political life, virtue understood as human excellence quite another. What he means by *moral security* is, I suppose, the virtual certainty that one lives among decent people, although its clearest meaning would be the belief in the rule of just gods. As to *"warmth,"* which he sets in quotes in order to indicate, apparently, that he despises it, it is Holmes's aesthetic replacement for the noetic purpose of the classics. But let us add that the term cannot but remind of the domestic hearth.[85] Friendship, like Aristippus, he does not mention. When Holmes says that the downgrading of the political sphere in modernity, the patent consequence, be it noted, of the preeminent concern for rights in contradistinction to virtue, means that "human engagement can only be partial and incomplete,"[86] he merely echoes Aristotle. He even indicates that "modern civic 'uprootedness'" has a much greater problem than did Aristotle in "condemning suicide."[87] Holmes's assault on "either-or" disjunctions,[88] such as good or bad, noble or base, compounds this dilemma. As the confusion over purpose becomes clearer, the wrongness of suicide grows dimmer. This exquisitely unsocial and irresponsible act is indeed the epitome of the "religion" of rootlessness.

"Christianity" and "capitalism" have caused "the whole/part schematization of society" to become, Holmes claims, "definitely anachronistic."[89] Yet how could anything be "definitely" anachronistic unless Holmes knows the future?[90] As it turns out, Holmes is the prophet of the religion of rootlessness. "As a direct result, the basic moral claims found in the political writings of Plato and Aristotle (such as the emphasis on duties instead of rights and the subordination of the individual to a single overarching community) lost their initial core of rationality."[91] Holmes's insight into the will of the liberal Zeus overturns the old rationality. Holmes concludes that "the originally convincing principles of the moral *polis* came to be enlisted in ideological support of what Mill aptly called the moral police." The liberal Zeus, who is a private or household god, will offer no rational support to morality or politics. The religion of love and the religion of greed are not, it would appear from Holmes's account, fond of "the moral police." But what are we to think of the rationality of Christianity and capitalism? Unfortunately, Holmes does not inform us. He merely and perhaps piously takes them for granted. What is more, it seems to be enough to believe that the perpetuation of these institutions is assured if we can only forget the rational origins of more that two millenia of Western civilization. Strikingly, Holmes the romantic acts as if he never heard of romanticism.

Let us conclude with a single remark on the practical implications of his position. Modern principles, according to Holmes, pretend to no superiority over ancient ones, perhaps because all are derivative from the will of Zeus. The dissimilarity stems from this: "the relatively undifferentiated character of the ancient city would have made it absurd to conceive the polity as an expansionistic 'subsystem' which needed to be obstructed from eroding the differentiation of society, that is to say, from repoliticizing religion, economy, art, law, sport and so forth."[92] This statement exemplifies how Holmes's allegedly liberal, but actually romantic heedlessness of piety misconstrues the intent of classical political philosophy. For domestic religion *was* an "expansionistic subsystem" which *always* needs to be prevented, according to the classics, from barbarizing or re-barbarizing religion, economy, art, law, sport, and above all politics. Holmes himself gives us vivid evidence of this point in his anecdote about Giovanni Gentile's account of the homecoming of the Italian soldiers after World War I and of the rise of fascism in Italy: "there was nothing more natural than for those young men to retain their uniforms and set about recasting Italian society in a *familial* mode (with a charismatic *pater patriae*)."[93] Such is not the political freedom of the classical republicanism of Plato and Aristotle, which Holmes considers dangerous, but the still more ancient tyranny of the *oikoi* or of the old houses, now made anew in a rootless, modern world.

Notes

1. *Greek Lyrics* Richard Lattimore, trans. (Chicago: The University of Chicago Press, 1960) pp. 55, 77.

2. *American Political Science Review,* Vol. 73, no. 2 (March, 1979) pp. 113–137. Holmes's article is entitled "Aristippus in and out of Athens," pp. 113–128. James H. Nichols wrote a reply to Holmes, pp. 129–133, and Holmes in turn wrote "A Reply to Nichols," pp. 134–137. All references to Holmes are to this journal.

3. However disdainful Nichols may be of Holmes's misreading of classical thought, Holmes notes that by arguing with him—by his action, we could say—"Nichols admits the disputable and hence nontrival character of my (Holmes's) analysis." Holmes, p. 134. It does not seem to me that Nichols has clearly enough brought out why it is nontrivial or, as one might say, what we have to learn from Holmes.

4. Cf. his *Spinoza's Critique of Religion* (New York: Schocken Books, 1965), pp. 332, 351, and "Preface," pp. 1–31, also printed in his *Liberalism: Ancient and Modern* (New York: Basic Books, 1968) pp 224–257; and his *Thoughts on Machiavelli* (Seattle: University of Washington Press, 1969) p. 173.

5. Cf. Nietzsche, "On the Thousand and One Goals," *Thus Spoke Zarathustra* Pt. I, ch. 15.

6. Holmes, p. 114, n. 3.

7. (Ithaca: Cornell University Press, 1963) pp. 194–195.

8. Holmes, p. 115.

9. (Chicago: Rand McNally, 1964) p. 63; cf. pp. 127, 129.

10. Holmes, p. 115.

11. Holmes, p. 117. As though hens could stop the feisty Hitler! But the manly Churchill did. After Britain had held out valiantly for two years against Nazi attacks, even though it had been predicted that Hitler would wring the neck of the British chicken in a matter of weeks, Churchill crowed: "Some chicken! Some neck!"

12. Why does Holmes place the term *totalitarian* in inverted commas unless he has no reason to oppose such regimes?!

13. Holmes, p. 117.

14. (Chicago: The University of Chicago Press, 1953) pp. 252–54, 277–78, 293–94.

15. pp 2225–226. Cf. Harry V. Jaffa's comment on Strauss's work in his *The Conditions of Freedom* (Baltimore: The Johns Hopkins University Press, 1975) p. 6: "Hitler's romantic longing for the Middle Ages was an irrational longing for a noble past purged of the reality its struggle with reason and revelation. The Jewish problem was, in the end, the human problem."

16. Holmes, p. 117.
17. Holmes, p. 117.
18. Holmes, p. 118.
19. Xenophon *Memorabilia* I 1.1–2; Plata *Apology* 19b; 23d.
20. Holmes, p. 118.
21. Socrates was accused of being a "busybody"; *Apology* 19b.
22. Holmes, p. 118.
23. Holmes, n. 14.
24. Holmes, p. 119.
25. Holmes, p. 119.
26. Holmes, p. 119.
27. Holmes, p. 119
28. Holmes, p. 120.
29. Holmes, p. 120.
30. Holmes, p. 120.
31. On the difference between the two forms of piety, consult Fustel de Coulanges, *The Ancient City*, especially I 4, III 3 and 6, a book which Holmes cites.
32. *The Ancient city* III 3; cf. Thucydides II 15–16.
33. Holmes, p. 116, n. 7.
34. Holmes, p. 120.
35. Holmes, p. 113, n. 2.
36. "On Human Prudence," *Thus Spoke Zarathustra* Pt. II, ch. 21.
37. Holmes, p. 120.
38. *Ethics 1177*b 24.
39. Holmes, p. 120, n. 26. cf. *Ethics 1177*b 24.
40. p. 49.
41. Holmes, p. 122; cf. pp. 115, 118.
42. *Plato's Apology* John Burnet, ed. (Oxford: At the Clarendon Press, 1967) p. 90; Gilbert Murray, *A History of Ancient Greek Literature* (New York: Frederick Ungar Publishing Co., 1966) pp. 175–176. I can discern no special reason to agree with Murray that the poet Meletus was "probably a fanatic," if by that he means to distinguish him as being inordinately susceptible to the "religious terrors" to which the body of the *demos* was "keenly awake." Besides, the threat of "divine vengeance" may be real. At least, so the modern rationalist Thomas Jefferson thought. Contemplating the existence of slavery in the United States Jefferson, in his *Notes on Virginia*, said: "I tremble for my country when I reflect that God is just."
43. Seventh Letter 324d–325a.
44. Fustel, III 17, quoted by Holmes, p. 122, n. 31.
45. Fustel, III 17, quoted by Holmes, p. 122.
46. Fustel, I.2.
47. Compare the similar instance at Teheran when Churchill walked off from the conference table over Stalin's suggestion that the Allies round up and "summarily execute" 50,000 Nazis and did not return until the idea was dropped. Winston S. Churchill, *Closing the Ring* (Boston: Houghton Mifflin Company, 1951) pp. 373–374. Since this incident concerned enemies, not fellow citizens, we must say that Churchill here appealed to the natural law.
48. Holmes, p. 122.
49. Fustel, III 6.
50. Holmes, p. 122.
51. Cf. Fustel, III 6: "because two cities happened to apply the same name to their god, we are not to conclude that they adored the same god. There was an Athena at Athens and there was one at Sparta; but they were two goddesses." On pan-Hellenic religion, compare Thucydides' mention of the war "called sacred" over control of the temple at Delphi (I. 112.5); the Spartans' exclusion from sanctuary, sacrifices and games at an

Olympian festival during the Peloponnesian war—note the reference to "the Olympic law" (V 49); and the Athenians' discovery of the plans about Chios at an Isthmian festival in Corinth which took place during that war (VIII 10).

52. Fustel, III 6.
53. Holmes, p. 122.
54. Holmes, p. 122.
55. Cf. Holmes, p. 119.
56. Holmes, p. 123.
57. Holmes, p. 123.
58. Religion presents moral imperatives; "Thou shalt not . . ." Aristotle's arguments are conditional; "If you would be happy . . ." See Harry V. Jaffa, *Equality and Liberty* (New York: Oxford University Press, 1965) pp. 204–205. "The ancient law never gave any reasons. Why should it? . . . it existed because the gods had made it." Fustel de Coulanges, III 11. Cf Nietzsche "The Problem of Socrates," *Twilight of the Idols*, aph. 5 and Plato *Republic* 331d, where the pious Cephalus leaves laughing at Socratic dialogue. Nietzsche sympathizes with Aristophanes' ridicule of Socrates in the *Clouds*. He agrees but also disagrees with the poets: "On Poets," *Thus Spoke Zarathustra*, Pt. II, ch. 17, a dialogue on why "we" poets "lie too much" or on the problem of "memory." The Greek word for "truth," *aletheia*, means in its component parts, *not forgotten*, i.e., *unforgetting*. Let us recall Holmes' poetic advice to forget.
59. Cf. Holmes, p. 126, n. 47.
60. Holmes, p. 123.
61. Cf. Simonides, "The city is the teacher of the man." *Greek Lyric Poetry* Willis Barnstone, trans. (New York: Schocken Books, 1972) p. 137. One would have to start from the importance of habituation to understand the "amusing claim" (Holmes, p. 116) that the classics anticipated "modernization" and rejected it in advance. Xenophon's Socrates does his best to teach moderation (*Memorabilia* I. 2.14–18.) prior to rhetoric, which, to the extent it is morally neutral, becomes a two-edged sword that prefigures the self-destruction of modern rationality: Aristophanes' Socrates, who forgets the city while teaching rhetoric, has his "think-tank" burned down by a former student. One could learn a good bit merely by following throughout the pages of Thucydides the impious and problematic character of "anticipation" itself, *prokatalambein*, as it implies an amoral knowledge (science) which is *practical* to boot, i.e., applied, as opposed to theoretical. "Anticipation," "grasping beforehand," or "apprehending beforehand," rooted in the "effectual truth," to use Machiavelli's phrase, of factionalism (*stasis*) and ultimately in the passion of *philonikein* or Machiavellian "private competitiveness," tends in practice toward the dissolution of trust and toward savagery or, to say the least, toward lowered human standards—Thucydides III 82. This chapter and its context, a scathing and penetrating account of revolutionary innovation, displays most vividly the classic view of amoral applied science, of "carrying thoughts far to the extreme of modernization (*kainousthai*)," both in "super-artfulness (*peri-technesei*) of assaults," eg., the modern nuclear weapons systems, which happen to be available to barbarians thanks to technology, and in "utopianism of revenges," eg., the mass murders committed by the Nazis and Communists, which were in no small part facilitated by technology. What Thucydides lacks in detail he envisions or anticipates most lucidly in principle or in *theoria*.
62. Holmes, p. 124.
63. Holmes, p. 124.
64. "I do not shut myself up in the four corners of a *politeia* but am a stranger in every land." Xenophon, *Memorabilia* II 1.13. Cf. Fustel de Coulanges, II 9: "In Plutarch's time they still said to the egoist, You sacrifice to the hearth. This signified, You separate yourself from other citizens; you have no friends; your fellow-men are nothing to you; you live solely for yourself and yours. This proverb pointed to a time when, all religion

being around the hearth, the horizon of morals and of affection had not yet passed beyond the narrow circle of the family."

65. If the sociology that Holmes prefers teaches that "independence and interdependence" always "increase simultaneously" (Holmes, p. 134, n.1), and if this means that individual freedom depends on political freedom, that political freedom depends on political responsibility, and that political responsibility in turn depends on individual freedom or the choice of virtue, if freedom is good for man, as Holmes contends, then man is political as Aristotle states.

66. Though Holmes may seem, by the time he answers Nichols, not to "conceive the political system as 'equal' to all other sectors of society" (Holmes, p. 134, n. 1), and thus to cast doubt on whether he ultimately disagrees with Aristotle, his disagreement is sustained by his use of inverted commas around the term *equal,* implying that all such evaluations are relative and ultimately equal.

67. Holmes, p. 124.

68. Holmes, p. 124 (Italics added).

69. Holmes, p. 125.

70. Holmes, pp. 135–136, n.3.

71. Cf. Plato *Euthyphro* 7 b–e.

72. Holmes, p. 135.

73. *Cooper Union Address,* 1860.

74. Holmes, p. 136.

75. Holmes, pp. 113–114.

76. Cf. Holmes, p. 116, where Holmes states that totalitarianism desires "to swallow 'subsystems,'" but then goes on to add, "there could not have been any Greek totalitarianism." It seems we must re-evaluate Plato's powers of anticipation, however "amusing" the thought! See note 61 above. Aristotle, to be sure, in his comment on the *Republic (Politics* II ch. 2–5) soberly explains that in fact communism is the sub-system of the family swallowing up the political sphere. In a word, communism no less than Fascism is fundamentally familial or racist.

77. Cf. Plato *Apology* 19c.

78. Holmes says (Holmes, p. 127) that in Greece "art was largely civic art, religion was civic religion." Hegel, whom Holmes calls "Athenian at heart" (p. 123, n. 35), identifies Greek religion with art religion and treats Aristophanes' comedies as the culmination of Greek religion—cf. "Comic Poetry," *Aesthetics* and "Religion as a Form of Art," *Phenomenology of the Mind.* Considering Holmes' mocking of piety (cf. p. 119 top right) while at the same time apparently defending it, one could perhaps be led to wonder if Holmes, imitating ancient comedy, is not more civic-minded than Socrates.

79. Holmes acknowledges (Holmes, p. 118, n. 14) that the supposition of Plato's enthusiasm for politics "must be modified, of course, by consideration of the solitary, almost entranced, quality of Platonic *noesis* and the small-scale and apolitical character of Socratic *elenchos.*" He is to be admired for not running altogether roughshod over the points which counteract his case. Thus he sees (pp. 118–119) that "if we abstract for a moment from Plato's appeal to the timeless Forms" we can more readily inveigh against Plato's supposed political enthusiasm.

80. *Ethics* 1141a 21–23.

81. *Liberalism: Ancient and Modern* pp. 227–231.

82. Cf. Holmes, p. 126, n. 50 on "that arch anti-Aristotelian" Hobbes and his agreement with Aristotle.

83. Holmes, p. 126.

84. Holmes, p. 126.

85. See note 64 above.

86. Holmes, n. 46.

87. Holmes, n. 48.

88. Holmes, p. 136.
89. Holmes, p. 127.
90. On page 113 Holmes says "essentially anachronistic," which carries the same implication. Yet, by the time he makes his reply to Nichols in the subsequent debate, his faith may have been slightly shaken. At any rate, at that point he merely says "wildly anachronistic" (p. 134). Cf. Matthew 27:46.
91. Holmes, p. 127.
92. Holmes, p. 136.
93. Holmes, p. 137. (Italics added to "familial.")

23

FROM FACTIONS TO PARTIES
AMERICA'S PARTISAN EDUCATION

Donald V. Weatherman

Factions stir the passions of men, but parties introduce the conflict of opinion.
FREDERICK GRIMKE

HAS AMERICA'S PARTY SYSTEM BECOME OBSOLETE? BEFORE RENDERING judgment, let us consider the past nature and functions of political parties. There is no shortage of printed matter on this topic, but previous works, with surprisingly few exceptions, have either ignored or misinterpreted some of the most pertinent aspects of the history of our party system.

Historians and political scientists alike have failed to distinguish between the origin of American party politics and the origin of America's party system. They have over-emphasized the former at the expense of the latter, and this oversight has caused many students of politics to view America's party history as a sequence of different party systems (e.g., the Jeffersonian party system, the Jacksonian party system, and the Lincolnian party system). Such categorization provides a valuable and convenient, albeit somewhat oversimplified, blueprint of America's party history. Implicit in such categorization is the understanding that there is no significant distinction among these systems; there are new players and new issues, but little else has changed. This approach to the study of political parties has helped produce some of the confusion which has contributed to our inability to recognize their overall importance. By retracing the origins of America's party system, some of the important differences between the so-called Jeffersonian and Jacksonian "party systems" will emerge. Clarification of these differences should produce a better understanding of the multifaceted role that parties have played in the American political system.

Richard Hofstadter's *The Idea of a Party System* is one of the premier historical accounts of the origins and development of America's party system. Most works on the origins of our party system concentrate exclusively on the events that led to Jefferson's victory in 1800. Hofstadter, by contrast, considers the development of political parties into the 1840s. But while he acknowledges that the ideas and actions of the 1820s signaled a new period in the development of parties, it is not clear that he ever comprehends the full importance of that period. Hofstadter clearly recognizes the critical periods in our party development and he has an admirable grasp of the different attitudes and beliefs that prevailed during these periods; what he lacks is a recognition of the broader implications of the philosophical foundation of these attitudes and beliefs.

Retracing America's party development requires that we cover some fairly common ground; however, I hope that some new observations made along this familiar path will provide a better understanding of the essential function of political parties.

There appear to be three overlapping yet discernible stages in the maturation of the American party system. The first of these can be readily identified as the anti-party stage. The first two chapters of Hofstadter's work consider this stage, yet he fails to note its most important aspect: that parties in the 1770s and 1780s were nothing more than interest groups; they were indistinguishable from factions and were considered the greatest threat to our young republic. The two best known, if not the clearest expressions of thought on this first stage are James Madison's *Federalist* 10 and George Washington's *Farewell Address*. Madison believed that "curing the violent effects of faction" was the most difficult task before the founders; Washington dreaded nothing more than the "baneful effects of the spirit of party." They were not alone in this belief. Thomas Jefferson is often quoted; "If I could not go to heaven but with a political party, I would not go there at all."

Madison and Washington provided a more detailed explanation of the arguments and attitudes which produced this strong anti-party feeling. In *Federalist* 10, Madison argued: "Complaints are everywhere heard from our most considerate and virtuous citizens, equally the friends of public and private faith, and of public and personal liberty; that our governments are too unstable; that the public good is disregarded in the conflict of rival parties." His definition of parties or factions further clarified this understanding of them:

By a faction, I mean, a number of citizens, whether amounting to a majority or a minority of the whole, who are united and actuated by some common impulse or passion, or of interest, adverse to the rights of other citizens, or to the permanent and aggregate interest of the community.

This narrow definition of party was further refined:

...the most common and durable source of factions, has been the various and unequal distribution of property. Those who hold, and those who are without property, have ever formed distinct interests in society....A landed interest, a manufacturing interest, a mercantile interest, a monied interest, with many lesser interests, grow up of necessity in civilized nations.

Washington's *Farewell Address* emphasized some different aspects of parties, but managed to reach a similar conclusion. Washington's primary concern was with parties of "geographical discriminations," yet all parties are to be feared because they may be used to destroy the constitutional power of the people. He claimed that parties "serve to organize faction, to give it an artificial and extraordinary force; to put in the place of the delegated will of the Nation, the will of a party; often a small but artful and enterprising minority of the Community." The foremost characteristic of parties during this first stage of development is that they are always in opposition to the permanent and general interest of the community. Usually, parties are designed to increase the personal gain of their members; these selfish policies are to be pursued with little or no regard to the interest of other segments of the society. We can sum up this earliest view of parties by calling them greedy, selfcentered, and myopic. Such a pessimistic view of parties meshes with the cynical tone set by the *Federalist Papers* in general.

Hofstadter's second chapter, "A Constitution against Parties," takes on new meaning once we have clarified the understanding of "parties" that existed during the constitutional writing and ratification period. Hofstadter criticizes Madison for not realizing what parties might become:

Envisaging political parties as limited, homogeneous, fiercely aggressive, special interests, he failed to see that parties themselves might become great, bland, enveloping coalitions, eschewing the assertion of firm principles and ideologies, embracing and muffling the struggles of special interests; or that they might forge the coalitions of majorities that are in fact necessary to effective government into forces sufficiently benign to avoid tyranny and sufficiently vulnerable to be displaced in time by the opposing coalition.[1]

Hindsight is a wonderful thing, yet Hofstader himself seems to be the person at fault for not recognizing how important this stage was to the later development of political parties. Indeed, the passions and factions Madison described in *Federalist* 10 have continued to exist. To argue that such factions "might become great" implies that the "special interests" which produced them would cease to be "actuated by some common impulse of passion"; this has not happened. While the "limited, homogeneous, fiercely aggressive, special interests" Madison described are still with us today, they have not become political parties as Hofstadter implies. Nevertheless, the motives that produce these special interests cannot be ignored by political parties. They are an important feature of parties, but only one feature.

The maturation of parties into something beyond mere factions characterized the second stage of party development. As political tensions widened the gaps between different groups in the government, Madison and others began to realize the short-sightedness of their belief that the public good is always disregarded "in the conflict of rival parties." Indeed, they began to recognize that there were times when a partisan movement was essential to preserve the public good. Surely, Madison and Jefferson did not believe that their activities in the 1790s were "actuated by some common impulse of passion, or of interest, adverse to the rights of other citizens, or to the permanent and aggregate interest of the community." In light of this realization, their old beliefs about parties proved inadequate.

Jefferson and Madison's "new" understanding of parties was little more than an acknowledgment that the oldest form of partisan division, the one most of the founders felt would be avoided by the establishment of a truly popular government, did exist in the United States. In his later years, a reflective Jefferson wrote to John Adams: "We broke into two parties, each wishing to give the government a different direction; the one to strengthen the most popular branch, the other the more permanent branch, and to extend its permanence."[2] Jefferson further indicated that these parties are natural and that "the terms of Whig and Tory belong to natural as well as to civil history."[3]

What is significant about this stage in the development of political parties is that it is a transitional period—a kind of adolescence. The transformation was considerable: the strong anti-party rhetoric mitigated, and two of the most outspoken opponents of parties were now recognized leaders of a partisan movement. Yet there was still no mass movement to embrace partisan division as a desirable element of popular government. The renewed understanding of the nature of parties still did not make them popular.

The second stage of party development produced a very ambivalent attitude toward parties, which had at least two causes. In the 1770s and 1780s, parties or factions did tend to be of a "geographical discrimination" and focused on concerns other than the national interest. There was a strong propensity toward personalized, seemingly self-serving factions; the Burrites and Clintonians are but two examples. By the 1790s, however, it was recognized that these were not the only kind of opinions that produced partisan divisions. What distinguished Federalists from Republicans was not impulse, passion, or interest, in the narrowest sense, but rather a conflicting notion of the kind of interpretation needed to make the new Constitution succeed. Each side believed its position to be the only one that could preserve our popular institutions. With this new, philosophical foundation, parties became something quite discernible from mere factions.

The second cause of ambivalence toward parties was the decline of the Federalists. During this second stage of Party development, we find the practice but not the advocacy of party politics, because the partisan conflict of the period was viewed as a passing event in American politics.

Jefferson and his followers considered the partisan battle of 1800 to be as important as the battle of 1776. For Jefferson, the Republican victory of 1800 signaled a philosophical break from English Royalism. Indeed, Jefferson believed that his election accomplished in fact what the Revolutionary War had accomplished symbolically: a full and complete break from English domination.

According to Jefferson, some members of the Federalist party were nothing more than Tories cloaked in American rhetoric. The fundamental difference between Republicans and Federalists was whether "the power of the people or that of the aristoi should prevail."[4] The Federalists were clearly at odds with the principles of the new Constitution. In a letter to Benjamin Rush, Jefferson wrote:

You remember the machinery which the federalists played off...to beat down the friends of the real principles of our Constitution, to silence by terror every expression in their favor, to bring us into war with France and alliance with England, and finally to homologize our Constitution with that of England.[5]

Generally, Republicans believed that the election of 1800 kept the Federalists from institutionalizing an American monarchy; if the Federalist could be thwarted for a few years, the Republicans would have no trouble sustaining their control over American government. This sentiment, which is found in Jefferson's First Inaugural Address, received its most succinct expression in a letter to Madison:

I know there are those among us, who would now establish a monarchy. But they are inconsiderable in number and weight of character. The rising race are all republicans. We were educated in royalism; no wonder, if some of us retain that idolatry still. Our young people are educated in republicanism; an apostasy from that to royalism is unprecedented and impossible.[6]

The Federalists, then, were simply the last vestige of a passing era —those who preferred the security of the past to the hope of the future. However, Jefferson apparently believed that once the transition was made from the old era to the new, from royalism to republicanism, something akin to Washington's unanimity would again emerge.

For this reason, stage two parties, like those of stage one, were quite different from the political parties that eventually evolved. Two differences can immediately be discerned. First, Jefferson used the word "party" in its most general sense. To him, the Federalists and Republicans were not two legitimate political organizations competing for control of the governmental apparatus; they were simply the names Americans had given to the two natural political opinions that occur in every society but are openly voiced in those nations which tolerate freedom of expression. As such, these parties are truly philosophical parties.[7] Second, that these opinions were natural made them neither equally desirable nor in the best interest of republican government. This is why Jefferson's First Inaugural Address called for "the union of opinion which gives to a nation the blessing of harmony and the benefit of all its strength." With this interpretation, the position of all true American patriots was recognized as a partisan position, and yet there was only one acceptable partisan position; all others fell into the category decried by Washington and Madison during stage one.

Stage two produced what is generally considered to be the origin of party politics in America. Yet it is clear from Jefferson's First Inaugural Address and other statements by him which we have cited that a party system was neither anticipated nor desired. The one-party politics espoused by Jefferson was obviously a by-product of the Enlightenment. Thus, Hofstadter is only half-right when he argues:

> Gone, now that Madison is a party leader, are the old references to the turbulence and violence of faction. Gone too, now that Madison is the leader of a party which he is convinced can soon well command the loyalty of an overwhelming majority, are his speculations about the best way to check the most dangerous of all factions, the majority faction.[8]

Hofstadter is accurate in his assertion that Madison was no longer concerned about the "violence of faction" or the potential power of "the majority faction" because the Constitution he was advocating in 1787 had been ratified. With this ratification came all of the auxiliary precautions that Madison credited to the new Constitution, and these institutional checks and balances obviated his concern over the "violence of faction." Simply stated, having argued that the Constitution would eliminate the problem of a majority faction, Madison was not inconsistent to cease worrying about majority faction once the Constitution had been adopted.

Furthermore, as we noted earlier, since parties were no longer synonymous with factions, the party Madison led in the 1790s and later was not a faction. Hofstadter errs, therefore, when he accuses Madison of modifying "his theoretical system;" in reality, it was America's understanding of the nature of parties which had changed and would continue to change.

The founding of America's party system fell upon the next political generation. This third stage in our partisan development was distinct from the second, in part because we find party politics being practiced and even defended. Here we see arguments attached to actions, and —even more important—the ideas expressed not only justify but also improve partisan activity. The paramount difference between the two political generations was captured by Van Buren's declaration:

In a government like ours, founded upon freedom in thought and action, imposing no unnecessary restraints, and calling into exercise the highest energies of the mind, occasional differences of opinion are not only to be expected, but to be desired. They rouse the sluggish to exertion, give increased energy to the most active intellect, excite a salutary vigilance over our public functionaries, and prevent that apathy which has proved the ruin of Republics.[9]

These "occasional differences of opinion" were of consummate importance to Van Buren and his teachings on political parties. Political parties become the superintendents of these differences and, as such, have the responsibility for insuring that the opinions over which people differ are those which produce a "salutary" effect upon the overall workings of governments.

What characterized this third stage of development was more than just a defense of practice; indeed, the changes that took place in party activities were the product of two significant factors. The first and most obvious was a more complete understanding of the potentials of party politics; the second factor was a significant change in public opinion and, therefore, the responsibilities confronting political parties and their reciprocal relationship to that opinion.

In his *Inquiry into the Origin and Course of Political Parties in the United States*, Van Buren explained how the early development and practice of party politics influenced American government; he argued that this influence was one of the most positive aspects of our early political development. Echoing many of the views expressed earlier by Jefferson and Madison, Van Buren took their arguments a step further because, to some extent, he was faced with a new challenge: the maintenance or, as Lincoln described it, "the perpetuation of our political institutions." The political problems that developed primarily during the administrations of James Monroe and John Quincy Adams made Van Buren realize that the threat facing America was quite different once the revolutionary zeal had abated.

Van Buren believed that the establishment and maintenance of a permanent party system were crucial to the establishment and maintenance of popular government. The ill-named "Era of Good Feeling" produced a false sense of security, rendering the public sluggish and indifferent and leading to uncertainty and political stagnation. If this

were not justification enough of a permanent party system, Van Buren
further pointed out that lack of public supervision allows those in power
to abuse their power:

But knowing, as all men of sense know, that political parties are
inseparable from free governments, and that in many and material
respects they are highly useful to the country, I never could bring myself
for party purposes to deprecate their existence.... The disposition to
abuse power, so deeply planted in the human heart, can by no other
means be more effectively checked; and it has always therefore struck
me as more honorable and manly and more in harmony with the
character of the People and our Institutions to deal with the subject of
Political Parties in a sincere and wiser spirit—to recognize their
necessity, to give them the credit they deserve, and to devote ourselves to
improve and to elevate the principles and objects of our own and to
support it ingenuously and faithfully.[10]

The natural spirit of parties was finally recognized as permanent.
Van Buren's reverence for Jefferson was probably what kept him from
pointing out the absurdity of Jefferson's position on political parties.
How Jefferson ever convinced himself that he was the founder of the
party to end all parties, when he also believed that party divisions are a
natural part of all free societies is quite perplexing. What Hofstadter
refers to as Van Buren's heresy is really no more than an acceptance of
the full consequences of the belief that parties are a natural part of free
societies.[11] From this standpoint, the only possible justification for the
orthodox Jeffersonian position would be a belief in the "new science of
politics" conquering the old nature of politics. This was clearly the
position expressed by James Monroe in an 1816 letter to Andrew
Jackson. After acknowledging the existence of parties in the ancient
republics and England, Monroe argued that their presence was due to
"certain defects of those Governments" and that "we have happily
avoided these defects in our system." He concluded by declaring:

[To] exterminate all party divisions in our country and give new
strength and stability to our Government, is a great undertaking, not
easily executed. I am nevertheless decidedly of the opinion that it may
be done, and should the experiment fail, I shall conclude, that its failure
was imputable, more to the want of a correct knowledge of all circumstances claiming attentions, and of sound judgment in the measure
adopted, than to any other cause.[12]

Van Buren opposed this position on all counts: not only is it impossible
to rid popular government of political parties, but, even if it were
possible, such actions would be undesirable.

The advantages Van Buren attributed to healthy party competition
are directly related to the natural causes of party divisions. In the first
chapter of his book on the origin of political parties, Van Buren attacked

the opinion that party divisions in America originated over the "conflicting prejudices and preferences of the people for and against Great Britain and France at the commencement of the present government."[13] Such attempts at attaching party development to some single controversy or set of controversies were grossly misleading:

> Party divisions which have extended to every corner of a country as large as our own, and have endured so long, could not spring from slight or even limited causes.[14]

All such temporary issues are either settled or lose their interest, and the organizations which grow out of these issues are "equally short-lived."[15] Political parties in America are the result of radical differences of opinion on fundamental political issues such as the proper form of government, how governments should be administered, the best way to promote the happiness of citizens, and, most important of all, "the capacity of the people for self-government." With such issues at the heart of America's partisan division, Van Buren concluded that "we may well look for party divisions and political organizations of a deeper foundation and a more enduring existence."[16] This should not, however, be interpreted to mean that specific controversies or transient issues are not an important part of partisan controversies. A note of caution was present in Van Buren's analysis of the first partisans: "The foundation of preferences and prejudices in respect to England and France, was, no doubt, true, but to suppose that these constituted the foundation of their own divisions is to mistake for the cause one of its least important effects."[17]

The perceived cause of party division remained unchanged from the second to the third stage of our party development. What did change was the expected outcome of the party division. Jefferson expected that the party battle between the Federalists and Republicans would expose the Federalists for what they really were, which would ultimately lead to their total and complete abolition. In a sense, Jefferson was right. The Federalist party did die. Van Buren, however, recognized that the demise of the Federalist party was not caused by the victory of republicanism over royalism; what really ended the Federalist party was the willingness of Republican administrations to adopt Federalist policies.

Jefferson's victory in 1800 was a genuine Republican victory: complete in that the Republican Party won and republican principles won. The later Republican victories, while more decisive in terms of a winning margin, were less decisive in terms of principles. Van Buren believed that the Republican victories of J. Q. Adams and Monroe were not the product of America's increased education in republicanism. (This was especially true of Monroe's sweep of the Electoral College in 1820.) If anything, the elections of Adams and Monroe were the product of compromised principles which produced policies that were designed to offer something to everyone. Monroe's amalgamation policy could only come about by compromising the Republican creed. Van Buren observed:

We shall find as a general rule that among the native inhabitants of each State, the politics of families who were federalists during the War of 1812, are the same now—holding, for the most part, under the name of Whigs, to the political opinions and governed by the feelings of their ancestors.[18]

The move to reestablish party competition in the 1820s was motivated by two distinct yet interrelated desires. The first of these was the reaffirmation of the "pure and self-denying" principles of the old Republican party.[19] According to Van Buren, the majority of the American people have always decided in favor of the Republican creed when they were presented with a clear choice: "That creed required only that unity among its friends should be preserved to make it the ark of their political safety."[20] A clear demarcation between political principles is all that is required to produce that unity. Like Jefferson, Van Buren considered all partisan struggles in America to be little more than a continuation —or an effect—of the original partisan battle between Hamilton and Jefferson.[21] In this light, partisan antagonism exists between those who support special or exclusive privileges and those who support the principles of the United States Constitution.[22] Since the former group is invariably smaller in number, it is to its advantage to denigrate party competition and to blur party distinctions. It was this belief that produced Van Buren's strong opposition to James Monroe and John Quincy Adams. To him, their fusion or amalgamation policies posed a greater threat to the old republican creed than did open antagonists like Daniel Webster and Henry Clay.

Van Buren's belief that the partisan division in America was between the landed interests and the moneyed interests or, as he put it, "between those who live by the sweat of their brow and those who live by their wits," led him to a different conclusion than Jefferson had reached. Since the moneyed interests rely on special privileges and are usually concentrated in the cities, they have no need for caucuses and conventions "to preserve harmony in [their] ranks."[23] On the other hand, the landed interests which consist of farmers, planters, and laborers, have a definite need for such unifying or harmonizing devices. For this reason, politicians who call for an end to party battles and refuse to cooperate with the party organization are undermining the only institution that allows the "large majority of the people" to check the "influence of the money power." Van Buren believed that political organizations were the savior of republican government. Political organizations would educate the majority of the people, but not in the manner described by Jefferson. Van Buren realized that political education was an ongoing process; it could not, as Jefferson thought, be accomplished once and for all. In this sense, Van Buren was more of a student of Jefferson's actions than he was of Jefferson's words.[24]

The second lesson Van Buren posited for reestablishing party competition was that such competition has a moderating effect on the political system. When they function properly, political parties curb the appetites of political aspirants and provide positive direction for the energy of the political masses.

Political aspirants who realize that their future depends on the success of the political organization will find it easier to suppress personal animosities than will those who place their personal ambition before all else. Van Buren took this argument a step further and declared that the most successful individuals have been those who place party harmony before personal gain:

A review of the history and fact of parties and factions will shew that it has been those...who refrained the most from suffering their personal feelings from being inflamed by their political rivalries and were most willing to leave the question of their individual advancement to the quiet and friendly arbitrament of their political associates have in the end been the most successful.[25]

This attribute, which recalls Tocqueville's self–interest rightly understood, is a general characteristic of political parties. Not only is it more noble to work for a political organization which stands for timeless principles than to work for one's own personal gain, but it is easier to extract political concessions and compromises when the battles are of a less personal nature.

Van Buren believed that this has a positive effect on regional antagonisms as well. He sincerely felt that a strong two-party system was the perfect cure for America's sectional rivalries. As he stated in a letter to Thomas Ritchie on January 13, 1827:

Party attachment in former times furnished a complete antidote for sectional prejudices by producing counteracting feelings....Formerly, attacks upon Southern Republicans were regarded by those of the north as assaults upon their political brethren and resented accordingly.[26]

Granted, political parties do not insure that all politicians will place party principles before personal gain, but they at least provide an incentive for doing so. In those less noble politicians not motivated by principle, the lure of patronage (provided it is allocated along party lines) will often produce the desired behavior.

Patronage, according to Van Buren, strengthens our democratic institutions by "giving full effect to the will of the majority." Van Buren defended Jefferson's patronage policy by arguing that it carried the spirit of the majority's preference into every branch of the public service. Thus, patronage should not be used to punish "obnoxious opinions" or to "gratify personal antipathies," but "to give full effect to the will of the majority, submission to which [Jefferson and Van Buren] regarded as the vital principle of our Government."[27]

Clearly, the third stage of America's party development, that which establishes an ongoing party system, was motivated by interests quite distinct from anything cited in Hofstadter's work. Hofstadter's subtitle, "The Rise of Legitimate Opposition in the United States," is wide of the mark. The notion of "legitimate opposition" was foreign to all of the political figures he discusses in his work. The phrase was as much an oxymoron to Van Buren as it was to Washington, Madison, and Jefferson. Van Buren encouraged opposition because of its illegitimacy. As long as the opponents of the old republican principles are organized and active, he argued, the majority of Americans will rally in support of our true principles; it is only when the choice is not clear that we make the wrong or bad decisions.

Van Buren further realized that the driving passions behind both stage one and stage two parties would continue to be a permanent part of American politics. He understood the desires which had produced each stage and realized that the most difficult task of our party system would be to reconcile the petty interests of the former with the highly principled interests of the latter.[29]

Notes

1. Richard Hofstadter, *The Idea of a Party System* (Berkeley: University of California Press, 1969), pp. 72–73.
2. Adrienne Koch and William Peden, eds., *The Life and Selected Writings of Thomas Jefferson* (New York: The Modern Library, 1944), p. 628.
3. Ibid.
4. Ibid., p. 637
5. Ibid., p. 609.
6. Ibid., p. 464
7. Two works that definitively establish the philosophical schools that parallel these parties are Harry V. Jaffa, *Equality and Liberty* (New York: Oxford University Press, 1965), especially Chapter 1, and John Zvesper, *Political Philosophy and Rhetoric* (Cambridge: Cambridge University Press, 1977).
8. Hofstadter, p. 84.
9. *The Autobiography of Martin Van Buren*, John C. Fitzpatrick, (Washington, D.C.: Government Printing Office, 1920), p. 512.
10. *Autobiography*, p. 125.
11. Hofstadter, p. 226.
12. John Spencer Bassett, ed., *Correspondence of Andrew Jackson* (Washington, D.C.: Carnegie Institution of Washington, 1929), II, 268.
13. Martin Van Buren, *Inquiry into the Origin and Course of Political Parties in the United States* (New York: Hurd and Houghton, 1867), p. 10.

14. Ibid.
15. Ibid.
16. Ibid., p. 11.
17. Ibid., p. 270
18. *Autobiography*, p. 125.
19. Ibid., p. 313.
20. Ibid., p. 124. See also Van Buren, *Origin and Course*, pp. 267, 349.
21. Van Buren, *Origin and Course*, p. 237.
22. Ibid., p. 224.
23. Ibid., p. 226
24. Ibid., pp. 221–23. Hofstadter covers Monroe's position on this topic in his chapter "The Quest for Unanimity." See also Robert V. Remini, *Martin Van Buren and the Democratic Party* (New York: Columbia University Press, 1959), especially Chapters II and VIII.
25. *Autobiography* p. 519n.
26. Martin Van Buren Papers, Library of Congress.
27. *Autobiography*, p. 123.
28. January 20, 1813, Martin Van Buren Papers.
29. I would like to thank the Earhart Foundation for funding most of the research and writing of this paper.

24

TIME OUT OF MIND
BURKE'S CONSTITUTION

Francis Canavan, S.J.

ONE OF THE MORE PUZZLING PASSAGES IN THE WRITINGS OF EDMUND BURKE is his statement that "our Constitution is a prescriptive Constitution; it is a Constitution, whose sole authority is, that it has existed time out of mind."[1] Taken in isolation, these words say or seem to say that the legitimacy and binding force of the British constitution derive solely from the length of time that it has existed. A number of commentators on Burke have understood him to mean just that, and their understanding of him has had far-reaching effects on their interpretation of the rest of Burke's political thought.

Thus, for example, Paul Lucas says that Burke "believed that prescription possessed an immanent justification," and that in his mind "time alone became the material and efficient cause of prescription."[2] Frank O'Gorman concludes that, since the mere passage of time was enough to confer authority, Burke's constitution was independent of any higher moral order: "He specifically denied that the British constitution rested upon a Natural Law foundation because 'it is a prescriptive constitution whose sole authority is, that it has existed time out of mind.'"[3] To put it in other terms, for Burke the constitution as it revealed itself in historical practice was cut loose from dependence on or control by the principles of moral, legal or political theory.

If this is so, then Burke made a clean break with the Western tradition of political philosophy which, in both its ancient and its modern versions, sought the source of political authority in Nature and Nature's God. The late and great Leo Strauss offers us a more sophisticated interpretation of Burke's words, one which nonetheless tends in the same direction. Strauss sees Burke as having made a last-minute attempt to return to the pre-modern conception of natural right and natural law.[4] He acknowledges that Burke "does not tire of speaking of natural right, which, as such, is anterior to the British constitution."[5] Yet he finds that Burke's statement about the prescriptive constitution denies the superiority of natural standards of right and justice to the constitution. For all of his devotion to natural law, Burke was sliding into historicism.

415

"Prescription," Strauss explains, "cannot be the sole authority for a constitution, and therefore recourse to rights anterior to the constitution, i.e., to natural rights, cannot be superfluous unless prescription by itself is a sufficient guaranty of goodness." To say that existence time out of mind is the sole authority of the constitution is implicitly to affirm that the standard for judging the goodness of a constitution is inherent in the historical process by which it evolved. Burke's statement "is, in fact, a preparation for Hegel."[6]

A more recent writer, Michael Freeman, resolves the contradiction between Burke's natural-law doctrine and his theory of prescription by holding that he did not fully mean what he said about the prescriptive constitution. "There is," says Freeman, "a natural-law basis to his well-known doctrine of prescription."[7] But this means that "prescription is not the ultimate ground of political institutions." Prescription furnishes Burke with "a weapon to destroy the radical doctrine of the [natural] rights of man." But

Burke does not dare to rely on prescription alone. Although prescription is the *sole* authority of the British constitution; although it supersedes every other title; he needs other grounds for attacking the pretended rights of man. The other grounds are 'justice', 'lenity' and 'beneficent government', concepts redolent of both natural law and Utilitarianism.[8]

From the above it is clear that interpreting Burke's assertion that the British constitution's "sole authority is, that it has existed time out of mind" has caused scholars some difficulty, and that the difficulty arises precisely from the word "sole." I have myself written elsewhere and at length on the meaning of Burke's doctrine of prescription,[9] and there is no need to repeat what I said there. Here I should like only to make a small contribution to clarifying what Burke meant by setting his dictum on the prescriptive constitution in the context in which he made it.

The statement occurs in a document entitled "Speech on a Motion made in the House of Commons, the 7th of May 1782, for a Committee to inquire into the state of the Representation of the Commons in Parliament."[10] *The Parliamentary History of England* reveals that such a motion was made on that date by William Pitt the Younger; the motion was followed by a debate; and the debate was followed by a vote, in which the motion was defeated. The whole matter was disposed of in a single day, yet the record of the debate contains no speech nor any remarks at all by Edmund Burke.[11] According to Carl Cone, "Burke did not speak, having been persuaded by his friends against stirring bad feelings."[12] But he did write a speech, and one may surmise that he wrote it after the debate. Some of his remarks, at any rate, seem to be directed against statements that Pitt made in introducing his motion for a committee to study and report on reapportioning the right of the people to vote for members of the House of Commons.

The demand for "parliamentary reform" was comparatively recent in 1782, but the situation that provoked it was an old one. The allocation to counties and boroughs of representatives in the House of Commons had varied little in centuries. The result was a glaring disproportion between the population of constituencies and the number of members they returned to Parliament. Possession of the right to vote itself varied widely from one constituency to another, particularly in the boroughs.[13] The electorate was, in fact, a small and haphazardly random sample of the population and, as a result, electoral corruption was rife. "Even such as it was," says George Stead Veitch, "the representation was shamelessly bought and sold."[14]

One might well question, then, to what extent the House of Commons represented the people. William Pitt, in the speech introducing his motion, said that the House "had fallen so greatly from that direction and effect which it was intended, and ought to have in the constitution, he believed it would be idle for him to attempt to prove." The departure from the principles of the constitution, he charged, consisted in this, that "the representatives ceased in a great degree to be connected with the people" because they were "either dependent on the crown or the aristocracy." This was particularly true of members returned to Parliament by the boroughs. There were, he said, boroughs "absolutely governed by the Treasury, and others totally possessed by them, or boroughs contested only by the Treasury and powerful men, decayed boroughs that were controlled as private property, and boroughs that sold their votes, sometimes to Indian potentates, in no sense the electors of representatives of the interests of the country."[15]

Organized agitation for reform of the representation began in the late 1760s. A decade later, according to John Cannon,

it is necessary to distinguish three campaigns—however much they were inter-related in practice. One was the campaign for moderate parliamentary reform, organized by Christopher Wyvill, and having as its main objective a substantial increase in county representation. The second was the more radical movement, which revived and gained new impetus, with John Jebb, John Cartwright and the Duke of Richmond taking over the work of Beckford, Sawbridge and Wilkes. The third campaign, and the only one to achieve any immediate success, was the agitation for economical reform, championed above all others by Edmund Burke.[16]

Burke, then, was himself a reformer, though very much in his own fashion. In May, 1782, he had risen as high as he ever got in government. Lord Cornwallis's surrender at Yorktown the previous October had caused the fall of Lord North's government on March 20, and had forced a very reluctant George III to bring in an uneasy coalition government headed by Burke's parliamentary patron and leader, the Marquis of Rockingham. Burke himself was not deemed suitable for a cabinet post and was appointed to the relatively minor position of Paymaster of the Forces. But he was a leading spokesman for the Rockingham Whigs and, under the Marquis's administration, was able to introduce and see enacted into law the so-called economical reform.

This promoted "economy" in the royal household, that is to say, it sought to reduce the influence of the Crown on Parliament by abolishing a number of patronage offices and by bringing royal expenditures under control. The premise of the measure was that, once Parliament's independence from the Crown was thus assured, no further reform of the House of Commons was needed.

The Commons had given leave for Burke to introduce his economical reform measure on May 6, the day before Pitt made his motion. This doubtless explains why Burke's friends were anxious lest he stir up bad feelings with an attack on Pitt's proposal. There was no point in alienating men who would support economical reform by criticizing their own more far-reaching parliamentary reforms.

Most of the reformers were moderate in their proposals (despite Burke's allegation, which we shall see below, that nine tenths of them argued on radical, natural-right grounds). "Some, like Pitt," says Carl Cone, "thought the weight of the counties should be increased by disfranchising the smallest boroughs and enlarging the number of county members."[17] According to Veitch, English parliamentary reformers by and large were practical men who "demanded only practical and immediate reforms, such as an increase of county members or shorter Parliaments, which they considered the proper remedies for specified abuses." They "had not, as a rule, much taste for spinning theories of the State."[18]

Some of them, however, developed such a taste and advocated universal manhood suffrage on the ground that every man had a natural right to vote. These were the "radicals," and it was characteristic of Burke that he took them as the principal object of his attack and identified the bulk of the reformers with their views. It was precisely against the radical argument for reform that he made his statement that the sole authority of the British constitution was that it had existed time out of mind.

He was aware, however, that not all the proponents of parliamentary reform were radicals. In his Speech on the Reform of the Representation of the Commons in Parliament he said that among the reformers "there are two parties, who proceed on two grounds, in my opinion, as they state them, utterly irreconcilable." One party argued on juridical grounds, "the supposed rights of man," the other on political grounds, i.e., "that the Representation is not so politically framed as to answer the theory of its institution."[19]

The juridical (or radical) party had at least the merit of speaking "plain and intelligible" language. Their case was founded on "an absolute right" from which it followed that every individual must be personally represented in Parliament. The right was an individual one because it was a natural right, and "all *natural* rights must be the rights of individuals; as by *nature* there is no such thing as politick or corporate personality; all these ideas are mere fictions of Law, they are creatures of voluntary institution; men as men are individuals, and nothing else."[20]

The radical case thus rested on what we may identify, in words taken from Michael Oakeshott, as "the so-called nominalism of late medieval scholasticism, . . . a philosophy for which the world is composed of *individuae substantiae*."[21] It rejected the Aristotelian thesis that man is by nature a political animal. On the contrary, it held, man by nature is simply an individual, endowed indeed with natural rights, but with rights that can belong by nature only to individuals. Men can join together to set up civil societies and can transfer authority to them. But civil societies are in no sense natural entities; they are "mere fictions of Law" and "creatures of voluntary institution." Products of the individual wills that made them, they have no rights and no powers save those conferred on them by the only natural entities involved, individual men.

This theory postulates, according to Burke, an absolute right belonging by nature to the individual. What is this right? It is the original right of the individual to govern himself. The proponents of the juridical argument, says Burke, "lay it down, that every man ought to govern himself, and that where he cannot go himself he must send his Representative."[22]

The argument, as presented by Burke, is considerably telescoped. Spelled out, it would run as follows. Every man is a naturally sovereign individual endowed with an absolute right to govern himself. Only he can transfer that right to a government and even he cannot transfer it totally. The only civil society that he can legitimately enter is one in which the individual's natural right of self-government becomes the natural and imprescriptible right of every man to take part in the government of society.

It is further assumed that, since all men are by nature equal in their right to govern themselves, their right to take part in the government of society translates itself into the principles of political equality and majority rule. Civil society is an artificial institution, but its basic structural principles are dictated by the nature of man as a sovereign individual. It must be emphasized that this was the fundamental point on which Burke took issue with the democratic ideology of the age of the American and French Revolutions. He did not assert that civil society was independent of natural law, but he flatly denied that the natural and prepolitical right of the individual to govern himself determined the political constitution of society.

To return to the natural-right argument, civil society ideally should be a direct democracy in which every individual voted in person on the laws. But since direct democracy was impossible in a large state, he must at least have the right to send his representative to vote on them. Even this, however, is overstating what is required by natural right, since an individual might well vote for a losing candidate and so have to be content with being "represented" by someone for whom he did not vote. Everyman's right thus turns out to be the right to vote in a parliamentary election, but that right, at least, is absolute.

Let us now quote in full Burke's summary of the natural-right argument for personal representation.

As to the first sort of Reformers, it is ridiculous to talk to them of the British Constitution upon any or all of its bases; for they lay it down, that every man ought to govern himself, and that where he cannot go himself he must send his Representative; that all other government is usurpation, and is so far from having a claim to our obedience, it is not only our right, but our duty, to resist it. Nine tenths of the Reformers argue thus, that is on the natural right.[23]

Burke did not attempt in this speech to refute the premises of this argument. Instead he drew out its logical implications and showed that the natural-right argument proved too much. It was used to justify a demand for universal suffrage in elections to the House of Commons. But that house was only one third of a Legislature composed of King, Lords and Commons and formed no part at all of the Executive. If the whole people, told by the head, were acknowledged to have a natural right to vote in elections to the House of Commons, one would have to ask: "How came they neither to have the choice of Kings, or Lords, or Judges, or Generals, or Admirals, or Bishops, or Priests, or Ministers, or Justices of Peace?" There was no ground, Burke argued, on which one could stop short of complete popular sovereignty and republican government, once "the right of self-government in each individual" was admitted.[24]

Having shown the conclusions to which the natural-right argument necessarily led, Burke proceeded to offer the prescriptive nature of the constitution as the answer to them.

Why, what have you to answer in favour of the prior rights of the Crown and Peerage but this—our Constitution is a prescriptive Constitution; it is a Constitution, whose sole authority is, that it has existed time out of mind. It is settled in these *two* portions against one, legislatively; and in the whole of the judicature, the whole of the federal capacity, of the executive, the prudential and the financial administration, in one alone. Nor was your House of Lords and the prerogatives of the Crown settled on any adjudication in favour of natural rights, for they could never be so partitioned. Your King, your Lords, your Judges, your Juries, grand and little, all are prescriptive; and what proves it, is, the disputes not yet concluded, and never near becoming so, when any of them first originated. Prescription is the most solid of all titles, not only to property, but, which is to secure that property, to Government.[25]

In presenting the above argument, Burke did not reject the doctrines of natural law or even of natural rights that he asserted in so many
other places in both earlier and later years. He was only rebutting "*this*
claim of right, founded on the right of self-government in each individual."[26]
It was, and still is today, quite possible to believe in natural law and natural rights without believing in a pre-political state of nature in which the
individual had an absolute right to govern himself, which right, when
carried over into civil society, determines society's constitution. Burke offered
prescription as an answer to *that* claim, not to the idea of natural rights as
such.

Faced with this particular natural-right argument, Burke simply
pointed to the existing constitution. Not one part of it, not even the House
of Commons,[27] was based upon the alleged principle of natural right. Yet
no loyal subject of the Crown could deny the legitimacy of the existing
constitution. In later years, when Thomas Paine, who was not at all a
loyal subject, attacked the constitution in root and branch, Burke was
forced to explicate the philosophical premises of his theory of the constitution.[28] Here, however, it was enough to point out that men who accepted
the constitution as legitimate in principle could not demand a change in
one part of it on the ground that it violated an asserted natural right.
Logically, one had either to conclude that the whole constitution violated
natural right or to abandon the alleged natural right.

The issue between Burke and his natural-right opponents was the
question of the government's title and right to authority. He did not
maintain, as Leo Strauss thought he did, that prescription was a sufficient
guaranty of the *goodness* of the constitution. That was a distinct question,
to which we shall turn later. He did maintain that prescription guaranteed the *authority* of the constitution against the contention that authority
could be conferred only by the wills of a majority of the present generation of the people.

For Burke, the existing constitution enters the field, so to speak, with
an antecedent claim upon the obedience of the people. They do not
create it; it is already there and already enjoys authority. This is a weak
argument if used in favor of a recent constitution established by foreign
conquest, domestic revolution or even by a close and bitterly-fought election.
But if the constitution, no matter how questionable its origins, has existed
since time immemorial, it is a very strong argument; for Burke, a simply
conclusive one.

Pushed to the full logical implications of its radical individualism,
the natural-right argument issued in the conclusions that the only legitimate constitution is a democratic one and that the only legitimate government is one chosen by the electorate in a democratic election. That is to
say that the title to political authority is ultimately individual consent.

Burke's theory of prescription took men as being by nature social and political. Since their natures could not develop to the perfection that the Creator intended for them without civil society, and since society cannot perform its function without political authority, men have a natural need for authority and a natural obligation to submit to it. They are therefore antecedently obliged to accept the existing constitution, at least until it is lawfully and legitimately changed. It can be changed—Burke did not deny that—but men do not have a natural right to change it at pleasure, nor is its authority contingent upon their present will as expressed in a majority vote.

On the other hand, since authority exists for them, and not they for it, they have a natural right to be governed for their own benefit and welfare. For Burke, political authority was a power held in trust for the good of the community. The trustees were therefore bound by natural law and by the ancient and settled laws of the state which defined their trust (and these included the inherited and established liberties of the people). If the trustees grossly and incorrigibly violated those laws, they forfeited their trust and could be relieved of it, by force if necessary.

But until they abdicated their trust by their abuse of it, they were its rightful holders and the constitution under which they held it was the rightful constitution. Their and the constitution's authority was not open to question on the ground of the individual's natural right of self-government. One could say, then, as Burke did, that the constitution's sole authority was that it had existed time out of mind. This was to say that the question of the *title* to authority was already settled. We do not need to conclude, with Freeman, that Burke was not fully confident of what he said. He was sure of what he said, but in the context in which he said it.

Burke used a variation on the same theme in replying to the "political" argument for reforming the representation. In a passage which seems to be directed against the speech with which Pitt introduced his motion for a committee to study the representation, he addressed himself to the question "whether it [the House of Commons] continues true to the principles, upon which it has hitherto stood;—whether this be *de facto* the Constitution of the House of Commons, as it has been since the time, that the House of Commons has, without dispute, become a necessary and efficient part of the British Constitution?" The question, he replied, was absurd:

A prescriptive Government, such as ours, never was the work of any Legislator, never was made upon any foregone theory. It seems to me a preposterous way of reasoning, and a perfect confusion of ideas, to take the theories, which learned and speculative men have made from that Government, and then supposing it made on those theories, which were made from it, to accuse the Government as not corresponding with them.[29]

If we assume that Burke was answering Pitt, he rather missed Pitt's point, possibly because he chose to miss it. Pitt had argued that when the

Crown summoned members of Parliament from the shires and boroughs, it summoned them to represent the people in whose name they consented to taxes and took part in making laws. But members whose election had been bought or otherwise controlled by the Crown itself, or by "powerful men," or even, God save the mark, by Indian nabobs, could hardly be said to represent the interests of the people. The House of Commons had deviated from its principle and original purpose by becoming "dependent on the crown or the aristocracy." Now, Burke proposed his economical reform in order to reduce the influence of the Crown on Parliament, but he was not eager to diminish the influence of the aristocracy. He believed that "powerful men," such as the Marquis of Rockingham, were the natural trustees for the people. He therefore refrained from meeting Pitt's argument head on.

Instead, he seized upon the notion of theories of the constitution and refuted that. The British constitution, he said, and truly enough, had not been framed on any antecedent theory of what a constitution ought to be. On the contrary, in Great Britain constitutional theories were abstracted from the historically-evolved constitution that in fact existed. There were no constitutional theories, prior and superior to the constitution, by which it could be judged and found wanting. So long, therefore, as the House of Commons remained in structure what it had always been— and Burke insisted that it did—there was no ground on which one could accuse it of having deviated from its constitutional principle.[30]

But it is noteworthy that, having said this, Burke immediately added:

> It is true, that to say your Constitution is what it has been, is no sufficient defence for those, who say it is a bad Constitution. It is an answer to those, who say that it is a degenerate Constitution. To those, who say that it is a bad one, I answer, look to its effects. In all moral machinery the moral results are its test.[31]

Now, at last, we come to the question of the goodness of the constitution. Prescription, Burke admits, does not answer that question but only the question whether a constitution which remains the same has degenerated from its principles. Similarly, prescription establishes the authority of the constitution against claims based on the individual's alleged natural right to govern himself. It does not establish the proposition that mere existence time out of mind makes a constitution good. It therefore does not make the constitution independent of natural standards of justice and right, and it does not render practice superior to theory.

To answer the question whether the constitution is good, says Burke, we must look to its "effects" and "moral results." But the effects of the British constitution are in fact good ones, as is shown by "the happy experience of this Country of a growing liberty and a growing prosperity for five hundred years."[32] Even the vilified representative system, for all its inequality in representation, has sound moral results for, Burke asks, "what advantage do you find, that the places, which abound in representation, possess over others, in which it is more scanty, in security for freedom, in security for justice, or in any one of those means of procuring temporal prosperity and eternal happiness, the ends, for which society was formed?" His answer is, of course, none, because the House of Commons serves the nation as a whole. "You have an equal representation, because you have men equally interested in the prosperity of the whole, who are involved in the general interest and the general sympathy."[33]

We need not discuss how convincing Burke's defense of the unreformed House of Commons was. It is sufficient to note that his ultimate criterion for judging a constitution and a government was the service they rendered to "the ends, for which society was formed." Prescription is indeed, as Burke was to say in a later writing, a part of the law of nature,[34] but for that very reason it is subordinate to the ends of society, which at their highest level are set by the same law of nature. The prescriptive constitution is presumed to be one that is serving those ends. When we hear Burke say that the sole authority of the constitution is that it has existed time out of mind, we must not forget that it is of the British constitution that he speaks. His case for prescription comes down to this, that men are obliged to obey a good government and are not exempted from that obligation by the allegedly superior right of every individual to govern himself or to choose those who will govern him. His case falls, if fall it does, with the proposition that the eighteenth-century constitution of Great Britain was a good one.

Notes

1. *Speech on the Reform of the Representation of the Commons in Parliament*, in *The Works of the Right Honourable Edmund Burke* (16 vols.; London: Rivington, 1803–1827), X, 96. All subsequent references to Burke's *Works* are to this edition.
2. "On Edmund Burke's Doctrine of Prescription," *Historical Journal*, XI (1968), pp. 40, 62.
3. *Edmund Burke: His Political Philosophy* (Bloomington and London: Indiana U. Press, 1973), p. 52.
4. *Natural Right and History* (Chicago and London: U. of Chicago Press, Phoenix ed., 1965), pp. 294–95.
5. Ibid., p. 319.
6. Ibid.
7. *Edmund Burke and the Critique of Political Radicalism* (Chicago: U. of Chicago Press; Oxford: Basil Blackwell, 1980), p. 20.
8. Ibid., pp. 94–95.
9. "Burke on Prescription of Government," *Review of Politics* XXXV (1973), pp. 454–74.
10. *Works*, X, pp. 92–108. It has the same title in several other editions of Burke's works that I have consulted.
11. *The Parliamentary History of England from the Earliest Period to the year 1803*, XXII (London: Hansard, 1814), pp. 1416–38.
12. *Burke and the Nature of Politics: the Age of the French Revolution* (Lexington: U. of Kentucky Press, 1964), p. 49.
13. For a more detailed description of the representation in the eighteenth-century House

of Commons, see Cannon, John, *Parliamentary Reform*, 1640–1832 (Cambridge: at the University Press, 1973), pp. 29 ff.

14. *The Genesis of Parliamentary Reform* (Hamden, Conn.: Shoe String Press, Archon Books, 1965), p. 3.

15. *Parliamentary History*, XXII, pp. 1417–19.

16. Cannon, p. 72.

17. Cone, p. 48.

18. Veitch, p. 43.

19. *Works*, X, 93–94.

20. Ibid., p. 94.

21. Hobbes, Thomas, *Leviathan*, ed. with an introduction by Michael Oakeshott (Oxford: Basil Blackwell, n.d.), p. lv.

22. *Works*, X, 95.

23. Ibid., 94–95.

24. Ibid., 95–96.

25. Ibid., 96.

26. Ibid., 95; emphasis added.

27. Ibid., 97–98.

28. See my "The Burke-Paine Controversy," *Political Science Reviewer*, VI (1976), pp. 389–420. The reader may consult this article and the one referred to in note 9 above for documentation of the statements I make here about Burke's political theory which extend my argument beyond the speech under consideration in this essay.

29. *Works*, X, 98–99.

30. Ibid., 98.

31. Ibid., 99.

32. Ibid., 100.

33. Ibid., 101–02.

34. In *Reflections on the Revolution in France*, he quotes a French jurist as making this statement "with great truth." *Works*, V, 276.

CONTRIBUTORS

Ernest L. Fortin, BOSTON COLLEGE

David Tucker, THE CLAREMONT INSTITUTE

John Adams Wettergreen, SAN JOSE STATE UNIVERSITY

Peter W. Schramm, THE CLAREMONT INSTITUTE

Larry Peterman, UNIVERSITY OF CALIFORNIA, DAVIS

Charles R. Kesler, CLAREMONT MCKENNA COLLEGE

Edward J. Erler, CALIFORNIA STATE COLLEGE, SAN BERNARDINO

Jeffrey D. Wallin, UNIVERSITY OF DALLAS

Harvey C. Mansfield, Jr., HARVARD UNIVERSITY

Grant Mindle, LAKE FOREST COLLEGE

Patrick J. Garrity, CENTER FOR STRATEGIC AND INTERNATIONAL STUDIES, GEORGETOWN UNIVERSITY

Thomas G. West, UNIVERSITY OF DALLAS

L. P. Arnn, PUBLIC RESEARCH, SYNDICATED

Ken Masugi, THE CLAREMONT INSTITUTE

Dennis J. Mahoney, THE ENCYCLOPEDIA OF THE AMERICAN CONSTITUTION

Thomas Engeman, LOYOLA UNIVERSITY OF CHICAGO

Christopher Flannery, THE CLAREMONT INSTITUTE

John Zvesper, UNIVERSITY OF EAST ANGLIA

Wayne C. Thompson, LYNCHBURG COLLEGE

Harry Neumann, SCRIPPS COLLEGE

Thomas B. Silver, PUBLIC RESEARCH, SYNDICATED

Sanderson Schaub, CLAREMONT GRADUATE SCHOOL

Donald V. Weatherman, ARKANSAS COLLEGE

Francis Canavan, S. J., FORDHAM UNIVERSITY

THE WRITINGS OF
HARRY V. JAFFA

1949
Letter to the Editor, "War Powers Under the Pact, Scope of Presidential Authority in Event of Attack Discussed," *The New York Times*, April 4, 1949.

1952
Thomism and Aristotelianism: A Study of the Commentary by Thomas Aquinas on the Nichomachean Ethics (Chicago: University of Chicago Press, 1952), 230 pp. Reprinted by Greenwood Press, 1979.

Review of Alan Gewirth, *Marsilius of Padua, The Defender of the Peace*, *Social Research*, March 1952, pp. 117–121.

1953
Review of Max Hamburger, *Morals and Law, The Growth of Aristotle's Legal Theory*, *The American Political Science Review*, June, 1953, pp. 546–547.

1954
Review of Giorgio Del Vecchio, *Justice: An Historical and Philosophical Essay*, *The Journal of Criminal Law, Criminology and Political Science*, Volume 45, Number 4, November-December 1954, pp. 463–464.

1955
Review of John Bowle, *Politics and Opinion in the Nineteenth Century: An Historical Introduction*, *Annals of American Academy of Political and Social Science*, Volume 297, January 1955, pp. 155 and 156.

Review of Kurt Von Fritz, *The Theory of the Mixed Constitution in Antiquity: A Critical Analysis of Polybius' Political Ideas*, 7 pages typescript.

1957
"Expediency and Morality in the Lincoln-Douglas Debates," *The Anchor Review*, Number 2, 1957, pp. 179–204. Also Bobbs-Merrill Reprint Series No. H-111. Also reprinted in *American Political Thought*, eds. Morton J. Frisch and Richard G. Stevens (New York: Charles Scribners and Sons, 1971), 2nd ed. (Dubuque, Iowa: Kendall/Hunt, 1976).

"In Defense of the Natural Law Thesis," *American Political Science Review*, March

1957, pp. 54–66. Reprinted in *Equality and Liberty.*

"The Limits of Politics," *The American Political Science Review,* Volume LI, Number 4, June 1957, pp. 405–427. Reprinted in *Shakespeare's Politics* and in *The Conditions of Freedom.*

1958

"Slavery—A Battle Revisited," a review of Paul M. Angle (ed.), *Created Equal: The Complete Lincoln-Douglas Debates of 1858, The New Leader,* August 18–25, 1958, pp. 21–23. Reprinted in *The Conditions of Freedom.*

"'Value-Consensus in Democracy': The Issue in the Lincoln-Douglas Debates," *American Political Science Review,* Volume LII, Number 3, September 1958, pp. 745–753. Reprinted in *Equality and Liberty.*

1959

In the Name of the People, Speeches and Writings of Lincoln and Douglas in the Ohio Campaign of 1858, edited with an introduction by Harry V. Jaffa and Robert W. Johannsen (Columbus: The Ohio State University Press, 1959), 307 pp.

Crisis of the House Divided: An Interpretation of the Issues in the Lincoln-Douglas Debates (Garden City, N.Y.: Doubleday and Company, Inc., 1959), 451 pp. Reprinted by University of Chicago Press, 1982. Chapter XVIII, "The Natural Limits of Slavery Expansion," reprinted in the Bobbs-Merrill Reprint Series H-112.

1960

"The Case Against Political Theory," *The Journal of Politics,* May 1960, pp. 259–275. Reprinted in *Equality and Liberty.*

Reply to Allan Nevins' review of *Crisis of the House Divided, The New Leader,* June 20, 1960, p. 30.

"En contra de la teoria politica," *Revista de Ciencias Sociales,* Volume 3, Number 4, Diciembre 1959, pp. 563–578. (Spanish translation of "The Case Against Political Theory.").

1961

"The Case for a Stronger National Government," *A Nation of States,* ed. Robert A. Goldwin (Chicago: Rand McNally, 1961), pp. 106–125.

"Agrarian Virtue and Republican Freedom: An Historical Perspective," *Goals and Values in Agricultural Policy,* The Iowa State University Press, Ames, Iowa, pp. 45–62. Reprinted in *Equality and Liberty.*

"The U.S. and Revolution," published by the Center for the Study of Democratic Institutions, Fund for the Republic, Inc., June 1961, pp. 11–13.

"The Nature and Origin of the American Party System," *Political Parties, U.S.A.,* ed. Robert A. Goldwin (Chicago: Rand McNally, 1961), pp. 59–83. Also reprinted in *Equality and Liberty.*

"Strauss on Political Philosophy," Communications, *The American Political Science Review,* Volume LV, Number 3, September 1961, p. 599.

1962

"Aristotle," *History of Political Philosophy,* eds. Leo Strauss and Joseph Cropsey

(Chicago: Rand McNally, 1962), pp. 64–129. Reprinted by University of Chicago Press, 1972 and 1981. Reprinted in *The Conditions of Freedom*.

Review of Robert W. Johannsen (ed.), *The Letters of Stephen A. Douglas, Journal of Southern History*, Volume 28, Number 2, May 1962, pp. 251–253. Reprinted in *The Conditions of Freedom*.

"Patriotism and Morality," review of Donald W. Riddle, *Congressman Abraham Lincoln, Chicago Review*, Summer-Autumn 1962. Reprinted in *Equality and Liberty*.

1964

Shakespeare's Politics, by Allan Bloom with Harry V. Jaffa (New York: Basic Books, Inc., 1964), Chapter V, pp. 113–145. Reprinted in *The Conditions of Freedom*.

"On the Nature of Civil and Religious Liberty," *The Conservative Papers*, ed. Melvin A. Laird (New York: Doubleday Anchor, 1964), pp. 250–268. Reprinted in *Equality and Liberty* and in *Did You Ever See a Dream Walking: American Conservative Thought in the 20th Century*, ed. William F. Buckley, Jr., (Indianapolis and New York: Bobbs-Merrill, 1970), pp. 221–238.

1965

Equality and Liberty: Theory and Practice in American Politics (New York: Oxford University Press, 1965), xv, 229 pp.

"Reconstruction, Old and New," review of Kenneth M. Stampp *The Era of Reconstruction 1865–1877, National Review*, Volume XVII, Number 16, April 20, 1965, pp. 330–332. Reprinted in *The Conditions of Freedom*.

"Lincoln and the Cause of Freedom," *National Review*, Volume XVII, Number 38, September 21, 1965, pp. 827, 828 and 842. Reprinted in *The Conditions of Freedom*.

1966

"The Virtue of a Nation of Cities," *A Nation of Cities*, ed. Robert A. Goldwin (Chicago: Rand McNally, 1966), pp. 115–128. Reprinted in *The Conditions of Freedom*.

1968

"Natural Rights," *International Encyclopedia of the Social Sciences* (New York: The Macmillan Co., 1968), Volume II, pp. 85–90.

"The Limits of Dissent," review of Abe Fortas, *Concerning Dissent and Civil Disobedience, National Review*, Volume XX, Number 36, September 10, 1968, pp. 911–912.

1969

"Reflections on Thoreau and Lincoln," *On Civil Disobedience, Essays Old and New*, ed. Robert A. Goldwin (New York: Rand McNally, 1969), pp. 33–60. Reprinted in *The Conditions of Freedom*.

1970

"Political Obligation and the American Political Tradition." Prepared for delivery at the 1970 annual meeting of the American Political Science Association, 25 pp. Reprinted in *The Conditions of Freedom*.

"Spokesman for the Political Tradition," review of Jim G. Lucas, *Agnew, Profile in*

Conflict, National Review, Volume XXII, Number 39, October 6, 1970, pp. 1060–1062.

"Weathermen and Fort Sumter," *National Review*, Volume XXII, Number 51, December 29, 1970, pp. 1403 and 1419.

1972
"The Conditions of Freedom," Inaugural Lecture as Henry Salvatori Research Professor, March 2, 1972, *Claremont Journal of Public Affairs*, Spring 1972, pp. 41–56. Reprinted in *The Conditions of Freedom*.

"Tom Sawyer: Hero of Middle America," *Interpretation*, Spring 1972, pp. 194–225. Reprinted in *The Conditions of Freedom*.

"What Is Equality?" Essay for The Center for Constructive Alternatives, Hillsdale College, Hillsdale, Michigan, September 1972. Reprinted in *The Conditions of Freedom*.

1973
"Partly Federal, Partly National: On the Political Theory of the Civil War," *A Nation of States*, revised edition, ed. by Robert A. Goldwin (New York: Rand McNally, 1973). Reprinted in *The Conditions of Freedom*.

Crisis of the House Divided, Paperback Edition, with a new Introduction (Seattle: University of Washington Press, 1973), 451 pp.

"Contra Herndon," review of Elton Trueblood, *Abraham Lincoln: Theologian of American Anguish*, *National Review*, Volume XXV, Number 13, March 30, 1973, pp. 376–377.

"Portrait of a Patriot," review of Robert W. Johannsen, *Stephen A. Douglas, National Review*, Volume XXV, Number 21, May 25, 1973, pp. 587–589. Reprinted in *The Conditions of Freedom*.

"The Truth About War," review of Frederick Woods (ed.), *Young Winston's Wars: The Original Despatches of Winston S. Churchill, War Correspondent 1897–1900, National Review*, Volume XXV, Number 31, August 3, 1973, pp. 847–849. Reprinted in *The Conditions of Freedom*.

"Full-Scale versus Large-Scale," a reply to Professor Alexander Bickel, *National Review*, Volume XXV, Number 39, September 28, 1973, pp. 1054–1055.

"Amoral America and the Liberal Dilemma," *A Symposium*, The Committee for Academic Freedom, Claremont, California, Fall, 1973. Reprinted in *The Conditions of Freedom*.

"Leo Strauss," A Memorial Address delivered at Bridges Chapel, Claremont, California, November 3, 1973. Published in *National Review*, December 7, 1973, pp. 1353–55. Reprinted in *The Conditions of Freedom*.

"What About the Dardanelles," review of Martin Gilbert, *Winston S. Churchill, 1914–1916: The Test of War*, and Martin Gilbert (ed.) *Winston S. Churchill: Companion Volume III, National Review*, Volume XXV, Number 47, November 23, 1973, pp. 1307–1310. Reprinted in *The Conditions of Freedom*.

1974

"The Sinking of the Lusitania: Bungling, Brutality, or Betrayal?" *Claremont Journal of Public Affairs*, Spring 1974, pp. 3–24. (A condensed version of the foregoing appeared in the *National Review*, March 15, 1974, "Torpedoing the Lusitania Thesis," p. 322.) Reprinted in *Statesmanship: Essays in Honor of Sir Winston Spencer Churchill.*

1975

"How to Think About the American Revolution: A Bicentennial Cerebration." Prepared for delivery at the 1975 annual meeting of the American Political Science Association, for a panel chaired by Irving Kristol, "American Political Thought," 113 pp. Revised and expanded in *How to Think About the American Revolution.*

The Conditions of Freedom: Essays in Political Philosophy (Baltimore: The Johns Hopkins University Press, 1975), 280 pp.

"Can There Be Another Winston Churchill?" Public Lecture, January 9, 1975, printed in *Statesmanship: Essays in Honor of Sir Winston Spencer Churchill.*

"Time on the Cross Debate: But Not Redeemed," *National Review*, Volume XXVII, Number 11, March 28, 1975, pp. 341–342.

"Equality as a Conservative Principle," *Loyola of Los Angeles Law Review*, Volume 8, Number 2, June 1975, pp. 471–505. Originally prepared for delivery at the 1974 annual meeting of the American Political Science Association, for a panel chaired by William F. Buckley, Jr., on the theme "Conservatism's Search for Meaning." Reprinted in *How to Think About the American Revolution.*

1976

Editorial: "Lincoln and the Bicentennial," *Lincoln Herald*, Fall 1976, Vol. 78, Number 3, p. 93.

1977

"A Phoenix from the Ashes: The Death of James Madison's Constitution (Killed by James Madison) and the Birth of Party Government." Prepared for delivery at the 1977 annual meeting of the American Political Science Association, Washington, D.C., 44 pp.

"The (OKAY) Imperial Presidency," review of Joseph P. Lash, *Roosevelt and Churchill, 1939–1941: The Partnership that Saved the West*, *National Review*, Volume XXIX, Number 4, February 4, 1977, pp. 160–162. Reprinted in *Statesmanship: Essays in Honor of Sir Winston Spencer Churchill.*

"Equality, Justice, and the American Revolution: A Reply to Bradford's 'The Heresy of Equality,'" *Modern Age*, Volume 21, Number 2, Spring 1977, pp. 114–126. Reprinted in *How to Think About the American Revolution.*

"Democracy, Good and Bad," *National Review*, Volume XXIX, Number 18, May 13, 1977, p. 553.

"Political Philosophy and Honor," *Modern Age*, Volume 21, Number 4, Fall 1977, pp. 387–394. Reprinted in the Appendix of *How to Think About the American Revolution*.

"On Mano's Jews for Jesus: An Exchange," *National Review*, Volume XXIX, Number 48, December 9, 1977, p. 1433.

1978

"Comment on Professor Lewis S. Feuer's 'The Problems of a Conservative Democrat.'" Prepared for delivery at the Conference on the Philosophy of Spinoza, The Jewish Theological Seminary, N.Y., 32 pp.

Los Requistos de la Libertad (Mexico City: Editores Asociados, 1978), (Spanish edition of *The Conditions of Freedom*), 166 pp. Chapters 2, 7, 11–13, 15, 16 and 19 of the original are reprinted.

How to Think About the American Revolution: A Bicentennial Cerebration (Durham: Carolina Academic Press, 1978), 183 pp.

"Human Rights," June 23, 1978, a syndicated column distributed by Public Research, Syndicated.

"What Happened at Camp David?" October 21, 1978, a syndicated column distributed by Public Research, Syndicated.

1979

"Looking at Mr. Goodlife," typescript, 19 pp. Reprinted in *American Conservatism and the American Founding*.

1980

"Foreword" to Harold W. Rood, *The Kingdoms of the Blind*, Studies in Statesmanship Series, general editor, Harry V. Jaffa (Durham: Carolina Academic Press, 1980), p. ix.

Letter to the Editor, "The Sally Hemings Story," *Yale Alumni Magazine and Journal*, March 1980, p. 2.

"Another Look at the Declaration of Independence," *National Review*, Volume XXXII, Number 14, July 11, 1980, pp. 836–840. Reprinted in *American Conservatism and the American Founding*.

"Has Reagan Promised Too Much?" August 1980, a syndicated column distributed by Public Research, Syndicated.

1981

Statesmanship: Essays in Honor of Sir Winston Spencer Churchill (Durham: Carolina Academic Press, 1981), editor and contributor, 279 pp.

"On the Necessity of a Scholarship of the Politics of Freedom," Introduction to *Statesmanship: Essays in Honor of Sir Winston Spencer Churchill*, Studies in Statesmanship Series, general editor, Harry V. Jaffa, pp. 1–9. This is a general introduction to the Studies in Statesmanship Series.

"Foreword" to Jeffrey D. Wallin, *By Ships Alone: Churchill and the Dardanelles*, Studies in Statesmanship Series, general editor, Harry V. Jaffa (Durham: Carolina Academic Press, 1981), pp. xi-xvi.

"Chastity as a Political Principle: An Interpretation of Shakespeare's *Measure for Measure*," eds. John Alvis and Thomas G. West, *Shakespeare as Political Thinker*, (Durham: Carolina Academic Press, 1981).

"The Unity of Comedy, Tragedy, and History: An Interpretation of Shakespeare's Universe," *Shakespeare as Political Thinker*.

"Inventing the Past: Gary Wills' *Inventing America* and the Pathology of Ideological Scholarship," *The St. John's Review*, Volume XXXIII, Number 1, Autumn 1981, pp. 3–19. (An abridged version was also published in *The Conservative Historians Forum*, Number 6, May 1982, pp. 2–4.) Reprinted in *American Conservatism and the American Founding*.

"The Wisdom of the People Must Correct the Folly of the Court," November 27, 1981, a syndicated column distributed by Public Research, Syndicated.

"The 1980 Presidential Election: A Watershed in the Making," *Current*, Winter 1981. Reprinted in *American Conservatism and the American Founding*.

"A Conversation with Harry V. Jaffa at Rosary College," *The Claremont Review of Books*, December 1981, pp. 5–14. (An abridged version also appeared in *The Newsletter*, University of Dallas Politics Department, Volume IV, Number 1, Spring 1981, pp. 1–4.) Reprinted in *American Conservatism and the American Founding*.

"For Good Government and the Happiness of Mankind: The Moral Majority and the American Founding." Prepared for delivery at Loyola University of Chicago, December 1981. Reprinted in *American Conservatism and the American Founding*.

1982

"Human Rights and the Crisis of the West." Prepared for delivery at the Toqueville Forum on Public Policy, Wake Forest University. (An abridged version appeared in *Grand Strategy: Countercurrents*, Volume 2, Number 5, March 1, 1982.) Reprinted in *American Conservatism and the American Founding*.

"Foreword" to Thomas B. Silver, *Coolidge and the Historians*, Studies in Statesmanship Series, general editor, Harry V. Jaffa (Durham: Carolina Academic Press, 1982), pp. ix–xv.

"In Defense of Political Philosophy: A Letter to Walter Berns," *National Review*, Volume XXXIV, Number 1, January 22, 1982, pp. 36– 44. Reprinted in *American Conservatism and the American Founding* along with "A Letter to Walter Berns of January 14, 1981" and "'In Defense of Political Philosophy' Defended: A Rejoinder to Walter Berns" of November 1982.

"Preface" to the University of Chicago Phoenix edition of *Crisis of the House Divided: An Interpretation of the Issues of the Lincoln-Douglas Debates*. The "Preface" to the original Doubleday printing, 1959, was inadvertently dropped by the publisher from the Phoenix edition.

"Needed: Conservative Voice on Israel," *Washington Times*, June 4, 1982.

"July 4, 1982: The 110th Anniversary of Calvin Coolidge's Birth," June 23, 1982, a syndicated column distributed by Public Research, Syndicated.

"Behavioral Science and the Hinckley Verdict," July 15, 1982, a syndicated column distributed by Public Research, Syndicated.

"The Primacy of the Good: Leo Strauss Remembered," *Modern Age*, Volume 26, Numbers 3–4, Summer/Fall 1982, pp. 266–269. Reprinted in *American Conservatism and the American Founding*.

"Old Left Right Out or the Whose Ox is Gored School of Constitutional Jurisprudence," October 1, 1982, a syndicated column distributed by Public Research, Syndicated.

"The Declaration and the Draft," October 29, 1982, a syndicated column distributed by Public Research, Syndicated.

1983

"Leo Strauss's Churchillian Speech and the Question of the Decline of the West." Prepared for delivery at the 1983 annual meeting of the American Political Science Association, Chicago, Illinois, 18 pp.

"The Doughface Dilemma or The Hidden Slave in the American Enterprise Institute's Bicentennial," Occasional Paper Number 5, The Claremont Institute, January, 1983, 53 pp. Reprinted in *American Conservatism and the American Founding*.

"The Birthday of Abraham Lincoln," February 4, 1983, a syndicated column distributed by Public Research, Syndicated.

"The Birthday of George Washington," February 15, 1983, a syndicated column distributed by Public Research, Syndicated.

"Marxism 100 Years After the Death of Marx," March 4, 1983, a syndicated column distributed by Public Research, Syndicated.

"Martin Luther King, Jr. Remembered," March 22, 1983, a syndicated column distributed by Public Research, Syndicated.

Letter to the Editor, "The Conflict between Slavery and Freedom," *Americans for the Reagan Agenda Report*, Volume 2, May 1983.

"Protectionism Ahead," May 4, 1983, a syndicated column distributed by Public Research, Syndicated.

"On the Education of the Guardians of Freedom." Prepared for delivery at the thirtieth anniversary of the Intercollegiate Studies Institute, Washington, D.C., September 1983, 21 pp.

"The Death of 007," September 9, 1983, a syndicated column distributed by Public Research, Syndicated.

"The Massacre of the Palestinians: What Lessons Can We Learn?" October 1, 1983, a syndicated column distributed by Public Research, Syndicated.

"Municipal Defense Policy: The Latest Attempt at Nullifying the Constitution," November 22, 1983, a syndicated column distributed by Public Research, Syndicated.

"Detente: The Opiate of the Democracies," November 29, 1983, a syndicated column distributed by Public Research, Syndicated.

1984

"Foreword" to Francis Canavan, *Freedom of Expression: Purpose as Limit*, Studies in Statesmanship Series, general editor, Harry V. Jaffa, (Durham: Carolina Academic Press, 1984).

American Conservatism and the American Founding (Durham: Carolina Academic Press, 1984), 262 pp.